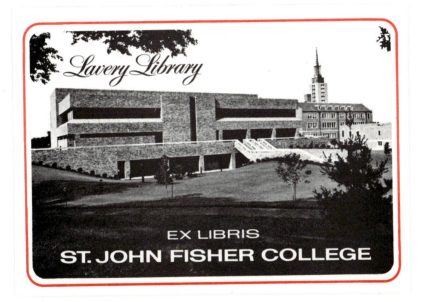

The Cultures of Work Organizations

Harrison M. Trice
New York State
School of Industrial and Labor Relations
Cornell University

Janice M. Beyer
College of Business Administration
The University of Texas at Austin

PRENTICE HALL, Englewood Cliffs, New Jersey 07632

Library of Congress Cataloging-in-Publication Data

TRICE, HARRISON MILLER,
  The cultures of work organizations / Harrison M. Trice, Janice M.
Beyer.
    p.   cm.
  Includes bibliographical references and index.
  ISBN 0-13-191438-3
  1. Corporate culture.   I. Beyer, Janice M.   II. Title.
HD58.7.T74   1993
302.2′5—dc20   92-9291
                                                        CIP

Acquisition Editor: Alison Reeves
Editorial/production Supervision
  and Interior Design: Esther S. Koehn
Marketing Manager: Sandra Steiner
Copy Editor: Sandra DiSomma
Cover/jacket Designer: Bruce Keneslaar
Jacket Painting: Merle Krumper
Prepress Buyer: Trudy Pisciotti
Manufacturing Buyer: Robert Anderson
Editorial Assistants: Diane Peirano, Reneé Pelletier

© 1993 by Prentice-Hall, Inc.
A Division of Simon & Schuster
Englewood Cliffs, New Jersey 07632

Printed in the United States of America
10 9 8 7 6 5 4 3 2

ISBN 0-13-191438-3

Prentice-Hall International (UK) Limited, *London*
Prentice-Hall of Australia Pty. Limited, *Sydney*
Prentice-Hall Canada, Inc., *Toronto*
Prentice-Hall Hispanoamericana, S.A., *Mexico City*
Prentice-Hall of India Private Limited, *New Delhi*
Prentice-Hall of Japan, Inc., *Tokyo*
Simon & Schuster Asia Pte. Ltd., *Singapore*
Editora Prentice-Hall do Brasil, Ltda., *Rio de Janeiro*

For Richard, Catherine, Claire, and Andrea

for lessons in cultural change

Contents

8 Cultural Interchange Between Organizations and Environments   299

9 Managing and Maintaining Organizational Cultures   355

Preface

Cultural processes underlie much of what happens in modern organizations. Culture filters the ways in which people see and understand their worlds. Culture prescribes some behaviors and forbids others. Culture colors the emotional responses that people have to events. Given the central role of culture in channeling human behavior, its relative neglect in the study of organizations is unfortunate. However, as we surveyed the literature, we found that this neglect had been somewhat exaggerated. Since the 1930s, a small but steady stream of research on organizations has been carried out from a distinctly cultural perspective, primarily by sociologists and anthropologists.

The Aims

The first aim of this book is to integrate these largely ignored findings with those from the more recent and larger body of research on organizational cultures. We have tried to be inclusive, in the sense of considering research from all disciplines, but have also been selective, in that we have focused on research we judged to be genuinely cultural. Not all of the research that claims to be about cultures is consistent with the distinctive demands and values of this approach.

A second aim in writing this book was to begin to integrate the cultural approach to studying organizations with what might be called the mainstream theories and ideas current in the study and analysis of organizations today. As our readers will see from the sampling of results we report in this volume, taking a cultural perspective reveals many aspects of organizational life missed by the predominantly rational theories of organizations and management. Looking exclusively at organizations through the lens of the abstracted, rational categories incorporated in such theories can be misleading because each theory so greatly simplifies the complexities and diversity of organizational life. Cultural research tries to apprehend and analyze larger chunks of reality and preserve the *context* in which it occurs as an integral part of that reality. In effect, it tries to encompass more of the complexities and messiness of real life—including its nonrational aspects. Because of this inclusiveness, cultural research yields results that are rich, concrete, and interesting to scholars and practitioners alike. While we hope to demonstrate that the cultural approach to the analysis and study of organizations can provide many distinctive insights, we do not see it as antithetical to other approaches used to analyze and study organizations. Indeed, we have incorporated into the chapters that follow many ideas from mainstream organizational and management theory.

Our third aim was to begin to fill in the theoretical gaps that became apparent as we struggled to integrate discrete cultural concepts and findings with each other and with those from other approaches. The writing of this book was spread out over a seven-year period. During that interval, the study of cultures in organizations was maturing and producing many new ideas and results. At the same time, our own ideas were developing as we pursued other research and professional activities. In particular, we both taught courses on organizational cultures regularly during that interval and found ourselves confronting, with the stimulus provided by our students, many basic questions that remained unanswered. Many of these we have tried to resolve in the pages that follow.

Finally, we aim to convince the readers of this book that the study of organizational cultures is not just a fad. Because its popular resurgence in the 1980s lacked a strong theoretical and empirical foundation, some scholars were quick to dismiss the ideas advanced. Many managers also became discouraged when the promises of the popular resurgence were not quickly realized. In this book we have tried to provide a broad scholarly grounding that can inform both application and research focused on the cultures of organizations. In particular, we have tried to convey, in an easily accessible form, the richness of detail and sense of reality that can be gained from qualitative research bearing on the cultures of organizations. While we have been able to present only a sampling of the fascinating accounts of the complexities of organizational life that have been generated by researchers, these excerpts breathe life into the concepts presented and help to make this a more engaging text than most. At the same time, we have tried to be careful not to sacrifice rigor for interest. We have drawn examples primarily from the research literature rather than the popular press. We have tried to make our arguments and conclusions as consistent as possible with the findings of empirical research, and when we have ventured beyond them to provide a coherent framework, we have tried to do so in a spirit that is consistent with what has been found and with prevailing theory. We indicate where our analysis is most speculative, but acknowledge that some degree of theorizing has been necessary at many points to pull the many discrete sets of results and ideas about organizational culture together.

We have used drafts of the chapters of this book with students at three levels: advanced undergraduates, and graduate students at both master's level and doctorate level. It was understandable and interesting to students at all three levels. These included students from psychology, sociology, anthropology, education, communication, law, nursing, public administration, business, and industrial and labor relations. We have made special efforts to include materials of interest to MBA students, but have not limited ourselves exclusively to business examples. While we recommend that students using this book have at least one prior course in organizations or in a related behavioral science, it may not be absolutely necessary at the graduate level. We have tried to present the ideas and findings in a way that does not require prior knowledge of concepts and theories. Of course, those who have such background will more thoroughly understand many of the points presented than those who do not. The book could be used as the central text for an elective course or as a supplement to a more conventional text in a survey course on organizations and organizational behavior. Because of its comprehensive review of the relevant literature, the book could also be useful in Ph.D. courses, especially those surveying various theoretical perspectives on organizations or those that seek to focus specifically on organizational cultures.

The Execution

In an era when many books seem to be almost tossed off in a year or less, we would like to make it clear that this book is the product of a much more sustained and extensive effort. We found that writing a textbook in an area that has not yet been comprehensively surveyed or integrated is a much more time-consuming and demanding task than either of us imagined at the start. The initial planning and work on the book began with great excitement in 1984, when an outline for the whole book and first drafts of two chapters were completed. Unfortunately, after Janice began her editorship on the *Academy of Management Journal*, she found that working on the book required more intellectual energy and effort than she had available. Other, equally demanding offices in the Academy followed. Fortunately, during that interval, Harry was able to sustain his commitment and continued working on the book. Over the next five years, he collected, read, sifted, and began the integration of the theories, data, and examples that provide the scholarly grounding of the book. He and his associates not only found but also kept track of the extensive bibliography. When Janice found time to rejoin his efforts, he had prepared rough drafts of most of the chapters. She added materials from her own knowledge of the literature—particularly the mainstream literature on organizations and management—pruned, organized, refined, and further developed the ideas and frameworks in Harry's drafts, and, working in close collaboration with Harry, wrote new drafts of all of the chapters. Each chapter was then refined and rewritten several more times, always adding new ideas and materials. The second-to-last draft profited from inputs from Ph.D. students; the last draft was refined in response to comments and suggestions of scholars who are experts in specific topics covered in the book and were kind enough to read those chapters.

When the rest of the book was almost in final form, we embarked on the most difficult task we had set for ourselves—writing the two final chapters on managing and changing cultures in organizations. These chapters both summarize the key ideas presented throughout the book and translate them into prescriptions for practice. They represent our efforts to come to grips with the familiar "so what" question that practical students and practitioners often ask. We offer these prescriptions to bridge the gap between research and practice and to stimulate others to think through the same difficult issues that our attempts had to confront.

Although Harry carried the main burden of the work for a long time, this book could not have been written without the complementary and extensive efforts and skills of both authors. Either of us alone would have written a different and probably much less valuable book. What appears between these covers is the fruit of an extensive and satisfying intellectual collaboration. We are excited by how much we have learned, by the new ideas we have generated, and by how much this field of study has developed, and how much it can tell students and practitioners about organizations.

Acknowledgments

Over the years that we have been working on this book, we have been assisted in many ways, large and small, in our efforts to complete it and, more generally, in our efforts to learn about the cultures of work organizations. We cannot possibly remember or acknowledge every helpful input that has been made to our learning or to the book itself, but we are thankful for them nonetheless. Over the years, Harry had perhaps a dozen undergraduate students working on his library task force searching out many of the sources used in this book. Among the scholars who kindly responded to our request for citations and materials were Lisa Berlinger, Alfred Chandler, Carolyn Dexter, Janet Dukerich, Peter Feuille, Jim Frederickson, Bill Glick, Dawy Greenwood, George Huber, Sirkka Jarvenpaa, Dave Moore, Denise Rousseau, Sim Sitkin, George Strauss, Kerri Strayer, David Throop, Karl Weick, Alan Wilkins, Robin Williams, and James Worthy. Sheldon Hochheiser from AT&T, Bob Tripolsky from the Saturn Corporation, and Ginger Shearburn from Southwest Airlines were also kind enough to share materials and information with us. As already mentioned, we owe special thanks to four scholars and friends who read one or more chapters and provided us with extensive and extremely helpful comments: Meryl Louis, Jim Meindl, Claudia Schoonhoven, and Bob Sutton. In the last months of completing the book, Tamar Terzian, Roland Chanove, Lynn Scott, and Audrey Chia were especially helpful in finding needed materials in our libraries.

We also wish to acknowledge the supportive role played by our respective universities and schools—the New York State School of Industrial and Labor Relations at Cornell, and the College of Business Administration at the University of Texas at Austin. Both provided stimulating and helpful colleagues and students and the sustained staff support necessary to pursue this kind of scholarly effort. At both schools, the assistance of particular people was especially crucial and important. At Cornell, the efforts and contributions of Shirley Foster were central at all times, but particularly in locating and keeping track of the voluminous amount of library materials consulted over the years. At the University of Texas, Kellie McCurdy, Kim Novak, and Lisa Hancock were skilled, cheerful, and patient in typing numerous drafts of the chapters. Special thanks are also due to Dean Robert Witt and to Edwin and Rebecca Gale, whose generosity provided practical assistance through Janice's endowed professorship. Roland Chanove, Audrey Chia, Michael Evans, Beth Laughlin, Gervaise Nix, Patty Sias, Anil Singh, and Joan Stuller, as students in a Ph.D. seminar on organizational cultures, provided much encouragement as well as helpful comments on Chapters 1 through 8. Finally, we want to acknowledge the highly professional and pleasant support and help of the Prentice Hall staff, especially Alison Reeves, Esther Koehn, and Sandra Steiner. We also want to thank Gordon Brumm for an exceptionally fine and useful index.

Until now, the study of organizational cultures has suffered from a lack of integration and coherence brought about by the multidisciplinary affiliations of its researchers and from internal schisms about theory and epistemology. One unfortunate result has been confusion among scholars with other interests and among practitioners about what organizational culture is and what a cultural perspective has to offer in terms of either understanding or practice. Another result has been a tendency to dilute the distinctive concepts and approaches that cultural analysis can provide and treat organizational culture as just another variable, much like any other, that can be studied with the same methods that are used to study any other phenomena in organizations. When culture is relegated to the status of a variable, much of the unique value of the cultural perspective is lost. Our loftiest hope in writing this book was that it could provide some of the integration and coherence that the cultural analysis of organizations needs to progress and continue to be distinctive and, at the same time, that this book could connect this type of analysis in useful and interesting ways to mainstream organizational and management research. If we have to any degree fulfilled this hope, all of the years of effort have been worth it.

Harrison M. Trice
Janice M. Beyer

1

How and Why Organizations Are Cultures

Humans build their cultures, nervously loquacious, on the edge of an abyss.

KENNETH BURKE*

Human cultures emerge from people's struggles to manage uncertainties and create some degree of order in social life. People in organizations face many uncertainties. Their environments change due to economic conditions, technological developments, or the actions of competitors. To compete in a fast-developing global economy, people in organizations must deal with different types of customers and a large array of possible new competitors. Concerned citizen groups and legislatures ask them to deal with problems of environmental pollution, environmental preservation, deterrence of drug and substance abuse, and even elder and child care. Meanwhile, the explosion of information and knowledge means they must try to coordinate the activities of specialists with many different kinds of expertise when each does not fully understand the other and when their diverse views often conflict. They must do all this even as the social order within their organizations and their boundaries are changing due to mergers, reorganizations, and downsizing. From all of these uncertainties, many ambiguities arise. It is often far from clear what is the best course of action for managers and others to take to ensure their organizations' survival and continued prosperity. If they fail, they face other threats and uncertainties, including loss of job, social status, and self-esteem. Thus, it is not surprising that, like people in other settings, people in organizations develop cultures.

Their cultures provide organizational members with more or less articu-

*Quote attributed to Kenneth Burke by Clyde Kluckhohn, "Myths and Rituals: A General Theory," *The Harvard Theological Review* 35 (1942): 45–79.

1

lated sets of ideas that help them individually and collectively to cope with all of these uncertainties and ambiguities. People in organizations, as in social life generally, generate ideologies that tell them what is, how it got that way, and what ought to be. Such ideologies form the *substance* of cultures. They are not rationally based belief systems. Rather they are relatively implicit sets of taken-for-granted beliefs, values, and norms. Also, ideologies are more emotionally charged and resistant to change than rational beliefs because they give people some sense of confidence in facing the threats posed by uncertainties, and because they arise in the very circumstances that cannot be fully understood or predicted by rational means. In addition, by endorsing some actions and forbidding others, ideologies channel people's actions so that most of the time they repeat apparently successful patterns of behavior, mesh together in predictable ways, and avoid certain dangers and conflicts. Table 1–1 gives some examples of ideologies that have grown up at Southwest Airlines, an organization that has faced and surmounted many uncertainties.

Cultures also help people to cope with uncertainties by providing them with accepted ways of expressing and affirming their beliefs, values, and norms. Cultures have repertories of cultural *forms* that members use to express the substance of their cultures. Table 1–1 also gives examples of some of the cultural forms used at Southwest Airlines. Cultural forms imbue actions and other entities with meanings; they enable people to communicate and celebrate their ideologies in many different ways. This is possible because most human actions have dual consequences—they both accomplish certain technical and practical ends and express some subset of cultural meanings (Leach 1968).

To summarize, cultures are collective phenomena that embody people's responses to the uncertainties and chaos that are inevitable in human experience. These responses fall into two major categories. The first is the *substance* of a culture—shared, emotionally charged belief systems that we call ideologies. The second is *cultural forms*—observable entities, including actions, through which members of a culture express, affirm, and communicate the substance of their culture to one another. Clearly, people in organizations develop both cultural substance and cultural forms. Out of these processes, cultures grow. Cultures are a natural outgrowth of the social interactions that make up what we call organizations.

Culture's Role in Managing Chaos

Human beings lack the genetic programming other animals have to ensure that they will behave in predictable ways that promote collective survival. Instead, humans have a relatively open nervous system that permits individuals to behave in many different ways (Geertz 1970). By comparison, many animal species, especially the lower forms, have quite closed and fixed central nervous systems. Amazing performances are made possible by inborn genetic programs that pattern actions within narrow, predetermined ranges of behavior. There is an amaz-

TABLE 1–1

EXAMPLES OF IDEOLOGIES AND CULTURAL FORMS
AT SOUTHWEST AIRLINES

Distinctive Ideologies[a]

As expressed by Herbert Kelleher, CEO of Southwest Airlines:

Failure is a natural result of the competitive process.

One organization's problem can become another organization's opportunities.

Competition and conflict are inevitable and can be turned to an organization's advantage.

One way to compete is to make work fun.

The crucible of competition made our employees very dedicated, very mission oriented, close knit, and high-spirited.

We give the best service in the business.

Examples of Cultural Forms

Once each quarter, officers of the company work as baggage handlers, ticket agents, and flight attendants.[b]

Employees traditionally wear costumes on Halloween, Valentine's Day, and other special occasions and don "fun uniforms" every Friday.[c]

One Christmas Day, at a time of intense competition with America West, SW flight attendants on a flight out of Phoenix donned red spandex pants, sweatshirts with a candy cane design, necklaces of jingle bells and tree bulbs, and headbands with sprigs of mistletoe.[d]

The entrance hall to corporate headquarters at Love Field in Dallas is covered with plaques earned by employees for outstanding contributions to the company.[e]

Every Friday at noon, employees in Dallas gather in the parking lot for a cookout.[f]

---

[a]Adapted from Freiberg 1987, pp. 152–55.

[b]From Farnham 1989, p. 78.

[c]From Carey 1988, p. 6F.

[d]From Lucas 1988, p. 28.

[e]From Freiberg 1987, p. 309.

[f]From Jarboe 1989, p. 104.

---

ing precision, an almost breathtaking exactness, about the web building of the black widow spider and the nest building of the oriole.

Because human behavior is less specifically regulated by genetic programs, it exhibits greater variability and pliability. Throughout human history, cultures have provided much of the additional guidance needed for human beings to collectively survive, adapt, and achieve. For what the genetic code does not provide, human beings have developed cultural codes. "We are, in sum, incomplete or unfinished animals who complete ourselves through culture—and not through culture in general, but through highly particular forms of it." (Geertz 1970, p. 61). To be human

is not just to talk; it is to utter the appropriate words and phrases in the appropriate social situations in the appropriate tone of voice. . . . It is not just to eat; it is to prefer certain foods cooked in certain ways and to follow a rigid table etiquette in consuming them; it is not even just to feel, but to feel certain quite distinctive emotions—patience, detachment, resignation, respect. (Geertz 1970, p. 64)

The potential diversity of human behavior can lead to chaos. It usually doesn't because human beings interactively create and perpetuate social order and some measure of control over events by means of their cultures. Without cultures, human life would be harsh and the qualities that we associate with being human would not exist. By producing some degree of orderliness and regularity from baffling, precarious, and disorderly circumstances (Leach, 1976b), cultures smooth human life and allow people to get on with the necessities of living. This ongoingness, in turn, permits the accumulation of human learning over time. Each generation does not need to discover anew the solutions to recurrent uncertainties and problems. But chaos always threatens because new uncertainties arise. Thus some analysts suggest that cultures only cover up the ultimate disorder of existence (Moore and Myerhoff 1977, p. 17) and construct a precarious social reality that keeps chaos at bay (Berger and Luckmann 1966, p. 103). Indeed, scientists of all kinds now realize that "chaos seems to be everywhere" (Gleick 1987, p. 5).[1]

Organizations, like other social collectivities, tend to produce and preserve shared responses and shared experiences of uncertainty and chaos. People who belong to a given organizational culture share to some degree its basic properties: its substance and its forms. Collectively, they hold certain ideologies about how to deal with recurrent problems and uncertainties. They arrive at their shared ideologies through collective experience and repeated social interactions over time. They use cultural forms to communicate and reinforce these shared ideologies. Organizational cultures, like other cultures, develop as groups of people struggle together to make sense of and cope with their worlds.

What's Different About Cultures

While cultural anthropologists who studied tribal societies tended to include all aspects of social life as part of cultures, their all-encompassing approach does not seem suited to the analysis of modern, complex organizations. Research in management fields like organizational behavior, human resources, and strategy, and in the social sciences disciplines of sociology, psychology, and political science has already developed many useful ways of looking at people in work organizations. Each of these approaches, however, greatly simplifies reality by treating only selected aspects of human behavior in organizations. Thus, each offers

---

[1]A new interdisciplinary branch of science developing to study chaos has underlying assumptions that are radically different from those of traditional science. Seeing the world as a chaotic place focuses scientists' attention on process rather than state, or becoming rather than being. The cultural approach to studying and analyzing organizations has similar potential to question traditional scientific assumptions and focus attention on the process of people becoming organized.

only a partial explanation—and one that can sometimes be misleading to the degree it ignores valuable insights provided by other approaches or misses important aspects of behavior. Cultural approaches to the study of organizations tend to be more encompassing, but because life in modern work organizations is so multifaceted and complex, cultural approaches do not try to encompass everything. We believe a cultural approach is most useful for organizational analysis when (1) it calls attention to and helps explain various aspects of organizations that are neglected or overlooked by other approaches; and (2) it pulls in and helps to integrate various concepts developed by these other approaches with cultural approaches. These were our aims in writing this book.

The purpose of this introductory chapter is to set the stage for the more detailed examinations in later chapters by briefly discussing some of the general features of cultures. Some of these features are unique to cultures; others have a distinctive twist when looked at from a cultural perspective. Together they delineate what makes this perspective different from others. We will begin by outlining some characteristics and consequences of cultures on which most analysts agree. We will then discuss briefly other characteristics over which there is considerable controversy. We will end this section with a discussion of some features that organizational cultures do *not* have but that are sometimes ascribed to them.

Characteristics of Cultures

Table 1–2 lists six major characteristics of cultures on which most analysts agree. Some of these were already mentioned in our general description of cultures. The words in Table 1–2 are seldom used in traditional analyses of organizations and management. They describe phenomena that are largely ignored in other approaches to analyzing organizations. Together they capture the essence of what makes cultures different. All will be described briefly here and revisited many times throughout this book.

Collective. Cultures cannot be produced by individuals acting alone. They originate as individuals interact with one another. Individuals may originate specific ways of managing the fundamental insecurities of life, but until these specific ways come to be collectively accepted and put into practice they are not part of a culture. Cultures are the repositories of what their members agree about. Persons who do not endorse and practice prevailing beliefs, values, and norms become marginal and may be punished or expelled. Belonging to a culture involves believing what others believe and doing as they do—at least part of the time.

TABLE 1–2
SOME CHARACTERISTICS OF CULTURES

Collective	Inherently symbolic
Emotionally charged	Dynamic
Historically based	Inherently fuzzy

Emotionally charged.   Because cultures help to manage anxieties, their substance and forms are infused with emotion as well as meaning. To some extent, all culture is a "gigantic effort to mask" life's fundamental insecurities (Kluckhohn 1942, p. 66). People cherish and cling to established ideologies and practices because they seem to make the future predictable by making it conform to the past. People's allegiances to their ideologies and cultural forms thus spring more from their emotional needs than from rational consideration. When ideologies and cultural practices are questioned, their adherents react emotionally. They may be able to advance elaborate rationales for them, but the depth of the feelings they bring to their arguments indicates that more than rationality is at work. Members of a culture rarely dare to question core beliefs and values.

> ... man [sic] dreads both spontaneity and change. ... Conventions and institutions ... originate as group expedients which have some social value at some time, but they remain the objects of passionate adoration long after they have outlived their usefulness. Men fight and die for them." (Ferguson, 1936, p. 29)

Cultural ideologies and forms also help to channel emotions into socially accepted channels. As one analysis of myths pointed out, "Emotion is assisted by the repetition of words that have acquired a strong emotional coloring, and this coloring again is intensified by repetition" (Hocart 1939, p. 208). The performance of rites and rituals heightens awareness of shared sentiments. Rites and rituals may also provide ways for individuals to sublimate antisocial impulses (Kluckhohn 1942, p. 74).

Historically based.   Cultures cannot be divorced from their histories and they do not arise overnight. To develop a culture, people need to spend time together to interact and share with one another common uncertainties and some ways of coping with them. Thus, a particular culture will be based in the unique history of a particular group of people coping with a unique set of physical, social, political, and economic circumstances. Once individuals in a cultural group come to share some set of ideas and cultural practices, these ideas and practices begin to have a kind of life of their own. They often persist within that group after the uncertainties that gave rise to them are no longer present, and their originators and early proponents have left. Thus, a thorough examination of a culture will usually uncover residues of cultural ideas and practices that originated at earlier points in its history to deal with uncertainties that may no longer be present. Even though these historical residues are buried under current preoccupations and relatively hidden from awareness, they can still have powerful effects in guiding current behavior.

Inherently symbolic.   To say that cultures are symbolic is to emphasize the expressive, rather than the technical and practical side of human behavior. While, as pointed out earlier, human actions both do and say things, it is their expressive side that cultural analysis explores. Symbolism plays a very important role in cultural communication and expression. Things often stand for other things.

Symbols so infuse cultural communication that they are considered the most basic unit of cultural expression (Turner 1967). They occur frequently as part of other cultural forms. Thus, while in one sense symbols are a specific type of cultural form, they are, in another sense, the most general and pervasive of cultural forms. Some organizational theorists therefore focus on symbolism in organizations rather than on the broader concept of culture (Pondy et al. 1983; Pfeffer 1981a; Turner 1990a).

Dynamic. While cultures create continuity and persist across generations of members, they are not static, but dynamic. Cultures continually change. Some of the reasons follow.

First, no communication is ever perfect, Thus, all members do not learn exactly the same things about what a culture endorses and expects. Even if they intend to conform perfectly to what others expect, their understandings of a culture may be too imperfect to make that possible. Second, individuals have considerable discretion, even in very traditional cultures, to create their own variants of expected behavior. The degree of individualism varies across societies and over time but is probably always sufficient to produce some degree of innovativeness and creativity in responding to life's problems and challenges. Third, so much of culture is taken for granted that its transmission and reception occurs at a nonconscious level. Members are often unaware of what their cultures really say about a specific issue or event. As one common expression notes, "It would hardly be fish who discovered the existence of water." Fourth, the fact that so much of cultural communication is symbolic makes it inherently imprecise. Symbols often have more than one meaning (Turner 1990b). What members receive from their cultures is often more like a series of clues than direct messages; they must often translate and extrapolate from these clues to get at core meanings. Fifth, organizations, in particular, must often assimilate new groups and practices to deal with new demands and opportunities in their changing environments. New importations, whether they involve techniques, equipment, or people, are likely to carry with them some cultural baggage that will affect existing cultures.

While not exhaustive, this list of reasons helps to show how and why cultural persistence is imperfect and why there is considerable change in how any culture manifests itself over time.

Inherently fuzzy. Not only are cultures inherently symbolic, they are inherently fuzzy (Leach 1976b; Gluckman 1963a; Pierce 1977; Moore 1975) in a variety of other ways. A leading anthropologist provides an instructive metaphor:

> ... The appropriate image ... of cultural organization is neither the spider web nor the pile of sand; it is rather more the octopus, whose tentacles are in large part separately integrated, neurally quite poorly connected with one another and with what in the octopus passes for a brain, and yet who nonetheless manages to get around and to preserve himself, for a while anyway, as a viable, if somewhat ungainly entity. (Geertz 1966, p. 66)

Cultures are not monolithic single sets of ideas, but rather incorporate contradictions, ambiguities, paradoxes, and just plain confusion. Anthropologists characterize modern cultures as "deeply ambiguous" (Keesing 1987, p. 162) and characterized by "enormous multiplicity" (Geertz 1983, p. 161). The more complex and fragmented the circumstances a human group confronts, the more likely it will mirror these elements in its culture with fuzziness.

Since modern organizations often operate in uncertain and confusing environments, observers have noted how the cultural elements they encounter in them are rather miscellaneous (Riley 1983), full of double binds (Cameron and Quinn 1988, p. 2), multiple meanings (Young 1990; Chatov 1973), ambiguous ceremonials (Mechling and Wilson 1988), and stories and metaphors (Feldman 1991). Some contradictions undoubtedly arise from residues of the past and from imperfect cultural transmission; others arise because of the many subcultural influences in organizations that emanate from occupational groups with different work-related uncertainties and experiences. Still others arise from the emergent, interactive nature of cultures and organizations; organizations and their cultures are perpetually in the process of becoming organized (Weick 1985). As actions go forward, people often discover some lack of shared and coincident meanings that needs to be worked out.

One analyst divided cultures into their core or central elements and those that are more peripheral. Fuzziness marks the peripheries, while the central elements and core values generate sufficient consensus to produce some cooperation and coordination and to permit members to "recognize their common identity through time and across lines of conflict" (Shils 1975, p. xii).

Consequences of Cultures

Table 1-3 lists the most prominent and distinctive consequences of cultures about which most experts agree. The words on this list do sometimes appear in traditional treatments of management and organizations. But, with the exception of *uncertainties* and *commitment*, the words are infrequently used. While the other consequences listed are central to understanding what cultures are about, they play a very minor role in most noncultural analyses. Considering each in some detail should therefore contribute to our understanding of what makes cultures different.

Management of collective uncertainties. Through ideologies and cultural forms, cultures supply "fixed points in a world of bewildering change and disappoint-

TABLE 1-3
SOME CONSEQUENCES OF CULTURES

Management of collective uncertainties	Encouragement of ethnocentrism
Creation of social order	Generation of dual consequences
Creation of continuity	Technical and expressive
Creation of collective identity and commitment	Latent and manifest
	Functional and dysfunctional

ment" (Kluckhohn 1942, p. 68). Even in contemporary U.S. society, where change itself is highly valued and pursued, conformity to core cultural expectations is considered a virtue. People do not want everything in their worlds to change at the same time. They want to be able to take some things for granted. Ideologies and cultural forms grow up particularly around "those sectors of experience which do not seem amenable to rational control and hence where human beings can least tolerate insecurity" (Kluckhohn 1942, p. 68). They persist because they "reduce the anticipation of disaster" (Kluckhohn 1942, p. 69). It is not hard to see how the ideologies and forms listed in Table 1–1 help managers and employees of Southwest Airlines to face the uncertainties engendered by the fierce competition and fluctuating environmental demands in the airline industry.

The ideologies and associated forms that cultures develop vary in the degree to which they are grounded in some sort of practical experience and confrontation with reality or based in purely imagined events and superstitions. Obviously, ideologies that match realities imposed by the physical world and other circumstances will serve to help members of a culture adapt to and perhaps surmount those realities better than ones that do not. Also, of course, it can be dangerous to misunderstand genuine threats or to rely on magic to dispel them. Cultures that persist in unrealistic beliefs jeopardize their very survival.

Creation of social order. Cultures create social order from the potential chaos that emanates from the open-ended nature of the human nervous system. Recurrent patterns of behavior form; people begin to see them as right and proper ways to behave and become emotionally attached to them. The result is norms–quite specific and taken-for-granted expectations for how people should behave in a myriad of circumstances. Norms control behavior because members of a culture will sanction violations of their norms with disapproval and more concrete punishments.

The degree of social control that cultures produce, however, varies across societies and time periods. Cultures never completely control individuals; some refuse to conform and become deviants. Also, most cultures are pluralistic, with each subculture having only partial control over members. While the social control that cultures produce can be used for sinister ends and all cultures can be seen as constraining individual freedoms to some degree, people do not reach their full potential as human beings nor live happily and contentedly without cultures. Examples of people living outside their cultures are provided by individuals who reject or lose contact with the norms of any social groups in their societies. This social condition, known as anomie, greatly increases the probability of suicide (Durkheim 1964). Also, frequently occurring accounts of feral children (Shattuck 1980)—children growing up outside human society, usually raised by animals—attest to the anxieties people have and the negative consequences they ascribe to being without culture.

Creation of continuity. Human cultures so uniformly generate continuity of their beliefs and practices that a special term is used to refer to this process. The ways in which cultural substance and forms are passed from member to member over time is called socialization. To socialize someone is to impart to that person how to think and behave to conform to a social group's needs and to attach emotional significance to those thoughts and behaviors. Thus, individuals are shaped to fit within and continue the prevailing social order. Failures to socialize are costly to cultural continuity and social order. Social life is disrupted when individuals do not know how or refuse to conform to important expectations. If disruptions are serious and widespread, the prevailing culture may be pressured into change.

Many agencies and institutions in modern society—most notably religions, the family, the schools, and peer groups—socialize members for their general social roles. Schools and higher education play an especially important role in socializing members for work roles. To the degree that these agents instill values and behaviors consistent with the past, some degree of cultural continuity is assured. To the degree that they fail, cultural continuity is imperiled and the general level of uncertainty will rise because people cannot count on one another as they used to do.

Creation of collective identity and commitment. Members of cultures come to be bonded together not only by shared views of the world, but by many social ties and commitments. People come to know themselves as well as others in terms of their place within a culture. They assume a certain social identity within the cognitive, emotional, and social frameworks provided by the culture. To a great degree this identity is acquired reflexively as people interact with others and interpret others' reactions to them (Mead 1934). People develop an image of themselves as part of a particular social group with particular cultural beliefs and practices. If they move to a new social group and become part of its culture, their self-image will change.

Wilthin social groups that persist long enough to form cultures, members also develop a sense of a common identity. They are aware, at some level, of the similarities that they and other members share and how this makes them different from others. They, in effect, develop some degree of consciousness and pride in what makes their group unique (Martin, et al. 1983). Cultural groups also become reference groups for their members. People look to other members of their cultures for emotional support and confirmation of the meanings they ascribe to events. They also look to them for approval and disapproval of their and others' behaviors. From these reactions and from the models other members' behaviors provide, people construct their understandings of their worlds.

People's dependence on each other for emotional support and for making sense of their worlds also builds commitment to their cultural groups. They come to depend on other members of their culture to help them get through life's uncertainties and difficulties. They do not want to disrupt the ties that provide them with these assurances and so become committed to their continuity. Members' experiences in the culture pile up positive rewards and hurts avoided that increase their positive attachments to their cultures.

Encouragement of ethnocentrism. The next characteristic of cultures listed in Table 1–3—that they encourage ethnocentrism—calls attention to some unpleasant possibilities associated with cultures. People who endorse one set of ideas often come to distrust, fear, and dislike people with other ideas. The stronger and more emotionally charged the ideas, the more likely that their adherents will come to have intolerant and emotionally charged reactions to people who hold other ideas. They very term *ideology*, which we use in this book to represent the substance of cultures, has an unpleasant connotation because of its association with groups who use their ideas to justify their domination of other groups of people. While it seems clear that ideologies are not used exclusively to advance selfish interests (Beyer, Dunbar, and Meyer 1988), it also seems clear that they carry the danger of enhancing feelings of group superiority. For example, the residues of the caste system of India and racist ideologies everywhere provide rationales for some ethnic groups to mistreat others. But many other cultural and subcultural differences that occur in organizations—especially occupational, departmental, and status boundaries—can also produce ethnocentrism. In organizations, as elsewhere in society, such feelings are likely to interfere with cooperation and coordination among groups and lead to such phenomena as passing the buck or blaming the victim.

Generation of dual consequences.   The consequences of cultures include at least three dualities that have rather different implications for organizations. The first of these—*technical and expressive* consequences—has already been mentioned. While some cultural analysts, especially cultural anthropologists, might consider all of the technical activities and ideas of organizations as part of their cultures, the approach followed in this analysis is to focus on the expressive side of activities in organizations as the essence of their cultures. Other approaches to analyzing organizations focus on their technical and practical side. We do not intend, by focusing on the expressive, to deny that orgnizational activities have technical or practical outcomes. Nor do we feel that most activities have exclusively one or the other set of consequences. Rather, these dimensions represent dual consequences in the sense that both are present in most situations.

The second set of consequences of cultural activities is their *latent and manifest* consequences. Latent consequences are those that are hidden from view; manifest consequences are those that are evident. This duality means that cultures operate simultaneously at various levels of awareness. While some components of culture may be deeply buried and unconscious, others are relatively close to the surface and more accessible to examination (Schein 1985). Although there is some controversy on this point, it seems unlikely that core cultural elements are so unconscious that they never come to the surface of people's awareness. If this were so, people would not know when their or others' actions violated basic cultural assumptions. It does seem likely, however, that much of culture is taken for granted and unexamined most of the time. It takes something out of the ordinary, something that makes a specific element in the culture salient, to make people become aware of what is ordinarily latent (Louis 1980, 1985a).

The third duality along which cultural consequences can be arrayed is their *functional and dysfunctional* aspects. In social science terms, functional consequences are those that are beneficial, useful, and help to maintain current social arrangements; dysfunctional consequences are harmful, not useful, and tend to upset current social arrangements. Because many early cultural anthropologists tended to analyze features of tribal societies in terms of how they helped to maintain those societies, their work was criticized as one-sided and as providing rationales for the continuance of current societies with whatever imperfections and injustices they included. Similarly, some early treatments of organizational cultures treated them relatively uncritically as functional (Peters and Waterman 1982). Whole areas of organizational and management research have tended to focus on discovering and explaining what is functional in organizations and thus ignored their dysfunctional aspects (Pondy and Mitroff 1979). There has been a strong tendency in analyses of organizational cultures to "overemphasize the integrative and cohesion-producing side of culture" (Van Maanen and Kunda 1989, p. 49).

Other analyses of organizational cultures have suggested that considering only the positive aspects of culture is misleading. Cultures can be "equally dysfunctional" (Trice 1985, p. 248). They have many downside risks and costs, even in companies that are admired for both their performance and cultures. Some of the general drawbacks of corporate cultures identified in a recent study of firms in the electronics industry include:

- making employees vulnerable to burnout from working too hard
- making people unwilling to change what they do
- coloring the interpretation of information and events
- encouraging behaviors that few people do well
- encouraging ego involvements that heighten the emotionality of events

Many other drawbacks were identified for specific types of corporate cultures in this industry (Jelinek and Schoonhoven 1990, pp. 370–402).

In general, most activities in organizations can be seen to have both functional and dysfunctional consequences. This is illustrated by such popular expressions as "the trade-off is . . . ," "the other side of the coin," and "the folly of good intentions." Sometimes activities have functional consequences for one set of people and dysfunctional ones for another set. Sometimes activities have both sets of consequences for the same people. An awareness of this duality raises the important question of how functional and dysfunctional consequences are distributed. History is replete with cultures that espoused ideologies that oppressed members of certain groups to the advantage of others. This third duality warns us that the same possibilities exist for organizational cultures. Also, organizational cultures that were functional for one period of time can become dysfunctional as the environment or other circumstances change (Starbuck, Greve, and Hedberg 1978; Miller 1990).

Some Controversial Characteristics of Cultures

All scientific fields give rise to controversies. So it is not surprising that anthropologists and other researchers of cultures disagree on some basic issues. In addition, the study of organizational cultures is relatively new. Those working in the area were trained in a variety of social science disciplines and thus bring different perspectives to their research. They, in effect, come from a variety of scientific subcultures. Table 1–4 lists several major issues on which the experts on organizational cultures do not agree. Each is important as well as controversial.

Single culture vs. multiple cultures. The revival of cultural analysis of organizations in the 1980s was sparked by a few popular books written largely for a managerial audience (Peters and Waterman 1982; Deal and Kennedy 1982; Ouchi 1981). These books gave the general impression that whole organizations can have distinctive cultures and that top management has a great deal of say in shaping those cultures. Some managers, many consultants, and perhaps a few scholars still hold to such views. Several organizational scholars reacted to these popular treatments by emphasizing how pervasive and important subcultures were in organizations (Gregory 1983; Riley 1983; Barley and Louis 1983). This multicultural perspective is dominant today (Trice and Morand 1991). Few scholars doubt the presence of subcultures in organizations, but some doubt that organizations have organizationwide umbrella cultures.

The perspective to be taken in this book is that many organizations have both. While subcultures undoubtedly grow up more readily than organizationwide cultures, the testimony of various careful scholars indicates that some organizations have distinctive organizationwide cultures (Clark 1970; Pettigrew 1979; Whipp, Rosenfeld, and Pettigrew 1989; Child and Smith 1987; Hackman 1984). The disputes over this point may stem from different conceptions of culture.

Consensus vs. dissensus. Many scholars agree that some consensus about cultural substance and forms is a distinguishing feature of cultures, but disagree about whether to include within the term *culture* rather fragmented, shifting collections of people with different, even conflicting, views. A recent analysis suggests that there are three perspectives on organizational cultures: integrated, differentiated, and fragmented (Meyerson and Martin 1987; Martin and Meyerson 1988; Meyerson 1991; Martin 1991). The integrated view emphasizes organizationwide consensus, internal consistency, and clarity; the differentiated view emphasizes consensus within subcultures, inconsistencies between them, and clarity only within subcultures; the fragmented view emphasizes a lack of consensus both organizationwide and in subcultures, a lack of either clear consistency or inconsistency, and the pervasiveness of ambiguity.

TABLE 1–4
CONTROVERSIAL ASPECTS OF ORGANIZATIONAL CULTURES

Single culture	vs.	Multiple cultures
Consensus	vs.	Dissensus
Distinctive	vs.	Universal elements
Rigid	vs.	Malleable cultures

It is important to note that the first perspective is the same as the organizationwide approach already mentioned. The second is close to the multicultural approach already mentioned. The two really differ only in the level at which cultures occur; in both, cultures are characterized by substantial consensus.

The third perspective departs from traditional definitions of culture by its emphasis on ambiguity and dissensus. While this view has some basis in the literature on culture (Turner 1969; Moore 1975), it so emphasizes ambiguity and confusion that it is hard to see how such a set of relationships could form the basis of a culture. If ambiguity and fragmentation are the essence of relationships, and if the feeble and transitory consensus that does form fluctuates constantly with various forces, there is no culture as most scholars (e.g. Moore 1975; Jones, Moore, and Snyder 1988; Schein 1990) define one. Such a culture, if it can be said to exist, would do little to help people grapple with ongoing uncertainties. Also, from a dynamic perspective, such a set of relationships seems likely to either degenerate over time into a collection of individuals, each doing his or her own thing, or develop mechanisms for resolving conflict and ambiguity (Trice 1991) and thus produce some consensus. What enables cultures to arise in such situations is not the pervasive confusion and ambiguity, but the presence of a minimal degree of consensus and clarity about some issues.

For example, an observer of social workers in hospitals described their cultures as fragmented ones, yet they were observed to use special, unstructured meetings in which "anything goes" to express their anxieties and reduce tensions and conflict (Meyerson 1991b, p. 264). Furthermore, attendance was especially good at these meetings, strongly suggesting that they had some shared value to the participants. These meetings undoubtedly functioned as rites of conflict reduction that helped members cope with the ambiguities that seemed to permeate their occupational roles. If nothing else, the social workers shared an understanding that they could share their perceptions of ambiguity on these occasions. Thus, there was some consensus about how to handle ambiguity even in this fragmented occupational subculture. They also shared some basic orientations and knowledge about their occupation, faced similar problems, and had comparable experiences (Meyerson 1991a, p. 131; Feldman 1991).

Perhaps the best resolution that can be made for this issue is to acknowledge that all of these perspectives have some truth, but that none is the whole story. As already discussed, organizational cultures have various characteristics that produce ambiguities, conflicts, and dissensus: they reflect history and carry forward residues of the past; they are inherently symbolic and fuzzy; they are dynamic and not static; they include multiple, often contradictory, sets of ideas; and they have dual sets of consequences. It is therefore unlikely that any single culture will fit completely into any of the three perspectives identified. All cultures have areas of dissensus, and all cultures have at least a core of consensus. Also, cultures have centers and peripheries; some members and some ideas are more marginal than others. Some degree of dissensus and ambiguity among marginal members must be expected (Shils 1975).

> Consistency, consensus, harmony, and integration do occur even though in the midst of inconsistencies, ambiguities, conflicts, disruptions, and dissolution. These

two sets of forces appear to be reciprocal to one another. It is even conceivable that they somehow are essential to each other. Such a condition is the ultimate paradox in the puzzle of organizational behavior. (Trice 1991, p. 304)

To avoid endless confusion, it seems sensible to reserve the term *culture* for situations in which there is some core of consensus. Because people try to reduce uncertainties, organizations will have pockets of consensus somewhere within them if any members are around long enough to share some of the same uncertainties and their ways of coping with them.

Distinctive vs. universal elements. Anthropologists developed two very different schools of thought about the relative uniqueness of the substance and forms of cultures. To simplify a bit, one school argued that certain universals occur in all cultures (Levi-Strauss 1963; Leach 1970). Applying this idea to organizations would argue that some commonalities can be found across various organizational cultures. The other anthropological school argued that to generalize beyond a single culture would be inaccurate because this would rip the cultural elements out of the social context that gave them their meaning (Geertz 1973). To apply this idea to organizations would argue that we cannot generalize from research conducted in one organization to anything in another. This controversy presents especially thorny issues for the analysis of organizational cultures because users of such analyses often want to be able to apply results from one organization to another. Managers and management researchers, in particular, seek results from which generalizations for theory and practice can be drawn.

The methods that cultural researchers use reflect this controversy. Researchers who believe that there are generalizable properties in organizational cultures often use *etic* methods, in which they apply a typology or explore some prior set of concepts in one or more organizations. Some of them use methods like questionnaires or structured interviews that yield quantified measures. Researchers who believe that cultures are unique and specific to a particular group will use *emic* methods—unstructured interviewing, observation, and other qualitative techniques—designed to elicit the "native point of view."[2] Emic researchers try hard to avoid imposing their own category systems or other ideas on a culture, seeking rather to bring to the surface category systems and ideas that members of the culture themselves use to think about their worlds (Naroll and Naroll 1973). Emic researchers are likely to study one organization or one group in an organization at a time.

Clearly, both of these approaches have value. The middle ground is to realize that without etics, comparisons lack a frame; without emics, comparisons lack

---

[2]The two types of research spring from different research traditions and have different aims. Quantitative research typically employs statistics to test hypotheses or to determine the probability of events. This procedure requires deciding in advance what is important and how it will be measured. Qualitative research is more exploratory and open-ended. Qualitative researchers typically observe and interact with groups of people in their social settings over a substantial period of time in order to discover the participants' perspectives and understand their social worlds as they do. Some qualitative researchers are content to produce rich descriptions of social life while others use their observations to develop new theory.

meat. Emic and etic data do not constitute a rigid dichotomy, but instead often present the same data from two points of view (Harris 1976). Thus, the most sensible resolution of this controversy appears to be to avoid carrying either approach to an extreme, except when the research or practical question at hand clearly demands that approach. Rather, some combination of these approaches seems advisable, with the particular mix depending on how much is known about the group under study in advance and what sorts of issues the researchers are interested in exploring. There seems to be room for both explorations of general properties of cultures and for explorations of specific cultures yielding relatively unique insights.

We will not try to categorize all past research on organizational cultures in terms of this controversy. Table 1–5, however, presents a partial listing of various types of organizational cultures that management researchers have advanced and discussed. Such typologies imply an etic orientation in that they seek to generalize some cultural properties across more than one organization. Their diversity suggests, however, that they were devised using emic methods. Obviously, the theories of researchers are not always consistent with their methods in terms of the issue of universality. Also, this controversy is clearly far from resolved in the management field. The contents of Table 1–5 illustrate that little consensus has emerged about how to categorize cultures, even though there is some overlap on the kinds of issues on which they might be categorized. If organizational cultures have universal properties, they have not yet been convincingly demonstrated.

Rigid vs. malleable cultures.   A few observers fear cultures are so unchanging as to confront managers with "unbridled rigidity" (Bennis and Nanus 1985, p. 138). For reasons already explained, however, most analysts agree that various characteristics of cultures internally generate some amount of spontaneous change on a pretty continuous basis. This change may be gradual, it may be sporadic, but over time it nonetheless produces significant amounts of change.

There is less agreement on whether cultures can be deliberately changed, especially in a relatively short time. Some cultural researchers argue that, because cultures emerge spontaneously from informal interactions, any changes must also emerge spontaneously (Dorson 1971). Such a stance implies that cultures cannot be deliberately managed or planned. Other analysts argue that cultures can be deliberately changed, but only a little, or only with great difficulty. Some suggest, for example, that managers may be able to "slightly modify the trajectory of a culture" (Martin and Siehl 1983, p. 53). Another view is that changing cultures cannot be accomplished without replacing existing social learning processes (Schein 1985, 1990)—no simple or quick undertaking.

Still other reasons that have been identified as making deliberate cultural change difficult include: that cultures are too elusive and hidden to be accurately diagnosed, managed, or changed (Uttal 1983); that the techniques and skills involved are rare and take too long to make deliberate change practical (Uttal 1983; Schwartz and Davis 1981); and that the many subcultures existing in most organizations act against coordinated change (Barley and Louis 1983). Undoubtedly the most basic reason that analysts expect deliberate cultural change to be difficult

TABLE 1–5

SOME EXAMPLES OF TYPOLOGIES OF ORGANIZATIONAL CULTURES[a]

Types of Organizational Cultures	Dominant Ideologies	Authors
Type A	Hierarchical control, high specialization, short-term employment, individual responsibility, individual decision making	Ouchi and Jaeger, 1978; Ouchi, 1981
Type J	Clan control, low specialization, lifetime employment, collective responsibility, collective decision making	
Type Z	Clan control, moderate specialization, long-term employment, individual responsibility, consensual decision making	
Process	Low risk, "cover your ass" mentality, tight hierarchy	Deal and Kennedy, 1982
Tough-guy–Macho	High risk, quick feedback, fluctuating structure	
Work-hard–Play-hard	Moderately low risk, race to the quick, flexible structure	
Bet-your-company	Very high risk, slow feedback, clear-cut hierarchy	
Sensation-thinking	Impersonal, abstract, certainty, specificity, authoritarian	Mitroff and Kilmann, 1975
Intuition-thinking	Flexible, adaptive, global notions, goal-driven	
Intuition-feeling	Caring, decentralized, flexible, no explicit rules or regulations	
Sensation-feeling	Personal, homelike, relationship-driven, nonbureaucratic	
Apathetic	Demoralizing and cynical orientation	Sethia and Von Glinow, 1985
Caring	High concern for employees, no high performance expectations	
Exacting	Performance and success really count	
Integrative	High concern for employees with high concern for performance	
Paranoid	Fear, distrust, suspicion	Kets de Vries and Miller, 1984
Avoidant	Lack of self-confidence, powerlessness, inaction	
Charismatic	Drama, power, success, abject followership	
Bureaucratic	Compulsive, detailed, depersonalized, rigid	
Schizoid	Politicized, social isolation	

[a]To save space, the table summarizes only some of the points used by these authors to describe their types.

is that cultures help to sustain people through life's difficulties (Beyer 1981; Boje, Fedor, and Rowland 1982), and people therefore hold onto their cultures with some tenacity.

Other analysts treat cultures as if they can be readily manipulated, suggesting that direct, intentional actions not unlike those used in other management tasks can be used to change corporate cultures (Peters and Waterman 1982; Deal and Kennedy 1982; Kilmann 1982). For example:

> Can every company have a strong culture? We think it can. But to do that, top management first has to recognize what kind of culture the company already has, even if it is weak. The ultimate success of a chief executive officer depends to a large degree on an accurate reading of the corporate culture and the ability to hone it and shape it to fit the shifting needs of the marketplace. (Deal and Kennedy 1982, p. 18)

Again, both positions have some validity. Cultures are undoubtedly resistant to change—especially changes that do not emerge from within the cultural group. If they were too malleable, cultures would not provide the continuity and certainty that people come to depend on to give their lives order and meaning. On the other hand, cultures *do* change, and sometimes that change occurs as the result of deliberate interventions. The large-scale changes produced by charismatic leaders like Martin Luther King, Jr., and Mahatma Gandhi illustrate that people's deliberate efforts can change cultures dramatically. If such changes can be accomplished in whole societies, it is certainly conceivable that organizational cultures can be deliberately changed.

Recent thinking suggests some of the variables that need to be considered in assessing how difficult it would be to change a given culture. Three factors identified as likely to affect cultural persistence are: the fluidity of current ideologies, members' commitment to them, and the availability of alternative ideologies (Wilkins and Dyer 1988). The greater the fluidity and availability of alternatives, and the lower the members' commitment, the easier it will be to effect cultural change.

Obviously, to say that change is possible is not the same as saying it is easy or frequent. Because organizations are complex and their managers tend to think more in terms of ostensibly rational rather than expressive processes, planned cultural change is not a simple matter. It requires a thorough understanding of how cultures work, what factors about them are likely to produce what sorts of resistance to change in a given situation, and what levers cultures offer for producing change.

The rest of this book is devoted to explaining how organizational cultures work. Some of the chapters—those on ideologies, subcultures, and occupational subcultures—focus on aspects of culture likely to produce resistance to planned change. Others deal with levers for cultural change—cultural forms, socialization, leadership, and environments; all involve social processes and circumstances that shape cultures and over which managers or others have some control. Chapters 9 and 10 deal directly with the issue of how all of the various aspects of culture figure into efforts to manage and change cultures.

What Cultures Are Not

As already stated, one danger in using a cultural perspective is that every-thing in human behavior will be viewed as culture. For the purposes of management research and practice, we favor using the term relatively narrowly. Thus, it may help to eliminate some confusion by pointing out what organizational cultures are not. While some may view the issues we raise in this section as still controversial, we feel there are sufficient reasons to decide them in the directions indicated. As before, our motive is to reserve the culture concept for phenomena that are distinctive and not encompassed in other, more traditional approaches.

Not climate.   In the management literature the concepts of culture and climate are sometimes confused. The two concepts, however, have distinctly different origins that give them rather different meanings. As originally conceptualized, organizational climate referred to psychological environments in which the be-haviors of individuals occurred. Studies focused on individually perceived, rather immediate experiences of organizational members (Campbell et al. 1970; Hellriegel and Slocum 1974). Attitudinal reactions or perceptions of these expe-riences were measured by items in questionnaires. The appeal of the climate construct was that it seemed to give researchers a way to combine a broad array of variables already studied into a single omnibus concept that would simplify the process of characterizing and comparing the psychological environments of individuals. Thus it focused on measuring the perceptions of individuals about their organizations, rather than beliefs, values, or norms shared by groups of people. While others have since argued for and applied the concept at a collec-tive level (Joyce and Slocum 1984), the measures used continue to be anchored in individual perceptions and thus reflect individual rather than shared experi-ences (Jackofsky and Slocum 1988). Although statistical techniques can then un-cover clusters of people holding similar perceptions, alone they cannot tell us how individuals who perceive their climates similarly arrived at their shared per-ceptions.

Another basic difference between climate and culture is that the primary techniques used to measure climate were developed to measure attitudes. They are etic techniques that hold the danger of imposing researchers' views of the world on those being studied. In addition, it is far from clear that what they ask about is cultural, either in the sense of emerging from shared experiences, or in the sense of reflecting people's core understandings of their organizations. If attitudes reflect culture at all, they do so at only the most superficial level. For good reason, the traditions of cultural research call for intensive data collection using primarily emic methods over a substantial period of time. Otherwise, the subtleties that characterize cultures, as listed in Tables 1-2 and 1-3, cannot be uncovered or understood.

Still another difference between the concepts of climate and culture is that climate lacks unique indicators. So many different variables have been subsumed under the climate concept by various researchers that it overlaps with most con-structs in organizational behavior (Glick 1985, p. 606), as well as with structure, technology, formalization (James and Jones 1974), and effectiveness (Lawler, Hall, and Oldham 1974). By contrast, culture has many unique indicators like myths, symbols, rites, and stories. Recent attempts to link climate to culture assume that employees' reports of what they perceive to be prevalent organizational procedures and practices are somehow equivalent to these rich cultural manifestations (Schneider 1990). This seems highly unlikely.

Although some researchers use methods and concepts similar to those used in research on climate to study culture (Hofstede 1980b; Cooke and Rousseau 1988; Hofstede et al. 1990; Rousseau 1990; O'Reilly, Chatman, and Caldwell 1991), other experts on culture feel such attempts are bound to miss the essence of what culture is all about. We will revisit this issue in the next chapter.

Not groupthink. A misplaced emphasis on the notion that shared meanings, by themselves, are the essence of culture can create some confusion between the concepts of groupthink and culture. Groupthink describes situations where people behave in certain ways that tend to not only make them think similarly but also hide any differences in how they feel and think (Hellriegel, Slocum, and Woodman 1986, pp. 249–52). It consists of "a collective pattern of defensive avoidance, lack of vigilance, unwarranted optimism, sloganistic thinking, suppression of worrisome defects, and reliance on shared rationalizations ... " (Janis 1972, p. 399). While the phenomenon of groupthink resembles culture in some respects, it is usually used in reference to relatively small, face-to-face groups. Thus, the concept has some overlap with subcultures, but seems inappropriate to apply at the more encompassing level of a large subunit or organization. Most important, the phenomenon of groupthink lacks such cultural characteristics as a historical base, symbolism, dynamism, fuzziness, cultural forms, and the duality of technical and expressive consequences. Nor do the descriptions of groupthink portray the kinds of ongoingness and inclusiveness that characterize cultures.

Not social structure. Another controversy concerns the relationship between culture and social structure. While cultures pattern behaviors, and social structure is often defined as recurrent patterns of behavior, cultures are *not* the same as social structures. Social structures in societies, organizations, or other collectivities consist of the tangible and specific ways that human beings order their observable relations with each other. Cultures, on the other hand, consist of systems of abstract, unseen, emotionally charged meaning that organize and maintain beliefs about how to manage physical and social needs. A clear illustration of the difference between social structure and culture and their relative independence of each other is " ... the existence of highly organized insect societies with at best a minimal rudimentary component of culture ... " (Kroeber and Parsons 1970, p. 87). Human societies, however, do not yield examples where the two are so clearly independent.

The structure-culture controversy revolves around how closely the two are related to each other in human society. If they are inextricably intertwined and highly interdependent, then it would be hard to argue that they are separate entities (Radcliffe-Brown 1952; Singer 1968). Most analysts conclude that culture and social structure are "distinct, though interrelated: neither is a mirror reflection of the other—each must be considered in its own right" (Keesing 1974, p. 83). One important reason that culture and structure cannot be too interdependent is that such a relationship would leave little possibility for change; the two would be interlocked in a static state, in which neither could change because it was constrained by the other. In reality, much social change arises from the relatively loose interplay of culture and structure (Geertz 1957).

Not metaphor.   Finally, culture is not merely a metaphor for describing organizations or other cultural groups. Cultures exist; they are naturally occurring, real systems of thought, feeling, and behavior that inevitably result from sustained human interactions. They occur in nations, corporations, occupations, unions, gangs, and scientific research laboratories.

One advantage of the cultural approach to organizational analysis is that it can displace two old metaphoric notions that have prevailed in organizational analysis—that organizations are like machines or like organisms (Lundberg 1985a, p. 197). But to adopt a metaphoric view that organizations are *like* cultures implies that culture is something an organization *has* (Smircich 1983). To reject the metaphoric view is to assert that "organizations don't *have* cultures; they *are* cultures . . . " (Weick 1983, p. 27). This seems to us the more valuable perspective. The purpose of this book is not to describe another way of looking at organizations; it is to describe what organizations are that other treatments have missed.

Not necessarily the key to success.   A recent analysis of the literature on organizational cultures from 1980 to 1985 indicates that over time academic researchers became more concerned with the relationship of organizational cultures to organizational success (Barley, Meyer, and Gash 1988). The practitioner literature, which paid little attention to culture until the 1980s, was understandably always concerned with how cultures might improve organizational performance. At least four different positions can be identified in the writings on this issue by academics and practitioners.

The first of these identifies *certain cultural configurations* that characterized excellent companies (Peters and Waterman 1982) and thus presumably provide formulas for success. This line of reasoning and the evidence for it, while attracting practitioners, did not persuade many academics (Pfeiffer 1984; Carroll 1983; Johnson, Natarajan, and Rappaport 1985). Data showed the exemplary companies identified were not superior to other Fortune 1000 companies in terms of performance or in terms of following the so-called principles of excellence (Hitt and Ireland 1987). Also, examination of the performance of Peters' and Waterman's "excellent" firms just a few years later showed that several were experiencing many difficulties (*Business Week* 1984). Apparently, cultural configurations associated with success at one point in time are not necessarily succesful at other times when environmental conditions have changed.[3]

---

[3]Perhaps the most telling criticism of the Peters and Waterman approach, from a cultural perspective, is that it ignores the differing environmental contingencies and other contextual circumstances of organizations, apparently assuming that similar cultural features are equally plausible and likely to be successful in all circumstances.

In a more amorphous way, early comparisons of U.S. and Japanese organizational cultures also implied that certain cultural components were associated with high levels of organizational performance (Ouchi 1981; Pascale and Athos 1981). Managers and consultants were quick to embrace some Japanese ideas and practices, and such devices as quality circles proliferated in U.S. firms. Their success has been mixed at best (Lawler and Mohrman 1987).

The second position is that *strong cultures* lead to success; it is exemplified in the earlier quote from Deal and Kennedy's book (see p. 18), which begins with a chapter entitled "Strong Cultures: The New 'Old Rule' for Business Success." Unfortunately, these authors failed to clarify what they believe constitutes a strong or a weak culture. This gap was filled by another analyst, who suggested that the strength of a culture is determined by its thickness, extent of sharing, and clarity of ordering (Sathe 1985, p. 15). He suggested strong cultures have many ideologies that are widely shared and clearly ordered in terms of their relative importance. Also, according to this analysis, strong cultures produce more intense behaviors. Since studies show that influential cultures can be dysfunctional and thereby detrimental to overall organizational success (Starbuck, Greve, and Hedberg 1978; Miller 1990), it seems dangerous to assume that having a strong culture always insures success. The very strength of a culture could serve to discourage needed change.

The third position is the other side of the coin; it argues that some cultures are sick—*neurotic* is the term used. The central idea of this analysis is that cultures may derive unhealthy modes of functioning from the psychopathological problems of their chief executives (Kets de Vries and Miller 1984). The implication is that strong cultures, in the sense of influential or powerful ones, are not necessarily healthy. While the authors do not directly address the issue of success, it is hard to imagine that the neurotic firms they describe are financially successful for very long.

The fourth position on the relationship between culture and organizational success tries to set forth certain conditions under which cultures are more important for and conducive to success. One analysis assesses whether cultures are efficient means of control in terms of how well they govern needed transactions. It concludes that cultures are more efficient when (1) transactions occur under conditions of ambiguity, complexity, and interdependence; (2) enough people share the same set of ideas that set forth appropriate orientations; (3) the costs of maintaining the culture are not too high; and (4) subunits do not develop cultures that operate to the detriment of a larger organization lacking in culture. From this perspective: "Some organizational culture will presumably be irrelevant to performance; some forms of culture will promote and some will inhibit efficient operation, depending on the conditions listed above" (Wilkins and Ouchi 1983, p. 478).

Another analysis specifies three conditions that must be met before a culture will contribute to sustained superior financial performance: (1) the culture must be valuable in the sense that it leads the firm to behave in ways that lead to high sales, low costs, high margins, and other factors adding financial value to the firm; (2) it must be rare in the sense that other firms do not have the same or very similar cultures; and (3) it must not be easy to imitate so that competitors cannot readily change their cultures to include the same advantageous characteristics (Barney 1986, p. 658). This analysis clearly envisions culture as a possible source of competitive advantage.

The works cited are only examples of these four perspectives. Each implies that organizational cultures tend to contribute "in some way to the systematic balance and effectiveness of an organization" (Smircich and Calas 1987, p. 237). Although the last perspective makes the relationship between culture and success contingent on certain conditions, it still tends to oversimplify. Cultures can vary on many different characteristics (Table 1–2) that these analyses gloss over. Also, financial or other kinds of practical success are not the only criterion by which organizational cultures can be assessed, nor is it necessarily the most useful and insightful perspective from which to examine them. A thorough and exhaustive review of the relevant studies concluded that " . . . these studies have not definitely established an empirical link to financial performance . . . if we continue, either explicitly or implicitly to use culture as yet another determinant of performance related outcomes, we will fail to realize the full potential of studying culture" (Siehl and Martin 1990, pp. 30, 34). We would rather see the cultural perspective on organizations liberate researchers and managers from past assumptions and ways of thinking about organizations and suggest new paradigms for their study and management (Beyer, 1984; Barley, Meyer, and Gash 1988; Smircich and Calas 1987).

A Brief History of Cultural Research on Organizations

Cultural research on organizations is not a recent development. While it became more prominent in the 1980s following the publication of popular books like *In Search of Excellence* and *Theory Z,* there had been a fairly steady stream of research on cultural phenomena in organizations dating back to the 1930s. Especially influential were the activities of a group of scholars at the University of Chicago who interacted extensively with the business community. Other efforts were scattered. All of this research did not come from a consistent theoretical perspective, but much of it has yielded valuable insights that have been important for the study of organizations. Thus, it may be useful to describe some of this research and summarize its findings to underline in still another way how the cultural approach is distinctive. This review will also provide a background for the more detailed discussions to follow in later chapters.

The Pioneers

The first systematic attempt to understand modern work organizations in cultural terms occurred in the early 1930s during the last phase of the well-known Hawthorne studies at the Western Electric Company in Chicago, Illinois. In this, as in so many other ways, these studies proved to be seminal for the study and understanding of human behavior in work organizations.

The Hawthorne studies began with experiments on the relationships between productivity and the physical work environment. This phase of the studies grew naturally out of the concerns of industrial engineers employed by the company. When the results of these experiments proved puzzling and not explicable in purely technical terms, the company decided to turn to behavioral scientists and incorporate them into the program of ongoing research.

Elton Mayo, a faculty member in the Harvard Business School, was hired as a consultant by Western Electric. He, in turn, had to persuade the business school dean to allow him to employ an experienced, but still young assistant professor from the anthropology department to assist him in the Hawthorne studies. The young anthropologist was W. Lloyd Warner. Mayo argued that Warner would adapt the anthropological methods he had employed to uncover social structure and belief systems in tribal societies to the current work community within the Western Electric plant. This had never been done before—no wonder the dean needed persuading. The result of Mayo and Warner's discussions was the famous bank wiring room observation study, which began in November 1931 and lasted until May 1932. Careful analysis indicates that "this study was primarily designed by W. Lloyd Warner" (Moore 1989, p. 3).

Warner did not come to this new challenge totally unprepared. He had not only done classical anthropological fieldwork among the Murngin of Northeast Australia, he had also recently begun an extensive ethnographic study of the community of Newburyport, Massachusetts. One of the purposes of the community study was "to shed light on the way in which behavior, values, and attitudes that had shaped the community influenced the behavior, values, and attitudes of employees in the workplace" (Moore 1982, p. 117). This classic and very influential research, begun in 1929 and not completed until 1937, was eventually published in six volumes, known as the Yankee City Series. In one of these volumes Warner focused on how a community's culture shaped the cultures of workplaces within it (Warner and Low 1947). At Western Electric he focused on how workgroup cultures affected worker behavior and productivity in a specific work setting.

Undoubtedly because of Warner's influence, a new phase in the Hawthorne studies began. The bank wiring room study introduced anthropological field methods of observation and interviewing into the Hawthorne studies; the kinds of data collected were very similar to those usually collected by cultural anthropologists. Observations and interviews were aimed at describing three kinds of social relations occurring in the room: the technical, the social, and the ideological (Roethlisberger and Dickson 1946; Moore 1982). Technical relations arranged the flow of materials to machines, tools, and their output. The social structure organized the work, both formally in terms of specific designated relations, and informally in terms of those friendships and cliques that naturally formed outside the formal, prescribed relationships. The third kind of relations, the ideological, concerned the workers' culture—their shared beliefs and understandings regarding the work setting.

An observer, seated at the back of the room, made records of what he heard and saw. An interviewer talked to each employee on a regular basis. Their data showed that the social structure in the room informally broke into two cliques, and that this division came about largely because of differences in tasks. In addition, the investigators detected a well-defined status structure in which, for example, selector-wiremen were decidedly superior to soldermen, connector-wiremen were decidedly superior to soldermen, and connector-wiremen were superior to selector-wiremen. The ideologies these workers shared were extracted from the interviews; they consisted of beliefs about fairness, a living wage, and the right to work. Workers used these ideologies to justify and explain why they restricted output, pressured fellow employees to withhold production, and frequently violated company rules. This phase of the Hawthorne studies marked the first well-publicized cultural explanations for workers' behaviors in the management literature (Roethlisberger and Dickson 1946).[4]

Warner went on to complete his research for the Yankee City Series (Warner and Lunt 1941) and joined the faculty of the University of Chicago in 1935. From there he and his students began another community study—this time of the Deep South (Davis et al. 1941). Unfortunately, Warner himself did not continue to do anthropological studies within work organizations. However, he stayed at Chicago, where he and one of his students, Burleigh B. Gardner, began a consulting firm to help employers deal with personnel problems. An influential businessman in Chicago, who was a trustee of the University of Chicago, learned of their consulting firm and convinced Warner and Gardner that their efforts should be under the aegis of the university. Gardner was offered a full-time position in the School of Business after completing his Ph.D. degree. He taught the first course in applied industrial anthropology at the University of Chicago business school in 1942 and continued to do so until the end of World War II. Gardner also wrote the first textbook that took a cultural perspective on work organizations (Gardner 1945).

Meanwhile, in late 1942, the Committee on Human Relations on Industry was established at the University of Chicago with Warner as chairperson and Gardner as executive secretary. Faculty from various departments became members of the Committee. A young sociologist, David G. Moore, introduced Gardner to James C. Worthy, a senior personnel executive of Sears Roebuck, who was trying to figure out how to study the personnel side of that organization (Muhs 1989). Almost immediately, Gardner began to collaborate with Worthy on a study of the effects of a simple, flat store organization. After four years Gardner left the university to do full-time consulting. The position of executive secretary of the Committee was filled by another student of Warner's—William Foote Whyte.

Whyte carried the cultural approach forward until after World War II. After finishing a famous community study of north Boston called *Street Corner Society*

---

[4]Although Professors Elton Mayo and W. Lloyd Warner played major roles in the initiation and collection of data in these studies, it was another Harvard Professor, Fritz Roethlisberger, and William J. Dickson, at the time Chief of Employee Relations Research Department at Western Electric, who analyzed the data and undertook to write a full account of the research studies (Trahair 1984). For a retrospective view of the research effort, see Roethlisberger (1977).

(Whyte 1943) that became his Ph.D. dissertation, Whyte returned to the University to Chicago in 1944 and carried out an ethnographic study of the restaurant industry at Warner and Gardner's invitation. In it Whyte focused primarily on the informal social structure, as he had done in *Street Corner Society,* but also analyzed organizational symbols (Whyte 1948).

All of this research occurred more than three decades before popular books made organizational culture a management fad in the early 1980s. It was made possible by an unusual degre of close cooperation between the progressive managers of two major corporations—Western Electric and Sears Roebuck—and a group of capable and respected academic researchers. Without the long-term access to workplaces, provided by these corporations' managers, such research is not possible. Writing in 1978, Whyte commented, "This strong beginning justified hopes that organizational studies would become a major field for applied antropologists, yet in succeeding years, very few anthropologists joined these pioneers" (Whyte 1978, p. 130). Unfortunately, Warner and Whyte moved on to other interests and pursuits—Warner to further community studies, Whyte to the study of social values and economic development in Peru. We can only speculate that managers and the dominant forces in academia were not sufficiently receptive to their pioneering work on organizational culture to make its continuance attractive to them. As a consultant, Gardner continued to research the social organization of work for Sears Roebuck (Worthy 1991). Much of this work, however, consisted of quantitative surveys—a technique which was then being developed to measure employee morale. Moore worked with Gardner and completed his dissertation during this period (Moore 1954), but Gardner's research for Sears was not published.

Other than Warner, cultural anthropologists had shown little interest in the workplace. Under the influence of Claude Levi-Strauss, the trends in anthropology moved toward examination of exotic and distant cultures rather than those close to home. Even Warner himself had done little actual fieldwork in work organizations. While Whyte did extensive fieldwork, his work focused mostly on group phenomena and only peripherally on cultural matters—specifically on symbolism. In organizational sociology there was a steady decline of interest in small groups and a concomitant turn toward formal structure. The promise inherent in a cultural approach to the study of organizations had only been partially implemented; descriptions and interpretations of cultural forms in the workplace, such as myths, stories, or rites, were rare.

At the same time, the qualitative field methods that characterize the cultural approach were being supplanted by the heady attractions of the computer. High-speed computing permitted the collection of large bodies of quantitative data and the flowering of the techniques of the social survey. The trend had begun with research carried out on the military during World War II; the statistical approaches developed for that research (Stouffer et al. 1950) could now be diffused and practiced by anyone with appropriate training and access to a high-speed computer. Soon a torrent of quantitative studies appeared; they encouraged research into other questions. The structural and psychological variables and theories that lent themselves to quantification became the dominant trends in organizational research from the 1960s to the late 1970s.

But there had been a beginning for the cultural approach. "In five short years there was an unusual flourishing of anthropological and sociological research ... a unique combination of circumstances involving academia, business, a great industrial city, and the times" (Moore 1982, p. 121). It did not revolutionize all of the research on organizations or all of management thought—as quantitative methods and the computer did later. But it did provide the foundation for a modest stream of insightful research and writing on work and organizations done primarily by industrial ethnographers (Gamst 1977).

Scattered Efforts

During the 1950s and 1960s, a few American researchers continued the anthropological tradition begun by Warner and his students. Perhaps the most sustained efforts were made by Donald Roy (1952, 1953, 1954, 1960), who used participant observation to study culture within small work groups and produced results resembling those from the bank wiring room in the Hawthorne studies. Undoubtedly the best-known work from this period was Melville Dalton's *Men Who Manage* (1959). Dalton, who worked in the two companies he studied, focused his research on the extent to which subcultures naturally emerged from workers' needs and documented how these informal groups actually governed much of what happened in these companies. In his accounts, the formal system of rules, titles, and the like served as a backdrop for the real dynamics of social life in industry.

Somewhat related and far more influential in mainstream organizational research was the work of scholars like Philip Selznick, who described the interactions of affected communities and the fledgling Tennessee Valley Authority[5] in terms of how institutions respond to changing circumstances (Selznick 1949). Selznick used the term *institution* to indicate that organizations were more than rational instruments—they were infused with value beyond the technical requirements of tasks (Scott 1987; Selznick 1957). Although a sociologist, Selznick conducted his research much like a cultural anthropologist, gaining his insights on cooptation and institutional leadership from long-term observations and extensive interviewing in the organizations and communities studied.

Meanwhile, in England, a group of social scientists known as the Tavistock Institute began to do research on organizations as cultural systems (Jacques 1951). They experimented in introducing various innovations into organizational cultures, especially beliefs about the positive value of worker participation in organizational decision making. A U.S. researcher in this tradition was F. L. W. Richardson (1955, 1961), who showed how the stress and conflicts generated

---

[5]The Tennessee Valley Authority was created by the U.S. federal government in 1933 to develop the Tennessee River and its tributaries in order to promote inexpensive electrical power, irrigation, and flood control.

by the structuring of work relations affected social interactions, employees' feelings, and productivity in a large electrical design and manufacturing concern.

A few cultural studies of atypical workplaces also appeared during this period. For example, Hortense Powdermaker (1950) did extensive observation in the motion picture industry on the relations of film making crews with those behind the scenes—writers, producers, and studio executives. William Caudill (1958) studied the day-to-day personal relations of doctors, ward personnel, and patients in a psychiatric hospital. Jules Henry's (1963) study of public schools documented how the schools acted as the cultural transmitters of the values of thrift, industry, competitiveness, and cleanliness.

But it was not until the late 1960s that the efforts of several researchers broke through the relative obscurity to which cultural research had been relegated in organizational and management studies. In the United States, a team of researchers led by Harrison Trice interpreted their observations of personnel practices as cultural rites and ceremonials (Trice, Belasco, and Alutto 1969). In England, Barry Turner (1971) wrote a book explicitly exploring both the substance and forms of organizational cultures. His analysis relied heavily on the concepts of British cultural anthropologists. Somewhat later, Andrew Pettigrew, an English sociologist, studied a large retail firm on a long-term basis. His detailed study of the introduction of computers into a retail firm (1973) not only continued the anthropological tradition of participant observation, but also capitalized on multiple methods and sources of data collection to achieve added confidence in the results of his qualitative observations. A few years later, in a highly influential article, he went on to delineate the concept of organizational culture for management research:

> In the pursuit of everyday tasks and objectives, it is all too easy to forget the less rational and less instrumental, the more expressive social tissue around us that gives those tasks meanings. Yet, in order for people to function within any given setting, they must have a continuing sense of what that reality is all about in order to be acted upon. Culture is the system of such collectively accepted meanings operating for a given group at a given time ... and the offsprings of the concept of culture I have in mind are symbol, language, ideology, belief, ritual, and myth. (Pettigrew 1979, p. 574).

A second important study done in the United States at about the same time was Burton Clark's *The Distinctive College* (1970), which documented the importance of what he called organizational sagas in the long-term survival and relative prosperity of three of these institutions. His concept of saga is very similar to that of organizational culture; he may have chosen the term *saga* to emphasize the important role that founders and historical tradition played in these colleges (1972). In an earlier study, he had focused on how organizational values shifted as school organizations adapted to their environments (Clark 1956). Both of these studies used qualitative methods.

The work of another researcher focused attention on the value of qualitative methods *per se*. Quantitative methods had become so dominant in mainstream management research that it was almost revolutionary when Henry Mintzberg systematically observed managers at work. His reports of this research on *The Nature of Managerial Work* (1973) received considerable scholarly attention and were rewritten for several popular publications, including the *Harvard Business Review* (Mintzberg 1975). Although Mintzberg did not focus on organizational culture, his detailed observations of the daily activities of five managers uncovered some cultural aspects of the managerial role. Perhaps because of the topic, or perhaps because of the business-oriented academic circles in which he moved, Mintzberg's work made systematic qualitative methods—the primary tools for studying culture—once again respectable in many circles that had largely ignored qualitative work by sociologists and anthropologists.

The rediscovery of the benefits of qualitative methods, in turn, led to an influential special issue of the *Administrative Science Quarterly* (1979). While this issue did not focus on culture *per se,* the guest editor was John Van Maanen, a professor at the Massachusetts Institute of Technology, who specialized in studying occupational cultures.

The research findings of Pettigrew, Clark, and Mintzberg caught the attention of prominent organizational and management scholars. Their work was published in leading journals and their books were widely cited. Such was not the case for the industrial ethnographers who were active over the same period. They were based in anthropology or folklore departments, where their work was hardly the vogue, and where they had little contact with organizational researchers, who were in sociology departments or management schools. Five researchers of this type deserve mention. Frederick C. Gamst (1980a, 1980b) and Robert S. McCarl (1974, 1976) studied the cultures of colorful occupations. C. S. Holzberg and M. J. Giovannini (1981) integrated a broad range of prior research on work cultures from many different societies in an annotated bibliography. Marietta Baba (1986) summarized the practical implications of these and other studies for workplace cultures. An exception is Michael O. Jones, Director of the Folklore and Mythology Center at the University of California at Los Angeles, who not only encouraged cultural research in organizations, but reached out to address the issues of application that concern researchers in organizations and management (Jones, 1988).

Recent Revitalization

Although the study of organizational cultures was not new, it certainly received a big impetus in the 1980s. Two best-selling books were widely interpreted as saying that orgnizational cultures were important for organizational productivity and adaptability: Peters and Waterman's *In Search of Excellence* (1982) and Ouchi's *Theory Z* (1981). At about the same time, two other books on organizational cultures garnered widespread attention from managers and the press (Pascale and Athos, 1981; Deal and Kennedy, 1982). Many business and trade magazines featured articles on the topic. Between March 1983 and October 1984, five major conferences on corporate culture and organizational folklore and symbolism were held (Jones 1984, p. 8), many of them bringing managers and scholars together. The proceedings of three of these were published as books (Pondy et al. 1983; Frost et al. 1985;

Kilmann et al. 1985). Three academic journals—*The Journal of Management Studies*(1982), *Administrative Science Quarterly* (1983), and *Journal of Management* (1985), and one journal oriented to managers, *Organizational Dynamics* (1983)—published special issues on the topic. Two academically oriented textbooks on organizational cultures appeared in 1985 (Schein 1985; Sathe 1985). More recently, four books of readings (Jones, Moore, and Snyder 1988; Turner 1990c; Gagliardi 1990; Frost et al. 1991), another textbook (Ott 1989), a book-length research report (Denison 1990, and a book-length ethnography (Kunda 1991) have appeared.

During the early 1980s, meetings of professional associations like the Academy of Management and the Institute for Decision Sciences began to include special symposia on culture. Since 1980, an international group of scholars calling themselves The Standing Committee on Organizational Symbolism has held annual conferences in Canada and Europe and published a newsletter, *SCOS Note-Work*. Inevitably, new courses sprang up in degree programs at numerous colleges and universities. A listing of Ph.D. theses by the library of the Industrial and Labor Relations School at Cornell University revealed that between 1980 and 1985 nineteen doctoral dissertations dealing with some aspect of organizational culture were written. Researchers reported that in 1979 they found about fifty studies with the word *myth* in the title or abstract; by late 1981, they found more than five hundred such articles (Broms and Gahmberg 1982, p. 30)—an increase of more than 1,000 percent in just two years!

What made the concept of organizational culture suddenly so attractive to managers, the press, and scholars? Two sets of parallel developments led in this direction. One was the turbulence and difficulties that U.S. firms were experiencing in competing with organizations from countries with very different cultures. The second was a growing realization by some organizational scholars that structural-rational approaches to understanding organizations missed crucial aspects of how organizations functioned and how they affected the lives of their members (Pondy and Mitroff 1979).

Following World War II, the supremacy of U.S. management went practically unchallenged. Many other societies looked to the United States to solve major productivity problems of the world with technical and managerial knowhow. But in the 1970s, the superiority of U.S. managerial skills and ideas came into question as Japan, a country with a drastically different culture, became the United States' chief competitor for economic leadership of the world. The question on everyone's mind was whether it was cultural differences that accounted for the unparalleled productivity of Japanese organizations. The cultures of U.S. work organizations became candidates for blame. Environmental forces were demanding change and many U.S. managers began to see that past practices may have discouraged innovation, quality, and cooperation; they apparently even failed to achieve the high productivity to which they were oriented. Managers and analysts also began to realize that changing organizations would not be easy without an understanding of the cultures that had grown up within these organizations; they began to see culture as both an impediment to change and a possible vehicle for achieving it.

The downturn in the U.S. economy in the 1970s had generated much anxiety and conflict between workers and management. Many U.S. workers and managers were unemployed for the first time in their lives. Learning of the apparent harmony in Japanese workplaces, U.S. managers began to see culture as a way to integrate managers' and workers' concerns to create some consensus and cooperation in their organizations. Managers and workers needed reassurance; increasing the coherence of the internal cultures in their organizations seemed a good way to achieve it. And if harmony could be achieved, it was bound to contribute to managerial control, increase performance and profits, and generally help to make U.S. industry competitive again. Culture became in some managers' eyes just another seductive "quick fix" for their problems (Kilmann 1984).

Even before the 1970s, some organizational scholars were growing disillusioned with the assumptions inherent in largely rational, bureaucratic models of organizations. The rational model had been modified and stretched to its limits (Thompson 1967), and still something essential to the realities of organizational life was missing. Perhaps the most influential work to set forth an alternative, much more subjective, view of organizations was Karl Weick's *The Social Psychology of Organizing,* published in 1969. Weick emphasized how people's cognitive processes and social interactions shaped organizations in nonrational ways. Like its title, his analysis also emphasized the fluidity and emergent nature of organizational life. Other researchers had become frustrated trying to apply the bureaucratic model to universities (Cohen, March, and Olsen 1972) and to Japanese organizations. One set of researchers, who studied Japanese-managed organizations in the United States, reported: " . . . we cannot describe adequately how different the atmosphere is in an organization where 50 to 80 percent of the personnel have Japanese origins . . . " (Lincoln, Olson, and Hanada 1978, p. 834). By the late 1970s, several researchers had advanced theories that severely questioned the rational bureaucratic view; they suggested organizations were loosely coupled systems (Weick 1976) and were permeated with myth and ceremony (Trice, Belasco, and Alutto 1969; Meyer and Rowan 1977).

Closely aligned with models of organizations are the methods used to study them. Some researchers were also becoming disillusioned with quantitative methods and quasi-experimental designs (Ouchi and Wilkins 1985) because of the relatively trivial amounts of variance they explained, the lack of comparability of results across studies, their failure to achieve much predictive validity, and the incomprehensibility their sophisticated methods contributed to reports of research. Furthermore, causality was often indeterminate or so complex that managers could not gain much insight from such research into how to change organizations in beneficial ways (Van Maanen 1982). In addition, critics pointed out, quantitative methods encouraged researchers to separate themselves from the phenomena that made up organizational life and spend limited time—if any—in organizations to collect their data (Beyer 1984). The resulting reports seemed sterile; they missed the drama, excitement, and high emotion that characterizes much of what happens daily in organizations.

In an effort to be scientific, organizational researchers had reduced their phenomena to such simplistic models that it had lost its richness and human character. Managers were understandably suspicious of the relevance of such abstracted research because it ignored many of the specificities their experience told them were important; so they did not use its results. Research on utilization found that managers were more likely to use the results of more detailed, qualitative studies (Beyer and Trice 1982).

These dissatisfactions led to a revival of interest in qualitative methods as well as in culture. Each revival reinforced the other, for qualitative methods almost invariably surface something of cultural significance and the accepted ways of doing cultural research involve qualitative methods. While there has been a drop-off of managerial attention to culture since the early 1980s, organizational research seems to have been permanently transformed. More researchers have been doing more qualitative studies than in the past, and more of these focus specifically on cultural phenomena. The accumulated literature is already large and of sufficient quality to merit study by students aspiring to become managers and those aspiring to become researchers of organizations and management.

SUMMARY

People in organizations develop cultures as they interact and share ways of managing and coping with uncertainties. Cultures have two components: (1) substance, which consists of shared systems of beliefs, values, and norms; and (2) forms, which are observable ways that members of a culture express cultural ideas. By reducing the potential variability of human behavior, cultures provide some degree of order and continuity in social life. Cultures have many distinctive characteristics that highlight aspects of organizations missed by other approaches and that make the analysis and study of organizational cultures both fruitful and challenging. Analysts do not agree on all aspects of culture. There is some danger that the concept will be used so broadly that it will lose its value. Also, some confusion has arisen between related concepts and culture.

Cultural research in organizations is not a recent development. The Hawthorne studies at Western Electric in the early 1930s involved an anthropologist and included observations of workgroup cultures. This work stimulated a brief flowering of cultural research in work organizations and provided the foundation for scattered efforts by sociologists and anthropologists until the 1970s. The books of the early 1980s that made culture a popular fad among managers followed a series of influential studies and publications by English and U.S. organizational scholars that revived qualitative methods and illustrated their value with new insights. The revival of interest in organizational cultures has continued in academic circles throughout the 1980s and has produced a substantial body of research.

But many gaps remain in our knowledge of organizational cultures. Also, the cultural approach focuses primarily on the expressive side of organizations. Thus, in the chapters that follow we will integrate the findings of cultural research with those of other approaches to organizations. Our aim is to provide a richer, more accurate, and more insightful picture of organizations than has been available using other perspectives.

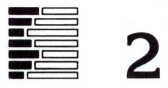

2

The Substance
of Organizational Cultures

As explained in Chapter 1, the actual content or substance of a culture resides in its ideologies. People are "meaning-seeking animals" (Geertz 1973, p. 140). These meanings are embodied in their cultures as ideologies—shared, interrelated sets of beliefs about how things work; values that indicate what's worth having or doing; and norms that tell people how they should behave.

Ideologies tend to be rather general sets of ideas, but they are powerful in specific situations because they link actions and fundamental beliefs. Ideologies are not mere intellectual theorizing about the world and how it works. They are emotionally charged, fundamental belief systems that impel people to act in certain ways. Ideologies also fulfill two major social functions: (1) the sharing of beliefs, values, and norms incorporated in their ideologies binds groups of people together and thus promotes their social solidarity; (2) the rationalized understandings that ideologies provide help to sustain individuals in enacting their social roles (Apter 1964).

For the purpose of analyzing decision making in organizations, a definition of ideologies was developed specifically to apply to organizational and managerial behavior (Beyer 1981, p. 166). For the purpose of analyzing the broader topic of culture, this definition must be expanded to include related values and norms. Ideologies, in a cultural sense, can best be defined as *shared, relatively coherently interrelated sets of emotionally charged beliefs, values, and norms that bind some people together and help them to make sense of their worlds.* While usually closely interrelated in actual behavior, beliefs, values, and norms are distinct concepts. Ideological beliefs express cause and effect relations; for example, that certain behaviors will lead to certain outcomes.[1] Values express preferences for certain behaviors or

---

[1]One theorist suggests that beliefs can describe nature, societies, or the believers themselves; can express why particular states of nature, self, or society occur; or can describe preferred states of

33

for certain outcomes. Norms express which behaviors are expected by others and are culturally acceptable ways to attain outcomes.

When beliefs, values, and norms develop over time into the relatively stable, unified, and coherent clusters that comprise ideologies, they provide causal models for explaining and legitimating collective and individual behaviors. Ideologies explain and justify existing social systems in ways that make them seem natural, logically compelling, and morally acceptable.

Max Weber's analysis of *The Protestant Ethic* provides a classic example of this process. The beliefs of the Calvinist doctrine provided the basis for the growth of this ideology. It taught that the impulses and desires of human beings must be subjected to God's will in order for them to attain salvation, but that each individual's fate was predestined. The only way to demonstrate that one was among "the chosen" was to accumulate tangible evidence of God's favor through unremitting work in a worldly calling. Such beliefs dictated both hard work and determined renunciation of enjoying the results of that work. Money and wealth could be accrued as signs of God's favor—but not spent lavishly in pursuit of worldly enjoyments. Instead, the wealth so accrued provided capital for the accumulation of further wealth and the exploitation of natural resources (Sahlins 1974). Thus the Protestant ethic laid the foundations of modern capitalism. This belief system carried with it associated values favoring rugged individualism and individual success and norms prescribing hard work and achievement as acceptable routes to success. Powerful residues of these norms and values persist within many Western societies including the United States (Jackall 1988).

The Protestant ethic also illustrates three important features of ideologies. First, through norms, ideologies often compel people to action. When people believe behavior *A* will lead to outcome *B* and they prefer outcome *B* to other possible outcomes for themselves and others, they are likely to feel compelled to exhibit behavior *A* and urge others to do so as well. Most Calvinists worked hard because this was the accepted way to demonstrate that they were among the chosen. The belief system was so strong that *not* to do so involved outcomes too threatening for most people to even consider. Second, the beliefs embodied in ideologies become imbued with strong emotions. People naturally cared very deeply about whether they would attain salvation and therefore wanted to believe that hard work and renunciations would ensure they were among the chosen. Third, ideologies provide consistent moral justifications for intended and past behaviors. Another interpretation of the role of the Protestant ethic is that it gave meaning to economic behaviors already underway (Poggi 1983) as the feudal systems of Europe disintegrated. The hard work, renunciation, and the accumulation of capital of a new class of merchants and artisans were made morally acceptable if they were God's will.

---

nature or being (Sproull 1981, p. 204). All, however, involve understandings about relationships between things or between things and their characteristics (Bem 1970). It is this relational quality of beliefs we think is especially central in ideologies in particular and cultures in general.

The Development of Ideologies

Beliefs: The Ideological Core

Because beliefs seem to form the core of ideologies, analyses of beliefs are highly relevant to understanding what ideologies are, where they come from, and how they work. A belief is "an understanding that represents credible relationships between objects, properties, and ideas" (Sproull 1981, p. 204). Beliefs result from people making sense of stimuli, and are heavily influenced by language and social interaction.

Since people's encounters with stimuli give rise to beliefs, behaviors can shape beliefs. Their own behaviors largely determine what range of stimuli people are likely to encounter. Also, their awareness of certain behaviors tends to unconsciously and involuntarily emphasize ideas justifying those behaviors and to deemphasize ideas that would make the same behaviors look irrational or wrong. In effect, people justify behaviors both prospectively and retrospectively by what they believe. These human tendencies have been well documented in a variety of natural settings (Garfinkel 1967), including business organizations (Nystrom and Starbuck 1984a), and in laboratory experiments (Staw 1976).

Beliefs, especially those incorporated in ideologies, come to be imbued with powerful emotions. The fervor with which many people hold their religious and political beliefs are good examples. But many other classes of beliefs provoke similar fervor. The historian Thomas Kuhn (1970) pointed out that, when faced with evidence inconsistent with their scientific theories, most scientists have usually fought to defend and try to fix up the old theories rather than accept new ones. A whole line of subsequent research has revealed the extent to which the amount of consensus in various scientific fields about scientific ideologies—which Kuhn called paradigms—affects the structuring of university departments (Lodahl and Gordon 1972, 1973a, 1973b; Beyer and Lodahl 1976); the use of power in university decision making (Pfeffer, Salancik, and Leblebici 1976; Pfeffer and Salancik 1974); the values placed on specific resources in times of scarcity (McKinley, Cheng, and Schick 1986); and the policies and practices of scientific journals (Beyer 1978; Pfeffer, Leong, and Strehl 1977). All of these studies show that scientific paradigms carry subjective and nonrational elements even though the overall ideologies of science encourage objectivity and rationality.

An interesting attempt to uncover corporate belief systems was undertaken by two doctoral students at the Massachusetts Institute of Technology (Dougherty and Kunda 1990). They analyzed photographs that appeared in the annual reports of five large computer manufacturers over a ten-year period and uncovered strong consistencies in the beliefs that these photographs conveyed about the nature of the customers of these firms and their relationships with them. IBM consistently portrayed its customers as service providers—clerical and secretarial workers, librarians, sales people, policemen, and middle managers. Digital Equipment portrayed its customers as complex networks and as engineering-oriented problem solvers and its workers as active, hard-working males, professionals, and technicians. Data General's customers were pictured as skilled laborers and technicians—more plain folks than professionals. Burroughs portrayed its customers as relatively isolated processors of information in work stations, control rooms, and other technological settings. Honeywell showed small groups of professionals interacting to monitor and control large projects and entities. Clearly, if these photos accurately reflect the beliefs of top management in these companies about their customers, they suggest and justify quite different marketing strategies and practices.

Multiplicity of Ideologies

Because ideologies develop gradually over time in response to specific uncertainties and circumstances faced by human groups, cultural differences arise. First, different people living at different times and in different places develop different ideologies that help them to understand and cope with the particular circumstances they face. Second, even within groups, subgroups develop unique understandings and "solutions" for the specific problems they face that they embody in their own ideologies. The ideas they develop for coping with these problems and uncertainties will not necessarily be communicated to those who perform other tasks—both because it is not necessary for group survival and because the possession of these task-specific ideologies has value and gives the subgroup a special and often advantageous status in the larger group. Because there are many possible solutions to many different problems and uncertainties, cultures incorporate a multiplicity of ideologies.

Single cultures have multiplicities of ideologies not only because of diversities, but just because ideas accrete over time. Although groups may face different problems and uncertainties during their history, they also have some continuity in their experiences. So they save parts of the old understandings and solutions even as they develop new ones. New ideological edifices are often constructed on basic understandings provided by the old. When the old understandings do not seem applicable to new circumstances, new edifices may be constructed without explicitly taking the old ideologies into account. But in the process, even those ideologies that are not needed anymore tend to be saved because people have imbued them with strong emotions. Also, particular strands of an ideology can become separated over time as new bundles of ideas are created. For example, the value of rugged individualism has become so separated from the Calvinist doctrine in American society that it can be used to justify the pursuit of individual enjoyment, as in lyrics of the song "I Did It My Way." In addition, as one analyst observed, patterns of behaviors consistent with the Protestant ethic have outlasted its ideas. The effects of its ideologies persisted by generating certain ways of organizing action that endured even after the "spur of the Calvinist quest for proof of salvation had been lost" (Swidler 1986, p. 276). The result of this accretion process is that the history of a group is carried forward in its ideologies, although sometimes in disguised and altered form. Some residue of the past remains and can be activated if circumstances call it forth from collective memories.

The multiple ideologies that cultures incorporate probably contribute to their adaptiveness and their persistence. Different sets of beliefs can be activated to deal with perceived threats to a cultural group. If one ideology isn't applicable or doesn't work, the group has other possibilities it can call upon.

The different ideologies contained within a single culture are not necessarily logically consistent with one another. Because they grow up over time in relation to differing circumstances, beliefs can be formulated in relative isolation from past understandings of problems seen as different. This process inevitably leads to internal contradictions among the ideologies that make up specific cultures. People are able to live with these contradictions because they don't usually feel impelled to resolve them. Instead, they hold their ideologies somewhat apart from one another. It's as if each set of ideas formed a separate bundle, and the bundles were stacked on one another as they were acquired. When something happens to make one or another bundle salient, all of the ideas that are in that particular bundle are unpacked and activated (Swidler 1986). Other bundles will lie dormant unless they too are somehow connected to the present event.

Of course, specific events can sometimes activate more than one bundle, particularly when different subgroups with somewhat different collective experiences and interests in the current event are involved. This is when ideological contradictions are likely to surface, leading to conflict within individuals or between subgroups within the culture. For example, incidents involving substance abuse can arouse quite different sets of values and beliefs, depending on the circumstances surrounding the incident. If illegal drugs are found in administrative searches of a student's locker in a high school, some parents and students will react with moral indignation and sentiments favoring punishment of wrongdoers; others will respond with concerns for due process and privacy. If the use of alcohol or drugs is documented in a ship, airplane, or train accident, people remember their ideologies about safety and performance. If a popular basketball player or entertainer publicly admits to drug addiction and voluntarily seeks treatment, many will view the episode in humanitarian terms tinged with moralism. If a company decides to begin involuntary drug testing, those who favor this practice will evoke ideologies about safety and performance; those who oppose it will evoke ideologies of mutual trust and rights to privacy.

Much of the time human groups manage to avoid direct confrontation between contradictory ideologies by such devices as decoupling, avoidance, good faith, discretion, overlooking, and mediatory myths (Meyer and Rowan 1977; Abravanel 1983). Decoupling minimizes or avoids formal inspection, evaluations, and control of activities and thus avoids confronting whether all are conforming to the same standards. People's confidence in one another is maintained by having faith in others' specialized knowledge and values, by allowing them discretion to pursue their own activities, and by overlooking anomalies that arise. Various myths arise to justify these practices and mediate relationships between units that might otherwise be in conflict.

Spontaneous and Emergent Characteristics

Ideologies generally emerge from social processes that are unplanned and spontaneous. Even ideologies associated with specific leaders—many religious and political ideologies, for example—were not formulated in a single day from a single mind. Similarly, although specific organizational leaders are often credited with the philosophies of their organizations, followers and historical circumstances usually played an important role in the gradual development of these ideologies, as is detailed in chapters 7 and 8.

> Successful institutions are usually able to fill in the formula, "what we are proud of around here is . . . ". Sometimes, a fairly explicit institutional philosophy is *worked out*; more often, a sense of mission is communicated in more *indirect*, but no less significant ways. (Selznick 1957, p. 151 [emphasis added])

New groups need to work out their ideologies over time because they cannot fully anticipate in advance the precise nature of the challenges and problems they will face. All groups need to adapt their ideologies to changing circumstances; their worlds continually present them with new uncertainties. People usually make sense of these uncertainties gradually and only partially by deliberate cognitive processes. To deal with new and changing circumstances, individuals act—they try out innovations, large and small, that can be adapted and imitated by others if they seem successful or their proponents are especially influential or persuasive.

While organizations are larger and more complex than groups, most undoubtedly develop ideologies over time. It is difficult to imagine an established organization that holds nothing in deep respect, holds no beliefs about what is valued and how to achieve it, treats all decisions as an open question, and sets no principles to guide and justify decisions. To the degree that organizations do these things, they have ideologies.

Implicitness

With the passage of time, ideologies tend to move from the forefront to the background of peoples' attention and conscious thought. As it is being formulated, an ideology may be highly articulated as a self-conscious belief system, complete with associated rituals and other cultural forms. After being acted upon and further articulated, the ideology begins to be taken for granted as an inevitable part of ongoing social life. In effect, it becomes part of the traditional way of interpreting and dealing with certain circumstances. Finally, with continuing expression and use, ideologies come to be viewed as nondebatable ways of understanding such events and as natural, undeniable guides for behavior. Data, evidence, facts, and proof are not required. By these largely nonrational processes, an ideology becomes a tradition, and finally "common sense" (Swidler 1986, p. 279).

Popular treatments of organizational culture differ greatly in their views about how easy or hard it is to uncover the ideologies implicit in these cultures. One extreme considers the ideologies that make up an organization's culture as so hidden and illusive that they can only be revealed—and then only partly—by outside specialists studying them for a long time. Another views these ideologies as so obvious that they can be easily uncovered. This book takes a stance between these extremes by suggesting that underlying ideologies can be detected and read from intimate knowledge of a culture and of the historical and social context in which a culture is embedded. Such knowledge takes a considerable time and sustained observations to acquire. A brief examination of each of these three views of culture should help to make their rationales more evident.

It's hidden.   Those who believe that cultural ideologies are very difficult to uncover argue that deep-seated and unconscious phenomena guide the construction of meaning and thus of ideologies. Because these phenomena reside outside human consciousness, they must be deduced from conscious expressions such as language (Pondy 1978), mental imagery (Mitroff 1983), or psychopathological behaviors (Kets de Vries and Miller 1984). This view of culture tantalizes with the promise of "deep" insights waiting to be discovered, but makes their discovery difficult and uncertain. Resulting insights tend to be rather abstract and amorphous.

One set of results from such deductions suggests symbolic archetypes—"highly charged, affect-ridden, intensively human personages" (Mitroff and Mason 1983, p. 153)—that help organizational members derive meaning from specific collective experiences. Examples are young man, young woman, the wise old man, the wise old woman, sorcerer, temptress, witch, priest, Adam, king, queen, hunter.

Another is a typology of neurotic cultures mirroring the deep-seated neuroses of their CEOs. Only psychoanalysis of the CEO can reveal whether he or she is paranoid, compulsive, histrionic, depressive, or schizoid (Kets de Vries and Miller 1984). The correspondence these analysts see between the CEO's personality and culture are briefly summarized in Table 1–5.

Perhaps the most extreme version of the view that the substance of culture is hidden and hard to discover is the theory offered by the noted anthropologist Claude Levi-Strauss. He analyzed myth and ideology in tribal societies in a search for a universally shared, unconscious order in human behavior. This order is presumed to come from a primitive, nonrational logic that is shared by all of humanity and that is expressed in its clearest, uncontaminated form in primitive myths (Leach 1980). The articulation and validation of this universal logic, which can be viewed as the basis of all culture, would require patient and painstaking analysis that is just beginning.

It's obvious.   The view that ideologies can be easily discovered is exemplified by writers who suggest that the substance of existing cultures can be discovered quite readily through a combination of such devices as surveys, informal conversations, unsystematic observations, direct participation, taped interviews, and analysis of "existing performance and bottomline results" (Silverzweig and Allen

1976, p. 36). One researcher used surveys of "individual perceptions of organizational practices and conditions . . . to characterize the culture" of individual organizations (Denison 1984, p. 8). These authors are not alone; many other examples could be cited. As explained in Chapter 1 in the discussion of organizational climate, while such methods may uncover some shared perceptions and practices, it is far from clear that what is uncovered is cultural. Often this view and its methods yield shallow insights because they tend to repackage familiar ideas about employee attitudes, interpersonal relations, and organizational structure with a few accounts of cultural features like myths, stories, and rituals.

Defining culture solely in terms of cognitions allows another group of researchers to argue that they can measure a culture and compare cultures with profiles of preestablished values or norms (e.g., Cooke and Rousseau 1988; O'Reilly, Chatman, and Caldwell 1991). Methods used in these studies assume that (1) members of organizations are sufficiently aware of their own values (or norms) and those of their organizations to give valid answers about them; and (2) that organizational cultures may have unique profiles but that the same values (or norms) can be used to characterize the cultures of many different organizations. These researchers in effect assume there is a generic, universal set of organizational values (or norms). While making such assumptions makes it possible to measure any organizational culture and compare it with any other, they are assumptions which many experts on culture do not accept.

A very carefully executed series of studies of this genre found that patterns of individuals' reported values remained quite stable over a period of 12 months. Also, key informants from accounting firms agreed quite well on which values characterized their organizations (O'Reilly, Chatman, and Caldwell 1991). The list of 54 values used to measure individuals' and firms' cultures in these studies was generated by the researchers without inputs from actual members of those firms; thus, the approach used was etic. The following are examples of some of the values used: opportunities, stability, respect for the individual, action oriented, precise, and competitive. Statistical techniques indicated that responses to these values clustered into interpretable groupings focused on 7 to 8 issues such as innovation, stability, and respect for people. The relative specificity and superficiality of these values is not consistent with the view of culture as emotionally charged, fuzzy, and embedded in a rich, historically based social context. Because of the different social contexts in which they are embedded, the cultural meanings of these terms probably varies across firms. Words, after all, can have many meanings. Also, because the list of terms presented to respondents is limited, it is not clear that they capture all that their cultures mean to members of organizations; unique elements may be missed. Attempts to probe organizational cultures more widely and deeply will be discussed in the next section. One possibility is to study the same culture with more than one type of method (Rousseau 1990).

It's possible to uncover.   Other researchers, including the authors of this book, believe that the substance of culture can be read with diligence, appropriate skills, and fairly extensive exposure to the social group involved. This view takes the position that although ideologies are implicit, they can be uncovered from explorations with members of the culture coupled with interpretations of cultural forms in use. While there is a gap between overt, superficial statements and actions and their underlying cultural meanings, this gap is not so wide that only a probing of people's unconscious will call it forth.

One approach, suggested by Edgar Schein (1985), is to assume that all cultures are based on a single, limited set of deeply hidden, underlying beliefs or assumptions that past research has already discovered. The task of the organizational analyst would then consist of collecting information that would allow the classification of each group or organization according to its position on each assumption. Because this approach assumes that the substance of different cultures concerns the same basic issues, it has some similarity to that of Levi-Strauss. It differs from his approach not only in assuming that universal underlying assumptions have already been discovered, but in not investigating whether the same assumptions could be generated in the settings currently being studied.

Schein (1985, p. 86) used the findings from a comparative study of five community cultures in the southwestern United States (Kluckhohn and Strodtbeck 1961) as the source of assumptions he applied to cultures of modern American work organizations. While a careful and massive study, this community study involved very different kinds of social units: (1) an off-reservation settlement of Navaho Indians, (2) a tiny on-reservation community of Pueblo Indians; (3) a Spanish-speaking village with a long history of economic decline; (4) a village of Mormon emigrants who came to the area to proselytize the local native Indians; and (5) a community of immigrants from Texas and Oklahoma who were rather successful homesteaders. All were located in a 2,000 square mile area called the Colorado Plateau and therefore constitute a rather unusual and localized population from which to derive a set of universal values.

The value orientations identified in these communities were modified slightly by Schein (1985, p. 14) to yield the following "basic underlying assumptions": (1) humanity's relationship to its environment; (2) the nature of reality, time, and space; (3) the nature of human nature; (4) the nature of human activity; and (5) the nature of human relationships. Applying these assumptions to organizations suggested to him the following kinds of questions.

- Does the organization attempt to dominate, find a niche, harmonize, or submit to its environment?
- What are the basic notions in the organization about time and space and how truth is determined?
- What does it mean to be human?
- What is the right thing for humans to do, given the above assumptions?
- What is the right way for people to relate to one another, to distribute power, and how cooperative and competitive should they be? (Schein 1985)

This list of assumptions and the very general questions they raise provide a possible starting point for exploring specific organizational cultures, but there are some limitations. First, the very generality of the assumptions puts them on a rather rarified plane that is very different from the everyday concerns and preoccupations of members of organizations. Second, this is a very logical, rational set of assumptions; people's most basic underlying beliefs are neatly divided into discrete categories that are unlikely to match the actual ways in which different people's cultural beliefs are tied or bundled together. Third, by making assumptions the underlying and most basic part of culture, Schein downplays the crucial role of symbolism.[2] Fourth, these assumptions seem to overemphasize the fixedness of human cultures in a way that may not apply to organizations; organization members may be able to change more specific organizationally-relevant beliefs and values considerably and not change their positions on these assumptions. Fifth, in its abstractness and orderliness, this formulation fails to acknowledge that cultures are charged with emotions and full of contradictions and ambiguities.

In addition, as discussed in Chapter 1, using categories developed elsewhere to apply to a culture constitutes what anthropologists call the etic approach, in which researchers supply the categories into which the subject's world is organized (Morey and Luthans 1984, p. 29). With these predetermined categories, researchers can range across many different cultures, attempting to place each relative to the others on each category. But such an approach assumes that the predetermined categories used are relevant to the culture at hand and that these categories will not miss any important part of that culture. In contrast, the emic approach attempts to develop categories and meanings for a culture on the basis of talking to and observing its natives.

Both approaches have their value. Using the etic approach facilitates generalizing across human groups in at least limited ways and making broad comparisons among them. Such an approach, for example, underlies the development of typologies—including a typology of six types of organizational rites and ceremonials (Trice 1985; Trice and Beyer 1984a) (to be discussed in detail in Chapter 3) that we developed from an examination of the literature on tribal societies and the literature on work organizations.[3] The emic approach attempts to uncover what is unique about each culture, and so largely eliminates possibilities for generalizing empirical findings to other circumstances. Concepts and theories generated in emic research provide ideas for future investigations.

Schein's approach involves a blending of both. In accepting categories obtained elsewhere, his approach is etic, but the methods he suggests for probing how organizations fit those categories are emic. He advocates prolonged expo-

---

[2]Schein does not directly address the many issues involved in symbolism as part of his analysis of culture; symbolism is not even listed in the index of his book. He does, however, deal with cultural forms in passing. The third and most visible level of culture in his conception of culture is labelled artifacts and creations; he specifies technology, art, and visible and audible behavior as belonging at this level. His view of culture is thus very different from ours and from that of many anthropologists, who assign symbols and cultural forms a more central role in culture.

[3]Using an etic approach to classify rites or other cultural forms is, however, different than using such an approach to study cultural substance. Cultural forms, by their very nature, have regularity, structure, and observability. Common features can thus be easily and reliably determined. The cultural messages carried by forms, however, may vary greatly across cultures and therefore require emic methods to uncover their particulars.

sure, interviewing, contact with informants, and other methods suited to emic inquiry. He also rejects the idea that cultures can be understood from responses to questionnaires (Schein 1985, p. 136). In general, he emphasizes the difficulty of uncovering underlying assumptions. He also suggests that they can probably only be understood by someone from the same national culture (Schein 1985, p. 117).

Like the assumptions that Schein focuses on as the basic substance of culture, ideologies are belief systems that have become so commonplace that people introduce their expression with phrases like: "It goes without saying that . . ." or "It's perfectly natural that . . .". They differ from Schein's conception of assumptions in that ideologies often involve more specific ideas and are not necessarily so deeply hidden as Schein argues assumptions are. People, however, do become so accustomed to their ideologies and so immersed in their symbolic expressions that they are not always fully aware of them and their significance. The sensitive observer, however, can often detect what is not obvious to the participants. It is relatively easy, for example, to detect the symbolic and its meanings in the lives of people different from ourselves. For ourselves it is more difficult—but not impossible—without resorting to psychoanalysis or convoluted analyses of unconscious meanings. This is because cultural meanings are not only in people's heads; rather they are ideas that are shared by social actors. They occur between, as well as in them. In this sense, cultural meanings have some public manifestations and therefore must be at least somewhat observable. Also, members of a culture cannot be completely unaware of its ideologies and prescriptions all of the time. If they were, how could they socialize newcomers to their culture? How could they live by it? And how would they know when it had been violated?

One analyst suggests that organizational cultures are likely to be more accessible at some times than at others (Louis 1985b, p. 133). Disruptions, for example, may reveal a culture through perceived violations of it. Corporate mergers and the entry of new members into work groups are examples of such disruptions. Another good opportunity to detect cultural ideologies is in situations of contrast. "Newcomers, for example, are likely to be more aware of understandings associated with both the settings they are entering and the settings they have left than are insiders in either place" (Louis 1985b, p. 134). In addition, rebels who challenge existing ideologies raise everyone's consciousness of them.

One of the preeminent examples of an emic approach to studying culture is the work of the anthropologist Clifford Geertz. Feeling that the quest for a set of universal meanings is futile, he worked to uncover the ideologies of cultures by careful observation and interpretation. He described his methods (Geertz 1973, p. 30) as follows: "[I tried] to keep the analyses of symbolic form as closely tied as I could to concrete social events and occasions, the public world of common life. And to organize it in such a way that the connections between theoretical formulations and descriptive interpretations were unobscured." His general strategy was to observe a sequence of relevant empirical events in detail from a number of perspectives. He called this strategy *thick description*. From these descriptions, he was able to then precipitate out recurrent beliefs and meanings.

It is important to note that Geertz used public events—not mysterious hidden fantasies or private attitudes of individuals—to generate his data. This makes his approach appropriate and practical for the study of organizations and management.

Classic Explanations of Ideologies

There are two major explanations for the origins and role of ideologies in human culture: interest theory and strain theory (Geertz 1964, p. 52). Interest theory sees ideology as a weapon in a universal and unending struggle among social classes, each seeking to advance certain interests its members hold in common. In particular, ideology is a vehicle for the capture and exercise of political power and economic advantage. This view has been most elaborated in Marxian thought and scholarship, which holds that the dominant ideology is that of the ruling class. Strain theory takes a broader view of ideology. Its general tenets are that (1) social life inevitably produces ambiguities, conflicts, and other strains; and (2) that people use ideologies to deal with the anxieties arising from those strains. Its proponents argue that interest theory neglects these basic functions served by ideologies. Accordingly, strain theory emphasizes "the role that ideologies play in defining (or obscuring) social categories, stabilizing (or upsetting) social expectations, maintaining (or undermining) social norms, strengthening (or weakening) social consensus, relieving (or exacerbating) social tensions" (Geertz 1964, p. 53).

Another scholar who found interest theory too limiting was Reinhard Bendix, who pointed out that ideologies "can be explained only in part as rationalizations of self-interest; they also result from the legacy of institutions and ideas which is 'adopted' by each generation much as a child adopts the grammar of his native language" (Bendix 1970, p. 67). That historical legacies are part of the make-up of ideologies is often overlooked by the proponents of interest theory.

Because shared belief systems can crystallize within virtually *any* long-lasting human group—including nation states, social classes, professional groups, formal organizations, organizational subunits, and others—it seems unduly restrictive to limit the use of the term *ideology* to only those beliefs, held by certain social classes, that are used to further their domination of other social classes. The broader view of ideology consistent with strain theory is more useful for analyzing organizations and can subsume the narrower conception of interest theory within it (Beyer, Dunbar, and Meyer 1988).

Strain Theory in Organizations

Basic to strain theory is the idea that all human societies suffer from chronic malintegration. Anxiety is inevitably produced because "no social arrangement is or can be completely successful in coping with the functional problems it inevitably faces" (Geertz 1964, p. 54). All cultures are permeated with insoluble contradictions, ambivalence, and puzzles. Liberty conflicts with political order, stability with incessant and inevitable change, precision with flexibility, and so on.

A penetrating analysis of the American business creed (Sutton et al. 1956) showed how inherent contradictions and ambivalences cause strains in the entrepreneurial role (Chatov 1973). For example, the creed's emphasis on the small businessman conflicts with the increasing size of corporations, its emphasis on individualism is incompatible with the structural bureaucracy of large companies, and the self-perpetuating management control found in many companies is at odds with the democratic ethos of the wider society. These and other contradictions produce considerable strain in individuals and in society that is managed by selective application and variants of the compensating, defensive beliefs embodied in the creed. Thus, although it is more myth than reality, the business creed provides ideologies to which many business leaders strongly adhere.

Ideologies lessen strain by fulfilling four functions: catharsis, morality, solidarity, and advocacy (Geertz 1964). The cathartic function is accomplished when emotional tension is lessened through projection of blame and anger onto symbolic enemies. The moral function applies when ideologies either deny chronic strain outright or else legitimize its existence in terms of higher values. Solidarity is realized when ideologies knit a group or social class together by creating a sense of community. Ideologies "lend dignity to everyday activities and elicit members' commitment by transforming formal organizations into beloved institutions" (Meyer 1982b, p. 47). Finally, ideologies perform an advocacy function when they articulate strains, calling attention to them, often polarizing them, and in the process making it difficult to ignore and neglect them.

While serving these important functions, however, ideologies may also have dysfunctions. The projection of blame upon symbolic enemies that ideology provides may encourage bitterness toward other groups in society. The uplift generated by the legitimation of strains may create such a wide gap between reality and ideology that people despair and give up. Ideological commonality may produce not only solidarity, but internal schisms. And the clash of ideologies that serves to surface social problems may also make them so controversial as to preclude efforts to ameliorate them.

In more general terms, the most basic function of ideology is to create some semblance of order and ongoingness in an incomprehensible, often chaotic world. *Ideologies serve to make social situations comprehensible and meaningful. People naturally tend to simplify what they perceive; ideologies act to structure that simplification.* But the world is a complex place; to deal successfully with it, organizations need to develop ways of complicating rather than simplifying (Weick 1979a). Ideologies are largely dysfunctional in this regard. Organizational ideologies can lead to distorted perceptions of the world, excessive deviance compared to other organizations, behavioral rigidity and stagnation, and the outside world seeing members as heretics and fanatics (Meyer 1982b, p. 60).

Extraorganizational Sources of Ideologies

Although the specific ideologies that form the substance of an organization's culture are developed within it, their content is heavily influenced and framed by the surrounding culture. Organizations are dependent on their environments not only for tangible resources like money and raw materials, but also for cognitive and symbolic resources like beliefs, values, and norms. Also, people are an important resource and they do not enter organizations without having some cultural conditioning elsewhere. Thus, organizations import cultural elements through their members and other people who enter them and through the ideas they acquire from outside their boundaries.

The ideologies that enter an organization from outside come from at least six external layers of its environment: (1) large-scale cultural systems or transnational cultures; (2) national cultures, (3) regional and community cultures; (4) industry cultures, (5) occupational cultures; (6) other organizations' cultures.

Transnational cultures. Three examples of ideologies that derive from cultural systems that transcend national boundaries have already been discussed in this chapter; they are the ideologies of science, capitalism, and Protestantism. Of these, the ideology of science is probably the most universally accepted and pervasive in its effects.[4]

Although various national states array themselves into hostile factions on the basis of political and religious ideologies, all seem to be relatively united in their belief in the value and efficacies of science. Furthermore, the international character of this ideology is well recognized. Faith in science unites countries that have other deep ideological divisions. Various groups consciously advance science as a way to provide some integration across these divides. Only when relations between them are extremely bad do governments stop scientific exchanges. The People's Republic of China, which tried to abolish much of the values and practice of modern science during its Cultural Revolution, soon regretted such actions and is now trying very hard to catch up with the rest of the developed world in science.

The core of the ideology of science is expressed in its preeminent cultural form: scientific methods, which consist of prescribed, presumably objective ways of proceeding with scientific investigation. Over time, the use and elaboration of such methods gave rise to certain normative beliefs, which include universalism, communalism, disinterestedness, and organized skepticism (Merton 1968). Universalism holds that scientific truth should be subjected to preestablished, impersonal criteria. Communalism in science means that research findings belong to the scientific community as a whole and must be communicated openly. Disinterestedness dictates that scientists must not allow their personal interests to affect their results. Organized skepticism prescribes that scientists must cultivate tem-

---

[4]While the political collapse of communism and embracing of capitalism in the former USSR has made capitalism seem very powerful, it remains to be seen how lasting this ideological switch will be.

porary suspension of judgment and detached scrutiny of their beliefs in terms of empirical and logical criteria. In practice, these norms come into conflict with other values, leading to various ambivalences about the norms (Merton 1976):

- make newfound knowledge available as soon as possible vs. do not rush into print
- avoid fads vs. be open to new thinking
- know the heritage vs. avoid too much reading to preserve originality and creativity
- knowledge should be shared universally vs. honor one's nation
- be an apprentice vs. be one's own person
- focus on major issues vs. give fastidious attention to detail

Thus, like other ideologies, those of science present some contradictions in practice. Nevertheless there *is* a coherent set of beliefs, values, and norms that prescribes a disciplined way of thinking about and studying physical and social phenomena. One way in which the pervasiveness of the ideology of science is evident is that physicists in the Soviet Union, France, and Canada proceed in similar ways to study similar phenomena. Thus, they can read and publish their findings in the same journals.

But it is at a more subtle level—it is by the manner of thinking that is conveyed by its ideologies—that science has pervaded modern society. People throughout the world believe in and value the scientific approach to solving humanity's problems. This faith in science denies the notion of a fundamentally unreasonable and capricious world; instead it sees the universe as a system whose underlying principles can be understood from rational analyses and then used to predict and control events. Applications of the method range form the exploration of space and weapons technology to personnel testing and brainwashing.

Common motives that cross national boundaries can help to create shared belief systems. For example, economic development is desired by most countries. The perceived link between scientific and economic development has no doubt helped to make the ideology of science so universally convincing and appealing. Another ideology that seems to encourage economic development is one that values individual achievement. David McClelland (1961) and his associates found that countries in which children's reading books positively expressed this value had higher rates of economic development. How did this happen? While hard to document, it seems likely that both this value and its associated motives were diffused across national boundaries not only through travel, exchange of workers and students, and the media, but also through conscious imitation by the poorer countries of what seems to have worked in the richer ones.

Other motives that give rise to transnational ideologies include problems and crises that have transnational origins and impacts. Environmental pollution, the dangers of nuclear technology and weapons, the threatened extinction of wildlife, and world hunger are four of the issues that have stimulated transnational movements and ideologies. Multinational firms in related industries are likely to find themselves increasingly confronting transnational organizations with militant ideologies. Observers have noted that the environmental movement is much more vigorous and militant in West Germany, Sweden, Norway, Holland, and Japan than in the United States (Kaprow 1985, p. 344). Many governments have created official agencies to monitor and deal with these problems. Regional and international governmental organizations are predicted to "play an increasingly important role" in policies related to pollution control (Gladwin and Walters 1976, p. 71).

A dramatic instance of a firm's culture coming into sharp clash with transnational ideologies occurred in the late 1970s when the Swiss-based Nestlé Company was accused by various church-related and other groups of ignoring infant welfare in selling its infant formula to mothers in underdeveloped countries. The company tenaciously maintained (at least in public) its belief that it had the right to sell a substitute for breast milk to any mothers who for personal or health-related reasons wanted to use their product, and who had the necessary means and information to use it properly. But opponents believed that this ideology was at odds with the reality of life in the underdeveloped world, where economic and hygienic conditions were not appropriate for its use (Sethi, Etemad, and Luther 1986). They pointed out that women in such countries often lacked the knowledge or means to sterilize water and bottles for formula, and often diluted the formula when they ran short of money to pay for it. Because breast milk dries up when nursing is discontinued, they often could no longer choose to nurse their babies at that point. With the backing of nutritional specialists, the coalition of interested groups organized an international boycott of the company's products; it was sufficiently successful eventually to win concessions from the company.

A variety of other organizations that operate across national boundaries are relatively autonomous and provide sources of extraorganizational ideologies. The Roman Catholic Church, World Council of Churches, international labor unions, and multinational firms are examples of transnational organizations that have important cultural impacts on other organizations (Keohane and Nye 1971). Such organizations generate private foreign policies that put pressure on national and organizational belief systems, pushing them toward more globalized ideologies. The increasing interdependence of national states creates background support for these autonomous cultures to grow and thrive. The emergence of English as an international language also facilitates the development and sharing of beliefs, values, and even cultural forms.

National cultures. Much research has been devoted to trying to identify distinct national cultures, focusing especially on those values that might be expected to be reflected in work organizations in different countries. Unfortunately, much of this research has used a relatively superficial etic approach (e.g., Hofstede 1980a). Despite this deficiency, the general result of these studies—that substantial differences exist among national value systems—cannot be ignored. First, everything we know about culture strongly suggests the likelihood of such differences. Second, our experience as travelers and business people soon reveals that some kinds of cultural differences create difficulties in transactions across national boundaries. Third, those emic studies that have been done also support the idea that there are distinct national cultures.

One leading scholar, for example, traced how the managerial ideologies in the United States and Russia are products of differing historical, cultural, political, and economic characteristics of each country (Bendix 1956). Another interpreted managerial and worker behavior in two French bureaucracies as products of that country's culture, which favors social isolation and formality (Crozier 1964). Another long-term study observed differences between Peruvian and U.S. workers in what they expected and valued in the behavior of their superiors (Williams, Whyte, and Green 1965). While U.S. workers valued superiors who behaved democratically, Peruvian workers had been socialized in their families and schools to value superiors who act authoritatively. Similarly, traditional authority patterns were observed to carry over from families into work settings in several cultures, including Japan, Turkey, Ghana, India, and Thailand (Kakar 1971a, 1971b). For example, the expectations carried in Japanese culture were that supervisors would behave like benevolent parents guiding their subordinates, who were expected to reciprocate with complete obedience and absolute loyalty. An analysis of child rearing practices, religion and philosophy, work values, and the practice of psychotherapy in Japan and the United States indicated that the Japanese culture favored secondary control, which involves harmonizing with the environment, while the U.S. culture favored primary control, which involves dominating the environment (Weisz, Rothbaum, and Blackburn 1984).

Because a substantial body of research exists on cross-cultural differences, many additional examples could be given. Further examination of these issues will, however, be reserved for Chapter 8, which deals in more detail with environmental influences on organizational cultures.

Regional and community cultures. The sociopsychological dimension of regionalism has been defined as "a set of attitudes and feelings" that constitute "an identification with area: a sense of certain distinctiveness from other areas; an attachment to a territory, its people, and institutions, . . . the process by which a particular geographic space is transformed into a social space . . . imbued with meanings and emotional connotations not attributed to other spaces" (Breton 1981, p. 58). To the degree that the meanings and emotions referred to in the latter part of this definition are shared, they become a cultural entity.

In his classic study entitled *Alienation and Freedom* (1964), Herbert Blauner explained a seeming paradox between the mindless, repetitive, boring work of textile workers and their apparent satisfaction with it by analyzing the cultural settings in which they lived. All of the plants studied were in the southeastern United States, and the workers came from small rural communities there. Ideologies in these communities included a fatalistic acceptance of one's destiny and submission to one's lot in life. Since they did not believe they could change their work circumstances, workers not only accepted them, but managed to feel satisfied and involved with their work.

Various other studies have found that rural- and urban-reared workers exhibit different reactions to work situations that appear to stem from different experiences and accompanying beliefs in middle-class values endorsing hard work as the route to success (Turner and Lawrence 1965; Blood and Hulin 1967; Trice 1961). Children reared in city slums may be taught the same values in school as children in small towns, but are likely to experience greater difficulties in their attempts to follow them. "Such frustration and negative reinforcement should extinguish behavior and beliefs consistent with American middle-class ideals" (Blood and Hulin 1968, p. 52).

A survey of ten French-Canadian industrial organizations in Quebec and ten English-Canadian companies in Ontario found differences in some cultural assumptions but not in others (Nightingale and Toulouse 1977). In particular, the two groups differed in their assumptions about the exercise of authority but not in their assumptions about human nature. French Canadians reported that their organizations more often permitted employees to use their own judgment, but also that their firms had more formalized procedures than were reported in the English-Canadian firms. Such regional differences "have acquired increased importance in Canadian economic, political, and cultural life [by creating] inter-organizational systems that embody cultural values and meaning." (Breton 1981, p. 57).

Another country with pronounced regional differences is Belgium. The country is divided into two regions that speak different languages—French and Dutch—and have different cultural heritages and history. Extensive research of government organizations in the two regions—Wallonia and Flanders—revealed markedly different cultural ideologies about authority and the meaning of work (Aiken and Bacharach 1979). Organizations in the two regions differed accordingly. In Wallonia, where French is spoken, the emphasis was on impersonal controls—rules and procedures, primarily—and little innovative behavior was evident. In Flanders, where Dutch is spoken, organizations relied more heavily on interpersonal control and less on impersonal rules and procedures, with the result that employees could be more innovative.

Another study documented the difficulties encountered in a business school when an innovative new curriculum and unconventional new faculty were seen by community benefactors as incompatible with the local culture (Dunbar, Dutton, and Torbert 1982). Benefactors threatened withdrawal of financial and other support for the university unless the business school returned to the status quo.

Industry ideologies.   Ideologies can also rise from the unique activities and problems encountered within industries. The competitiveness of an industry, its historical development, its dominant technologies, its customers' requirements, societal expectations, and other factors channel the experiences of those working in an industry in certain directions and not others (Gordon 1991). These experiences, in turn, color and shape the beliefs and values members hold. For example,

> . . . no matter when or by whom an electric utility is founded, a widely shared assumption is that the customer needs continuous, uninterrupted service. Based on

this assumption, a high value is placed on reliable delivery of the product, which manifests itself in forms designed to avoid either strategic or operational decisions that involve radical departures from known ways of doing things. Thus, the industry predisposes all the companies within it to develop cultures that encompass certain assumptions and values stemming from the nature of what the industry does or produces. (Gordon 1991, p. 402)

In effect, within industries, people develop shared beliefs about what are appropriate strategies (Huff 1982). These tendencies have also been documented in the English woolen industry (Whipp, Rosenfeld, and Pettigrew 1989), in the U.S. wine industry and fine arts museums (Phillips 1991), and in the computer industry (Weiss and Delbecq 1987).[5]

A study of the rodeo tied this unique cultural form to the ranching industry where the skills celebrated in the rodeo were used as a part of working life. Those working at ranches reported that the rodeo was "an integral part of the ranching way of life . . ." (Lawrence 1982, p. 84). The ideology of individualism is probably the most celebrated quality of rodeo performance. Its roots go back to the beliefs and practices cherished in frontier days. According to this study, current-day ranchers still harbor intense fears about loss of autonomy and "uniformly preach about the evils of government intervention in their lives and work" (Lawrence 1982, p. 105).

Very distinctive ideologies also pervade the direct selling industry. Examples of direct selling organizations (DSOs) are Tupperware, Mary Kay Cosmetics, Amway Corporation, Shaklee, Home Interiors and Gifts, Avon Products, and the Fuller Brush Company. In 1984, 5 percent of the U.S. labor market were members of DSOs selling $8.6 billion in goods and services. Women accounted for 80 percent of direct salespeople. Despite their impressive success, "nearly every familiar feature of corporate life is either distorted or missing" from DSOs (Biggart 1989, p. 16). They lack recruitment criteria, discourage competition among distributors, have few rules and managers, spawn charismatic rather than rational leadership, encourage friendly and even highly personal relations among co-workers, and encourage employees to incorporate spouses and children in their selling activities. These organizations also give a unique twist to the entrepreneurial ethic in that entrepreneurs usually run their own organizations while direct salespersons must be both entrepreneurial and operate within a national organization.

Other industries are less monolithic in their cultures. The publishing industry, for example, is so structured that the type of publication—trade, college text, scholarly, monograph, and university press—determines social networks, ideologies, and behavior. In the large publishing houses, social values and beliefs of subunits differ according to the type of publication each does (Coser, Kadushin, and Powell 1982).

Organization sets. Many organizations regularly interact with a limited set of organizations in their environment. The term *organization set* refers to such closely

---

[5]The latter study also showed that industry cultures may vary somewhat by region.

knit groups of organizations (Evan 1972). For example, social service agencies that deal with family problems must interact regularly with schools, police departments, drug and alcoholism treatment centers, hospitals, and churches. In an organization set, organizations are interdependent in various ways. They may supply clients or other inputs to one another, or they may accept and deal with some of the outputs of one another. Sometimes they simply provide know-how and other resources to one another. Occasionally, as in the United Way, Catholic Charities, or the United Jewish Appeal, one organization specializes in supplying financial resources for many others. Whatever its form, some degree of exchange of resources occurs among these organizations, which are therefore dependent on one another for those particular resources. Because of this dependency and because regular contact provides a convenient channel for it, cultural transfer is likely among organizations in the same organization set. Working together involves sharing aspects of the same problems, which is likely to lead to shared views of the world. Also, members of such organizations are motivated to try to influence one another or to accommodate to others' views to smooth working relationships. Mutual influence is facilitated by the fact that employees often share similar cultural roots and occupational training.

A study of defense contractors, who are highly dependent on the U.S. government for their business, showed that ideological concerns varied according to the degree of firms' dependency on the government, measured by the proportion of sales going to the government and the likelihood of enforcement pressures. Where enforcement pressures were most likely, the degree of concern with affirmative action was strongly correlated with the extent of the organization's dependency on the government (Pfeffer and Salancik 1978, p. 58).

Another study, focusing on bankruptcies in the computer industry, studied the reactions of key audiences, including other organizations, who were affected by and concerned about firms' failures (Sutton and Callahan 1987). These included customers, lawyers, journalists, stockholders, venture capitalists, competitors, suppliers, government officials, members of employees' families, and others. The researchers found that both bankrupt organizations and their managers suffered spoiled images. The stigma they aroused was expressed by a variety of negative reactions among their audiences that further crippled the firms. Most relationships changed, with the reactions of others ranging from disengagement, to reduction in the quality of participation and bargaining for more favorable exchanges. For example, suppliers refused to send parts unless they were promised some cash in advance and the rest on delivery. Vendors apparently cleaned out their defective merchandise by sending it to the troubled firm. Espoused evaluations of the firm among members of its audience also changed, primarily through denigration by rumor, but sometimes by denigration via confrontation. At a meeting of creditors, one creditor told a president to "quit making excuses for your incompetence" (Sutton and Callahan 1987, p 418). Such reactions reflected not only the actors' self-interests, but more importantly the general cultural ideology that "competent leaders are expected to exercise control over their organizations and that such control is expected to lead to organizational success" (Sutton and Callahan 1987, p. 405). When organizations fail to meet such expectations, they are discredited with other members of their organizational set.

Occupational ideologies.   The various occupations and professions that are represented by organizational members are another extraorganizational source of ideologies. Although members receive training and indoctrination after they join work organizations, much of the training and indoctrination in the most developed occupations and professions tends to occur prior to employment. Training sites range from union halls to special academies and universities. During their training, recruits are inevitably indoctrinated with beliefs, values, and norms specific to that occupation. In the most developed occupations—the professions—this indoctrination includes a professional code of ethics that puts client welfare above that of the employing organization. Such indoctrination has powerful effects on those who experience it. For example, although many who earn the Ph.D. degree do not end up as faculty at research-oriented universities or in other research-oriented positions, persons with this degree usually try to maintain the appearance of conducting research, writing, and publishing.

Because occupational subcultures are covered at length in Chapter 5, further discussion of them will be deferred until then.

Distinctive American Ideologies

Perhaps the best way to illustrate how ideologies are incorporated into work organizations is to trace the development of the national culture of the United States. Many of the examples used throughout this book are drawn from U.S. organizations and thus reflect U.S. ideologies. By setting forth the central substance of the U.S. culture from the beginning, the cultural content in the examples presented later will be more evident.

In order to understand a national culture and its potential influence on work organizations, an historical view is essential. All cultures are transmitted from generation to generation. Their distinctiveness arises from the particular ideologies and values that happen to emerge during these intergenerational transmission processes. Each generation tries to instill in succeeding ones certain ways of thinking, feeling, and behaving. The distinctiveness of national cultures persists despite enormous social changes. The pace of change "grows ever faster. . . . the first rockets were launched during the Second World War; today astronauts roam outer space"; yet "persisting traits, values, and folkways create a palpable national identity" (Schlesinger 1986, p. xi). Those who read de Tocqueville's *Democracy in America* (1877) today are "astonished to recognize the lineaments of modern America in this great work, though de Tocqueville visited a predominantly agricultural nation of thirteen million people a century and a half ago" (Schlesinger 1986, p. xii). Another analyst concluded that ". . . during the twentieth century, no completely new major value orientations have appeared [in the United States], nor have any main values completely disappeared" (Williams 1979, p. 34).

In his seminal work entitled *American Society,* Robin Williams (1970) identified a set of values that reflect the major ideological themes of American culture. While many other researchers have studied other sets of values of U.S. society, his is the most comprehensive and is well grounded in the relevant literature. Williams set out to describe what is unique about the American value system. He arranged dominant and subordinate values according to their extensiveness in the total society, their duration over time, the intensity with which they are pursued and maintained, and the prestige of those who express and behave according to them. The values he identified are given in Table 2–1, arranged in clusters so that related valued can be discussed together.

Value Clusters

Competitive achievement, work, efficiency, and rationality.   The first cluster emphasizes the importance of personal achievement within a context of strenuous and unremitting competition. The ideology does not encompass the complete range of people's achievements—only their practical accomplishments. Success should be sought in business and occupational life, the central preoccupations of the culture. "The 'success story' and the respect accorded to the self-made man are distinctly American, if anything is" (Williams 1970, p. 454).

An ironic example of how the deep-seated value of success affects U.S. organizations occurs in the antagonistic attitudes of American managers toward labor

TABLE 2–1
CLUSTERS OF AMERICAN VALUES

		Direction of Change 1945–1976[a]
I.	Competitive achievement and success	±
	Activity and work	−
	Efficiency and practicality	−
	Science and secular rationality	±
II.	Individual personality and value of self	±
	Freedom	−
	Equality	+
	Democracy	±
III.	Progress	−
	Material comfort	±
IV.	Humanitarian domestic mores	+
	Moral orientation	±
V.	Nationalism and patriotism	−
	Racism and group superiority	−
	External conformity	+

[a] + denotes increase, − denotes decrease, ± denotes evidence for both increases and decreases in different groups or in terms of different aspects of these values.
SOURCE: Adapted from Williams 1970, 1979.

unions. Their keen drive for individual success undergirds the resistance of U.S. managers toward unions having any control in workplaces. "Neither European nor Japanese managers display as deep an antipathy toward unions as is embedded in the value systems of United States managers and top executives" (Kochan and Barocci 1985, p. 497). This antipathy is especially notable since American unions have always accepted the ideologies of capitalism. In Europe, managers are more pragmatic; faced with the political power of unions and a greater working class consciousness, they accept and accommodate themselves to unions.

American unions themselves also reflect the predominant cultural values of competitive individualism. Compared with unions in Europe and Australia, they lack a

> sense of class solidarity and incline to pursue more narrowly, self-interested economistic strategies. They are also more militant, and often violent, in their tactics. . . . [reflecting] the strong emphasis on individual achievement and equality . . . [in] a highly competitive culture, and one that emphasizes ends—especially precuniary ends over means. (Davies and Weiner 1985, p. 357)

Because of the persistent antagonism between U.S. managers and unions that arises from deeply felt ideologies and values, it is difficult for them to overcome their tendencies to resist one another—despite various efforts at union-management cooperation and despite the obvious need for greater cooperative effort to meet competition in global markets from other countries with more cooperative labor-management relations.

American culture has historically given action and work a central place in the constellation of values, not only because of the legacies of the Protestant ethic, but because of value systems generalized out of unique experience. "Work was required for groups' survival along the moving frontier from the first settlements until the continent had been won" (Williams 1970, p. 459). Also important was that the early American population was largely recruited from the working classes of England and the European continent. As a result, there were few aristocrats around to stigmatize manual labor and commercial trade.

The continued centrality of work in the values of Americans has been documented numerous times. For example, research identified two themes in the work ethic in the late 1970s (Kanter 1978). The first, called the cultural or expressive, concerned work as a source of self-respect and material reward; of challenge, growth, and personal fulfillment; of interest and meaning; of the opportunity to advance and to accumulate; and of a chance to lead a safe and healthy life. The other, called political, concerned individual rights, power, equity, justice, and participation. A review of relevant social science research found "a continuing high involvement with work as a central focus of life. . . . there is some indication that work is becoming more important as higher proportions of the population seek paid employment" (Mortimer 1979, p. 16). Other analysts argued that, despite the appearance of a "new breed" of American worker, "both old and new values converge to reinforce the symbolic power of the paid job in our society. For those who remain faithful to the old values, a paid job is the classic road to self-respect . . . under the new values a paid job symbolizes independence, freedom, challenge, belonging, a chance for self-fulfillment. . ." (Yankelovich 1979, p. 17).

Arguing that the best indicator of a person's commitment to working was whether that person would continue to work after a large economic windfall, a researcher investigated whether lottery winners planned to continue working (Harpaz, 1986). Because research has been done on this question since the 1950s, he was able to compare results over time. The results suggested that the value attached to work declined during the late 1960s and 1970s, but that the decline was reversed during the 1980s. Results from U.S. respondents in the mid-1980s were close to those for the 1950s and early 1960s. In the U.S. samples, 88 percent of the winners wanted to continue working. Only one other country—Japan— exceeded this percentage, with 93.4 percent planning to continue work. As will be explored more extensively in Chapter 8, the Japanese culture also values work very highly.

The values of efficiency and practicality are closely allied. "Getting things done" is an American motto. To be thought of as impractical is a stigma. Adjectives like *useful, applied,* and *concrete* express positive valuations; expressions like *academic, ivory tower, theoretical,* and *abstract* are often used to comdemn something. U.S. values favor rational and immediate action over intellectual and aesthetic concerns. One result is that U.S. culture tends to lack a sense of history. Details of World War II are largely unknown to American youth as compared to their counterparts in Russia (Schlesinger 1986). Henry Ford's insistence that history is bunk expressed this ideology.

The high value placed on science stands in stark contrast to the place accorded history in U.S. culture. America's optimistic stance toward science is not an expression of positive sentiments toward intellectual endeavors and learning; rather it stems from the fact that, in the American experience and mind, science is wedded to practical technology. Thomas Edison rather than Albert Einstein is the popular image of the ideal scientist. Americans value science, not for its own sake, but as a way to produce technologies that will solve practical problems. To them, science epitomizes the mastery of the natural environment—a central goal in a culture that aspires to primary control.

In addition, as already mentioned, the ideology of science rejects caprice and unpredictability; disciplined examination can be used to produce explanations and control. Thus, the values of science are closely linked to what is often called secular rationality. The American culture places its faith in a rationalism that opposes traditionalism; it "does not accept things just because they have been done before" (Williams 1970, p. 502). Instead the culture orients its people primarily to the present and immediate future.

Individualism.   The second cluster of values in Table 2–1 concerns individualism and the supreme importance of the self. This concept of self as a unique universe unto itself is "a rather peculiar idea within the context of the world's cultures" (Geertz 1979, p. 229). For example, it stands in marked contrast to Japanese culture, in which groups are seen as the primary social unit, and individuals are seen as subordinate to organizations, communities, or states. The American culture places extraordinary importance on the individual personality and self, on the freedom of the individual from social and organizational controls, on the right of the individual to be part of any control patterns that may affect him or her, and on a basic presumption of equality between individual persons.

Indeed, an anthropologist born in China and educated in England concluded that there is *one* core value that catches up the many contradictory values in American culture. It is "self reliance, the most persistent psychological expression of which is fear of dependence ... the fear of dependence is so great that an individual who is not self reliant is an object of hostility and called a misfit" (Hsu 1961, p. 217). Dependence can get in the way of exercising individualism. All of the ideologies in American culture, "the mutually contradictory ones and the mutually suggestive ones, the evil ones as well as the angelic ones, spring from or are connected with self reliance" (Hsu 1961, p. 217).

Another anthropologist, living in a metropolitan suburb in Georgia, described life there as follows: "The individual is drawn apart, isolated from his fellows.... In the community where I worked, family life is thought to become perfect not as individuals perfect their knowledge and appreciation of each other, but as each member perfects his sense of self" (Greenhouse 1985, p. 262). A century and a half earlier, de Tocqueville (1877) observed much the same thing: individualism encouraged the isolation and self-withdrawal of Americans from one another. Consistent with these observations, the American business creed "commends to all, businessman or non-businessman, the virtue and necessity of self-reliance: each must take his [or her] own way, stand on his own feet, and fare as he deserves" (Sutton et al. 1956, p. 356).

In a popular book of the 1950s, William H. Whyte, Jr. (1956) expressed his fear that the rugged individualist would be displaced in corporate life by *The Organization Man,* who valued social approval and security more than hard work and individual accomplishment. That such a displacement was seen as dangerous to American society is further evidence of the centrality and potency of the ethic of individualism. More recent evidence of the persistence of individualism among contemporary Americans came from wide-ranging interviews with diverse groups of people. Their responses indicated that their notions of success were directly linked to individual accomplishments in their work lives (Bellah et al. 1985).

All of these analyses indicate that an ideal of individual separateness pervades the American culture and that the social identity of Americans comes from their selves, rather than from a matrix of relationships in a group, as it does in the Japanese culture. According to the U.S. value system, work organizations are primarily contexts for the expression and execution of individual goals, rather than entities for pursuing collective goals. The values of work and individualism are fused in the emphasis among new-breed workers upon self-fulfillment and job autonomy. These workers speak of "fulfilling their potential," "keeping on growing," and "duty to themselves" (Yankelovich 1979, p. 11). Apparently many types of American workers have come to feel that ordinary success is not enough. Unlike traditional notions of success as experiences outside the self, self-fulfillment is experienced within the self.

The relatively recent emphasis on striving for internal and vague states of being has opened up a wide latitude for job dissatisfaction. In the 1970s, workers in all occupations reported greater dissatisfactions with their jobs (Mortimer 1979, p. 16) than in the past. They also were more concerned about equity and justice in the workplace. These developments led to substantial changes in U.S. military organizations. When the draft was repealed, these organizations realized they had to modify their authoritarian practices and be more tolerant of individuality (Klein and Ritti 1984, p. 134) in order to attract new recruits. Even conceptions of romantic love have changed to incorporate the aspects of individualism concerned with self-development. In current U.S. society, a love relationship is often viewed as a route to personal growth rather than an end in itself, with the result that transitory relationships have become common and lasting ones the exception (Swidler 1990).

Strong ideas about freedom and equality dovetail with and support the core value of individualism. Freedom means that individuals are relatively autonomous, as well as morally responsible. Historically, the American colonies sought to emancipate the major sectors of community life—trade, religion, and property—from feudal control. In the process, freedom came to mean release from practically all restraints, a suspicion of established authority, and a deep-seated insistence on the right to be free of coercive controls. Freedom from explicit, well-defined patterns of social control was especially encouraged in the economic sphere and in the behavior of the quintessential individualist—the entrepreneur. Individuals had not only the right to own property, but to use it in any way they judged desirable as long as they competed freely and openly.[6] The U.S. political system of democratic government was an extension of this powerful belief in the sanctity of the individual. Faith in the perceptive power of the people, an aggregate of individuals voting freely and responsibly, was the bulwark of democracy. Such values are directly reflected in work organizations through current-day programs of employee participation (Locke and Schweiger 1990), workplace democracy (Rothschild and Whitt 1986), and employee ownership plans (Whyte, Hammer, Meek, Nelson, and Stern, 1983).

Progress and materialism.   The third cluster of dominant values in American culture concerns beliefs about the inevitability of progress in the human condition. One tangible expression of these beliefs lies in the value placed on high levels of material comfort. The American historian Henry Steele Commager put the progress theme in perspective when he wrote: "Throughout their history Americans have insisted that the best was yet to be.... Progress was not ... a mere philosophical ideal, but a commonplace of experience..." (Commager 1947, p. xi, xiv). This orientation fit the formation of a new country. In the beginning, America was promise, rather than past; hope, rather than accomplishment. "For a long period this promise was kept and the hope was fulfilled to a remarkable degree" (Williams 1970, p. 468). Citizens prospered and enjoyed their prosperity

---

[6]Initially, these property rights were confined to free men. It took centuries for blacks and women to win the same rights in even a legal sense.

in tangible ways. At the turn of the century, the economist Thorstein Veblen (1899) coined the term *conspicuous consumption* to characterize the enthusiasm with which Americans pursued material comforts and ostentation. By the 1960s, in an economy bolstered by consumer purchases and commercial advertising, the pursuit of consumption and hedonistic gratification—even of some illegal and potentially dangerous drugs—became symbolic of progress and individual success.

Humanitarianism.   The fourth cluster of values is in conflict with the first. It expresses a strong moral concern, which often focuses on humanitarianism in one form or another. To the degree that it favors helping others rather than letting them fend for themselves, it creates contradictions in the overall value system. An example of this moral orientation is the tendency for Americans to criticize and document the moral lapses in their own culture and history: slavery, the persecution of Native Americans, discrimination against women, child labor, lynchings, organized crime, and drug and alcohol abuse. Furthermore, eventually something is usually done about these lapses. The culture creates strong pressures to see things in terms of right or wrong, good or bad. Williams concludes that this value tends to produce moral overstrain (1970, p. 462). People have great difficulty making their actual practices fit with their moral pronouncements.

The practices of workplaces have occasionally picked up the humanitarian theme from this cluster of values. A current example is the proliferation of Employee Assistance Programs designed to help troubled employees deal with their personal problems. These programs and their predecessors will be discussed in a later section of this chapter that focuses on managerial ideologies.

Ethnocentrism.   The final cluster of values in Table 2–1 concerns the ethnocentric flavor of American culture. Americans attach much positive emotion to the idea of being an American. Although all cultures are ethnocentric by definition, the American culture seems to be especially so. Studies have repeatedly shown that, save for Australians, Americans express less desire to live in other nations than people from other cultures. Moreover, Americans are inordinately proud of their political institutions and consistently seek to have other countries adopt them. Their ethnocentrism seems to convince Americans that they have a unique mission in the world. This ethnocentrism made U.S. managers of the past presume that their ways were superior to those of other countries. These beliefs may have made them overconfident of their abilities to meet foreign competition and thus led them to embrace free trade.

Another disturbing feature of U.S. culture has been a theme of racism and group superiority. Throughout its history, the American culture has tended to define various groups—blacks, immigrants, women—as "different" and therefore not entitled to the same privileges that the dominant values confer on in-group members. While this ideological theme has been in flux and changed somewhat in recent decades, it remains beneath the surface with the potential to re-emerge. Since demographic data show that the U.S. workforce of the future will include more members of minority groups and women than in the past, many employers have embarked on programs designed to promote the positive values of multicultural diversity (Cox 1991).

Another expression of ethnocentric values in American culture is its emphasis on external conformity. De Tocqueville noticed this feature of American society and warned that a tyranny of the majority could dilute American individualism and freedom. He was referring to a noticeable uniformity, absent in Europe, in such things as dress, speech, housing, political ideas, and recreational activities. This warning was echoed by William H. Whyte in the 1950s (Whyte 1956) in his concern that work organizations were encouraging look-alike, think-alike conformity.

The external conformity of U.S. society may be largely a surface product of its other ideologies. The pressures for success and achievement make upward mobility highly desirable. Such mobility inevitably involves external conformity to the social practices of the reference group to which one aspires. Also, the very heterogeneity of U.S. culture promotes external conformity as a signal that diverse groups are willing to carry on needed collective efforts (Williams 1970, p. 486). Of course, some degree of conformity is expected in all societies.

Changes in Values

In the long run, cultural values tend to be responsive to changes in shared experiences. The right-hand column in Table 2–1 summarizes an analysis of changes in American values from the end of World War II to the late 1970s (Williams 1979). Evidence for these changes was culled from many sources.

There is substantial evidence that the strong emphasis given to achievement until 1945 has receded somewhat in importance while success has increased in relative importance. In effect, what has happened is " a shift in emphasis rather than a reversal of values. . . . achievement remains an outstanding value orientation" (Williams 1979, p. 35). The general emphasis on efficiency and practicality has also lessened.

Changes in the values connected with science and secular rationality have been mixed. The emphasis on applied science and technology has strengthened—certainly in the 1980s as a route to the continual economic prosperity of American society. But people have also become aware of the threats as well as the benefits posed by the products of modern science. "Life-saving discoveries appear side by side with environmental pollution, population explosions, and nuclear, chemical, and biological weapons" (Williams 1979, p. 36). Such awareness has decreased faith in progress as an inevitable outcome of hard work, even as the byproducts of science have made greater material comforts possible and taken for granted. At the same time, various aspects of religious beliefs have become secularized, creating some conflict between traditional religious values and scientific modes of thought. Many matters formerly considered part of religion have come under the influence of scientists and other secular professionals.

While the values of individualism, freedom, and democracy remain strong as generalized beliefs, these values are "severely strained by organizational centralization and the categorical and impersonal character of much of national life" (Williams 1979, p. 38). Equality has fared better; its increase is reflected in substantial changes in both national law and administrative policies establishing equality in political and civil rights. Economic equality, however, has not increased except for small segments of formerly disadvantaged groups.

As discussed earlier, the absolutist moral orientation of U.S. society created inevitable strains as people faced conflicts between various values and found they could not live up to all of them. Data show increases in deviant behavior of all kinds. Such absolute values as honesty and fidelity are probably less potent than they once were, but "the effective implementation of humanitarian values" has probably increased (Williams 1979, p. 37). Also, the prevailing ethics of personal relations are probably more kindly and less stern or punitive than they once were.

More recent data, collected on three generations of families in Southern California in 1971 and 1985, showed considerable similarity in four distinctive American values across generations and only slight variations in the relative importance of these values over time (Bengtson 1989). Compared to the generally strong endorsement of these values, differences between generations and across time periods were small. The greatest differences occurred in the generational rankings for the values of humanism and individualism. In 1985, the youngest generation expressed the lowest level of humanistic values—contrary to the expressed values of the youngest generation in the 1960s—and their grandparents were highest in endorsing humanism. The youngest generation was highest on individualism in both time periods. Materialism and collectivism showed very small differences between generations and over time. The researcher concludes that "the 'generation gap' cleavages which were so much a focus of the mass media during the 1960s seem not to be sustained over time" (Bengtson 1989, p. 49).

The fact that the dramatic expressions of dissent that occurred in U.S. society during the 1960s and 1970s are not reflected in marked differences in values across generations fifteen or so years later demonstrates how persistent cultural values can be in a society. It will be interesting to see which sets of values exert themselves in the formerly Soviet-dominated societies of Eastern Europe and in the now-defunct USSR. Will these societies find it hard to move beyond the communist ideologies that their rulers tried so hard to instill or will they easily revert to social and political values and beliefs present before the communist takeover of their countries?

Effects on U.S. Organizations

The U.S. culture has been described at some length for two reasons. First, it provides an extended example of ideologies with which many of our readers are familiar. Second, it provides the ideological context within which U.S. work organizations operate. As already pointed out, national cultures represent one of the several sources of organizational ideologies. Thus, we must expect the cultures of U.S. work organizations to be both influenced and framed by the American culture described. In the remaining chapters, the basic ideological themes just outlined will be revisited often. However, there are other ideologies and cultures that surround and are imported into U.S. organizations. Some of these have elements that conflict with elements in the American culture in one way or another.

Also, the American culture itself contains a variety of confusing and inconsistent elements. De Tocqueville noted some of these inconsistencies as follows: "An American attends to his private concerns as if he were alone in the world, and the next minute he gives himself to the common welfare as if he had forgotten them. At one time he seems animated by the most selfish cupidity; at another by the most lively patriotism" (1877, p. xiv). One possible source of these inconsistencies is, of course, the diverse cultural backgrounds that immigrants to this country brought with them.

Whatever their origin, many contradictions and conflicts are endemic in American ideology and culture. For example, some forms of humanitarian aid encounter resistance because many Americans believe that individuals are solely responsible for their own welfare and have the moral responsibility to take care of themselves. Strong beliefs about personal freedom are inconsistent with pressures toward conformity. Latent racism erupts while the society openly espouses nondiscrimination and civil rights.

Some of these conflicts and contradictions occur between individuals and groups; some occur within them. The ideological values identified are not absolutes that all hold to an equal degree. Specific values can be supplanted by those of other cultural groups to which individuals belong: regions, occupations, or dissident political groups, for example. They can also be muted or overshadowed by variations that arise due to such factors as ethnicity, age cohort, or social class. Various ideologies may be added to or removed from an organization as the participants in the organization change (Beres and Portwood 1979, p. 170). These variations make possible an almost unlimited number of combinations and permutations.

Another reason that U.S. organizations cannot be expected to simply mirror the U.S. culture is that the fuzziness of culture makes its transference unavoidably imprecise. Also, socialization of youths and adults is by no means standardized or uniformly effective because (1) communications are subject to distortions and omissions; and (2) the idiosyncratic personal experiences of individuals may blur the transference process. Consequently, the ideologies of a culture are only imperfectly transmitted from generation to generation. All cultures have some internal intergenerational contradictions and ambiguities for this reason (Beck and Moore 1985) and because people have different experiences at different times in history. Observers tend to feel, however, that the U.S. culture is especially rife with intergenerational contradictions.

Moreover, when we consider the likely effects of the surrounding culture, we must not overlook the powerful influence that many organizations themselves have on their members. Many organizations are economically and politically very powerful. They create, modify, and train the forces of production within a society

(Stinchcombe 1983). Given such a powerful role, organizations can modify the persistent strains of the external culture that they incorporate. How they do this is the subject matter for much of the rest of this book.

Examples of Ideological Elements in Work Organizations

Rationality: the arch-ideology in organizational life.   No set of beliefs has so permeated modern organizations and their environments as the ideologies of rationality and science. The traditional management literature "provides legitimacy for the position that managerial action is intendedly rational, that there is a science of administration, that leadership can be both learned and important, and that [organizational] structures can be rationally designed to achieve specific ends" (Pfeffer 1981b, p. 15). This ideology is not created by management writers, but is a reflection of what managers and others in the society already believe. Rationality is "expected, encouraged, and even enforced" in corporations (Moore 1962, p. 30). An analysis of children's literature showed that it contained "an orientation toward work life that could have been dictated by management textbooks, and that was fully consistent with the metamyth" of rationality (Adams and Ingersoll 1985, p. 231).

Other analysts argue that the ideology of rationality is so strong that organizations "attempt to create the illusion of rationality for their internal membership, although these behaviors may not, in fact, contribute to effectiveness" (Staw 1980, p. 64). An incisive analysis of management information systems in organizations pointed out that information has a symbolic value that "is a function of the social norms of society and of a belief in rational decision processes of a particular kind." Thus, "organizations systematically gather more information than they use, yet continue to ask for more" (Feldman and March 1981, p. 182). This behavior is explained by noting that "information use symbolizes a commitment to rational choice. Displaying this symbol reaffirms the importance of this social value and signals personal and organizational competence" (Feldman and March 1981, p. 182). In addition, maintaining the appearance of rationality helps to maintain organizations' legitimacy in the wider society and thus to ensure their continued practical support by their environments (Meyer and Rowan 1977).

Although later organizational theorists modified this view, the classic writers on management and organization—Weber, Taylor, Gulick and Urwick—and even the early work of Simon, portrayed modern organizations as rational systems in which people behave in purposeful and coordinated ways. Their portrayal not only reflected the beliefs of the times in which they wrote, but probably also helped to reinforce the ideology of rationality by broadcasting it and giving it a scholarly credence. "The language employed connotes this image of rational calculation: such terms as *information, efficiency, optimization, implementation,* and *design* occur frequently" (Scott 1987, p. 32). Even in the 1950s—long after the Hawthorne studies showed that people's emotions play an important role in how they behave in organizations—when James Thompson decided to found a new journal that would focus on the analysis of organizations, he called it the *Adminis-*

trative Science Quarterly. His initial editorial expressed the hope that: "An administrative science will be an applied science, standing approximately in relation to the basic social sciences as engineering stands with respect to the physical sciences, or as medicine to the biological" (Thompson 1956, p. 103).

Much of what is taught in the various subfields of business and management is based on beliefs in science and rationality. Human resources professors teach about scientific techniques for selection, job analysis, performance appraisal, and wage and salary determination. Accounting professors teach systems for determining the tangible resources that exist in the organization and how best to deploy them. Finance professors teach how to manage money scientifically to maximize profits and return on capital. Professors in operations research teach mathematical models that try to maximize the efficient flow of materials and finished products. And so on. The ideology of rationality is so pervasive in business schools that it is rarely questioned. And when it is, most students—especially those who are also working as managers—are not comfortable or pleased. No one enjoys having a cherished and central ideology surfaced and questioned.

The ideology of rationality refers to more than a belief in the use of reason in human affairs. The ideology includes a series of interrelated beliefs that emphasize efficiency, predictability, calculability, substitution of nonhuman for human technology, and control over uncertainty (Ritzer 1983). It holds that a series of actions can be organized in such a way that they lead to predetermined goals and at maximum efficiency. This general ideology of rationality has been carried to its logical extreme in what many call the rational model of organizations and management, which assumes that (1) goals are unified sets of purposes that are consistent among themselves and across the organization; (2) persons have knowledge of all relevant alternatives for achieving these goals and their probable consequences; (3) preexisting goals actually guide behavior; and (4) the formal structure of the organization makes the use of rationality possible (Thompson 1967, p. 54). It follows that managers, who control the formal structure, must possess superior knowledge and know-how in order to use scientific reasoning appropriately to coordinate and direct the collective efforts of others. While the model prescribes that managers should be selected and retained on the basis of such abilities, the model cannot assure that this happens. What actually happens is that managers and others often only presume they possess all of the requirements for rational action. This can lead to managerial myopia. A manager in one high-tech firm that experienced difficulties reflected,

> Our company's problem between 1964 and 1980 was our overemphasis on the rational-thinking function. We forgot about the visions and values that must be behind the objectives and strategies. . . . our corporate objectives reflected the narrower purposes of a small group of executives. (Hurst 1986, p. 22)

Despite its appeal, rationality is an ideal, not a reality, in organizations and social life generally. Herbert Simon (1957) was one of the first to systematically point out the practical limits on rationality. Individuals in administrative positions lack the information-processing capacities required to deal with the complexities they face. So organizations provide individuals with specific goals and formalized procedures that ensure at least *bounded rationality*. In addition, because individuals lack the motivation and resources required to search out all relevant information, they tend to *satisfice*—to look for a course of action that is good enough rather than one that is optimal.

Political factors in organizations also limit the use of rationality. Goals are seldom as unified as the rational model suggests because people's self- and sub-group interests create diverse goals, because communication and understanding are not perfect, and because abilities to resolve conflict are low. To pursue their goals and interests, individuals and groups use a variety of tactics to gain power over what happens: (1) they seek to control access to certain information or individuals; (2) they push for the selective use of objective criteria that favor their interests; (3) they try to control the agenda of what is considered; (4) they hire experts sympathetic to their cause; (5) they use red tape and a literal interpretation of the rules, and play other games with the formal features of the bureaucracy; and (6) they form coalitions and alliances (Pfeffer 1977; Daft and Steers 1986). All of these tactics break down the conditions necessary for rationality.

Nevertheless, organizational behavior is intended to be rational and in some respects does achieve a semblance of this ideal (Thompson 1967). Formal goals do often set at least the broad parameters within which organizations operate. Rules, procedures, and formal authority relationships do govern much of the behavior that occurs within them. And even cultural rites and ceremonies often have practical and rational, as well as expressive consequences. Also, as was suggested in regard to information systems (Feldman and March 1981), behaviors that are initially symbolic may lead to ones that are instrumental and rational when outcomes are favorable and so reinforce the behaviors involved.

One obvious conclusion from these analyses is that organizational behavior is both rational and nonrational. This duality is caught up in such expressions as "reasonable administrative behavior" (Van de Ven 1982) or "shrewdly irrational" behavior (Frank 1987, p. 21). The two "are equal partners, each providing the context within which the other can operate; neither makes sense alone" (Pondy 1983b, p. 181). In one analyst's approach to this duality, behavior "reflects simultaneously both the power of emotions and values and that of calculations of benefits and costs" (Etzioni 1987, p. 1). Many studies of general social phenomena document this duality. Crime rates are affected both by personalities and moral precepts and by the levels of punishment and opportunities for crime (Wilson 1983). Compliance with tax laws is determined both by the size of the payoff from cheating and by moral values (Song and Yarborough 1978).

Egalitarianism.   After the 1960s, a decade in which authority was widely questioned and expressions of individualism were rampant, an egalitarian type of organization emerged. These organizations attempt to realize egalitarian ideals by eliminating practically all authority relationships and operating as a collectivist democracy. They "generally refuse to legitimate the use of centralized authority or standardized rules to achieve social control. Instead, they rely upon personalistic and moralistic appeals to provide the primary means of control . . ." (Rothschild-Whitt 1979, p. 513). Egalitarian organizations eliminate formalization and status gradations wherever possible, deny the authority of office, and instead emphasize individual preferences and equality in decision making. Such organizational forms have emerged in food cooperatives, legal collectives, so-called free schools, child care centers, health food stores, commercial printing operations, cooperatively owned plywood mills, and alternative mental health centers. They remain, however, comparatively rare.

Although the egalitarian organizational form realizes one cherished American ideal, it stands in direct opposition to others, especially to those the society normally associates with the process of getting things done. Organizations that do not meet the expectations and values of their environments encounter many problems. For example, collectivist organizations studied encountered many constraints and social costs that made survival difficult (Rothschild-Whitt 1979; Rothschild and Whitt 1986). Chief among these was members' time. Meetings needed to carry out democratic ideals take lots of time, especially when individualistic preferences must be honored. An alternative newspaper devoted three full days each week to a wide variety of meetings. The emotional intensity of relationships was threatening and also time consuming. Headaches, trembling, and other signs of tension tended to accompany the many meetings needed to reach consensus. Also, agencies in the external environment often required specific behaviors that conflicted with organizational ideals and members' preferences. For example, staff in the free schools preferred not to keep evaluative records of students, but students could not transfer back to regular schools or apply for entrance to college without such records. The schools ended up complying with the environmental demands.

Another study of 12 egalitarian organizations in California also found that environmental constraints led to modification of the original structure. The dependence of these organizations on external sources for such things as federal grants and government contracts required the hiring of full-time salaried employees to handle these external relationships. As the employees became more powerful, a formal status hierarchy began to emerge. Thus the cumulative effect of the environmental pressures was to encourage the formation of hierarchies; "many of the collectives evolved into bureaucratic institutions—the opposite of what they had intended" (Newman 1980, p. 159).

Research on an alternative mental health center produced similar observations (Schwartzman, Kneifel, and Krause 1978, p. 102; Schwartzman 1981, p. 82). Treatment staff spent 50 percent of their work days in meetings; center management spent 80 percent. The weak formal authority structure, however, led to such intense conflict and such ambiguity of responsibilities and job duties that a more traditional authority pattern began to appear.

Other research buttresses the conclusion that ideologies do not usually overcome traditional authority structures, but only mute them. One program of research compared patterns of control in organizations in five countries—Italy, Austria, the United States, Yugoslavia, and Israel—chosen to represent a continuum of egalitarian ideologies but to be roughly the same in technologies. Hierarchy characterized all of the organizations, but was less pronounced in Israeli kibbutzim and Yugoslav plants. One interesting comparison was that in the American plants, individual achievement tended to predominate over egalitarianism. Americans wanted to move up the hierarchy, not eliminate it. Kibbutz members, on the other hand, had little or no desire to increase their formal status (Tannenbaum et al. 1974, p. 214).

Performance-oriented managerial ideologies. Managers are supposed to concern themselves with the productivity and efficiency in the organizations they manage. In the past century, at least six distinctive managerial ideologies directed at improving work performance have emerged in the American culture. Two conflicting ideological themes can be traced within them. The first and oldest is one of impersonal and unremitting authoritarian control of employees to ensure that they perform as expected. The second advocates a more humanitarian and compassionate stance as the best method to elicit employees' voluntary cooperation and effort. Both are, of course, consonant with values held in the wider society—the first with the first cluster given in Table 2–1, the second with the fourth cluster.

In order to be useful to managers, a managerial ideology must prescribe what they will accept as the *right way* to achieve some accepted goal. Historically, there has been no question about general social acceptance of the goals of efficiency and performance as appropriate for managers. The authoritarian control theme fits naturally with this performance goal. The humanitarian theme does not. To make humanitarianism relevant to the accepted managerial goal, the concern with performance has been grafted, with varying degrees of success, onto humanitarian values and beliefs to produce new ideologies. Historically, in response to general social trends, the pendulum of espoused ideology has swung from emphasizing one theme to the other. But neither theme has ever disappeared entirely, and various popular programs try to blend the two, usually by seeing humanitarianism as leading to higher employee performance (Trice and Beyer 1984b). This blending, however, took time. An outline of the historical unfolding of this development follows.

Social Darwinism. During the 1880s, Herbert Spencer applied Darwin's concepts to human societies, arguing that superior performance emerges from natural, impersonal, competitive forces. Allowing these forces to operate without interference should produce superior performance over time by weeding out the unfit (Hofstadter 1955). Justifying this competitive struggle was an alleged natural law that guaranteed gradual, but inevitable, progress via the process of natural selection of superior performers. When applied to the workplace, Social Darwinism discouraged any tolerance of poor performance; instead it encouraged managers to ruthlessly pit one worker against another in a relentless process of survival of the fittest. Employees were admonished to work hard and to accept defeat as an expression of an inexorable evolutionary process (Perrow 1972). Social Darwinism is alive today in beliefs that hostile takeovers provide needed discipline to managers and thus are, in the long run, good for the economy and the society.

Industrial betterment.   Around the turn of the century, a more humanitarian ideology that opposed Social Darwinism emerged. It was as if natural selection has been replaced by a helping hand—a hand that employers extended to workers because it was "good business" (Brandes 1970). Rather than relying upon the emergence of the fittest, the industrial betterment movement sought to promote job performance through paternalism. It advocated, for example, improving the ventilation, lighting, and general physical comfort of workplaces; and offering medical care, housing, education, opportunities for recreation, and even plans for saving and lending money to workers. These betterment efforts were aimed both at improving the lives of workers and reducing production costs and labor conflict.

The National Cash Register Company (NCR) provided a prominent example. Its president pioneered the idea of "welfare work" in mid-1889 along with the slogan "it pays" (Nelson and Campbell 1972, p. 3). Jane Addams, a well-known social worker in Chicago, praised NCR for its welfare program and used her influence to promote similar programs in other work establishments (Rodgers 1978). Indeed, the movement spread steadily during the first two decades of the 20th century, cresting during the 1920s. At its peak, it was warmly embraced by at least five hundred prominent employers, and until World War I, even organized labor supported its strategies (Brandes 1970). Post World War II scholars looking at this movement have referred to it as American welfare capitalism.

Scientific management.   During the same period, scientific management, which had considerable affinity with social Darwinism, was born. This new movement shared with industrial betterment the goals of reducing costs, labor conflict, and of generally improving worker performance (Nelson and Campbell 1972, p. 4). But its strategy for improving performance, initially developed and popularized by Frederick Taylor, emphasized individual competitive performance as measured by impersonal scientific techniques (Taylor 1911). Jobs were broken down into elementary operations so that the best and most efficient method of performing them could be determined scientifically. Superior workers were timed to measure how long it took them to perform the operations involved. Such measures were then used to set standards for all workers, who were paid according to how well their performance met the standards.

In contrast with the personal concern for employees expressed in the betterment movement, scientific management advocated impersonal and mechanistic controls as the best way to rationally engineer superior performance. The ideology associated with the movement viewed workers with suspicion because they were inherently given to shirking, which could be corrected only by the strict application of measures designed to ensure accountability. The growth of this movement helped to spark the subsequent rapid growth of labor unions.

Despite unionization, the movement survived. A familiar and highly successful example from the present day is provided by McDonald's restaurants. Each unit tries to achieve the ultimate in efficiency. Each job description reflects a time-and-motion study, and the training of new employees is explicitly geared to that job description. All procedures in performing specific jobs are standardized and formalized through written rules. Checklists and manuals spell out how to do each and every task in every job. For example, a new cashier gets a written sheet from McDonald's headquarters specifying exactly how to serve customers. Even the way to greet customers is completely specified. A checklist details how to perform each job in the restaurant. In addition, an operations manual specifies exactly how to manage all positions, including the precise amount of ingredients to put into drink dispensers and shake machines (Polisoto and Fernandez 1987). In every way, McDonald's is a prime example of scientific management as it is now practiced. Customers like the predictable quality, fast service, and low cost these procedures ensure. Most of the workers don't stay long, but they are relatively easily replaced.

The fields of industrial psychology, industrial engineering, and operations research extended and refined the impersonal, mechanistic control theme expressed in Taylorism (Braverman 1974; Leavitt 1965). These fields, in effect, comprise the modern-day manifestation of the scientific management ideology. As these fields developed, both jobs and workers were scrutinized ever more carefully with the aims of engineering better fits between the two and of removing all possible impediments to performance. A shared ideological premise is that better fits between the characteristics of employees and jobs assures higher productivity. Much of the work done in employee selection, training, job design, and human factors engineering is based on this premise. Another premise is that various workplace conditions can be impediments to performance. The scheduling of work flows and physical factors like ventilation and noise were therefore investigated and brought under closer control by management.

Human relations. The emergence of the Human Relations movement in the 1930s and 1940s gave managers another ideology to consider as they grappled with the rapid growth and new militancy of unions. This movement extended and refined the compassionate theme of the betterment movement, but suggested a shift in orientation and strategy. The techniques of Taylorism had not solved the problem of how to secure employees' best efforts. The well-known Hawthorne studies made this evident and provided some new ideas for solving the problem. The studies suggested that performance was affected by how employees were treated, and how they felt about their work and their supervisors (Roethlisberger and Dickson 1946). This idea became central to this movement. As one analyst suggested, it "reduced social and organizational issues to personal troubles" (Brown 1978, p. 367). From these tenets it followed that supervisors needed to be trained in social skills, listening techniques, and leadership patterns consistent with the emotional and social needs of workers (Roethlisberger 1977; Mayo 1945). Full-time counselors, who took a nondirective, listening role, were also advocated (Wilensky and Wilensky 1951).

The ideology of human relations attracted many adherents in subsequent decades, spawned the specialty called organizational development, and is still very much alive today. Its intellectual base has been extended and buttressed by the work of such well-known academics as McGregor (1960), Likert (1961), Argyris (1964), and Bennis (1966).

One of the theories of organizations best known among managers is the Theory X and Theory Y formulation of Douglas McGregor (1960). In these two theories, which he proposed as opposites, McGregor identified two clusters of managerial beliefs about the nature of human nature. Those who hold to Theory X, McGregor argued, believe that people dislike work, and are distrustful, lazy, unmotivated, and unwilling to work; they must therefore be coerced or bribed into working and appreciate being told what to do rather than thinking it out for themselves. In sharp contrast, Theory Y holds that people neither like or dislike work, but come to have feelings about it as a result of their experiences with work. Theory Y also says people want to grow; basically trust their surroundings and other people; and are self-actualizing, self-controlled, and self-motivated. Thus, people will set goals for themselves and pursue them energetically without being pressured by managers. Theory Y became an important codeword for referring to the human relations ideology.

Undoubtedly, the most important lesson of this framework for managers is that the exercise of hierarchical authority over subordinates is viewed positively by Theory X and negatively by Theory Y. While McGregor did not label Theory X as undesirable and Theory Y as desirable, his followers in the human relations movement and his readers ever since have. For it is no mystery which of the two sets of beliefs accords best with trends in the American culture, with its increasing emphasis on individualism.

McGregor was not the only theorist to advance ideas consonant with this cherished ideological theme. Earlier, Abraham Maslow, a clinical psychologist, developed a hierarchy of needs, which assumed that self-actualization was every person's ultimate goal. McGregor simply applied Maslow's ideas to managerial and subordinate roles in the workplace. Still earlier, the research at the Hawthorne plant of Western Electric had shown that workers prefer to participate in decisions about how they do their work and that, when management does not provide it, workers will wrest some measure of control over their work from management by establishing and enforcing their own standards of behavior (Roethlisberger and Dickson 1946). Since then, experts in this movement have advocated a variety of programs that clearly express the ideology of individualism so prominent in the U.S. culture. Examples include employee participation programs, the quality of work life movement, and most recently, strategies to facilitate employee ownership.

Because they incorporate this important ideology, human relations programs and theories tend to be emotionally charged. Studies of the efficacy of such programs show that employees like them, but results have not as yet provided clear evidence that the programs make any difference in productivity (Wall et al. 1986; Burke 1980). This does not deter most proponents from arguing on their behalf and continuing to mount such programs. As will be discussed in Chapter 3, most of these programs function largely as cultural rites that serve to strengthen existing systems of authority rather than change them in fundamental ways.

Quality of work life. As time passed, both of the ideological themes of performance-oriented control and humanitarianism became entrenched in management thinking, and the contradictions between them became more and more evident. Some sort of reconciliation and integration was badly needed. One such attempt is the relatively recent quality-of-work-life (QWL) movement. In many ways, QWL programs are continuations and extensions of ideas begun under the banner of human relations.

Although it emphasizes humanitarianism, this movement is also concerned with better engineering of the workplace in the sense that it applies social science formulations to suggest improvements. The ideology views many jobs as dull, repetitive, and meaningless, and as offering little challenge or autonomy. One tenet is that there are numerous "physical and emotional health costs of jobs as they are now designed" (O'Toole 1972, p. 11). The very structure of most workplaces, especially the more bureaucratic ones, is seen as repressive, leading to feelings of helplessness and alienation that decrease performance. QWL advocates favor strategies designed to alleviate these damaging conditions, including the formation of autonomous work groups, restructuring of jobs to enlarge and enrich them, and employee involvement in decision making through participative management (Cummings and Molloy 1977).

Employee assistance programs. Although the EAP movement is relatively young, it has also developed clear ideologies that reconcile the two major ideological themes and other parts of past movements. The theme of performance-oriented control is reflected in the EAP tenet that employees' job performance is decreased by their psychic pain and personal troubles, which then tend to be viewed as another impediment that can be eliminated or at least brought under the control of management. The humanitarian theme is reflected in the tenet that employees who suffer from such pain and troubles should be helped by their employer or union to secure treatment or other assistance. Expressed in these ways, the two themes are easily combined. Helping employees is good business because decreasing their pain and alleviating their troubles will improve their work performance (Trice and Beyer 1984b). If "... the fault lies in the employee ... it is the employee who must be changed" (Argyris 1957, p. 143).

By emphasizing individual-level causes of poor performance, rather than the effects of supervision, work groups, or organizational structure, the EAP movement differs from human relations and QWL and resembles Social Darwinism, industrial betterment, and scientific management (Trice and Beyer 1984b). But in its central concern with the welfare of workers, it incorporates the humanitarian flavor of human relations and QWL. A unique feature of the EAP ideology is its emphasis on causes of poor performance that emanate from *outside* the workplace. Employees enter such programs in two primary ways: (1) they can go to the program counselor voluntarily for help with a personal problem such as alcoholism, other drug abuse, divorce, sick relative, or disturbed family member; or (2) they can be referred to the counselor by their supervisor because their performance is visibly suffering because of their preoccupations with their personal problems. For example, an employee may be repeatedly late or absent or a chronically poor performer. No matter how employees enter the program, their entry and problems are confidential and not made part of their work record.

Summary.   Of course, variants of all of these general ideologies are likely to arise in specific company cultures. Each organizational culture will emphasize the common ideological elements just discussed to different degrees and add unique elements and practices of its own. While endless combinations are theoretically possible, certain elements are more compatible with others and seem to cluster together. The typologies listed in Table 1-5 are attempts to identify and describe such clusterings. However, no specific organization will have ideologies or cultures that exactly match any typology. All cultures embody some unique elements.

Some of the findings of studies of specific organizations should help to illustrate how generally held ideologies develop unique features in different organizations.

Examples of Specific Organizational Ideologies

One company's EAP.   Several separate worksites of a large corporation had started EAP programs without corporate approval or sponsorship (Trice and Beyer 1984b). During interviews, local managers involved in the decision to add these programs justified having them more in terms of how it helped supervisors to cope with disruptive employees than they did in terms of the official EAP ideology—namely, improving those employees' work performance. They did not disagree with the official ideology, but put more emphasis on the company's responsibility to help employees with their problems whether or not their specific productivity would be affected. They saw the most likely gains in productivity as coming from the removal of disruptions that could affect the work groups and supervisors of the troubled employees. The programs were also seen by these managers as natural expressions of the company's ideology—verified in a separate survey of a larger number of managers throughout the company—in which concerns with productivity and employee welfare were blended in an ideology we called humane pragmatism. Further details of that survey are worth considering because they illustrate how many strands from the general ideologies already discussed can be combined in a unique way within a specific company culture.

Since other work sites in the company had not adopted EAP programs, we asked a sample of 475 managers in 19 other worksites of this company whether or not they favored the expansion of an existing company program focused on helping employees with alcohol problems into a more general EAP program that would help employees deal with all types of personal problems. In addition, we asked these managers to respond to 18 statements reflecting beliefs and values relevant to management; these were factor-analyzed to see which covaried in coherent clusters that might reflect managerial ideologies (Beyer and Trice 1981; Trice and Beyer 1984a).[7]

---

[7]The purpose of this phase of the research was to study the implementation of a program designed to help employees with drinking problems. It was not a cultural study and did not focus on

Subsequent results indicated that those managers who favored the expansion of such programs expressed high agreement with five items reflecting the ideology of human pragmatism; for example, they agreed highly with separate items saying they wanted to be thought of as humane managers and as efficient managers and that helping employees was good business. They also expressed belief in the ideology of social responsibility—items saying that management should be concerned with responding to employee and social needs.

Statements reflecting the ideology of humane pragmatism received the strongest and most unanimous endorsement across the whole sample of managers, suggesting it was the most generally accepted and basic ideology within this company. Items reflecting other ideologies were less strongly and consistently endorsed across respondents. There were, however, a subset of managers who endorsed a Protestant ethic-like ideology expressed by agreement with items saying most people bring their troubles on themselves, that failure is usually deserved, and that providing many benefits and services tends to encourage employees to evade responsibility for their own affairs. These managers opposed extension of the alcoholism program into an EAP.

Together these results illustrate how the acceptance of new ideological appeals is conditioned by previously held beliefs and values. Those managers whose beliefs were consonant with the EAP ideology favored adoption of such programs; those who held beliefs that disagreed with the tenets of EAPs did not think they should be adopted.

Two hospitals. Other examples of strong organizational ideologies and their consequences were observed in a study of 19 hospitals in the San Francisco area (Meyer 1982a, 1982b). The two hospitals observed in most detail had very different ideologies. One, called Memorial Hospital, had a "lean and hungry" ideology that discouraged meetings, conferences, and memos, believing them to be frivolous. Setting up and maintaining a formal, bureaucratic structure was believed to be costly and therefore to be avoided; rather the hospital should rely upon tradition and efficiency to keep costs down. Consistent with this ideology, Memorial Hospital had a low ratio of employees to patients, the controller prepared and typed his own financial reports, the administrator answered his own phone, and meetings and outside relationships were discouraged. This organization was run as a tight ship.

The second hospital, dubbed Community Hospital, had an ideology of entrepreneurial pluralism, which emphasized the value of a loose federation within the hospital of semiautonomous parts, each centered on a distinct program or type of patient. Added to this belief in pluralism were beliefs favoring innovation

---

culture as a *major* explanatory variable. The study design, involving multiple locations and large numbers of respondents, did not allow for qualitative data collection except during the pretest phase and in the limited number of sites with "different" (EAP) programs. But we did not want to ignore ideology entirely as a possible explanatory variable; so we constructed a questionnaire scale as the only practical way to get ideologies in this study. Items were based on extensive interviewing done at multiple sites over a one-year pretest phase to provide the foundation for the structured instrument used in the final data collection.

and links with the outside environment; both were encouraged. Thus the administrator spent about 70 percent of his time managing relationships with community organizations and planning agencies. Internally, the hospital was rather a "chaotic place" with "impromptu agreements negotiated informally" rather than formally in board rooms (Meyer 1982b, p. 46–47).

The effects of these very different ideologies became evident when all of the hospital-based anesthesiologists in the community went on strike to protest an enormous increase in the cost of malpractice insurance. Most surgeons and referral physicians joined the strike, causing abrupt declines in hospital admissions, bed occupancy, and cash flows. For one month all hospitals in the community experienced an intense crisis—an environmental jolt.

Because it did not customarily watch its environment, Memorial Hospital did not foresee the strike. It did little to change to respond to the strike, and because its normally lean ways gave it a favorable cash position, it was able to continue more or less as if nothing had happened and still weather the strike. In effect the strike enabled Memorial to reaffirm the value of its self-reliance and lean ways and also to dramatize its commitment to its employees, none of whom were laid off during the strike. In contrast, Community Hospital anticipated the strike and used it as an occasion to experiment and learn new tactics in external relations. The strike therefore lead to permanent changes in Community Hospital. The researcher interpreted these events as follows:

> The cases suggest that jolts acquire meanings from ideologies that determine whether the jolts are perceived as dilemmas, opportunities, or aberrations. Memorial's leaders perceived the jolt as a decline in revenue, and thus they confronted an ideological dilemma: which is more crucial—our balance sheet or the commitment to our employees? Efficiency was valued, and inaction would jeopardize Memorial's cash flow. Self-reliance, however, was also valued, and members would regard unilateral administrative actions as improper, yet the members were inept at collaborative problem solving. The employees' interests finally prevailed because Memorial's leaders decided that the hospital's financial reserves exceeded those of the doctors. Community's leaders perceived the jolt as an upheaval in the environment, and they interpreted the upheaval as an opportunity for a drill, testing members' adaptive dexterity. The pluralistic ideology gave rise to an ad hoc coalition that constructed accurate projections of the strike's impact on the hospital. Supervisors planned for this contingency adroitly because authority was customarily delegated to foster novel solutions to unfamiliar problems (Meyer 1982, p. 530).

Ma Bell. Another company with a distinctive ideology that recently weathered a substantial environmental jolt is American Telephone & Telegraph. Its jolt, though long anticipated, was truly mammoth in its impact on the company. After years of legal arguments, a federal judge ordered AT&T to divest itself of all of its operating divisions (the so-called Baby Bells). Reactions of employees to this sundering will be discussed in a later chapter. More relevant to this chapter is to consider the unique ideology that had helped to make this company one of the "most consistently profitable, the most self-assured, and one of the best managed corporations in the twentieth century..." (Keller and Lewis 1988, p. 56).

A good picture of this culture comes from the writings of W. Brooke Tunstall, who served as corporate vice-president for organization and management systems at the time of the divestiture. He reports that Theodore Vail, the charismatic founder of the company, coined a six-word mission statement that became the foundation of the company culture. It was simply: "one system, one policy, universal service." A later president, Walter Gifford, added the aim of the "best possible service at the lowest possible cost, consistent with fair treatment of employees and shareowners" (Tunstall 1985, p. 146). Gifford expressed this ideology through the metaphor of the three-legged stool, with the three legs representing customers, shareholders, and employees.

Concrete manifestations of the concern for employees included the practice of promoting managers from the ranks and general policies that led to lifetime employment for most employees. In many segments of the company, layoffs never happened. As a result, managerial ranks were filled largely by insiders who were very loyal and committed to Ma Bell—as the company was affectionately called. Other outcomes were "extreme deference to the status inherent in each level of the managerial hierarchy ... also a powerful bias toward consensus management..." (Tunstall 1983, p. 21).

Concern for customers was expressed through a dedication to service, instilled during socialization of new employees and given teeth through a special measurement system that quantitatively evaluated managerial performance relative to the service ethos. In many offices, a picture of Angus McDonald—a 19th century lineman fighting to repair broken lines during a blizzard—adorned the walls. His determination and his status as company hero symbolized the lengths to which employees were expected to go to maintain customer service. Many stories attested to the fact that employees did, indeed, live up to this ideal (Tunstall 1983, p. 21).

The concern for shareholders, which included most employees, was expressed through the keen internal competition the company fostered between its divisions. The company consistently monitored productivity and emphasized technical and operational skills.

Like the other organizations discussed in this section, AT&T developed its culture around a somewhat distinctive ideology, which guided what people in the company did. Other firms express concern for customers, employees, and stockholders, but the particular ways they express these concerns and act upon them will differ somewhat from what happened at AT&T because each organization's ideologies and culture are products of its unique history, leadership, mission, membership, and context.

SUMMARY

The substance of an organization's cultures resides in its ideologies, which are emotionalized, shared sets of beliefs, values, and norms that both impel people to action and justify their actions to themselves and others. Cultures have multiple ideologies; the ideas they express sometimes complement and sometimes contradict each other. The substance of cultures emerges largely from informal social processes in spontaneous and unplanned ways. With the passage of time, ideologies tend to move away from the forefront of people's attention and become implicit and taken for granted. Although cultural substance is difficult to uncover, careful and sensitive efforts can reveal its major outlines.

While controversy exists over the role of ideologies in society, the arguments for interest theory can be incorporated into more general strain theory. People develop ideologies to help them deal with all kinds of uncertainties including how to advance their own interests.

Some of the ideologies in organizations are imported from at least six levels of their environments: transnational systems, nations, regions and communities, industries, occupations, and other organizations. The ideologies that have grown up in U.S. society include both complementary and contradictory elements. Most distinctive is the U.S. culture's strong emphasis on personal achievement, self-reliance, and individualism—reflecting the American adaptation of the Protestant ethic. Within most U.S. work organizations, rationality is the arch-ideology; only a small subset of organizations emphasizes egalitarianism.

Consistent with an emphasis on rationality, various managerial ideologies about how to promote efficiency and performance have emerged in this century. A somewhat contradictory ideology, humanitarianism, also emerged in various movements and was eventually reconciled with rationality, which however remains dominant. Specific organizations develop unique cultures from the amalgamation of ideologies they import and those they develop to deal with their circumstances and unique historical events.

3

Cultural Forms

While ideologies are abstractions—the emotionalized sets of beliefs, values, and norms that constitute the substance of cultures—cultural forms are concrete manifestations of culture. They consist of observable entities through which members of a culture express, affirm, and communicate cultural substance to one another. There are four major categories of cultural forms—symbols, language, narratives, and practices. Table 3–1 lists them in order of their complexity and gives some specific examples in each category. Although this list is more comprehensive and detailed than most treatments of cultural forms, it is not exhaustive. Other categories and examples probably exist.

To introduce the discussion of cultural forms, we will first describe and illustrate briefly the four categories given in Table 3–1. This brief treatment is intended to prepare the reader for an explanation in the next part of the chapter: how cultural forms contribute to sense-making processes and thus to the emergence and persistence of cultural ideologies. The rest of this chapter returns to the four categories of cultural forms, illustrating in some detail how various types differ from each other and the kinds of messages they can convey.

Symbols are listed as the first category of cultural forms because they are the most basic and "smallest" units of cultural expression (Turner 1967, p. 19). Also, other cultural forms usually incorporate symbols, making them the most frequently encountered form of cultural expression. The dictionary defines a symbol as "something that stands for or suggests something else ... (esp: a visible sign of something, as a concept or an institution) that is invisible" (Gove 1981, p. 2316). Organizations use all of the types of symbols listed in the table to convey abstract ideas. Prudential Life Insurance Company uses a natural object—the Rock of Gibraltar—to represent continuity and dependability. The uniforms worn by hospital personnel are manufactured objects that denote their wearers' skills and statuses. The spaciousness, plush carpet, and expensive furniture

TABLE 3–1
CATEGORIES AND EXAMPLES OF CULTURAL FORMS

Category	Examples
Symbols	Objects, natural and manufactured Settings Performers, functionaries
Language	Jargon, slang Gestures, signals, signs Songs Humor, jokes, gossip, rumors Metaphors Proverbs, slogans
Narratives	Stories, legends Sagas Myths
Practices	Rituals, taboos Rites, ceremonials

found in most executive offices provides a setting that represents power and high status. McDonald's used a clown (Ronald McDonald) as a performer in its advertising and promotions, probably to suggest fun and a welcoming stance toward children.[1]

Language is a shared system of vocal sounds, written signs, or gestures used by members of a culture to convey categorized meaning to each other. Language employs categories and rules through which people structure their perceptions and understandings of the world (Evered 1983, p. 127). In effect, language imposes a kind of "grid on experience" (Gowler and Legge 1989, p. 438). While written language consists of a series of symbols, these are only a shorthand way of conveying the totality of its meaning. This is because the categories and rules embodied in language provide more explicit meanings for written symbols and their relationships to each other than is possible from mere groupings of physical objects. They also make language more malleable and flexible than any set of discrete symbols by allowing words and gestures to be combined in an infinite number of ways to convey many different meanings. Thus, although like symbols in that it is basic to and contained in other cultural forms, language conveys meanings in a more complex and refined way than symbols do. Language thus makes possible a different array of cultural forms.

Organizations deliberately employ many of the language forms listed in Table 3–1 to create certain cultural images. They use metaphors (the company is like a "big family"), proverbs ("Everyone at Northrup is in marketing"), gestures (mandatory smiles at McDonald's), and songs ("I've got that Mary Kay enthusiasm") for this purpose. Also, companies and specific occupations have specialized jargon ("Are you wired in" at Western Electric) and slang ("flaming" among

---

[1]They have elaborated this symbol to convey a caring image through the establishment of Ronald McDonald Houses that provide subsidized housing for families near their hospitalized children.

computer programmers) that is understandable only to members. In addition, in most work settings, employees have their own informal languages, consisting of the jokes and gossip they tell each other about managers and other work-related issues, and the humor they employ to deal with work-related tensions.

Narratives, the next most complex type of cultural form, employ both symbols and language. Members of organizations, like people generally, use several kinds of narratives to make sense of their experiences and to express their feelings and beliefs. Myths are dramatic, rather vague, unquestioned narratives of imagined events, usually used to explain the origins or transformations of something. They deal with matters that are very serious or sacred in a culture. Myths often incorporate beliefs about the efficacy of something. A prominent myth that originated in the military and was carried over into industry and business education is that PERT (program, evaluation, and review technique) was instrumental in the efficient and timely development of the Polaris submarine. In fact, the technique was not employed until after the Polaris was successfully tested (Sapolsky 1972).

Sagas differ from myths in that they are based in a true account of events. They are historically grounded narratives that describe the unique accomplishments and beliefs of organizations and their leaders over a period of time—usually in heroic and romantic terms. Well-known examples include how Mary Kay founded a highly successful company in the process of struggling to support herself and her children, and how Lee Iacocca managed to save the Chrysler Corporation and repay its massive loans. Sagas involve whole sequences of events. They are, of course, prone to exaggeration and embellishment; thus, all of the details of the saga may not be entirely true.

Legends are also historical narratives; they differ from sagas and stories in that they incorporate some literally *wonderful* elements. For example, one account of an anniversary celebration of the Western Electric studies emphasized that the sun suddenly came out of the clouds on that very rainy day. This fortunate occurrence was interpreted by participants as another manifestation of the good fortune that had surrounded these studies.

Organizational stories are simpler and more mundane; they dramatize more ordinary, everyday events within organizations in order to convey important cultural meanings. Many stories are highly distorted and humorous accounts of true events; sometimes they are wholly invented. They often portray the enactment of ideologies in an extreme instance. For example, one story about General Motors tells how local managers were so eager to please a visiting manager from corporate headquarters that they knocked out the wall of a hotel room so they could fit in a refrigerator with his favorite snacks (Wright 1979). This story portrays an ideology of abject submission to authority and to the company as ridiculous.

The final and most complex category of cultural forms includes specific *practices* and behaviors that express cultural meanings. As already explained in Chapter 1, people's behaviors both say and do things (Leach 1968). Thus, many activities in organizations that are undertaken for instrumental purposes also carry important cultural messages to members and other observers.

The smallest and simplest unit of cultural practice is the ritual. Rituals are standardized, detailed sets of techniques and behaviors that the culture prescribes to manage anxieties and express common identities. Some rituals have lost any pretense of practical consequences. For example, during World War II, a time-and-motion expert observed that two members of a motorized gun crew in the British army stood at attention throughout the discharge of a large cannon. When he asked an old colonel of artillery why they did so, the colonel thought awhile and replied, "I have it; they are holding the horses" (Morison 1982, p. 84). Other rituals, whose efficacy is usually not questioned, may be practiced in an exaggerated form that exceeds any technical benefits. Before operating, surgeons typically scrub their hands for much longer than is required to achieve asepsis. Many other rituals are practiced as if they will have beneficial practical consequences, but seem to have largely expressive benefits. Letter writing and other paperwork frequently becomes a ritual in large organizations. An observer in one federal agency noted how letters were generated and sent to various bureaucratic links for redrafting and approval even when the information they contained had already been communicated over the telephone (Taylor 1979).

While rituals are behaviors people are supposed to do, taboos are behaviors that are forbidden. Taboos spring from powerful beliefs that certain acts are socially undesirable, even loathsome. These beliefs vary among social groups and change over time because they reflect the culture and the context in which the behavior would occur. For example, corporal punishment, once common on ships and in some schools, is no longer generally acceptable in either setting.

The final category of practices—rites and ceremonials—are the most complex and elaborate of the cultural forms because they typically consolidate several discrete cultural forms into one event or series of events (Gluckman 1962). In rites and ceremonials, various forms come to be "intimately associated and to influence one another" (Kluckhohn 1942, p. 65). Rites are dramatic, planned sets of activities carried out for the benefit of an audience; ceremonials are systems of several rites connected with a single occasion. Perhaps the most pervasive rites are those used to mark people's moving from one status to another; many managerial training programs are such rites of passage. Inaugurations of heads of state usually involve ceremonials consisting of many distinctive rites—the swearing-in ceremony, the parade, the inaugural ball, and so forth.

Although all cultural forms convey cultural meanings, the meanings received will be heavily influenced by the cultural context in which the form occurs, the prior socialization of receivers, and other factors. Analysts of organizational cultures refer to the process by which people derive meaning from cultural forms as sense making.

Sense-Making Processes

It is in the interplay between ideologies and cultural forms that cultures coalesce and maintain their existence. Cultural forms condense and make ideologies tangible and concrete. They serve as sense-making mechanisms by which members of cultures think out loud about themselves (Mukerji and Schudson 1986, p. 50). Analysts describe cultural forms as "sense making practices" (Gephart 1978, p. 553); as "sets of indicators and displayers of organizational sense-making" (Pacanowsky and O'Donnell-Trujillo 1982, p. 124); and as "culture in action" (Deal and Kennedy 1982, p. 59).

Definitions and Related Concepts

The term *sense making* refers to the processes through which people make their situations "accountable to themselves and others" (Morgan, Frost, and Pondy 1983, p. 24). The central idea behind the term is that reality in everyday life is an ongoing accomplishment that takes a particular shape and form as people try to create order and to make sense of the situations in which they find themselves (Mead 1934; Berger and Luckmann, 1967). The actual activity of sense making combines several processes that are often treated as distinct. Sense making is a cognitive process in that it involves knowing and perceiving, it is a behavioral process in that it involves doing things, and it is a social process in that it involves people doing things together.[2] While conceptually distinct, these processes are linked and often occur together.

Nonconscious process. Sense making occurs at multiple levels of consciousness. Social scientists from various disciplines agree that people cope with familiar, everyday situations in a "loosely preprogrammed, nonconscious way" (Louis 1980, p. 239). They develop cognitive scripts based in past experience that provide expectations about the usual sequences of events (Abelson 1976) and cultural tool kits that provide accepted sets of behaviors and emotional reactions (Swidler 1986) to use in routine decision making and action.[3] When people habitualize their thinking and behavior in these ways, they reduce uncertainty for themselves and others. They also narrow the choices they need to make and thus leave themselves time and energy for conscious deliberation and innovation (Berger and Luckmann 1967, p. 53) in coping with nonroutine circumstances and unexpected events.

Although cognitive scripts and habitual behaviors may have idiosyncratic

---

[2]Other terms used by social scientists to refer to some of the same processes are *noticing, interpretation, enactment,* and *learning* (Hedberg 1981; Weick 1977; Daft and Weick 1984; Starbuck and Milliken 1988). Noticing refers to the perceptual, automatic phase of the cognitive part of sense making. Interpretation is usually used to refer to the more deliberate, conscious cognitive part of sense making. Enactment refers to the behavioral part in that it focuses on actions. Learning is a more general term that is used to refer to the whole process.

[3]The term *cognitive script* is a metaphor scholars use to liken this process to learning the parts or roles in a play. A cognitive script tells people about a series of events and relationships among them. Another term often used to refer to such cognitive structures is *schemas,* defined as "... an abridged, generalized, corrigible, organization of experience that serves as an initial frame of reference for action and perception" (Weick 1979, p. 154). Tool kits are, of course, another metaphor likening cultural forms to the instruments people use to fix and build things. Since cultures have many forms they are like tool kits.

elements, much of their content is probably determined by people's cultures. How people drive their cars, clean their teeth, or greet other people was not always automatic for them; how to think about and do each of these things had to be learned at some point during their socialization, and perhaps relearned by those who moved into new cultures. Cultural forms—especially language, rituals, and taboos—guided thinking and behaviors, and in this way, helped people make sense of what they were doing. Similarly, in work organizations, cultural forms guide people in how to think and act by telling them "how we do things around here."

Conscious process.   Sense making becomes a more active and conscious process when people need to cope with uncertainties arising in nonroutine or unexpected situations. While it is not an entirely rational or necessarily orderly process, one way to visualize such active sense making is in terms of recurring cycles of behavior (Louis 1980; Hedberg 1981; Isabella 1990). One view of this process uses the metaphor "switching cognitive gears" to suggest that people must experience certain conditions to induce them to change from an automatic to a conscious mode of sense making (Louis and Sutton 1991). Novelties, discrepancies, and requests for active thinking are three of the conditions likely to produce a switch from automatic to conscious sense making. Examples of novel situations are mergers, technological change, and organizational birth. Discrepancies that could have similar effects include organizational deaths or criminal behavior. Requests for active thinking include career planning and environmental scanning (Louis and Sutton 1991, p. 65). Often events include more than one of these conditions.

Conscious sense making may occur before, during, and after such triggering events; its results will then feed back into the scripts and tool kits engaged in the next similar event. People bring anticipations, expectations, and assumptions to any situation from their past experiences, their personal predispositions, and their cultures. When people experience something novel or something that does not match their expectations, they actively seek ways to explain the discrepancy. There are two major paths to explanation:

1. They can use their past experiences and cultural understandings or look to other people and to their environment to arrive at interpretations on which to base choices of actions. (Louis 1980, p. 241)
2. They can simply act first and see what happens afterward. (Hedberg 1981; Weick 1988)

An important implication of the term *sense making* is that much of the meaning people derive from their situations is made up retrospectively. In effect, events and actions are given meaning by how people think about them afterwards. In many situations, the thinking people do *after* they act, to make sense of what they have done, is more consequential than any thinking that preceded their actions. But conscious sense making also has a prospective side; after infancy, people are unlikely to go into any situation without some expectations of what will happen.

Such expectations may shape the actions people do and do not take and thus constrain the raw materials available for retrospective sense making. People who avoid trying anything new are less likely to arrive at new cultural meanings than people who venture to act in novel ways.

Cultural forms help prospective, concurrent, and retrospective sense making by providing shared meanings that help people work out what they expect, what is happening, and what has happened to them. When confronted with an organizational change requiring new behaviors, for example, people often tell one another stories. They may invent new stories about new personalities or circumstances, or they may return to familiar myths and sagas in their search for meaning. Management often holds meetings that function as rites of various kinds. New buzzwords and slogans become popular and new jokes are told.

Individual and collective processes.   Sense making is both an individual and a collective phenomenon. Individuals try to make sense of their worlds in the ways already described. They may use their cultures to help them in the process, but their individual sense making cannot, by itself, create or change cultures. Because cultures involve shared views of the world, sense making that shapes cultures must occur between and among people. Somehow people come to share similar interpretations of familiar and unfamiliar situations (Beyer and Lutze, 1992). Observations of newly formed decision-making groups in a laboratory experiment led to the following description:

> A series of common experiences propels the group toward the development of a common definition of group behavior. Members integrate each succeeding event with the interpretation they have developed from previous experience. This process occurs concurrently for all group members; the subjective meanings that members place on actions within the group become more compatible, even if they are not identical. (Bettenhausen and Murnighan 1985, p. 356)

Such collective sense making involves more than the aggregation of individual interpretations (Daft and Weick 1984, p. 285). It involves *social* processes.

The persistence of cultural forms and ideologies after their originators are gone is evidence that cultures have collective properties that are not reducible to individuals. As people are born into or join a culture, they do not know the circumstances that gave rise to certain cultural interpretations. Existing interpretations have become a social reality they take for granted (Berger and Luckmann 1967; Louis 1980).

Social Processes Involved

Although we do not yet know exactly how dominant social realities develop (Isabella 1990, p. 35), various social processes have been identified as making collective sense making possible. Most obvious are shared experiences (Berger and Luckmann 1967); socialization (Beyer and Lutze, 1992); communication (Putnam and Pacanowsky 1983); other social interactions (Harris and Sutton 1986);

and the related processes of influence, power, and leadership (Smircich and Stubbart 1985). Less obvious but also important are habit forming and conditioning (Hedberg, 1981); reciprocity and negotiation (Berger and Luckmann 1967; Strauss 1978); imitation and role modeling (Hedberg 1981); and exploratory action (Hedberg, Nystrom, and Starbuck 1976; Weick 1988).

Perhaps the most important vehicles for sense making in relatively routine situations are shared experiences and conversations; people talk through various experiences and allocate them "a definite place" in their world (Berger and Luckmann 1967, p. 153). Language both objectifies the world and realizes it in the double sense that it enables people to apprehend and create their situations. People do not have to arrive at exactly the same interpretations of events to make collective sense making possible. In fact, some ambiguity in language and meanings can facilitate cooperation; organized action (Meyer 1984; Donnellon, Gray, and Bougon 1986); and subsequent sense making.

Some of the processes just listed seem to be especially important in the formation and maintenance of cultures. Forming habitual patterns of behavior contributes to both individual and collective sense making. When individuals develop habitual sets of behaviors, it makes subsequent behaviors sensible to them. Their habits contribute to collective sense making by helping to channel others' behaviors into reciprocal or complementary patterns. These collective patterns then become part of collective sense making. Behaviors can become habitual because of conditioning or other reinforcements, which are often supplied by other persons acting on cultural prescriptions. In organizations, standard operating procedures and work routines embody collective sense making.

Another way to coordinate individual behaviors into acceptable collective patterns is through the norm of reciprocity, which seems to emerge in some form in virtually all societies. Such norms, for example, dictate appropriate behavior in giving gifts, extending invitations, greeting others, exchanging favors, and the like. They are often powerful regulators of behavior in work settings. Still another possibility is through more explicit role negotiation. Members of a work group, for example, may negotiate so that each does certain tasks that further the collective welfare. Decision makers may negotiate from initially different ideological positions to arrive at shared premises on which to base choices (Walsh and Fahey 1986).

Imitation and role modeling shape collective behavior and subsequent sense making when groups of people consciously or unconsciously strive to behave like others they see as successful. Organizations often imitate what other successful organizations do; U.S. firms, for example, imitated the Japanese by adopting quality circles and continuous quality improvement programs. Junior managers and professionals often model their behaviors on what admired superiors do.

The social processes that are important in collective sense making become more explicit and intense when organizations are undergoing change or dealing with crises or threats (Berger and Luckmann 1967, p. 156; Bettenhausen and Murnighan 1985). Also, to the degree that greater uncertainty is involved, people's emotions are engaged and they become more active in their sense making. A study of 40 managers' interpretations of five key events in a financial service firm concluded that their "collective construed reality included both elements of fact and feeling and emotional reactions" (Isabella 1990, 33).

In crises or other situations of high uncertainty, "people often don't know what the 'appropriate action' is until they take some action and see what happens. . . . Understanding is facilitated by action, but action affects events and can make things worse." By changing the position of a switch or dial and watching to see what happens, an operator may be able to discover vital information about the nature of the problem and how to deal with it. Since "action is a means to get feedback, learn, and build an understanding of unknown environments," failure to act also has risks. It will eventuate in "less understanding and more errors" (Weick 1988, p. 306). In crisis situations, such as large-scale industrial accidents, those individuals or groups who dare to act can create information valuable for collective sense making.

Role of cultural forms.   Action in organizations inevitably involves some cultural forms—symbols, rituals, language, rite and ceremonials, and the like. A study of decision-making processes in hospitals observed that at one phase "language ceases to be a technology for processing information and becomes a process of ascribing meanings" (Meyer 1984, p. 12). Familiar language and other cultural forms help sense making by evoking similar past experiences on which to base interpretations of the current situation. Narratives and cultural practices also provide similar scripts for behavior. In nonroutine situations, cultural forms may occur in new combinations that help people to discover new meanings. The mere juxtaposition of forms and other acts is likely to affect the perceptual processes that feed into sense making. Psychologists have determined that people tend to form individual stimuli into meaningful patterns by means of four perceptual grouping processes: continuity, closure, proximity, and similarity (Hellriegel, Slocum, and Woodman 1986, p. 97). These processes indicate that people tend to perceive objects as continuous patterns, to complete objects so they form a logical whole, to see objects as related if they are near one another, and to group together objects they see as similar. Thus, new sequences of even familiar actions can lead to new interpretations.

Cultural forms not only aid sense making through the meanings they convey; they also aid the sense-making process through the emotional reassurances they provide that help people persist in their coping efforts. Forms provide a concrete anchoring point, even if the meanings they carry are vague and only imperfectly transmitted. Even partial and vague ideas are better than nothing. Sometimes even the wrong ideas are helpful because they reassure people and structure their actions in constructive directions.

> While on maneuvers in the Swiss Alps, a reconnaissance unit of the Hungarian army was caught in a snowstorm; members considered themselves lost until one of them found a map in his pocket. They calmed down, pitched a camp, lasted out the snowstorm, and with the aid of the map, discovered their bearings. Only later did their lieutenant find out that the map they had used was of the Pyrenees, not the Alps. (Adapted from Weick 1987, p. 222)

Also, many cultural forms involve the expression of emotion and, by this venting of emotions, help people to cope with stress (Harris and Sutton 1986; Isabella 1990). Finally, the mere doing of something is often reassuring, especially when people do what they know how to do best (Starbuck 1983).

Constraints.   Certain characteristics of organizations, however, will constrain collective sense making. The physical and cultural context will channel behaviors in certain directions. The physical context makes it easy for some people to interact and difficult for others. The cultural context focuses attention on certain actions and objects and provides a repertoire of established interpretations and emotional reactions. Tight or loose coupling between some work groups makes certain combinations of events and communications more or less likely. Resources may be lacking to collect information or provide meeting times or training that would facilitate sense making. And finally, people's investments in past enactments and competing enactments may make experimental actions or reaching a shared set of new meanings very difficult (Smircich and Stubbart 1985).

Despite these constraints, collective sense making does occur in organizations, and this sense making is greatly facilitated by the use of cultural forms. Examples of their uses in organizations should make this clear.

Symbols in Organizations

A symbol is a "concrete indication of abstract values" (Firth 1973, p. 54). Because virtually any object can become a symbol of something to someone, symbols are truly ubiquitous in human society.[4] Everyone, every day, confronts a literal swarm of symbols. The list is almost endless—signs, logos, pictures, insignias, style of dress, length of hair, type of automobile, office furnishings, size of dwelling, and so forth. Many of these objects convey some kinds of meaning to almost everyone, thanks to advertising and other means of mass communication, but these meanings may form only a peripheral background to our lives and activities.

One way to sort through the swarm is to become aware of which symbols matter and how they function. Some clearly play a more central role than others in creating meaning in a given culture. In effect, some are *key symbols* because they express the underlying substance of that culture "in a relatively pure form" (Ortner 1973, p. 1338). For example, in the U.S. culture, the figure of Santa Claus and a decorated evergreen tree are key symbols of Christmas and many of the meanings associated with this holiday. There are two kinds of key symbols: *summarizing symbols* and *elaborating symbols*. Summarizing symbols represent "in an

---

[4]Some writers on culture use the term *symbol* to refer to all cultural forms. Others use a variety of terms—but without clear consensus on their definitions. For clarity, we have grouped cultural forms into several discrete categories that subsume a large number of terms that appear in the cultural literature. Readers should, however, be aware that much of what we talk of in this chapter is subsumed under the terms *symbol, symbolism,* and *symbolic behaviors* by other authors.

emotionally powerful and relatively undifferentiated way" what an organization or other social group means to its participants. Elaborating symbols are more specific and help members to sort out and categorize their experiences so they are comprehensible and translatable into orderly action (Ortner 1973, p. 1339).

Because organizations use multitudes of symbols of various kinds, and all tend to be multivocal in that they can carry more than one meaning, separating them into specific types and giving them specific interpretations is a somewhat arbitrary process. Nevertheless, in the following sections we will try to illustrate the various types of symbols so readers can get a sense of how each can function.

Objects

Uniforms are common cultural artifacts—manufactured objects that serve as elaborating symbols in that they symbolize the notion that the uniformed person will conform to organizational norms. Uniforms mute individuality while providing an immediate identity and basis for interaction among persons who would otherwise be strangers. They symbolize a whole series of behaviors that make up specific organizational roles and carry implications that their wearers must behave in accordance with associated roles and not as they might choose to do (Joseph and Alex 1972).

Organizations use many different kinds of objects as summarizing symbols. A study of 122 public agencies of 4 kinds—police departments, public health departments, driver license examination stations, and armed forces recruiting offices—observed and recorded the presence of objects that symbolized ideologies of service or authority (Goodsell 1977). Symbols of authority included physical barriers between employees and clients, formal or informal dress of receptionists, and emblems of authority such as flags, seals, certificates, diplomas, photos of political leaders, and signs prohibiting certain behavior. Symbols of service included types of seating arrangements or other physical items denoting warmth. The presence of soft couches or chairs was considered warmer than hard straight chairs or benches, or no seating. Other symbols of warmth included the presence of reading materials, vending machines for clients, visible plants or flowers, decorative pictures or calendars, inducement signs ("walk-in"), service instructions ("apply here"), descriptions of services available, and badges giving the receptionist's name.

Overall, the four types of agencies had distinctive mixes of symbols. Recruiting stations had more symbols than any of the others—presumably because they wanted to both attract and impress clients. Police stations stood in marked contrast to the others in the predominance they gave to authority symbols. Especially distinctive were ceiling-to-floor physical barriers with counters and rails between the public and police employees. Also, police receptionists were typically uniformed, and service symbols were rare. Public health departments were the warmest of the four types of agencies, with informally dressed receptionists, reading materials, and potted plants. The symbols at drivers' license bureaus conveyed an ambivalence about ideology. They combined the most prohibitive signs with the most inducement signs and service instructions. They also had nonupholstered seating, little reading material, and few vending machines. This study treated all of the objects observed as summarizing symbols that expressed the dominant ideologies of such agencies.

Perhaps the most obvious summarizing symbols of organizations are the identifying signs they display and their logos. Designers are paid huge fees by corporations to create these distinctive symbols, which come to be imbued with many meanings associated with the organization they represent.

Settings

Similarly, the physical settings used by the McDonald's chain of fast-food restaurants seem to function as summarizing symbols. A study of these restaurants in the northeastern United States observed many similarities among them that seem so typical as to suggest a conscious intent to convey certain uniform cultural meanings. McDonald's restaurants are typically located in rectangular brick buildings with large windows to let in the sun and with neatly kept surroundings (Polisoto and Fernandez 1987). Parking lots are large and well paved, there is rarely any visible litter, and green shrubbery is mulched with wood chips or white stones. A drive-through window and sign means speedy service is available. The most prominent and obvious symbol of the chain is the golden arches sign, which towers over the building where zoning laws permit. This latter symbol has become such an effective summarizing symbol by itself that it effectively identifies the chain's restaurants and the kind of food and service they provide in many sorts of buildings throughout the world. In the United States, an American flag usually completes the exterior image.

Although less standardized, the interiors of McDonald's restaurants are invariably sunny, cheerful, and neat. Bright colors and healthy plants create a homey atmosphere. Glistening stainless steel appliances behind the counter provide an up-to-date, efficient, and sanitary appearance. Above all, everything is clean. The exceptional cleanliness is achieved by endless sweeping of floors and mopping, rapid garbage removal, instant collection of dirty trays and cleaning of spills, continual washing of windows to remove fingerprints, rapid cleaning of unoccupied tables, and the constant wiping of the counter. "Cleaning is a perpetual activity at McDonald's . . . when the store opens it is spotless . . . as soon as the first customer arrives, the cleaning commences" (Polisoto and Fernandez 1987, p. 9). Both the exterior and interior settings convey the central ideologies that dominate the culture of this organization—predictability, efficiency, speed, courtesy, friendliness, and cleanliness.

Office arrangements also serve as potent symbols. A study of employee reactions to a change from a closed to open office setting in a public bureaucracy found that open settings were symbols of egalitarianism to employees. The new open offices had no interior walls or partitions, considerably lessening the privacy of managers who previously had private offices. Lower level employees reacted favorably to this change, apparently feeling that the new setting had diminished status differences. Higher status managers evaluated the change unfavorably because they felt they had symbolically lost status (Zalesny and Farace 1987). A study of an insurance company's move to a brand new building in Manchester, England obtained complementary results. The building had been designed to have exclusively open offices, but this plan was never carried out because department managers and other high-status officials within the company insisted on the addition of partitions to provide them with private offices and meeting rooms (Manning 1965). Clearly, the configuration of space carries messages about status, and thus serves as an elaborating symbol.

The furnishing of a setting is also a potent status symbol. An executive promoted to a new job was moved to an office at company headquarters. His new office was well furnished with most of the symbols of a relatively high status manager. But before he was allowed to occupy it, his superiors ordered the maintenance department to cut a 12-inch strip from the entire perimeter of the carpet. In that company, wall-to-wall carpeting was a status symbol given to vicepresidents or above (Preston and Quesada 1978, p. 111).

Generally, in all organizations, large corner offices with good views, offices located near other powerful figures, and offices with private washrooms connote high status. According to one observer, there is substantial agreement that desks can be ranked into seven status levels, beginning with one-drawer steel tables and ending with a teak desk of any size. Other symbols of status include desk accessories, access to executive dining rooms and washrooms, automobiles, secretaries, master keys, private railroad cars and jet planes, and company-paid memberships in country clubs (Mound 1978). The pervasiveness of such status symbols in a given organization, of course, says a lot about its culture and ideologies. Organizations with greater status distinctions thereby express ideologies supporting hierarchy and bureaucracy; organizations that eschew status symbols probably subscribe to more democratic and participative ideologies.

Performers and Functionaries

In many instances, uniforms become part of summarizing symbols in that they identify their wearers as important cultural performers or functionaries who represent what their organizations mean to the public. The uniforms of military personnel, clergy, doctors and nurses, judges, and other highly valued occupations have this property. Costumes in general often signal what part the wearer is playing and what it signifies. It doesn't matter who is in the clown's costume—any performer in it symbolizes McDonald's. Using a specific individual as a symbol is a riskier proposition, as Kentucky Fried Chicken found out when its summarizing symbol—Colonel Sanders—threatened to leave his association with the company. Another wearer, in the same costume, might not express the same desired meaning. His person was an important part of the symbol.

While many other examples of symbols and their meanings could be given, those already discussed provide at least a sampling from the three types listed in Table 3–1. They also illustrate the distinction between summarizing and elaborating symbols.

Organizational Languages

Organizations have no objective reality, but rather are "created daily by the linguistic enactments of members in the course of their everyday communications [with] each other...." (Evered 1983, p. 126). Language structures experience by providing categories for things. Initially, as children, people lack categories and things have no separate identities. Through socialization, people are taught to impose on their environments a "kind of discriminating grid which serves to distinguish the world as being composed of a large number of separate things, each labelled with a name.... This world is a representation of our language categories ..." (Leach 1964, p. 34).

All organizations have their own characteristic languages that newcomers must learn in order to understand their cultures and to function effectively as members. All but the simplest and smallest organizations may have several different languages; members learn the languages they need to carry out their specific work activities and function in relevant subcultures. The military uses an especially rich mix of language forms.

Jargon and Slang

Like many organizations, the U.S. Navy uses jargon as a shorthand way to refer to things. Jargon is specialized language used by those in the same work and way of life; it must be learned and sets members apart from nonmembers. Like other members of military organizations, naval personnel customarily use an alphabetical jargon to refer to various formal groupings, designations, and locations. NEC (Naval Enlisted Classification), CC (Company Commander), NTC (Navel Training Center), and AFEES (Armed Forces Examining and Entrance Station) are just a few of these designations. In addition, each of 11 different occupational groups broken down into 70 different ratings has its own two-letter identification code; for example, DS means Data Systems Technician and SM means Signalman. Most of these formal labels also have an informal or slang equivalent: a signalman is also a skivvy waver. Other formal and informal jargon is based on the formal pay scales. For example, the enlisted ranks (E-1 through E-9) are white hats. Jargon is also used to refer to cultural symbols like badges, markings, awards, and insignia worn on uniforms and to specific rules and regulations. NAVREGS are naval regulations and UCMJ stands for the Uniform Code of Military Justice. Such designations "convey a whole universe of meaning to a navy person, but very little to a non-navy person" (Evered 1983, p. 131).

This relatively general jargon is not all that a member of the navy must learn, however. Because every craft, trade, and occupation also produces its own specialized language, the navy has literally hundreds of different jargons used by different subcultures. Also, there are informal, or colloquial, languages specific to certain subcultures that must be mastered. Different slangs are used in surface, aviation, and submarines. Even within these groups, specialized slang emerges; personnel on nuclear subs use different slang from those on diesel subs; supply people use different slang from operating fleet people; and a different slang has evolved on aircraft carriers from that used on destroyers (Evered 1983, p. 139). Clearly, a large part of being socialized into the navy culture is learning the languages appropriate to one's role.

Gestures, Signals, and Signs

In addition to these many verbal cultural forms, the navy uses a myriad of nonverbal forms of communication that have meaning only to those schooled in the navy culture. These include sounds (bells, buzzers, horns, gongs, sirens, whistles, and the traditional Morse code) and visual signals and signs (flags, hoists, semaphores, flashing lights, and pyrotechnics) that convey important and very specific information to the initiated (Evered 1983).

Nonverbal languages are not confined to the military. They are used on all kinds of ships, by railroaders, by construction crews, by airline ground crews, in sports, and in many other occupations and organizations. The meanings of many of the gestures and signals used are not self-evident; people must become acculturated before they can understand and use them correctly.

All cultures seem to have gestures that are used in certain common situations and carry important meanings. In a wide variety of cultures, handshakes are used in greeting people (Firth 1972). Other common gestures are winks, nodding or shaking heads, and bowing; the meaning of these latter gestures may, however, be more variable across cultures (e.g., Geertz 1973).

Songs

Formal discourses on organizational languages tend to overlook songs as examples of cultural forms. Adding music to words, however, clearly adds something to their meaning. Also, of course, music tends to arouse and express emotion. Mary Kay Ash understood this well and began a song contest soon after she started Mary Kay Cosmetics. One popular song, "I've Got that Mary Kay Enthusiasm" was written by a member to the tune of the hymn "I've Got that Old Time Religion." Another begins, "If you want to be a director, clap your hands," and ends, ". . . you've got to be a perfecter, so do all three: clap your hands, stomp your feet, and yell hoorah" (Ash 1981, p. 40). Such songs are rather direct expressions of the Mary Kay culture and fervently sung during various ceremonies within that company.

Songs are not, by any means, typical of all U.S. organizations. For example, their use at a company retreat in a high-technology firm engendered doubt among the cynics present about "the sincerity of those singing corporate songs" (Van Maanen and Kunda 1989, p. 45). In direct selling organizations, where customer relations constitute a persistent source of uncertainty and a threat to employee morale, songs are more prevalent and do not seem to engender the same cynicism. In general, the cultures of direct selling organizations encourage effusive and expressive behaviors (Biggart 1988, p. 4). Other organizations that use songs frequently are normative organizations that seek to foster high levels of loyalty and commitment; schools and colleges, churches, and fraternal organizations are examples.

As already pointed out in Chapter 2, managerial and work cultures in the United States value rationality very highly; songs are not expressions of rationality, and are often seen as rather naive, old-fashioned, and laughable. Most adults in the United States probably feel ridiculous singing a company song, although they might still feel okay about singing their old school song at an athletic contest because those ties are not supposed to be entirely rational. Songs may also be more acceptable among sales personnel than among other employees because salespersons have to face continual refusals and rejections by customers and thus need and are willing to accept the emotional support and bolstering that comes from singing songs together.

IBM's company song was a staple part of company sales meetings and campaigns earlier in this century; while it has fallen somewhat into disuse, it is sometimes still used in sales gatherings and is known to long-term employees throughout the company. Its words and titles are an unabashed assertion of the company ideology:

EVER ONWARD—EVER ONWARD

That's the spirit that brought us fame!
We're big, but bigger we will be,
We can't fail for all can see
That to serve humanity has been our aim!
Our products now are known in every zone,
Our reputation sparkles like a gem.
We've fought our way through—and new
Fields we're sure to conquer, too.
Forward, onward, IBM.
(Cleverley 1973, p. 37)

The poetry may be crude, but certain core values come through loud and clear—growth, confidence, service, prestige, conquest, persistence, and a competitive spirit. The company mission is made sacred, collective rather than individual effort is emphasized, and members are clearly urged toward hard work and perseverance.

The use of songs has been more frequent and accepted among unions and their members than among managerial and white-collar employees in the United States. Although songs about working go back to colonial times, their use was especially frequent within and characteristic of the union movement. It is noteworthy that unions are also organizations whose members need emotional bolstering to face a rather hostile and difficult environment. The fact that new songs keep emerging from within the labor movement to deal with new problems in workplaces strongly suggests that songs help union members to make sense of threatening changes in their worlds. Collectors have found recent union songs that comment on such issues as automation and discrimination (Green 1965, p. 52).

Some union songs are widely known throughout U.S. society. One of them—"We Shall Not Be Moved"—was modified to become the rallying song ("We Shall Overcome") of the civil rights movement in the 1960s. The lyrics of this militant song express the difficulties the coal miners had in forming their union and their determination to maintain it:

> ...John L. Lewis is our leader
> We shall not be moved...
> Just like a tree dat's planted by the water
> We shall not be moved.
> (Korson 1965, p. 315)

Another prominent theme in union ballads is we against them. The United Automobile Workers (UAW) songs fall especially into this mold, with titles like "Solidarity Forever," "Which Side Are You On," and "All Together" (Reuss 1983, p. 66).

Songs extolling company virtues are more common and probably more widely sung by managers and workers in Japan than in the U.S. The Japanese also see such songs as rather old-fashioned and laughable (Rohlen 1974, p. 35), but seem to get past those sentiments and sing them anyway—especially on very ceremonial occasions or very informal ones involving heavy use of alcohol. While the songs of unionized U.S. workers celebrate their determination to keep fighting to get their rights from managers presumed to be hostile, Japanese workers sing songs that portray their organizations as admirable and benevolent. Japanese culture accords a central place to the value of membership in a group and the obligations entailed in that membership. Many Japanese workers view their companies more like families to which they belong than as adversaries that must be continually confronted. This is exemplified in the words of the company song of the Hitachi Company, a large corporation with factories in numerous locations:

> Over hill, over valley, each calls and each responds.
> We are united and we have dreams,
> We are Hitachi men, roused and ready
> To promote the happiness of others.
> Great is our pride in our home produced products.
> Polished and refined are our skills.
> (Dore 1973, p. 52)

The ideologies expressed in this song have some similarities to those in the IBM songs; both emphasize a kind of pride in the company and its accomplishments. The Japanese song differs in its emphasis on the collectivity by its repeated use of "we" and "our" and its reference to the company as "home." Apparently this song is sung among Hitachi managers rather often, especially on drunken social occasions. But workers at the various company plants use this company song less frequently than ones that have been written for their specific locations (Dore 1973, p. 52). The fact that people in this company continue to write and sing such songs indicates that songs are vital expressions of collective experiences and values.

Humor, Jokes, Gossip, and Rumor

Another cultural form using language is humor. "It is generally agreed that humor is a unique type of communication in that it establishes an incongruent relationship or meaning and is presented in such a way as to cause laughter" (Duncan 1982, p. 136). Because it involves sets of meanings, humor is inevitably an expression of the culture and intimately tied into its values and norms. Its meaning also depends heavily on the context in which it occurs; the same acts are funny in one setting and appalling in another.

Humor is a "double-edged tool" (Malone 1980, p. 357); it serves to reduce social distance and express and control hostilities while, at the same time, preserving the status quo. It also tends to promote cohesion. A study of verbatim recordings of conversations in 24 staff meetings of a mental hospital revealed that high-status members used humor more frequently than lower-status members (Coser 1960). By its use, senior members created a temporary leveling of statuses and tentatively gave up some of their control to promote positive group feelings. Junior members used humor to ingratiate themselves, often making themselves the target of the humor. Such self-deprecation often earns group support and approval in return (Fine 1984). Junior members never made senior staff members the targets of their humor for that would be seen as an attack on the hierarchy and the status quo.

All humor does not involve verbal exchanges. Sometimes humor arises from the mere juxtaposition of actions or the occurrence of actions that do not fit a particular social context. An example repeatedly shown on television occurred when a professional baseball player, who obviously forgot he was in front of an audience and television cameras, revealed his underwear by pulling down his uniform pants in the process of cleaning them. Of course, retelling the incident as an anecdote also engenders humor. Actions can be funny at the time they occur and continue to be funny when recounted later.

Because humor is a general quality of events that makes them seem funny or ludicrous, it may occur inadvertently as well as deliberately. But humor frequently comes about by someone's planning and intent (Winick 1976). A field study of a small, family-owned corporation found a wide variety of deliberate uses of humor. These included puns, slapstick, jokes, anecdotes, and teasing (Vinton 1986). Jokes were of several types. Some were anecdotes of events that had happened. Some were bawdy; others involved aspects of the work or industry. The researcher observed:

> . . . many of the traditional psychological approaches to humor view humor as an act of aggression. At QRS, however, humor appeared to *create* bonds among the employees and facilitated the accomplishment of work tasks. . . . This bonding aspect of humor may have a significant impact on workplace productivity and employee levels of satisfaction. (Vinton 1986, p. 13)

Another study found that general managers spent considerable amounts of their time in talking exchanges that included joking, kidding, and bantering (Kotter 1982). Much of the humor observed in the staff meetings at the mental hospitals discussed earlier probably involved similar talk.

Sometimes the exchange of banter and jokes may become so habitual as to characterize certain relationships. Anthropologists call these joking relationships (Spradley and Mann 1975). A classic example is the exchange of quips and insults that often characterize interactions between bartenders and cocktail waitresses. In a London department store it was traditional for employees to engage in rather continuous banter and mutual teasing (Bradney 1957, p. 183). Joking relationships are most likely to emerge in situations where there are built-in conflicts that people must somehow manage; the bantering and teasing that goes on helps to reduce tensions by enabling people to air resentments in a way that is experienced as less hostile or aggressive than a more direct expression of them would be.

Another use of humor is to make the almost intolerable seem more tolerable. An observer of cowboys concluded that their distinctive humor helped them to deal with the trials of their hard lives. Within this occupation, stoicism is an important and necessary value. The following exchange between two cowboys illustrates this well:

Q. How deep do you reckon this snow is?

A. What the hell difference does it make? You can't see nothing but the top of it no how.

(Lawrence 1982, p. 73)

Such exchanges also relieve tensions produced by living together in close quarters over long periods.

Gossip consists of informal talk among friends and associates about other people they know and about recent related events. While such talk often provokes laughter and humor, it has a serious side because it frequently concerns supposed shortcomings, peccadillos, presumed scandalous behavior, and other negative aspects of the behaviors and lives of others. The judgments it embodies reinforce cultural values. Gossip usually begins with one person telling another something that is couched in uncertain terms; by the time it has been repeated several times it gains an aura of certainty.

Scholars who have studied gossip conclude, "the more exclusive the group, the greater will be the amount of gossip in it" (Gluckman 1963b, p. 309). Most gossip is directed at insiders, and thus helps to mark the boundaries of who belongs and who does not. The restricted nature and specificity of gossip distinguishes one group from another; it is one of the subcultural features of informal groups in organizations. In addition, the foibles recounted in gossip carry certain meanings in the context of a specific group culture; they would not have the same meanings in another cultural context. Those who hear gossip learn what the group culture approves and disapproves of. In this way, gossip surfaces and reminds people of taken-for-granted norms, values, and beliefs, and thus helps to maintain the cultural system (March and Sevon 1984).

Observations of managers as they worked revealed that they prefer action to reflection and oral communication to other forms (Mintzberg 1973). Much of the oral communication they attend to occurs informally and includes gossip and rumors. Rumors differ from gossip in that they focus on groups or individuals that are unfamiliar to the teller. Such informal communication is often referred to as the grapevine and can be a rapid means of communication.

> The grapevine operates fast and furiously in almost any work organization. It moves with impunity across departmental lines and easily bypasses superiors in chains of command. It flows around the water coolers, down hallways, through lunchrooms, and wherever people get together in groups . . . a study of 100 employees found that, if management made an important change in the organization, more employees would expect to hear the news first by grapevine than by any other method. (Davis 1969, p. 269)

Grapevines convey information in all directions, they include information not commonly available through formal channels, and the information they convey is 75 to 95 percent accurate (Davis 1953, 1973; Daft and Steers 1986, p. 541). Because top level managers deal with the unexpected and nonroutine, and because the information reaching them through formal channels is often heavily filtered, "the importance of 'hot' and 'grapevine' information increases with managerial level" (Hellriegel, Slocum, and Woodman 1989, p. 10).

Metaphors

Metaphors are comparisons by which people reach an "understanding and an experiencing of one kind of thing in terms of another" (Lakoff and Johnson 1980, p. 5). They are figures of speech in which a phrase or a word that stands for one kind of idea, object, or thing replaces another in such a way that a close similarity between them is implied. Usually the parallel drawn is one "that says something much more concrete and graspable—a rolling stone, a bird in hand is equivalent to the essential elements of another situation we have difficulty in grasping" (Fernandez 1971, p. 43). Metaphors are pervasive in everyday life, not just in language, but in thought and action. People's conceptual systems are fundamentally metaphorical in nature (Lakoff and Johnson 1980, p. 3).

Metaphors are very central to cultural sense making. They have certain virtues: (1) they are compact ways to convey complicated ideas; (2) they enable people to grasp distinctions for which there are no existing labels; (3) they are far more vivid and emotionally appealing than the abstract and generalized concepts they represent (Ortony 1975, p. 49). However, metaphors are not precise; something is lost in the translation process.

The power of metaphor is illustrated by the familiar saying, "Time is money." Because of the emphasis on efficiency and hard work in U.S. culture, time is viewed as a valuable asset. Thus, time is often equated with money, even though it is obvious that time does not in any physical sense consist of actual money. Yet Americans think of, and experience, time as something that is spent, budgeted, squandered, saved, and invested. Everyday workplace language reflects this ideology:

- "You're wasting my time."
- "This gadget will save you hours."
- "I don't have the time to give you."
- "I've invested a lot of time in her."
- "Is that worth your while?"

Other national cultures do not tie time so closely to money.

Like other people, management scholars, writers, and analysts use metaphors. The very word organization has the characteristics of a metaphor in that, to many people, it stands for order and orderliness (Krefting and Frost 1985, p. 156). Until 20 years ago, "the development of theories of organization [was] the history of the metaphor of orderliness" (Meadows 1967, p. 82). This metaphor originally led scholars and managers of organizations to think of them as rational and predictable.

The metaphor was more wishful thinking than reality. Although many scholars had pointed out various nonrational and inefficient aspects of organizations, it was not until a group of them imaginatively described organizational decision making in terms of garbage cans and referred to organizations themselves as organized anarchies that the field had new metaphors to express the conception that organizations are often disorderly, inefficient, and nonrational (Cohen, March, and Olsen 1972, p. 1). The metaphor of organized anarchies implies some degree of linkage, but not necessarily along expected lines. The metaphor of the garbage can portrays organizations as the capricious intermingling of problems, proposed solutions, participants, and choices. Which solutions become attached to which problems and involve which participants is a matter of chance when they are thrown together in no particular order. The metaphor thus implies that these factors haphazardly link up to form decisions.

Other writers and scholars have used other metaphors to try to capture the essence of organizations. Most portray organizations as orderly. Common metaphors liken organizations to machines or to living organisms, both of which are composed of many interrelated parts run by invisible forces. The machine metaphor portrays organizations as relatively efficient systems; the parts are engineered so they will fit together smoothly and with minimum friction. Clocks, cars, and computers are among the types of machines used as metaphors for organizations. The living organism metaphor expresses both the idea of a living, interdependent system and the idea that organizations must feed on their environments, compete with other organizations for survival, and adapt themselves to changes in their environments. Other metaphors provide a somewhat less orderly image of organizations. They liken organizations to political struggles for power (Pfeffer 1981b) or to theatres in which organizational actors act in dramas, scripts, and roles for the benefit of internal and external audiences (Goffman 1959).

Another common metaphor for organizational activities is the game. Games, of course, are orderly because they are played according to rules. The choice of game used in the metaphor conveys different meanings about the relative independence and number of the players. One analyst suggests there are baseball companies, football companies, and basketball companies (Keidel 1985). According to this analysis, baseball-like organizations contain employees who interact minimally as they carry out a variety of independent tasks that together produce results for the entire collectivity. The Mary Kay Cosmetics organization, with its many independent salespersons, is an example of a baseball-like organization. Football-like organizations are hierarchically controlled organizations with top-down direction, detailed plans, and exact, one-shot coordination and execution. While the problem in baseball is to manage independence, the problems in football is to manage dependence on the coach and the quarterback. Individualism is not as prominent in football as in baseball. McDonald's is the archetypical example of a football-like company, with every behavior planned in advance and every process rigorously specified, leaving little discretion to employees. Basketball-like organizations involve players who are directed in interdependent combinations of moves by a coach but must improvise on the general pattern to interact effectively. High-tech companies operate like basketball teams because they must rapidly and collaboratively enact an overall strategy by integrating the work of a small number of highly technical specialists.

Members of organizations seem to use different metaphors for their organizations than analysts do. A study of Canadian bank managers found that they thought the most appropriate metaphor for their organizations was the family (Beck and Moore 1985, p. 353). Another study of a medium-sized assembly and packaging plant found that employees thought of their organization in family terms; they saw themselves as children and thought that managers, like parents, were responsible for their behaving properly. In this cultural context, the resistance of line employees to management was compared to father-offspring conflicts because employees were treated "like children." Employees didn't "tell" on maintenance personnel because they were their siblings and they did not want to get in trouble with them. The family metaphor also helped members to reconcile with each other after their many angers and disagreements. One long-term employee said, "Like kids, we fight like the dickens, but we are really one big happy family" (Moch and Huff 1982, p. 55).

In four hospitals in the San Francisco Bay area, the metaphors used by members reflected very different organizational ideologies (Meyer 1982b). The metaphor of a mob was used in one hospital that operated like a loose federation of heterogeneous units; its ideology was entrepreneurial and allowed highly professional employees to build different clusters of programs around distinct types of patients. Members of another hospital called their organization "lean and hungry." This organization had very low ratios of employees to patients, no department head had an assistant or a private secretary, and all nursing supervisors periodically returned to direct patient care; its culture cherished "self-reliance and efficiency" (Meyer 1982b, p. 45).

Because so many different metaphors have been used to refer to organizations, the previous listing is not exhaustive. It begins to illustrate, however, just how ubiquitous metaphors are in people's thinking and analysis. The most important quality of metaphors is the way in which they condense a complex set of meanings into a single word or phrase. They can deliver a cultural message cogently, but not very precisely. Thus, they leave room for the imagination to fill in details and for people to find rationales for accommodation and change.

Proverbs and Slogans

Proverbs are brief, popular sayings—short statements of folk wisdom. They "capture something people in the organization deeply believe in" (Deal and Kennedy 1982, p. 24) and thus express genuine cultural meanings. Even though their catchy wordings must be invented by some imaginative and witty individuals at some time, the sentiments they express arise out of collective experience and sense making and thus reflect group learning. Proverbs often express the practical as well as the moral "wisdom of many" (Taylor 1981, p. 3). For example, in one municipal government, managers used the proverbs: "rules tie our hands" and "if only the union weren't so powerful." These sayings expressed their timidity and resignation to bureaucratic restrictions; they also provided ready excuses for not taking bold, innovative action (Wharton and Worthley 1981, p. 359). Even though brief, such proverbs carry enough meaning to contribute to sense making in ambiguous situations.

Slogans are similarly brief sayings that differ from proverbs in that they are usually exhortations deliberately invented by someone to persuade others to do something. They are more imposed than emergent; thus, they may or may not be accepted and internalized by members of the target culture. A regional manager in a microcomputer company attempted to change his organization's culture by the use of three slogans:

- "Feed it or shoot it."
- "Professionals think success."
- "We have a responsibility to the rest of the company." (Siehl 1985, p. 127)

With these slogans he attempted to introduce new ideologies that favored focusing on good long-term customers, acting successful and confident, and striving for group goals rather than individual success. He was modestly successful in getting organizational members to accept and internalize these ideas.

The line between slogans and proverbs can only be drawn if we know their origins. On the surface, they may appear the same. Tables 3–2 lists sayings that are popular in various specific companies; because of their pervasiveness, most of these appear to be proverbs, but since they sometimes originated with top

TABLE 3-2
EXAMPLES OF COMPANY PROVERBS

Company	Proverb[a]
International Telephone and Telegraph	Search for the unshakable facts
Cadbury, Limited	Absolutely pure, therefore the best
3M	Never kill a product idea
Mary Kay Cosmetics	You can do it
American Telephone & Telegraph[b]	Universal service
Price Waterhouse	Strive for technical perfection
Leo Burnett Advertising	Make great ads
Proctor & Gamble	Listen to the customer

[a]Could be slogans if not collectively held.
[b]Before the divestiture.

management, it is hard to say without studying the companies in detail if they are really part of these companies' cultures. The list does not include the many sayings that are expressed in advertising because they were most likely invented outside the company by advertising agencies to create a certain image, and thus are unlikely to express the actual internal company culture.

Proverbs arise in general social life, as well as in organizations. Sometimes people in organizations adopt these more general proverbs to help them with sense making in their work situations. A faculty committee in a large university was observed to use a variety of commonplace proverbs in the process of reaching decisions. Some of these were "half a loaf is better than none" (said in reference to a part-time position); "you can't look a gift horse in the mouth" (referring to a researcher willing to work on a project without salary); "lightning won't strike twice in the same place" (said of an event that presumably could not occur again); and "let sleeping dogs lie" (used as a warning not to bring up a certain matter again) (Arora 1988, p. 183). Common proverbs are also sometimes slightly altered to make catchy advertising slogans; for example, the slogan "Man cannot live by clothes alone" is used by Pierre Cardin cologne (Mieder and Mieder 1977, p. 313).

Some proverbs deal with issues that are crucial to all of the members of an occupation and thus diffuse across many organizations. One of these is the "publish or perish" saying that is a very real and potent part of academic cultures and so widely known among the general public that it was recently the subject of a cartoon in the *New Yorker* magazine.

Narratives

Some cultural meanings are too vague and complex to be expressed by a word or a saying. They require a more extended treatment to convey their subtleties and intricacies. There are several types of narratives that people use to carry such cultural messages: stories, legends, sagas, and myths. As the definitions given earlier in the chapter should make clear, they differ primarily in whether or not they are based on true events and in the nature of their content.

Stories and Legends

The most common cultural narratives in organizations are stories. People tell one another stories all the time; they become cultural forms when they are widely shared and come to carry distinctive cultural meanings. Stories are down to earth, sometimes even profane. They usually narrate a single event, often with levity and irony (Dandridge 1983). They are brief, simple, and punchy. They combine truth and fiction in such a way that those who hear them often cannot tell which is which. They involve ordinary people—which, in organizations, usually means rank-and-file workers. They are almost never written down, but spread by word of mouth (Georges 1969). They are universal; "the teller of stories has everywhere and always found eager listeners" (Thompson 1946, p. 3).

A typical story follows:

> The president of a large electronics firm was doing some photocopying after hours. He was wearing a white lab coat because he had been doing research in the company labs. A secretary who was closing up the laboratory saw him and asked him accusingly, "Were you the one who left the lights and copying machine on last night?"
>
> He replied, "Uh, well, I guess I did."
>
> "Don't you know that we have an energy-saving program in the company and that the president has asked us to be particularly careful about turning off lights and equipment?" she inquired in scathing tones.
>
> "I'm very sorry; it won't happen again," answered the president.
>
> Two days later the secretary passed the president, now dressed in a suit and wearing a name tag. . . ."Oh no," she thought, "I chewed out the company president." (Adapted from Wilkins 1984, p. 54)

The most important point for those who told this story was not that the president had forgotten to follow his own energy-saving policy, but that he didn't pull rank on the secretary. He felt bound by the rules like everyone else. There is also a subtheme in the story about the excitement of innovative work in that the company president was himself working after hours in the lab.

Although stories are often considered unique to the organizations in which they are told, research shows that many stories told in organizations have striking similarities (Martin et al. 1983; Wilkins 1984). Three reasons stories with similar themes might arise are: (1) people in many organizations face similar conflicts and concerns that are not easy to resolve; (2) they want to claim credit for organizational success and blame others for failures; and (3) they want to see their organization as unique—making it either benevolent so they can identify with it or bad so they can distance themselves from it (Martin et al. 1983, p. 452). Some of the common conflicts and concerns stories express center on inherent tensions surrounding the issues of equality, security, and control—value-laden issues for which individual employees and organizations may hold different preferences from time to time.

Table 3–3 lists seven types of stories that researchers heard in a variety of private and public organizations: each expressed a common concern. The stories were further grouped by the general tensions they expressed. The story recounted above about the president and the secretary corresponds to the first concern listed in the table. Other tension-producing circumstances may, of course, generate stories. One documented in the literature as producing stories with similar themes is the death of an organization (Harris and Sutton 1986; Sloate 1969).

Occupational groups also tell stories with common themes. One such story, initially told in shipyard occupations, was subsequently adapted and retold by automobile workers, railroad mechanics, and soldiers (Green 1965, p. 57). The initial story goes:

> A tough, hard-boiled foreman chewed out a worker who appeared to be loafing on the job. The man was sitting down near the launching ways on a keg of nails, a violation of a basic rule in many blue-collar jobs: never sit down. He continued sitting with his elbows moving in a peculiar fashion. Finally the boss descended upon him and kicked the keg from underneath him. Upon recovery, the worker knocked the boss down, exclaiming, "Listen, you s.o.b.; I don't work for Bethlehem [shipyards]. I'm a cable-splicer for Pacific Telephone and Telegraph." (Adapted from Green 1965, p. 57)

This story expresses the inherent conflicts between the hierarchical control in formal organizations and occupational ideologies, which favor members' controlling how they do their work. The specific concerns reflected are similar to, but not exactly the same as those listed in Table 3–3. In this story, the concern

TABLE 3–3
TENSIONS UNDERLYING COMMON CONCERNS
IN ORGANIZATIONAL STORIES

Tension	Specific Concern
Equality vs. inequality[a]	What do I do when a higher status person breaks a rule?
	Is the big boss human?
	Can the little person rise to the top?
Security vs. insecurity[b]	Will I be fired?
	Will the organization help me if I have to move?
	How will the boss react to mistakes?
Control vs. lack of control[c]	How will the organization deal with obstacles?

[a]Members must deal with status inequalities in organizations.

[b]Members desire security but organizations can threaten that security.

[c]Members wish to control events but are often unable to do so.

SOURCE: Adapted from Martin et al. 1983, p. 449.

expressed is that members of occupations must avoid and resist inappropriate managerial control. The great appeal of this story is obvious. It has many of the fundamental characteristics of a good story—simplicity, punch, ordinary people, and some humor—so it suffers little in the retelling (Mitroff, Nelson, and Mason 1974, p. 379). Also, it is a story that is easy to adapt to different work settings. Stories can also be used to allay concerns arising from threats in organization environments. Southwest Airlines was embroiled in legal battles with competitors from its inception. The following story relates an episode from one of these court battles:

> A witness favorable to Southwest was exhorted by Braniff's lawyer to speak up. The witness replied he could not because his collar was choking him. He further explained that he was wearing a borrowed shirt because Braniff had lost his luggage. (Adapted from Bancroft 1986, p. 5).

This story helps to dissipate feelings of insecurity by saying, in a humorous way, that the opposition makes mistakes.

Legends are more uplifting than stories. They portray literally *wonderful* events—events that presumably cannot be fully explained by ordinary and mundane circumstances. One such legend follows:

> Just before the turn of the century, Harley Procter, a son of the founders of Procter & Gamble Company, became concerned that the company's candle business was declining. One Sunday morning, while attending church services, he had a revelation as the minister read a passage about ivory palaces from the 45th Psalm. He went to the company's Board of Directors, composed of very religious men, and told them of his revelation. Using it, he persuaded them to call a new white bath soap Ivory. (Adapted from Wilkins 1977)

Another legend, which is told and retold within all of the Bell System companies, is wonderful in that it gives its protagonist superhuman qualities:

> A 19th-century AT&T lineman named Angus McDonald was confronted with a large blizzard in which many telephone lines were blown down. Despite freezing temperatures, heavy snow, and strong winds, he was able to climb poles and splice feeder lines to restore service. (Adapted from Tunstall 1983, p. 21)

Because it expresses a central ideology within the old Bell System—service at all costs—a drawing of Angus McDonald fighting the elements was frequently reproduced in company literature, and copies of it hung in many offices—at least before the court-ordered breakup of that system.

While they differ in the manner in which they present their cultural messages, stories and legends clearly have similar impact: both impart moral lessons that reinforce cultural ideologies and values.

Sagas

"Sagas are evocative narratives about heroic exploits performed in the face of adversity. They are ideological parables that express, enhance, and codify beliefs (Meyer 1982b). Sagas help perpetuate ideologies by anchoring the present in the past and lending meaning to the future. They intermix historical facts, retrospective justifications, and wishful thinking" (Meyer and Starbuck 1991, p. 4).

Organizational sagas often begin with their founders and celebrate the unique ideas they had that were subsequently embodied in the history and culture of their organizations. "A saga begins as strong purpose, introduced by a man (or small group) with a mission, and is fulfilled as it is embodied in organizational practices and the values of dominant organizational cadres, usually taking decades to develop" (Clark 1972, p. 178). Because they cover a period of history rather than a single event, sagas usually incorporate both trials and triumphs. Sagas are not, however, the mere history of the company; sagas, like stories and legends, are actually celebrated parts of the organizational culture that are told and retold to new members and others to explain the organization:

> When Bill Hewlett and Dave Packard founded the company that bears their names in the 1940s, they started out in Bill's garage and used the Hewlett oven to make some of their first products. Very early they became convinced that innovation was achieved through people, and that teamwork was the key. This ideology led them to decide that they would not be a "hire and fire company." The strength of their convictions was severely tested in the 1970s, when a business decline made some cut in costs imperative. Instead of laying off some workers, they adopted a policy whereby their staff took a 10 percent pay cut and worked 10 percent fewer hours. H-P's keeping its full complement of staff, while other companies were taking layoffs, conveyed the message that everyone on the team was valued and mattered to the company. (Adapted from Wilkins 1984, p. 46)

A less well known saga recounts the early history of Cadbury, Limited. Two brothers, George and Richard Cadbury, who ran the company from 1879 to 1899, succeeded in turning around a failing tea and coffee business and making chocolate a popular food. They adopted an ideology of cooperation, which was especially necessary during the company's struggling years. They embodied this ideology by working beside their workers and knowing all by their first names. They consequently built a new factory in the country, called "the factory in a garden," evoking the union of industry and nature. Besides being well lit, well ventilated, and clean, the factory was graced by acres of park and playing fields. "Everywhere Bournville boasted greenery and flowers. Even the approach to the railway station was attractive . . .". In these and other ways, Cadbury's became a "pioneer of progress, notable for social responsibility, industrial experiments . . ." and the purity of its products (Dellheim 1987, p. 31).

A study of three distinctive colleges in the United States revealed that all had sagas that narrated how their unique cultures developed (Clark 1970). In two cases, the convictions of visionary men who were their presidents set the tone for subsequent similar developments. Both Frank Aydelotte of Swarthmore and William T. Foster of Reed College believed that colleges should cultivate in their students a single-minded devotion to intellectual pursuits and excellence. These ideas were contrary to the emphasis on social pursuits, good times, and athletics that characterized much of U.S. higher education at the time. To realize their then radical aims, each recruited dedicated young faculty and selected students with great care and scrutiny. The academic programs they developed were tough, including such things as senior theses, but grades were deemphasized or discarded. At Swarthmore, a crucial battle was waged and won over the issue of athletics; their control had to be taken from alumni and put into faculty hands before athletics could become mere "friendly contests on Saturday afternoons with colleges such as Union, Amherst, and Hamilton . . ." (Clark 1970, p. 151).

Because they deal with central themes of their organizations' cultures, these sagas are serious and almost sacred to members of these colleges. They include many colorful details that we do not have the space to repeat here, but that are integral parts of these narratives. Those who hear these sagas can almost visualize how certain things came about.

While sagas are based on true events, it is likely that some of their details are embellished and distorted in the telling. Thus, some details of sagas may not be historically true. What is important is that they are sufficiently true and believed to become an exceedingly important part of organizational traditions and cultures where they exist.

Myths

Myths differ from stories in their "high seriousness" (Kluckhohn 1942, p. 47). They are used to explain the origins or transformations of things of great importance. In myths, explanations are placed beyond doubt and freed from argument. The explanations they provide stimulate, rationalize, and organize actions; they provide the "final warrant of authority" for much that occurs in social life (Kluckhohn and Leighton 1980, p. 194). For example, all human cultures have myths about the origins of their physical and social worlds that guide much of what happens in their societies.

Myths differ from sagas in that they are largely inventions—the events depicted in myths never happened; they were imagined. Nevertheless, myths have a kind of integrity and truth in that they must be deeply rooted in a set of cultural beliefs before they will have any power or grip on people. They express emotionally laden ideas that are fervently believed but difficult to validate in any scientific sense. They have been aptly called "things that never happened, but always are" (Pondy 1983b, p. 159).

Because the ideologies of rationality and science have become deeply infused into organizational life, organizational myths often buttress these central values. Frederick Taylor, widely known as the founder of the scientific management movement, apparently contrived a myth from a mixture of historical events and his own fabrications to explain the origins of that movement. The myth, which has been widely accepted and retold, narrates how a worker named Schmidt (actually, one Henry Noll) was persuaded and trained by Taylor to load pigs of iron (92-pound iron bars) into railroad cars at the Bethlehem Steel Company.

According to the myth, Taylor selected Schmidt scientifically, studying his habits, character, and motivations. Schmidt was notable because he had been observed to trot back home for a mile or so after work in the evenings "as fresh as he was when he came to work in the morning" (Wrege and Perroni 1974, p. 15). In addition, on his small wages he had managed to buy a small lot and was busy before and after work putting up the walls of a small house. Having made these observations, Taylor was confident that Schmidt would respond favorably to a chance to earn higher wages.

Using such exhortations as "Are you a high-priced man?" and presumably showing him a scientific way to do his work, the myth portrays Taylor as getting Schmidt to load 47 tons of pig iron in a day, almost four times the average. The myth also says that Schmidt was eager to do so and that Taylor scientifically recruited and trained a special force of men, including Schmidt, to load pig iron using his methods.

Business historians unearthed quite different facts from records at Bethlehem Steel. They found the original report, written by two managers, on the pig-iron loading experiments of 1899. The report made no mention of many of the procedures that Taylor claimed as integral parts of his scientific approach and as basic to his success with the pig-iron handlers. There is no evidence that pig-iron handlers were recruited systematically or selected scientifically; that rest periods were introduced, as Taylor claimed; nor that the workers complied willingly and happily with the new incentive system. On the contrary, the report told of a new strike because of the piecework system, of ethnic hostility among gangs, and that only Noll and three others initially persevered in the truly laborious work. Also, when the tensions in gangs lessened, the records show that several men actually outperformed Noll in loading pig iron (Wrege and Perroni 1974).

Several serious cultural messages that had a lasting impact on labor-management relations were conveyed by the myth Taylor invented. These messages appealed to managers because they fit their arch-ideology of rationality. The first was that the measurement of task performance that Taylor initiated was an objective and fair basis for ensuring justice in wage distributions. The second was that scientific selection and placement could put the right person in the right job—a claim that has patterned the actions of many U.S. employers in hiring and placing employees until the present. Third, the myth portrays workers as rational if they worked hard in the pursuit of individual gain and ignored group norms. Fourth and perhaps most important, it bundled all of these ideas together under the rubric of scientific management, thereby implying that workers could be controlled by managers more effectively if management used scientific methods.

The enthusiasm that these ideas provoked among industrial leaders and others has had long-lasting impacts on U.S. organizations. Because organizations must answer to various constituencies in their environments, they enact myths that correspond to the expectations and values of those groups. Managers themselves tend to believe these myths because, as pointed out in Chapter 2, they want to believe their actions are rational and have a scientific basis. If outside forces expect managers to behave scientifically, managers will take pains to appear to do so and often convince themselves in the process. Scientific rationales and facades that amount to rationalized myths (Meyer and Rowan 1977) about the effectiveness of certain actions and programs which actually have scant demon-strated effectiveness thus grow up and are maintained. For example, many of the procedures and techniques used in selection and placement of personnel in organizations lacks scientific verification but are nonetheless often treated as if they were scientific. They derive legitimation from the scientific-like procedures and jargon they use (Trice, Belasco, and Alutto 1969; Meyer and Rowan 1977). Similar myths rationalize the collection of more information and the generation of more reports than organizations ever use (Feldman and March 1981). The myth about the origins of PERT, already mentioned at the beginning of this chap-ter, also celebrates the supposed use of scientifically proven techniques in organi-zations.

In general, rationalized myths tend to grow up whenever people need to believe in what they do. Such myths are especially pervasive in the professions, whose members must take on the responsibility for exceedingly difficult and un-certain tasks with tools that do not ensure desired performance. In such circum-stances, professionals create myths about the efficacy of certain techniques or practices, and then do not measure actual outcomes, but assess performance in terms of behavior prescribed by the myths. They do not usually question the myths, unless they have new myths to replace them, because without myths to believe in, they would have little basis for believing in their own efficacy.

Practices

Another way that people use cultural forms to cope with their uncertainties is by following certain prescriptions and prohibitions about how to behave in certain circumstances. Behaviors become cultural forms when their efficacy is taken for granted and their appropriateness is rarely questioned.

Rituals and Taboos

Rituals are relatively simple combinations of repetitive behaviors, often car-ried out without much thought, and often relatively brief in duration. Even ani-mals use rituals. Male birds of many species wave their wings and heads, vibrate their bodies, and strike other colorful postures during courtship. Herring gulls engaged in disputes over territory attack the grass instead of each other (Day 1984). Like human rituals, these displays express to onlookers certain physical, attitudinal, or status conditions. The motions themselves make no practical dif-ference; their purpose is expressive and symbolic.

Many human rituals are much less emotional and become rather boring and routine. Some telephone behavior is a good example of this. Because people are generally expected to keep up their conversational obligations, they will utter certain ohs, grunts, and sighs as they listen to others. These sounds have ritual-ized meaning—by using them the utterer is conveying that he or she is continuing to participate in the conversation. By contrast, a sudden hanging up without some sort of ritual completion of the conversation is tantamount to "interactional suicide"; not only the conversation, but all future social interaction is in question after such unilateral action (Ball 1968, p. 64). Similarly, in many cultures, certain gestures have become rituals. For example, a handshake signifies that the two parties are willing to at least tentatively and minimally recognize and accept one another (Firth 1972, p. 2).

The introduction of new technologies is fertile ground for the development of ritual behaviors because such technologies give rise to new uncertainties that people must somehow manage. Technologists who operate CAT scanners have been observed to resort to rituals when they are uncertain how to make the technology work properly (Barley 1986). Even though they have been trained in the physics and mechanics of the machines, these workers often resorted to trial-and-error learning when confronted with problems. One such solution that was rapidly passed from one technologist to another and became part of the group culture was to repeat the last command to the computer to see if it would be accepted when entered the second time. Typically, this ritual was repeated several times before it was abandoned. When the previous ritual did not work (and it rarely did), technologists would resort to downloading their machines, a procedure that broke the link between the computer and their console. Even though neither of these behaviors was typically effective, they became rituals because they helped the technologists to manage their anxieties temporarily. The behaviors involved could fill this function because they typically did no harm.

The General Motors Corporation had many rituals that reinforced status distinctions and relieved anxieties about how to deal with them. Two of these were rituals of how people were met at airports and rituals of who ate where and with whom. "The bigger the boss, the bigger the retinue waiting at the airport terminal. A chief engineer required a show of at least one assistant engineer and perhaps a local plant official. A division general manager commanded more" (Wright 1979, p. 35). When in town, those executives with offices on the prestigious fourteenth floor of the General Motors headquarters building in Detroit were expected to eat together in the executive dining room; this ritual was characterized by great emphasis on proper, careful etiquette and decorum. Both rituals expressed how important and valued hierarchical position was in this company's managerial culture.

Perhaps the organizations with the largest number of rituals expressing status distinctions are military ones. In the U.S. Navy, there are established rituals concerning which visitors enter a boat first and which enter it last. The lower ranks enter first because it is presumed that persons in senior ranks should not have to waste any unnecessary time on board. When someone as important as a vice admiral visits, he is accorded a formation in dress uniform, an "admiral's march" music, full guard, a 17-gun salute on arrival, 15 on leaving, 3 drum ruffles and flourishes, and 8 "side boys" (Evered 1983, p. 134). Violation of such rituals is practically unknown, yet these practices have minimal practical benefits. Their main function is to express and reinforce the culture.

Rituals are not confined to the navy. It has probably been well over a century since mass formations of men were of any practical utility on the battlefield, yet every army drills its troops in how to march. This ritual of endless drilling says to the participants, in a very intense way, that orders have to be obeyed instantly, and that the soldier is not an individual but a part of a collective effort.

The negative counterpart to the ritual is the taboo. Taboos specify which behaviors are prohibited. Like rituals, taboos are usually unspoken and unwritten; they are thus excellent examples of how culture is taken for granted. Sports are rife with taboos. In football, it is taboo to have sexual intercourse the night before practice or a game (Arens 1975, p. 80).[5] In baseball, it is taboo to drop bats on top of one another or to fraternize with players in another team (Charnofsky 1974, p. 267). In boxing, it is taboo to have women in training camps or allow them to watch boxing practice (Weinberg and Arond 1952). Various other occupations have unusual taboos. Among longshoremen, there is a strong taboo against the use of profanity when women are present (Pilcher 1972, p. 104). Among high steel iron workers, who work high above the ground on the girders of tall buildings, there is an understandable taboo about talking about their fears of falling (Haas 1977, p. 167). Among funeral directors, there is a taboo against any boisterousness or levity in public (Van Maanen and Barley 1984, p. 304). Among loggers, there is a taboo against breaking a log jam on a Sunday (Santino 1978). Among striptease dancers, there is a taboo against bad-mouthing another stripper to a customer (Boles and Garbin 1977, p. 235). Finally, among managers there are taboos against mentioning the unthinkable—such possibilities as product tampering, harmful product defects, and other corporate disasters (Mitroff and Kilmann 1985). There are also taboos against open discussion of such unmentionables as the actual amount of salaries or stock options one receives (Steele 1975), and frequently, the expression of one's true feelings and emotions (Martin 1990).

Rituals and taboos are especially interesting and convincing illustrations of organizational culture because they rarely have practical consequences of any importance. Thus, the primary reasons they arise and persist must lie in their expressive consequences. Also, they demonstrate how even in rationalized settings like workplaces, people resort to nonrational behaviors to manage their anxieties and conflicts and dissipate their uncertainties. By doing as the culture prescribes, and not doing what the culture prohibits, people hope to avoid what they most fear.

Rites and Ceremonials[6]

As pointed out earlier, "a rite amalgamates a number of discrete cultural forms into an integrated public performance; a ceremonial connects several rites into a single occasion" (Trice and Beyer 1984a, p. 654). Rites and ceremonials

---

[5]This taboo is also common in tribal societies. However, scientific research shows that sexual activity may actually be beneficial to athletic performance because it encourages a restful night's sleep (Arens 1975, p. 80).

[6]This section is an expansion of ideas originally published elsewhere (Trice and Beyer, 1984a).

differ from most of the other cultural forms already discussed in that they often have technical or practical, as well as expressive outcomes. Like myths, they often have a sacred quality, and some rites are intimately connected with myths. Other features of rites and ceremonials include the following: they are typically enacted over and over, on similar occasions; they are social dramas, acted out "like parts in a play," (Moore and Myerhoff 1977, p. 7) with well-defined roles for people to perform; they are sufficiently elaborate and detailed to require preplanning; and they are invariably collective activities that have audiences. Rites and ceremonials are especially rich indicators of culture because they are elaborate and incorporate various forms, each of which carries meaning. As the anthropologist Clifford Geertz (1971) commented about the Balinese cockfight, while rites and ceremonials may not be a master key that unlocks all of the meanings of a culture, they are events in which much of the culture surfaces.

To recognize the expressive consequences of rites is not to deny that they also often have practical consequences. Many of the activities discussed in this section as rites can also have practical benefits. Sometimes, however, organizational members perceive few practical benefits of certain activities and lament their continuance. Committee meetings or employee training, for example, that seems almost useless in a practical sense may persist because of important expressive consequences. As usual, we will focus on the expressive side of rites in this analysis of their place in organizational cultures.

Our research identified at least six distinct types of rites that occur in both tribal societies and modern organizations. Each has different evident expressive consequences, as listed in Table 3–4. They fall into two groups: those that focus on specific individuals, and those that focus more on group functioning and welfare. Of course, the potential exists for all rites to have multiple purposes. A particular rite may accomplish multiple practical and expressive consequences at the same time. Some of these consequences will be latent and some will probably be unintended.[7] Most rites can be classified, however, as having a primary expressive consequence and so fit into the typology. Other researchers have identified a few additional rites that can be seen as distinct from the six listed in the table, or as subcategories of them. Examples of each should help to make the distinctions clear.

Rites of passage. Modern organizations usually have at least minimal rites to mark the passage of members from one status to another. Many readers will also be familiar from their own experiences with various initiation rites used in fraternities, some high school social groups, and other clubs.

The Dutch scholar Arnold Van Gennep was the first to observe commonalities across sets of customary behaviors that typically accompanied common and unavoidable events—like pregnancy and childbirth, the onset of sexual maturity, betrothal and marriage, and death—in many different tribal societies. Because such events create marked changes in roles and statuses for the individuals involved, he

---

[7]Unintended consequences occur because of the inherent uncontrollability of social life; they are so prevalent as to be more the rule than the exception (Merton 1936).

TABLE 3-4
SIX TYPES OF CULTURAL RITES

Type of Rite	Example	Manifest Expressive Consequences	Examples of Possible Latent Expressive Consequences
Individual Focus			
Passage	Induction and basic training, U.S. Army	Facilitate transition of persons into social roles and statuses that are new for them	Minimize changes in ways people carry out social roles
			Reestablish equilibrium in ongoing social relations
Degradation	Firing and replacing top executives	Dissolve social identities and their power	Publicly acknowledge that problems exist and discuss their details
			Defend group boundaries by redefining who belongs and who doesn't
			Reaffirm social importance and value of role involved
Enhancement	Mary Kay seminars	Enhance social identities and their power	Spread good news about the organization
			Provide public recognition of individuals for their accomplishments; motivate others to similar efforts
			Enable organizations to take some credit for individual accomplishments
			Emphasize social value of performance of social roles
Group Focus			
Renewal	Annual meetings	Refurbish social structures and improve their functioning	Reassure members that something is being done about problems
			Disguise nature of problems
			Focus attention towards some problems and away from others
			Legitimate and reinforce existing systems of power and authority
Conflict reduction	Collective bargaining	Reduce conflict and aggression	Deflect attention away from solving problems
			Compartmentalize conflict and its disruptive effects
			Reestablish equilibrium in disturbed social relations
Integration	Corporate Christmas party	Encourage and revive common feelings that bind members to a social system	Permit venting of emotion and temporary loosening of various norms
			Reassert and reaffirm, by contrast, moral rightness of usual norms

SOURCE: Adapted from Trice and Beyer, 1984a, p. 656.

called the accompanying sets of customary behaviors *rites of passage*. Modern societies also, of course, have sets of customary behaviors to mark such events.

Van Gennep classified the behaviors of such rites into three phases, which
he called rites of separation, rites of transition, and rites of incorporation (Van
Gennep [1908] 1960). While all three of these phases are evident in his and many
other tribal examples, their occurrence is less clear in organizations. Relatively
few accounts of rites of passage in modern organizations have all of these distinct
stages, a circumstance that will be discussed in more detail in Chapter 4. But
some examples do exist and can be summarized.

Rites of separation help persons to let go of old statuses and roles and
adopt new ones. They facilitate "unfreezing, moving away, or letting go as a necessary preliminary step to effecting change . . ." (Louis 1980, p. 231). These processes are especially evident in military organizations. In the U.S. Army, rites of
separation begin when recruits report to an induction center, step forward and
are sworn in, are assigned to groups with other recruits, are transported to a
camp some distance away, and receive uniforms and severe haircuts. In their first
days in camp, they are taught to make their beds in a ritualized fashion, are
repeatedly humiliated and told to behave differently than in the past, and are
generally stripped of past identities and statuses.

Some corporate rites of passage have equally distinct rites of separation.
For example, in the training program of a large U.S. corporation, trainees who
had been selected from rank-and-file employees were physically removed from
their normal work settings into assessment centers where they were tested and
evaluated for two weeks. This first phase of this corporate rite signalled to both
participants and the audience (other members of this organization) that recruits
had been identified as candidates to receive additional status and powers and
they they would be carefully screened and tested to be sure they were worthy
of assuming these additional powers. Such certification helped to dissipate the
tensions of the candidates about exercising their new powers and reassure those
who might be subject to those powers that they would exercise them appropriately (Conrad 1983). Also, of course, the rites meant that trainees would have to
give up practices associated with their old statuses.

The transition stage of rites of passage is characterized by liminality—a
kind of limbo in which newcomers are neither in their old roles nor in their new
ones. They are "betwixt and between" (Turner 1970, p. 354). This phase typically
includes humiliations and ordeals that presumably prepare neophytes for responsibilities associated with their new statuses. The transition phase of basic
training in the U.S. Army occurs when the raw recruits learn the skills associated
with their new identity—shooting guns, marching and saluting, and obeying
promptly and without question. Efforts are made to rebuild their bodies through
calisthenics, long arduous marches, and other physically demanding exercises.
They are repeatedly tested to determine what new permanent role they are capable of assuming.

In the corporate training program, the transition phase included a three-
day sensitivity training program, in which the trainees experienced the ordeals
of giving and receiving blunt feedback on one another's social skills and per-

formance in the group. Three candidates dropped out during this phase, and two others became very upset.

The incorporation phase marks the reentry of neophytes into the larger social group and their assumption of their new statuses. It often has a rather celebratory air about it. These rites begin at the end of basic training in the U.S. Army, when recruits are given relatively permanent assignments to a specific unit, followed by parades, a flag ceremony, speeches, and the issuing of awards to recruits who have performed exceptionally well. These rites culminate with the issuing of insignia designating each recruit's newly assigned, more permanent status. Recruits then usually receive a leave; they go home and discover that they have, indeed, been transformed in a variety of ways and have a new identity (Bourne 1967).

Trainees in the corporate training program were brought back to the plant, where an induction rite was held during a brief shutdown of regular work activities. The production manager made a few remarks, emphasizing the rigors of the training the new managers had just received. He then read the names and new positions of each of the new managers, thus formally assigning them their new status and power in front of the other employees. The rite ended with a cocktail party in honor of the new managers at a nearby club that evening to which spouses and other managers were invited.

Besides their intended and evident expressive consequences, all rites can have some unintended and latent cultural consequences. Rites of passage, for example, help to minimize changes in the ways people carry out customary roles. Army privates, after going through basic training, march and shoot much like others who have gone before them. In this way, cultural continuity is assured and the effects of turnover in important social roles are minimized. Also, these rites help to restore equilibrium in ongoing social relations that might otherwise be disturbed by persons moving from one status to another. All of the stages in the rite of passage for managerial trainees helped to convince them and onlookers that they were qualified to be managers, that their ascent followed fair and impartial rules, and generally that they and others should accept their new status as right and appropriate.

Like other cultural forms, all rites can also have unintended dysfunctional consequences. As will be explained in more detail in Chapter 4, rites of passage can produce a conservative conformity that interferes with adaptability and sometimes with the expressed intents of management.

Rites of degradation.   These rites act to strip individuals of powerful social identities and give them lesser ones (Garfinkel 1956). Because powerful social statuses tend to become closely attached to the identities of the persons who hold them, it is necessary to have some way to detach the two and make them separate again (Fortes 1962, p. 86). Only if they are detached can someone else assume the powers of the now-separated status. Like rites of passage, rites of degradation ideally have three stages: rites of separation, discrediting rites, and rites of removal.

Rites of separation usually begin when organizational members focus attention on persons to be degraded and publicly associate them with organizational problems and failures. An important part of this stage is the degradation talk (Gephart 1978) used to forge a link between a certain person and the failures. When Lee Iaccoca was president of the Ford Motor Company, Henry Ford II, who was chairman of the board at the time, called in a team of consultants to diagnose the causes of difficulties the company was experiencing. The consultants recommended that the company be run by a troika, thus implying that something was wrong with Iacocca's leadership. Ford then added a third member to the management team, which of course communicated to everyone that Iacocca must have failed in some way.

In the U.S. Congress, rites of degradation typically begin when someone makes public statements alleging that members have been guilty of serious wrongdoing. The press often plays an important role in this process. For example, in one instance involving the sexual misconduct of two members of Congress with congressional pages, the press quickly spread the accusations of the teenagers involved. The reactions of other members of Congress emphatically served to separate the alleged wrongdoers from them.

The second stage of rites of degradation often involves some kind of investigation or documentation of the focal person's wrongdoings or mistakes. In this process, the person is discredited. Lee Iacocca reported in his book (Iacocca 1984) that Ford raised questions about whether Iacocca was associated with the Mafia and authorized an investigation of these rumors. By taking the question seriously and spending money to investigate it, Ford threw an aura of suspicion around Iacocca. Ford also began to discredit Iacocca with other members of the board of directors.

In Congress, long public hearings and extensive debate are a standard part of rites of degradation. This gives ample opportunity for new and damaging information to be aired and broadcast to members and the wider society. Occasionally the allegations are found to be without substance and the hearings help to clear the person subject to them. In the sexual misconduct case, these hearings proceeded in typical fashion, with enough revelations to convince the committee members and others that the two accused members of Congress were guilty. Whether poor performance or wrongdoing has actually occurred is, however, not the point. What matters is that people have collectively constructed such an evaluation.

Iacocca's degradation at Ford moved into the third phase when Ford began to talk about resigning if Iacocca was not fired. Iacocca reported in his book (1984) that he had been attempting to ignore what had been going on, but the pressures on him became too great to make inaction a viable option any longer. He cut short the rite and resigned rather than be fired.

In the case of the discredited members of Congress, they were not actually removed from office. However, they suffered substantial decrements in their power since they were stripped of their committee posts. They also suffered loss of esteem and personal influence as they were publicly rebuked by the Speaker of the House in front of a national television audience and their assembled colleagues (*U.S. News & World Report* 1983, p. 48). The cumulative emotional impact of the whole rite was such that one of the members of Congress broke down in tears and admitted his guilt and remorse.

Corporate examples of rites of degradation are hard to detect in all but the final phases because of the secrecy surrounding much corporate conduct, especially any which might serve to depress the confidence of investors and thus the price of the firm's stock. Via the grapevine, however, insiders know what is going on. Rites of degradation of public officials are much easier to track because they generally are publicized heavily at all stages. All of the allegations against U.S. President Richard Nixon connected with the Watergate scandal were publicized by the press as soon as they surfaced, and the entire proceedings of the subsequent impeachment hearings were broadcast on national television. Other heavily publicized rites of degradation involve sports coaches, who are usually identified as having problems and then discredited heavily in the press before they are fired or resign. As the last two examples make clear, rites of degradation will be cut short when the focal person resigns.

Rites of degradation have several likely latent cultural consequences. They publicly acknowledge that problems exist and discuss their details. In this way, members of the organization or the public may become reconciled to bad news. These rites also define and defend group boundaries, by dramatizing the conditions for membership. Finally, they reaffirm the importance of the social role involved, saying, in effect, that poor performance in this role cannot be tolerated. Rites of degradation can be dysfunctional if the person degraded did not contribute to the problems and if the degradation becomes a substitute for doing something more effective to deal with the problems.

Rites of enhancement. Any public and ceremonious activities that enhance the personal status and social identities of organizational members are rites of enhancement. Frequently, the enhanced persons receive some concrete symbol of their enhanced status. These conferrals are common—both in organizations and in society generally. Some examples include the prizes awarded salespersons who reach certain quotas, the cash awards and certificates often given for good suggestions, and the prizes awarded by trade associations for those who serve the industry (Goode 1978). Not all awards, however, are conferred in public ceremonies. Those that are obviously have more cultural impact.

Few awards, however, are bestowed as ceremoniously as those of the Mary Kay Cosmetic Company, which gives to high-performing members a plethora of awards and titles that are clearly intended to enhance the identities of those who receive them. During elaborate meetings called Mary Kay Seminars, gold and diamond pins, fur stoles, and the use of pink luxury automobiles are awarded to saleswomen who achieve certain sales levels (Mary Kay Cosmetics 1982). The awards are presented in a setting reminiscent of the Oscar award dinners in the motion picture industry. They are held in a large auditorium, on a stage in front of a large cheering audience, with all of the participants dressed in as glamorous evening clothes as they can afford. Other direct sales organizations also have impressive award ceremonies. Amway has Rallies, Extravaganzas, and Family Reunions. Tupperware puts on an annual Jubilee. Shaklee has an International Convention (Biggart 1989, p. 127).

At a Diamond International plant in Massachusetts, the personnel manager devised a 100 Club to emphasize the cultural value of good performance. Employees were awarded points for such factors as their attendance, accident, and error records. On the program's birthday every year, a ceremony in which employees received awards according to the total number of points they had earned during the year was held. All those with 100 points or more were publicly recognized and presented with a jacket emblazoned with the company's logo and a membership patch to symbolize their accomplishments. Those with more than 100 points received additional rewards and recognition (*Time* 1983, p. 46).

Many other examples of corporate awards could be given. They include the "You Want It When" award, in which scrolls were presented to persons who exhibited exceptional efforts, like working overtime and late at night at Versatec (*Harvard Business Review* 1980, p. 111); bronze stars at Addison-Wesley Publishing Company; "Attaboy" plaques and "Gotcha" awards—the latter tributes signed by the head of a company's U.S. operations (Deal and Kennedy 1982, p. 61); and many smaller awards conferred for outstanding performance, like special parking places and being named "employee of the month." At the Tennent Company, "employees award each other teddy bears—known as Koala T. Bears—for taking the initiative in problem solving and achieving quality goals" (Knowlton 1990, p. 241). All of these say to the receivers and audience that someone's efforts are noticed and appreciated.

A double-edged and somewhat ironic example of an enhancing award is the Deming prize, which was established by the Japanese in 1950 to commemorate the work of Dr. William Deming, an American statistician whose methods and philosophy were adopted by the Japanese after World War II to improve the quality of their products. The prize recognizes a specific Japanese company for use of Dr. Deming's methods. In 1970, for example, Toyota Auto Body, a part of the Toyota Motor Company, won the award in an impressive ceremony that featured many references to Deming's contributions (Cole 1979). The ceremony was an explicit enhancement of both Deming, whose ideas had been ignored by U.S. managers, and the Toyota Auto Body organization. A further irony is that this particular rite, as well as Deming's philosophy about quality, has since been adopted by U.S. industry. The United States imitated the Deming Prize with the Malcolm Baldridge National Quality Awards, which take into account many aspects of a company's business. Since August 20, 1987, when they were instituted, only 9 out of a possible 18 awards have been given (Institute of Industrial Engineers 1991).

The awards involved in rites of enhancement vary considerably in their value and prestige. All, however, provide public recognition of people's accomplishments and thus may motivate others to similar efforts. They also spread good news about the organization involved and enable it to take some credit for individual accomplishments—at the very least, by saying that the organization has selected its members well. Also, like rites of degradation, they emphasize the social value of the role involved, saying, in effect, this organization benefits greatly from high performance in this role. Rites of enhancement can have dysfunctional consequences, however, if they reward and reinforce behaviors not in accord with the professed and desired culture. Like high grades to teachers' pets, undeserved rewards breed cynicism.

Rites of renewal.   These rites rejuvenate and reinforce the existing social arrangements and help to legitimate the current social order. In effect, they refurbish the status quo and help to keep it acceptable. They maintain the stability of organizations by "repetitive symbolic activities which continuously create and recreate the system. The ceremonials of authority have to be periodically staged in order to reassert its existence . . ." (Cohen 1976, p. 135). As the sociologist Everett C. Hughes (1958, p. 19) put it, "The ceremonies of renewal imply that faith and fervor cool and want reheating." Every 18 months, "to keep things in sharp focus," a company celebrated a Zero Defect Day with a magic show and other live entertainment. At the end of the all-day celebration, workers renewed their pledge to do their work correctly. "It sounds corny," said a security analyst, "but the corniness works" (Knowlton 1990, p. 241).

Various analysts have concluded that much of the planning and decision making that goes on at top levels of organizations has largely expressive consequences. The relevant research has been summarized as follows:

> An amazing amount of decision making in an organization is done symbolically— for the sake of decision making itself. The revealing studies of Lindblom (1959), March and Olson (1976), and Westerlund and Sjostrand (1979) show that a considerable number of major reorganization plans are never implemented or are implemented in another form than planned. But it would be hasty and unwise to try to accuse the body that makes these decisions by calling it the futile part of corporate activity. The planned structures give a sense of purpose and change. (Broms and Gahmberg 1983, p. 493)

Clearly, elaborate planning activities project an image of managerial competence and effectiveness to employees and other stakeholders. They symbolize rational, careful, and systematic preparation for the future (Cohen and March 1976). Thus, the enactment of specific steps and explicit procedures may readily become a ceremony that organizations use to maintain their legitimacy and thus their continuity. Also, as managers enact these steps, their confidence in their own competence is probably renewed. In this expressive sense, the process of planning and the symbolic meanings it generates may become more important than the practical worth of the plans generated.

Annual meetings are other common corporate rites of renewal. While they sometimes include some disputes, rarely do they result in actual changes in top management. The Polaroid Company, under the leadership of Edwin Land, held large and elaborate annual meetings to celebrate and renew its culture. Land used these occasions to reinforce the company's dedication to research and development; for example, he talked up and showed off new products (Deal and Kennedy 1982, p. 75).

By merely claiming scientific validity, performance appraisal and other personnel procedures also tend to serve as rites of renewal. Their main organizational value probably lies not in their actual or presumed validity to detect differences in jobs and job performance, but in their justification of existing salary structures and distributions of rewards (Trice, Belasco, and Alutto 1969). Performance appraisal activities in particular serve to buttress the current distributions of authority in organizations (Quaid 1992). Regardless of the procedures employed, implicit in their use is the recognition by both the superior and the subordinate of the relationship of their roles. The mere act of appraising performance reminds both participants of their respective statuses; it thus reinforces the superior's higher status and the subordinate's lower status.

Because organizations tend to subscribe to the myth of rationality, they frequently use research and the information it generates as rites of renewal. The findings of social science research can often be used to reinforce the power of decision makers and detract from their opponents' power (Edelman 1977; Beyer and Trice 1982). "Merely sponsoring research and analysis can be a ritual protection by giving the organization and its authorities the coloration of rationality and responsiveness" (Weiss 1981, p. 200). Organizations routinely collect much more research and other information than they use, suggesting that "information use symbolizes a commitment to rational choice . . . reaffirms the importance of this social value and signals personal and organizational competence" (Feldman and March 1981, p. 182).

Other examples of rites of renewal include most so-called organizational development (OD) activities: management by objectives, job redesign, team building, quality-of-work-life programs, quality circles, survey feedback, and the like. Any practical consequences of these programs tend to fine-tune rather than fundamentally change organizational systems (Bowers 1973; Jackson and Morgan 1978). Thus, even when they have intended practical consequences, at the expressive level they are renewing the status quo.

Rites of renewal have both positive and negative latent consequences for cultures. While they reassure members that something is being done about problems, they may sometimes disguise the real nature of problems or defer their acknowledgment. Also, by focusing attention on certain problems, they may deflect attention from others. Above all, there is general agreement that rites of renewal tend to legitimate and reinforce existing systems of values and authority, which can be dysfunctional when real change is needed.

Rites of conflict reduction. These rites are developed to reduce the pervasive conflicts emerging out of various features of organizational life that give more power and resources to some groups of persons than to others. Such features include hierarchies of authority, the division of labor, age and status groupings, and any other differences between persons that seem to matter. Many of these conflicts are endemic in organizations because they arise from their very characteristics. Since conflicts are potentially damaging and disruptive to social life, "in general, conflict generates pressures to reduce conflict . . ." (Pondy 1980, p. 492).

Collective bargaining is perhaps the clearest example of a rite of conflict reduction in U.S. industry. While there are often real disagreements between labor and management, each side takes care to present its proposals in exaggerated form to signal to constituents that its negotiators are tough and representing their interests (Bok and Dunlop 1970). What follows is a series of "alternating moves," in which "each side is expected to step toward the other's position—most simply demonstrated in percentage point moves of wage negotiations, each side offering a point in turn" (Glick 1983, p. 8). Sometimes, "false fights" occur and "tough stands" are taken, midnight sessions become necessary, and one side or the other unilaterally leaves the room (Blum 1961, p. 64). Despite these displays, the whole process usually entails considerable informal cooperation.

Because it is a cultural rite valued for more than practical reasons, should anyone try to avoid bargaining, the other side is likely to be aghast. An idealistic manager decided he was willing and "ready to give workers as much as his company could afford" (Deal and Kennedy 1982, p. 63). By making the offer, he bypassed the entire collective bargaining process. Union officials felt he was trying to destroy good-faith bargaining. They were so angered that they "immediately asked for 5 cents more than the idealistic executive had offered."

Another common conflict reduction rite in modern organizations is the committee. Organizations form labor-management committees, affirmative action committees, quality-of-work-life committees, and many others. Widely practiced rituals—agendas, minutes, motions, and votes—provide accepted ways for these committees to proceed. Committees do not need to make substantive changes to reduce conflict because their very existence and their activities symbolize the organization's willingness to cope with problems and discontents. They also provide a forum for participants to ventilate their grievances.

A prime activity of committees is to hold meetings, which by themselves often function as rites of conflict reduction. Meetings provide a forum for discussing social relationships in a way that frames them as "business" and thus legitimates dealing with social conflicts as part of that "business" (Schwartzman 1986, p. 247). In a large community mental health center,

> ... the significant feature of certain meetings was that nothing was "accomplished"—problems did not get solved, tasks did not get done ... instead, participants engaged in a ... commentary or critique of themselves and their relationships to each other. The commentary appeared in the guise of a discussion of a specific problem or issue and it would turn into a general discussion of all problems and issues ... [that] involved participants in specific types of complex and often confusing social negotiations. ... a lengthy list of problems developed ... [that] was always enthusiastically and dramatically discussed and then promptly forgotten, only to be "reinvented" at the next meeting. (Schwartzman 1981, p. 80)

The ideologies prevalent in a culture will serve to reduce or enhance the importance of meetings as a conflict-reducing technique. The more unacceptable conflicts are, and the more participants value democratic principles, the more frequently meetings may need to be held and the longer they may run without any concrete accomplishments. A study of so-called alternative, highly democratic organizations revealed that most of them spent much of their time in meetings. One such newspaper, for instance, spent three full days a week in meetings (Rothschild-Whitt 1979, p. 520).

Early in its history, the Securities and Exchange Commission (SEC) developed a rite that served very well in reducing conflict among potentially conflicting groups. There were three sets of actors in the potential conflict situation—the accountants and their accounting firms, the public, and the SEC, which was supposed to represent the public interest. In actuality, the accountants controlled the financial reporting standards, and the SEC made little effort to control them. Instead, whenever a persistent accounting controversy arose that upset the public, the SEC engaged in a "threat ritual," issuing a warning to do something about the controversy or it would take action. Following this threat, "there would be an appropriate period of grumbling back and forth. Then the relationship would continue with no major actions having taken place" (Chatov 1981, p. 500). Meanwhile, public discontents with the accountants had been dissipated.

Rites of conflict reduction sometimes involve "rituals of rebellion," in which factions protest against the established culture, ventilating the tensions the established culture produces. The interesting point about these rites is that they demonstrate that "conflict can be stated openly wherever the social order is unquestioned and indubitable—where there are rebels and not revolutionaries" (Gluckman 1963a, p. 130).

An annual dinner for psychology graduate students and faculty at a western U.S. university always featured skits spoofing the faculty. The skits were original each year, quite elaborate, and written and acted by students. They usually portrayed the faculty as having callous disregard for student feelings and unrealistically high academic standards. They provoked much merriment by exaggerating, in highly uncomplimentary ways, various personal mannerisms of the faculty. Another student-faculty party, observed in an eastern U.S. business school, featured rowdy, cutting, and derogatory caricatures of faculty by MBA students; poems, gifts, and humorous awards called attention to embarrassing faculty situations or characteristics. While students expressed considerable hostility and aggression toward faculty on both of these occasions, this happened without damaging the relations between faculty and students or changing anything else about the academic system. The whole was couched as humorous, and it was understood by all that it is better to laugh about collective predicaments than to despair over them.

Like rites of renewal, rites of conflict reduction have latent consequences. They can deflect attention from solving some problems. They also tend to compartmentalize conflicts and their disruptive effects by dealing with them apart from ongoing social life. Most importantly, they tend to reestablish equilibrium whenever conflict has disturbed ongoing social relations. They are dysfunctional if they paper over conflicts when revolutionary change is needed for system survival.

Rites of integration.   These rites enable potentially divergent subgroups within organizations to interact socially and thus revive shared feelings that bind and commit them to the organization as a whole. These rites are needed because, as organizations grow larger and their members become more specialized, they tend to form subcultures expressing their differences. The mix of participants is important; only if a rite successfully brings members of diverse subgroups to-gether under circumstances where they will indeed mingle and interact can it have an integrative effect. There are many intended rites of integration—like student-faculty mixers—where members of each status group barely speak to the others. Thus, the consequences of this rite depend heavily on its setting, the activities involved, the richness of the cultural tradition of the event, and the divisiveness present in the overall culture.

Company Christmas parties are familiar and important examples of in-tended rites of integration held in many work organizations.[8] They usually in-clude some of the symbols and rituals associated with Christmas myths—a Christ-mas tree, traditional food and drink, and the giving of gifts. While many participants may feel that Christmas parties are relatively routine and not very meaningful anymore, this may be because people are not sensitive to their cul-tures until their expectations are violated. In one large company, a cost curtail-ment effort caused a drastic cutback in the size and quality of the annual Christ-mas party. "In the months following the holidays, a series of unexplained conflicts and erratic behaviors stimulated the CEO to investigate the causes. The problems were traced back to the changes in the Christmas party, an event that earlier had signalled that the company cared for its employees" (Deal 1985, p. 311).

One of the important features of rites of integration is status leveling. Com-pany picnics are ideal for this purpose. During them, managers and workers of all statuses and ages interact in settings and activities that lessen the social dis-tance between them. They may, for example, play softball or engage in other sports together.

> At such a picnic, where participants wore name tags with only their first names, an employee saw an older, silver-haired man pitching horseshoes. He asked if he could join him and then proceeded to brag at some length to the stranger about his pres-ent job and a probable promotion he expected. At the same time, he soundly beat the older man at horseshoes. A few minutes after the game was over he learned he had been playing the CEO! (Adapted from Ritti and Funkhouser 1977, p. 9)

Whether at picnics or parties, eating, talking, and drinking together expresses equality and community. The use of alcoholic beverages at these events lowers inhibitions, permitting less guarded interactions than are usual among persons of divergent statuses. Participants often engage in backslapping, hugging, kissing, and other gestures of affection and approval rarely used in regular work settings. Under such circumstances, a temporary sense of closeness can be achieved.

Sometimes status leveling occurs through participants taking unaccus-tomed roles. For example, in a southern trucking company it was customary for the CEO to personally give turkeys to employees at Christmas time. One year a strike prevented this event. In subsequent months grievances increased and

---

[8]During the Christmas of 1984, for example, Advanced Micro Devices spent $100,000 on a single party for 10,000 guests, and Apple Computers spent $110,000 for 19 parties (Bellew 1984).

productivity decreased. Although no direct link could be isolated, a number of people suggested that "things haven't been the same around here since last December's fiasco. That has always been the highlight of the year. The CEO himself gave out the turkeys. It was a special event. It was really missed and people are still pissed" (Deal 1985, p. 312).

Sometimes status leveling is achieved through role reversal. In a toy company, where the plant was closed shortly after Thanksgiving Day until after the Christmas holiday season, there was a long-standing tradition for management to finance and employees to prepare a Thanksgiving dinner held in the production area of the plant. Role reversal occurred when managers served food to the employees as they filed by (Dandridge 1983).

Another common feature of rites of integration that helps to produce status leveling is humor. It is hard to maintain status distinctions when people appear ridiculous. The same company that had the Thanksgiving dinner just mentioned had another rite of integration called the Great Race. Outlandish vehicles, built especially for the occasion and powered by teams of six people, were raced against one another for prizes on the company parking lot (Dandridge 1983).

By themselves, increased familiarity and interactions can increase social cohesion (Homans 1950). One California company sponsored a year-long ethnic festival in which members of all ethnic groups were encouraged to engage in activities that explained and expressed their ethnic heritage to other employees. The presentations occurred once a week during extended lunch hour periods on the company grounds. Various groups prepared and sold foods, performed dances and music on a central stage, and prepared booths displaying cultural artifacts (Samuelson 1983). Through sharing their cultural backgrounds with one another, employees could find underlying similarities on which to base feelings of cohesion.

Companies known to have cohesive cultures often have memorable rites of integration. One of the many lessons Tom Watson, Sr., founder of IBM, learned from John H. Patterson, the energetic, long-time president of the National Cash Register Company, when Watson worked for Patterson, was the value of bringing geographically scattered sales personnel together for conventions. These conventions

> unified the far-flung company, bound it into a family with the factory serving as home and the officers as the center of loyalty. The sales convention was Patterson's . . . way of maintaining unity as the NCR stretched to the far corners of the country, of keeping a small company spirit along with big company organization and dividends. (Belden and Belden 1962, p. 54)

Watson developed similar but more encompassing rites of integration at IBM to unify both field and factory personnel. Huge conventions were held in an elaborate tent city constructed on 30 acres near the IBM factory at Endicott, New York. Paved streets ran between the tents, and terraces planted with flowers surrounded them. Meetings were held in a Barnum and Bailey circus tent. There were many ceremonial events: the group picture, tours of the factory, awards, songs of praise, and visits by distinguished guests. By 1950, however, even with the "tent flaps raised," there was no longer room for the swelling ranks of the company (Belden and Belden 1962, p. 251).

One set of researchers observed both functional and dysfunctional uses of the rites of integration at the Atari Corporation during a time of intense competition and decline. Sales of home videos had dropped 30 percent and the company had lost more than half a million dollars. Some managers used rites of integration effectively to maintain morale; one manager, for example, held wine parties on Friday afternoons in which he and his employees would "hash over" what had been good and bad about the past week. Another rather lavish party for managers backfired, however, when attendees interpreted the "fancy setting, nice dinner, and free drinks . . . as symbols that things were getting better" (Sutton, Eisenhardt, and Jucker 1986, p. 27). When a marketing manager got up and announced that things had turned even worse, the party-goers were understandably upset. The manager "was not sufficiently sensitive to the unspoken messages conveyed by the ceremony" (Sutton, Eisenhardt, and Jucker 1986, p. 27). Given the firm's straitened circumstances, a less lavish spread or a simple meeting would have been more culturally sensitive and more consistent with the bad news to be delivered.

The latent consequences of rites of integration include expressions of emotion—including unacknowledged conflict—that are not allowed on other occasions. Letting off steam doesn't count in the same way it would on another occasion, nor do expressions of intimacy. Such occasions thus provide a break from the strict codes of behavior normally enforced, and they tend to reassert the importance and rightness of these codes by the clearly temporary and exceptional basis on which the usual prohibitions have been lifted.

Potential for change.   While the discussion thus far has emphasized the ways in which rites and other cultural forms help to promote cultural maintenance and continuity, it would be misleading to fail to point out that all cultural forms have potential for promoting cultural change as well. Leading anthropologists suggest that rites, in particular, can do more than "mirror existing social arrangements and existing modes of thought. They can act to reorganize them or even help to create them. . . . [That] the ceremonial form should make and mark change as often as it celebrates repetitions and continuities is one of the many paradoxes that the form encompasses" (Moore and Myerhoff 1977, p. 10). The ceremonial process is active and dynamic—not simply a passive restatement of the status quo (Turner 1969).

Rites and other cultural forms probably most often help to promote gradual cultural change. Celebrants or others may make minor changes from time to time that carry new meanings to participants and to their audiences. Adaptations or alterations of existing rites could come about either inadvertently or intentionally. Either way, to the degree that members of audiences detect changes, they will be stimulated to engage in new sense making and thus will be likely to arrive at somewhat altered understandings. Rites have special potential for making and marking changes in culture because they can carry so many different meanings through the various forms they consolidate and because they are planned and often dramatic events.

An interesting instance of this capacity of cultural forms to carry multiple meanings simultaneously comes from an analysis of Picnic Day on the campus of the University of California at Davis (UCD). The university, which began as an agricultural campus of the state university system, had recently become a major research center. This development created an unresolved duality in the campus culture, which was represented symbolically by the coexistence of "the UCD mustang and the Cal Aggie cow ... in campus iconography" (Mechling and Wilson 1988, p. 315). Not only were animals used as symbols, but the meanings they carried were central elements in the culture. The demands of animal scientists' work made it inappropriate for them to develop affection for animals used in experiments; rather scientific values and norms dictated that they treat animals with coldblooded detachment. Agricultural activities, on the other hand, included nurturing animals; thus treating animals with affection was appropriate in that culture. Cultural ambiguities deepened when animal research began to employ animals used as pets—monkeys, dogs, cats. Picnic Day, a sort of public festival, became a ceremonial way to disguise the duality, conflict, and ambiguity present in the campus culture by permitting various rites and ceremonials to express both sentiments about animals in the same public event.

The six types of cultural rites listed in Table 3–4 do not exhaust all possibilities for the kinds of rites that may occur in work organizations. Because all of the rites included in the table occur in both tribal societies and modern organizations, this list only begins to identify rites in modern work organizations. The social conditions and world view of tribal societies and modern organizations differ dramatically. Many of today's organizations must function in very complex societies and frequently cope with rapid changes in technologies, markets, and economic conditions. Such circumstances are likely to spur modern organizations to give birth to types of rites that do not occur in relatively simple and static tribal societies.

Indeed, three additional types of organizational rites have been documented in some detail; they are rites of creation, rites of transition, and rites of parting. Rites of creation (Trice 1985; Trice and Beyer 1984a) help to create new ideologies favorable to change. Rites of transition help managers and other members to manage the passage of organizations from one set of cultural arrangements to another (Deal 1985). Rites of parting (Harris and Sutton 1986) help organizational members cope with the dissolution of roles and statuses that occurs when organizations die. In all of these sets of circumstances, managers and other members have been observed to use rites to help them to make sense out of organizational changes to which they must adapt.

Rites of creation. These rites have emerged in organizations where members, especially management, strongly believe in the necessity of remaining flexible and adaptive to change. Such rites celebrate change as a positive development and thus communicate to organizational members ideologies and values that favor change itself rather than status quo. Rites of creation work in at least three ways: (1) they can make a change tangible and thus facilitate its acknowledgment and acceptance; (2) they can specifically encourage and recognize creative, new behaviors; (3) they can create and legitimate new roles designed to promote cultural change.

Various organizational analysts have suggested that organizations must create metasystems of ideologies and values that favor change itself if they are to prosper in rapidly changing environments (Beyer 1981). Their prescriptions say that organizations should become self-designing systems (Hedberg, Nystrom, and Starbuck 1976; Weick 1977) or chronically unfrozen systems (Weick 1977) that encourage second-order change (Watzlawick, Weakland, and Fisch 1974); double-loop learning (Argyris 1976); and overturning stable states (Schon 1971). While these prescriptions have merit, they seldom explain how organizations can achieve such cultures or how members of organizations can cope with such continual change. Rites of creation can help to do both.

One of the possibilities that has been documented involves the creation of new roles designed specifically to bring about change. The incumbents of such roles are expected to question or overturn the status quo by what they say or do. One model that could be followed is the devil's advocate role, sometimes used in group decision making. The role is filled by one or more persons who are expected to challenge, criticize, and seek alternatives to dominant trends that have emerged during decision making (Janis 1982). Sometimes the devil's advocate role is filled by members of the group, sometimes by outsiders. Outsiders probably find it easier to detect and object openly and vehemently to unchallenged assumptions and other taken-for-granted elements in a group's decision making. When the use of this role leads to new strategies and ideas and operates relatively publicly and ceremoniously, it becomes a rite of creation.

A more dramatic example is provided by a company that appointed a vice-president for revolutions. In this capacity, he "stepped in approximately every four years and shook up operations by transferring managers and reorganizing responsibilities. When asked how he decided what changes to make, he answered that it made little differences so long as the changes were large enough to introduce *new perspectives*. . . . The vice president for revolutions injected unexpected and somewhat random question marks about operations that otherwise would have grown smug and complacent through success and would have lost opportunities and alertness through planning" (Nystrom and Starbuck 1984b, p. 61 [emphasis added]). By his actions, this vice-president forced members to engage in new sense making and thus increased the possibilities that new cultural understandings would emerge. Also, he encouraged members to cross the "thresholds of their normal relationships with each other, making it possible to change social structure" (Turner 1990a, p. 93).

Very different rites of creation emerged in the American Telephone & Telegraph Company (AT&T) following the divestiture ordered by the courts and the Federal Communications Commission. The breakup of the company called for considerable cultural change because it meant that AT&T would be faced with much more intense competition than it had dealt with in the past. One device that managers used to broadcast, legitimate, and reinforce new ideas and values was to give awards in recognition of change-oriented behaviors and accomplishments. In effect, they used rites of enhancement specifically to encourage behaviors consistent with new desired ideologies. An Eagle award was given for new marketing ideas or supersales and a Golden Boy award for exemplary customer service. In addition, a program was introduced to give cash-equivalent awards for ideas that were successful in cutting costs (Tunstall 1985, p. 156).

In dealing with a doctors' strike, a hospital administrator who had anticipated the strike deliberately avoided formalizing procedures after it happened. Instead he employed rites of creation by encouraging informal cliques and coalitions to form and come together to consider how to mitigate the strike's impact (Meyer 1982a). These informal negotiations not only created tangible, technical consequences, but also created new understandings among staff members.

Rites of transition. Somewhat less extensive and drastic actions can serve as rites of transition, not producing change itself, but easing its acceptance.

> At a large newspaper, the introduction of computers did not have the anticipated result of reducing the time required to produce a story. After a series of training sessions had failed to produce any improvement, a consultant was retained to investigate what was happening. He spent two days observing and talking with individuals and groups. He then went to the publisher and asked for an old Remington typewriter, the name of a local firm that bronzed baby shoes, and the scheduling of a Friday beer party in two weeks. The consultant arrived at the beer party with a bronzed Remington typewriter and presented it to the oldest reporter, who served as the employees' informal priest. There was stunned silence when he placed the bronzed Remington on his computer console. The act was then greeted with a loud ovation. In successive weeks, the typewriter was passed from desk to desk. Eventually the efficiency of the computerized process was realized. The transition event helped the reporters to acknowledge their loss and move ahead. (Deal 1985, p. 310)

A more common device is for various levels of management to hold meetings to explore and acknowledge cultural change and its consequences. In an electronics firm that had recently experienced many changes, management conferences became vehicles for surfacing managers' views of their culture. The managers used such imagery as "afloat in a stormy sea without an anchor," clearly expressing tension and uncertainty; they felt they were still in a state of transition. Groups were then encouraged to address the issue of loss by listing what they had lost; the list included values, symbols, rituals, ceremonies, priests, and heroes. "As people contributed specific losses, someone got up and dimmed the lights. Emotion was obviously high" (Deal 1985, p. 321). The rite ended with a discussion of the positive features of the changes the company had made and a closing speech by the CEO. The whole event served as a sort of collective rite of passage for all of the managers who attended; through it they were separated from the past culture and better able to move ahead within a new one.

Rites of parting. Sometimes organizational members must face the permanent loss of their organizational cultures because their organizations cease to exist.

Researchers observed rites they called parting ceremonies in six of eight dying organizations they studied. In various ways, these rites helped organizational members cope with the "imminent breaking of social bonds" formed in their organizations (Harris and Sutton 1986, p. 6). They had many common elements. All were parties that involved eating, drinking some sort of alcoholic beverages, and animated conversations concerning the loss of their organizations. Employees consistently expressed sadness and anger over the death, examined its causes, and blamed it on someone else—usually the parent organization. They told stories about the "old place," and invited former members to attend. They exchanged names, addresses, and phone numbers, promising to write and keep in touch; in addition, they took photographs of one another. They discussed their futures, exchanged information about job searches and new jobs, and told one another, "I guess this means it's really over" (Harris and Sutton 1986, p. 15). In most instances, employees, rather than management, initiated and sponsored the rites.

The commonality of so many elements in these rites is striking. Apparently people find similar ways to deal with similar personal disasters. By means of the various elements in these parting ceremonies, stranded employees not only gained emotional support from one another, but managed to rearrange their perceptions and understandings of the death sufficiently to make it easier to bear and accept. This happened on three levels: through collective sense making, displaced members could revise (1) their cognitive scripts of the history, attributes, and fate of their organizations; (2) their self-concepts as reflected in their personal histories within the dying organization; and (3) their ideas for dealing with the imminent role transitions.

The personal experiences of a manager caught in another organizational death shows that appropriate rites do not always happen on such occasions. A successful store manager with the W.T. Grant Company learned of his company's closing from a customer's report rather than from his own management. At the time, he was in the middle of reorganizing and repainting his store at the direction of company headquarters. Rumors spread rapidly, but the manager tried to reassure employees. Then, the day his redesigned store opened, he learned from other managers that creditors had forced the firm into bankruptcy. Because he knew little of the details, he could not explain the reasons behind the decision to the 80 employees who worked under his supervision. They were angry and behaved "irrationally." Close to tears, the manager said, "What can I say? It was a great company" (Loving 1976, p. 113). Without social events in which emotional support could be given and received and in which events could be reexamined and given new meanings, this manager lacked cultural supports to help him or his employees deal with his organization's death.

Because they involve imminent role transitions, parting ceremonies might be thought of as part of a rite of passage. They would, however, be only a partial rite because they involve only the separation from the old role, and do not include arduous preparation for or incorporation into a new one. Thus, it is probably best to consider these a separate type of rite.

SUMMARY

Cultural forms consist of observable entities people use to express, affirm, and communicate the substance of their cultures. Many kinds of behaviors and objects can function as cultural forms; they can be classified into four categories: symbols, language, narratives, and practices, with symbols the most basic form of cultural expression and practices the most complex. Each category includes many specific types of forms.

Cultural forms condense and make cultural ideologies concrete. They serve as sense-making mechanisms by which members of a culture can either consciously or unconsciously derive meaning from their situations. Sense making occurs at both individual and collective levels. Collective sense making involves many social processes, including communication, influence, leadership, habit formation, conditioning, reciprocity, negotiation, imitation, role modeling, and exploratory action.

Symbols are everywhere and form a sort of cultural background to everyday life. Key symbols are those that express the underlying substance of a culture, either by summarizing its overall meaning to participants or by elaborating its specifics. Objects, settings, and functionaries of various kinds often function as symbols.

Language structures experience and gives it meaning by providing systems of categories for things. The representations provided by language come to represent people's worlds to them. All organizations have characteristic languages that are used to express meanings specific to their cultures. They include jargon, slang, gestures, signals, signs, songs, humor, jokes, gossip, rumors, metaphors, proverbs, and slogans.

Narratives are used to convey relatively subtle and intricate sets of cultural meanings. They also have important emotional effects; they release tension, entertain, reassure, and provide cautionary lessons. Some are true or based in historical fact, others are wholly invented; some deal with sacred matters, others with the profane. The various labels given to narratives distinguish them on these and other characteristics. They include stories, legends, sagas, and myths.

Various practices become cultural forms when their effectiveness is taken for granted and their appropriateness is rarely questioned. These practices can be categorized as rituals, taboos, rites, and ceremonials. Of these, rites and ceremonials are the most complex in the sense that they typically incorporate other cultural forms. Many management practices with ostensibly practical aims also function as cultural rites with a variety of expressive consequences. Six types of rites occur in both tribal societies and modern organizations: rites of passage, degradation, enhancement, renewal, conflict reduction, and integration. Organizations may, however, employ other rites. Research suggests three additional types: rites of creation, transition, and parting. Rites and other cultural forms are concrete manifestations in which the ideologies of a culture surface in organizational life.

4

Organizational Passages and Cultural Continuity

One of the distinguishing features of human cultures is their continuity. Because human beings have language and manipulate symbols, they can pass on to succeeding generations their understandings of the world so that (1) new members of cultures do not need to make all of the same mistakes and discoveries; and (2) they will know how to fit in and not disrupt group life. The process by which persons are inculcated with the substance and forms of a culture is called socialization.

Although the most basic and primary socialization that humans experience happens during their infancy and childhood, socialization is a lifelong process. Especially in modern societies, people move in and out of different social roles, with associated sets of cultural expectations and demands, throughout their lives. Socialization processes help to ensure that people accomplish these passages with minimal disruption to the fabric of social life. Socialization helps to ensure that they know how to behave in their new roles.

Of course, socialization is not always equally successful and never perfect. New members are not cultural clones of the old. They bring with them individual differences and they have had different experiences that color the way they receive the cultural messages sent to socialize them. Socializing agents and events also vary in their efficacy; some are more persuasive, coherent, and inspiring than others. Thus, cultural continuity is not absolute, and variations in socialization are one of the factors producing cultural change.

Many work organizations outlive their initial membership. They must import new members from time to time and socialize them to fit into the ongoing life of the organization. Most work organizations also expand and develop new patterns of activity over time. Existing members move up the hierarchy or laterally into new roles with different expectations than were attached to their old

129

roles. Thus, socialization processes in organizations are not confined to newcomers, bur reoccur throughout members' work lives.

Definition and Nature of Organizational Socialization

Organizational socialization consists of social processes through which organizations transmit to members the expectations associated with their roles. In particular, members of established cultures communicate to newcomers systematic sets of expectations for how they should behave. Ideally, all members internalize these expectations so that they will voluntarily and willingly perform the role behaviors expected of them. Organizations deliberately employ a variety of socialization practices to achieve these aims. For example, they use various mixtures of cultural forms to transmit cultural values and expectations to new and existing members. However, all socialization is not deliberate or planned. Much of it arises spontaneously within informal social groupings of various kinds. For example, many organizational recruits "learn the ropes" from fellow workers. Because of the multiple sources of socialization, individuals are usually exposed to diverse socializing influences.

Typically the process of socialization proceeds through a predictable set of distinct stages, to be discussed later in the chapter. Individuals go through these same stages many times in their work lives as they change roles within an organization, as they move to different organizations, as they change occupations, or as their organization changes its expectations of them. While the same stages tend to occur in each socialization cycle that individuals experience, several factors modify the ways in which these stages unfold and their effects on the individuals involved. First, the relative intensity of these stages is likely to differ somewhat at various stages of people's careers. First-time workers may spend more time and energy anticipating their first job than experienced workers do their next. Second, individuals respond differently to socialization practices because of differences in their personalities and personal histories. A dogmatic person may reject tips and advice from experienced co-workers. A member of an underprivileged social group will probably react differently to training than a person from a privileged group. These and other personal characteristics modify the ways in which socialization occurs and its effects on the individuals involved.

The human capacity to change makes repeated socializations possible. People have few deep-seated patterns of behavior that continue throughout their lifetimes and over all social experiences (Brim 1966). The meanings that constitute people's reality are constructed anew in each social setting. Consequently, people are always in the process of becoming—they travel through life's passages by adjusting their understandings and behaviors as they go along.

The most basic and probably the most powerful socialization that individuals experience occurs during childhood. One reason is that childhood socialization works on a relatively blank slate. When children learn the expectations associated with various roles, or are exposed to certain human values, they can adopt them relatively easily because they have no store of competing expectations or values; they have little or nothing to unlearn. Second, children have few options; they can seldom choose which roles they will take on or the socializing agents who will prepare them for those roles. Third, much of the content of childhood socialization is very general; it seeks to civilize children to fit into ongoing society. Experiences in school, church, and family prepare children in a general way for adult roles but cannot possibly anticipate much of the specific learning those roles will entail. Thus, the bulk of socialization into organizational life and work roles occurs during adulthood. Adult socialization inevitably differs from childhood socialization because it may involve unlearning and must confront competing role expectations and values previously acquired.

Socialization can have both positive and negative consequences. People sometimes learn the wrong expectations or acquire countercultural values. One reason is that learning is never perfect. Another is that people are usually exposed to multiple socialization influences. In particular, individuals in work organizations find themselves the targets of influence from friendship and work groups, occupational subcultures, and various political coalitions. Despite these mixed messages, socialization helps individuals to navigate life's many passages. Each passage involves some degree of reality shock (Hughes 1958). "There is no gradual exposure and no real way to confront the situation a little at a time." People making a passage "are simultaneously inundated with many unfamiliar cues." Socialization helps them "to construct maps . . . specific to the new setting" and suggests ways to perform in new roles and relationships (Louis 1980, p. 230).

Types of Organizational Socialization

Organizations clearly have a stake in seeing that members fit into ongoing routines and conform to organizational cultural expectations. There are many different ways in which organizations introduce newcomers to their cultures and attempt to inculcate them with their ideologies, values, and norms. Much of this variety has been captured in the typology shown in Table 4-1, which describes socialization tactics by polar opposites along six different dimensions (Van Maanen and Schein 1979, p. 232). Actual socialization efforts usually combine several of these tactics and may mix elements that fall at different points along a single dimension. For example, socialization of new recruits inevitably involves some informal processes, and most organizations use at least rudimentary formal processes, as well. Thus, it is unlikely that any socialization process fits just one part of the typology. The utility of the typology lies in providing reference points for describing a particular socialization process or comparing different processes in the same or different organizations.

TABLE 4–1
A TYPOLOGY OF SOCIALIZATION TACTICS

	Institutionalized		Individualized
Context	Collective	vs.	Individual
	Formal	vs.	Informal
Content	Sequential	vs.	Random
	Fixed[a]	vs.	Variable[a]
Social aspects	Serial	vs.	Disjunctive
	Divestiture[a]	vs.	Investiture[a]
Likely Effects:	Custodial role orientation		Innovative role orientation

[a]Predictions of researchers differ for these tactics.
SOURCE: Adapted from Van Maanen and Schein 1979, p. 232.

The logic underlying the typology also suggests likely effects of different kinds of processes on role performance. The typology essentially lists twelve different tactics—one at each end of the polar opposites—and orders them according to their logical effects, listed at the bottom of the table. The more that a socialization process employs the tactics listed under one or another column, the more likely it is to produce either a custodial or innovative response. A custodial response is one in which the person being socialized subsequently performs in ways that preserve and continue the prevailing culture. An innovative response is one in which the person being socialized subsequently behaves in ways that differ from and thus could change the prevailing culture. Such differences are not necessarily deliberate and the resulting changes may be relatively minor.

Responses to Socialization

Persons undergoing socialization will respond both cognitively and emotionally (Van Maanen and Schein 1979; Jones 1986). First, they will to various degrees receive and understand the cultural messages being sent to them by socializing agents. Both cognitive processes are essential for accurate cultural transmittal. Second, they will to various degrees agree with and emotionally accept those messages—as they understand them—as appropriate for themselves and their organizations. Without some degree of emotional acceptance, cultural content is unlikely to be internalized to guide future behavior.

Figure 4–1 depicts these responses in terms of a flow diagram and shows how these two sets of responses are likely to produce different role behaviors and effects on an existing culture. If messages about cultural expectations and content are not received, persons being socialized must invent their own role behaviors. Such behaviors are unlikely to exactly reproduce the behaviors of past occupants of the same roles, and in that sense, the behaviors are innovative. Even when messages are received, they may not be fully understood. To the degree that understanding is incomplete or imperfect, persons being socialized will also

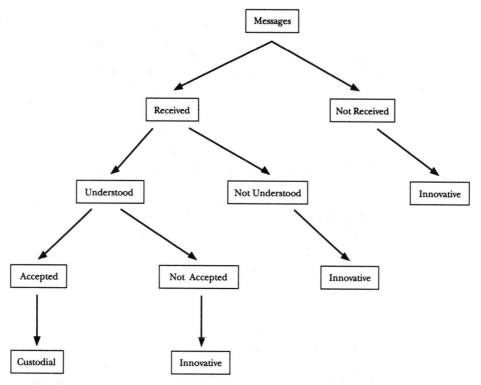

FIGURE 4–1
FLOW DIAGRAM OF COGNITIVE AND EMOTIONAL RESPONSES
TO SOCIALIZATION INFLUENCES

end up doing something different from what was expected. In this sense they are also innovative. Even when messages are received and understood, they are not necessarily compatible with individuals' personal value systems, aspirations, or abilities. Thus, all or part of the messages sent during socialization may not be accepted at an emotional level by those being socialized. If individuals do not accept such messages, they are also likely to innovate by behaving differently from what the culture prescribes. Only when all three conditions are satisfied— individuals receive, understand, and accept cultural messages sent—are they likely to make a custodial response. Even in this situation, however, they may adapt expected behaviors to local situations in ways that could produce a degree of cultural innovation.

Breaking down the process in this way shows how unlikely it is that cultural transference will be perfect; variations can occur through flaws in either the cognitive processes or the emotional responses involved. From this analysis, pure custodial responses and flawless cultural continuity appear to be the *least* likely effects of socialization.

While responses to socialization are unlikely to be totally custodial and to produce perfect continuity, they usually do produce some continuity. A variety of factors, described in more detail throughout this chapter, act to produce at least partial reception, understanding, and acceptance of cultural messages sent during socialization processes. Most basic is that those being socialized and those doing the socializing often share the same overarching societal culture. Also, many people in the same society experience similar socialization experiences, like schooling, that prepare them somewhat uniformly for adult roles like work roles. Thus, the range of behaviors they are likely to use to innovate in a role will usually be greatly constrained by general societal expectations. Finally, as mentioned earlier, socialization processes usually involve several tactics and a variety of socializing influences; this multiplicity of influences and experiences increases the probability that a match will occur—that those being socialized will receive, understand, and agree with at least *some* of the role expectations others in an organizational culture have of them.

With some understanding of the basic cognitive and emotional processes involved, and an appreciation of how other factors can modify those processes, we can now return to the specific tactics in Table 4–1 to see how and why specific tactics tend to produce primarily custodial or innovative responses.

Socialization Tactics

A socialization process is collective when a group of persons goes through common experiences as they collectively face entry into an organization or into a new role. These collective experiences are often arduous and thus provide a basis for building strong social bonds and cohesion between cohorts of peers. Collective experiences are also likely to produce similar understandings of an organizational or occupational culture, through shared indoctrination and through social interactions among the recruits as they collectively struggle to understand their new role. Examples include MBA and law school programs that keep students in the same groups for different courses, classes in police and firefighting academies, and boot camps in the military. Such collective processes are sometimes prolonged by small groups of recruits passing into the same employing organization or unit after graduation. Business firms and law firms may hire several Harvard students from the same graduating classes; groups of recruits from the police or firefighting academies may end up at the same station.

When organizations combine collective tactics with other tactics listed in the center column of Table 4–1, they are likely to achieve especially strong custodial responses. Socialization that is collective is often also formal, sequential, and fixed. Formal tactics separate those to be socialized from other members and indoctrinate them into cultural expectations with well-structured programs. Sequential tactics involve passing persons through well-defined steps that lead to a specific role. Fixed tactics involve specific and known timetables required to complete a particular passage to a particular role. The examples already given conform to all of these tactics, as do medical school, seminaries, Ph.D. programs, and many other programs that train professionals in this society. Such collective programs often also use serial and divestiture tactics.[1] Serial tactics involve using experienced members of the culture to serve as role models and otherwise groom newcomers into established role expectations. Divestiture tactics are aimed at changing cultural content; they act to weaken previous identities and dilute the impact of past role prescriptions.[2]

At the other extreme are socialization processes that handle individuals separately. Such tactics involve inducting members singly and isolating them from others in similar passages so that each has a relatively unique set of socializing experiences. Examples include most one-on-one training that occurs on the job and most apprenticeship programs. When organizations combine the individual tactic with the others listed in the right-hand column of Table 4–1, they are likely to produce some kind of innovative response in the person being socialized. Socialization is informal when no structured program of training or indoctrination is set up for the newcomer, who must learn the new role through individual experience, guided by self-selected socializing agents and by trial and error. It is random when the steps that lead to a specific role are ambiguous and undefined. It is variable when there are few or no clues as to how long it will take to complete the passage to the new role. It is disjunctive when the setting lacks role models and offers the recruit opportunities to be free of past expectations associated with the new role. Finally, a socialization process involves investiture when newcomers are accepted without having to alter past identities or shed past role expectations. Some of these tactics give the persons being socialized opportunities to vary from past expectations associated with the role they are assuming; others almost require them to innovate and create meaning for their new roles.

The typology given in Table 4–1 best applies to the entry of new members into organizations. Organizations obviously have control over these processes. Also, socialization processes used at entry probably provide the clearest and most dramatic illustrations of how organizational socialization occurs. While the same processes occur as insiders progress through different roles, they are at that point more embedded in other organizational processes and thus likely to be less distinct in their operation and effects. The typology is even less applicable to what happens as people anticipate moving into new roles or what happens as they leave them. Much anticipatory socialization occurs outside the employing organization and thus is largely outside management control. Similarly, such passages as quitting or retirement take the passenger outside the organization.

Because it aims for generality, the typology also ignores factors that may

---

[1]There is some theoretical disagreement about whether the divestiture tactic is more individual or institutional. The many descriptions of ordeals that strip members of past identities in collective rites of passage among police, firefighters, smokejumpers, and military recruits argue for its placement under the institutional category.

[2]It is clear that new roles do not entirely erase old ones. When returning to a prior cultural context, many people experience role revival—that is, they find themselves behaving as they did in an earlier role learned in that context. One likely reason is the continued presence of role senders with whom the old role prescriptions were developed.

moderate the effects of socialization. Considerable research has accumulated, however, showing that personal characteristics affect how individuals respond to socialization.

Personal Characteristics

To balance the emphasis on organizational strategy and context reflected in the typology of tactics, the characteristics of newcomers themselves must be considered. Numerous observers have pointed out the importance of individual differences in the probable outcomes of socialization experiences. The personal characteristics most often shown to affect socialization fall into two clusters: relevant past experiences and feelings about self. The first cluster includes variables that reflect past experiences that somehow prepare the individual cognitively and emotionally for the new role. These usually involve similar or comparable life events. A psychiatrist who studied the reaction of recruits to basic training in the U.S. Army found "past experience with any remotely comparable event . . . to be the major factor in ameliorating the high level of stress during this period . . ." (Bourne 1967, p. 190). Research on organizational identity in the U.S. Forest Service found that recruits with a prior service orientation, plus high affiliation and security needs, tended to develop stronger organizational identities than those without such characteristics (Hall, Schneider, and Nygren 1970, p. 176). A study of freshmen lawmakers in the California legislature concluded that "the swiftness and ease with which the rules were learned suggests a carryover from previous life experiences, as well as the efficacy of veteran legislators and others in advising the newcomers" (Bell and Price 1975, p. 156).

The second cluster concerns feelings of confidence, competence, self-esteem, and self-sufficiency. In a study of new manufacturing, sales, and service employees, the self-esteem of recruits moderated the degree to which successful and competent supervisors served as role models in the recruits' learning their organizations' cultures (Weiss 1978). Low self-esteem reduced the efficacy of the transfer process between role models and their subordinates. Another study showed that managers who made successful adaptations to new role demands had higher self-esteem, were more flexible, and showed more openness to new ideas than those who did not adapt as well (Morrison 1977).

From a careful review of the individual variations that contributed to convictions about personal competence, one researcher hypothesized that individual employees vary greatly in how they perceive their personal competence to manage change, new tasks, and new roles; he called these perceptions their "self-efficacy expectations" (Jones 1983b, p. 472). Individual differences in these expectations moderate or accentuate the reality shock of entry into an organization and affect the way in which recruits react to the types of socialization they encounter. If newcomers view themselves as competent, they will perceive new situations quite differently from those who do not feel competent. And, if their past experiences have provided them with realistic notions about organizational life, this experience will favorably moderate their reactions to entry (Jones 1983b).

A longitudinal study of MBA graduates of a major midwestern university tested whether or not self-efficacy does actually moderate responses to the various types of socialization described in Table 4–1 (Jones 1986). The outcomes assessed included custodial versus innovative role orientation, role conflict and ambiguity, job satisfaction, intention to quit, and organizational commitment. Tactics were divided into the two basic categories—institutionalized and individualized—as shown in Table 4–1.[3] Institutionalized tactics were expected to produce custodial orientations and individualized tactics to produce innovative role orientations.

Results indicated that institutionalized tactics did indeed generate custodial role orientations among these new MBAs. Moreover, those who experienced institutionalized tactics reported less role conflict and ambiguity, and greater job satisfaction and commitment than other graduates. Individualized tactics also produced innovative role orientations, as predicted. However the level of self-efficacy moderated the effects of the various tactics on the way recruits came to view their role. Recruits who were high in self-efficacy tended to shape their own definitions of the situation even when the tactics they experienced were highly structured as institutionalized practices. Those with low levels of self-efficacy, on the other hand, conformed to the tactic experienced.

Although these results have not yet been replicated on other populations, they strongly reinforce the results of earlier studies. The structure of socialization —the tactics employed—matters, but because of differences in self-perception and experience, individuals will vary in how they respond to those tactics.

An important test of whether socialization has succeeded is whether new recruits stay with an organization or leave soon after entry. Research suggests that, if experiences after entry do not match their expectations, new employees are not likely to stay. One study found that rural-reared workers had significantly higher rates of turnover than urban-reared employees (Trice 1961); one reason was that the expectations of the rural-reared that their high school educations would be used in their work were not met. Another study of how job turnover was influenced by socialization found that incompatible combinations of job conditions, personality, and biographical features induced employees to leave their jobs (Trice and Penfield 1961, p. 13). Other researchers found that when employees' individual career plans matched those of their organizations, they expected to succeed and had high job satisfaction; if the two sets of career plans did not match, they were likely to search for other jobs (Granrose and Portwood 1987).

---

[3]Results, however, showed an investiture tactic to be associated with a custodial orientation. Further research on more extreme instances of investiture vs. divestiture may be needed to resolve this point.

TABLE 4–2

EXAMPLES OF FOUR TYPES OF CULTURAL CONSEQUENCES
OF TRAINING NEW MANAGERS

	Technical Consequences
Manifest	A thorough evaluation of candidates' potential and an improvement of their administrative skills so as to promote only the best qualified to management rank in the system.
Latent	The relative priorities placed upon various areas of performance in the company are communicated and reinforced; members of management who act as trainers sharpen and reinforce their own skills; new and old managers size up one another's strengths and weaknesses.
	Expressive Consequences
Manifest	The transformation of the social identities of successful candidates among an immediate audience and a widely dispersed audience.
Latent	The enhancement of the prestige of the managerial role within the company; the motivation of nonmanagement personnel to perform according to the priorities made evident; the development of social and emotional bonds among managers.

SOURCE: Adapted from Trice and Beyer 1984a, p. 656.

Cultural Forms in Organizational Socialization

As was pointed out in Chapter 1, people cannot do only one thing at a time. Human actions both do and say things, and thus they have both technical and expressive consequences. Also because people are more aware of some consequences than others, their actions have both manifest and latent consequences. The common organizational ceremonial of training new managers provides a good illustration of these distinctions. Table 4–2 shows four types of consequences managerial training can have. Such training also often has many of the features characterizing rites of passage.

Rites of Passage

As explained in Chapter 3, classical rites of passage consist of three distinct stages (Van Gennep [1909] 1960). The managerial training in one company we observed illustrates these stages. *Separation rites* consisted of several days of testing and screening a large group of candidates self-selected from nonmanagerial employees and three days at an off-site, live-in assessment center. *Transition rites* included a week of formal instruction and sensitivity training for those who passed the initial screening. *Rites of incorporation* occurred at the completion of the training, with a welcome-back speech by the production superintendent on the shop floor and a cocktail party that evening.

As this example suggests, rites of passage are no less important in complex modern life than they were in simpler societies of the past (Kimball 1960). Perhaps the most perceptive manager of the 20th century, Chester Barnard (1938, p. 180), recognized this, observing that

> ceremonials of investiture, inaugurations, swearing-in, induction, and introduction are all essentially appropriate methods of making known who actually fills a position and what the position includes as authority. In order that these positions may function it is often necessary that the filling of them should be dramatized ... to [help] inculcate the sense of organization.

In fact, rites of passage are probably the most universally potent cultural form found in many different cultures.

In terms of the socialization tactics discussed earlier (Table 4–1), rites of passage tend to be institutionalized, even when they are used to ease the passage of a single individual. Inauguration ceremonies, baptisms, and funerals are examples of highly institutionalized ceremonials that usually mark individual passages. Because the typology was developed to describe socialization in modern organizations, it does not neatly incorporate rites of passage. These rites bear the strongest resemblance to the tactic of divestiture because they tend to strip away prior identities, statuses, and roles in order to replace them with new ones. Almost never do rites of passage conform to the investiture tactic, which in effect says, "We like you recruits just as you are and want no changes."

The most important cultural feature of rites of passage is that they involve more than a mere acquisition of new social position; they make and signal an essential change in the identity of the persons involved in the passage. This feature is especially evident in the extensive managerial training used in many medium-sized and large Japanese organizations.

A U.S. anthropologist observed trainees at several Japanese banks as they went through an extensive set of rites (Rohlen 1973). Their rites differed markedly from those we observed in a U.S. organization and described at the beginning of this subsection. At the Uedagin Bank, trainees and their parents were invited to an entrance ceremony, during which the president of the bank gave a speech congratulating the parents on raising such fine children and reassuring the trainees and their families that taking a job at this bank was like joining a large family that takes good care of its members. The presence of current trainees in uniform, the prominent display of the company logo, the singing of the company song—all symbolized the cohesiveness and continuity of the trainee's new "family." This event functioned as a rite of separation.

Next were several rites of transition, each demanding that the trainees submit to new ordeals. First came a two-day trip to a nearby army camp where the trainees were subjected to some of the rigors of basic training. Marching under the direction of a sergeant and sweating their way over obstacle courses, they wore castoff army fatigues that symbolized their shared lowly status. They were told that a large company required a high degree of order and discipline, that military training was the best way to teach this, and they accepted this explanation. Periodically, they were also taken to a Zen temple for a two-day session in meditation and other Zen practices. Here they were also subjected to a strict regimen that included tasteless gruel for meals and a whole series of rituals that had to be meticulously observed.

Perhaps the most arduous ordeal of all was a 25-mile marathon walk held at the end of the training. Trainees were told to walk the first nine miles together in a single body, the second nine in designated groups, and the last seven alone and in silence. Past trainees monitored their conformity to the rules and tempted them with cold drinks, which they were not allowed to accept. The first part, walking and talking together was relatively pleasant. During the second part, intergroup competition emerged, leading the trainees to escalate their pace even though competition had not been encouraged. The result was that many trainees could not stand the pace and had to drop out. The final part of the walk was very painful and difficult; any who finished took great personal pride in that accomplishment. The marathon walk taught the values of perseverance, self-denial, and rejection of competition as the route to collective accomplishment. In addition to all of the ordeals mentioned, the trainees were expected to study bank operations and pursue a variety of other scheduled activities. Every day except Sundays were filled with 14 hours of supervised activity.

Rites of incorporation were not described in this research report and so may have been less ceremonial. They would include whatever events occurred as trainees reported back to the bank for their initial work assignments and were absorbed into work groups and activities.

Because they are so common, many variants of the phases of rites of passage occur in modern organizations. A more detailed examination of each and how it works is needed to fully appreciate their prevalence and powerful cultural consequences.

Separation. "Unfreezing, moving away, or letting go is a necessary preliminary step in affecting change at both individual and group levels" (Louis 1980, p. 231). Rites of separation ease entry into new roles because they facilitate letting go of current statuses and roles. When MBA students move from the student role into managerial positions, they must unlearn their reluctance to deal with other people and learn the selling, compromising and politicking necessary to get their ideas adopted (Schein 1978, p 95). In effect, the unlearning involves leave-taking from the well-organized, highly structured, well-understood role of being a student to a much less structured and equivocal role. New managers are apt to find that matters move more slowly and less rationally than they expect, and that it may be necessary to participate in carving out their own job. Furthermore, having an immediate boss contrasts sharply with the autonomy of student life.

It seems likely that the rigorous interviewing and selection processes (Trice, Belasco, and Alutto 1969; Pascale 1984) used by many companies help to unfreeze recruits from their old roles and set the stage for them to accept new realities. In some cases, actual physical separation from the company setting symbolically dramatizes the letting go of former roles and the necessity to go through a transition before the new role can be assumed. Travel to a new location signals entry into this transition phase. The use of off-site assessment centers is a good example; they combine both separation and seclusion to help recruits to leave old understandings behind in preparation for assuming a new role.

The letting go involved in the separation phase is especially well illustrated by the extreme form of this rite used in military organizations. In Navy boot camps, within an hour after arrival,

> The new recruit is told to remove all his civilian clothes, his jewelry, religious medals, etc., and place them, along with wallet, comb, key ring, and the like into the shipping box that has been given him. He stands there nude and wraps and addresses the box containing the accouterments of his civilianity. When finished he proceeds through a line in which he is issued his naval attire. (Zurcher 1967, p. 91)

During the paper processing prior to this stripping process, the recruit is still called Mister; following it he becomes a "boot"—because the leggings he wears resemble actual boots. A shaved head completes his separation from his prior identity.

> There he and his company mates stand in their ill-fitting, stiff dungarees, arms still burning from shots, heads cold and itching from the haircut, tired, lonely and lost. (Zurcher 1967, p. 91)

No one would doubt that separation processes have occurred.

Now unlearning begins. Suddenly, the recruit cannot talk with nonrecruits, cannot leave the physical isolation of the base, and must do most things in a mass formation that contrasts dramatically with the freedom of individual movement experienced in civilian life. In officer training in the U.S. Coast Guard, additional practices facilitate unlearning past behaviors: the new recruit discovers that it is taboo to discuss personal wealth or background and, further, he cannot receive any additional money from home (Dornbusch, 1954). While practices in the military have been softened somewhat in the years since these observations were made, the essential outlines of separation rites remain.

Very explicit rites of separation are also used in other occupations where physical dangers are endemic to the occupation: police (Van Maanen 1973); municipal firefighters (McCarl 1980); and forest firefighters who parachute to remote locations (McCarl 1976). It is interesting to note that the Japanese managerial training already described, in its arduousness and explicitness, also resembles military rites. While such physically arduous and demeaning rites are probably not suitable for U.S. managerial recruits, as already pointed out, managerial recruits are sometimes physically isolated as they go through training, and separated from other employees by such devices as assessment centers and testing of various kinds. The more unique the culture an organization seeks to inculcate in recruits, the more important are separation rites.

Transition. The second phase, transition, produces liminality—a limbolike state in which the initiate is marginal, neither in an old role, nor in the one toward which the passage is leading (Turner 1969). The initiate experiences an ambiguous, unstructured state of being "betwixt and between." Many tribal versions of this liminal period are marked by the initiates' names being taken from them; each is instead called by some generic phrase that refers to everyone in the neophyte category (Turner 1970, p. 358). The use of the term *boot* in the U.S. Navy is an example. During this phase, initiates are sociologically naked, stripped of past identities and lacking new ones. They have physical, but not social being.

Debasement experiences, of one kind or another, tend to characterize the transition phase of rites of passage. They reinforce separation by requiring the abandonment of old responses, and by underscoring the need to acquire new roles and responses. They act to open up the newcomer to the influences of the social group or organization. These experiences and the social processes involved grind the newcomers down "to be fashioned anew and endowed with additional powers to cope with their new station in life" (Turner 1970, p. 362).

Again, the military provides the most explicit and dramatic examples. During basic training in the U.S. Army, it is during rites of transition that raw recruits learn the skills associated with their new identity—shooting guns, marching, and obeying promptly and without question. Efforts are even made to rebuild their bodies through calisthenics, long arduous marches, and other physically demanding exercises. Debasing rituals include the wearing of fatigues, frequent inspections, and endless saluting of those of superior status. Typically, noncommissioned officers treat the recruits with contempt. Toward the end of the transition period, recruits are repeatedly tested, presumably to determine what new permanent roles they are capable of assuming.

In modern work life, debasements may be relatively mundane. One set of observers described the following example:

> Stanley, a new junior level manager, found that he had to walk all the way around the building from the parking lot and then walk all the way back through the plant to get to his office. He soon discovered that there was another possible way to go between his office and his car—a door at a loading gate at the back of the building presided over by a security guard. Stanley felt relieved until he learned that only those on his supervisor's list could use that door. A forthright inquiry with the boss's secretary established the fact that Stanley would be informed when, and if, he got on this list. In the meantime, he had to truck back and forth twice every day rain or shine, four times a day if he went out to lunch.
>
> Months later his boss asked him into his office for his semiannual review. During this session he told Stanley about a raise for him, and incidentally, that he was putting him on "the list"—"just tell the guard who you are." At the end of the day he confidently went to the guard, told him his name, and in a few seconds was at his car. (Ritti and Funkhouser 1977, p. 5)

This mildly debasing experience set the stage for Stanley's full membership in the organization; he was liminal until he got on his boss's list.

Various "up-ending experiences" used to initiate brand new engineers also create liminality. In one firm, the strategy was to get the new employee deeply involved in some task that "violates his or her expectations about self or the organization in order to teach certain 'realities' quickly and dramatically" (Schein 1978, p. 106). One engineering manager gave every new graduate entering his group the task of analyzing a circuit that should not work, but did. When the recruit said it would not work, he was shown that it did and asked to explain why. Because few newcomers could explain, they were left chastened and skeptical of their education by this experience. One summary of such liminal experiences catches their flavor: "You are in kindergarten as far as what you know about this organization" (Pascale 1984, p. 30).

As the examples illustrate, rites of passage are sometimes collective and sometimes individual. When the separation and transition phases of these rites are collective, as they often are, strong comradeship emerges from the common experiences undergone during the passage together. A sense of equality permeates these experiences and comes to transcend differences in social rank, age, kinship, and accomplishment. Recruits from the same police academy training class experience this sense of camaraderie years after they enter the police force. Similarly, cohorts in graduate schools develop deep friendships that grow and flourish from the shared liminality of going through rites of transition together.

Incorporation.   As mentioned earlier, clearly demarcated rites of incorporation are often missing from modern organizations. However, in tribal cultures, they are quite obvious. Among the Andaman Islanders, rites of incorporation for young males consisted of a series of intricate dances performed by adult males in which initiates were welcomed and saluted with bundles of sacred twigs. The initiates responded with a vigorous acceptance dance. Subsequently, under close observation to assure they adhered to numerous taboos, the initiates slowly assume their adult roles—but only after weeks of monitoring by adults (Radcliffe-Brown 1964, p. 94). One description of how successful companies put new managerial recruits into the field and give them "carefully monitored experience" (Pascale 1984, p. 30) following rites of transition bears considerable similarity to the incorporation rites of the Andaman Islanders. The recruits are similarly isolated and made to question prior beliefs and values.

A rite of incorporation ideally gives two sets of messages relevant to socialization: (1) it tells the initiate "you are one of us"; and (2) it shows the initiate "this is how it really is." Both are well illustrated by observations of the clear-cut incorporation phase police recruits experienced. It followed "harsh and often arbitrary discipline" (Van Maanen 1973, p. 410) during their transition phase, which had taken place in an academy physically isolated from ongoing, everyday police work. Incorporation began with initial assignment to a real department and a field training officer (FTO) who introduced the recruit to the complexities of street work. FTOs were experienced officers who treated the recruits as apprentices, teaching them the most basic and simple aspects of police work. Following six weeks of apprenticeship, most recruits got assignments to permanent partners and were "considered to be real (albeit rookie) policemen" (Van Maanen 1975, p. 210). During the incorporation phase, recruits tended to undergo dramatic changes in the high motivations they had displayed at the time of graduation from the academy. They entered their new departments motivated to achieve and highly committed to their new organizations. As the incorporation phase continued, however, they encountered the complex bureaucratic arrangement in which their work was embedded. These encounters produced a perspective that stressed "lay low, don't make waves" (Van Maanen 1975, p. 207).

Often, the most visible aspects of the incorporation phase are welcoming induction ceremonies. The incorporation phase of one managerial training program already mentioned began with a short speech by the production manager on the shop floor during a brief shutdown. This speech emphasized the rigors of the training the initiates had just been through. The rite ended with a cocktail party in honor of the new managers that took place that evening in a management club nearby. The next phase, learning the realities, was less explicit and fixed. The new managers reported to various experienced superiors, who took a variety of roles relative to them.

Incomplete rites.   The correspondence between rites of passage and training in modern organizations was overlooked until the late 1960s (Trice, Belasco, and Alutto 1969). One likely reason is that such training often misses or abbreviates one or another of three consecutive rites. Other times, one phase of the total rite is so dominant it obscures the others (Myerhoff 1982, p. 116). In organizational and occupational training the middle transition phase often dominates and is relatively prolonged. The initial separation phase, even when it lacks ceremony, is usually detectable because it must occur to get into the pervasive transition phase. The last phase, that of incorporation of trainees into their new roles, is often skipped over and handled on an informal, individualized basis. The literature on work organizations describes very few instances of truly ceremonial incorporation practices. No wonder assessments frequently find that training is not applied after trainees return to their regular duties. Without a rite of incorporation, whatever new identity may have been gained in the training is likely to be lost. No matter which phase is neglected, organizations lose some of the socialization potential of training programs when they fail to develop them as full-fledged rites of passage.

Absence of rites.   As the examples used illustrate, rites of passage are not entirely lacking in modern life; their benefits and importance, however, are often overlooked, especially in business organizations. Yet "there is every reason to believe that rites of passage are as important now as they have always been for our social and psychological well-being. Indeed, given the fragmented, confusing, complex, and disorderly nature of modern experience, perhaps they are more important ..." (Myerhoff 1982, p. 129).

At least one anthropologist (Turnbull 1984, p. 88) feels that "Western culture is lacking in effective mechanisms for socialization" because of its lack of effective rites of passage. Although college fraternities and noncollegiate fraternal organizations like the Masons have elaborate initiation rites, they apparently do not function as effective rites of passage. One reason is that the new statuses they confer do not have much meaning in the wider society. Initiates do not feel they have assumed important new identities (Raphael 1988).[4] In effect, they are cultural forms without much cultural substance. Religious rites of passage like bar mitzvahs and confirmations have lost much of their significance in modern secular societies, probably because they happen at too young an age to be able to mark the passage to adulthood. Gang rituals may be more potent, but do not confer statuses accepted within the wider society. The disadvantaged in modern society may be especially deprived by the lack of such rites—not only to help them enter work roles, but also to help them cross the boundary between childhood and adulthood. High school is the only relatively universal rite of passage provided in present U.S. society (Leeman 1972; Burnett 1969), and many of the disadvantaged do not complete high school. For others, its impact may be minimal. Some commentators, seeing this lack, have suggested the cultivation of new rites of passage to help to prepare young males from disadvantaged groups for constructive roles in society.[5]

In general, recent changes in expectations of adult male and female roles and the confusion and conflict accompanying these changes make assuming adult roles a difficult and uncertain process for all young people in the United State and probably in other modern societies. The development and use of meaningful new rites of passage could conceivably help to ease this transition and further desired cultural continuity (Van Biema 1991).

Other Rites

Because they carry cultural messages, all of the other rites identified in Chapter 3 may contribute to socialization. But some will play a more direct role than others. Rites of integration help newcomers to feel a part of the larger social group they are joining. Already mentioned was a cocktail party that finished a corporate welcoming ceremony by socially mixing new managers with the old. During such prevalent rites of integration as office Christmas parties or picnics,

---

[4]Besides occupational training, the one rite of passage that might be expected inevitably to confer a new identity is marriage, which traditionally involved assuming a new adult status and responsibilities. Marriage may still have this function for some, but a penetrating analysis of love and adulthood indicates that marriage no longer marks having arrived at a new societal status so much as opening another opportunity for personal growth and change. This observer's analysis suggests that there is no clear adult status in current modern U.S. society (Swidler 1990). If there is no adulthood, there can be no rites of passage into it. Interviews designed to uncover rites of passage men had experienced revealed that some had invented personal ordeals that helped them achieve the feeling that they were now adult men (Raphael 1988). Such private rites, of course, cannot carry cultural messages to a cultural group.

[5]Although most tribal cultures have demanding rites of passage to transform boys into men, they lack comparable passages for their female members (Gilmore 1990). A variety of the explanations that have been offered suggest that becoming a man is considered more problematic in most societies. Chief among these are that the male role is more strenuous, and that men must be induced to achieve high levels of performance in the struggle for survival. They must be tempered and toughened to perform well in the productive activities of society. The two primary explanations for the lesser importance of such rites for women is that biology equips women to play their complementary role of reproduction, and that women, being physically weaker, are easier for the society and men to control (Gilmore 1990).

newcomers have the opportunity to learn about and participate in common feel-ings that bind members together and commit them to the celebrating group.

Rites of enhancement and degradation also have socializing influences. When new Mary Kay saleswomen attend one of the company's seminars, they learn from the recounting of others' accomplishments what the organization ex-pects. The lavishness and public nature of the ceremony conveys how important these accomplishments are to the organization. Such latent messages, along with the awards and recognition given, help to motivate all observers, but especially those there for the first time, to greater efforts. Many organizations hold similar public rites of enhancement, especially for their salespeople. Rites of degrada-tion, although they occur less often, help any newcomers who observe them to learn what behaviors are not tolerated and which are the wrong role models for the current culture.

Rites of renewal can also be used to socialize members. RCA (Radio Corpo-ration of America) used a formal research project that gathered data about its culture as an explicit training tool to assist the socialization of newcomers (Kreps 1983). The research team uncovered actual metaphors, a saga, legends, stories, rites, and symbols being used in the company and then incorporated them in a video tape used for employee orientation. Prominent among their findings was the saga of David Sarnoff, the visionary inventor who developed the radio music box—a forerunner of radio and television. He founded RCA and guided it into a major corporation. Some of the metaphors were: "RCA as an idea company," "RCA as a tradition on the move," and "RCA as a family." Significant symbols included Nipper, the faithful white dog, listening to his master's voice on an RCA phonograph. The script was repeatedly submitted for feedback from RCA employees "at different hierarchical levels . . . ranging from hourly employees to top executives. . . . the process of critique and refinement resulted in a written script that reflected organization members' perceptions about RCA culture" (Kreps 1983, p. 253). Thus, research intended to renew the company became a device for socialization of new members.

Stories and Sagas

As narratives based on true events, but distorted to incorporate fictional embellishments, stories graphically and quickly communicate emotionally charged beliefs to newcomers. They are apt to be entertaining and, as a conse-quence, are sometimes far-fetched. An often-told story in the National Cash Reg-ister Company (NCR) expressed the intense commitment to the company in-grained in employees:

> The NCR Paris office of the Champs Elysees was on the line of march when Hitler's Wehrmacht rumbled into the capital of France in 1940. A tank swerved from the column and halted before the NCR door. Out leaped a German soldier. He pounded for admittance. Finally our French employees decided that discretion required that they open to him. The German smiled and said, "I'm from NCR in Berlin. I just wondered if you made your quota last year." (Dyer 1985, p. 215)

The allegiance to NCR transcended national boundaries even during war time.
Observers have noted that corporations that socialize well have numerous retold stories that point in a single ideological direction:

> "In the old Bell system, story after story extolled Bell employees who made heroic sacrifices to keep the phones working. The Bell folklore was so powerful that when national disaster struck, all elements of a one million-member organization were able to pull together, cut corners, violate normal procedures, even do things that would not look good—all in the interest of restoring phone service." (Pascale 1984, p. 34)

Despite the breakup of the Bell system, such values persisted in 1990 when an obscure computer programming error eliminated much of AT&T's long-distance capacity worldwide (Sims 1990). Service was slowed down, but not totally interrupted. Programmers and managers managed to locate the malfunction in less than seven hours and were able to restore full service in nine hours. Engineers subsequently worked around the clock to be sure the problem would not recur.[6] So accustomed is the public and AT&T employees to no interruption of service that this slowdown in service was treated by the press as a major black eye for AT&T. In a press interview, Robert Allen, AT&T's chairman, said:

> Even though it was a one-time hit to the network, it was certainly the most far-reaching service problem we've ever experienced. . . . We didn't live up to our own standards of quality. We didn't live up to our customers' standards of quality. It's as simple as that. That's not acceptable to us. (Sims 1990, p. A1)

Two additional stories further illustrate the potential of stories as socializing agents (Wilkins 1984, p. 46). One could be called the "Beat Up" story, since it told about how a highly rated young manager was humiliated when he made a presentation at a series of meetings. Senior managers sharply criticized his arguments and seriously questioned his intelligence and background. This story was interpreted as meaning that top management expected managers to be able to take criticism and really cared about quality decision making. The second story was used "to quiet the anxiety of concerned newcomers" about probable cutbacks. It told of how the company (Hewlett-Packard) avoided a mass layoff in the early 1970s, when other companies in the industry were forced to lay off employees in large numbers. According to the story, top management avoided such layoffs by asking everyone in the company, including themselves, to take a 10 percent cut in salary and work only nine out of ten days.

Research has demonstrated the efficacy of stories in transmitting cultures and generating commitment to organizations. One researcher (Wilkins 1978, 1983a) studied stories in two organizations—one with high and the other with low employee commitment to the organization. In the one with high commitment, there was a significantly greater number of favorable stories told to newcomers about the unique features of the company than in the company with low

---

[6]Unfortunately, however, AT&T has experienced significant interruptions of service since then.

commitment. In an experiment to determine if organizational stories were more persuasive than quantitative data in introducing a company to newcomers, stories proved more vivid and influential (Martin and Powers 1983).

Sagas differ from stories in that they are embellished, but true. They are historical narratives that describe the unique accomplishments of a group and its leaders, usually in heroic terms. A well-known instance is the saga of Bill Hewlett and Dave Packard of Hewlett-Packard. New recruits are often shown a slide presentation of how Bill and Dave started the company in Bill's garage and used Hewlett's stove and oven for making some of its original products. Other company sagas carrying heroic narratives about unique accomplishments have been recorded for Robert W. Woodruff of Coca-Cola (Walters 1978); Lee Iacocca of Chrysler (Tichy and Ulrich 1984); and George and Richard Cadbury of Cadbury, Limited, in England (Dellheim 1987).

Organizational Jargon and Language

Closely akin to organizational stories is the unique language that grows up in work settings. "Organizational talk" is both a feature of the work setting and descriptive of the setting. As they are socialized, new members need to learn "the language used to talk about actors' roles, vocabularies, normal usage, etc., as a sign of competence" (Manning 1970, p. 250). A new recruit's encounters with the U.S. Navy illustrates this point well. Recruits walk into a blizzard of new language, much of it technical jargon and administrative designations.

> They enlist at the AFEES (Armed Forces Examining and Entrance Station), otherwise known as a home town recruiting station. They then go to a RTC (Recruit Training Command) at the nearest NTC (Naval Training Center). Here the Navy puts them through the transition from civilian to military life with a very busy schedule of lectures and drills on the Navy's traditions, customs, and regulations. Here they learn the first key words in their new vocabulary, such as CC (Company Commander), the POD (Plan of the Day), BI (Barracks Inspection), EPO (Educational Petty Officer), MD (Military Drill), TOD (Term of the Day), TAD (Temporary Additional Duty). Newly enlisted recruits are given three tests: the ASVAB (Armed Services Vocational Aptitude Battery), the NFQU (Nuclear Field Qualification Tests), and the FLAT (Foreign Language Aptitude Test). They also receive a four digit NEC (Navy Enlisted Classification), which codifies their incoming skills, qualifications, and aptitudes. (Adapted from Evered 1983)

There is another language, an informal language, that the Navy recruit must also learn. The obscenity of this language is sometimes explained in terms of aggression, negativism, and need to express hostility. While these factors may indeed be operating, the "importance of role expectations must not be overlooked . . . the obscene terms come into universal and relatively indiscriminate usage and thus loose their original sexual significance. The words merely become the language of a social group" (Zurcher 1967, p. 95). In effect, the recruit is expected to swear; it is the argot of the informal organization.

Learning organizational language, especially technical terms, is a prominent part of the socialization of newcomers to railroad work. The newly hired member of a train crew must learn a whole vocabulary of terms, gestures, and signals to become "a rail" (Kemnitzer 1973). There is an informal language and a formal language used in the Book of Rules and official bulletins. A third language, the technical language, is used in everyday relations with officials, inexperienced men, and often in union agreements, grievances, public relations, and job descriptions.

Signals—hand, lantern, and whistle—are all classified as formal and described in the Book of Rules; they are part of the official language of the organization. However, informal forms of these signals gain currency and must also be learned.

Each of the verbal languages is appropriate in some contexts and not others. Among rails themselves, informal language predominates. Between experienced and inexperienced workers, technical language prevails. Between rails and officials, when no accusations of rule infraction is under consideration, an informal, mildly jocular language pertains. When, however, these two groups face a conflict situation—which is rather frequent—only formal or technical language is used.

In effect, the new railroad recruit must come to understand an organizationally based set of languages and signs on four different levels. On the cognitive level, "rails" must learn terms for objects and technical operations. On the technical level, they must learn complex communication systems in order to carry out technical tasks. On the affective level, all messages carry craft or community implications. Finally, on the cultural level, words and signals carry messages regarding the socialization and identification of senders and receivers.

Only when recruits know its culture's language and jargon can they fully understand jokes and humor unique to an organization. In turn, the content of jokes reflects the degree of socialization of the tellers and listeners. In the beginning of a training program for new managers of a sales division of a large corporation, laughter and jokes were few. Moreover those that did occur were understandable to outsiders, consisting largely of sexual innuendo and foolish mistakes. At the end of the training—some ten weeks later—an outsider would have had difficultly understanding the humor. Jokes were now directed toward out-groups such as competitive companies or other subcultures in the company (Siehl 1985). The trainees had developed a clear sense of "we" and "they"—an ethnocentrism that marks subcultural development.

In this training program, various cultural forms tended to emerge in a predictable sequence: jargon, stories and humor, shared interpretation of stories, and ideological language. A grasp of jargon and technical language provided the foundation for jokes and humor, which were followed by more complicated stories. A common interpretation of these stories came about somewhat more slowly than did the cultural effects of the earlier-used forms. Individual differences and uneven exposure produced some variations, but in aggregate, these forms helped to develop a series of ideological orientations that had become relatively tacit by the end of the training period.

Many other behaviors and practices that are explicit cultural forms contribute in one way or another to socialization. Examples include role models, mentoring, and supervision. We will illustrate these practices and their role in socialization as we consider two more important features of socialization—that it proceeds in stages and that in unfolds differently at different points in people's life cycles and careers.

Stages of Organizational Socialization

One frequent way that theorists have analyzed socialization is as a sequence of stages. However, if taken too literally, this approach can be misleading; the process of socialization is a continual one and the demarcations between any set of stages is bound to be fuzzy and imprecise. However, it also seems clear that there is some kind of progression within any instance of socialization, and a sequence of stages is a convenient way to represent it.

While the labels given to these stages vary, most analysts identify four stages of a complete cycle of socialization, which we will call anticipatory socialization, encounter, assimilation, and departure (Feldman 1976; Louis 1980; Jablin 1987). Members pass through these stages as they move from being outsiders to being insiders, as they move from role to role within an organization, and as they leave an organization. Each passage from one role to another usually entails a complete cycling through these four stages although, in some instances, some of the stages may be abbreviated and rather unobtrusive. When stages are abbreviated and receive little attention, the entire passage is likely to be damaged; the passenger will not be as well socialized as one who has undergone a more complete experience at each stage.

Anticipatory Socialization

During anticipatory socialization, while still outside their new role, people anticipate, often without much evidence on which to base their projections, what will happen to them, who the major persons will be with whom they must interact, what problems and rewards will materialize, and generally what their new role will be like. At least two sets of anticipations can arise: expectations about their life in the organization they are joining, and expectations about the specific role they will assume. While children and adolescents may develop images of what occupations and organizations are like, their knowledge is too vague and imprecise to qualify as anticipatory socialization. This stage typically begins when there is a realistic possibility that persons will actually assume specific roles. It is only then that they are likely to try to visualize the expected changes in their life in some detail.

The literature on anticipatory socialization has focused on the passage of persons entering their first job or entering a specific occupation. Clearly, however, persons moving to new jobs within an organization or moving from one organization to another after they are established in a career will also experience some degree of anticipatory socialization. In fact, it is reasonable to expect that their anticipations will be more specific and more accurate because of their past experience in similar roles.

To the extent that anticipatory assessments are accurate, they facilitate adjustment after entry. To the extent that they are inaccurate, they may interfere with constructive adjustments after entry. If recruits have anticipations that are quite inaccurate, unpleasant misunderstandings will result. In effect, the stage is set for unmet expectations (Dunnette, Arvey, and Banas 1973)—a gap between anticipatory expectations and the actual experiences recruits have on the jobs. In particular, inaccurate anticipations may cause recruits to find far less of a desired feature than expected. Research shows that the less realistic the anticipations, the more likely newcomers are to quit their jobs (Wanous 1977).

To increase the accuracy of anticipations, practitioners have therefore developed the realistic job preview (RJP). The RJP is a conscious attempt to acquaint the applicant with negative as well as positive aspects of the job and organization. Such information is usually conveyed by an interviewer and embedded in selection interviews, which are "the most common form of job preview that applicants receive from organizations" (Jablin 1987, p. 689). The central idea behind RJPs is that they function much like medical vaccinations. Vaccinations inject people with a weakened dose of germs so that the body can develop a natural resistance to infection. Similarly, analysts argue, presenting applicants with a small dose of organizational reality will inoculate them against some of the disappointments they would otherwise encounter and thus reduce the likelihood of their leaving the organization soon after entry (Wanous 1980; Reilly et al. 1981; Popovich and Wanous 1982). The accumulated evidence from the many studies of RJP effectiveness suggests that the inoculation does indeed occur, but it only modestly increases newcomer retention (Premack and Wanous 1985). One reason is that interviewers presenting RJPs cannot possibly fully anticipate the expectations of potential members about how they will personally react to and function in their new roles. After entry, newcomers may therefore experience considerable surprise in these areas. Also, other factors that kick in after entry, such as the influence of peers and role models, apparently also influence newcomers' staying or leaving.

There is also some evidence that the preexistence of values that fit the ideologies of the organization to be entered also affects role adjustment after entry. For example, studies of the American soldier during World War II (Stouffer et al. 1949) showed that those recruits who initially understood and accepted the official values of the military were far more likely to be promoted. In their civilian lives, these recruits had apparently undergone complementary orientations by persons of significance, who had socialized them into accurate and favorable anticipations of military life. More recent research indicates that entry-level auditors whose values matched those of the public accounting firms they joined adjusted more quickly, were more satisfied, and intended to stay with their firms longer (Chatman 1991). Socialization experiences, however, also mattered; firm-sponsored social activities and contact with mentors were related to the match between personal and firm values in this study.

Encounter

The second stage is the entry into and encounter with the new role (Van Maanen 1975; Louis 1980). During this period, recruits first come into regular direct contact with their new workplaces. The phrase *breaking in* graphically describes this stage. Like young horses experiencing the bridle, saddle, and rider for the first time, neophytes often are both puzzled and frightened. Even experienced workers, when first encountering drastically different responsibilities and expectations, will experience reality shock (Hughes 1958). An extreme example of such shock was observed by Bourne (1967, p. 188) in new recruits to the U.S. Army. During basic training they were deprived of civilian comforts and placed in a strange and unfamiliar setting in which they had no control over their environments. They reacted by becoming stunned, dazed, and frightened.

The key features of the encounter experience include change, contrast, and surprise (Louis 1980). Change includes any objective difference between new and old settings. The more elements that are different, the more the newcomer has to cope with during encounter. Such changes include publicly noted and knowable facts like changes of location and address, phone number, title, and salary. In addition, newcomers may have changed role expectations, new statuses, and different working conditions. Most crucial, co-workers and informal social networks change; research shows that newcomers rely heavily on information from co-workers when they are new to a job (Feldman 1981; Feldman and Brett 1983).

All of these changes contribute to the other characteristics of the encounter stage—contrast and surprise. Contrast involves noticing certain features of the new job against a background provided by past experience. The changed circumstances of the newcomer often contrast sharply with immediate past experience. A new set of understandings are called for in the new setting. But vivid memories remain of the old roles left behind as encounter proceeds. The letting go of old roles is gradual and continues well into the socialization process. Of course, surprise accompanies change and contrast. It consists largely of unmet expectations—the differences between anticipations held upon entry and actual experiences in the new setting. Numerous forms of surprise occur: conscious expectations are unfulfilled, expectations about self are unmet, features of the job are unanticipated, and newcomers rely on assumptions about the culture of the new setting only to discover that it is unique and largely unknown (Louis 1980, p. 237).

During the encounter period, newcomers search for accurate information to clarify their roles. The types of socialization tactics employed will help to determine where information is found and how it is used. When highly individualized tactics are used, newcomers must rely heavily on their own personal resources. They may sometimes have to develop their own role prescriptions. For example, they may, to varying degrees, be able to choose role senders from whom to solicit role prescriptions. Other times, they may negotiate a set of role pre-scriptions with relevant role senders by acting and seeing how they react. Or, if they bring idealized conceptions to their new role, they may try to enact those. There are other instances when roles are tightly prescribed by formal proce-dures, and the major problems for newcomers are to detect and learn these pro-cedures.

Newcomers must learn about role prescriptions at two levels. They need to find out what the formal organization and its culture expects of them; they also need to find out about subcultural expectations emanating in informal groups, especially the expectations of co-workers and immediate superiors. The latter part of this exploration is likely to be the most difficult and prolonged because informal expectations are likely to be more hidden, dense, and multifaceted than are formal ones. Collective tactics help newcomers to learn more quickly about some of the informal expectations connected with jobs. Recruits come out of these experiences already part of some informal networks and attuned to the issues they are concerned with. For a long time to come, they can also fall back on friendships made during collective experiences to help them make sense of the face-to-face groups into which their new formal roles thrust them.

However, it takes time before the full extent of the gap between anticipa-tions and realities sinks in. The more intense the anticipations, the more likely they will lead to subsequent feelings of "broken promises" and to quitting (Wa-nous 1977). The types of socialization tactics used and the personal characteris-tics of recruits can speed up or slow down inclinations to quit. If the gap is considerable, the tactic very individualized, and the recruit rather naive and low in self-efficacy, quitting becomes likely and relatively swift. The organization, of course, loses its investment in the process. Such turnover can, however, have some benefits. To the degree that the gap is irreconcilable, the organization may be better off seeking new recruits than trying to continue to socialize those who have highly incompatible expectations. When tactics are collective, even large gaps are easier for recruits to tolerate or reconcile. They may very well realize the gaps sooner, and the collective sense making that occurs assists them in find-ing ways to close gaps or rationalize them away.

In summary, during the encounter stage, newcomers usually must adjust themselves to differences between reality and anticipations. Unrealistic anticipa-tions are commonplace, but will lessen under favorable conditions. If newcomers feel competent and accepted; if details of role definitions can be agreed upon in terms of tasks, priorities, and time allocations; and if feelings of trust in co-workers emerge, unmet expectations will likely fade. Overall, this stage involves the clarification of roles plus the confrontation and acceptance of organizational realities.

Assimilation

The third stage can be designated as a settling-in process in which newcom-ers become accepted participating members of their organizations. During this period, expectations become more fixed and actual role performance occurs.

Some reasonable congruence between self-appraisals and organizational appraisals emerges. For army recruits this is the period in which actual training occurs, anxiety levels drop, the newcomer's self-image is altered, and successes are experienced with credit and rewards attached to them. Newcomers resolve or adapt to ambiguities that have come to light. Alterations in the newcomers' self-images are reinforced by established organizational members.

Research on the process of becoming a successful manager showed that the first year was critical. High company expectations of good performance during the first year seemed to produce internalization of positive job attitudes and high performance in later years. The researchers concluded that trainees were uniquely ready to develop in the direction of the company's expectations during this critical first year. "Never again will there be so 'unfrozen' a situation, one high in readiness to learn and adapt" (Berlew and Hall 1966, p. 222). Another study of new managers describes "companies sending the new humble recruits into the trenches, pushing them to master one of the disciplines at the core of the company's business" (Pascale 1984, p. 30).

In this stage the outsider clearly moves toward becoming an insider. Responsibility for and autonomy in role performance becomes more pronounced, privileged information is more frequently shared, and informal networks come to at least partially include the now not-so-new newcomer. An organizational role and a newcomer are joined. These developments signal the beginning of the longest stage in socialization. Socialization continues with all of the many subsequent experiences people have in their work roles. The process is, at bottom, a lifelong one, both in work organizations and other dimensions of human life. Increasingly, signs of mutual acceptance appear. Evidence of dependability and recognition thereof mounts, and commitment to both job tasks and to the organization grows.

Often, however, people change their roles again. They get transferred or promoted, they quit and move to a new organization, they change occupations, or they retire.

Departure

A fourth stage, often overlooked, can be thought of as letting go of old roles to permit recycling and socialization into new roles, either in the same organization or in a new one. This stage marks the end of one passage and sets the stage for a new passage; it involves departing from a role and usually, except in the case of death, involves assuming a new one. Because it is the final stage of a cycle, this stage takes place somewhat later in work life, when the passenger is more experienced and personal characteristics may be relatively less influential.

Research shows

> ... there is a high and rising rate of management mobility—there are still some managers whose careers are stable and orderly, but their numbers are dwindling. Most can expect to change jobs at least once every three years, and for the great majority, job change also means a change of job function. More often than not job

changes involve either a change of status, a change of employer, or both, for over half of all management job change is "spiralling" in character, involving simultaneous functional and upward status changes. (Nicholson and West 1988, p. 69)

Managers are not the only ones changing jobs. With the recent rash of organizational downsizing, mergers, and failures, many employees have no choice but to change jobs, employers, or occupations. In this sense, work life for most people constitutes a sequence of roles connected by transition mechanisms that link the old to the new (Nicholson 1984; Trice and Morand 1989). Socialization into new settings and new relationships is thus a continual process throughout adult life (Louis 1980).

Because of the historically high rates of mobility in U.S. society and the insecurities inherent in the large numbers of organizational changes that have occurred recently, many young people enter their first jobs preprogrammed to leave them. Indeed, recent developments in corporate America may lead workers of all ages to fear for the organization's future and thus to feel they must position themselves to move on relatively favorable terms at any time (Hirsch 1987). The lure of upward mobility is also potent and may still be the most influential factor in job switching.

As job incumbents move into the departure stage, they are likely to begin to search out and weigh alternatives more carefully and notice new role models. Their aspirations may grow; their commitment and involvement in their present role may lessen. The old disappointments with the current role resurface, and additional factors may provoke dissatisfaction. In the initial stages of this psychological withdrawal process, employees tend increasingly to avoid communication with others. When they do interact, talk will likely emphasize differences and distinctions between themselves and other organizational members. In the final phase of withdrawal, communications focus on the leaver's preparing co-workers for his or her departure from the role (Jablin 1987, p. 723).

Most of the research on socialization has focused on young recruits moving into their first jobs. Much less emphasis has been put on the fact that, following the first job, people inevitably recycle into other jobs that require additional socialization. Many persons are likely to experience several passages in their lifetime; some will experience many passages. We will now turn to the question of how these passages may differ at different career and life stages.

Career and Life Stages

Early Career

Many discussions of organizational socialization use the term "*the* organization" as if workplaces were collectivities marked by cultural homogeneity, and as if there were typically an overall culture that acted organizationwide to overcome diversity and ambiguity. Far more realistic is the view that organizations contain cultural diversities that are more powerful influences than any overall "blanket" culture (Dubinskas 1988, p. 219). When socialization is viewed from this perspective, it can be seen as a cluster of multiple influences playing unevenly and often ambiguously on a new arrival.

This cultural diversity will be especially difficult to cope with for persons early in their careers. At this stage, they are still learning the specifics of what their jobs require. Even those who come in with prior occupational socialization still need to learn many specifics as they come to grips with the realities of actually doing the job. Now they must also learn, often for the first time, about a specific work organization. Those who have had more experiences with other organizations—from college, graduate school, military service, part-time jobs, voluntary activities—will probably be less overwhelmed than those with fewer experiences.

Of the many influences people encounter in organizations, six play especially important parts in socialization of individuals early in their careers. These are occupational socialization, other training, peer influences, mentoring, role models, and leaders.

Occupational socialization and other training. Many employees receive occupational training and socialization early in their careers. Some of it, notably college and university training, occurs before being hired for a specific job. Other occupational socialization, like police and firefighting academies, occurs after hiring and is thus potentially more under the control of the employing organization. Many studies document the rigors and potency of the socialization that occurs in both settings. We have already provided several examples from military and police training. The rigors and unique features of law and medical training have been documented both by extensive research and in popular literature, movies, and television series. Less well known are the distinctive features of MBA programs and the differences in socialization within different programs.

One study documented the drastically different cultures in two elite graduate schools of management: the Sloan School of Management at the Massachusetts Institute of Technology (MIT) and the Harvard Business School (Van Maanen 1984). The latter socialized MBA students "in splendid isolation from both the undergraduate and other graduate schools of the university." The school's campus lies across a river from Harvard's central campus, and, in practically every way, is "literally a self-contained educational plant" (Van Maanen 1984, p. 219): bookstore, press, libraries, pub, health center, administrative offices, recreational facilities, post office, barber shop, and living quarters—all owned by the business school. The class schedule was in no way synchronized with other Harvard schools and is quite "incomprehensible to outsiders" (Van Maanen 1984, p. 219). It is possible for a student to go through and finish a two-year course and never encounter a Harvard student from another school. During their first year, all students must take the same classes, at the same time, and in the same order with 70 other beginning students. In the second year, the same pattern tends to repeat itself. Further, students come to "own" a lecture room since a given group frequently has a series of back-to-back classes in it while professors rotate in and out. Student name tags gave students a personal identity and professors were expected to address students by name. Participation in class discussions was also expected and emphasized. As a result, absences were readily visible. These various features spawned a sense of community among students that was reinforced by studying and partying together. A strong collective identity was the chief outcome of this socialization.

The Sloan School at MIT set up their MBA experience in a remarkably different pattern. Few courses were restricted to Sloan students; approximately a quarter of the students in most courses were from outside the school. No special facilities save a modest snack bar were available to them. Nor was the building in which the school was housed exclusively for them; it included economics and political science departments. Because they carried courses in other schools, many students had to dash to far-away classrooms instead of remaining in one building for all their classes. Another contrast was the open-ended nature of the Sloan program, which offered a large number and variety of courses. Students thus individually organized and selectively arranged their own graduate programs.

Perhaps because the Harvard MBA program was far more uniform and structured, providing little individual choice, a master's thesis was not required. At MIT, the MBA degree required each student to write and defend an individually chosen thesis in a specific area of concentration. This highly personalized requirement stood in sharp contrast to the commonly reached solutions shared among many Harvard MBA students in their informal student groups. In cultural terms, the Sloan School valued individual performance, especially in those courses believed to be most demanding. Individual eccentricities were easily tolerated and isolation from student study groups and cliques generated little, if any, comment or sanctions. The formal grade was the chief symbol for differentiation between students. Friendships were largely accidental, and if they caught on, tended to be based on common interests outside the classroom.

Differences in the student cultures were also reflected in relations with faculty. At the Sloan School, students had, in effect, been divided and conquered, leaving them vulnerable to guilt feelings about their individual performance in various courses. The collective student subculture at Harvard created feelings of being in the same boat and a siege mentality vis-à-vis the faculty. A collective paranoia about certain courses and professors came to predominate most student interactions. Informal study groups coalesced and provided social support and a sense of need for each other as students faced the barrage of work and cases assigned by faculty. These groups tended to control performance by controlling "rate busters" as well as "rate shirkers." Despite faculty admonition to "do your own work," students divided the work so as to provide each member with the benefits of the specialization of other members. While these two programs probably represent the extremes of MBA programs, other programs also differ in important ways that create different socialization values and experiences.

Sometimes, organizations sponsor training that socializes newcomers primarily into subcultures rather than directly into a larger organizational culture.

Dramatic instances have been reported in the U.S. Air Force, where two military subcultures engaged in radically different socialization techniques to produce commissioned officers. One, the Aviation Cadet Pre-Flight Training School (ACPFTS), "used harsh techniques to inculcate heroic values and eliminate the 'unfit.'" The other, the Officers Training School (OTS), used "low-key techniques" and treated trainees in the same manner as managerial supervisors related to subordinates during management development (Wamsley 1972, p. 399).

The OTS attempted an orderly transition into military life and, unlike the ACPFTS, did not isolate the recruit behind a "khaki curtain." ACPFTS trainees were denied all civilian contacts; for four months their cadets' only contacts were strictly within the military unit. Called "raunchies," the ACPFTS cadets were routinely tormented, insulted, discredited, and deprived of the most basic forms of respect. Often these torments were administered by noncommissioned officers. Fire drills interrupted their sleep. "Lights out" cut preparation time drastically. Such tactics screened out those men whom the trainers believed would not conform to the subculture's strict and authoritarian code. Those predisposed to neurotic behavior soon cracked under the pressure (Wamsley 1972).

OTS trainees suffered none of these harassments and indignities. Superiors did not "chew out" or "stress" the officer trainees; noncommissioned officers were largely removed from the training; hazing was explicitly forbidden; each trainee was expected to act "as a gentleman" and behave accordingly with fellow recruits. Repeated efforts were made to avoid "washouts" and the introduction to the military was thought of as gradual rather than sudden and traumatic. A demerit system (17 for a second class cadet; 10 for a first classman) involved possible restriction to base; even then, however, the officer trainee had access to club, pool, gym, and library. Among the officer trainees, the "cocksure aggressiveness" of the ACPFTS was lacking, but was replaced by a general enthusiasm and "can do" spirit (Wamsley 1972, p. 412).

A potent symbol that differentiated the two training subcultures centered around uniforms: among the ACPFTS cadets no civilian clothes were permitted at any time; even their presence in closets was forbidden. Although the military uniform was typical attire among OTS trainees, uniforms would be replaced by civilian clothes on those occasions when the recruit visited with relatives or friends. The presence of civilian clothes in OTS closets was a matter of no concern; among ACPFTS cadets it was absolutely taboo. The OTS and ACPFTS coexisted side by side in the air force of the late 1960s and early 1970s. Later, the OTS subculture began to be increasingly accepted by various commands and soon dominated air force training activities.

When training is viewed from the standpoint of these examples it becomes clear that the expressive outcomes of training may be as prominent—possibly even more so—than the technical outcomes. Clearly, evaluation of training outcomes should look beyond official technical goals (Chen and Rossi 1980) to indications of "ceremonial results [that] could justify the entire effort" (Trice and Roman 1973, p. 11).

One rigorously controlled experiment that evaluated supervisory training demonstrated that the technical outcomes of training on newly recruited managerial trainees was relatively important, but the expressive effects were also sig-nificant (Belasco and Trice 1969a, 1969b). Another qualitative field study con-cluded that a testing and training program for new supervisory recruits persisted because management valued its expressive effects (Trice, Belasco, and Alutto 1969, p. 47). Specifically, the lengthy supervisory training program studied pro-vided a long-lasting camaraderie that enabled newcomers to share similar prob-lems with each other; it showed the organization genuinely cared and knew about them; and it symbolized the importance of supervisors and supervision to partici-pants and others in the organization.

Subsequent research and observation have borne out and refined these early findings. A longitudinal qualitative study found that formal training in a police academy for a large city's police force produced rather irrelevant and weak technical outcomes. But the subsequent expressive outcomes of the training were highly consistent with later occupational ideologies of autonomy, pragma-tism, and "don't rock the boat" (Van Maanen 1975). Other observers commented that "surprisingly, the ceremonial effects of training may represent a more po-tent change agent than the intended effects of training," and went on to describe how the conduct of training sessions "off-site" maximized the opportunity to develop organizational bonds with trainees (Rosenthal and Mezoff 1980, p. 105).

A study of "winner" companies revealed that their socialization of neophyte managers tended, in part, to be in the form of experiences and training "calcu-lated to induce humility" and to make them question prior behavior, beliefs, and values. By lessening the recruits' comfort with themselves, the companies "hoped to promote openness toward their own values and norms." This sounds remark-ably like the transition phase of rites of passage, especially since the humility induced is brought on by long hours of intense work that carry recruits close to their limits. "Everyone has so much work to do" that they don't have time to see people outside the company or "re-establish a more normal social distance from co-workers" (Pascale 1984, p. 30). Such requirements create an exceptionally mar-ginal identity in which the trainees are outside most normal life rhythms and are cut off from their own pasts and futures. It seems that "if entry into an organiza-tion is a result of success in a series of difficult trials, then membership in that system must be valuable" (Trice, Belasco, and Alutto 1969, p. 46). One observer summarized the entire process of training new managers by saying that it is the "organization's rough equivalent of a *bar mitzvah*" (Gordon 1979, p. 23).

Peers.   The most ubiquitous socializing agents in work organizations are a new-comer's peers. Peers are those who have equal standing in the organization with the newcomer, although they may have been in the organization somewhat longer. People who are just beginning their careers are likely to look to their peers for information about their roles and about the organizational culture. For example, both new and old lawmakers in the California legislature were peers in that each had a role, was on a committee, and had an office. The freshmen legislators were often influenced by the veterans. "There was a clear tendency among the freshmen to change their perceptions toward those of the veterans when there was a substantial difference between the two groups at the outset" (Bell and Price 1975, p. 155).

Sometimes newcomers belong to a cohort of recruits undergoing a common boundary passage from outsider to insider. There may be a common "fellowship suffering" among them. They may have actually been members of the same off-site collective training group and bring into the organization the relationships established during that period. Also, they will have shared certain binding, emotional experiences during their collective socialization. Even if these conditions do not prevail, there are demographic forces that are apt to produce peer influences on those new to a career, regardless of prior situations. Many times peers are those with roughly the same tenure in the organization. Another potent factor in peer influence is age. Falling within an approximate five-year age span seems to produce a consciousness of kind, probably because of similar life experiences.

Studies of peer influence consistently use this age-span as a criteria to identify peers (Kram and Isabella 1985, p. 119). They have found three different types of peers: the information peer, the collegial peer, and the special peer. The information peer provides a "friendly exchange" and is quite common. Although the relationship contains a low level of trust, there is nevertheless an exchange of information about work and the organization. This relationship demands little of those in it, yet yields considerable information—sometimes accurate, sometimes inaccurate. The collegial peer involves more trust and "increasing levels of self-disclosure" in the relationship. As a result there are greater amounts of self-expression than in the information peer relationship. In addition, there is more "direct, honest feedback." All of these qualities, and more, enter into special peer relationships (Kram and Isabella 1985, p. 120). These have the qualities of a "best friend" relationship with a strong sense of bonding between the peers involved. Special peer relationships provide many opportunities to "express one's personal and professional dilemmas, vulnerabilities, and individuality" and also provide a "wide range of support for family and work issues" (Kram and Isabella 1985, pp. 122–23).

Another study, although it did not divide peers into specific types, nevertheless throws considerable light on the role of peers in the socialization of newcomers. The study focused on the initial work experiences of undergraduate business school graduates from both a small private university on the West Coast and a large public East Coast university. "Daily interaction with peers while working was the most important factor in helping newcomers to feel effective. Further, interaction with peers was available to respondents more than any other aid, and was significantly correlated with job satisfaction, commitment, and tenure intention" (Louis, Posner, and Powell 1983, p. 863).

Mentors.   Mentorship is a special intense form of role modeling, less prevalent than either peer relations or more ordinary role modeling. Traditionally a relationship between two males, one perhaps 10 to 15 years younger than the other, mentoring takes on the form of informal sponsorship. The mentor acts as teacher, guide, and even exemplar for the younger person. Such relationships can be especially valuable to those just beginning their careers.

Typically lasting three to five years, mentoring is a transitional relationship, facilitating the realization of career hopes and dreams for the younger person (Levinson 1978). It is also one of intense, nonsexual friendship, "best understood as a form of love relationship" (Levinson 1978, p. 100). Others liken it to the intense qualities of child-parent relations (Kram 1983), with the younger person moving through phases of initiation, cultivation of planned opportunities, and separation as the drive for independence becomes more and more intense.

Data from young managers throw light on the unique nature of the mentoring process (Kram 1983). An initiation phase consists of strong positive fantasies about the older manager, often reinforced by that person's concrete behavior. The senior person quickly recognizes the junior person as someone with much potential, someone who would provide him or her with continued status and recognition during a period of probably waning influence. These highly positive features move the relationship toward the cultivation phase, which could last as long as five years, but is more likely to be two to four years. The positive hopes held by both are regularly tested by reality; both thus discover the genuine, real advantages of the relationship. The interpersonal bond grows, characterized by considerable trust, mutuality, and much coaching and counseling on career, reflecting the mentor's insider view of how to nourish career development. As one young manager expressed it: "He has given [me] an awful lot of confidence in myself that I lacked before. I had almost begun to feel that I was not really of much value. . . . Now I feel that I am being pushed, advised, growing" (Kram 1983, p. 616). For the older manager there was "substantial satisfaction in knowing that he had positively influenced a younger individual's development." Clearly, each person in a mentoring relationship changes in complex ways. Younger members become more confident and optimistic about their careers, and feel more legitimate and dynamic because of the counseling to which they are exposed. Not only do they "learn the ropes" of organizational life, but they receive confirmation and support for an emerging new self-image. Presumably those newcomers not in mentoring relationships are at a disadvantage.

Somewhere between two and five years along in the relationship, the junior member wants more independence and autonomy, and the senior member reassesses the relationship. Both structurally and psychologically, separation occurs. Promotion, or geographical separation may erect structural barriers that end the relationship for all practical purposes. But sometimes the separation phase is stormy and emotional.

> The mentor—who only yesterday was regarded as an enabling teacher and friend—has become a tyrannical father or smothering mother. The mentor, for his part, finds the young man inexplicably touchy, unreceptive to even the best counsel, irrationally rebellious, and ungrateful. (Levinson 1978, p. 101)

In any case, the drive toward autonomy and independence that characterizes American culture begins to express itself in the behavior of the junior member. As one junior member expressed it,

"... I really didn't want others to think that he was the reason I got my new job and that he was a crutch. I had to prove to myself and everybody that it was me, that I stood alone, and that I no longer needed his support." (Kram 1985, p. 57)

Ironically, it is after the termination that the most value may be realized for the younger member. The older person readily becomes an admired and internalized role model, and a major source of development in adulthood. For the older managers there was a sense of loss; reactions ranged from pride and satisfaction in having been a part of something that was over, to behaviors that resisted the change, such as blocking promotion for the younger person. On balance, however, the separation phase was less stressful for the senior member.

Role models and leaders.   Because people sometimes model their behavior after that of other persons they find attractive and admire, role models are another socializing influence in organizations. Persons early in their careers are especially likely to adopt role models as a way of being sure they will meet expectations and not violate crucial norms. While mentors and peers may provide role models to some neophytes, others may turn to more distant figures to emulate. Leaders, both formal and informal, provide a natural source of role models.

Studies consistently show that newcomers' relationships with their initial supervisors have long-term consequences in terms of subsequent success in organizational and professional careers (Katz 1980; Jablin 1987). Research on mid-career executives revealed that in their early career they had observed leaders they perceived as well-liked, benevolent fathers who were friendly, encouraging, gave advice, and shared knowledge with subordinates (Bass and Avolio 1985). Such leaders can serve as both role models to emulate and as inspirational leaders who can heighten the motivation of subordinates to perform expected tasks (Yukl and Van Fleet 1982, p. 90).

Another study found that successful and considerate supervisors served as role models for newly hired younger managers (Weiss 1978). The data, however, suggested that filling this function was dependent upon a supervisor's possessing considerable competence plus warmth and affection for the newcomer. Thus these relationships probably happen more often by chance than design, which would limit their occurrence.

One analyst argues that "nothing communicates more powerfully to younger professionals within an organization than the example of peers or superiors who are recognized as winners and who also share common qualities. The protege watches the role model make presentations, handle conflict, and write memos, then tries to duplicate the traits that seem to work most effectively" (Pascale 1984, p. 34).

While role modeling of face-to-face leaders is quite common, perhaps the most effective role models are exceptionally attractive cultural leaders at the top of organizations. Founders of small entrepreneurial organizations readily become role models for new employees and retain this role as the organization grows. Alfred Fuller, founder of the Fuller Brush Company, is a well-known example. He was a supersalesperson who provided a strong role model for new employees. Although he was not the first to sell door to door, Fuller perfected the techniques for doing it and personally trained his followers in his approach. Mary Kay Ash, the founder of Mary Kay Cosmetics, is another example. Not only is her example as a supersaleswoman emulated, but many of the sayings and symbols in the company culture are based on her personal philosophy and experiences.

Role models, however, do not always represent the official or dominant values of the organization. Many organizations have subcultures and countercultural leaders that express ideas and values opposite in some ways to the organizational culture. If persuasive and likeable, countercultural leaders can also serve as role models. John DeLorean became a countercultural role model when he could not get his ideas accepted within General Motors (Wright 1979; Martin and Siehl 1983). He had initially been very successful as a manager, and his personal magnetism won a substantial group of followers to his ideas (Haddad 1985). Later, disillusioned with GM top management and its culture, he defied their norms and values by adopting nonconservative clothes, behaviors, and decor in his office. It is not clear how many of his followers were in early career stages and how many were more established in their careers. But clearly, such leaders may serve as the role models for both.

Mid-Career

Comparatively little attention has been devoted to what happens to insiders—often veteran organizational members established in their careers—as the organization goes about socializing newcomers. Yet it is clear that actions taken to recruit and induct new members often have a socializing effect on insiders as well. Sophisticated selection and socializing procedures, for example, increase "the value of organizational membership not only for the new initiate, but also for the currently employed organizational member" (Trice, Belasco, and Alutto 1969, p. 46). Entry procedures provide evidence to insiders of the selectivity exercised by their organization—that only those of presumed ability are accepted.

One likely reason why these effects have received so little attention is that it is much easier to detect changes in newcomers than among established insiders. Yet the values, norms, and beliefs of newcomers definitely have a potential to change those who are already organizational members. The particular role taken by a newcomer may trigger changes in the roles of established insiders. "Even if the newcomer may be 'alone' in the sense of being the only newcomer, the groups joined are themselves changed during the assimilation process ..." (Wanous, Reichers, and Malik 1984, p. 671). The potency of this newcomer effect was dramatically demonstrated by the observation of freshmen lawmakers in the California legislature already mentioned. "In the assembly, with almost one-half of the members freshmen, the leadership made every attempt to placate and accommodate itself to the new power factor. In a sense the large bloc of new legislators also socialized the veteran legislators" (Bell and Price 1975, p. 166). The socialization process is not a one-way street.

The effects that newcomer socialization have on veteran members of the organization can be conceptualized as similar to the effects emanating from minority influence (Sutton and Louis 1984). Researchers found that "... a consistent minority is able to exert a remarkable degree of influence even when it is not equipped with such characteristics as power, status, and competence ..." (Maas and Clark 1984, p. 428). Interviewing prospective new employees and setting up other socialization experiences for them makes explicit to insiders various features and attributes of their organizations that might otherwise go unrecognized. For example, engineers who believe they have basic state-of-the-art knowledge could discover from a candidate, or a newly hired engineer, that they are ignorant of some recent technical developments in their own work (Sutton and Louis 1984). Professors who proclaim to a newly hired Ph.D. that close working relationships characterize their department may be moved to actually carry out their depiction of themselves.

Empirical studies of selection interviews consistently reveal low reliability and validity for selecting the better recruits. Then why does the interview persist in view of this evidence? The reason is that it carries cultural meanings. "The interview is not valid, but it does other things well" (Arvey and Campion 1982, p. 314). While few if any selection procedures select the "right" person for the job, they have the latent functions of reinforcing the favorable perceptions and commitments of current members, many of whom are in mid-career, resolving their questions concerning the competency and dependability of new employees, and establishing a self-fulfilling prophecy by setting up expectations that foster exceptional performance by all who are involved in the process (Trice, Belasco, and Alutto 1969, p. 46). These functions are some of the "other things" that selection interviews and other socialization devices do, even when they are ineffective technically.

Organizational selection and socialization activities can have four latent effects on current organizational members:

1. The process of becoming truly committed to an organization is accelerated by participation in their planning and execution.
2. Participation in them stimulates judgments about employing organizations as well as about candidates and newcomers.
3. They may prove useful in scanning the organization's environment and lead current members to discover which new skills and knowledge they should learn.
4. Current members may be alerted to previously unrecognized internal and external demands. (Sutton and Louis 1984)

It should be noted that these indirect socialization experiences of mid-career workers tend to be personal and individual.

Workers going through mid-career passages like promotions or role changes also seem to do so alone, experiencing little of the collective and formal tactics so often used in earlier socialization (Glaser and Strauss 1971; Brett 1984). This aloneness parallels the general experience of adulthood in present-day U.S.

society. The trend is for adults to find that "one's self is one's only resource . . . adulthood provides no resting place from demands on the self . . ." (Swidler 1990, p. 134). For example, by midcareer time in their organizational and occupational lives, people have become enmeshed within organizational departments and hierarchies, with the result that each person is in a somewhat unique position. Work-related role passages in midlife are consequently individualized, only occasionally having collective features. Formal individualized socialization is rare and of relatively brief duration when it occurs. Research on job changes and job transfers found that relatively few of the people involved were shown the ropes by the new boss or the previous incumbent. According to one researcher, ". . . the old incumbent is seldom around, and if he or she is, he or she is too busy learning his or her new job to be of much help to the new incumbent. It seems almost as though the companies we've been studying have a policy against using the old incumbents to socialize the new ones" (Brett 1984, p. 175).

One exception is training, which is often used with employees in midcareer. While the context of such training is sometimes technical, much training is aimed at improving rather general managerial skills. Especially in the case of such managerial training, the act of training itself, rather than the content, may well be responsible for improved managerial performance (Guyot 1977, 1978). Managers who have undergone such training may expect that they should perform better, and other insiders may have the same expectations of them because of the training. Rarely, however, is such training followed by rites of incorporation that dramatize changes in the trainees.

If people's entire careers are viewed as rites of passage, the mid-career stage is the transition stage. A prominent feature surrounding mid-career socialization is the ordeal of intense competition for hierarchical position. As the career progresses, there are relatively few chances for advancement. Accountants, for example, have to compete for advancement within a highly competitive and flat hierarchy (Faulkner 1974). In general, hierarchies for professions tend to be flat, while hierarchies for managers can be relatively tall. Tall hierarchies create many possibilities for promotion. The situation for managers has been likened to a tournament (Rosenbaum 1979) or horse race (Forbes 1987). Individual aspirants face increasingly selective competitions. To the extent that hierarchical promotions fit this metaphor of a contest, the process is one of unremitting elimination of an ever-increasing number of losers. For example, a study of promotions in a large corporation found that promotion rates for foremen and low-level managers, which had been high during their late twenties and early thirties, declined rapidly through the ages of forty and fifty and totally disappeared by age sixty (Hall 1986).

Studies of the career paths of managers in one firm in their second decade of work life showed that those who were promoted earlier than others had a significantly more rapid career path later on (Rosenbaum 1979, 1984). A later study of managers in an oil company found that some of the "losers—those passed over in the early periods—were later able to move up quickly." Thus, in this firm the contest was more like a horse race than a tournament: "position out of the gate had relatively little effect in comparison to position entering the home stretch" (Forbes 1987, pp. 121–22). While the process may vary somewhat across firms, mid-career passages generally involve increasingly individualized contests. Competition and advancement take place on the basis of individual accomplishments, successful informal and political manipulations, and competitive endurance. Accordingly, socialization for these competitions is likely to be a product of individual experiences in which each competitor is prepared for the contest largely in isolation from other competitors.

But cultural understandings about age and careers largely determine the meaning of these individual experiences. Research in a public utility showed that organizational members developed shared beliefs about the ages typical for each hierarchical level to create "a cognitive representation of an entire career" (Lawrence 1988, p. 333). In the process, they consistently overestimated the youngest age and underestimated the oldest age for each level, probably because they see typical managers more often than they see those ahead or behind the expected schedule. Managers apparently believed they were on an age-based career ladder when, in fact, it was unclear that such a ladder existed. Although these shared beliefs were clearly affected by actual age distributions, managerial performance ratings were significantly related to the expected career progression and not to actual age. Managers ahead of schedule tended to be rated higher than those on schedule, who tended, in turn, to be rated higher than those behind schedule. However, because actual age distributions appear to drive the development of age norms, they can change over time and differ across organizations.

In related research, a sample of managers who read the *Harvard Business Review* were asked to make decisions about three specific situations:

1. a manager who responded too slowly to customer complaints,
2. a request by a manager to attend a production seminar at company expense, and
3. a request to be considered for promotion.

Half of the respondents received a version in which the manager was described as "older" and the other half received a version in which the manager was described as "younger" (Rosen and Jardee 1977, p. 98). In those instances where the manager was described as younger, the respondents were much more willing to offer opportunities for training, promotions, and constructive feedback. The researchers concluded:

- Managers perceive older employees to be relatively inflexible and resistant to change. Accordingly, managers make much less effort to give an older person feedback about needed changes in performance.
- Few managers provide organizational support for the career development and retraining of older employees.
- Promotion opportunities for older people are somewhat restricted, particularly when the new position demand creativity, mental alertness, or capacity to deal with crisis situations. (Rosen and Jardee 1977, p. 98)

Subsequently, another researcher replicated this study with almost a thousand Harvard students, finding "that those who thought the employee was younger were more willing to help him or her and provide opportunities" (Sonnenfeld 1988, p. 14).

Whatever the norms and their unique and personalized set of socializing experiences, most managers will, at some time, stop progressing further up the ladder. Most middle managers

> do not make it to top management and resign themselves to a career of being "betwixt and between": a guy is sixty years old and has lost every battle along the way and says "F—— it" and waits until retirement. . . . Liminality is inherently stressful and protracted liminality is protractedly stressful. (Schrier and Mulcahy 1988, p. 148)

Late Career

As the tournament continues, more and more managers must drop out of the competition. For a vast majority of managers there are fewer and fewer passages to be made as they move into their later work years. Their prolonged liminality will soon lead to retirement. It is problematic to describe socialization during later work life since there are few, if any, distinct new roles for which aging employees can be prepared and subsequently enter. So-called preretirement counseling programs may be short and superficial; they often last only an hour or so and are offered one to five times during the five years prior to retirement. "Virtually nothing is done to prepare the worker for a distinctive retirement role and help him [or her] find meaningful substitutes for work" (Rosow 1974, p. 26). For many, retirement at any age entails giving up a valued role without acquiring a new one. Nevertheless, many people retire voluntarily, apparently believing they will find their roles in their families, communities, and leisure life sufficiently involving to give their life continued meaning.

Amendments to the Social Security Act have made retirement at age 62 viable for both men and women. This "... resulted in a dramatic increase in the proportion of workers leaving the labor force before the normal retirement age" (Blau, Oser, and Stephens 1983, p. 116). While the proportion of early retirees rose from 20 percent in 1962 to 44 percent in 1974, so has the proportion of retirees returning to the work force, which suggests many retirees do not find satisfying roles to fill after retirement. A study of a thousand middle-level managers and professional and technical workers from three companies in manufacturing, utilities, and retailing who had retired and then returned to work reported that reasons given for reentry were typically noneconomic rather than economic (Gray and Morse 1980). Three out of five reported they returned because they liked working, a third said that they wanted contact with people rather than the social emptiness of retirement, and a quarter believed their health would be damaged by remaining in retirement. When interest rates fall or pensions and savings are lost in restructuring of the economy, a larger proportion may feel compelled to return for economic reasons.

It is obvious that "retirement from the labor force at some arbitrary fixed age is a *social invention*, not a biological imperative" (Blau, Oser, and Stephens 1983, p. 101). The original Social Security Act, in effect, set up the category of retirement in the 1930s. At the turn of the century the idea of retiring from work roles scarcely existed. Ultimately, Social Security came to include both male and female workers. It presumably provided sufficient income for workers aged 65 or over to meet their basic needs without working. Moreover, retirement at that age was made mandatory. Subsequent legislation, mentioned earlier, made retirement at age 62 possible. In recent years, the mandatory cutoff has been raised to age 70, and other legislation has furthered weakened the idea of an absolute cutoff age. Nevertheless, the idea of retirement based solely on chronological age has become firmly fixed in U.S. culture and workplaces. Despite considerable evidence that many workers over 70 continue to be competent performers in work roles, widely accepted rationales continue to favor retirement. In effect, retirement has become a cultural category into which workers of advanced age *should* be placed. Workers in late life who continue to work are therefore viewed as marginal, even deviant, if they continue "too long."

One widely accepted rationale for the retirement category is expressed in the theory of disengagement put forward by Elaine Cumming and her associates (Cumming et al. 1960; Cumming and Henry 1961; Cumming 1963). They insisted that American society must disengage from workers as they become older because they are approaching death. Hence people must give up their social roles so that at the time of death society will not suffer sudden discontinuity. Thus Cumming (1963, p. 385) wrote: "When a middle-aged, fully engaged person dies, he [or she] leaves many broken ties and disrupted situations. Disengagement thus freed the old to die without [contributing to serious social] disruption." According to this rationale, disengagement, especially from work, is functional for society even though at times it may be grossly unfair to those who do not fit the assumption of being near death.

A graphic, even dramatic account of the potency of the retirement category comes from a description of an elaborate retirement dinner for a municipal firefighter in Washington, D.C. During this dinner, other firefighters reminded one another of the memorable fires in which the retiree had been involved. In the process, they confronted him with his misdeeds and indiscretions, as well as complimenting him on his past valor and successes. The retiree responded in various ways to these reminders intended to sum up his career as a firefighter. At the end of the dinner, the retiree stood up in front of fellow firefighters as a person who was no longer a firefighter. He was forced to realize the inevitable change—his isolation from the others—that was happening before his and others' eyes. The dinner had moved him "symbolically from being a member of the group to a nonactive status as a retired firefighter . . ." (McCarl 1984, p. 417). So embedded are such cultural practices that he, and his co-workers, had held expectations about this dinner throughout his career.

Even though some recent trends have begun to blunt its rationale, the retirement category remains alive and well. As the example of the firefighter's retirement dinner suggests, the category functions to generate a somewhat stigmatized status with little or no work expectations. It becomes an invidious stereotype associated with nonwork and old age. It inevitably acts to separate "useful" younger workers from those retired. For millions, it is the end of working life. Apparent exceptions are those who, because they can claim generous pensions after set years of service rather than at certain ages, retire from military and government posts at relatively early ages and pursue another career. Such persons may not enter the cultural category of retirement because, within their occupations, a second career is not unusual but expected.

Until work life is structured to contain identifiable roles for older workers to enter and perform, there can be no socialization strategy directed toward them by work organizations. Even the deviant roles accorded to those who wish to continue to work are ill-defined and ambiguous. Now that the baby boom has moved out of high school and college, there is a shortage of younger workers to fill part-time jobs. Some employers are hiring retired workers for the same jobs recently held by teenagers. While some of those filling such jobs may take them primarily for economic reasons, chances are that most simply prefer to work at least part-time rather than staying home all of the time. Nevertheless, retirement remains a category occupied by those who have been urged to think of themselves as nonworkers rather than as the workers they have been for the largest part of their lives. Cultural categories can change, of course, and the presence of increasing numbers of previously retired persons in the workforce may slowly lead to such change in cultural assumptions about older persons as workers.

Other Career Interruptions

Sometimes even prior to mandatory retirement, members may be suddenly and irrevocably forced to withdraw from an organization's culture. Organizational death can produce such a situation, forcing employees to cope with the demise of the organization to which they have become to some degree committed and on which they depend. They are, in effect, forced into involuntary departure and passage into some new role in some unknown organization. Mergers and restructurings can have the same effects.

As discussed in Chapter 3, well-structured "parting ceremonies" may come into being in response to the impending death of an organization (Harris and Sutton 1986). Eleven parties, picnics, and dinners occurred in six private and public sector organizations just prior to or during their demise. Although the classical three phases of rites of passage did not emerge in these ceremonials, their function was clearly to facilitate the passage of employees from the dead organization into a transition period. In this sense, these parting ceremonies functioned as the separation phase of the employees' passage. Names attached to these rites—"the last supper," "the last hurrah," "the wake," and the "final party"—clearly expressed their function (Harris and Sutton 1986, p. 13–14).

The similarity of these rites strongly suggests potent cultural forces at work. The departing employees were apparently attempting to bring their experiences into some form of control. Their behaviors acted to provide emotional support for the parting that was imminent and initial frames of reference for how to behave and how to perceive what was happening to them.

According to the researchers, "organizational death packs an emotional wallop" (Harris and Sutton 1986, p. 16), one that calls for emotional support from outside the individual psyche. Of the forty-four informants in the study, twenty-three felt that the closing experience was worse for them than a serious illness, and nine of those reported that the parting experience was equivalent to divorce or the death of a spouse. Seven of the eleven constant elements found by the researchers served to provide emotional support. For example, exchanging names and addresses, mutual sadness and anger, and the presence of former members helped members to gracefully break their current social bonds with the organization. Sharing meals symbolized a sense of common grief and sadness and an open expression of these emotions. Alcohol use helped to produce a sense of community. In short, the parting ceremonies provided a sanctioned setting in which members could openly grieve together for the death of their organization.

In addition, these parting ceremonies were the occasion for the telling of "summary" stories about the organization, stories that caught up the organization as members recalled it. When combined with other stories, these provided a cognitive schema of the social system for the parting members. Also, discussions of causes of the organization's death during the ceremony provided an opportunity for members to firm up a causal explanation for the demise. Moreover, the ceremony was a symbolic confirmation that the organization was truly dead, thereby avoiding a denial of a closing—a common feature of organizational deaths. Added to these features were those that helped members face the realities of role transitions. By talking with former members who had already made successful transitions to new roles, the soon-to-be-displaced members began to cope with the transition they inevitably faced. They talked at length about how to cope with the future.

Dysfunctions of Organizational Socialization

So far the emphasis has been on the functional nature of socialization—on how it incorporates outsiders into an organization so that they become insiders, and how it eases other role transitions. Practically nothing has been said about the way dysfunctions of these actions affect either the individual worker or the organization itself. Dysfunctions are those consequences that are harmful, disruptive, and tend to weaken rather than strengthen the system and those in it. Recall that in Chapter 1, the nature and extent of the dysfunctions of culture were explored. What follows is an application of those points to organizational socialization.

One of the most pervasive negative outcomes is the possible encouragement of a custodial orientation in newcomers. Some analysts (Van Maanen and Schein 1979, p. 253) believe that socialization has a strong tendency to reinforce the status quo if it comes from the sequential, fixed, serial, and divestiture processes (Table 4-1). Given the enormous pressures for change that currently permeate the environments of most organizations, such consequences can be truly dysfunctional. Most organizations need employees who have innovative orientations to help them adapt to their ever-changing environments. However, as the analysis summarized in Figure 4-1 suggests, such fears may be somewhat exaggerated. Lack of innovative behaviors may have other causes.

Another danger from the institutionalized processes listed in Table 4-1 is that they tend to make the organization myopic, even incestuous. This dysfunction may be an especially likely outcome of well-defined rites of passage, which often produces recruits who are remarkably like older members and who thus may engage in excessive conformity. Such socialization was vigorously attacked by W. H. Whyte, Jr. in *The Organization Man* (1956). He warned that managers' conformity to the corporate norms would squash innovation and the creative capacity of individuals and organizations. Prevalent cultural values in the 1960s decreed that individuals should be permitted and encouraged by their employers to develop according to their innate capacities.

This concern has weakened considerably as the full impact of Japanese competition has been felt by many U.S. companies. Japanese success in motivating employees and generating commitment has caused a reexamination of socialization processes in U.S. organizations and a search for ways to make them more effective. Thus, some work organizations may be tempted to create completely new rites of passage. One danger is that ceremonial practices that are new, freshly contrived, and imposed on the system may be seen as trivial, or even ludicrous, by all involved. Building on already existing practices seems likely to reduce the likelihood of such dysfunction. If some part of the ceremonies is part of the existing cultural fabric, additions will be better accepted and probably will be functional. Sometimes formalizing and expanding on existing informal practices may be effective.

At the individual level, socialization practices can produce hostility between recruits and socializers. Affected individuals may then leave, or become increasingly rebellious if they stay. For example, in a mentoring relationship, the younger person may feel undermined, held back, and prevented from exposure to the main stream. Or the senior member—the mentor—can be threatened by the protege's continued success and advancement. Some relationships may be destined to be vitiated by the unintended consequences of pent up resentments on both sides. Other probable dysfunctions stem from the demoralizing consequences of tournament-style socialization, especially on those who are losers in midlife competition. Managers socialized to believe in and hope for high positions are likely to later become frustrated and disappointed as they plateau and cease to advance. Any exclusion can also negate socialization processes and seriously jeopardize subsequent performance. One study (Trice and Roman 1971) showed that those left out of technological change and its passages were more emotionally hurt than were those who experienced the trauma of adapting to the changes. Alternatively, people in the mid-career stage can become so complacent that merely getting by becomes the major norm for work behavior.

Finally, it should also be pointed out that the consequences of training can always be dysfunctional for organizations if they do not prepare members to deal with realities. The ceremonial effects of training can be so consuming that trainees and others are blinded to environmental forces that require adaptation for organizational survival. A dramatic example of such dysfunction comes from the training of U.S. ground forces in Hawaii just prior to the Japanese attack on Pearl Harbor in 1941. In an effort to train troops for expected threats—internal sabotage and native Japanese uprising on the Hawaiian Islands—Lt. General Walter C. Short, and to a lesser extent, Admiral Husband E. Kimmel, focused intensive training efforts on tactics to prevent and contain such eventualities. General Short became "tremendously preoccupied with training for its own sake . . . he got so wrapped up in the training business that he could not see the other issues at stake . . . he was so busy honing his own blade that he forgot its sharpness mattered little unless it was ready to hand" (Prange 1981, p. 730). At the time of the Japanese surprise attack, mobile guns had no ammunition and were not in field positions. Radar installations were understaffed and their reports were ignored. All of the training had focused upon internal subversion; its ceremonial effect was one of reassurance and certainty about what the dangers were. This mistaken certainty was very expensive in human lives.

SUMMARY

The continuity of human cultures is made possible by socialization—social processes by which members are inculcated with the substance of their cultures. In organizations, socialization is especially crucial for new members because they must learn and ideally internalize expectations associated with their work roles in order to behave effectively within these roles. They come to their organizations, however, already socialized by prior experiences in their families, schools, occupational training, and prior work settings.

Also, people's socialization to a particular organization begins even before they accept employment as they anticipate what the organization and their job will be like. Other steps of socialization include employees' actual encounters with their new roles, their assimilation into their new roles, and their eventual departures, usually to assume new roles of some kind. Most people cycle through the four stages of socialization many times in their lifetimes as they assume new positions or as their organizations change drastically around them. In one sense, the three stages of people's work lives—early career, mid-career, and late career—can be looked at as the last three stages of socialization writ large. In another sense, at every stage, people cycle through all four stages as they anticipate, encounter, get assimilated to, and then leave specific roles.

Through all of their many socializing experiences, people rely on cultural forms to help them make sense of what is happening to them and to enable them to cope emotionally with losses, threats, and challenges. Rites of passage are especially valuable in easing transition for both the persons undergoing passages and the social groups to which they belong. Unfortunately, such rites are often missing or truncated in modern society generally and in many work organizations.

Like all human endeavors, organizational socialization has both functional and dysfunctional consequences, often simultaneously. There is a high likelihood that outcomes will be a mixture of both. On the positive side, socialization makes organizational life less capricious, helps to reduce problems of coordination, and supports at least a modicum of shared values in organizational life. Most important is that socialization, even when only partly effective, assists new members in learning how to become insiders and how to perform new roles in new settings and in new relationships.

5

Occupational Subcultures

Although organizations have distinctive cultures, it would be a mistake to think that any particular organization has only a single homogeneous culture.[1] As various scholars have observed, most organizations have multiple cultures (Riley 1983; Louis 1985b; Gregory 1983; Dalton 1959). It is customary to call the cultures within an encompassing culture subcultures. Organizational subcultures consist of distinctive clusters of ideologies, cultural forms, and other practices that identifiable groups of people in an organization exhibit. They differ noticeably from the overall organizational culture in which they are embedded, either intensifying its understandings and practices or diverging from them. Subcultures also differ noticeably from each other.

Modern organizations are so internally diverse that some scholars feel that there is only a small degree of overlap among the ideologies shared by various subcultures within them (Van Maanen and Barley 1985; Jermier et al. 1991); others believe that there may be considerable overlap (Schein 1985; O'Reilly, Chatman, and Caldwell 1991). A good way to reconcile these viewpoints is to look at organizations as composed of a multiplicity of discrete subcultures that are held together, more or less strongly, by an overall culture. An overall culture consists of some number of cultural elements that are embraced by practically everyone in an organization. Organizations can have both an overall culture and a multiplicity of subcultures. Organizations differ in the potency and pervasiveness of their overall cultures and in the conflict and divisiveness generated by their subcultures. In order to understand why these differences occur, we need to consider

[1]Portions of this chapter extract and adapt materials from *Occupational Cultures in the Workplace* by Harrison M. Trice, forthcoming, ILR Press, Ithaca, N.Y.

those features of social life and modern organizations that give rise to subcultures.

Characteristics of Subcultures

Some people have the romantic notion that simpler societies than our own had single, homogeneous, harmonious cultures. This is far from the case. Tribal and pastoral societies have secret associations, clans, and distinct sex and age groupings that display all of the characteristics of subcultures (Sapir [1915] 1966; Warner 1937). For example, four tribes of the Northwest Coast Indians, who lived on the western coast of what is now Canada, were subdivided into a considerable number of clans; each had its own crest in addition to a more general crest designating a group of clans to which it belonged (Sapir [1915] 1966, pp. 41–42). These divisions were sufficiently important to be portrayed and symbolized in the totem poles outside members' lodges. In modern U.S. society, even street gangs in large cities—notorious for their cohesiveness—have subgroups and cliques, usually formed around age groupings (Monti 1991).

Although subcultures have probably always been a feature of all but the most primitive and tiny of human societies, the great complexity of modern societies undoubtedly encourages their formation. "Multiculturalism is the normal experience of most individuals in the world today, for they are perforce drawn into the microcultures of administrators, teachers, physicians, and others who have power over them" (Goodenough 1978, p. 79). Subcultures are apt to be especially plentiful in American society because of its great diversity and its strong emphasis on individualism, democracy, and freedom as cherished values. Individualism encourages the development of idiosyncratic belief systems; democracy and freedom encourage people to band together with like-minded individuals to express and further their beliefs in all sectors of social life. The dominant values, in effect, encourage the formation of both socially concerned interest groups and street gangs of youths.

Subcultures have the same elements that cultures have: distinct patterns of shared ideologies and distinctive sets of cultural forms. They also exhibit the characteristics of cultures listed in Table 1–2. The degree of distinctiveness of subcultural elements varies, however. Some subcultural elements resemble the overall culture in which they are embedded in many ways, and others deviate markedly from it. The more unique the elements of a subculture, the more it encourages members to loosen their commitment to the overall culture and generate shared rationalizations that allow them to violate significant aspects of it.

Organizations are typically multicultural, meaning that they have multiple subcultures within them. Members can belong to more than one of these subcultures; in fact, belonging to multiple subcultures may be more the rule than the exception. Subcultures represent distinct "symbolic domains," with some members frequently and routinely switching between domains, while others stay in one domain and thus in one subculture (Schultz 1991).

Factors Encouraging Formation of Subcultures

Some social conditions are more likely to give rise to subcultures than others. Three facilitating conditions are frequent social interaction, shared experiences, and similar personal characteristics. All contribute to the development of social cohesion, which provides fertile ground for the growth of subcultures over time.

Differential interaction.   The basic foundation of subcultures is differential interaction. The degree to which some people engage in interactions with one another more frequently than with others provides the basis of subcultures. Work organizations create structural and other conditions that produce differential rates of interaction among their members. So do communities, industries, occupations, and whole societies. In organizations, many factors facilitate interactions among some organizational members and inhibit it among others. These factors include the size of an organization, its geographical dispersion, how departmentalized it is, the division of labor present, hierarchies of authority, work flows and technological processes, channels established for lateral and vertical communication, physical locations of workers, rules and regulations, unionization, occupational mix, and demographic characteristics of workers. In other social units, similar factors operate to encourage more interactions among some individuals than among others. Such differential association is important because the more people interact, the more they tend to develop similar feelings and understandings (Homans 1950).

Shared experiences.   As discussed in Chapter 1, people do not develop their cultures quickly or easily. They need relatively long periods of close association to develop the distinctive ideologies that mark subcultures. Also they need shared experiences that stimulate collective sense making. When people live or work in close proximity to one another, they can communicate frequently on a face-to-face basis about how they view their world and how they cope with it. They can interact to accomplish shared goals and to manage shared problems and uncertainties. Shared problems and uncertainties, in turn, can stimulate shared reactions and solutions. So do situations that require close coordination of activities and behaviors. In effect, as people interact over time within a common context, they develop shared patterns of behavior and belief that coalesce into subcultures. Work situations without close proximity or interdependent tasks are therefore much less conducive to the development of subcultures.

Similar personal characteristics.   The development of distinctive ideologies in a group is also facilitated if people share personal characteristics associated with cultural differences—age, ethnicity, occupational training, education, and social class. Such similarities encourage the formation of subcultural ideologies because members do not need to displace their old beliefs and values very much to find common ground with one another. Similar personal characteristics also form a ready basis for shared identities, self-images, and reference groups.

Cohesion.   The ongoing demands of work processes in organizations shape the formation of the three conditions that facilitate the growth of subcultures. By doing so, they also encourage friendliness and social cohesion among some members but not others. Social psychologists have identified a large number of additional factors that tend to produce cohesiveness in interacting groups of people: agreement on group goals, small size, tasks requiring interdependence, physical isolation from other groups, performance success, performance failure or crisis (Schermerhorn, Hunt, and Osborne 1982, p. 249), threats from outside the group, and similarity of members' characteristics, interests, values, and personalities (Lott and Lott 1965). When groups are cohesive, members are attracted to and come to like one another, tend to spend time together outside of work, and in many ways influence one another. Especially relevant for the formation of subcultures is that cohesive groups tend to develop strong norms to govern the behavior of members.

While social cohesiveness provides fertile ground for the growth of subcultures, it is not the same as nor sufficient by itself to produce subcultures. Individuals in relatively temporary proximity can develop strong cohesive groups. A group of people on a plane hijacked by terrorists, neighbors piling up sandbags to ward off the flood waters threatening their homes, or a crowd listening to a charismatic speaker may be very cohesive for a time. But when the circumstances that temporarily brought them together are ended, the mutual influence and strong emotional bonds that linked them also ends. Subcultures are more enduring. Like all cultures, they form to provide some measure of continuity in social life.

One of the particular values of subcultures is the close social support they provide to members facing uncertainties. Subcultures are important bulwarks in people's lives. A study of coal miners observed that they became psychosomatically ill when their long-standing work groups were disbanded because of a technological change (Trist and Banforth 1951). Because of the continual threats these workers faced, their work groups had undoubtedly become more than cohesive groups; they had become subcultures.

Diffuse Subcultures

Although subcultures seem to emerge naturally from face-to-face interaction, their formation does not require such interaction. Other forms of interaction can become the basis of more diffuse subcultures. In modern society, a wide variety of linkages facilitate the spread of subcultural substance and forms among people who are geographically distant (Fine and Kleinman 1979). These linkages include overlapping memberships, weak social ties (Granovetter 1973), computers and other communications media, and linking roles. In organizations, people who belong to two groups will carry subcultural understandings from one to the other. In more general society, occupational memberships often provide the basis for casual yet ongoing relationships between widely dispersed persons who are not in regular, face-to-face contact (Katz 1958). Computer mail and bulletin boards give their users access to a wide variety of other people with whom they share some set of interests. The more general media—magazines, newspapers, television, films, music, and other arts—generate rather indirect but wide-ranging communication interlocks. Their chief function may be to create and reinforce common identities, self-images, and reference groups for like-minded people. The media also create opportunities for opinion leaders to arise and create subcultures. Finally, the activities of people in certain roles link different groups and so further subcultural diffusion. Examples include consultants, agricultural extension agents (Beyer and Trice 1982), salespeople and marketers of all kinds, and such countercultural roles as itinerant evangelists and dealers in illicit drugs (Fine and Kleinman 1979).

Occupational Subcultures

The most highly organized, distinctive, and pervasive sources of subcultures in work organizations are people's occupations. As such, they provide a good starting point for an examination of subcultures in organizations. They illustrate clearly how the conditions that facilitate the growth of subcultures work. Because they are the most frequently studied form of organizational subcultures, their characteristics are well known. Many examples of occupational subcultures have been documented in some detail. They provide a rich pattern against which other subcultures can be assessed.

Occupations give rise to subcultures at two levels: (1) they provide the basis for diffuse subcultures in the general society; and (2) their members often form face-to-face subcultures within the organizations that employ them. From an organizational perspective, occupations are imported subcultures; they carry ideas that have their origins outside organizations. Furthermore, the ideas they carry are, like those of organizational cultures, focused on work-related issues. Thus, occupational subcultures often compete with specific organizations' cultures for members' minds and hearts.

When organizations include multiple persons from a single occupation, those persons can form internal, face-to-face subcultures. The cohesiveness and potency of such subcultures will likely depend on structural and other factors encouraging or discouraging social interaction among members of an occupation. But occupational subcultures can have important impacts on organizations even in the absence of a face-to-face subculture. Members of organizations can be influenced by their occupational subcultures even when they are relatively isolated from colleagues and few in numbers. Such persons may maintain their occupational identities and ideologies through memberships in occupational associations, diffuse networks of friendships, and other communication interlocks. Doctors, lawyers, and accountants who are employed by corporations are classic examples. Members of these occupations receive intensive and lengthy socialization into certain beliefs, values, norms, and practices. These socialization experiences typically result in members' internalizing rather detailed sets of expectations for their behavior in their work roles. These subcultural expectations are then made rather sacred by the professional label given to them. Thus, organizations who employ professionals find that they must accommodate to some degree to the mandates of their occupational subcultures.

In many important ways, all established occupations compete with management for control over members' work behaviors. In effect, they create alternative, potentially conflicting bases of control in organizations. One reason that occupations can be influential in organizations, and in modern societies generally, is that people derive much of their distinctiveness as persons and their social status from their occupations. When people are introduced or first meet, they usually soon exchange information about their respective occupations. In news accounts, people are identified by their occupations. Clearly, occupations give people who have them a major portion of their identity. However, not all workers belong to well-established occupations. Certain things must happen in order for an occupation to become established as such.

Origins and Development of Occupations

In a general sense, an occupation consists of a line of work or set of tasks. In well-developed and recognized occupations, members *claim exclusive rights* to perform and control those tasks. Occupations usually come into existence by social processes that are internal to them—that is, instead of being formally created, occupations emerge spontaneously within groups of persons performing like tasks. Occupations thus are cultural entities. They emerge whenever tasks are the nucleus around which groups form. Persons who share task-related demands and uncertainties develop shared ways of coping with them. They come to believe in and value what they have learned through sense making based in their own work-related experiences. They pass on their ideas to others performing the same or related tasks. The groups that form around these ideas provide important social support and emotional reassurances to members. As their sense of identity as an occupation develops, members come to believe that, because of their technical knowledge, they collectively know best how to cope with certain task-related demands. They also come to see the demands of those outside the occupation as representing significant sources of uncertainty for them. In particular, administrative attempts to control their work create uncertainty because such attempts often spring from different ideologies and concerns than those of the occupation. Thus, to reduce their uncertainties and realize the ideologies they have developed about their work, as occupations develop "members seek autonomy and control over their particular and distinctive work" (Freidson 1982, p. 54).

As occupations develop distinct identities and influence in society, several things happen within them:

- workers begin to perform certain defined and logically interrelated tasks on a full-time basis;
- performers of such tasks systematize them and cooperate to set up special training programs—when practical, outside employing organizations;

- performers of these tasks form occupational associations to promote and strengthen their claims to exclusive rights to perform them;
- performers of these tasks begin persistent political agitation to secure recognition of their exclusive rights through formal licensing;
- rules are derived by members of the occupation to eliminate the unqualified and unscrupulous, and a formal code of ethics emerges. (Wilensky 1964a)

Research suggest, however, that specific occupations do not follow any particular sequence in these events (Abbott 1988). The development of rules and a code of ethics, however, is usually considered the hallmark of the fully professional occupation. From a perspective outside the occupation, sets of tasks do not become full-fledged occupations until the labor market recognizes those who hold them collectively and society accords them certain rights in the performance of them (Child and Fulk 1982, p. 156). Obviously, these developments also promote the growth of shared ideologies and cultural forms and thus of occupational subcultures.

The occurrences in the previous list have a cumulative effect; each contributes to the development and distinctiveness of an occupation. Obviously, many sets of tasks never set in motion *all* of these occurrences. Numerous tasks, however, give rise to one or more of these developments. Although some specialists who study them consider only tasks that have undergone certain of these developments occupations, a more inclusive definition is desirable in order to consider all of the possible effects of occupational subcultures. For the purposes of this chapter, therefore, tasks that include any of the developments in the list will be considered as having potential to spawn occupational subcultures.

In the process of claiming rights to perform certain tasks, members of occupations naturally tend to emphasize what makes them like one another and different from other workers. As they interact and work together, members of occupations come to share a similar view of their work and, more generally, of the world in which they perform it. Over time, members create self-definitions, ideologies, and values that help them to sustain their occupational identities and justify their rights. Occupational myths, rituals, symbols, rites, and other cultural forms emerge to help to express and affirm these distinct sets of understandings to current members, new recruits, and those outside the occupation. These processes mark the emergence of occupational subcultures. The degree of influence that occupational subcultures have over members varies widely. Their influence depends not only on how distinctive and developed the occupation is, but also on social and psychological factors that accompany belonging to an occupation.

Characteristics of Occupational Subcultures

Belonging to a distinct occupation structures people's lives in many ways. In some instances, members' lives become so permeated with occupational relationships and ideologies that even their nonwork lives are strongly influenced by their occupational identities (Gerstl 1961). Researchers call the social groups that arise from such intense occupational ties occupational communities (Van

Maanen and Barley, 1984). People in occupational communities build their lives around their work. These communities, in turn, produce particularly clear manifestations of occupational subcultures. Many occupations have at least some of the features of occupational communities in that the subcultures generated have influences that carry beyond the work setting to members' personal lives. Thus, much of what has been learned about occupational communities has relevance for all kinds of occupational subcultures and, indeed, for other subcultures as well.

Occupational communities have been described in terms of certain characteristics: (1) members share a "consciousness of kind"; (2) members of the occupational group take each other as reference points in deriving meaning from their experiences; (3) members have in common certain unusual emotional demands of their work; (4) members' self-images and social identities are enhanced by their work; (5) members extend their social relations into nonwork life (Salaman 1974; Van Maanen and Barley 1984). Members of a particular occupation can be said to belong to an occupational community when their subculture exhibits all of these characteristics to some degree. Occupational subcultures lacking some of these characteristics are not full-fledged occupational communities. Because all occupations have at least some of these characteristics, they provide a useful way to describe occupational subcultures in general and how they work. In discussing each characteristic, we will therefore use examples from a range of occupations rather than just from occupations that tend to form occupational communities.

The subcultural characteristics associated with occupational communities are not necessarily confined, however, to occupational subcultures. They are discussed here because they are especially typical and evident in occupational subcultures. In the next chapter we will discuss their relevance to other types of subcultures.

Consciousness of kind. The most basic characteristic of occupations is that persons in them must think of themselves as part of the occupation and identify themselves with other members of that occupation; just doing a certain kind of work is not enough. Self-definitions of members—and not any organizationally conferred job title, census classification, or even government license or certification—determine the boundaries of occupations and of occupational communities. Official distinctions thus provide only approximate indicators of their boundaries (Gusfield 1975; Van Maanen and Barley 1984).

Structural conditions sometimes make the boundaries of occupational communities almost inevitable. For example, persons who work in conditions that cut them off from much of the rest of society cannot help but be conscious of their differentness and therefore identify with those members of society with whom they share their isolation. People who work after dark find their life styles very different from that of daytime society; they therefore become aware of having an identity separate from that of daytime society and think of themselves as "night people" (Melbin 1978). Jazz musicians, who share the constraints of both night work and transient engagements, define themselves as different from those who inhabit ordinary society. They see the world outside their own occupation as hostile, and therefore avoid contact with it, beyond that which is required to perform for it (Becker 1951). Until recently, the occupation of printing also had structural characteristics conducive to a consciousness of kind. Printers had a status somewhere between that of manual and nonmanual workers, they often could substitute for one another on specific jobs, and they frequently did their work at night. All of these conditions heightened their interactions with each other and decreased their interactions with other members of society (Lipset, Trow, and Coleman 1956).

Reference groups.   Members of occupations come to share beliefs, values, and norms in a variety of ways, many of which have already been discussed in the previous chapters. In addition, members of occupations develop shared ideologies by using one another as reference points. Members look to one another for support and confirmation of the meanings they ascribe to events around them and for approval and disapproval of patterns of behavior. They incorporate what they learn from the reactions and role modeling of others in the occupation into their beliefs, values, and norms. When individuals use a group as a referent, their ideologies will come to resemble those of that group.

One sign of an occupation is that members, as they become integrated into it, increasingly tend to compare their own behaviors and values to other members of that occupation. One study found that "sandhogs"—members of an occupational community of mining workers who specialize in digging tunnels—disapproved of fellow workers whose levels of drinking were not comparable to their own. Abstainers were not fully accepted and thus became marginal members of the occupational community (Sonnenstuhl and Trice 1987). Similar observations were reported for dockworkers (Mars 1979). In these occupational groups, belonging meant heavy drinking.

Members of occupations that are not full-fledged occupational communities also exhibit this tendency to look to other members of their occupations for signals about the appropriateness of their behavior. Another study found that, although beginning nursing students expected to have the value of their nursing performance confirmed by appreciative patients, advanced nursing students looked to their nursing supervisors and doctors for assurance about their performance (Simpson 1967). Similarly, when computer data processors were asked to whom they looked for an evaluation of their work, well over 60 percent of them reported they looked to other data processors rather than to members of management, senior management, or user groups to find out how they were doing (Hebden 1975).

Unusual emotional demands.   The nature of the work in many occupations makes unusual emotional demands on the people doing it. These demands vary widely from unusual compassion and gentleness to fierce aggression and hostility, from extreme friendliness to extreme remoteness, from genuine sincerity and caring to the most expedient manipulations and exploitation of others, and so on. Sharing emotional demands tends to create a sense of common fate and a strong impetus to find and exchange ways of managing these demands. Many occupations use cultural forms to help members manage their emotions appropriately. Language, stories, myths, songs, rituals, taboos, and rites, in particular, help members to both vent their emotions and learn ways to frame their activities so emotions do not overwhelm them or interfere with their carrying out their duties. Doctors and nurses learn not to become emotionally involved with patients. Pilots who bomb targets during a war learn to think in terms of missions accomplished and collateral damage, and not in terms of people who might be injured or killed. Many of the examples already given in this book also illustrate how cultural forms help people deal with emotional demands of doing their work.

In addition, people are increasingly being paid to exhibit and provoke specified emotions. This commercialization of human feelings requires members of some occupations "to produce an emotional state in another person—gratitude or fear, for example" (Hochschild 1983, p. 149). Bill collectors deliberately instill fear and seek to produce angry responses in order to get delinquents to admit that they are tardy in their payments. Flight attendants must deal with anxious and often rude and demanding passengers while maintaining an official demeanor of calmness, friendliness, and unfailing courtesy; they are expected to have "a managed heart" (Hochschild 1983, p. 147). Funeral directors and morticians must learn to adapt to and deal not only with cadavers, but with grieving and sometimes hysterical relatives. Research identified a number of ways in which morticians framed ongoing events so as to minimize the distressing emotional content of them. For example, after a person died at home, the funeral staff rearranged the room in which the death had occurred "to reconstruct what the room may have looked like before it became a death room and to suggest that a removal [of the body] did not occur" (Barley 1983, p. 407).

Favorable self-image and social identity.   Members of many occupations derive favorable self-images and social identities from their work that are then projected to others as an important part of their presentation of selves. Three features of work contributing to favorable occupational identities are facing danger, using esoteric skills, and providing socially valuable services (Van Maanen and Barley 1984).

Some occupations face obvious dangers; members of these occupations can therefore lay claim to exceptional traits of character, particularly persistent courage. High-steel ironworkers, policemen, soldiers, firefighters, demolition workers, deep-sea divers, and underground miners are good examples.

The possession of esoteric skills also contributes to a positive occupational self-image. In modern society, the possession of such skills is often certified by examinations that must be passed to acquire a license or other certification. Specialized university education is necessary to pass many of these examinations, but other occupations receive training in specialized colleges and schools, in community colleges, in apprenticeship programs, and on the job.

Members of occupations also bolster their self-images by emphasizing the social value of their work. When other peoples' health, safety, or welfare is highly dependent on how members of an occupation perform, they can easily construe their work as having great social value. Air traffic controllers, nurses, doctors, firefighters, and locomotive engineers feel important because other people's safety and well-being depend on how they perform their jobs.

Occupations without these characteristics often construct ideologies that confer such value on their work. Garbage collectors manage to devise favorable occupational self-images by emphasizing the public health benefits of their work (Lasson 1971). Nightwatchmen see themselves as surrogates for absent managers and project a self that stands constantly ready to manage crises at late hours (Trice 1964). Ward attendants in mental hospitals think of themselves as therapists since it is they, and not the psychiatrists, who interact frequently with patients (Simpson and Simpson 1959).

Extension into nonwork life.   Members of certain occupations tend to spend leisure time together, live near one another, link their families through marriage, and encourage their children to follow the same occupation. Such social relations make the label of occupational community especially fitting. Pilcher found that nearly all nonfamily associations of longshoremen in Portland, Oregon were with other longshoremen, that they had many kinship ties, and that they felt that "another longshoreman is a sort of kinsman" (Pilcher 1972, p. 19).[2] Fishermen, police officers, prison guards, and lumberjacks are examples of occupations whose members tend both to live and work near one another (Van Maanen and Barley 1984). Small communities dominated by single industries or organizations provide conditions conducive to the growth of occupational communities. Isolated college towns, military bases, and the concentration of computer firms in the so-called Silicon Valley of California are examples.

As already mentioned, some occupations involve working conditions that isolate their members from other members of society. Fighter pilots, submariners, intelligence agents, and carnival people are examples. Persons pursuing these occupations have little alternative but to associate with one another or forego social relations altogether. In other cases, the working conditions in an occupation prevent members from associating even with one another. One study showed how tight schedules and regulated work hours for railroad engineers and firemen made it difficult for them to have much social interaction with others (Cottrell 1940). In such occupations, it may be hard for occupational communities to form.

Ethnocentrism.   Among the subcultures that occur frequently in organizations, those forming around occupations seem especially prone to ethnocentrism. The consciousness of kind members develop makes "us" seem very different from "them." Those who do not belong are viewed as outsiders and treated with some suspicion. Membership is seen as conferring immediate superiority over others—at least in the relevant task domain. "Our ways" of doing things become the only "right ways." When occupational subcultures become communities—that is, when they exhibit the five characteristics just discussed—they are also bound to

---

[2]Throughout this chapter, the traditional masculine form of the names of various occupations will be used when virtually all members of those occupations were male in the time period studied.

develop some amount of ethnocentrism. The more intense the five characteristics just discussed, the stronger the ethnocentrism is likely to be.

Ethnocentrism sets the stage for conflict with other occupational groups and with management, who likely have their own ideas about what is the right way to organize work processes. If workers feel that they know better than management, they will often refuse to carry out or cooperate with management edicts. One researcher observed a group of machinists who joined with other groups in a factory to resist the implementation of new production controls (Roy 1954). Similar instances of so-called resistance to change are often found and discussed by those who try to implement various changes in organizations. Resistance of this sort is usually attributed to such factors as individuals' motives to stay with what is familiar or to group motives to protect prerogatives. Such explanations may be part of the story, but they fail to take into account how the culturally ethnocentric views of various occupational groups can undermine change efforts that originate outside their groups. Members of occupational groups frequently feel they know best.

Occupational ethnocentrism can also become a formidable barrier to understanding and cooperation among groups in work settings. Librarians, for example, are well known in universities as "being in a world all their own." Despite overt policies to the contrary, they believe in tight control of "their books" and are uncomfortable with scholarly needs for flexibility in scheduling their use (Wallace 1989; Reeves 1980). Technical workers in Silicon Valley who were interviewed showed ethnocentric tendencies, referring to one another in terms of the occupational subcultures to which each belonged:

> "Hardware," "software," "engineering," "marketing," "PAC division" and "scientist" orientations were often mentioned. . . . Employees holding such contrasting viewpoints may try to interact and coordinate their actions to produce computer products, but may find that their conflicting cultures complicate these attempts or even make direct coordination unproductive. (Gregory 1983, p. 372)

This example is interesting because it illustrates the strong tendency of groups of workers to differentiate themselves from one another by the kind of work they do. Workers in organizations draw such distinctions whether or not they correspond to distinct, recognized occupations.

Such self-labeling and labeling by others provides fertile ground for the growth of ethnocentrism, which may precede the development of either a genuine, distinct occupation or an occupational community. By itself, therefore, ethnocentrism is not an indicator of subculture, nor is the presence of subcultures or occupational communities necessary to produce ethnocentrism.

Competing Forms of Control

Occupational Principle vs. Administrative Principle

Because one of the impulses behind the banding together of members of occupations is to seek autonomy and control over their work, the development of distinct occupations poses a threat to the power and authority of management in work organizations. Members of each group—occupation and management— may think they know best how work should be organized and carried out. Both can have the same goals of achieving good work-related outcomes, yet differ substantially in the specifics of how they think work should be done. Members of an occupation usually feel they need discretion to use their work-related expertise appropriately; members of management feel they must exercise some measure of control to ensure efficiency and prevent opportunism. Each sees work-related issues from the framework provided by their own experiences and ideologies.

One way to describe the situation is in terms of the distinction between the occupational principle and the administrative principle (Freidson 1973, p. 19). According to the administrative principle, management dictates the division of labor in work organizations by deciding the way that tasks are divided and who will do them, and then trains and indoctrinates workers to perform according to those decisions. According to the occupational principle, certain workers have exclusive rights to perform certain kinds of work, to control training for the access to doing that work, and to control the way it is performed and evaluated (Freidson 1973, p. 22). When members of occupations are successful in establishing such control, management decisions are significantly constrained. Managers cannot divide the work in any way they like. Perhaps even more telling, since they do not provide the training that members of the occupation need to perform their work, management has no direct control over the work procedures that workers learn, nor over the values and ethical principles that are bound to be inculcated at the same time. Furthermore, since workers do not need to depend on work organizations for their training, but instead on outside organizations or groups, they enter employing organizations as relatively independent agents who have allegiances to occupational groups outside the organization.

The traditional crafts provide an excellent example of how occupational control can powerfully constrain administrative control. In crafts like those in the construction industry, unions do much more than bargain with management for members' welfare and rights. They actually do some of the administrative work needed to coordinate and control work processes that is done by management in mass-production manufacturing firms. For example, craft unions set up jurisdictions over certain sets of tasks, actually fill jobs from lists of available members, and train members in how to perform their work. One result is that administrative structures are smaller and less elaborate in the construction industry than in manufacturing firms. Another is that decision making is more decentralized in construction work:

> Decisions, which in mass production were made outside the work milieu and communicated bureaucratically, in construction work were actually part of the craftsman's culture and socialization and were made at the level of the work crew. (Stinchcombe 1959, p. 180)

The most studied and discussed examples of how occupations constrain management control are provided by the professions. In the 1960s, scholars who studied scientists in industry documented conflicts that arose between the demands of employers and the expectations and values instilled during scientific training (Kornhauser 1962; Pelz and Andrew 1966). Physicians provide the extreme example by the degree to which they have succeeded in establishing control, not only over their own work, but also over the hospitals that provide facilities and equipment they need; over the medical schools that train new members of the profession; and over the procedures that license new members and enforce professional standards of conduct. Their hegemony, however, is not without limit. Given sufficient reason to do so, society can limit the autonomy and controls it has conferred on occupations. Recent concern over rising medical costs has prompted increased public scrutiny of medical practice and new government controls. How successful these attempts will be to increase societal control over medical practice remains to be seen.

Other professionals—professors, lawyers, accountants, engineers, architects—also enjoy substantial control not only over their immediate work, but also more generally within the organizations in which they work. In U.S. society, which values individualism and autonomy so highly, such control is a prize that many seek. Thus, all sorts of occupations that lack the standard requirements for professional status try to claim its benefits by calling themselves "professional." The word itself has come to have a very favorable connotation and is applied to activities as diverse as cleaning septic tanks, cutting hair, and advising people about investments.

Unions and Professional Associations

Clearly the existence, activities, and power of unions and professional associations help to strengthen occupational claims for control in the crafts and professions. Because the boundaries of the occupation and the union or association largely coincide, their interests also coincide; there is no dilution or conflict of interest between them. Although they vary in their practical power, occupational associations generally devote some efforts to maintaining boundaries against interlopers and buttressing the claims of members' control of their area of work competence over that of rival claimants.

In the case of industrial unions, however, the situation is different. Industrial unions usually represent most of the workers, regardless of occupation, in a given industry. The boundaries of industrial unions therefore do not coincide with those of single occupations, and they are not in a position to provide training for all of their members, nor to establish the exact work processes that members use to perform tasks. The diversity of types of work done by their members tends to dilute the ability of industrial unions to establish such controls, and probably also to develop strong, distinctive subcultures. Such unions also usually represent workers in less developed occupations. Members of the developed occupations who work in industrial settings—carpenters, electricians, pipefitters, tool and die makers, machinists, plumbers, security guards—are usually represented by their own craft unions and not by the industrial unions that represent the other workers in those settings.

Arenas of Conflict

Access to knowledge intrinsic to the performance of tasks is the fundamental basis for occupational control over the conduct of work (Child and Fulk 1982, p. 159). To the extent that management can reduce its dependency on workers for such knowledge, it can better maintain its own control over work processes. The primary way that management has reduced occupational autonomy and control is through the standardization and routinization of work. Occupational work is broken down into discrete tasks that can be done by workers with less training or by machines, robots, or computers. Management planning and decisions determine exactly what work is done, when, and how. The processes of mechanization, automation, and computerization have thus eroded the power of some occupational groups and increased the power of management. This process of reducing the skills required to do work is referred to as "deskilling" (Braverman 1974). Its effects are most evident in large-scale, batch-production industries (Form 1987). Other industries exhibit mixed patterns of both upgraded and reduced sets of skills.

Table 5-1 summarizes how the amount of control that management and occupations have attained relative to each other is likely to affect relations between their respective subcultures in specific kinds of organizations. Management control depends on the extent and elaboration of managerial control devices like management hierarchies, rules and regulations, and standardization of

FIGURE 5-1

A FRAMEWORK FOR CONSIDERING RELATIONS BETWEEN MANAGEMENT
AND OCCUPATIONS IN ORGANIZATIONS

		Control by Administrative Principle	
		Predominant	*Subordinate*
Control by Occupational Principle	*Predominant*	1 Mutual tolerance and accomodation Lawyers and doctors in corporations Skilled craft workers	3 Assimilation of management by occupation Universities Social work agencies Hospitals Police departments
	Subordinate	2 Assimilation of occupation by management Accountants Engineers Pharmacists Deskilled occupations	4 Egalitarian relations Food cooperatives Alternative schools Health collectives

SOURCE: Adapted from Sonnenstuhl and Trice 1991.

work. Occupational control depends on the extent and elaboration of occupational control devices like occupationally controlled training and socialization, occupational associations or unions, licensing, and codes of ethics. Also important in determining the relative control of each group is how scarce and valuable the skills of occupational members are and how heavily management depends upon them.

Cell 1 portrays the likely relationship in organizations where devices for both occupational and management control are strong and well developed. In effect, the administrative and occupational principles are balanced; neither subculture prevails. Members have strong occupational identities and professional associations. They also possess scarce and valuable skills. Their employing organizations are also in a relatively strong position—in the case of corporations, because the doctors and lawyers they employ are few in number and thus cannot readily form internal subcultures. Mutual tolerance and accommodation in these situations works something like this. The doctors and lawyers retain considerable control over how they carry out their corporate work; after all, management doesn't have the legal or medical knowledge required to give them detailed supervision or to second-guess many of their decisions. But management can control the conditions of their employment, their remuneration, what resources they will have in carrying out their tasks; can give them assignments and influence the values and priorities that govern their activities. One physician described his reactions to such influence as follows:

> ... physicians accept production as a priority, too; we do work in that situation, and that priority to a lesser or greater degree takes priority over health. You just have to bargain, to sort of push health a bit; they push production, and you bargain. (Walters 1982, p. 2)

As already mentioned, skilled craft workers often work out similar accommodations. Management assigns them jobs and sets general deadlines and priorities, but traditionally carpenters, plumbers, and electricians have performed their various tasks without much direction and control from management, and have operated within performance standards set more by the craft than by management (Stinchcombe 1959). Historically, although mechanization and automation often disrupted the patterns of skills within craft occupations, workers in many crafts have managed to acquire the new skills required and thus retained their autonomy (Form 1987).

Cell 2 represents situations where management has managed to dilute the control of occupational subcultures by providing career tracks that lead occupational members into management or by simply reducing the skills required and thus the distinctiveness of an occupation. In such situations, the administrative principle predominates and members of occupational subcultures are assimilated into the prevailing management culture. Accountants and engineers, for example, often seek and are promoted into general management positions. The printing trade provides a prime example of how management, by the use of computers, has substantially deskilled members of an occupation (Wallace and Kalleberg 1982). When printing technology was mechanized and used lead type, linotype operators, usually men, were still considered highly skilled craft workers with high status in their trade. Now operators with more commonly held sets of skills, often women, operate the keyboards of much more sophisticated computerized equipment. This equipment not only requires less judgment to operate, but can also eliminate steps in the production process—and thus jobs. In producing newspapers, reporters and editors, using the computers on their desks, type their own stories directly into printed form and edit them. Professors both write and print their papers on their computers, thus bypassing the secretarial pool. Soon, scientific journals will be accepting papers on computer diskettes, rather than on typed pages that need to be set into type in a separate operation. When this happens, the services of two white-collar workers—typist and typesetter—will either be eliminated or reduced to making a few corrections and changes in format here and there.

The occupational autonomy of even the traditional professions could conceivably be reduced by recent developments in computerization and other technologies. As standardized protocols, flow charts, and computer programs are developed to make diagnoses from patient symptoms and case histories, and more and more automated processes are developed to analyze blood and other samples, hospitals and patients may become less dependent on doctors for the discretionary skills they once held exclusively. Other developing technologies enable administrators to exercise greater oversight over physicians' caseloads, their speed of service delivery, and the costs of medical care they provide. In addition, the actual location in which many tasks are performed has moved from the doctor's office or patient's bedside, where the doctor has ultimate control, to centralized labs and administrative offices, where hospital administrators have greater control. These developments open the door for increased control of the provision of health care by the administrative principle. Similar developments are foreseeable in the practice of law, where computer programs already exist for case retrieval and sophisticated accounting of costs and profits associated with cases.

In some instances, the deskilling process has led to intense and prolonged conflict between workers and management; in other instances, very little. The advent of mechanization further devalued the skills of unskilled workers and greatly reduced their autonomy. These developments not only produced the Industrial Revolution but eventually led to widespread and bloody labor-management conflict and the emergence of trade and industrial unions that institutionalize that conflict. The more recent computer revolution has not yet produced such intense or prolonged conflicts. In white-collar occupations, workers are not sufficiently organized to mount effective resistance. Also, many probably believe that using a computer upgrades their skills. In the skilled trades, incumbents eventually accepted what seemed inevitable to protect some jobs and retain some vestiges of control over them (Wallace and Kalleberg 1982). In industrial settings, the introduction of computerized equipment that allows flexible manufacturing probably leads to an upgrading of operators' skills.

Cell 3 represents the situation where occupational groups generate their own administrative structures to plan, direct, and control their work processes

(Freidson 1973). In effect, the organizations involved grow up around the skills of members of that occupation and the organizations that result are made up almost entirely of members of that occupation. In such situations, the occupational principle predominates. While members may have to take orders, these orders are usually given by a member of the occupation who has been chosen to be an administrator rather than from someone trained in general management. The administrators of social work agencies and police departments are drawn from the ranks of members of those occupations. In other occupations, special schools under the influence of the occupational culture have grown up to train people for administrative posts. Examples are schools of hospital administration, schools of educational administration, and administrative tracks in schools of social work and nursing administration. Within law firms and accounting firms, members accept technical supervision only if it is carried out by a senior respected member of the occupation (Montagna 1973; Spangler 1986).

Despite the assimilation by members of these occupations of their administrators, differences in the subcultural values between the two groups remain sources of conflict. Even in these settings administrators may feel obliged to enact the administrative principle. As long as occupational members believe that their administrative colleagues have the group's interests at heart, they show goodwill and cooperate with their directives. If, however, an administrative colleague is perceived as pursuing administrative interests to the detriment of the group, members will revolt and seek to replace the administrator (Feldman 1987). Such instances are dramatic reaffirmations of the proper order of things. The welfare of the occupation comes before anything else.

Also, professional values usually emphasize the interests of individual clients. The code of ethics of physicians says they must put the welfare of patients above all other concerns; thus, the costs of treatment are peripheral concerns to the doctor. To the hospital administrator, costs are a much more central concern. Similarly, to the basic scientist, contributing to scientific progress is the ultimate goal; scientific norms thus dictate the full sharing of new findings and techniques with the rest of the scientific community. But private firms who employ scientists and have financed their research naturally want to preserve the secrecy of their discoveries and obtain patents for them so they can realize a financial return (Kornhauser 1962). Such conflicts may be especially pronounced in the professions (1) because professions have more developed ideologies and values than other occupations; and (2) because their professional norms and codes tend to include certain absolutes that powerfully constrain them in bending to practical concerns.

In organizations whose main purpose is to provide professional services, the esoteric levels of skills and the vital nature of the services provided will probably enable professional workers to hold their own against administrators despite the computer revolution. The knowledge and skills on which professions rest are not fixed, but continually develop and expand by efforts of those within the profession. Thus, administrators will always have to rely on professionals for new knowledge and skills that have not yet been systematized or routinized. Also, professional tasks have important expressive consequences for clients and the public. Standardization of these tasks often involves the dilution or the disappearance of these reassuring and satisfying consequences and may not be acceptable to clients or the public for that reason. Patients want to talk to a doctor; students want to see a professor in person.

Cell 4 portrays a situation where, either because of ideology or structural situations, the control of both the occupation and management are weak. For example, food cooperatives depend on members to do important aspects of the work and to support them financially, but these members lack any collective identity or occupational subculture. Much the same situation arises in extremely egalitarian organizations like free schools, where neither occupations nor management can have strong influence because norms and values favor individuality and shifting preferences over any organized effort. Health collectives often also fall into this quadrant because their ideologies and practices favor demystifying medical practice by teaching nonprofessional volunteers to perform some services and patients to take care of themselves as much as possible (Rothschild and Whitt 1986). Such ideologies and practices greatly weaken the occupational principle. The administrative principle is weakened by these organizations' tendencies to view decisions as "morally binding only if they reflect the will of the collectivity and are arrived at through a process of democratic consensus" (Rothschild and Whitt 1986, p. 50). These collectives often provide services to disadvantaged groups—poor blacks and Hispanics, counterculture youth, raped women, AIDS victims, and the like—who are themselves represented in the staff and therefore in decision making. Lacking a dominant culture, life in such organizations can be chaotic. One member of such an organization called what she experienced ". . . undignified, unprofessional, just plain craziness, but it was fun in a way" (Schwartzman 1984, p. 90).

Arenas of Commonalities

Of course, the relations between management or administrators and members of occupations are not wholly conflictive. These two groups also share common interests and values. Most basic, they are united in their interests in preserving the organizations and industries that provide them with their livelihood. To a considerable extent, each needs the other to be able to continue to do what they do. When it comes to matters pertaining to the welfare of the auto industry, the United Auto Workers and the management of the automobile companies find considerable areas of agreement. When the funding for higher education is being decided, professors, students, and administrators forget their differences and lobby together.

In a more general sense, members of management and members of occupations need one another to maintain their organizations' legitimacy in the wider society. Legitimacy helps to insure continued support of organizations by their environments. In order to maintain their legitimacy, organizations must conform to some degree with what are called institutional rules or expectations. These include four types of conformity: categorical conformity, structural conformity, procedural conformity, and personnel conformity (Scott 1987, pp. 194–98). Examples of each follow. First, organizations must comply with certain basic taken-for-granted categorical distinctions like management and worker, research and development, or student and teacher. Second, funding agencies, regulatory agencies, and foundations require that they comply with expectations or requirements that they have certain departments or structural features. Third, these and other groups may also require that certain procedures are established and followed. Finally, state laws, client expectations, and general societal expectations may force organizations to hire certain workers with certain kinds of training and certification. Note that some of these forms of conformity depend primarily on management skills; others depend more heavily on occupational skills and training.

Some overlap also exists between occupational and managerial subcultural values and practices. Both insist on universalistic standards, explicit definition of tasks, and evaluation of competence on the basis of actual performance (Blau and Scott 1962, pp. 60–62). Also, some occupational and professional values are not very different from those of management. Studies of engineers suggest that their goals are in more accord with those of management than with those of basic scientists (Ritti 1968, p. 129). Other studies show that many engineers initially aspire to management positions (Perrucci 1971, p. 492). Some occupational groups have so influenced the development of management ideologies and values that there is little disagreement between them. Accountants are probably the prime example. Their occupation provides "a form of moral and technical reckoning, where the careful husbandry of scarce resources is not only treated as a sign of managerial competence, but also of moral superiority" (Gowler and Legge 1983, p. 210).

Occupational Socialization

A Means of Control

Training and indoctrination are important aspects of organizational control and coordination. "Training refers to the processes by which job-related skills and knowledge are taught, while indoctrination is the process by which ... norms are acquired" (Mintzberg 1979b, p. 95). Because much occupational training and indoctrination occurs outside employing organizations, occupations rather than management sometimes control the initial socialization of new members into work roles. Even when occupational socialization occurs inside the organization after the recruit has joined, it will often be carried out by an experienced member of that occupation. During occupational training, recruits are inevitably indoctrinated into the ideologies, values, and norms of the occupation as they are learning technical skills. The combination of technical training and cultural indoctrination becomes socialization—the process by which people learn how to perform specified social roles in a way that is acceptable to members of a relevant cultural group and come to internalize those expectations.

Socialization is a very potent and relatively long-term form of control. Once people have learned and internalized certain ideologies, values, and norms, the maintenance of their self-esteem depends upon behaving in conformity with them (Brim 1966). Thus, they are likely to resist others' attempts to require them to behave in ways counter to their internalized expectations or to change those expectations. In addition, control achieved through socialization has the advantage of being implicit; effective control is often achieved without power holders having to make explicit demands. Because the controls internalized through socialization are largely taken for granted, they may seem less onerous than following direct orders.

Becoming a Member

Socialization in an occupation differs in important ways from organizational socialization. Entering a defined occupation is apt to involve a lifelong commitment, yet it is one that individuals often drift into gradually. Entering an organization frequently involves only a temporary commitment and has a well-demarcated beginning. Thus, different processes appear to be relevant to describing how people become members of occupations and organizations. Entering occupations involve five, somewhat overlapping processes: attraction, access, adjustment, identification, and commitment.

First, a person must know about and feel attracted to something in the occupation. It could be specific members to whom they are attracted; it could be the activities of the subculture; it could be the kinds of extrinsic and intrinsic rewards it appears to offer. Caprice operates here, in the sense that persons' experiences expose them to selected information about some occupations and not others. Moreover, they are not aware during these experiences that what is happening may affect their choice of an occupation. Often, people do not set out consciously to join a specific occupation. They become aware of education, training, or job opportunities, they take advantage of the opportunities seen as most attractive, and are gradually drawn into the activities of the occupation. Sometimes people drift into or grope toward the occupation without much conscious intent. Other occupations, like the professions, require definite choice points and must be approached more deliberately.

Second, various structural factors will affect whether a person has access to and can successfully enter an occupation. People may want to join an occupation but find that they cannot realistically do so. A variety of factors enhance and discourage individuals' access to particular forms of occupational life. The structure and makeup of American society leaves some persons shut off from and oblivious of many occupations while it encourages others to become interested in an array of occupations. Social class sets severe limits on both a child's knowledge about, and aspirations for, a given occupation. Parental education, income, and occupations channel childhood fantasies and expectations about various occupations so that children from higher socioeconomic backgrounds learn about and aspire to many more occupations than do children of lower socioeconomic backgrounds (Shapiro and Crowley 1982; Brinkerhoff and Corry 1976). Similarly, gender and race can restrict occupational awareness and aspirations (Sewell 1969; Sprey 1962). Labor market conditions, educational requirements, family obligations and expectations, personal abilities, and historical events block certain people from entry and channel others in specific directions. Rural backgrounds also restrict opportunities for young people to explore a wide range of occupations to which they might be attracted. Some analysts observe that by the time race, nationality, family, area of residence, and gender are taken into account, the range of occupations to which individuals might realistically aspire is severely restricted (Miller and Form 1980).

Third, as persons become acquainted with an occupation and its beliefs, values, norms, and activities, they need to come to terms with whether they will fit within that occupation. Do they already or can they enthusiastically espouse the occupation's ideology and values? Are they willing to conform to its norms? Do they have the intellectual and physical equipment to carry out its activities? Does their personal temperament enable them to deal with the emotional demands of the occupation's pattern of activities?

Fourth, persons become identified both socially and psychologically with the occupation. As the attraction process goes on over time, it eliminates other alternatives. Because it is impossible for a person to pursue all alternatives at once, as a person focuses on one occupation, other opportunities disappear or fade from awareness. Also, as a person carries out initial activities associated with the occupation, other people begin to identify that person with that occupation. The person also begins to identify himself or herself with the occupation. Two factors facilitate psychological identification: using other members of the occupation as reference points (Hebden 1975), and developing a self-image as someone performing the tasks of the occupation (Simpson and Simpson 1959; Trice 1964).

Fifth, over time members become committed to occupations. They accrue certain benefits from being in the occupation that they would lose if they left it (Becker 1960; Ritzer and Trice, 1969b). They develop certain patterns of behavior in which they are inclined to persist (Salancik 1977). Also, they develop loyalties to other members of the occupation (Ritzer and Trice 1969a), much as members develop loyalties to employing organizations (Mowday, Porter, and Steers 1982).

Occupational associations play an important role in promoting identification with and commitment to occupations. They do this in three ways: by providing a broader, more extensive reference group; by providing organized, political influence at a state or national level; and by giving members a recourse outside the employing organization to which they can turn. Within the occupational association, members form extensive networks that provide friendship, advice, and knowledge about work activities. They lobby for legislation and regulation that favors their occupation. Above all, they feel protected by their membership from complete reliance on the employing organization. If this employer proves to be unsatisfactory, another can be found through contacts within the association.

Formal and Informal Socialization

Occupational socialization occurs both formally and informally. Educational and training programs aimed explicitly at imparting technical knowledge used in the occupation and at indoctrinating aspirants into the cultural expectations of occupational roles constitute the formal side of socialization. Occupations vary widely in the amount of formal socialization acquired before members enter employing organizations. The professions require the longest period of formal socialization; other occupations require far less formal socialization.

On the other hand, as illustrated repeatedly in Chapter 4, informal socialization is extensive in all occupations. It occurs in conjunction with formal training and continues as members work within their occupations. Like many other aspects of culture, informal socialization practices seem to emerge spontaneously as people interact in carrying out occupational roles. Even in the medical professions, where formal socialization is so elaborate, informal socialization plays a very crucial part in transforming students into doctors. Two classic studies of medical students found that (1) they learn their self-conceptions as doctors from experiences with patients (Merton 1957); and that (2) interaction with other students and faculty serves to break down initial idealism of students and replace it with more realistic aspirations that enable graduates to cope with the reality of private practice and hospital bureaucracies (Becker et al. 1961).

Learning the Culture

An important part of informal socialization is learning the culture of an occupation, particularly the ways in which members cope with work-related anxieties so that they can continue to perform required tasks confidently and safely despite them. For example, most of the informal socialization of high-steel ironworkers revolves around managing the anxieties produced by working high above the construction activities "protected from certain death only by their skill in balancing on slender beams" (Haas 1977, p. 148). The beams range in width from four to twelve inches. Adverse weather conditions—rain, sleet, snow, ice, and particularly high winds—increase the danger. The safety of individual workers depends heavily on trustworthy and competent behaviors of fellow workers.

In this dangerous and skilled occupation, there is little formal training. New recruits—called "punks"—are initially assigned to "firewatch"—standing below on the ground to watch for bits of welding material that might but rarely do fall to the ground. Since not much happens that requires their intervention, recruits have plenty of opportunity to watch the experienced ironworkers going about their tasks above them. After an indefinite period, experienced workers decide a recruit is ready to be called to help or "punk for" the experienced workers above. This happens "without any orientation or training and any practice he gets in walking the steel comes while he carries out his work" (Haas 1974, p. 99). A punk must respond to a variety of demands for help from the scattered ironworkers who demand that tools, equipment, and materials be brought to them.

Once the punk goes up to join experienced workers, an informal, yet well-institutionalized, pattern of socialization begins. Experienced workers assign the punk demeaning, almost insulting work and frequently subject the punk to blistering personal attacks and verbal degradations. Punks are constantly questioned about their personal life and activities and reviled for the slightest shortcoming. At the same time, however, the experienced workers provide technical information about the work.

Through the ordeals to which the punk is subjected, experienced workers determine whether the confident front automatically assumed and carefully maintained by all—including the punk—will break down under pressure, and whether the punk can casually accept the trauma of constant danger. It is taboo to discuss or otherwise remind others of the dangers all are confronting; these workers appear to believe that talking about the dangers makes accidents more likely. Repeatedly, they observe the punk's trustworthiness, self-control, and emotional reactions. Each individual apprentice must live down the punk label through consistently satisfactory performance—both technical and emotional— before becoming a full member of this unusual and demanding occupation.

Ideologies and Forms in Occupational Subcultures

Perhaps the richest and most colorful of cultural forms associated with work life are celebrations of occupational subcultures. All of the cultural forms already identified and discussed are common within occupations.

Myths and Fictions

While symbols are viewed as the central cultural form in cultures in general, myths seem to occupy a central place in occupational subcultures. This is because such myths are used to justify the very existence and continuation of occupations. Although they are unconfirmed, self-serving myths are accepted as truth within occupations and often by the public, as well. Researchers who study occupations have described such myths for such diverse occupations as accountants, personnel managers, computer programmers, carpenters, bricklayers, and cowboys.

The "myth of principles" that undergirds the accounting occupation began with the Securities Act of 1933, which gave accountants the right to perform necessary audits of firms' bookkeeping records.

Because of a belief in its expertise ... the profession implied that this expertise encompassed a body of generally accepted standards, principles, and practices, and that audit judgments would be based on good reason. These were deceptive myths, for the profession had yet to create a codified body of knowledge or to define appropriate practice.... These myths gave rise to a technology of standard setting by three quasi-legislative boards.... By mimicking legal procedures a body of accounting principles [would] emerge that is analogous to common law. (Boland 1982, p. 118)

This particular occupational myth has been remarkably impervious to objective analysis. Accountants manage to avoid surveillance of their practice despite their strong tendencies to be influenced by the interests of large corporations (Chatov 1975). Recent bank crises, like that of the Penn Square Bank in Oklahoma City, revealed how little public protection is sometimes afforded by the principles and expertise of accountants and auditors (Singer 1985). In testimony before the House of Representative Commerce Committee, one expert witness remarked:

> If one were starting from point zero today, it would be madness to invent a system where the one to be audited hired the auditor, bargained with the auditor as to the size of the fee, was permitted to purchase other management services from the auditor, and where the auditor in turn has the social responsibility for setting the rules and for enforcing them and applying sanctions against themselves. (Klott 1985, p. 22)

One analyst described the situation most succinctly as "unaccountable accounting" (Briloff 1972, 1981). Despite these and other criticisms, the occupation has flourished with the myths of its principles intact.

Another widely accepted occupational myth was that of the boy apprentice, which was held without question among carpenters and bricklayers in the 1930s. The myth visualized a boy "growing up in the trade," dedicated to a course of action "involving patience, abstinence, and the arduous acquisition of high skill" (Myers 1948, p. 333). The myth served these trades by justifying severe restrictions on the number of apprentices who could enter training and thus kept the skills of these occupations in relatively short supply. The extent to which this myth was fiction was partly revealed in a 1941 study of the building trades in the Great Lakes area. Researchers discovered that 40 percent of the sample had entered their trade when they were 25 years or older, and 42 percent indicated they had received no formal, apprentice-like training (Myers, 1948). Perhaps because it was so patently untrue, this myth eventually died out.

Perhaps the most generalized of occupational myths is that surrounding professionalization. Professional occupations promulgate myths that actions taken by members of those occupations are based in highly specialized, tested areas of knowledge, and that they are rational, disinterested, and oriented primarily to the interests of clients or the public. Relatively few professions begin to approximate this ideal, although many try to claim the status. Many of these occupations have knowledge bases that are "too general and vague or too narrow and specific for achievement of exclusive jurisdiction and autonomy of a profession" (Wilensky 1964a, p. 141). In others, some systematic base of knowledge exists but is still too controversial to justify the status of professional. Many of the applications of behavioral science to the workplace—organizational development efforts, selection and testing, training, counseling—are examples of activities that are often labeled as professional but do not meet the ideal.

A particular type of myth has grown up recently in human service occupations aspiring to professional status. Current increasing claims of burnout and stress associated with such occupations as nursing, social work, counseling, and clinical psychology provide "a perfect vehicle to convey the symbolic virtues of an occupation not yet recognized as professional" (Van Maanen and Barley 1984, p. 319). Nearly ten times as many articles deal with job stress in police and nursing periodicals as appear in comparative periodicals in law or medicine (Terry 1981).

Some occupational myths have been created more by the media than by members of the occupation itself. The myth of the cowboy is one of these. Perhaps what is most remarkable about this myth is that it celebrates the activities of relatively few people over a relatively brief period of time—from about 1880 to 1885. The mythical image of the cowboy hero was deliberately concocted by theatrical spectacles, like Buffalo Bill's Wild West Shows of the 1890s; by novelists like Owen Wister, whose popular novel *The Virginian* was published in 1902; and by artists like Remington, who portrayed both cowboys and their traditional enemies, the American Indians.

> The mythical cowboy worked in an occupation that permitted him to gain his livelihood outside the constraints of conventional society; he relied chiefly upon himself; he was stoic and uncomplaining, humorous and droll; he enjoyed nomadic freedom, and was completely unfettered by the past. Women and family life were largely irrelevant; horses took priority and symbolized personal freedom—one of the major ideologies embodied in the myth. The realities of cowboy life were much less glamorous. Their lives were almost exclusively tied to the habits and foibles of droves of dumb animals—to jobs with low pay, excessively long hours, and demanding, autocratic bosses. They were seen by themselves and others as uninhibited nomads who eschewed the institutions of community life and who relieved long periods of monotony and loneliness with large doses of whiskey, gambling, and tainted women. (Adapted from Lawrence 1982, p. 46)

Equally popular and profitable to the media is the more recent myth of the police hero. This myth ascribes to the police the power to prevent crime and catch most criminals (Manning 1977). Research shows a great divergence between what the public believes the police do, on the basis of this widely promulgated myth, and what they actually do. However, new stages of mythmaking may be underway for both of these occupations. Recent movies and television programs often portray cowboys and policemen and women in almost an anti-heroic vein. This new myth may be as inaccurate as the old, and, like the old, may reflect more about the current values and beliefs of the overall society than about these occupations.

Other undocumented beliefs about occupations are not as well developed and elaborate as myths, and have been called fictions (Dubin 1951; Smith 1962). Examples include the fiction that staff managers, like personnel managers, do not give orders (Ritzer and Trice 1969a, p. 84), and that computer programmers need to be free of time constraints to operate effectively (Pettigrew 1973, p. 151). Such fictions have a kinship with occupational mystiques and the control of information. One researcher described how skilled French maintenance workers managed to keep secret the details of how to repair equipment and thus made other workers and even management heavily dependent on them (Crozier 1964, p. 153). Another study documented how industrial relations specialists protected their influence by deliberately keeping union-management agreements as secret or vague as possible (Gouldner 1961).

Although many occupational myths can be seen as self-serving, they should not therefore be judged as reprehensible or undesirable. Instead they should be understood as ways in which members of occupations organize their behaviors and support them socially, emotionally, and cognitively. The complexities of environmental demands make the emergence of internal contradictions within many organizations inevitable; to try to rationally reconcile and remove such contradictions would be counterproductive, for they enable organizations to attend to various parts of the environment and so maintain their legitimacy (Beyer 1981, p. 184). One way that organizations manage incompatible external demands and internal components is by decoupling: they focus on good human relations rather than on formal rules, emphasize professional autonomy and decentralization, make inspection and evaluation into ceremonies, and state ambiguous goals while attending to means (Meyer and Rowan 1977, p. 357). The second is to maintain certain "rationalized myths" that enable specialists to get on with their tasks without attending closely to how they fit with those of others. For example, members develop a special kind of fiction—"the logic of confidence and good faith," which helps to maintain legitimacy despite a lack of technical validation of their activities (Meyer and Rowan 1977, p. 358). Confidence is maintained through professionalization and displays that dramatize ritual commitments to noncontroversial elements of organizational structure (Meyer and Rowan 1977; Trice, Belasco, and Alutto 1969).

Ideologies

As is evident from the examples already given, occupational myths are closely allied with occupational ideologies. Whether myths are expressions of existing ideologies or whether they actually give rise to ideologies is not clear. Most likely is that the two emerge in tandem. If ideologies consist of beliefs about how to accomplish certain ends (Beyer 1981), then the myths just described can be seen as prescribing effective ways to achieve those ends. Ideologies and myths thereby justify traditional occupational behaviors.

Occupations also give rise to ideologies through task performance itself. Members learn specific techniques and processes, explicit modes of reasoning, and certain ways of interacting with others. They perform repetitively according to these learned routines and often receive positive feedback for that performance. Consequently, the routines become associated with positive feelings over time and are internalized. They come to be seen and believed in as *the* way to accomplish certain ends.

Another way in which occupations affect members' ideologies is through the socioeconomic status that the occupation confers on its members. To the degree that relative wealth or poverty, relative power or powerlessness, and relatively high or low social status determine people's ideologies, their occupations are a major factor in determining them. In many countries, including the United States, certain types of workers tend to belong to particular political parties. In the United States, for example, blue-collar workers are traditionally Democratic, although they will not invariably vote that way. Similarly, high-status professionals and managers are traditionally Republican, but may occasionally support Democratic candidates. In other countries, where class divisions are more pronounced, deviations from party loyalties are probably rarer. Members of certain occupations and certain classes may almost automatically belong to a traditional political group. Of course, the occupations in which persons end up depend heavily on their initial socioeconomic status, especially in countries where the social stratification system is more rigid than it is in the United States. Thus, it is most accurate to think of socioeconomic status and occupation as dual, usually reinforcing, factors that help to shape people's ideologies. However, when individuals leave their initial socioeconomic status because of choice of occupation, it seems reasonable to suppose that occupation will have the stronger effect on their ideologies.

Most occupational groups develop ideologies that justify the work they do and the way they do it. Accountants, for example, believe that "only the independent public accountant can properly deal with problems of materiality and remain both competent and objective while doing so" (Montagna 1973, p. 142). In business schools, this belief may lead to the faculty's placing an exaggerated value upon earning the status of certified public accountant or CPA. One student we knew remarked that students who failed to get a job with a CPA firm at graduation felt they had "failed to get to heaven." Accountants also believe that they are "designers of order." They assume they play a crucial role as reducers of ignorance and preservers of order and the status quo. Accounting procedures and data help to generate consensus within organizations and facilitate the governance of organizations by means of rational knowledge and fact. Such beliefs carry with them an essentially conservative orientation and generate theories of social life that emphasize conflict, strain, and power struggles (Goldner 1970; Montagna 1973).

In the field of advertising, by contrast, the dominant ideologies concern "creativity and challenge" (Gerstl 1961, p. 44). What is sold, and how it affects society is not prominent in this ideology—but rather that it be sold with a certain style that will be effective in convincing the public to buy. The ideology says that past tried and true approaches are not sufficient—that creativity must continually be employed to find ways to make products and services attractive to consumers. More generally, marketing specialists justify their activities by reference to the free market and the benefits that untrammeled competition provides to consumers and society.

Among actors, the chronic uncertainty of employment structures occupational ideologies. For male actors in particular, this uncertainty inhibits the growth of an esteem system by which actors can invidiously compare their accomplishments to that of other actors (McHugh 1969). Actors have instead developed strong beliefs that no one can claim full credit for what he has done because someone else might have done as well, given the opportunity. This ideology is often expressed by successful actors in interviews with the media and more generally within the occupation through sentiments favoring egalitarianism in social relations with other actors.

It would seem that occupations that involve illegal or socially unacceptable behaviors would have difficulty in justifying their activities. However, studies show that members of these groups are quite successful in developing sets of beliefs that justify their activities to themselves, if not to others. For example, researchers find that prostitutes subscribe to an ideology saying that they perform socially valuable functions. They point out that they provide comfort, insights, and sexual satisfaction to their customers, and thus, they believe, they help to insure the permanence of many marriages (Bryan 1965).

Rites of Passage

All occupations make emotional demands on their members. To carry through the activities of an occupation demands a certain emotional stance. Rites of passage prepare members for the emotional demands associated with an occupation by teaching newcomers what it is like to belong to that occupation. In some occupations, the events that occur around the entrance and incorporation of new members take the form of relatively complete rites of passage. In others, relatively little attention is paid to a newcomer. Passages into occupations range from very complete sets of ceremonial activities that mark the movement of aspirants into various degrees of membership to no ceremonial activities attending such transitions at all.

The occupations of college professor and public school teacher have been contrasted in this regard (Lortie 1968). The repeated ordeals of graduate school that lead into the professoriate resemble puberty rites practiced in tribal societies. "Progress calls for clearing all sorts of hurdles such as course examinations, language tests, general examinations, and completion of a dissertation" (Lortie 1968, p. 257). Data collected after general Ph.D. examinations at the Massachusetts Institute of Technology indicated that these rites influence the self-images of those who successfully pass the examination. Comparisons of data collected two weeks before the examination with data collected afterwards showed that gaps the graduate students reported between themselves and professors had narrowed significantly.

Even after earning the Ph.D. degree and winning the initial professorial appointment of assistant professor, however, further ordeals lie ahead for the aspiring professor, who must publish, teach, and participate in administrative duties so as to satisfy senior professors and administrators. Only thus will the aspirant, after five or six years, earn tenure, and after another five or six, the coveted rank of full professor. Many aspirants never make it all the way. In this sense, the rites of passage into the professoriate diverge sharply from puberty rites in tribal societies. Almost all boys in tribal societies eventually succeed in making their passage into male adulthood. But a good proportion of assistant professors fail to achieve tenure, and another considerable proportion never reach the rank of full professor even though they stay in academic careers until retirement.

This is another way in which occupations vary: some have rites of passage structured so that most aspirants will succeed; other have rites of passage designed to weed out a goodly proportion of aspirants. It is logical to suppose that the unusualness of the demands of the occupation would be the major factor determining the degree to which rites of passage serve as filters, but we know of no research specifically addressed to this issue.

Entry into public school teaching has always been much less difficult than entry into the professoriate. Practice teaching is the major hurdle, and it is not nearly as demanding or uniform as the various hurdles leading to the Ph.D. degree. Student teachers are eased into teaching gradually. Although they may see some of their experiences in practice teaching as ordeals, these are individualized experiences and not organized, collective experiences undergone by all aspirants to the occupation. During the practice period and later in their first real job, the experience of the new teacher is one of sink or swim. Consequently, teachers come to feel like teachers as a matter of individually defined attainment rather than by crossing hurdles specified by a well-organized occupational group. Consistent with these relatively undeveloped socialization experiences are two other factors: (1) the lower status accorded to teachers; and (2) the fact that this occupation has been traditionally a temporary role in which women work while in transit to more rewarding social positions as wives and mothers (Lortie 1968, 1975). It is probably fair to conclude that more aspirants make it through the rite of passage leading to the teaching occupation than make it through the passage to the professoriate. One question that could be raised about the teaching occupation is whether its rites of passage are rigorous enough, given the very heavy emotional and other demands of the teaching role in today's public school systems. Existing rites do not seem to match current realities in the teaching occupation.

Occupational socialization does not need to be formal to include rites of passage. Observations by participants (Vaught and Smith 1980) indicate that becoming an underground miner involves all three stages of the classical rites. The separation phase is symbolized by the portal of the mine, which marks the boundary between the life on the outside and the new one to be experienced far below. Passing through it is the way in which a new miner journeys from the ordinary world into a new world. Because miners go through this portal daily on their way underground, and again when they return to the surface, certain rituals are repeated daily. First is the dressing rite, in which putting on work clothes symbolizes the removal of the outsider role and the assumption of the minor role. This rite is characterized by warm, boisterous greetings and the exchange of recent experiences. In this social milieu, the new recruit dons a sort of uniform—new overalls, mining belt, boots, a bright orange hat, and lamp. The newness of the uniform marks the newcomer, and during the first trip down the "slope" in a car with fellow workers and for a period thereafter, the newcomer is subjected to a variety of indignities: "beating the hat, pulling the recruit's lampcord and belt, kicking dents in the shiny new dinner bucket, and generally calling attention to the trappings of the occupation" (Vaught and Smith 1980, p. 166). These crude indignities serve to dramatize to the newcomer that he or she is entering a select group that inhabits a different world. Crowded into the car taking a "man-trip" below, with personal space invaded and personal freedom of movement restricted by close proximity to other workers, the newcomer is lowered into "an environment that is noisy, dark, dusty, and illuminated only by shifting beams from miners' cap lamps. He is in truth a 'new man' . . . abjectly dependent upon these boisterous strangers to lead him around and show him what to do" (Vaught and Smith 1980, pp. 166–67). During the separation phase, newcomers are also often talked about by others as though not present.

During the transition phase, the older miners fill out their understanding of newcomers by becoming very inquisitive about details of their private lives—what they did before coming to the mine, what they do outside, and any other details they can be provoked to divulge. From this information, older miners form opinions of the new miners in terms of their potential reliability, loyalty, beliefs about mining, and capacity to control their tempers when frustrated. Colorful nicknames are typically given to newcomers during this period, reflecting gaffes or mistakes, peculiar personal traits, or stunts or incidents in which the newcomer has been involved. Examples observed included Jackhouse Jones, Smooth Mouth, Maggot Mouth, Plunger Lip, and Dynamite (Vaught and Smith 1980, p. 167). The uniqueness of these nicknames symbolizes being in another world where normal identities and names do not count. Miners can work together for years without knowing each others' real names.

The rite of "making a miner" marks the end of the rite of transition. Everyone asks everyone else whether the newcomer is a miner yet. The ritual answer is no. Once consensus is expressed on that point, the newcomer—whether male or female—is grabbed and subjected to "several swaps" on the posterior with a "capboard." The process is repeated until all groupings of miners are satisfied. This humiliating degradation confronts newcomers with the solidarity of the group and forcefully impresses upon them the necessity to conform to the group will.

Other rites of incorporation practiced by miners involve gross violations of bodily privacy. One rite involved grabbing a victim without warning, removing his trousers, coating his genitals with grease, and throwing handfuls of rock dust on the greasy genitals. Another involved a "pretty pecker" contest, in which mock judges proceeded to evaluate the genitals of five or six of the initiates to choose the "prettiest" (Vaught and Smith 1980, p. 168). Such traditions, of course, make the incorporation of women into this occupation extremely difficult. Also, in light of these traditions, it is not surprising that there have been allegations of sexual harassment by women working in the mines.

Other occupations that involve extreme bodily danger—the police (Van Maanen 1973), the military (Trice and Beyer 1984a), municipal firefighters (McCarl 1980), and smokejumpers who fight forest fires by parachuting to them (McCarl 1976)—also exhibit rather pronounced physical ordeals during rites of passage. Undoubtedly these are intended to be toughening or jolting experiences that help to prepare the recruit for the rigors of the new occupation.

Other Rites

Although rites of passage are especially prominent in occupational life, all of the other types of rites sometimes occur. Occupational subcultures use rites like those discussed in Chapter 3 to replace key members, enhance the social identities of exceptional performers, refurbish social structures, reduce conflict and aggression, and celebrate shared feelings that bind members together.

The military provide the most dramatic examples of rites of degradation. Tradition decreed that when an officer was cashiered from the U.S. Marine Corps, for example, all of his ranking officers were assembled and stood at attention to watch the ceremony. While the drums played a prolonged drumroll, the commanding officer read a formal declaration, stripped the symbols of rank from the uniform of the discredited officer, and broke his sword. He was expected to stay in place until all of the others had marched away, leaving him standing there alone (Young 1965; Joseph and Alex 1972).

In general, rites of degradation are probably confined to the most prestigious and powerful of occupations; such rites are not necessary to dissolve the relatively modest power of members of most occupations. Also notable is that members are usually ejected from an occupation by other members of that occupation, and not by the public at large or by management. Thus, the rite of degradation expresses and reinforces occupational members' control over how the tasks in their occupation are carried out. In the professions, when the competence or ethical-moral conduct of members is brought into question, committees of peers formally meet to judge the competence or conduct of that member. Such committees have various sanctions available to them, but rarely use the extreme sanction of removing the offender from the profession. Most denominations of clergy also have provisions for removing severely deficient members. In representative governments, legislators can often be removed from office, for cause, by their peers.

Rites of enhancement occur more frequently than rites of degradation in all sorts of occupational subcultures. Whenever some members are given awards or special status for their performance by their peers, the more or less elaborate rites involved enhance the social identities and power of the persons receiving them. Again, however, what distinguishes occupational rites from organizational ones is that sponsorship is by the occupation and the rite is carried out exclusively by members of the occupation. For example, members of professional associations confer the special status of fellow on those of their members who are judged by their peers in the profession as behaving consistently in especially meritorious ways. The criteria used to judge this performance will vary from one professional association to the other, but typically involve both exceptional competence and performance in the profession and service to the profession, often defined as service to the professional association itself. The new status is only conferred on those who are voted into this select group by those who are already fellows; it is often conferred with some pomp and ceremony in a dinner or other gathering of the assembled fellows.

The Pulitzer Prize for excellence in journalism and the rookie-of-the-year award in baseball are other well known examples of occupational rites of enhancement. These prizes are highly valued because the judges who make the decisions are considered by members of those occupations to be both competent and fair (Goode 1978). The Oscars given by members of the motion picture industry are not exactly occupational rites of enhancement because members of a variety of different occupations within the industry vote on the awards—many outside their particular area of competence. As a consequence, the Oscars are not uniformly valued as a sign of exceptional merit by members of these occupations, but are viewed more as the result of a popularity contest with strong political overtones. The occasional refusal of a recipient to come to the Oscar award dinner to receive the award is evidence of the lack of consensus within the occupation about this award's value.

Examples of occupational rites of renewal are common. Perhaps the most prevalent examples are committees of occupational associations that regularly meet to consider factors affecting that occupation. To the extent that problems are detected, talked about, and somehow resolved so that the existing structure is strengthened, the activities of these committees function as rites of renewal.

A more dramatic example is provided by many of the events of rodeos, which serve to refurbish the image and ideology of the cowboy. The event of calf roping, for example, reenacts the prelude to cattle roundups—branding and castration. Other events—steer wrestling, bull riding, bareback bronco riding, and wild horse racing—assert the dominance of cowboys over animals and nature. For the rodeo cowboy, these events revitalize the entire complex of activities and ideologies associated with the occupation of cowboy in its heyday.

Sometimes, when an oldtimer in a closely knit occupational subculture dies, the social structure of the occupational group is disturbed. One researcher observed members of manual craft occupations respond to this disturbance by a special kind of rite. They held auctions of the deceased's expensive, often ornate tools and gave the proceeds to members of the immediate family (Green 1965). These events served as rites of renewal because they expressed the central role of the craft in the personal and work life of the deceased and his family and celebrated the solidarity of those who remained.

A rite of conflict reduction that is effective and frequently used in work organizations is the joking relationship. Anthropologists have described the joking relationship as a mode of interaction meant to bond together persons who have problems cooperating with one another because of some structural or role conditions. The interactions are framed as humor as a device for reducing conflict. Within this framework, actions that would otherwise be an insult or attack become play or a joke that helps to dissipate endemic feelings of conflict and frustration. Often these rites of conflict reduction develop to manage relationships across occupational boundaries or between statuses within a single occupation. The example of bartenders and cocktail waitresses has already been mentioned. Researchers observed that the public exchange of ritual insults between members of these occupations reduced and managed the conflict created between them. Factors contributing to this conflict were constant interaction in a confined situation, the rushed pace of their work, the circumstance that a lower status person—the waitress—gave orders to the bartender, and the male macho myth that permeated the tavern (Spradley and Mann 1975).

Joking reduces conflict not only by releasing tensions and expressing hostilities in acceptable ways, but also because joking tends to set up and maintain social interactions. Joking by one party carries with it the expectation and license for the other to respond in kind. "Joking takes on a reciprocal quality in which the exchange of words, much like the exchange of gifts, creates and solidifies the social ties between bartender and waitress" (Spradley and Mann 1975, p. 90).

A clear-cut example of rites of integration within occupations are the annual meetings of occupational associations. All associations seem to have them and many members attend, so they must be reasonably successful events. These meetings, of course, have other avowed purposes—like educating members in the latest developments of their occupation, sharing practical ways to deliver services most effectively, and keeping members abreast of the latest knowledge relevant to their work. Whether these technical consequences are realized or not, most members will admit that they enjoy going to meetings to see old friends and acquaintances and to meet others in their occupation. Such meetings are often held in resortlike locations, families are sometimes brought along, and many of the activities, both scheduled and unscheduled, have a distinctly social flavor—luncheons, dinners, cocktail parties, receptions, and the like. Through these shared experiences, members of the occupation renew their sense of common identity and celebrate their membership in the occupation. Such meetings are more successful as rites of integration if they draw attendance from all of the subcultures within the occupation. If the occupational association boundaries are too narrow or specialized to encompass all members of the occupation, the annual meeting cannot provide an overall, integrating function.

The Academy of Management serves as a well-regarded occupational association for faculty members from the fields based on the behavioral sciences in colleges of business and management. This association, however, does not attempt to attract all types of business and management faculty to its ranks. The fields of economics, finance, accounting, and marketing are not included in the boundaries of the Academy. Thus, this association cannot integrate faculty from all of the subfields of business.

Embedded within the overall rite of the Academy's annual meeting are other rites of integration. For the last ten years or so, various divisions within the Academy of Management have held special programs before the annual meetings for Ph.D. students; more recently, divisions began holding a similar preconvention program for relatively new assistant professors. Both programs are obviously intended to help neophytes become integrated into the academic profession, as well as to acquaint them with ideas that will help them to carry out their teaching and research activities. These programs bring well-known, successful senior and junior faculty together with the neophytes to inform, inspire, and mix with them. To assure that the two groups will interact and get to know one another, small discussion groups that combine students and faculty are a prominent part of the programs.

Rituals and Taboos

The two cultural forms—rituals and taboos—are used to prescribe or pro-scribe certain behaviors at certain times; both help to manage shared anxieties. Occupational rituals are expected, detailed, standardized behaviors that members of the occupation carry out at certain times even though they have no evident technical consequences. Occupational taboos are behaviors that are compulsively avoided and viewed by members of the occupation as prohibited.

The way surgeons prepare for surgery takes the forms of a ritual:

> They "scrub down" for about seven minutes before an operation. Most doctors will argue that germs are destroyed in thirty seconds—but the ritual is faithfully upheld. To do otherwise is to "break scrub"—a signal that the surgeon is ill-prepared. By following this and other rituals, the surgeon stays within cultural boundaries that provide security during a high-risk operation. (Deal and Kennedy 1982, p. 68)

In a similar vein, young lawyers follow rituals that allay their anxieties: They look up "all past cases, the art of arguing out all possibilities are gone through, even though lawyers know that the decision will be made upon simpler—perhaps also a sounder—basis" (Hughes 1958, p. 95). The record keeping of school teachers, and the meticulous measurements of pharmacists and nurses also serve as ritualistic protection, through their punctiliousness, against possible mistakes.

Taboos often seem curious to persons outside the particular culture in which they occur. Taboos are taken for granted by members and yet the prohibited behaviors are not logically likely to produce any dire consequences. Taboos apparently emerge from historical coincidences that brought feared events and the prohibited behaviors into association with each other. Loggers have a strong taboo against trying to break up a log jam on a Sunday; one of their most revered ballads ("The Jam on Merry's Rocks") tells of the violation of such a taboo and the death of the loggers involved (Santino 1978). Cowboys insist on "meeting all circumstances with humor . . . displaying . . . stoicism . . . and have . . . taboos against complaining" (Lawrence 1982, p. 96). High-steel ironworkers' strongest taboo is against talking about their fears. "The fact that they didn't talk about their fears, if they had any, was suggestive . . . that an important understanding was not to reveal one's fears" (Haas 1977, p. 167). All of these dangerous occupations deal with realistic fears of injury or death through their taboos.

Although they may not be life threatening, other occupations face other threats and uncertainties. Boxers, who risk losing their fights and being severely injured in the process, insist that if a woman watches them train, it is a bad omen; women are therefore taboo in boxers' training camps (Weinberg and Arond 1952). Baseball players scrupulously avoid mentioning that a "no-hitter" is in progress, and also meticulously avoid dropping bats across other bats already on the ground. Tuna fishermen, who spend long periods of time at sea away from their families and homes, have a taboo against taking pictures of their families with them on long voyages. Apparently, such pictures are thought to make their owners homesick, and collectively, these fisherman try to avoid expressing this shared emotion. "One who dwells on his family or friends ashore is generally chided for being homesick or 'whipped'" (Orbach 1977, p. 274).

Stories and Songs

Through their stories and songs, members of occupations derive a sense of kinship with the past and share present common experiences that provide instructions, or inferences, about how to feel and behave in carrying out their tasks and responsibilities. These cultural forms, however, do not have the sanctity of occupational myths; they are often told, or sung, for amusement or entertainment.

"The Mines of Avondale" is probably the most famous mining ballad; it was sung by miners in barrooms, down in the mines, and in miners' homes (Dorson 1973). It describes a fire that started in a Pennsylvania mine shaft in midmorning of a September day in 1869 and swept rapidly throughout the chambers of the mine, blocking all exits. As a result, 111 miners and boy helpers perished. The song vividly portrays the dangers of injury and death in this occupation—dangers still experienced by miners over a century later.

Occupational stories often carry grim reminders of occupational hazards. An example is a story told by a high-steel ironworker to other workers:

"I remember I was on this job putting this bridge over the seaway and this stupid s.o.b. is up there and he has his hat on backwards, so this wind comes and lifts the peak up and the hat starts flying off his head. So this guy comes and reaches up with both hands and grabs his hat and goes overboard with it . . . he should have known better and left the g.d. hat drop. So there he is falling down through the air one hundred feet still holding on the g.d. helmet . . . I don't know how stupid guys can be." (Haas 1977, p. 163)

Welders tell stories that carry obvious lessons about electrocutions because of spilled coffee on the floor, and partial blindness because of cracks in helmet glass (McCarl 1974).

Stories are not, of course, always true. Some stretch the credulity of listeners, but still carry their messages about occupational uncertainties and how to manage them. A popular and funny story among Mormon missionaries expresses the idea that divine protection may save them from the dangers they face in carrying their religious message to sometimes hostile people:

Two elders, who were going from door to door distributing Mormon literature, were invited into a woman's house and urged to have a meal with her. She requested, after the meal, that they return on a specified date and time, for she was looking for the true church and wanted to be baptized. When the missionaries returned on the appointed day, she immediately asked to be baptized without further discussion. When asked why this instant conversion, she replied that she had earlier fed them poisonous food, yet they were unharmed, showing that they were true servants of the Lord. (Adapted from Wilson 1981)

Stories also communicate to members how they can deal with management so as to achieve their own ends, how the occupation fits within the organization, how members should interact with clients and customers, and generally how members should behave in their occupation. Stories are very common and probably very potent socializing devices in occupational life. They also release tensions and express shared feelings about issues.

A widely told story among railroad employees relates how a trainman got around management—at least for awhile. At the least infraction, a foreman was apt to send the offending trainman to see the general foreman, who never got to work before nine o'clock. The trainmen, however, had to report for work at seven o'clock. The story tells how a particular trainman, after discovering that the general foreman's office was air-conditioned and had comfortable chairs, deliberately engaged in some minor infraction just after reporting to work in order to enjoy an hour or more respite waiting for the general foreman in that office. After a number of these episodes, the general foreman told the trainman; "You'd get fired once a week, at least. Look, if you don't stop getting fired, and wasting all this time in my office, I am really going to fire you" (Byington 1978, p. 185). Not to be outdone, railroad engineers have their own story about an engineer who ordered high steam pressure built up and then backed the engine near the office and released the pressure so that water from the boiler spilled all over the office floor (Santino 1978).

A story airline flight attendants tell one another was related by Studs Terkel: "The stewardess asks if he'd [a male passenger] like something to drink, him and his wife. He says, 'I'd like a martini.' The stewardess asks the wife, 'Would you like a drink?' She doesn't say anything, and the husband says, 'I'm sorry, she's not used to talking to the help.'" The stewardess who told Terkel the story also reported: "When I started flying that was the first story I heard" (Terkel 1972, p. 78). Terkel interprets the story as conveying the message that the customer is always right. The story also carries a clear message about status.

In general, flight attendants feel that customers are frequently abusive to them. This feeling has been crystallized in what they call the "smile war," in which they are on one side, and the customers, on the other, expect them to smile.

> A young businessman said to a flight attendant, "Why aren't you smiling?" She put her tray back on the food cart, looked him in the eye, and said, "I'll tell you what. You smile first, then I'll smile." The businessman smiled at her. "Good," she replied. "Now freeze, and hold that for fifteen hours." Then she walked away. (Hochschild 1983, p. 27)

Many of these stories also reflect the preoccupation of members with the central issue of occupations: their members' control over their own work. The story recounted in Chapter 3 of a foreman confronting a man sitting on a keg of nails and then finding out he is not his employee is another example.

Clearly, there is no dearth of occupational stories. They are probably the most frequently used cultural form within occupations. Their ubiquity suggests that they are effective in helping members of occupations to express and share their feelings about how they manage many aspects of their work.

Symbols, Gestures, and Language

Symbols are the catchall term among cultural forms; practically any object, word, act, emblem, or personal quality can stand for and signify certain ideas and so be considered a symbol. Careful observers of human behavior have noted that it is couched in an endless array of manners, speech, etiquette, dress, and manner of eating and drinking that differ by groups and social settings (Goffman 1959). Because the term is so inclusive, symbols are present everywhere in social life. Occupational life is no exception, and we therefore cannot possibly enumerate or give examples of all of the symbols found in occupational subcultures. Instead we will focus on five of the most evident of occupational symbols: dress, titles, setting, language, and gestures.

Distinctive dress often gives notice that the wearer fills a special occupational role. In many instances, a person's wearing of an official uniform is sufficient to induce others to comply with occupationally based authority. A standard device in dramas of various kinds is to put someone in uniform or dress that gives the person a different status. Shakespeare uses this device frequently in his plays; Mark Twain employed it in *The Prince and the Pauper*. Modern television dramas often portray characters who succeed in posing as members of certain occupations—doctors, nurses, repairpersons, athletes, soldiers, or police officers—by donning the appropriate uniform. The presumption is that other people will accept the uniformed person's actions as appropriate because they are legitimated by the occupational status associated with the uniform. Thus, uniforms and other distinctive dress serve as symbols to those outside the occupation of its legitimated domain of action and authority.

Uniforms and other occupational dress are also heavily symbolic for those who wear them. In many occupations, donning the uniform becomes symbolic to members of the assumption of the occupational role, with all of its rights and obligations. Police officers feel more like police officers when they are in uniform. The same can be said for soldiers, professional athletes of all kinds, airline pilots, waiters, the clergy, and nuns. Clowns could not be clowns without their funny dress; rodeo riders would not evoke cowboys without wearing the distinctive cowboy dress; and no one would be likely to televise the hand signals of someone not in the uniform of a professional baseball umpire. Some occupations do not have an explicit uniform, but nonetheless require suitable dress. The near-black suit of undertakers and the conservative business suits of bankers are good examples.

In organizations we have studied, members of different occupational groups wore distinctly different clothing. Engineers invariably wore shirts with ties, but not suitjackets. Middle managers or above, while they would often sit at their desks in shirt sleeves, invariably put on their suitjackets when they left their offices. Both thereby differentiated themselves from each other. Shop floor employees wore coveralls distinctive to their occupational group, clothes that washed easily, or simply casual clothes if their work involved little dirt. Shop floor managers—who wore sports shirts and sweaters of sports jackets—dressed differently from both their subordinates and from higher level or staff managers.

Most women employees in these groups dressed similarly, but there were often notable exceptions, suggesting that the norms for women are less codified and less clear. In effect, the general status and occupational grouping of almost any employee was symbolized by the clothes worn.

Uniforms or special items of dress have the important technical consequence of differentiating persons of one status from those of another with whom they are dealing continually. Referees at athletic matches must wear distinctive clothing so that participants and fans can identify them readily, and also to protect themselves from being mistaken for a player and treated roughly.

Often, parts of uniforms have special significance to their wearers and others. Nurses used to wear caps that symbolized the school where they received their training. Likewise, professors have doctoral hoods that symbolize their Ph.D. degree and are worn over academic gowns on ceremonial occasions. Soldiers wear medals, patches, and other insignia to denote campaigns they participated in, special skills or recognitions received, and rank earned.

Some occupations have uniforms or dress that are worn only on certain formal occasions. The academic gown of the professor has already been mentioned; others include the wigs worn by British barristers in court and the vestments or robes worn by the clergy of some religious denominations. During World War II, British chaplains wore both a clerical collar and their military uniform. "The basic regulation [uniform] identifies the chaplain as a military officer, while the collar is a constant reminder that he is, after all, a clergyman" (Zahn 1969, p. 100).

Titles are an obvious way that people denote membership in an occupation. Lawyers list themselves as Attorneys-at-Law on their office doors and business cards. Physicians usually list their specialities as well as their degree. Thus, their office door and cards will usually say something like: John Doe, M.D., Ophthalmologist. The forms of address used in writing or talking to members of certain occupations also reflects their occupational status and the respect accorded it by others. Clergymen are typically called reverend or father, university teachers are called professor, and physicians are called doctor. In England, nurses, like nuns, are called sister.

Abbreviations following names often denote titles (and membership in an occupation) because the established professions have their own corresponding academic degrees. Thus, J.D. denotes a lawyer; M.D., a doctor; Ph.D., a professor or scientist; D.D.S., a dentist; D.V.S., a veterinarian; and so on. All of these designations have practical utility in identifying members of the occupations to others, but also have strong symbolic value in that they stand for and represent all of the skills, values, obligations, and social status attached to that occupation. Their symbolic value is evidenced by the fact that literally hundreds of new abbreviations appended to names have appeared in the last decade. Some we have encountered include Ph.B., C.A.C., A.C.E., and P.D. Surely the public at large does not know what all of these abbreviations mean. But they must have some symbolic value to those who use them within some occupational subculture. Apparently many members of occupations—like the scarecrow in *The Wizard of Oz*—feel that an abbreviation after their names signifies learning and status.

Occupational settings also potently symbolize members' tasks and status. Some of these symbols are byproducts of occupational activities. An example is the table used in a chiropractic clinic:

> Central to the adjustment area itself was the adjustment table.... Technically known as the Zenith-Thompson-Pneumatic Terminal-Point Chiropractic adjustment table, it presented a formidable appearance to the new patient. [When the viewer was] standing upright, it was seen to be constituted of four vinyl-covered sections—[called] the foreward motion headpiece, the dorsal-lumbar section, the pelvic section, and the . . . ankle support section. (Cowie and Roebuck 1975, p. 56)

Most people only have to think about a dentist's chair to have a fairly marked series of reactions.

Other settings are consciously manipulated by members of occupations to achieve certain desired effects. As already mentioned earlier in this chapter, funeral directors arrange the settings in which they work to minimize the distress of the bereaved. In a household in which death has just occurred, they escort all persons present into other rooms away from the death scene, and then quickly rearrange the setting so that it looks as ordinary as possible. After removing the body as quickly and silently as they can, they rearrange the death scene by opening shades, curtains, and windows, replacing bedding, and generally tidying up the room. In the funeral parlor itself, they try to create a comfortable, peaceful, homelike atmosphere. They furnish the rooms as if they were the living rooms of private homes, arranging the furniture to provide niches for small groups to converse. If the behaviors of any mourners become too agitated, the funeral director will escort them to another room where they are expected to stay until they compose themselves (Barley 1983).

Every craft, trade, occupation, and, recently, every technology, has its own specialized language and argot. Argot refers to the relatively informal specialized vocabulary and idioms that those in the same type of work use to communicate with one another. Occupational language may be more formal; it involves the technical terminology that those trained in the occupation must know in order to work within it. We have already given numerous examples in other sections.

It is interesting to note that the work vocabularies of manual occupations draw on a few major sources of imagery (Meissner 1976, p. 265). The names of animals provide an entire galaxy of argot. All sorts of dogs stop or hold objects, while bulls denote strength. Body parts like knuckle, elbow, belly, head, and toe are used in the names given to various tools. Other argot uses sexual imagery: objects fitting into one another—clutches, pipe fittings, shafts, and bushings—are designated male and female.

White-collar occupations also use familiar images in their argot. A whole plethora of colorful terms has grown up to refer to the actors and circumstances in takeover attempts: For example, the cowboy myth has spawned the terms *white hats, black hats, shootouts, tombstone hill,* and *code of the west* (Hirsch 1980). Other colorful language used to refer to takeovers is based on sexual conquest, warfare, or the image of the medieval knight in armor.

Gestures frequently accompany spoken language (Bocock 1974) and are sometimes used as substitutes for verbal communication when circumstances make verbal communication impossible or difficult. Sawmill workers, police officers who control traffic, and sailors are examples of occupations that substitute gestures for language. Other gestures avoid verbal confrontations, and may be more acceptable and at the same time more emphatic than words would be. Researchers described the practice of "binging" (hitting another person on the upper arm) as a way in which production workers expressed antagonism and regulated one anothers' output (Roethlisberger and Dickson 1946, p. 421). A rodeo cowboy's hat often comes off during his ride; he then walks slowly over to it, picks it up jauntily and casually, and, as a lone single figure, puts it on his head and walks out of the arena (Lawrence 1982).

Cultures of Labor Unions

Just as occupational cultures have been largely overlooked in the revival of interest in organizational cultures, so the cultures of labor unions have been largely ignored. The translation of the concept of culture to organizations has been primarily in terms of managerial or corporate cultures. Four scholarly volumes on organizational cultures have either no mention or only incidental mentions of the cultures of occupations or labor unions (Pondy et al. 1983; Schein 1985; Sathe 1985; Kilmann et al. 1985). Other popular books have focused exclusively on corporate cultures (Deal and Kennedy, 1982; Peters and Waterman 1982; Ouchi 1981). Yet unions are increasingly coming to be viewed as administrative organizations (Kochan 1980b; Child, Loveridge, and Warner 1973). Local unions, as well as national ones, evolve administrative bureaucracies similar to those in manufacturing organizations (Pugh et al. 1968).

Obviously, labor unions are organizations and can have their own cultures, like any other organization. Only a few researchers have focused on the cultures of unions. Two researchers described in some detail the rites of integration used by unions to achieve solidarity during a strike in a northeastern city in the 1940s. They included "speeches by which workers' sentiments were reinterpreted . . . in union terms, parties, entertainments, flag-waving, bands" and "can-days"—days set apart by the union for contributions for families of the strikers. These and other devices—committees, picketing, and parades—were designed to produce a festive spirit of comradeship and "to make the workers feel they were doing something to accomplish their ends" (Warner and Low 1947, p. 41).

Certain unions have been identified as consistently strike-prone on the basis of their unusually high degree of ethnocentrism: "The miners, the sailors, the longshoremen, the loggers, and, to a lesser extent, the textile workers form isolated masses, almost a 'race apart.' They live in their own separate communities . . . [they] have their own codes, myths, heroes, and social standards" (Kerr and Siegel 1954, p. 191). Another detailed analysis looked at labor unions as organizational cultures that grew from a stream of history that featured heroes (John L. Lewis), saints (Mother Jones), and martyrs (Joe Hill); and from union songs, stories, and accumulated traditions forged in battles (often physical) with owners and managers (Miller and Form 1980). A sense of ideology, identity, and common, shared understandings emerge from these cultural components.

As pointed out earlier in this chapter, occupational and union boundaries sometimes coincide—most notably in craft unions and some professional associations that bargain on behalf of members—but for other occupations and unions they do not. When occupations and unions have the same boundaries, occupational subcultures will pervade the union, and the two subcultures should merge and reinforce one another. The likely result is a strong and powerful joint culture in which genuine occupational communities are likely to emerge.

Structural Characteristics of Unions

American labor unions, despite ideological differences from management, have developed formal structures and cultural forms that resemble those of corporations. That they have so much in common can be attributed to "iron law of oligarchy" (Michels [1911] 1949), by which control in voluntary organizations tends to become more and more concentrated over time in ever smaller groups of members. In effect, even in unions, hierarchies of power and privilege emerge that resemble the status hierarchies of business organizations. Although Michels' law was derived from observations of German trade unions and political parties, similar observations have been made regarding U.S. voluntary associations in general:

> In their trade unions, professional societies, business associations, and cooperatives ... men have learned, and learned again every day, that the clauses in the constitutions which set forth the machinery for translating membership interests and sentiments into organizational purpose and actions bear little relationship to the actual political processes which determine what their organizations do. (Lipset, Trow, and Coleman 1956, p. 2)

The iron law of oligarchy works in the following way: Once an elite group of leaders emerges, it becomes self-perpetuating over time. Those in power come to be increasingly concerned and exert more and more of their efforts into maintaining their own influence, and become less and less enthusiastic about pursuing the original purposes of the association. This loss of missionary zeal also encourages the growth of bureaucracy. Feeding this development is the lack of political restraint on the emerging oligarchy by the rank-and-file members. For example, union constitutions rarely impose barriers on long tenure for their officers and typically fail to provide executive boards and conventions with enough power to balance that of union presidents (Barbash 1967; Brett 1980). And, even though union ideologies presumably favor democracy and equality, two-party political systems almost never arise in them. One usual byproduct is political apathy by rank-and-file members. In contrast, officers accumulate experience and develop bargaining skills in office; consequently, they come to possess greater political savvy than the rank and file—a fact not generally appreciated by the membership. This further entrenches officers' hold on their formal offices. All of these factors together produce oligarchy—the concentration of power in the already ruling elite.

The actions of most local unions in the United States are directed by a local president, a business agent, and an executive committee. Long tenure in these offices is common. Not only are incumbents much more likely to be elected than members who have never been officers before, but they also have much better chances to run for other offices, such as delegates to international conventions, and to be considered for appointed positions, such as international representative. At the higher levels of office holding, like international presidencies, incumbents in U.S. unions are rarely defeated in elections. Many have been in office for 20 or more years.

Overall, careers in the hierarchies of unions are not too different from those in the hierarchies of management. At the bottom of the hierarchy are union stewards—the union's counterpart to first-line supervisors. Both are caught in the middle between various groups (Sayles and Strauss 1953). In particular, union stewards must balance the expectations and demands of the specific work groups they represent with those of company and higher-level union officials. They enjoy no buffers to insulate them from the immediacy of face-to-face conflict with and between members of these groups. In contrast, higher status union officers enjoy a variety of mechanisms that shield them from the fray. For example, screening committees act as filters that prevent poor grievance cases from reaching formal grievance procedures. In addition, like the shop supervisors, union stewards have steadily lost power to higher status officers and union staff specialists over the last two decades. Thus, like line supervisors, theirs is a job with a high potential for role conflict and relatively little power.

As in management, advancement within the union hierarchy tends to be limited to a fortunate few. Although they are often ambitious to move into the officer ranks, stewards are usually prevented from such advancement by their modest occupational status and their lack of formal education. Studies have repeatedly shown that those aspirants to union office who have higher incomes and higher occupational status are more likely to win votes than are lower status aspirants (Dalton 1962).

Cultural Characteristics of Unions

The beliefs and values that characterize U.S. unions include some that are markedly different and others that overlap considerably with the beliefs and values of management. The unique history of the labor movement in the United States helps to explain why this is so. An important precursor of today's labor unions in the United States was the Knights of Labor, founded during the 19th century. Originally, membership in the Knights included practically anyone—except bankers, professional gamblers, and makers of intoxicating liquors (Kochan 1980a). The great trade union leader Samuel Gompers, however, disagreed with this policy and attacked the Knights for admitting employers. Under his leadership, American labor organized according to craft—excluding farmers because many of them were employers. Symbolically, this exclusion set an ideological foundation for the American union movement. The ideologies from which American unions subsequently grew emphasized the exclusion of all but rank-and-file workers. Also, this exclusion set the stage for a pragmatic emphasis on job security realized through control of the immediate, tangible terms and conditions of work within the craft, and later, within the industry. Because of these ideologies, U.S. unions, by and large, did not try to influence the content of work itself, but rather attempted to control the terms and conditions of work through collective bargaining and the power of the strike. Political action and ideology became secondary to concerns with work rules about hiring, firing, layoffs, apprenticeship training, allocation of work hours, and other issues concerned with job ownership (Perlman 1949). Unlike the ideologies of European socialists and the unions they fostered, American unions came to espouse the "legitimacy of both worker and employer interests in industrial society" (Kochan 1980a, p. 8) and therefore the equal accommodation of these two basic interests. The entire structure of modern American industrial relations incorporates these ideologies.

Thus, union ideologies in the United States recognize a certain commonality with the interests of management. However, while there is probably more overlap between the two groups' ideologies in the United States than in Europe, U.S. unions certainly do not hold ideologies identical with those of management. The distinctiveness of union ideologies is evident in the cultural forms and symbols used to set union members apart from management. A frequent name for unions is *brotherhood*—as in the Brotherhood of Electrical Workers and the International Brotherhood of Teamsters. One observer interprets the widespread use, both formal and informal, of this term within the labor movement as a cultural classification; namely, "the category of those who are parties to the same species of industrial subordination and who therefore have the same status position" (Turner 1977, p. 114). Since the designation of brotherhood does not occur in the context of professional associations or other occupational groups, members of brotherhoods share a unique status.

Another prevalent union symbol is wearing the union button. Wearing it is a deliberate way to symbolize the workers' capacity to act independently of superiors (i.e., management) (Turner 1971). Also, the wearing of the button links the wearer with other wearers since only those who share a common status can wear this insignia.

Like management cultures, unions are likely to have numerous subcultures. Large-scale industrial unions embrace numerous jobs and occupations, resulting in a more diverse occupational mix than in craft unions, which by definition include only variants of single occupations. Even in craft unions, however, distinctive subcultures can arise along occupational lines. A classic example was the bitter division between train engineers (the hogheads) and the conductors (the captains) that existed among railroaders well into the 1960s (Cottrell 1940; Kemnitzer 1977). Originally these two groups of workers had belonged to different unions, and their subsequent merger did not remove established subcultural differences.

Located in work situations with many jobs and occupations, industrial unions are organized around the central principle of seniority. One important result is that during bad times some workers lose their jobs to others with higher seniority in a process called bumping. Understandably, workers try to maximize the number of jobs below them in their occupational category so that they will have a reservoir of positions into which they can be bumped if it becomes necessary. Likewise they seek to minimize the number of employees qualified to bump from above into their job category. The structural conditions that follow from the organizing principle thus operate to divide members along lines of self-interests within the ranks of industrial unions. Local unions are often honeycombed with such conflictual subcultures.

Cultural Consequences

The formation and persistence of elites within unions creates conditions conducive to the emergence of distinct subcultures that set union elites apart from their rank and file. Primary among these conditions are the high levels of interactions and the interdependencies union elites have with managerial elites. During ongoing processes of negotiation and joint decision making, local union presidents, international representatives, and business agents engage in a form of cultural interchange with their counterparts in management ranks. Each side must understand the position of the other, and from such understanding, some amount of mutual influence is likely to grow. For example, "sometimes . . . top union leaders speak in the same disparaging terms that management people tend to use about the intelligence and lack of understanding of the rank and file" (Whyte 1949, p. 18).

Another factor operating to produce cultural interchange between the top officers in both unions and management is their common participation in rites of conflict reduction, generally referred to as collective bargaining (Garfield and Whyte 1950; Trice and Beyer 1984a). During these rites both sides of the table engage in ceremonial behaviors that temporarily reduce or resolve differences that cause disruptive and potentially damaging conflict. As described in Chapter 4, collective bargaining rites proceed almost as if they followed a standard script and typically require mutual cooperation between the supposedly hostile parties.

The intended, manifest, technical purposes of the union in this rite are to conduct collective bargaining negotiation and to generate explicit, visible techniques whereby they can protest and redress conditions they believe to be unfair to members. From a cultural viewpoint, these technical actions can be seen to produce expressive and unintended consequences that are not immediately apparent. For example, formal grievance procedures often become so legalistic, so cumbersome, and so slow, that management and union together generate other informal, relatively hidden procedures to manage many complaints and differences. There are many unofficial ways in which local management and union people cooperate to resolve important local issues and grievances outside the formal, written contract. The various parties usually reach an accord orally, make sure the resolution is not written down, and in this fashion, remain locally autonomous despite national industrywide contracts. The many advantages of settling disputes informally and orally are self-evident, since the resolutions take place among those close to where the conflict arises (Kochan 1980a, p. 396). Moreover these unofficial mechanisms usually deal with important tensions and conflicts employees face on their jobs, leaving less important ones to be resolved by the conventional and explicit procedures.

A keen observer noted three other ways that formal union contracts are often circumvented. First, individual workers use their own initiatives even though they are unionized: "they had a tradition of getting things done and advancing themselves privately," that is, "politicking for oneself" (Dalton 1959, p. 111). Second, managerial expediency produced unofficial settlements between first-line supervisors and union stewards; tacit exchanges reduced the filing of grievances in return for exemption from such things as dirty and monotonous tasks. Third, production pressures inevitably operated to encourage unofficial exchanges not sanctioned by the contract. These pressures encourage actions outside the formal contract. For example, we were recently told about how first-line supervisors in an automobile company covered up the absences of subordinates with unusual skills in exchange for those subordinates being willing to work extra hard and overtime when upper management exerted pressures for extra production.

Importation of Occupational Cultures

Structural Conditions

The boundaries of occupational cultures do not usually coincide with those of employing organizations. Occupational cultures usually encompass persons working in many different organizations. Also, many important occupational activities, like those of occupational associations and the network interactions of members of occupational communities, occur outside organizational boundaries. Because important parts of these cultures arise outside employing organizations, occupational cultures are vehicles for importing certain environmental influences into work organizations. Members of occupations bring their cultures with them when they take employment in an organization.

Furthermore, members of occupations possess skills that are transferable across organizational boundaries. As they move from one employing organization to another, they bring not only their skills, but their culture to each. Their mobility thus becomes a force operating to homogenize aspects of different employing organizations. These homogenizing influences can be relatively conservative, as when they protect occupational privileges and status in ways that are costly to employers and society, or they can be innovative and a positive force for change, as when scientists or technicians bring knowledge about new developments into one organization from another.

When members of occupations control recruitment, hiring, and induction into employing organizations, their cultures are especially likely to influence those of employing organizations. This usually happens in one of two ways: (1) the union takes over some of the personnel functions of employing firms, as happens in the construction industry (Stinchcombe 1959) and among the dockworkers (Pilcher 1972); or (2) members of the occupation already employed within organizations exercise practical control over personnel decisions relating to other members of their occupation, as happens among doctors in hospitals, partners in law firms, and professors in universities. In the former case, the hiring hall serves as the vehicle through which members of the occupation gain entry into employing organizations. Although the union does the actual hiring, its discretion may be severely limited by rules requiring that members with most seniority are hired first and specifying which qualifications members must have to fit certain jobs. In the second case, members of occupations succeed in establishing control over internal recruiting, hiring, promotion, and other personnel decisions; they thereby exercise considerable discretion over which members of their occupation are hired and which are retained by their organizations. They are thus in an excellent position to preselect new members to fit within or reinforce preferred elements of their occupational culture, whether or not these coincide with elements in the overall organizational culture. These practices are most prevalent among professional employees, who tend to maintain contact with other selected professionals through professional networks. Given the usual forces operating, like the attraction of similarities, the influence that professional cultures have over personnel matters is likely to operate so as to preserve the status quo.

Effects on Organizations

Complexity and diversity. In some instances, organizations consist largely of persons from the same occupational culture. This is the case in most police departments, accounting firms, law firms, primary schools, architectural firms, and some government bureaus such as air traffic control and forest management. Most organizations, however, employ persons from many distinct occupational groupings. When organizations include a diverse mix of occupations, they face difficulties in managing and coordinating conflicting subcultures that inevitably compete over resources and power. Organizational researchers have investigated these tendencies under the rubric of organizational complexity. They have found that in organizations where there are relatively large numbers of highly trained craftsmen or professionals who control their work operations, there tends to be significantly more supervisory levels to coordinate their efforts (Hage and Aiken, 1967; Meyer 1968). In effect, the complexity arising from occupational mix appears to lead to proliferation of supervisory levels. Also, other researchers found that greater occupational mix occurs in larger organizations (Beyer and Trice

1979; Blau and Schoenherr 1971), although more recent longitudinal research on universities indicates that growth itself is not a sole determinant of the amount of occupational mix (Cullen 1986).

Occupational mix and accompanying cultural diversity also affect organizational decision making. When collective decisions become necessary, the ideologies and vested interests of specific occupational cultures are likely to surface. For example, in university faculties there are at least four decision points at which occupational subcultures usually emerge: (1) hiring decisions; (2) tenure decisions; (3) curriculum changes; and (4) resource allocations. Of these, curriculum changes may be the most revealing of cultural diversity derived from occupational mix, since the decisions made either enhance or threaten each occupation's access to the major raw materials in a university—namely, students. Severe internecine conflicts are thus usually expected and taken for granted in curriculum changes and the changes made may operate to reflect power shifts in the occupational mix of faculty rather than the needs of students.

Dual loyalties.   Since occupations command such allegiance from their members, the question naturally arises as to whether the presence of occupational cultures dilutes the allegiance of members of those occupations to their employing organizations. For example, a prominent sociologist argued that professionals belonged to two camps—cosmopolitans whose main orientation and presumably allegiance was to their larger profession outside the employing organization, and locals whose main orientation was to their immediate employing organization (Gouldner 1957). He found that individual professionals could be classified as having one of these orientations, but the findings of later research questioned the underlying assumption that professionals were not simultaneously concerned about both their larger professional community and their employing organizations.

For example, one study examining the organizational and occupational commitments of a large sample of personnel managers found that the two types of commitment were positively, not negatively, related (Ritzer and Trice 1969a). Furthermore, most personnel managers expressed about equal commitment to their occupations and organizations. Similarly, many analysts have expressed concern that organizational members who are loyal to their unions may therefore be less loyal to their companies. Research indicates that dual loyalty, however, is more prevalent than are competing loyalties. Researchers found a positive relationship between union and organizational commitments among unionized workers in a newspaper and in a pharmaceutical company (Fukami and Larson 1984). Another study found that among workers who perceived the union-management climate in their companies as positive, union and company commitments were positively related, but among workers who perceived the union-management climate as negative, these two forms of commitment were negatively related (Angle and Perry 1986). Thus, whether or not employees feel dual loyalties or experience competing allegiances may well depend on the general climate of conflict or cooperation between occupations, unions, and employing organizations.

Relative potency. Another obvious question that arises is how much control occupational subcultures exert over their members compared to that exerted by overall organizational cultures. Three simple structural indexes into the relative potency of an occupational subculture are the number of occupational members present in the organization, its relative isolation from other occupations, and the multiplicity of cultural forms that carry that occupation's ideologies. The number of members is important because only one or two members of an occupation cannot provide enough support for one another to form a potent subculture. Such relatively isolated occupational members are likely to be treated like tokens (Kanter 1977). On the other hand, more than a handful of members of the same occupation can probably provide enough support to one another to form a viable subculture. Second, the more their roles enable them to interact with other occupational members in relative isolation from the rest of the organization, the more powerful their occupational identity and subculture is likely to be. Interaction inevitably includes cultural content, and such exclusive interactions thus serve to repeatedly affirm and reinforce occupational subcultures. Third, when occupations manifest many different cultural forms, they are likely to have greater effects on their members than when they do not. Well-defined rites of passage; numerous and popular occupational myths, heroes, jargon, rituals and taboos—all help to sustain the sense making and continuance of an occupational subculture.

Another way to assess the potency of occupational subcultures is to consider the arduousness of demands involved in attaining and maintaining membership in the occupation. For example, some occupations require much longer and more arduous training than others. Others require members to face constant danger. When members increase their investments by meeting arduous demands, they experience increased commitment to the identity that made those demands. A study of utopian communities found that six factors cumulatively increased members' commitment to these communities: sacrifice, investment, renunciation, communion, mortification, and surrender (Kanter 1968, p. 499). All these factors have some relevance to the strength of occupational commitment.

First, the presence of sacrifice in some form requires that members give up something as a price of membership. Such sacrifices make membership more valuable and meaningful. The time, the extent of ordeal, and the sacrifice in personal resources involved in mastering a body of occupation-based knowledge—all symbolize the extent members are willing to go to belong to that occupation. Since these sacrifices require investments in the occupation, leaving it after making them becomes painful and costly. Such investments become "side-bets" (Becker 1960), which accumulate unobtrusively as the member continues through socialization and into early stages of occupational life. Commitment continues to grow as members find themselves renouncing relationships that might be disruptive to their occupational life and success. Friendships with persons of lesser status, parenthood, and even marriage may be given up as unsuitable or interfering. As the member continues to work in the occupation, opportunities to participate in occupational rituals and regularized contacts with other members of the occupation accumulate. These activities provide a sense of communion with other members of the occupation. Finally, members of many occupations experience varying degrees of mortification as part of their socialization and early work experiences. Those for miners and high-steel ironworkers have already been described earlier in this chapter. Varying degrees of mortification are also prominent in the socialization of athletes, firefighters, military personnel, and other physically demanding or dangerous occupations. The sixth factor—surrender—is likely to occur only in religious or other morally based occupations since it requires believing that transcendent power and meaning reside in the occupation. In general, although such beliefs occur in moral movements, the awe and wonder required for an attitude of surrender to the collectivity is absent from most occupational life.

Relations among subcultures.   Understanding organizational behavior requires analyzing the subunits of the organization and their relations with one another (Tushman 1977). Most such analyses focus on units grouped together according to task and reporting relationships. However, as this and the previous chapter have emphasized, it is the subcultures that emerge within organizations—which may or may not coincide with the boundaries of subunits—that probably matter most. Also, of course, occupational subcultures may not fit neatly within the prescribed boundaries of subunits drawn by organizational designers. Thus, we would argue, understanding organizations requires analyzing the relations of subcultures and not just subunits with each other.

In particular, seeing organizations as constellations of separate occupational subcultures focuses attention on the processes of accommodation that permit coordination of effort and joint decision making despite differences in objectives and preferences and strong desires by occupations to control their own work. Some analysts therefore see organizations as examples of negotiated order in which compromise and accommodation are *the* basic social processes (Strauss et al. 1964; Strauss 1978). Coordination arises from continual series of informal, temporary accommodations that are reached by persons representing various occupational subcultures. Studies have revealed how physicians, psychologists, social workers, and nurses negotiate informally over how to handle patients (Strauss 1978); how construction workers work out compromises when it is necessary to hold off some tasks until others are completed (Applebaum, 1981); and, how managers collude to transform what were supposed to be surprise inspections into quite predictable ones along agreed-upon routes (Dalton, 1959). "The negotiated order in any given day could be conceived of as the sum total of the organization's rules and policies, along with whatever agreements, understandings, pacts, contracts, and other working arrangements currently obtain" (Strauss 1978, pp. 5–6). This perspective emphasizes the temporariness of social agreements. The informal contracts reached are understood to have a limited time span. Also, negotiation processes that occur take many forms: overt or covert, periodic or extraordinary, standardized or novel, general or specific. Whatever their form, the agreements reached enable members to get on with the activities involved in playing their parts in organizational life. These agreements range from explicit ones that specify the ways in which tasks will be coordinated for a specific time period to tacit understandings that are ill-formed and vague in content and duration.

Other analysts have described these negotiations as "integration through a political process" (Bucher and Stelling 1969, p. 12). "From a political perspective, decisions are *not* made in a pattern of rational compromise, accommodation, and bargaining . . ." (Tushman 1977, p. 207, [emphasis added]). Rather, decisions made in a political arena are often compromises reached by partisans of different interests. In such circumstances, who is involved in making a decision affects its content, and different viewpoints and issues are focused on at different times. In this way, a variety of interests can be attended to over time. The resulting decision processes have been called "disjointed incrementalism," "muddling through," and "garbage cans" to emphasize their nonrational, emergent character (Cohen, March, and Olsen 1972; Lindblom 1959, 1965; Braybrooke and Lindblom 1963).

Ideological and other divisions between occupational subcultures can also be of benefit to organizations. The diversity they incorporate can help organizations to cope with the diversity of their environments. For example, a study of the adaptation of hospitals to a doctors' strike concluded that the hospital with the most pronounced internal divisions adapted rapidly and comprehensively (Meyer 1982a). These issues will be addressed again in subsequent chapters.

SUMMARY

Modern organizations are multicultural. Although some organizations lack detectable overall cultures, all but the smallest include evident subcultures. Distinctive ideologies, cultural forms, and practices of subcultures make them differ noticeably from overall organizational cultures and from each other. Factors encouraging the development of subcultures include differential interaction, shared experiences, similar personal characteristics, and social cohesion.

Occupations provide the basis for the most highly organized, distinctive, and pervasive subcultures in work organizations. Because the boundaries of occupations span organizations, occupational cultures represent both internal and external influences. Also, in various ways, occupations compete with management for control over members' work-related behaviors.

Occupations form around defined, interrelated tasks that members come to feel they should have the exclusive right to perform. Over time, members create self-definitions, ideologies, and values that help to sustain their identity with an occupation and to justify their rights. Member-controlled training programs and occupational associations help to systematize the work and their claims. Rules and codes are sometimes developed to ensure qualified and ethical performance of duties.

Members of occupations often share a consciousness of kind, use one another as reference points, share unusual emotional demands, develop favorable self-images and identities from their work, share extensive social relations, and develop ethnocentrism. Occupations with all of these characteristics tend to have very influential subcultures called occupational communities.

The ideologies of occupations and those of managers are in conflict in some respects and have underlying commonalities in others. The primary conflict concerns control over how work is done. The mechanisms for control that specific occupations and organizational managements have established, and the scarcity and value of occupational skills, are likely to determine the outcomes of this conflict in specific organizations. The mutual dependencies of the two groups on each other and the overlap in some of their values and practices moderates their competition for control.

Occupational socialization occurs both formally and informally. It begins when people enter an occupation and continues throughout their work lives. Entering an occupation includes five processes: attraction, access, adjustment, identification, and commitment. All of the cultural forms identified in Chapter 3 are common in occupational subcultures and help to socialize members and maintain their commitment. Myths, rites, rituals, taboos, stories, songs, and other forms also help members to express and deal with the emotional demands of their work. Occupational ideologies concern the way work is done and what it seeks to accomplish. These ideologies usually also provide the justification that the work or services performed has important social value.

Like other organizations, labor unions can have distinctive cultures. When occupational and union boundaries coincide, the occupational subculture will pervade the union. When they do not, the same conflicts identified as occurring between management and occupation can arise within unions. In general, unions, like other organizations, tend to become bureaucratized and to develop strong hierarchies of power and privilege. Union officials, who have substantial contact with members of management, tend to develop their own subcultures within unions.

Because of their history, U.S. unions have ideologies that generally emphasize job security, controlling the conditions of work, and seniority. Collective bargaining and contracts focus on these issues. Many other issues are handled informally at a local level.

Because the boundaries of occupations and employing organizations do not usually coincide, occupations import environmental influences into organizations. Some of these influences are conservative; others help to produce innovation and change. Seeing organizations as constellations composed of discrete occupations and their subcultures helps to expose processes of conflict, assimilation, and accommodation within them.

6

Other Subcultures in Organizations

Many other differences besides occupational ones can give rise to subcultures in organizations.[1] Work demands encourage and allow social interaction among some people and not others. Organizational structures divide people into work units and establish various status levels. Memberships and identification with social groupings that transcend organizational boundaries are carried into organizational life. Mergers, internal discontents, and other factors breed countercultures that resist and even oppose the dominant cultures in organizations. Because so many potential sources of subcultures exist, few organizations lack subcultures. And, because of differences in their ideologies and practices, the presence of multiple subcultures tends to create conflict within organizations. This conflict is often disruptive and difficult to manage but, like any diversity, can have some positive outcomes if managed well. Indeed, there is currently a rising sentiment that increased diversity, especially in terms of gender, race, and nationality, "is an opportunity and not a problem" (Cox 1991, p. 42). In order to realize such positive sentiments, however, managers will need to recognize, understand, and learn to manage the conflicts that arise from subcultural differences.

Subcultures as Sources of Conflict

An example of how damaging the conflict between subcultures can be was observed in a hospital laboratory (Brown 1983). An experienced black laboratory technician had started a small, temporary laboratory when the hospital first opened. She hired six other technicians; most were black and had only high

---

[1]Portions of this chapter expand ideas originally published elsewhere (Trice and Morand 1991).

school degrees. When the hospital later expanded its services, a young white woman was hired to manage and expand the laboratory. She hired only certified technologists; certification required a college degree. All of the new hires had college degrees and were white. Three years later,

> the laboratory had expanded to a staff of fifteen, which was split into two antagonistic groups. One group, led by the original supervisor included the original staff and other minorities (six blacks, a Polynesian, and a first generation Jewish immigrant). All these members of the "old guard" were technicians, with less professional training than the technologists. The other group [led by the white supervisor] included the five newly hired white technologists. (Brown 1983, p. 180)

Soon it became obvious that the group of technicians was rapidly becoming an angry counterculture, while the technologist group was a reflection of the dominant managerial culture. This became evident when the laboratory jobs were reclassified to correspond with the system's other health care facilities. In the new classification, the job titles and definitions of the technicians were unchanged, while those of the technologists were upgraded. Several of the technicians received no raises, causing an outcry of racial bias: "Now new people with less experience get more pay for doing the same work as the Old Guard" (Brown 1983, p. 181). The technicians became a clear counterculture when they began to retaliate and show defiance by slowdowns and minor insubordination. The white supervisor responded with disciplinary actions. She formally disciplined the original supervisor for eating lunch in the laboratory. In addition she transferred a member of the counterculture against her will, causing suits against the hospital for racial and religious discrimination.

The management of the hospital subsequently caved in to the Old Guard (the counterculture), and settled out of court, which caused much rejoicing and planning for new attacks on the hospital's management among the Old Guard. "Meanwhile laboratory performance declined seriously. Tests were misperformed, samples were lost, and the medical staff increasingly protested low quality work ..." (Brown 1983, p. 182). In this example, differences in racial and ethnic background, education, status, and tenure in the organization became the basis for the growth of different sets of interests and ideologies. The actions of the laboratory manager and the personnel department served to heighten the differences and create grievances that solidified the technician subculture and turned it into a counterculture.

Subcultures and even countercultures can, however, have positive effects on organizations. The military provides two examples:

> ... in the late 1950's Brigadier General Hutton (faced with official opposition based on written agreements among the Department of Defense, the Army, and the Air Force) developed the armed helicopter. Starting with baling wire and lashing machine guns to the frame, a group of young, middle-ranked officers evolved the quick-strike mobile air cavalry.... The Army's air force is now the third largest in the world. (Zald and Berger 1978, p. 824)

This counterculture violated rules, procedures, and even formal orders and thus challenged the efficacy of existing practices.

Similarly, the famous Flying Tigers of the late 1930s became highly successful by becoming a counterculture. The group's orders were to use fighter planes, as was traditional then, as an auxiliary to infantry and artillery movements. They operated in the China theatre as World War II approached. Most members initially came from the disintegrating Chinese Air Force, but a few Americans served with them. They were under the command of U.S. General Claire Chennault. Deliberately defying orders from above, Chennault and his group developed and put into practice fighter pilot tactics. They engaged enemy planes at every opportunity and perfected the techniques of air-to-air combat. To celebrate their differentness, they employed such dramatic symbols as painting flying tiger sharks on their planes and wearing cowboy boots instead of regulation military boots (Love 1964).

The counterculture that developed the armed helicopter helped to justify the development of the Army's own air force. This counterculture exaggerated the ideology of its parent organization, the Army, in opposition to the official ideologies embodied in a joint-services agreement. Official ideologies provided for reliance on a separate organization—the U.S. Air Force—for air support of ground combat. The formation of the counterculture of the Flying Tigers also incorporated an exaggerated version of general military ideology. Neither differed from the general military culture in its aims; they disagreed with prescribed ways to achieve those aims and, by defying military authority, succeeded in demonstrating the efficacy of what they believed in. In the case of the Flying Tigers, the ethnic differences and national loyalties of members probably encouraged the growth of countercultural sentiments in support of General Chennault's radical ideas.

All of the factors discussed in Chapter 5 as encouraging the formation of subcultures contribute to the potential for conflict between subcultures. Differential interaction leads to different sets of people developing different understandings of their worlds. Shared experiences within groups provide members with materials for sense making that others do not share. Similar personal characteristics provide a ready basis for interaction and shared interpretations among some people and not others. Such similarities also tend to attract people to one another in the first place and contribute to a common sense of identity. Social cohesion reinforces cognitive and emotional bonds between subgroup members and tends to raise barriers between them and others, who are seen as outsiders or different. As distinctive ideologies, norms, and other cultural practices coalesce from these similarities, they are viewed by those who hold to them as natural and right. Other ideologies, norms, or practices that differ are therefore likely to be seen as strange or wrong. Thus, when the formation of organizations brings the substance or forms of different subcultures into contact, misunderstandings and conflict may arise. Decisions about such matters as the allocation of resources, future goals, changes in practices, and criteria used to evaluate performance seem especially likely to promote conflict because they can be seen as affecting the relative welfare of groups.

Much of the time, however, subcultures coexist relatively peacefully in organizations because practices have grown up to promote mutual tolerance and minimize direct confrontations (Meyer and Rowan 1977). It is when organizations must apparently choose among different subcultural beliefs, values, or norms as the basis for action that the differences become salient and subcultural conflicts surface. As the examples already given illustrate, however, such conflicts are not always damaging to the performance of organizations. Conflicts can give rise to useful innovations.

As already described and discussed in Chapter 5, occupational subcultures can come into conflict not only with management, but also with each other. It is important to recognize that other groupings of individuals also provide bases for the growth of subcultures and thus for the generation of subcultural conflict that has both functional and dysfunctional consequences.

Groups as Bases for Subcultures

Groups in organizations are often described as formal or informal. The distinction refers to the origins of groups. Informal groups arise spontaneously without direction from formal authorities. Formal groups are those that arise because formal authorities group people in certain ways. Managers thus have more control over the formation of formal groups than informal ones. Informal groups often interact on a face-to-face basis. But informal groups with members who never see one another are also possible. Members of an informal computer network are an example (Finholt and Sproull 1990). Similarly, some formal groups interact on a face-to-face basis while others do not.

Both kinds of groups are common in all kinds of work organizations. Both have important influences on their members and thus on organizational functioning. As one observer put it, "Management . . . is not related to single workers but always to working groups. . . . workers have, whether aware of it or not, formed themselves into a group with appropriate customs, duties, routines, even rituals . . ." (Mayo 1945, p. 81).

Informal Groups

Friendship groups. The work units that are formally created by management often become the basis for informal friendship groups. However, boundaries of the two do not always coincide. A single formal work group may have more than one friendship group within it, or only one friendship group from which some of the formal group members are excluded. Research showed that high-status employees in work organizations tend to base their friendships on status characteristics and symbols, while those in lower status positions tend to base friendships on proximity (Lincoln and Miller 1979). For both, however, individual preferences for friends are channeled and restricted by formal arrangements.

Friendship groups engage members' personal interests, liking, and social intimacy. Because friends significantly affected people's evaluations of fellow employees on culturally relevant criteria, one set of researchers concluded that friendship choices are sources of workplace cultures (Krackhardt and Kildoff 1990).

The existence of cultural forms like ritualized humor and joking relationships are one sign of subcultures in friendship groups. They clearly demonstrate the existence of shared understandings. In routine factory work, for example, workers often use horseplay to help to make their days interesting and to cement friendship groupings. In one factory, at the same time each day a worker playfully "stole" a banana or other fruit from the lunch pail of another; the mock theft permitted playful scuffling between the workers involved. The mock dispute then often spread to disagreement over how far to open the windows, with different workers alternately going over to open or shut them (Roy 1960). In another factory, machinists secretly painted the controls of a fellow worker with dye; when the worker used his hands to operate the machine, they picked up the dye and he then inadvertently spread it to his clothes and face, causing much merriment in the group. Different workers were the butt of this joke at different times (Boland and Hoffman 1983). One observer noted that such jokes and the eruption of laughter they produce represent a shared understanding and temporary alliance between the initiator of the joke and the audience, directed against the joke's target (Dwyer 1991). We suspect that such jokes are more likely to be initiated by powerful members of groups and directed against less powerful ones—like newcomers.

Such ritualized displays seem childish and senseless unless we look at them as expressions of strong underlying cultural consensus among group members. By such horseplay a group affirms that its members are so strongly bound together that they will tolerate certain indignities from one another. The horseplay also sets status limits; anyone in the group could presumably be the target and is thus informed not to feel superior to other group members. Such antics also help to define the boundaries of the group (Radcliffe-Brown 1940; Lundberg 1969). The imminent acceptance of new group members is often marked by playing such a joke upon them (Boland and Hoffman 1983). These same jokes would never be used on strangers to the group, who, it is understood, would be subject to another class of jokes altogether.

Gossip also helps to maintain group boundaries by asserting group values and marking those who are insiders from those who are outsiders (Gluckman 1963b; Sparks 1983). The revelations of personal, intimate details that gossip often entails mark the object, the sender, and the receiver as part of a group of persons who care about what happens to one another. The evaluations of group members of these revelations also communicate shared group values about the behaviors in question. Gossip differs from the stigmatization often directed by group members against outsiders in that the discussion is much more detailed, thorough, and widespread throughout the group.

Cliques. When group members exchange more than friendship among themselves, they often form cliques. Cliques differ from friendship groups in their calculated power seeking; members consciously use collective resources to further both individual and collective aims. Cliques are smaller than friendship groups, and members typically resemble one another closely in social characteristics (Tichy 1973). Cliques also give social support in job activities, informally socialize newcomers, help members to escape unpleasant situations or annoyances, and offer defensive protection against dominant elites.

A good example is provided by an instance where corporate headquarters sent auditors to a location to determine the extent to which a specific policy about the use of trucks had been implemented (Dalton 1959). A clique of middle managers supported one another in misleading the auditor and successfully evading the policy by deliberately moving and camouflaging trucks so that there appeared to be more trucks than actually existed. In this way, they were able to use money allocated for trucks in their budgets for ends they had decided were more important; namely, to boost their sales. The implicit understandings that united these managers in evading official corporate policy provided a good basis for the development of a subculture. Unfortunately, the account of the particular incident is not complete enough for us to judge whether such a subculture already existed or developed later.

Cabals and coalitions.   Cabals and coalitions differ from cliques in that members are dissimilar in social characteristics and are drawn together by mutual interests. Cabals and coalitions differ from one another in their size and duration. The term *cabal* is usually used to describe a small number of individuals who join together to realize some temporary, highly explicit objective through political maneuvering (Bacharach and Lawler 1981). Because the group's purposes are narrowly defined, because its life is usually short, and because members have little in common to begin with, cabals do not provide fertile ground for the growth of subcultures. They are unlikely to produce the close understandings and implicit structure that is characteristic of cliques.

Coalitions differ from cabals in that they last for longer periods and can include a large number of individuals, or even groups. Coalitions are "interest groups which are committed to achieving a common goal" (Bacharach and Lawler 1981, p. 9) that requires concerted member action (Stevenson, Pearce, and Porter 1985). Coalitions emerge when the bargaining and negotiations of cliques and cabals uncover common ideologies and subjective definitions among them (Druckman 1977). It is these bargaining activities that, in turn, produce the political strength and power needed to influence an organizations' culture and goals. Coalitions of students supported and thus helped to bring about radical changes at Reed and Swarthmore Colleges during the 1920s (Clark 1972), and at many colleges and universities during the civil rights and antiwar movements of the 1960s and 1970s. Most recently, coalitions of university students and faculty have sought to bring about curricular changes reflecting multiculturalism. Because the formation of coalitions often rests upon some discovered common understandings, they provide more fertile ground for the formation of subcultures than do cabals.

Formal Groups

Technology and work flows.   The technologies used in work processes form groupings of persons by similarity of task, interdependence of tasks, and physical proximity. Technologies may encourage or discourage the formation of subcultures.
They involve not only machines, tools, equipment, and computers, but also the
knowledge that people employ when they use them to produce a product or
service (Woodward 1980). Some technologies allow people lots of opportunity
for informal interaction because their hands are busy, but the work does not
require much concentration; other work demands the entire attention of individuals. Obviously, features of the work that permit interaction and put people in
close proximity or allow them to move around so they can contact one another
are more conducive to the formation of subcultures than the reverse.

Management often has some discretion in which technologies to employ,
and how to deploy them within the work setting. Management also decides which
workers should be grouped together for the administrative purposes of supervision and coordination; workers are designated as belonging to certain subunits
under the supervision of certain managers (Mintzberg 1979b). Depending on the
work to be done and many other factors, these formally created groups typically
vary in size from two or three to over thirty workers. Some features of such formal groups that make them especially likely or unlikely to become subcultures
are interdependence of tasks, group-level evaluation and rewards, and anxieties
associated with uncertainty.

Task interdependence means that workers depend on one another for the
completion of tasks, which creates power differences and potential conflict
among them. Three types of task interdependence have been identified: pooled,
sequential, and reciprocal (Thompson 1967). Pooled interdependence is the
lowest level of interdependence; workers depend on one another only in the
sense that they share resources. A typing pool or the lawyers in a law firm are
examples of pooled interdependence. In sequential interdependence, one set of
workers must complete their tasks before another group can do theirs. Assembly
line manufacturing is the classic example, but many other kinds of tasks involve
some degree of sequential interdependence. For example, maintenance people
must repair defective equipment before workers can use it again. Work that involves the continuous alternation of who is working on the task creates reciprocal interdependencies. Hospitals and medical services in general are classic examples of reciprocal interdependence. Doctors, nurses, and medical technicians
of various kinds provide services for patients at various times. Thus the performance of each is partially dependent on what one of the others has or has not
done for the patient.

The greater the interdependence, the greater the power enjoyed by groups
that others are dependent on. Maintenance men in a French factory acquired
power over both workers and management through their exclusive control over
the knowledge of how to repair machinery (Crozier 1964). Computer programmers in a group of English department stores that was just beginning to comput-
erize its operations became very powerful and developed their own subculture

(Pettigrew 1973). Elaborate self-serving ideologies and myths grew up within this group to justify their newly found power. For example, they came to believe, and propagated the myth, that they were exclusively qualified to perform computer-related tasks and must be free of all time constraints in order to operate effectively. To the degree that task interdependence creates clear power differences and intergroup conflict, it encourages the growth of subcultures that divide workers along the same lines.

Group rewards probably also stimulate the development of subcultures. Sports teams provide a clear example in which the evaluation of the group's performance has powerful effects on individual members. Football players on the teams that play in the Super Bowl make a lot of money and have an opportunity to make still more if they win. When sports writers refer to teams as having personalities, they are really describing distinct team subcultures.

Another factor encouraging subculture formation is a high level of uncertainty. People become anxious in the face of uncertainty and tend to develop shared ways of dealing with shared uncertainties. Extremely threatening uncertainties create strong emotional bonds and shared beliefs among those facing the same threats. As pointed out in Chapter 5, workers in dangerous occupations develop taboos. People in threatening circumstances also develop strong irrational beliefs that are widely shared and not questioned. During World War I, the famed Rainbow Division developed a myth that a rainbow always appeared in the sky to accompany their attacks on the enemy; to make sure, they carried rainbow symbols with them on their gun barrels and other equipment, even though carrying such symbols had been prohibited (Linton 1924). The presence of their symbol apparently reassured the members of this division, who shared the hope that it would protect them from harm and assure their victory.

Departmentalization. Departments may be created administratively along various lines, such as function, geographic location, or product or service produced (Woodward 1980). Departments or other subunits based on function or geographic location are more likely to produce strong subcultures than product-based departments. After all, grouping workers by function puts people together who already have similar occupational interests, ongoing experiences, and educational backgrounds. A common supervisor, social interaction, shared identities, and shared experiences facilitate the elaboration of occupational ideologies already shared into unique departmental subcultures within organizations. One common result is the tendency for such groups to develop a kind of ethnocentrism, in which group goals and identity become all important and cooperation with other groups is minimal (Mintzberg 1979b). In the Oregon Fish Commission, hatchery workers ignored the recommendations of biologists; in meetings and even in social activities, each set of specialists stuck to themselves, and only the biologists attended the research division picnic (Price 1968). A study of industrial firms in the 1960s found that "sales and production were 'natural enemies' of each other; that production was also highly critical of R & D" and that different levels of management were more or less critical of production, finance and accounting, and sales (Perrow 1970, p. 88). A more recent study of Sears Roebuck found a gulf between the sales part of the organization and the buyers and corporate staff (Katz 1987). In some large organizations, members can tell which function other members belong to by the clothes they wear. To the extent that functional groups build upon shared understandings to develop their own unique cultural forms and norms, they are subcultures.

Even within functional groupings, subcultures may emerge based on finer distinctions between products produced or work performed that presumably produces differences in point of view. As mentioned in Chapter 5, employees in Silicon Valley computer firms not only distinguished between the functional groupings of engineering and marketing, but also between hardware and software types in each group (Gregory 1983).

Many organizations develop product-based groupings and hybrid forms like matrix structures to overcome the lack of coordination and cooperation often evident in functionally departmentalized structures. To the extent that such structures force or encourage interaction with persons with dissimilar rather than similar experiences and backgrounds, they discourage the formation of subcultures along departmental lines.

All kinds of geographic groupings probably encourage subcultures. The relative geographic isolation of groups from the rest of the organization channels interaction to others in the same unit. The greater the isolation the more members are forced into exclusive interaction with each other. Some kinds of work requires workgroups to be away from the parent organization to perform their tasks, and others require groupings of workers to be dispersed to serve scattered clientele. Conditions that force or encourage workers to interact exclusively with each other are highly likely to produce subcultures. For example, forest rangers develop tight subcultures even though they don't see one another very often (Kaufman 1976). Similar feelings of social isolation can arise from feeling different from the surrounding societal culture and will tend to produce strong bonds with others seen as similar. Expatriates of various kinds are notorious for sticking together.

Line and staff distinctions.   Like functional groupings, line and staff distinctions have traditionally tended to undermine cooperation and coordination as each group develops its own subcultural values and norms. Departments that produce the main outputs of the organization, whatever they are, are considered line departments. In manufacturing organizations, production, sales, and service are line departments. Traditional staff departments are those that provide services that help to maintain the organization itself. Internal accounting, finance, information systems, and personnel departments are examples. Each group usually feels superior to the other and develops beliefs and rationales to support its superiority. Membership in each is carefully marked by different dress, language, grooming, and behaviors. Line managers tend to resist staff recommendations as impractical or unrealistic because they represent threats to their exclusive power and control; staff experts, who are often powerless to enforce their recommendations, respond with disdain for the backwardness and ignorance of line managers (Dalton 1959). "Street" cops in the New York City police think of themselves as very different from the planners and computer specialists hired by "management" cops to rationalize work procedures (Reuss-Janni 1983).

Because they have different responsibilities, pressures, and bailiwicks to protect, line and staff managers often fight over organizational resources and over rules. The more freedom staff members are given to intervene in line affairs, the more they are feared and resented by line management. The less autonomy staff has and the more they are required to sell their services to line managers, the more jealousy and resentment staff members feel (Jackall 1988, p. 34). Matters in which staff think they have some measure of control seem to produce especially sharp conflict. To the alarm and dismay of industrial relations specialists, line supervisors often develop their own collective interpretations of the union contract in collusion with the local union (Miller and Form 1980). Purchasing agents will ritualistically "go through the motions" of complying with line managers' requests for materials that they know are unavailable rather than take the time and risk associated with explaining the true situation to the line managers (Strauss 1962). Other examples of issues that produce sharp line and staff conflict and provide ready materials for subcultural interpretation include quality control, safety regulations, and other administrative constraints placed on managers that are administered by staff experts.

Hierarchical differences.   Nearly all formal organizations have a hierarchy of statuses that specifies who has authority over whom. The status differences so created can also provide a basis for the formation of subcultures. The most basic distinction in status is that between supervisors and those they supervise. The formal authority accorded supervisors tends to create social distance between them and their subordinates. Supervisors can be friendly with subordinates, but the two are not equals, and thus supervisors are generally not part of informal friendship groups that arise among their subordinates. However, supervisors can be part of, and even leaders in, subcultures that include their subordinates, as the examples of the military countercultures described earlier in this chapter illustrate.

The physical separation of supervisors from each other that is usual in most organizations militates against their forming their own, organizationally specific subcultures. They simply do not interact enough with their peers to make it likely. There are, however, exceptions; military officers are perhaps the most prominent one. In all but the smallest organizations there is, however, one rank of management whose members do interact extensively with one another. This is what is often called the top management team or the dominant elite—those top managers who together make the key decisions for an organization (Thompson 1967).

Research observing top managers shows that they spend a great deal of time interacting with each other. This interaction occurs both in informal, unscheduled face-to-face encounters and in relatively formal meetings of larger groups. Although some time is spent with immediate subordinates, and some top managers make it a policy to tour their organizations and talk to other workers, it seems fair to observe that most top managers interact most frequently with their own kind. Moreover, they tend to spend a great deal of this interaction in oral communications. "Managers seem to cherish 'soft' information, especially 'gossip,' hearsay, and speculation" (Mintzberg 1975, p. 52). As already discussed, such communications enhance the cohesiveness of subcultures.

One description of managerial life in General Motors dramatically describes the posh isolation of those who spend their time in the executive suites of large corporations (Wright 1979). The entrance to the fourteenth floor was protected by a thick glass door that was controlled electronically by a receptionist. "The hallways were awesomely quiet and usually deserted" (Wright 1979, p. 20). Undoubtedly such surroundings help the occupants of the offices to believe in their own importance, and also insure they are rarely bothered by those of lesser status. In effect, the physical isolation of top managers can become social insulation (Kanter 1977). Top managers may end up surrounded by flatterers who react to their every word and insulate them from realities. Thus top management can build an unrealistically self-approving subculture.

Other factors already mentioned also encourage the formation of subcultures among top-level executives. First, these executives probably do need to meet and talk to each other frequently to keep in touch with what is going on in their environments and in their organizations. Observers find that executives value information obtained orally over that obtained in formal reports, probably because they often find they need information that is not in the formal information system or because they need more up-to-date information than the formal system can provide (Mintzberg 1979b; Feldman and March 1981).

Second, everyone agrees that top managers deal with the most uncertain sets of problems in their organizations. When lower levels of management don't know how to handle a problem, it is passed up the hierarchy (Mintzberg 1979b). Top managers are also responsible for dealing with present and future uncertainties produced by the environment that may affect their organizations. Social trends, consumer preferences, economic and political conditions—all of these and many other factors must figure into how top managers make decisions. Like other people, top managers need the reassurance provided by ideology and culture to enable them to cope with these uncertainties. Managers, especially those at upper levels, have faced many uncertainties and successfully made their way through them. These experiences and other commonalities encourage the formation of subcultures that preserve and celebrate their accumulated learnings. Managers also share certain economic interests and beliefs in the administrative principle that legitimate their roles and tasks. Numerous observers agree there is a generalized management culture based upon ideologies and cultural forms shared across organizations (Sutton et al. 1956; Guth and Taguiri 1965; England and Lee 1974; Knudsen 1982). In specific organizations, some elements of this general management culture are likely to be given more emphasis than others, and unique variants of the generalized belief systems develop over time in response to social and other changes that particularly affect that organization (Trice and Beyer 1984b).

Third, top managers are socially similar to one another. In some corporations, many come from the same ethnic groups (Ouchi and Johnson 1978) and have similar religious backgrounds and education. A sample of leading U.S. corporations in 1977 yielded the following composite picture of the typical chief executive officer: "a white, middle-class Protestant male with a college education. He is about fifty-six years old; most likely, he was in military service during World War II; he attended and usually graduated from a university" (Scott and Hart 1980, p. 174). Although exactly comparable data are not available for more recent periods, there is no reason to suspect the picture has changed much except for a trend toward longer education, especially MBA degrees. Respondents to a recent survey of CEOs of Fortune 500 companies were in their mid-50s, and the majority (66 percent) had earned a graduate degree—mostly in business administration (Chandy 1991). While this survey did not report on the gender of the CEOs, we know from other sources that only rarely are any of the very top executives women (Spiller and Cryer 1991). The functional experience of corporate presidents, however, has varied across time in the U.S. Early in the century, presidents who came up through manufacturing were common; by the 1950s, presidents tended to come from sales and marketing; by the 1970s, presidents increasingly came from finance and accounting (Fligstein 1987). The most recent survey reported "a heavy concentration of quantitatively oriented majors such as finance [39.5 percent] and accounting [21.4 percent]" (Chandy 1991, p. 19).

One reason for the similarities among top executives, of course, is that the selection processes that allow some individuals to reach the top tend to be based on positive valuations of similarities. People tend to trust other people who are similar to themselves. Since much of top management's work is so uncertain and unpredictable, it is important that they can trust their immediate subordinates and peers to do what they would have done in the same circumstances. Also, those who are at lower rungs in the status ladder tend to consciously and unconsciously model their values and behaviors after that of their superiors. The result is what one observer called reproduction "in kind" (Kanter 1977, p. 68)—male top managers reproducing themselves through purely social and cultural processes. Another reason is that managerial elites often belong to social networks outside their organizations that reinforce subcultural values. Some of these provide the kinds of weak ties described as providing the basis for diffuse subcultures in Chapter 5; others consist of strong and closer bonds. Trade associations are one vehicle for forming ties. Others result from interlocking directorates among the boards of directors and top managements of many firms. In addition, there are the social contacts made through intermarriage, belonging to the same exclusive social clubs, and serving together on community action boards, church boards of trustees, and the like (Domhoff 1971; Useem 1979).

Subcultures that Transcend Organizational Boundaries

As the example of occupational subcultures illustrates, all subcultures that exist within formal organizations are not necessarily encompassed within organizational boundaries. Various subcultures that occur in work and other formal organizations have their origins and most of their membership in the environment. Furthermore, they derive their major supports from resources and ideologies that are part of the environment and not unique to particular organizations. Thus, a few other distinctions that give rise to cultural differences in the environment and thus to imported subcultures within organizations will be mentioned. Our list is not intended, however to be exhaustive. The possibilities are too numerous.

Many of these imported subcultures form a latent basis for members' behaviors and values; they can create difficulties for the management of organizations because those who hold them derive some of their understandings from cultures other than that of the work group in which they are at the moment participating (Becker and Geer 1960, p. 305).

Managerial Subcultures

The practice of management was not viewed as a distinct work activity until around 1880, when the separation of ownership and management began to occur with some frequency. Since that time, observers have noted some shifts in the managerial ideologies that support managerial activities (Bendix 1956). But certain themes have also been persistent. Chief among these are themes exalting rationality and achievement. Both themes help to justify the large power differences between those who manage and those who merely work for organizations.

Other themes that are part of the American value system, however, tend to be undercut by the ways in which organizations, and the practice of management, have developed. In particular, an ethnographic study of managers in three large organizations found that the moral imperatives incorporated within the Protestant ethic had been diluted in these firms (Jackall 1988). A central tenet of the Protestant ethic was that hard work was rewarded in this life as a sign of divine favor in the afterlife. Failure to work hard and to fulfill one's personal and social obligations were therefore both a sin against God and a threat to one's self-interest. By breaking apart such elements of the Protestant ethic as the ownership of property from its control, substance from appearances, action from responsibility, obligation from guilt, language from meaning, and notions of truth from reality, the researcher concluded,

> bureaucracy and the ethic it generates undercuts the crucial premises of this classic ideology and strips it of the powerful religious and symbolic meaning it once had. Most important and at the bottom of all of these fractures, it breaks apart the older connection between the meaning of work and salvation. In the bureaucratic world, one's success ... [and] economic salvation [depend on] ... the extent that one pleases and submits to new Gods, that is, one's bosses and the exigencies of the impersonal market (Jackall 1988, pp. 191–92).

By tying managers' success to their moral choices, "bureaucracy makes its own internal rules and social context the principal moral gauges for action ..."(Jackall 1988, p. 192).

The result is a kind of relative morality, in which managers have no recourse but to

> turn to each other for moral cues for behavior and . . . to fashion specific situational moralities for specific significant others in their world. But the guidance that they receive from each other is as profoundly ambiguous as the social structure of the corporation. What matters in the bureaucratic world is not what a person is, but how closely his [her] many personae mesh with the organizational ideal; not his willingness to stand by his actions, but his agility in avoiding blame; not his acuity in perceiving falsity or errors, but his adeptness at protecting others; not his talent, his abilities, or his hard work, but how these are harnessed with the proper protocol to address the particular exigencies that face his organization; not what he believes or says, but how well he has mastered the ideologies and rhetorics that serve his corporation; not what he stands for, but whom he stands with in the labyrinths of his organization.
>
> In short, bureaucracy creates for managers a Calvinist world without a Calvinist God, a world marked with the same profound anxiety that characterized the old Protestant ethic, but one stripped of that ideology's comforting illusions. (Jackall 1988, p. 193)

This analysis of managers suggests that they face similar pressures in their work organizations and learn to deal with them in similar ways. Because U.S. managers, especially at early stages of their careers, are highly mobile, the ways they develop for coping with the pressures placed on them in their work roles are likely to spread from one organization to another.

Another way that managerial subcultures spread is through common socialization experiences in universities and other training programs outside their employing organizations. Many top managers today receive part of their socialization for management in universities. To the degree that entry into the lower rungs of the managerial hierarchy and later paths to promotion are dependent on specialized management education,[2] academic and managerial subcultures are mutually reinforcing. Both picture the world as something that can be controlled and manipulated—a very different world view from that held by many other cultures. These images derive from ideologies favoring rationality and extolling modern science, which has accomplished so many impressive feats. With the growth and accomplishments of modern science as a backdrop, it is not surprising that Western managerial ideologies presume that the disorder and confusion of the social and physical worlds can be molded into effective and productive routines with the help of managerial techniques. Associated myths portray effective management as a deductive, linear, rational-technical process.

An analysis of the images of management projected by management textbooks found: "There is a very strong resemblance between the characteristics perceived as defining effective managers of today and old hero-descriptions from Greek mythology or medieval times" (Gustafson 1984, p. 34). The mythical mes-

---

[2]Despite the growth of this education, scholars of occupations do not consider management a distinct occupation. Among their reasons are that the scope of the work performed by managers is exceedingly broad and that they do not band together to claim exclusive rights to perform these tasks.

sage is clear—managers are the heroes of today; they represent the current ideal-ized conceptions of human excellence. Such idealization of managers gives spe-cial significance to the moral relativism and self-protecting norms observed in Jackall's study of the way managers deal with difficult pressures in their work lives. To the degree that managers are or become heroes for others, their situa-tional morality is likely to be emulated and so affect conceptions of morality in the wider society.

Two researchers (Gowler and Legge 1983) analyzed spontaneous remarks that practicing managers had made in executive classes and in letters to the edi-tor in popular British management magazines. They found three persistent themes in these letters: management-as-hierarchy, management-as-accountability, and management-as-achievement. They see all these themes as supportive of what they call the "rhetoric of bureaucratic control" (1983, p. 215). The first theme links power differences to expertise, and thus helps to legitimate "the right to manage" by linking control and efficiency. The second helps to put management within a moral framework that equates management with "the responsible con-duct of human affairs" (1983, p. 215). The third theme also helps to justify mana-gerial position by assuring that only those who achieve in a superior way advance to positions of authority. Managerial ideologies thus clearly portray managerial control as a way to achieve high levels of performance.

However, as already discussed in Chapter 2, managerial ideologies also in-clude other themes. A prominent one advances humanitarianism and compas-sion as a way to obtain employees' voluntary compliance (Trice and Beyer 1984b). To make it acceptable, this other theme must be seen as enhancing, or at least not diluting, managerial control over the things that matter. Most new variants of this theme are advanced by arguing that being considerate to employ-ees will lead to higher levels of some kind of performance—quality, productivity, service, or innovation—that management wants to achieve.

Subcultures Based on Fields of Knowledge

In the U.S. system of values, science and rationality are linked. But the real-ity is that scientists are not always rational. Their methods are supposed to be objective and their stance detached, but scientists are people. They become pas-sionate about their theories and work and sometimes refuse to discard old theo-ries in the face of new evidence (Kuhn 1970; Mitroff 1974). Also, scientific fields have become very specialized. Each develops distinct paradigms that focus on different phenomena, with the result that theories, methods, and viewpoints often do not mesh readily across fields or subfields. Thus, scientific specialities become subcultures with distinctive ideologies and cultural forms.

In a world in which technological advance is the preoccupation, scientific subcultures occur in many kinds of organizations. Many business and govern-ment organizations employ scientists, and thus import the scientific subcultures to which these scientists belong into their organizations. Also, other fields of specialized knowledge follow the same pattern as the sciences; they develop their own ideologies and cultural forms. The various management-related fields of inquiry taught in business schools—accounting, economics, finance, human re-source management, organizational behavior, marketing, management informa-tion systems, and business policy—are not exempt. Their practice is rationalized by paradigms that are based more in ideology than in proven facts. Paradigms are powerful precisely because, like other elements of culture, they are so taken for granted that they become implicit and thus are seldom subject to critical scrutiny.

Demographic Groupings

The demography of human populations provides another basis for im-ported subcultures in organizations. Most obvious among these are the divisions created by age, gender, ethnicity, and social class. Each has the potential to create latent, imported subcultures, but this potential will be realized to different de-grees in different settings within organizations. It seems likely that these very general subcultures will tend to operate most strongly when other subcultures are weak or absent. Some of the issues related to these social groupings will be discussed in more detail in Chapter 8. Others are pertinent here.

Age is undoubtedly the most pervasive among the demographically based subcultures. Age segregation is common among U.S. adults in many arenas of social life. Popular media and advertising help to create and broadcast blatant role models for youth-based subcultures. To the degree that young adults retain the often countercultural values of a youth subculture, it becomes an impedi-ment to the continuity of American culture by making cultural transfer from one generation to the next uncertain and incomplete. Such tendencies may be especially prominent when demographic bulges occur. If the ratio of young per-sons to older persons is large, contact with older socializing agents may be less than it would be with a more balanced ratio. Schools, families, and other socializ-ing institutions become crowded (Perrow 1979).

Since age tends to be closely related to seniority within organizations, age-based subcultures often form around distinctions between old-timers and new-comers. For example, two factions emerged in a village fire department with 36 members. Each tried "to outsmart" the other and "direct the course of the department" (Perkins 1987, p. 345). The younger, more educated group was more training-oriented. The old guard was composed of older members and in-cluded the founders. The latter bemoaned the movement of the department from being a "servant" to the community to a "county" department. Other re-search found that old-timers in a large manufacturing plant held ideologies fa-voring conformity, commitment, and loyalty to the company, while newcomers espoused ideologies that were more concerned with personal experiences, enjoy-ment of their feelings, and authentic personal relationships (Friedman 1983).

These values are clearly related to those in the wider society. In particular, the values of the newcomers paralleled values held by youth who battled the establishment in the 1960s and by the age-cohort of youth just before them (Burns 1955). Observations of the 1960s support the view that the so-called gener-ation gap became markedly wider during the decade (Perrow 1979, Myerhoff

1975). Perhaps such sharp cleavages also existed between age groups before the 1960s; they certainly must be expected to occur in current organizations as a residue of that period of social upheaval. In an extreme instance, young editors on a large newspaper bitterly challenged senior editors—even denouncing them in ads in their own newspaper (Raelin 1987).

Subcultures based in gender, race, ethnic, and social class differences are also possible. They may arise through friendship groups or through occupational segregation of some demographic groups from others. The example of the counterculture within the hospital laboratory given earlier in this chapter illustrates how the presence of several demographic differences between groups—race, education, and status—provided fertile ground for the growth of subcultures. The demographic make-up of the Flying Tigers also differed substantially from that of the rest of the U.S. Army Air Corps.

Scholars have suggested that women have historically lived in a separate subculture within the wider society because they have consciousness of kind, as well as customs, traditions, mores, dominant activities, ways of talking, sex roles, and values that differ from those of men (Faragher and Stansell 1975; Bernard 1981; Tannen 1990). Traditionally, female socialization encourages the development of such values as unselfishness, altruism, and self-sacrifice—summed up as the love-and/or-duty ethos (Bernard 1971). To the degree that women do indeed inhabit a separate subculture within the wider society, they cannot help but bring aspects of that subculture into their work roles and organizations. And to the degree that they are numerous enough in workplaces and inclined to associate more frequently with one another than with men, the ground is laid for the development of female subcultures within work organizations.

The fact that most women still work in sex-segregated occupations (e.g., secretaries and nurses) or in sex-segregated settings within other organizations (e.g., assembly processes in high-tech manufacturing) means that their gender coincides with other commonalities already discussed that often form the bases of subcultures. Nurses are not only usually women; they belong to an occupation with distinct emotional and skill demands. These demands coincide with ideologies and values associated with femininity—caring, empathy, and service to others. The work demands and subcultures of traditionally male-segregated occupations like police, firefighters, high-steel ironworkers, and miners, on the other hand, reflect values and ideologies normally associated with manhood—bravery, risk taking, and so forth. Settings are also often segregated by gender. Women assemblers working in the clean rooms of the semiconductor industry also belong to different subunits with different supervisors than men working in the same facility. In such situations, it is hard to untangle which characteristics of any of the subcultures formed derive from other factors and which derive from gender. One scholar, for example, argued that the unique value orientations of parochialism, timidity and self-effacement, praise-addiction, and emotionality that she observed in secretaries in one corporation grew out of the way their work was structured rather than their gender (Kanter 1977).

Cross-cultural research, which looks for differences across national boundaries, has documented substantial differences in values, beliefs, and work-related attitudes from one country to another. Religious beliefs, which are often histori-cally an important part of national cultural identities, probably tend to reinforce such differences. These differences apparently occur despite similarities in the way work is organized both in relatively developed and in undeveloped countries (Lincoln, Olson, and Hanada 1978; Kiggundu, Jorgensen, and Hafsi 1983). It therefore seems reasonable to expect that in a polygot society like the United States, the country of national origin of employees may play a role in producing subcultural differences within organizations. Evidence on the point is sparse, however. One study found that Japanese-Americans working in Japanese-run plants in California had attitudes that more closely resembled that of their Japa-nese managers than did other American workers at the same plants (Lincoln, Hanada, and Olson, 1981). Other evidence indicates that ethnic cultural differ-ences persist despite acculturation over time to the U.S. culture. For example, research showed that persons of Jewish descent continued to deal with the drink-ing of alcohol differently than other ethnic groups in the United States and thus have lower rates of alcoholism than the general population (Glassner and Berg 1980).

Environmental Supports

A variety of structures and mechanisms provide practical and ideological support for imported subcultures. Basic to the operations of this support is the presence of communication linkages with other members of the subculture out-side the organization. As described in the beginning of Chapter 5, these linkages support diffused subcultures by spreading information and ideological under-standings across organizational boundaries.

One set of researchers identified four types of what they called communica-tion interlocks: overlapping membership in other groups, weak ties among brief acquaintances, structural roles positioned in intergroup relations, and diffusion via mass media and entertainment (Fine and Kleinman 1979, p. 8). Given its recent proliferation, electronically mediated communication should probably be added to this list. Although linkages in general were discussed briefly earlier, some examples of different types may help to illustrate their variety. Overlap-ping memberships include those in professional and scientific associations, se-cret fraternal societies, political groups, religious sects and churches, and various activist organizations. Weak ties occur through the exchange of correspondence, written documents, phone calls, and even holiday greeting cards among persons who have enjoyed only brief, but ideologically compatible acquaintance. Inter-group roles include various kinds of boundary-spanning and go-between roles like marketing researchers, salespeople, purchasing agents, public relations agents, trainers, consultants, guest lecturers, and brokers of all kinds.

More research has been done on the role of mass media in diffusing subcul-tures than on the other communication interlocks. Findings reiterate what seems obvious: These media are very influential in subcultural diffusion. Studies of a rock music concert at Woodstock, New York that occurred in the summer of 1968 showed, for example, that thousands who did not attend but followed accounts avidly on the media used this event, like the participants did, to express shared values that favored extreme individualism and impulsiveness (Myerhoff 1975). Other observers have noted the importation of sports terms used by the media into the talk of managers, who apparently see many of their activities as contests (Jackall 1988). More generally, popular television programs and movies provide reinforcement for certain beliefs about the roles of the sexes in marriage, the relationship between supervisors and supervised, the power of money, and the dedication (or lack thereof) of various occupational groups. The pervasive influence of these media are evident in the frequency with which the events portrayed in them become the subject of conversation, even in work settings. By such means, subcultural understandings are transmitted to large masses of people without the necessity of face-to-face interaction.

Research on electronic mail in an office products firm revealed that "electronic group mail was used throughout the organization for many kinds of group communication" (Finholt and Sproull 1990, p. 59). The researchers found that four different sets of users had distinctive ways of communicating and that they exhibited the group processes of interaction, influence attempts, and identity maintenance. Through these processes, subcultural differences among the groups emerged. One group of users, dubbed Captain Developers, who were developing a new operating system together, communicated with extreme brevity and efficiency. Even expressions of emotion were brief and tied to task-related successes or failures. There were no messages about non-work-related issues, nor about work not related to the new operating system. The communications of another group who called themselves Rowdies focused on extracurricular activities, humor, and gossip. The messages "displayed complex stylistic conventions, including closing messages, with a Rowdy number and a run-on commentary" (Finholt and Sproull 1990, p. 53). These commentaries were often sarcastic. Rowdies sometimes referred to each other by special names called "handles." They also issued membership lists giving their handles, birthdates, and favorite drinks; included persons from their revels as honorary Rowdies; and tended to express clear opinions about each other and the larger community. On one occasion, when three new members dropped out after only two days, one member's reaction was, "They weren't Rowdy material. Keep up the good work" (Finholt and Sproull 1990, p. 54).

It is interesting to note that the subcultural features shown by each electronic mail group were relatively narrow and specialized. The required, work-related group only exchanged information and feelings pertinent to their shared task. The discretionary group focused only on extracurricular matters. In situations of face-to-face interactions, groups and subcultures are usually not so specialized. A bit of gossip or humor often creeps into work-related discussions, and shoptalk often occurs in friendship or other socially oriented groups.

Countercultures

Formal organizations clearly have the potential to produce countercultures—subcultures whose basic understandings question and oppose the overall culture in some way. Three examples were given at the beginning of this chapter—a hospital laboratory, the U.S. Army group that developed the armed helicopter, and the Flying Tigers. However, accounts of countercultures are relatively sparse compared to accounts of less divergent subcultures, probably because they occur less frequently and tend to persist for shorter times than other subcultures.

One study indicated that industrial conflict, from which countercultures might emerge, contained much less worker resistance than might be expected (Edwards and Scullion 1982). Once they entered the workplace, young discontents adapted to its demands and became relatively conformist. Also, a study of activists from the youth movement of the early 1970s estimated that only 15 percent were actually committed to a counterculture (Horn and Knott 1971). Moreover, it seems unlikely that countercultures would emerge in work organizations unless they expressed ideologies that somehow responded to something in the immediate organizational situation of members. As one observer puts it, countercultures "express the situation from which they emerge—pushing away from it, deploring its contradictions, caricaturing its weaknesses, and drawing on its neglected and underground traditions" (Yinger 1978, p. 496). Thus, countercultures are expressions of situations, and some situations are more likely to produce them than others.

Mergers

Dominant managerial values in the United States once deplored the hostile takeover. However, in 1973, the number of takeovers suddenly nearly tripled the number in 1972. In 1973 and subsequent years, an average of 75 to 80 such takeovers occurred yearly until the mid-1980s. Approximately 25 percent of the takeovers involved tender offers of $75 million or more. A study of those events (Hirsch 1986) suggests that what were initially countercultural values came to be gradually accepted by the dominant managerial and business subcultures. An analysis of language used in the media about such takeovers showed how they came to be gradually associated with less threatening and hostile imagery. In effect, dominant managerial ideologies changed in the same period so that takeovers are no longer considered questionable practices but are now a relatively respectable strategy. This is evidenced by their use by many Fortune 500 firms.

These recent trends toward takeovers and other mergers in U.S. industry virtually guarantee at least a short life for one kind of counterculture. When organizations with disparate cultures are merged, the culture of the acquired organization often represents a potential counterculture for the acquiring firm. As one set of observers of mergers commented, "There is the possibility (and even probability) that *subcultures,* i.e. groups of people who share common systems of beliefs that distinguish them from the majority of organizational members, and *countercultures,* i.e. groups of people whose behavior rejects that of the dominant culture . . . evolve out of mergers and acquisitions" (Buono, Bowditch, and Lewis 1985, p. 497). Examples of the emergence of such subcultures will be presented in Chapter 8.

Members at all levels of the hierarchy of an acquired organization often

feel that it is being plundered, exploited, and occupied (Jones 1983). They frequently react with anxiety, paranoia, and hostility toward the acquiring firm. At
the same time, the acquirer is understandably concerned to establish clear control and instill its own cultural values in its new employees. Thus, various new
forms of scrutinizing are introduced by the acquirer (Jones 1983), and the acquired firm's entire top management group is often removed (Pfeffer 1981a).
One latent reason to get rid of such executives is to forestall the possibility of
potent subcultures by removing their potential leaders. Despite such measures,
sometimes the two cultures are never successfully integrated.

One analysis of mergers suggests, however, that the degree of cultural integration sought after the merger should vary according to what capabilities the
acquiring firm expects to gain from the merger. Three degrees of integration
are described: absorption, symbiosis, and preservation (Haspeslagh and Jemison
1991, p. 157). As the labels suggest, only the first type would find high levels of
cultural integration desirable. In such situations, management in the acquiring
firm would be wise to "move as fast as possible" (Haspeslagh and Jemison 1991,
p. 158) to fully integrate the two firms. In preservation acquisitions, the acquired
firm should be granted more autonomy because such acquisitions are "essentially experiments and opportunities for learning" (Haspeslagh and Jemison
1991, p. 159). An example of such an acquisition involves a firm acquiring
another in order to develop a platform in a new area of business. A symbiotic
acquisition requires "an adaptive attitude on behalf of both organizations"
(Haspeslagh and Jemison 1991, p. 160). The main capabilities transferred in such
mergers revolve around functional skills such as R&D, marketing know-how, and
product design. Continual testing of the benefits of such transfers is required
because the actual benefits may be quite different from those originally expected.
Thus, in symbiotic mergers, both cultures may be allowed to continue to exist
until some degree of integration occurs.

Rebels

Old, established organizations may give rise to countercultures when determined innovators feel they have to oppose the dominant culture to try to achieve
changes they envision. The U.S. Army Air Corps helicopter group and the Flying
Tigers exemplify this type of rebellious counterculture and show that it can have
constructive outcomes.

John DeLorean's later career in General Motors is a well-known example
of another kind of outcome. Researchers have analyzed how he deliberately set
out to undermine the dominant culture's core ideologies in a variety of ways
(Martin and Siehl 1983). The Corvair automobile was considered one of GM's
finest achievements; it was both a bold innovation and a financial success with
great market appeal. DeLorean took this cherished success story and turned it
into a vehicle for attacking the dominant culture. He retold the story to emphasize the number of deaths the Corvair had caused, the faulty axle construction
at its center, and the suppression of owner complaints that had occurred during

its promotion. He thus openly defied the dominant culture's emphasis on blind loyalty to the company.

DeLorean also created new organizational stories that ridiculed the strong deference to authority that was part of the dominant culture, and eliminated symbols of deference where he could. For example, he refused to go along with the usual practice of being met at airports by large retinues of underlings. He also expressed nonconformity by dressing differently from other General Motors executives: by wearing continental-cut suits, wide-collar shirts, and wide ties. He deliberately developed other new symbols for his own ideology, which empha- sized brisk efficiency. He redecorated offices with bright, bold colors and mod- ern furniture, thus encouraging the expression of independence and individual- ism in office decor as well as dress. In these and other ways, DeLorean promoted a counterculture based on the values of independence, productivity, and individ- uality. Soon thereafter he was asked to leave the company (Wright 1979). Thus the counterculture he started lived only a short time.

It seems likely that genuine countercultures in top management ranks would have short lives in most business organizations. Their existence at top levels is simply too threatening to the dominant culture to be allowed to persist. Top management has two obvious options—either to get rid of the countercul- tural leaders, as GM did with DeLorean, or to try to coopt them and turn their ideas into ones acceptable within the general framework of the established cul- ture. Smart managements probably always try coopting first and only resort to removal if cooptation fails. Many so-called organizational and management inno- vations—quality-of-work-life programs, organizational development inter- ventions, employee assistance programs—can be seen as rites of renewal that attempt to refurbish existing arrangements and culture just enough to make them acceptable to disaffected persons and groups (Trice and Beyer 1984a, 1984b). These innovations may contain elements of a countercultural ideology, but rarely are implemented in a way that produces radical change.

Employee Discontents

The prospect of sustained countercultures among nonmanagement em- ployees seems somewhat greater than among managers. Countercultures may de- velop as a way to handle and express severe, shared employee discontents. For example, in a new center for emotionally disturbed children, employees ex- pressed their anger at a manager's demands for control (and also their anxieties over the difficulty of the tasks facing them) by referring to the manager as the dwarf Rumpelstiltskin (Smith and Simmons 1983). In the fairy tale of the same name, Rumpelstiltskin demanded a high price for his assistance in turning straw into gold. The denigrated manager was soon fired. Another example is provided by machinists who resisted and violated company-promulgated rules governing production procedures because they thought the rules made no sense (Roy 1954). They joined together with other informal groups and blocked a series of attempts by management to implement a new production-control program.

Countercultures based on employee grievances are not likely to last beyond the issues that provoked them. Only if management is determinedly inflexible to employee grievances are there likely to be enough strong emotions in the situation to sustain a rebellious counterculture over a long period. The counterculture already described in the hospital laboratory appeared to be such an instance. Another is the group of women who tried to form a union at a bank in Wilmar, Minnesota.[3] The trigger for their discontent was that they were again going to be asked to train a new male employee who knew nothing about their work to supervise them. At enormous personal costs, these eight women formed a counterculture that survived several years of picketing and unemployment. It persisted despite lack of significant support from the community. However, when the National Labor Relations Board's decision on their case went against them, the group gave up and their counterculture died. We suspect that such persistent countercultures are rare because management usually (1) placates dissatisfied parties sufficiently to undermine support for the counterculture; or (2) coopts the leaders. A third possibility is that dissatisfied employees, having given voice to their discontents without effect, will choose the other option of exit and leave the organization (Hirschman 1972).

Another factor militating against the persistence, if not the emergence of countercultures, is that management and workers have shared interests that tend to override their divisions. This is most evident in established U.S. unions, which may form a kind of imported subculture within organizations but rarely form genuine countercultures. Sharp divisions between unions and dominant cultures simply cannot be maintained. As already discussed, top managers and top union officials grow to resemble one another as they interact, bargain, and deal with common problems in their industries. Also, both sides recognize that theirs is a symbiotic relationship in which their respective interests and welfare are joined. The very processes that enable them repeatedly to come to agreements militate against their forming opposing cultures. In other countries, where there are class-based, ideological and political traditions in unions, they may have the potential for becoming the basis of genuine countercultures.

Although there was widespread concern that the youth movement of the 1960s would produce a generation that was resistant to prevalent work-related norms and values, there was little evidence in the 1980s that these fears were realized. Surveys of young workers showed that they were as committed to and satisfied with their work and employing organizations as were previous generations (Yankelovich 1979). One reason may be that some of the most disaffected among them chose different career paths than their parents did.

A study of the "sixties kids" indicates that a relatively high proportion of them entered the professions. While the overall rate of workforce participation in the professions decreased by 1.3 percent from 1970 to 1980, that of the 1960s cohort increased by 18.4 percent (Raelin 1987, p. 24). The professions offered the best institutional opportunity to promote social change and work in occupational settings compatible with the cultural values that distinguished the youth

---

[3]These events were publicized on the television program "60 Minutes" and by a documentary film produced and directed by actress Lee Grant called *The Wilmar Eight*.

movement of the 1960s: defiance of authority, participation in decision making, a service ethic, and anticareerism (Raelin 1987, p. 25). The analysis also suggests that few of these professionals, however,

> even if they were radical during the 1960s, are radical today. They are at best "progressives" who have come to terms with the evolutionary nature of social change in a democratic society, and who are content to make subtle changes in the institutions of which they are a part. Some have discarded their outwardly defiant personas and have joined with other Americans to pursue the almighty dollar and the articles of conspicuous consumption that go with it.... Yet it is my contention that the '60s kids do not believe they have "sold out." Some, in fact, are continuing their public interest work within the professions.... Others joined the government and went to work for a new breed of social regulatory agencies.... [But] the vast majority of the '60s New Class professionals are simply working as salaried workers in relatively large organizations, seeking to make a buck *like everyone else*. (Raelin 1987, p. 27 [emphasis added])

It is hard to maintain countercultural practices and values while participating in the wider society. Genuine countercultures seem to require some degree of social isolation to survive for any extended period of time.

Also, an analysis of the youth culture of the 1960s has shown that it carried within it the seeds of its own destruction. Its emphasis on individualism militated against the kind of collective concerns that are typical of lasting countercultural movements (Myerhoff 1975). The persistent countercultures that this movement did spawn—drug cultures, cults, and other deviant subgroups—tend to stay as far away from traditional workplaces as they can. Thus, their penetration into most work organizations is minimal and likely to be short-lived.

The only organizations in which genuine countercultures flourish and become established as a persistent part of ongoing social life are ones in which members have overwhelming discontents, often because their interests conflict with those of management. Prisons, for example, typically have a secondary system of government that is run by the inmate counterculture. The counterculture sets prevailing norms for inmates' behavior, sanctions violations, and generally governs most of the informal life in the prison (Cloward and Ohlin 1959). Individual inmates band together in numerous cliques—a necessity for coping with this social milieu. There are even occupational subcultures within the inmate counterculture; for example, in one prison studied, there was a separate thief subculture.

Deviant Behavior

Some subcultural groups within organizations develop various forms of deviant behavior and, in the sense that their deviance is counterproductive to their organizations and opposed to its dominant norms, these groups harbor countercultural elements within them. Examples of such behaviors include drinking alcohol when officially prohibited, the use of illegal drugs, stealing, sabotage, gambling, and organized evasion of work. Many of these groups are not really countercultures, however, because their deviant behaviors are not intended to interfere with the primary values of the dominant culture.

Research in a large utility revealed that the supervisors and medical department independently arrived at similar estimates of the occurrence of drinking problems in subunits of that organization (French and Trice 1972). The differences between units were striking, strongly suggesting that subcultures within some units were much more tolerant of problem drinking than were others. Various work-related factors in workplaces encourage the development of norms that tolerate or even encourage heavy drinking and the use of illicit drugs (Trice and Sonnenstuhl 1988). Substance abuse, moreover, is often promoted as facilitating work or as making it more tolerable. Also, scholars who study alcoholism have noted that alcoholics seek out other persons with similar levels of drinking to normalize their own heavy consumption of alcohol (Trice 1965); that is, their own drinking seems normal when it fits within the drinking patterns exhibited by those around them (Lemert 1967). Thus, it seems likely that heavy drinkers could also end up in the same work groups by self-selection and processes of recruitment.

An organizational researcher observed that drinking norms varied among two groups of London police and thus helped to distinguish the subculture of one group from that of the other. The drinking norms of the plainclothes detectives who worked in Scotland Yard supported heavy drinking (Van Maanen 1986). Although the researcher does not specify this, it seems likely that drinking while on duty was officially prohibited. Of course, detectives were less likely than regular uniformed officers to observe regular working hours. Thus, it is perhaps not surprising that they were observed to engage in occasional heavy drinking in informal parties at the office. Such parties involved supervisors as well as regular detectives. Uniformed police sometimes appeared briefly at these events but soon came to understand that they were not really welcome. The detectives also drank heavily on "pub tours" (Van Maanen 1986, p. 217). These drinking bouts were a way to express the unique identity they shared and to ventilate the dangers and difficulties they all faced that differentiated them from uniformed officers. The latter group also drank, but less heavily. The researcher suggests that both groups used drinking as a temporary and accepted "time out"—a small and relatively brief lapse from the normal, onerous controls that their formal organization and work imposed upon them.

A striking, well-documented example of deviant behavior is the pilfering of cargo that Newfoundland dockworkers regularly practiced (Mars 1982). A work gang of 12 to 20 workers self-selected themselves to unload a specific freighter. They could then cooperate in very systematically pilfering the most desirable parts of its cargo. Their pilfering involved an elaborate division of labor and required complete cooperation and trust among members of the group. First, certain members who customarily worked in the hold and therefore had unhindered access to the cargo identified certain crates as desirable to steal. Next, other members of the team "accidentally" dropped and thus damaged these same crates. Since they were now damaged, they were routed to special teams in the sheds who could go through the crates relatively undisturbed and take out some of the contents. To facilitate this, forklift truck drivers stacked other cargo so as to block the supervisor's vision of the pilfering process. This group was so well-organized that they even constructed a "fitting room" where members could try on pilfered suits and other garments. The loot was distributed at after-work drinking celebrations in which older members reinforced group understandings and socialized carefully selected new members by telling stories of other, particularly successful lootings.

The most telling examples of behaviors with deviant countercultural elements come from the literature on occupations. It may be that the strong ties that bind members of an occupation together provide a set of conditions that is especially conducive to the development of some countercultural norms and behaviors. Alternatively, it may be that such instances have come to researchers' attention because those who study occupations have done the kind of long-term and close observation needed to reveal such behaviors. Readers probably recognize that the types of deviant behavior these investigators describe are not too unusual in work organizations.

Another type of deviant behavior highly likely to produce countercultural groups is the use of illegal drugs, including marijuana. At one point in the 1980s, the popular press was full of stories about the smoking of marijuana on Wall Street. According to such popular reports, the use of cocaine was also becoming widespread among young professionals, such as lawyers, during this period. In addition, some researchers of drug use report that the sale of illegal drugs is commonplace in factories (Runcie 1980), as it is in many schools. Given the apparent prevalence of these behaviors in the wider society, some prevalence in work organizations must be expected.

When people band together and develop countercultural norms to support and protect deviant practices, a counterculture can develop. However, in most instances, the countercultural norms developed will probably focus on the particular forms of deviant behavior members want to engage in and protect, and not on matters of more general importance to their organizations. However, the potential exists for such groups to generalize their counterculture beyond the particular deviant acts that brought members together.

Social Movements

Large-scale social changes also have the potential for generating countercultures in organizations. De Tocqueville observed long ago that as people become more equal, they find the remaining inequalities harder and harder to tolerate. The 1970s and 1980s have produced a steady mounting of discontents within U.S. society among those who have experienced some broadening of their opportunities but feel they are not yet fully equal (Boudon 1982). Individuals tend to grow more discontented with their social system as it offers them, on the average, better opportunities for success and promotion than they have enjoyed in the past. In particular, women and minority group members seem ripe for this type of discontent.

Pressures from the civil rights and feminist movements have helped to fuel a recent trend toward programs that promote multicultural diversity in work-places. Growing awareness of demographic projections indicating that white males will be a minority in the workforce by the year 2000 have undoubtedly also contributed. Proponents of the multicultural perspective suggest that the cultivation of ideologies favoring pluralism would be consistent with the increas-ing diversity of employee backgrounds. The objective of such efforts is to "ensure influence of minority-culture perspectives on core organization norms and val-ues" (Cox 1991, p. 41). Specific techniques to realize such objectives have prolif-erated recently. They include training directed at managing and valuing diver-sity, new member orientation programs, multiple language training, inclusion of diversity in key committees and mission statements, and groups to advise top management on issues of cultural diversity.

Other analysts have identified what they call the "deauthorization" syn-drome—marked by a sharp increase in people's frustration with "life's possibili-ties, hopes, dreams, and actualities" (Yinger 1978). People who feel this way begin to question the American dream and the legitimacy of the various authorities that have been buttressed by it. Such sentiments may lead members of work orga-nizations to question not only supervisory authority, but also the authority usu-ally vested in age, experience, and expertise.

The deprofessionalization of everyone is a current social trend (Stewart and Cantor 1982). It started in the late 1960s (Hall and Engel 1974) with the burgeon-ing of questioning by clients and lay groups of the expertise of professionals (Haug and Susman 1969). Some fuel was probably added to this movement by other occupational groups that tried to claim equal status with professionals by denigrating the expertise that traditional professional groups hold. Social change, of necessity, involves the disparagement of old ideas and privileges.

However, as mentioned earlier when discussing the youth culture, it is not clear that large-scale social movements such as these produce countercultures in organizations. The surrounding dominant culture tends over time to dilute the efforts of even the most determined alternative organizations—collectivist and egalitarian organizations (Newman 1980; Rothschild-Whitt 1979); utopian socie-ties (Kanter 1968); and worker-owned firms (Hammer and Stern 1980, Wachtel 1973). Their dependence on the surrounding environment creates the necessity to cooperate and coordinate their activities with it. In the process, alternative organizations inevitably begin to grow more like traditional organizations. If, where the counterculture is protected by formal organizational boundaries, such countercultures cannot survive for long, it seems very unlikely that they can per-sist as splinter groups within ongoing organizations with only informal bounda-ries to protect their uniqueness.

SUMMARY

The existence of many kinds of differences among members of organizations can give rise to subcultures. They are often sources of conflict, which can have positive as well as negative effects. Factors encouraging the formation of subcultures contribute to underlying conflicts between subcultures. Most of the time, subcultures coexist peacefully. Conflicts between them are likely to surface when organizations must choose among subcultural ideologies as bases for action.

Both formal and informal groups in organizations have the potential to become subcultures. Friendship groups, cliques, functional or geographically based departments, and top management teams tend to create conditions conducive to the development of subcultures. Subcultures are less likely to emerge in cabals and coalitions, product-based departments, or other levels of management. Some factors encouraging subculture formation are interdependencies created by technology and work flows, group rewards, and line-staff distinctions.

Various subcultures occurring in organizations originate in their environments: a general managerial subculture, subcultures based on fields of knowledge and demographic groupings, as well as the occupational subcultures discussed in Chapter 5. These subcultures are supported by communication linkages between members such as overlapping memberships, weak social ties, linking roles, mass media, and electronic communication.

Countercultures arise to oppose the dominant cultures in organizations in certain situations. Mergers, rebellious innovators, chronically discontented employees, and illegal or other deviant behaviors involve some countercultural norms and practices and thus may encourage the formation of countercultures.

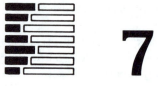

7

Leadership and Organizational Cultures

Leadership is probably the most studied and analyzed aspect of work organizations (Stogdill 1974; Bass 1981, 1990). Popular treatments also abound (Peters and Austin 1985; O'Toole 1984; Wall 1986). Despite some studies showing negligible effects of leadership on practical organizational-level outcomes (Lieberson and O'Connor 1972; Salancik and Pfeffer 1977), the importance of leadership is generally unquestioned by most management scholars and practitioners. This persistence of widespread beliefs in leaders and leadership has ideological overtones.

Like other preoccupations, the attention accorded to leadership arises from people's cultural beliefs and values.[1] Social groups that highly value rationality and predictability need to be able to believe that events have discernable and controllable causes. Members of such groups will attribute to leaders many factors that they do *not* want to attribute to luck, chance, or other circumstances beyond human control or understanding. Leaders thus become an important avenue for humans to act out and continue to believe in their own efficacy as a species. In many cultures, leaders symbolize humanity's control over its world. However, the ideologies of different cultures will produce somewhat different conceptions and beliefs about the role of leaders that structure how people understand what the people who lead them do. Cultural forms also affect and reflect conceptions of leadership.[2]

---

[1] This chapter is an expansion of ideas originally published elsewhere (Trice and Beyer 1991).

[2] For example, the Japanese, Chinese, and Korean languages lack a word that is equivalent in meaning to the English word *leader*. Their closest equivalent has a meaning more like *coach* in English. The German language has no word exactly corresponding to the meaning of the term *manager* in English. Present-day Germans also avoid using the German word for leader (*führer*) because of its association with Hitler. Management analysts in those countries therefore resort to using the English

One set of researchers coined the term the *romance of leadership* to refer to people's tendencies to attribute to leaders heroic qualities that justify putting faith in them to resolve uncertainties. This faith becomes evident when people give leaders credit or blame for organizational outcomes when true causes cannot be determined (Salancik and Meindl 1984; Meindl, Ehrlich, and Dukerich 1985). Experiments showed that MBA students who were also managers evaluated the same, positive organizational performance as more favorable when it was attributed to leaders' efforts than when it was attributed to events not under management's control (Meindl and Ehrlich 1987). These results suggest that managers exaggerate the positive effects of leadership on events.[3] They are probably not alone; even casual attention to the U.S. popular media reveals a preoccupation with leaders and leadership as a key determinant of events.

Despite the importance given to leadership in general analyses of organizations and management, the role of leaders in the cultures of organizations has thus far received only scattered attention (Schein 1985; Sergiovanni and Corbally 1984; Hunt 1991). Most scholarly analyses of leadership treat organizational cultures only peripherally (House and Baetz 1979; House and Singh 1987; Yukl 1981; Bass 1981, 1985a; Conger and Kanungo 1988; Conger 1989). Also, many analyses of organizational cultures pay only minor attention to leadership (Deal and Kennedy 1982; Frost et al. 1985; Kilmann et al. 1985; Jones, Moore, and Snyder 1988; Ott 1989; Denison 1990). Thus, the part that leadership plays in organizational cultures has not been systematically explored.

Leadership and Culture

Most applications of leadership theory to organizations have tended to emphasize the instrumental consequences of leadership—how leaders influence the accomplishment of the work of organizations (Daft 1983). But as we've pointed out repeatedly, most behaviors have dual consequences in that they both do and say things (Leach 1976a). A cultural approach to leadership should illuminate the other side of leadership—how leaders influence the development and expression of culture in their organizations.

Specific cases of leadership may involve both instrumental and cultural consequences, but all instances of leadership do not necessarily involve both. Thus, leadership may best be viewed in terms of two continua: the one for instrumental leadership indicates the degree to which instrumental ideas and behaviors are affected by leadership; the second, for cultural leadership, indicates the degree to which cultural ideologies and expressive behaviors are affected by lead-

---

words when they want to discuss leaders or leadership. We thank Wonsick Lee and Hans Schollhammer for this information.

[3]This study did not examine the circumstances under which leaders may be blamed for failures. Clearly this happens, as when sports coaches are made scapegoats for their teams' losses.

ership. Such an approach does not make a priori assumptions about whether either form of leadership can exist without the other, but allows for that possibility (Trice and Beyer 1991).

Human cultures, of course, largely grow from and reside in the expressive side of human behavior. As already explained, over time, through social interaction and behavior, people develop shared understandings and practices that help them to cope with and manage the uncertainties they face (Moore and Myerhoff 1977; Kluckhohn 1942). It is hard to imagine that the social processes needed to create and sustain cultures could occur without the efforts of cultural leaders. Someone in a culture has to originate or recognize sets of ideas that reduce people's uncertainties, make those ideas understandable and convincing, and communicate them widely and repeatedly so that others come to share them. Such efforts are not confined to designated leaders or one leader at a time. Rather, different persons located in different roles in the same or different subgroups can take cultural leadership roles at the same time or at different times. A comprehensive consideration of cultural leadership must therefore provide for multiple cultural leaders.

Theories of Leadership

Four Major Instrumental Approaches

Over the years, organizational researchers have studied leadership from four rather different perspectives. All were instrumental in the sense that they viewed leadership as a way to accomplish desired practical goals. Although none of the studies explicitly considered cultural leadership, they can nonetheless be helpful in delineating what is involved in leadership in general.

The first perspective has been labeled the *trait approach.* It attempted to identify which personal traits characterized leaders and made them more or less effective. Work along this line showed, for example, that cognitive skills and self-assurance are much more important than some of the traits commonly believed to be important to leaders, such as need for power, or initiative (Hodgetts and Altman 1979, p. 184). Clusters of traits were found to "differentiate leaders from followers, effective from ineffective leaders, and higher echelon from lower echelon leaders" (Bass 1990, p. 87). However, results obtained differed sufficiently from study to study that many considered this line of research inconclusive. Although debate continues on the effects of traits in leadership (Lord, DeVader, and Alliger 1986; Bass 1990), it seems safe to conclude that traits are not the whole story.

The second perspective used was the *behavioral approach,* in which researchers attempted to identify certain sets of behaviors, called styles of leadership, that leaders manifested and then to assess their effects on followers. They identified two contrasting styles of leader behaviors—variously called initiating structure versus consideration, autocratic versus democratic, task oriented versus socioemotional, or production centered versus employee centered. Research in this tradition did not usually actually observe the behaviors in question, but asked subordinates to report how their managers typically behaved and then categorized managers' leadership styles by those reports. Recent theories of transactional and transformational leadership (Burns 1978; Bass 1985a) emphasize subordinate reports of leader behaviors and thus continue this general approach.

Next, researchers tried a *contingency approach* to leadership, in which they argued that the effectiveness of specific leadership behaviors depends upon the situation in which the leader and followers interact (Fiedler 1978; Vroom and Yetton 1974; House and Baetz 1979). Researchers' attention then focused on discovering which aspects of situations are crucial and on determining which leadership behaviors are effective in them.

Recently, some researchers argued that the primary determinants and effects of leadership are in the minds of the followers, who attribute to certain other persons the ability to lead and thus consider them leaders. According to the *attribution approach,* "leadership exists only as a perception" (Calder 1977, p. 202). From such theory it follows that it is what followers think, rather than what leaders actually do, that determines who is a leader.

A cultural version of an attribution approach to leadership focuses on the symbolism inherent in managerial action, which amounts to focusing on how followers and others perceive leaders' behaviors. Research accumulating during the 1960s and 1970s indicated that instrumental models of leadership were not fully accurate nor a complete description of what managers actually did. Summarizing and integrating that research, one organizational theorist proposed that more attention be paid to the symbolic side of leadership:

> Much of the activity occurring in organizations is motivated more by sentiment than by rational calculation. Rationality is likely to be retrospective, so that we make sense out of what has already occurred. Thus, a task of leadership in organizations and in nations is to *make activity meaningful and sensible,* and in so doing, produce positive sentiments, attitudes, and feelings among those in the organization. In this pursuit, symbolism and symbolic activity, including the use of language, ceremonies, and setting, is all-important. There is increasing evidence that effective managers implicitly or explicitly recognize the importance of symbolic activity and use it with great success. (Pfeffer 1981a, pp. 2–3, [emphasis added])

As this quote illustrates, viewing leadership as a symbolic activity emphasized its sense-making function and thus began to link leadership with culture.

Application to Organizational Cultures

All of the instrumental approaches to leadership can contribute to understanding how cultural leadership in organizations works. First, they remind us that cultural leaders may have distinctive personal traits and exhibit distinctive sets of behaviors, and that the emergence and effectiveness of cultural leadership may vary according to the situation and the willingness of followers to attribute leadership to their leaders. Also, these approaches have in common an underlying presumption: that leaders are those persons who are successful in influencing others. The presence of leadership is usually inferred by effects on followers; it is not inferred from the behaviors, qualities, or position of a leader alone. Thus, leadership is both defined and known from its consequences. In addition, these approaches cumulatively recognize that leadership is a social process[4] that entails some persons' influencing other persons in certain social situations. All three—leaders, followers, and situations—are essential components of the social process of leadership (Hollander 1978).

Since formally designated managers are not always successful in influencing others in desired directions, some may not be leaders at all. Leadership and management or supervision are not synonyms (Dubin 1979, p. 225). Leaders and managers may be different types of people, and the "conditions favorable to the growth of one may be inimical to the other" (Zaleznick 1977, p. 5). Only under certain conditions should supervisors or managers be viewed as leaders (Kochan, Schmidt, and DeCotiis 1975, p. 291). These cautions apply even more stringently to cultural leadership. Managers are not automatically cultural leaders because only some are successful in influencing the shared ideologies their subordinates hold and the expressive behaviors they exhibit.

Also, persons do not have to be managers to be leaders. Informal leaders tend to emerge from within all social groups, often to fulfill functions that their designated, formal leaders perform poorly; other times to pursue goals and norms specific to that group. Thus, cultural leadership can be exercised both by designated and by emergent leaders. Persons who are emergent leaders can become designated leaders if relevant authorities recognize their influence and give them formal authority. A person who is the designated leader of one group (such as a manager) may simultaneously also be an emergent leader in another (an informal group of managers). Ignoring such differences creates confusion about what leadership is and how it works. To analyze cultural leadership in organizations adequately requires identifying not only the leader but the relevant group of followers, and how the situation affects the leadership process. Clearly, the leader's status in the organization and group is an important part of the situation.

Charismatic Leadership

The great German sociologist, Max Weber, described a fifth type of leadership that provides a useful starting point for analyzing cultural leadership. His seminal analysis of charisma recognized that leadership is crucial to both continuity and change. While charismatic leaders provoke social and cultural change, such change does not endure without the efforts of successors who maintain and further the visions of charismatic leaders (Weber 1947). Thus, cultural leadership

---

[4]The term *social process* refers to an ongoing series of acts or events that involve groups of people, that extend over some period of time, and that are often marked by changes or developmental stages.

involves not only leaders who originate new cultures or change existing ones, but also subsequent leaders who carry forward others' cultural innovations. The social mechanisms through which leadership operates to create *cultural innovation* are not the same as those Weber identified as producing *cultural maintenance.* Thus, at least two basic types of cultural leadership apparently occur. This insight is important because existing analyses of cultural leadership have focused on cultural innovation, portraying leaders as founders of cultures (Clark 1970, 1972; Schein 1983b, 1985) or as changers of them (Bass 1985a, 1985b; Roberts 1985; Conger and Kanungo 1988).

Weber identified four circumstances that occur together in instances of charisma: (1) a leader with exceptional personal qualities (2) emerges during a time of social crisis (3) with a vision that provides a solution to the crisis through a radical break with the past and (4) attracts a set of followers who come to believe in that vision because they attribute powers beyond ordinary experience to the leader. Another scholar observed that in order for charisma to be more than a transitory phenomenon, a fifth circumstance is needed: the leader's gifts and vision must be validated by what followers consider repeated successes (Friedland 1964). All five of these elements are present to some degree in genuine charismatic leadership (Trice and Beyer 1986).

The celebrated civil rights leader, Martin Luther King, Jr., fits Weber's description of charismatic leadership very well. He had "a dream" and succeeded in winning many followers to that dream by his dominant personality, courageous example, the strength of his convictions, his unshaken confidence despite repeated adversity, and his eloquence. U.S. society, which has never resolved the deep social crisis resulting from slavery and the subsequent lack of equality for black Americans, needed a solution to this persistent and shameful contradiction of cherished social values. Thus, many blacks and whites eagerly embraced Rev. King's dream; they marched, faced arrest, and demonstrated peacefully their belief in his vision of the future.[5] Despite his assassination, U.S. society continues to move slowly toward realizing his dream. As it does so, he and his visions for the future remain potent symbols of the meaning of civil rights and how they can be achieved.

Before applying the central ideas about charismatic leadership to organizations, it is important to dispel three common misunderstandings about charisma. First, the extraordinary qualities of charismatic leaders should not be confused with mere personal charm or likableness. Nor are charismatic leaders saintly. Like everyone else, they have personal flaws and may be very difficult and demanding at times. The charismatic leader wins followers not by being nice to them, but by inspiring them with a new radical vision of what is possible. Second, charismatic leaders are not always forces for good. The grip that charismatic leaders have on followers may induce them to act in socially destructive ways (Musser 1986). History is replete with frightening examples. Adolph Hitler was

---

[5]Rev. King, of course, was not the only leader of the civil rights movement. Others may be functioning today as cultural maintenance leaders by routinizing his charisma and keeping his vision a vital part of that movement.

undoubtedly a charismatic leader. So was the Reverend Jim Jones, who persuaded his followers to commit mass suicide by convincing them that the outside world was going to try to destroy the way of life they had established at the People's Temple in Guyana (Lindholm 1990). Third, charismatic leadership involves more than the personal qualities of the leader. To use the term *charisma* as loosely as it is often used in popular parlance is to reduce the scope of this unusual leadership to just personal traits. General leadership theory has progressed beyond trait theory, and so should theories of charismatic and other cultural leadership.

Weber's conception of charisma anticipated all of the four major, instrumental approaches to instrumental leadership described earlier, and he added an additional element that is crucial in explaining cultural leadership. The personal qualities involved in charismatic leadership seem to include not only unusual *traits* in a leader, but also a *style of behavior* that followers find compelling. The *contingency* involved is that the social group to which the leader appeals perceives itself as facing some sort of crisis. Charismatic leadership also depends on followers who *attribute* exceptional qualities and success to a leader. What is distinctive about charisma, and makes it especially pertinent to cultural leadership, is that the content of charismatic leadership—the leader's *radical vision*—becomes the ideological basis of a new culture. It is in this sense that charismatic leadership creates culture.

> What is new and different in our enumerative definition of charisma and not easily subsumed under past approaches to leadership is the charismatic mission—the radical and novel visions and prescriptions of the charismatic leader. This component of charisma addresses the *content* of leadership—what the leader is trying to accomplish and is influencing the followers to do—an element not yet incorporated into general leadership theories. (Trice and Beyer 1986, p. 133)

The importance of success to charismatic leadership was observed in an empirical study of a union leader in Tanganyika, which concluded that the charismatic vision must be validated with "some victory" (Friedland 1964, p. 24). Without repeated successes, the position of a charismatic becomes unstable (Trice and Beyer 1986, p. 131). Because cultural leadership rests heavily on the acceptance and approval of some set of followers, it probably cannot endure without followers' attributing their own successful performance to the influence of their leaders. In organizations, followers can be any set of stakeholders, including the board of directors, stockholders, lower-level managers, or rank-and-file workers.

Of course, charismatic leaders probably often *are* successful. A recent study of the U.S. presidents concluded that those who were charismatic had better performance on several dimensions including economic and social performance (House, Spangler, and Woycke 1991). They were not better, however, on their performance in international relations, suggesting that presidential charisma may not be as effective abroad as it is at home. Also, of course, international relations over the years studied must have involved many factors outside presidential control, especially since the United States was not always a world power.

Another expansion of Weber's ideas was made by a scholar whose theory of charisma specified behaviors likely to characterize charismatic leaders (House 1977). This theory and later empirical work (Howell and Frost 1989; House, Woycke, and Fodor 1988; House, Spangler, and Woycke 1991) identified a variety of behaviors and effects on followers that people attributed to persons they considered to be charismatic leaders. This approach has won a number of adherents, who tend to focus on followers' and other observers' perceptions of qualities and behaviors that differentiate presumed charismatic leaders from others (Conger and Kanungo 1988; Puffer 1990; Ehrlich, Meindl, and Viellieu 1990).[6]

Because Weber and others (Roberts 1985; Roberts and Bradley 1988; Trice and Beyer 1986, 1991) have suggested that a situation of crisis is essential to charismatic leadership, two recent empirical studies have attempted to ascertain whether crises and charisma occur together. A laboratory study on attributions of charismatic leadership found that undergraduate students saw more charismatic appeal in a leader who was portrayed as managing a situation of crisis than the same leader with the same traits portrayed in a situation with no crisis (Pillai and Meindl 1991). A study of U.S. presidents found that those who faced crises were more likely to be described in charismatic terms by persons who worked closely with them, by biographers, and by contemporary editorial writers for *The New York Times* (House, Spangler, and Woycke 1991).

All of the elements of charismatic leadership just discussed might be expected to apply to leadership that initiates cultural innovations. Weber's analysis, however, extended beyond the initiating stage of charisma to specify conditions under which its effects are likely to persist. He called the process by which charisma achieves some lasting effects its routinization. His analysis of the routinization of charisma suggests additional elements pertinent to cultural leadership in general: administrative structures and actions needed to carry forward the charismatic mission; the transference of charisma to others by means of rites, symbols, and other cultural forms; and the incorporation of the charismatic's vision and mission into the written and oral traditions of the organization (Weber 1947). The ultimate test of routinization is whether the radical vision endures—whether the organization "continues to express, to work toward, and to cohere around the charismatic message and mission of the founder (or reformer)" (Trice and Beyer 1986, p. 134).[7]

Although elements derived from theories of charisma provide a useful starting point for analyzing cultural leadership, the two concepts are *not* identical. Cultural leadership is a more general and common phenomenon than charisma. Charismatic leadership is best viewed as a relatively rare subset of cultural leadership—one destined to produce cultural innovation. However, as will be seen in the discussion that follows, all innovative cultural leaders are not necessarily charismatic.

---

[6]By downplaying or ignoring the importance of the situation in defining charismatic leadership, these studies miss what has been learned from contingency approaches to leadership—namely, that the kind of leadership that is effective depends on the situation in which it is manifested.

[7]One other element of routinization—the selection of a successor resembling the charismatic leader (Weber 1947)—is not pertinent to cultural leadership as discussed here.

Linking Elements of Leadership to Its Consequences

The first column in Table 7–1 lists ten likely elements of cultural leadership distilled from Weber's conception of charisma and the extensions of his ideas just discussed (Friedland 1964; House 1977; Trice and Beyer 1986). The next two columns present expected differences in these elements between leadership that produces cultural innovation and leadership that produces cultural mainte-nance. Cultural innovation occurs when *new* sets of shared beliefs, values, and norms emerge within a social group. New ideologies can arise through the rela-tively direct influence of leaders who communicate new ideas, or more indirectly when leaders use cultural forms or their behaviors to carry new cultural messages to members of a group. Most often both occur and mutually influence one another. Leader's ideologies influence their use of cultural forms and other be-haviors. Their use of cultural forms and behaviors shapes their own ideologies. Both influence followers' shared ideologies and behaviors. Cultural maintenance occurs by the same social processes, but eventuates in the continuance and rein-forcement of *existing* sets of shared ideologies and practices.

The specifications of elements for cultural innovation leadership in the ta-ble were derived and adapted from the scholarly literatures on charisma and on cultural change. Since there is little relevant literature, the specification of ele-ments for cultural maintenance leadership are more speculative. Some were de-rived theoretically as contrasts to those expected to produce innovation; others followed logically from our definition of cultural maintenance. Detailed ac-counts of such leadership in the popular and scholarly literatures also consist-ently portrayed such contrasts. For other elements, there were no compelling theoretical reasons to posit differences for the two types of leadership. Nor did descriptions in the literature of cultural maintenance leaders vary from those of innovation leaders. Entries in Table 7–1 thus reflect both similarities and differ-ences between leadership that produces cultural innovation and leadership that produces cultural maintenance. Whether cultural leadership must display all of these elements to be effective is an open question requiring additional research to answer. It seems likely that the more of these elements an instance of leader-ship has, the more effective it will be in establishing, changing, or maintaining a culture. But all of these elements are probably not necessary to produce some degree of cultural leadership.

Four Types of Cultural Leadership

Since the presence of leadership is usually known from its consequences, one way to approach the analysis of cultural leadership in organizations is to identify a set of cultural consequences that occur repeatedly in descriptions and analyses of organizations. Such an approach can be especially useful in providing reference points for describing specific instances of leadership. We have already done this by suggesting that cultural leadership involves both cultural innovation and cultural maintenance. Further analysis of the literature revealed another set

TABLE 7-1
ELEMENTS OF CULTURAL LEADERSHIP AND CONSEQUENCES
FOR ORGANIZATIONAL CULTURES

Elements of Cultural Leadership	Consequences for Cultures	
	Innovation	*Maintenance*
1. Personal qualities	Self-confidence	Confidence in group
	Dominant personality	Facilitator
	Strong convictions	Strong convictions
	Evangelist	Catalyst
	Dramatic and expressive	Persuasive
2. Perceived situation	Crisis	No crisis or a manageable one
3. Vision and mission	Radical ideology	Conservative ideology
4. Follower attributions	That leader has extraordinary qualities needed to deal with crisis	That leader represents existing values that were successful in past
5. Performance	Repeated success in managing crisis	Continuation of success
6. Leader behaviors	Effective role model	Effective role model
	Creates impression of success and competence	Creates impression of success and competence
	Articulates ideology	Articulates ideology
	Communicates high expectations, confidence in followers	Communicates high expectations, confidence in followers
	Motivates	Motivates
7. Administrative actions	New structures and strategies; or radical changes in structures and strategies	Refurbishes and strengthens existing structures and strategies; or incremental changes in structures and strategies
8. Use of cultural forms	Communicates new cultural ideologies and values	Affirms and celebrates existing cultural ideologies and values
9. Use of tradition	Establishes new traditions	Continues existing traditions
10. Persistence over time	Change is institutionalized	Continuity is made appealing and vital

SOURCE: Adapted from Trice and Beyer 1991, p. 153.

of distinctions, however, that can be subsumed under these two general categories.

Our analysis of accounts of numerous organizations revealed four types of cultural consequences (Trice and Beyer 1991): leadership can create, change, embody, or integrate the cultures of organizations. Two of these consequences—creating and changing cultures—involve cultural innovation in that such leadership creates and inculcates new cultural substance and forms. The other two—embodying and integrating cultures—involve different ways in which existing cultures are maintained. Although specific leaders could conceivably play a role in achieving more than one of these consequences, we did not find such accounts in the literature. Individual leaders usually are portrayed as influential in achieving only one of these consequences for one specific organizational culture. However, it may be possible for a given leader to figure in more than one of these types, especially in different organizations or over long periods of time.

In keeping with the U.S. cultural emphasis on individuals and their achievements, most accounts of leadership focus on individual leaders rather than on the social processes they set in motion. We have nonetheless been able to discern in various of these accounts the outlines of the social processes involved, which inevitably include followers and situations as well as leaders. The following specific cases of each of these types of leadership were selected to illustrate the elements listed in Table 7–1. They also show that the four types of leadership involve rather different sets of problems and likely solutions, listed in Table 7–2.

Leadership that Creates Cultures

Organizational cultures are created when leaders set social processes in motion to achieve their visions of what their organizations should be like and what they should try to accomplish. In effect, leaders' visions provide the substance of new organizational cultures. Such leaders may emerge from the general society to

TABLE 7–2
FOUR VARIANTS OF TWO BASIC TYPES OF CULTURAL LEADERSHIP

	Innovation		Maintenance	
	Create	*Change*	*Embody*	*Integrate*
Core Organizational Problem	To attract followers and unite them	To weaken and replace elements of the old culture	To keep existing culture vital	To reconcile diverse interests of subcultures
Possible Solutions	Personal qualities	Personal qualities	Rites of renewal	Rites of conflict reduction
	Rites of integration	Rites of degradation		

SOURCE: Adapted from Trice and Beyer 1991, p. 163.

found new organizations that carry out their visions, or they may be persons who have such visions and are appointed by others to found or head organizations. Charisma is clearly one route to the creation of culture. But is not, by any means, the only one. The literature provides examples of apparently effective culture creation that lack some of the distinctive features of charisma.

Charismatic Foundings

Because the visions of charismatic leaders are radical, they often are founders of new organizations. Such leaders usually emerge from within an existing organization and its culture, but find they cannot carry out their vision within it. Thus, they are forced to found new organizations to realize their aims. Many different types of organizations have been founded through the operation of charismatic leadership. The examples that follow were chosen to illustrate some of that variety.

John L. Lewis, the founder of the Committee for Industrial Organizations (CIO), is a particularly good example. Lewis was a leader within the American Federation of Labor (AFL), and even president of one of its affiliated unions—the United Mine Workers (UMW)—during the 1930s. The country was in the middle of a deep depression. Labor and management were locked in bloody battle, but the AFL was not addressing the widespread unrest. The vision Lewis advanced to AFL leaders was to expand the federation to organize all industrial workers; the AFL only included craft unions at that time. Lewis's idea of a union encompassing all of industry was a solution to the crisis because it could give the large mass of previously unorganized workers the power to negotiate with large companies. His proposal was, however, bitterly opposed by leaders of the other craft unions belonging to the AFL.

Nevertheless, confidently defying the old guard in the AFL, Lewis joined with a handful of followers in November 1935 to create a new union—the Committee for Industrial Organization (CIO)—to represent and thus answer the pleas of many unorganized mass production workers. His eloquent advocacy of this cause was immediately successful in winning thousands of followers from the automobile, rubber, and steel industries.

> Despite one of the worst blizzards in Ohio history, thousands of workers packed meeting halls in Cleveland and Akron; indeed, in both cities the halls were too small to contain the crowds, and thousands stood in the streets outside in the driving snow and numbing temperatures to listen to Lewis over a loudspeaker system. (Dubofsky and Van Tine 1977, p. 228)

At the 1936 convention of the UMW, by asking those who agreed with him to rise, Lewis directly confronted William Green, the president of the AFL. The delegates rose en masse and applauded for 15 minutes.

Despite Lewis' strong following, the political wrangling continued, and in September of that year, the CIO was kicked out of the AFL. The two groups did not reunite until 1955. Lewis never wavered from his cause and was rewarded by seeing industrial workers accepted into and represented in the newly merged AFL-CIO. His vision left a lasting impact on the American labor movement and created a markedly different culture within it.

A less well known example of a charismatic founding is provided by the Oneida Silver Company, which originated within a utopian community. Alfred Noyes was the charismatic founder of that community, located in upper New York State. His radical visions included the sharing of everything—property, capital, sexual relations, and children. His followers accepted his radical visions and lived happily for decades putting them into practice. To support the community, his followers manufactured animal traps. They were a hard-working and prosperous people, and therefore tolerated by their more conventional neighbors for a while. However, the community eventually foundered over its opposition to exclusivity in sexual relations; young people in the community fell in love and wanted to marry. Also, the surrounding communities became increasingly outraged by the community's practice of free love. As the community began to break up, Noyes urged his remaining followers to use their metal-working skills to make silverware. During the first half of the 20th century, his son Pierrepont Noyes carried forward the routinization of his father's charisma into a new organization. He formed a joint stock company to use the community's acquired skills to manufacture silverware on a bigger scale. By his enthusiasm and example, Pierrepont Noyes managed to infuse the group with an organizational harmony similar to that which had prevailed in the original Oneida community (Carden 1969). He was a remarkable salesman who made an effective role model. The company quickly grew into a very profitable manufacturing concern.

When Reed College was founded, William T. Foster became its first president. Foster turned out to be a genuine charismatic. He was a "high-minded reformer" who "did not want to be limited by established institutions, all of which were, to his mind, corrupt in practice" (Clark 1972, p. 180). His visions were taken up by his new faculty and routinized through a radically new and demanding curriculum. The students that this new college attracted also fell under Foster's spell; together the faculty and students established traditions that embued the college with the radical visions of its founder.

Mary Kay, the founder of the cosmetic company that bears her name, is widely recognized as a charismatic leader who established a company culture based on her own ideologies and values. Her radical vision was that women could be successful in business and in their families at the same time. Her direct-selling company has built an elaborate system of cultural forms around her experiences, preferences, and beliefs.

> During elaborate meetings called Mary Kay seminars, jewelry including gold and diamond pins shaped like bees, fur stoles, and even the use of pink Cadillacs are awarded to saleswomen who reach certain levels of sales. The awards are presented in a setting reminiscent of the Miss America pageants—in a large auditorium, on a stage in front of a large cheering audience, and with all participants dressed in glamorous evening clothes. Underlying this impressive and dramatic rite is the story of Mary Kay and how her personal determination and optimism enabled her to support herself and her children successfully as a saleswoman after her husband

left her, and later to use those experiences as a basis on which to found her own company. The bee-shaped pin is a symbol of the founder's ideology that with help and encouragement, everyone can "find their wings and ... fly." This optimistic ideology permeates this organization, which has become notably successful. The pink Cadillac clearly is a symbol of exalted status; Mary Kay herself drives one. Everyone who joins the company is given literature detailing the saga of Mary Kay, her company's rise to success and her belief that "women can succeed beyond their greatest dreams—if just given the opportunity." (Trice and Beyer 1984a, p. 660)

Several other direct-selling organizations also had charismatic founders (Biggart 1989).

While there are some exceptions, there is not enough detailed information available on most contemporary founders of new businesses to enable us to tell which are genuine charismatics and which are not.[8] Our last example of a well-known recent charismatic founding must therefore be somewhat speculative. Among several entrepreneurs interviewed in 1986 for a television program on the Public Broadcasting System, Steve Jobs, the cofounder of Apple Computers, presented the most charismatic qualities. He expressed a radical vision: to transform society and the way people learn with computers. The first half of his vision involved inventing and selling the personal computer to the masses in society. Together, he and Steve Wozniak accomplished that vision (Butcher 1988). The second half of his vision involves making computing power equivalent to that of mainframe computers readily available at low cost to researchers and students in universities. This vision is close to being realized.

Jobs clearly has had dedicated followers; he was not only able to attract many of them to work for Apple, he was also able to attract some of his old employees away from Apple, after he was ousted from that company, to join him in a new company called Next. The crisis to which his visions are responsive is the growing complexity and interconnectedness of human activities, which requires better ways for more people to process and communicate information more rapidly than in the past. His extraordinary personal qualities were evident as he discussed his vision and conducted a meeting with his staff. He is an articulate, charming, persuasive speaker who exudes energy, conviction, and a drive to dominate events. In addition, of course, he possesses legendary technical and marketing genius. His vision has clearly been successful, not only as measured by the success of Apple computers, but more importantly because the personal computer has revolutionized the way many people do business, write, study, make decisions, and communicate with each other. Like Martin Luther King Jr., he is not the only advocate of his vision, but he is clearly its best-known champion and symbol.

Cautions. Although space considerations prohibit illustrating each of them in each example, our analysis indicates that the cases of charismatic leadership already summarized included all of the elements listed in Table 7–1. But genuine

---

[8]Two exceptions are Donald Burr, founder of People Express Airlines, and Herb Kelliher, cofounder of Southwest Airlines. Both are discussed elsewhere in this book.

charisma is rare. Although many people may have the potential to develop the personal qualities that mark the charismatic leader, the meeting of *all* of the conditions needed to produce genuine charisma is unusual (Roberts and Bradley 1988). Social crises of one kind or another are common, and many people have visions, but few can translate those visions into a message that will attract followers and persuade them to follow. Fewer still will realize success in following their visions. Without all of these happening, a potential leader's extraordinary qualities will not be noticed, or will languish and fade for lack of support. While some analysts believe charisma can be cultivated by training and other means, such efforts are likely to encounter various difficulties, as will be discussed later in this chapter.

Also, for charisma to eventuate in a new organizational culture, it must be routinized in various ways. The routinization of charisma is itself a demanding process. It involves administrative actions that help to realize the radical vision and mission but do not interfere with it, the expression and celebration of the vision in cultural forms, and the embodiment and preservation of the vision in a durable tradition that produces persistence of the vision and tradition over time. The routinization process will be described and discussed more fully later in this chapter when we address the issues involved in attempting to stimulate charismatic leadership. Probably potential charisma often remains unrealized because it is not routinized appropriately. Many potential new cultures and new organizations die aborning.

Other Foundings

Other founders have been effective creators of cultures without their leadership exhibiting all of the elements in Table 7–1. Alfred Fuller, the founder of the Fuller Brush company, was an entrepreneur who provided a heroic role model for his followers (Carson 1986). Fuller was a supersalesman, but not a radical reformer in any sense of the word. His leadership was not so much a response to crisis as to the opportunities he saw. He was an innovator in that he envisioned the possibilities of selling brushes to housewives. He was not the first to sell door to door, but he perfected techniques for doing so. The main way in which his ideologies were embodied in his company was in terms of his codification of how to do door-to-door selling. Fuller was exceptionally good at attracting salespeople to his organization, training them with his own approach and techniques, and then keeping them loyal to his organization through building a strong company culture. The company was especially notable for its numerous rites of integration—dances, parties, and picnics—which helped to unite his far-flung employees and gave them a sense of belonging to a cohesive group. For members of his door-to-door salesforce, who faced many abrupt refusals and rejections every day, these frequent social gatherings undoubtedly provided important emotional and social support.

Persons who are chosen by relevant authorities to head new organizations also have exceptional opportunities to create new organizational cultures. They can imprint their organizations with their own personal ideologies and values

(Schein 1985). The dean of a new medical school believed that medical education lacked adequate contact between actual practitioners and students. In effect, he saw and communicated a sense of crisis in medical education. His vision called for the hiring of practicing physicians as teaching faculty and for a high ratio of faculty to students as remedies to this crisis. The supporters of the new school accepted this vision and the dean's other ideas. "The school's early development cannot be understood without some knowledge of the ambitions, strengths, and weaknesses of its first dean . . . his personality, his dreams, his flaws, and his talent are largely responsible for the school's early structure and results" (Kimberly 1979, p. 454).

Cautions.   While founders clearly have opportunities to create cultures, they are not always successful in doing so. On the basis of their research into Silicon Valley firms, researchers at Stanford University argued that founders may some-times be credited with more influence into the formation of their company's cultures than is warranted by what actually happens. In one firm, they compared what the founder reported with what subordinates from different subgroups in the firm reported about ideologies each held during the founding period. They found that there was considerable disagreement between the reported values of the founder and those of his employees. He favored individual accountability, for example, and they favored a more bureaucratic dispersion of responsibility. As time passed, the founders' ideologies faded and those of his employees pre-vailed (Martin, Sitkin, and Boehm 1985).

   This research reminds us that organizations do not necessarily automati-cally build their cultures around the ideologies and values of the founders—probably because all founders are not equally successful in winning over others to their ways of thinking. Cultures may instead form around the values of sub-groups or other leaders within organizations.

   One observer suggested two criteria for deciding whether a particular founder created a distinct organizational culture (Schein 1983b). His analysis of three entrepreneurs who founded organizations led him to conclude that they had lasting impacts on their organizations' cultures because (1) their personal ideologies were prominently shared by other members of the organizations they founded; and (2) this influence continued even after the organizations had grown much larger, changed the nature of their products, and even changed leaders. Such lasting influence probably requires that most of the other elements of cul-tural leadership listed in Table 7–1 be present.

Leadership that Changes Cultures

Cultural change occurs when something causes the basic elements of a culture to become different. It inevitably involves both ideological change and change in prevalent cultural forms. Since the two reflect one another, a change in one provokes a change in the other. Two aspects of this definition of cultural change, however, require clarification. The first concerns the causes of change; the second concerns how much of a difference must occur before a culture is considered changed.

Because cultures are not static, but in a constant state of flux, cultural change might be considered endemic. Such endemic change, however, is not what managerial researchers and practitioners usually mean when they use the term. Rather, when researchers or practitioners refer to cultural change, they usually mean change that was sought and consciously intended. When referring to leadership that changes cultures, then, we mean leadership that consciously promotes different ideologies and cultural forms.

Also, some changes involve slight differences and others profound ones. The social processes involved probably differ. Gradual, almost imperceptible, cultural evolution and the relatively minor changes involved in cultural revitalization are not as demanding or difficult as revolutionary or radical cultural change. To avoid confusion, cultural change of some magnitude and consequence must be separated from minor adjustments and inevitable inconsistencies. Indicators of how substantial a cultural change is include what proportion of people and activities are affected, what proportion of resources are displaced, and how different new understandings and behaviors are from those already present in the culture. While analysts could improve our understanding of cultural change by being more specific about how substantial the changes they discuss are in terms of such indicators, what really matters in concrete instances is how leaders and followers perceive their situation. Situations defined as crises or great opportunities engender change; those defined as ongoing success or business-as-usual encourage maintaining a culture. The issue of distinguishing between situations calling for change and for maintenance will be addressed in more detail in Chapter 9. Because of these ambiguities in what is meant by the term *cultural change,* we want to clarify from the outset that, when referring to cultural leadership that changes cultures, we mean leadership that involves intended and substantial cultural change.

Cultural change can conceivably be initiated at the top of the management hierarchy of organizations or by people in other positions. The first kind of change is more or less mandated; formal authority buttresses its influences. The leaders of the change are usually those designated by relevant authorities to head the organization. They may be newcomers to the organization or part of the existing management. The second kind of change is more revolutionary; it emanates from within and might involve overturning existing designated leaders. The leaders of such changes are emergent leaders in the sense that they emerge from the general membership to lead a particular change effort. Examples of cultural change leadership found in the literature fall into three groups: turnaround leadership, transformational leadership, and reform from within. The first two involve designated leaders; the last is an example of emergent leadership.

Turnaround Leadership

Lee Iacocca provides the best-known example of a designated leader whose leadership drastically turned around an organization's culture. His leadership at Chrysler, at least in his early days there, exhibited all of the features of charismatic leadership. In this connection, it is interesting to note that Iacocca showed many of the personal characteristics while at Ford that later enabled him to be successful at Chrysler, but he did not have the supporting circumstances at Ford to allow his charisma to reach full fruition. Iacocca's best-known success at Ford was his heading of the team that built the small, sporty Mustang. When unveiled at the New York World's Fair in 1964, the Mustang "proved a sensation . . . and became an instant classic. It racked up record sales and it created, virtually on its own, a major new sector of the U.S. car market" (Lacey 1986, p. 513). Even in the pre-Mustang days, Iacocca

> had the ability to switch on, to light up. . . . In a group, he might appear awkward. But then you put him on a platform, and he came to life, swelling with his feelings about the car. . . . It was quite extraordinary, we all felt it, so much so that we wanted to go back to the office and work some more, to put in another couple of hours that night if we could. (Lacey 1986, p. 514)

Clearly, this was inspiring leadership, but Iacocca had not yet advanced a radical vision or surmounted a deep crisis, as he was later to do at Chrysler.

So it was the crisis at Chrysler and his coming up with radical solutions to it that enabled Iacocca to become a genuine charismatic. Soon after Ford fired Iacocca in 1978, people at Chrysler became interested in hiring Iacocca as their savior. The Chrysler Company was in deep crisis, and only some radical, dramatic action could transform it from imminent bankruptcy to solvency. During the mid-1970s Chrysler had consistently lost money, had acquired unprofitable foreign companies, and, during the recession of 1974 to 1975, had laid off valuable engineers, resulting in the production of flawed models that produced massive recalls (O'Toole 1984). Actually, the crisis was even deeper than these external signs indicated. One writer described the company as a "mess" and "operating chaos" (O'Toole 1984, p. 210) when Iacocca took over as chairman and chief executive officer in September of 1979 (Iacocca 1984, p. 145). The crisis was so deep that even the elimination of $1 billion from operating expenses, which included the closing of eight plants and concessions from the union on wages and salaries, plus the introduction of front-wheel-drive cars and a complete reorganization of the company were not sufficient to solve it.

Under these circumstances, very few believed Chrysler could survive. Both *The Wall Street Journal* and the then CEO of General Motors, Thomas A. Murphy, argued that Chrysler was no longer a viable business. But Iacocca had a vision that said otherwise. His outstanding success with the Ford Mustang apparently primed him with enough confidence to generate a vision of a new Chrysler—one free of debt and actively competing in the national and international markets. He generated an infectious vision of success, mobilizing many other key managers to carry out that vision despite the enormous odds against it. "As employees caught the vision . . . they became more committed to the future success of Chrysler" (Tichy and Ulrich 1984, p. 260).

To pull Chrysler out of its deep crisis, Iacocca now turned to more radical steps. He first attempted a daring but not unprecedented step—to get the United States government to use its immense resources to prop up a failing, privately held company. He proposed and succeeded in getting the U.S. Congress to lend the full faith and credit of the U.S. government to guarantee bank loans to Chrysler of $1.5 billion. To achieve this step, he agreed to give the federal government a sizeable amount of control in monitoring the company. His next step *was* unprecedented. He succeeded in getting Douglas Fraser, president of the United Auto Workers (UAW), appointed to the Chrysler Board of Directors as a part of a deal for further union concessions. Also, he used advertising to appeal to the American public in a personal way to adopt his vision of a new Chrysler. He prepared and delivered television commercials that phrased his vision in simple, compelling language to both the public and employees of the company. The personal appearance of the CEO of a large corporation in TV commercials was highly unusual and provoked considerable skepticism among advertising experts. Critical reactions in the press at the time show that this and the other steps Iacocca took were seen as radical (O'Toole 1984, p. 212). But, by using them, Iacocca was enormously successful. By 1983, he had dramatically eliminated debts, produced deep cutbacks, manufactured a profitable new car, and paid back the government-guaranteed loans a year early.

Along the way, from 1979 to 1982, symbolism, myth, rites, and Madison Avenue sales techniques played a prominent role in establishing Iacocca's charisma. For example, in 1979, as the crises multiplied, he announced that he had cut his salary from $360,000 to $1 per year. Also, in 1982, as a symbol of confidence, he built Dodge and Chrysler convertibles—something none of the U.S. auto makers had done for years. Such moves dramatically convinced both insiders and outsiders that he was personally deeply committed to his vision of a new Chrysler. The members of the UAW symbolically sacrificed more than a billion dollars in wages and benefits in response to his confident vision (and the realities of the crisis the company was in). After awhile, the myth became one that said that Iacocca has saved Chrysler single-handed. This, of course, was not true, and union members later expressed some anger that their contribution was not recognized. The myth, of course, helped to power Iacocca's charisma.

Several other features of charismatics can be illustrated by Iacocca. The first is that they are not necessarily likeable persons up close. Nor does everyone fall under a particular charismatic's spell. Iacocca has gotten into wrangles with others besides Henry Ford II. One was his apparent conflict with Donald Hodel, then Secretary of the Interior, over the celebrations surrounding the renovation and birthday of the Statue of Liberty. For reasons never made public, Hodel fired Iacocca as chairman of the Statue of Liberty–Ellis Island Centennial Commission. Charismatics probably appeal most to those persons caught up in the crisis to which their vision is a solution. Uninvolved onlookers may be puzzled by the charismatic's attraction for such persons. Clearly, however, Iacocca's appeal generalized beyond those working for Chrysler. His autobiography had sold over two and a half million copies by June 1986, making it the best-selling nonfiction hard-cover book in history up to that time (Spitz 1986).

Iacocca also illustrates the difficulties of sustaining charisma in large business organizations. According to Weber's and others' analyses of charisma, the personal characteristics of charismatics have a transcendent quality; they are seen by followers as somehow separate from and outside their normal, everyday experience. When the charismatic founder of the National Council on Alcoholism became closely involved in administrative detail as its chief operating officer, she was resented and eventually forced to leave; her charisma was never routinized (Trice and Beyer 1986, p. 113). Similarly, involvement in the business dealings and administration of large business firms necessitates practical and mundane behaviors that may undermine the exceptionality of charismatic business leaders. Another factor making charisma especially hard to sustain in business organizations is that the uncertainties of business keep changing; continued success is thus extremely difficult to achieve. Without it, followers may lose faith in a charismatic leader and others may be able to justify overthrowing him or her. Iacocca suffers considerable diminution of his charisma when Chrysler's financial performance sags. Steve Jobs was forced out when his wizardry no longer produced commercially successful products.

Although Iacocca is the best-known recent example, there may be other turnaround leaders who have charisma for their followers but are relatively unknown to the general public. The turnaround situation is ripe for the emergence of charisma because it is, by definition, a situation of crisis. The best indicators of whether the leaders who head organizations in crisis are charismatic is whether they propose genuinely radical visions with conviction and persistence, and whether their persuasiveness succeeds in winning followers to share their visions. To do all this they must exhibit exceptional personal qualities. The final test is whether their vision is validated by success—at least as defined by their followers.

Transformational Leadership

Not all leaders who change their organizations radically do so in response to crisis. Some may see benefits in and push for major cultural change before the organization experiences a crisis. For example, many credit Alfred P. Sloan's innovations at General Motors (GM) for the phenomenal success that company enjoyed for many years. Like Iacocca, Sloan moved through the ranks of his organization and rose quickly to the top. He was also a reformer of sorts; he opposed the autocratic type of management that prevailed in corporate life at that time. He believed that decentralized management would work better and eventually succeeded in reorganizing GM along those lines. He devised a structural system in which each divisional manager ran that division as a separate, autonomous organization (Sloan 1963). The divisions were held together and their managers' self-interests curbed through centralized financial controls. As company president, he gave up operating control of these independent units to an array of officers, enabling them to develop via the opportunities they seized and the talents they used in capitalizing on them. Sloan saw decentralization as a way to make managers' pursuing their own self-interests work for the benefit of the company (Sloan 1963). In essence, he "combined a decentralized manufacturing system with a centralized policy and financial control. . . . the GM model . . . remains as the major organizational model, not only in the United States, but throughout the industrial world. . . . it was compelling and long lasting" (Bennis and Nanus 1985, p. 130). The document in which Sloan recorded his innovations in 1920, called the "Organizational Plan," was an important cultural form within the company and has become almost a sacred text in many management circles (Dale 1956).

Another leader who radically changed his organization even though it was not in crisis was General Robert E. Wood, who formally headed Sears, Roebuck and Co. from 1928 to 1953. When Wood took over as CEO of Sears, the company was in the doldrums. Its chief competitor and imitator, Montgomery Ward, was making inroads on its mail-order business. Sears's market share had slipped for the prior four years.[9] Wood got the idea to go into new markets and not rely exclusively on the rural, mail-order business. He consulted the U.S. Census, read the population trends accurately, and opened retail stores in suburban areas. He foresaw the changes in consumer habits that the automobile would produce. By 1954, when Wood retired, Sears had well over six hundred retail stores and had retained a commanding position in the mail-order business with 11 mail-order plants and 570 catalog sales offices (Worthy 1984, p. 54). Although Montgomery Ward also imitated Sears's movement into the retail business, it was never as successful.

Wood was a commanding and confident leader, who had had a successful military career and had worked briefly for Montgomery Ward before joining Sears. He was a quartermaster general in World War I, running the entire supply arm of the American Expeditionary Force. Before the war, he was in charge of supplying the workforces, both civilian and military, that built the Panama Canal (Worthy 1984).

His basic philosophy was one of humane pragmatism (Trice and Beyer 1984b). Wood insisted on demonstrating that human values were not in conflict with economic and business values. "In his thirty years at Sears, he proved that with proper care and nurture they can be made mutually supportive" (Worthy 1984, p. 259). Few other companies at that time went as far as Sears did to protect and preserve humanitarian values. One basic expression of this ideology was Wood's distrust of authoritarian control from upper levels of management. Although he was a military man, he usually gave wide discretion to his store managers in their selection of merchandise and what to charge for it. He devised a flat organizational chart that radically reduced the number of hierarchical levels in

---

[9]Such performance was not viewed as a crisis at that time, perhaps because it was before the heyday of hostile takeovers and programmed trading by huge investors. Chapter 8 deals with these issues.

the company. His ideology was also evident in his willingness to cooperate with behavioral science research at a time when such research was almost universally rejected, or tightly controlled by management. Near the end of World War II, he urged his personnel department to improve its employee survey program. In response, the department developed an ongoing relationship with the newly formed Committee on Human Relations in Industry at the University of Chicago in 1944. Sears become one of the first corporate supporters of this highly innovative academic venture.

Designated leaders who transform their organizations' cultures in substantial ways through innovation without the impetus of a crisis are probably more common than charismatic leaders. To be successful, such leaders need to have more than innovative ideas, however. Besides having many of the elements listed in Table 7–1, they undoubtedly also need some sensitivity for the existing culture so that they can build upon what is there without totally disrupting it.

Reform from Within

The leader who emerges from within an organization and succeeds in changing its culture is probably a charismatic. Existing cultures tend to be conservative in that they "celebrate and diffuse shared meanings based on past experience" (Trice and Beyer 1984a, p. 665). Only someone with a radical vision and enormous persuasiveness is likely to be able to emerge from the membership of an organization and lead a drastic change in its culture. John L. Lewis might be thought of in this way. We discussed him as a culture creator instead because, although he did emerge from within the ranks of the labor movement and from within the ranks of officers in the AFL, he was not able to realize his vision within that organization. Instead he founded an entirely new and independent organization. In more recent times, Lech Walesa has played a similar role in Poland, and, for a while, so did Mikhail Gorbachev in the Communist Party within the former USSR.

What is remarkable about emergent cultural change leaders is that, although they do not have a designated position of power from which to effect the changes they have in mind, they succeed in doing so within the organization in which they developed these visions. To do this, they need truly exceptional personal qualities and probably also the same kinds of supportive followers and contextual circumstances discussed in connection with charismatic founders. Some elements of the existing culture may conflict with the new vision, and these must be weakened or dismantled. Its adherents are often fired or encouraged to retire, as Blount did when he set about transforming the Post Office. But, as should be evident from previous chapters, we do not believe any culture can be totally changed; residues of the old culture always remain. Smart cultural change leaders try to connect their new ideas to old ones that are already accepted.

During the decade of 1910 to 1920, Antioch College was in a "crisis of decay" (Clark 1972, p. 180). A sense of failure pervaded the organization, and there was a general consensus that incremental changes were insufficient. In 1919, Arthur E. Morgan, a member of the Antioch Board of Trustees, who was a "charismatic utopian reformer" took over as president and instituted a radical program that "overturned everything" (Clark 1972, p. 180). Antioch is a clear-cut example of social processes and charismatic vision coming together to produce lasting and radical change. What is radical and different about Antioch is its particular way of combining the scholarly with the practical. Students at Antioch work part time while pursuing their studies. This requirement not only enables them to help to support themselves, but, more importantly, to juxtapose practical experience with academic learning. The jobs they hold are not just any jobs; their jobs are integral parts of their college experience and must be approved by the faculty. This unique combination apparently appeals to a large enough body of potential students to enable Antioch to continue to prosper.

Although there may be others, this is the only well-documented example of organizational cultural reform from within that we located in the literature. Even in this case, Morgan was a relative newcomer to the board, who had been placed there by interested outside parties to protect their interests when it became evident the college was floundering. While he was an insider, he had been one for only a year when he was named president. The board had accepted the first part of his vision for the school, "A Plan of Practical Industrial Educational," just six weeks after he joined them. "At this point, he became *de facto* head of the college" (Clark 1970, p. 19).

Cultural reform from within may be a genuinely rare phenomenon. That's not to say that there are not numerous attempts made by emergent leaders to try to change their organizations' culture. Most are probably unsuccessful. John L. Lewis failed to reform the AFL. John DeLorean, as already discussed in the countercultures section of Chapter 3, failed to reform General Motors. The sad stories of whistle-blowers provide additional examples of members' failing in their attempts at cultural reform of their organizations (Glazer and Glazer 1989).

Leadership that Embodies Cultures

Another important role for cultural leadership is to preserve and embody existing cultures. By their actions, some leaders help to advance, put into practice, and protect the prevailing ideologies of their groups. Such leadership performs three important tasks: (1) it sustains the mission, distinctive role, and basic commitments of the organization; (2) it embodies its purpose by actually implementing its mission and, in the process, gives shape to its culture; and (3) it maintains organizational values and identity by defending the culture's integrity and making its ideologies as secure and stable as possible (Selznick 1957, p. 62). Embodiment leaders are also important symbols. Since people have difficulties in dealing with abstractions, they often reify—that is, treat an abstraction as a material object (Lopreato 1984). Leaders are handy targets for reification and thus come to symbolize their cultures.[10]

---

[10]We wish to thank Roland Chanove for calling this point to our attention.

Institutional Leadership

The term *institutional leader* was coined to refer to leaders who specialized in refining the mission and role of a social group, and in promoting the ideologies that support its activities (Selznick 1957, p. 27). The term seems especially appropriate to apply to formally designated leaders who embody their organizations' cultures. They are likely to be long-term members who know their cultures well.

George Washington is a telling example of a leader who emerged from within a social group as a representative of its interests and later came to embody his culture's most cherished principles and values as its designated leader. He provides an instructive contrast with the charismatic leader.

> Washington showed little if any confidence in his ability to lead the colonial forces in their rebellion against England. There is good evidence that he actually sought to avoid leadership, even though subsequently appointed to it. (Trice and Beyer 1986, p. 123)

Despite his reservations, he heroically defended and preserved the ideologies of the patriots and merchants who broke away from the English crown and founded the United States. He was "virtually deified" by his generation as a collective representation of "the values and tendencies of his society, rather than a source of these values and tendencies" (Schwartz 1983, pp. 21, 30).

Washington's leadership provided continuity for political, economic, and social structures and practices firmly rooted in English tradition (Padover 1955). He was the symbolic embodiment of prevailing ideologies, rather than their originator. Washington was a conservative, not a radical. "In addition . . . Washington displayed few, if any, extraordinary talents, or the superhuman or supernatural qualities usually associated with charisma, nor did he accomplish any unusual political or military triumphs of personal heroism or magnetism" (Trice and Beyer 1986, pp. 123–24). He thus illustrates how embodiment leaders can be heroic figures and very popular with followers without having the personal qualities of charisma. Perhaps their very ordinariness is what enables them to represent *prevailing* ideologies so well.

Thomas Watson, Jr., the CEO of International Business Machines for many years, is a good example of a corporate institutional leader. Despite some basic father-son differences, he preserved and carried forward the major missions and ideologies of the company that his father had played a key role in founding. He made it his personal responsibility to continue IBM's strong emphasis on service to customers and aggressive marketing, on "high standards of performance and meticulous attention to detail, on high moral and ethical standards" (Levinson and Rosenthal 1984, p. 206). Once he discovered that IBM's tax accountants had made a minor error in the company's favor on tax returns two years after the fact. He "personally called on the head of the IRS [Internal Revenue Service] in New York to report the mistake; sometimes Tom Jr. thought business ought to pay more taxes and said so" (Levinson and Rosenthal 1984, p. 206). Other instances of Watson's reinforcing the dominant ideologies were his efforts to make sure that small vendors did not become too dependent on IBM. He instituted a rule that no vendors could rely on IBM for more than 30 percent of their business. Also, to avoid IBM dominating a community, he inaugurated a policy that his company would never exceed a certain percentage of the community workforce—typically no more than 6,000 employees.

Watson also embodied his father's concern for treating employees fairly and used many of the same communication devices that his father did, like seeking personal contact with employees at all levels and making frequent speeches to IBM employees in many locations. When his father died, Watson "went to every one of the plants, and held meetings with all of the employees. He talked about what he thought, what he planned to do, and what he hoped for the business" (Levinson and Rosenthal 1984, p. 212). These visits clearly functioned as rites of renewal. So did a plethora of other practices. Under Watson's leadership, the well-known open-door policy established by his father became thoroughly institutionalized. According to this policy, employees could go to their bosses at any time with their concerns and complaints; if their doing so did not produce a resolution, employees had the right to go directly up the line, to whomever they chose, even to Watson himself. For employees who preferred to deal directly with Watson himself from the beginning, there was the Dear Tom letter, which was typically used by older employees who had been hired by Watson's father. These letters usually began: "Dear Tom, When your father hired me . . ." (Foy 1975, p. 125).

Both of these alternatives provoked awe and fear among line managers, who knew that regardless of where Watson was, he would immediately act upon an employee's concern or complaint—often with a slight bias against the manager involved. One manager remarked, "A lot of companies have Open Doors, but I doubt if many have the hard attitude that the employee is right unless proven otherwise. Injustices were done . . . but it was basically good for the company" (Foy 1975, p. 125). Tom Watson, Jr., estimated he spent 25 percent of his time on the open-door policy and felt it was "well worth the while" (Levinson and Rosenthal 1984, p. 213). For one thing, it was not an empty ritual, but something for which the managers had to be thoroughly prepared at all times. Particularly if an employee was to be discharged, the open-door policy was put into practice.

Without Tom Watson, Jr.'s efforts to preserve and reinforce the cultural legacy of his father, it is unlikely that IBM would be known as a company with a distinctive culture today. The son did not create the culture, but his role in embodying it was crucial to its continuance and vitality.

Philip Caldwell, who was CEO of the Ford Motor Company from 1980 to 1986, is another example of a leader who both embodied and solidified the organization's existing culture. The culture at Ford is very different from that at IBM. Starting with Henry Ford, and continuing with his son Edsel, his grandson Henry Ford II, and later Lee Iacocca, the company developed a culture of confusion and internal struggle that was surmounted to achieve efficiency. This culture undoubtedly developed in response to Henry Ford's tendency to enact his own convictions of the moment, no matter how much they upset ongoing events. Ford was notorious for reversing the decisions of others to whom he had presumably delegated authority. His son Edsel was the unfortunate chief target of his caprice. During World War II, Edsel had committed the company to build airplane engines, especially for Great Britain. As the Battle of Britain approached a climax, the British asked President Roosevelt for help with the urgent production of 6,000 Rolls Royce Merlin engines for Spitfire fighters. Roosevelt's commissioner for industrial production, William S. Knudsen, secured from Edsel Ford a commitment to build them with all deliberate speed. Henry Ford initially agreed and permitted the arrangements to be made public. When, however, the British hailed the development as a "major step," Henry Ford suddenly reversed himself. The Ford Motor Company never made the engines; both Edsel Ford and Knudsen were deeply embarrassed (Lacey 1986, p. 388).

Such capricious interventions set a tone for the company. Efficiency came about under such circumstances *despite* confusion and unforeseen obstacles—it was not the product of rational planning and smooth implementation of plans. But rationality was never completely forgotten. How could it be in the company that introduced the assembly line?

Caldwell was picked by Henry Ford II to become CEO after a time of unusual strife, even for the Ford company. Lee Iacocca and Ford II had been locked in battle for several years, culminating in Ford's firing Iacocca in 1978. Ford, who was CEO, had consistently turned to Caldwell as a way to blunt the power of Iacocca, who, as president, was a clear threat to the established culture and perhaps to Ford's power. Iacocca agitated for change. Caldwell represented the current culture's determination to produce in predictable fashion despite turbulence and confusion. This is what he had done all during his career in unglamorous arenas like trucks and commercial vehicles and international operations. In effect, Caldwell personified the assembly-line mentality. As one analyst put it, he was "the uncharismatic Caldwell" (Lacy 1986, p. 660).

Under Caldwell's leadership, Ford became a smooth working organization that produced "a proper, long-term, planned product cycle, with new medium-sized cars, the Taurus and the Sable, which are the first Ford products since the Mustang and the Falcon to give General Motors serious grounds for concern" (Lacey 1986, p. 661). That Caldwell was a successful leader is evidenced by the performance of Ford during his reign. The company gained in market share even faster than did Chrysler, headed at the same time by the charismatic Iacocca. Furthermore, the Ford company did this without outside help, even though it was in almost as serious a financial plight as Chrysler was when Iacocca got the government to guarantee its loans. While Iacocca was doing a dramatic turnaround of Chrysler by changing it from top to bottom, Caldwell apparently achieved equally good, perhaps even better results by consistent embodiment leadership. Caldwell acted so as to preserve company traditions, not to transform or radically change them. He found within the existing culture beliefs and values he could reinforce to achieve improved performance.

Numerous other examples of designated leaders who embodied their company's cultures could be cited. They include Charles Steinmetz of General Electric and Robert W. Woodruff of Coca-Cola. Steinmetz was one of those leaders who "embody the values of the culture and pass along important lessons in business success and motivation" (Deal and Kennedy 1982, p. 45). A crippled Austrian immigrant, Steinmetz worked in Thomas Edison's laboratory and took over its leadership after Edison left. In this role, he continued the exploratory, inventive spirit of that lab, extending it into present-day life at G.E. by hiring eager, young engineers and then attending carefully to their socialization and development. Some even lived in his home with him. In this way, he implanted the culture into succeeding generations of G.E. engineers and managers. Robert Woodruff took control of the Coca-Cola Company in 1923. He immediately decided that the best way to sell Coca-Cola was to emphasize the traditional taste of the drink. He therefore undertook extensive efforts to improve the quality of the existing syrup and instituted a quality control program to ensure uniformity of taste. He also took a personal interest in the company's already extensive promotion and advertising programs, sharply increasing the budget allocations and stimulating more creative approaches. In the process, he refined the traditional marketing strategies, making them more coherent, purposeful, and focused (Walters 1978, p. 135).

An important role for embodiment leaders is to express a mission or set of values that give meaning to a group's customary activities. A brothel manager who was considered an effective leader expressed such a mission for his organization with great conviction:

> We have a mission here. We contribute to society. I show society that this business can have positive aspects. One example: I just fully equipped this place so it's accessible to the handicapped. Handicapped people don't get a fair shake in society when it comes to the freedom to have sexual relationships. They're ostracized. Here it's really refreshing to see a paraplegic come in. The women are sensitive to his needs, and they send him out feeling like a whole man. (Wall 1986, p. 26)

To be an institutional leader in an organizational sense is not always the same as being a pillar of society.

Group Leadership

Informal leadership that emerges in small groups usually involves embodiment leaders because such leaders tend to be conformists to the prevailing cultures in their groups, rather than nonconformists or reformers. Why this occurs was explained by a theorist who suggested that groups accord their members idiosyncrasy credits corresponding to the positive regard in which they are held (Hollander 1958). Deviance and poor performance reduce the credit balance, while conformity and good performance increase it. Only a member who reaches a certain threshold of credits attains a leadership role. Thus, persons who respect the existing culture and represent it by their behaviors tend to be accorded group leadership roles.

Another explanation for why some persons become the informal leaders of small groups comes from laboratory experiments: "some of the most consistent, compelling, and powerful results in the leadership literature" support what is affectionately known as the "babble hypothesis," namely that those persons who emerge as leaders in small groups are also among those who talk the most (Sashkin and Garland 1979, p. 83). These leaders tend not only to be verbally proficient, but to have dominant personality traits (House and Baetz 1979, p. 351) and to represent the interests of group members to outsiders.

Leaders of small groups are often cultural leaders because their efforts are sure to reinforce prevailing group norms and cultural practices. They also help to articulate shared rationales for advancing their groups' interests and maintaining group boundaries. The defense of group interests and boundaries is especially crucial among the powerless. In an interview, a leader of a group of winos explained how he defended his group:

> "I negotiate with the police. They leave us alone if we stay down here. Once in a while you have trouble with blacks coming down here wanting to start a fight or something. I fight them or just tell them to go on. Then we all get up and there's more of us than them so they don't fight. We're all going to help each other." (Wall 1986, p. 39)

Observations of another group of winos—a so-called bottle gang—showed that its leader enforced group boundaries and norms by first collecting money from each member who shared the bottle and resisting attempts to include any persons who did not have the full amount of money decided on (Peterson and Maxwell 1958). He then either purchased the bottle himself or deputized someone else to do so. Finally he monitored how much each member drank out of the communal bottle and intervened if anyone tried to drink more than his fair share. The leader also represented the gang in any brushes with the police.

Observations of employees in restaurants and of street-corner gangs revealed the same tendencies: Both kinds of groups had definite status structures headed by informal leaders who customarily originated action for their groups and exercised major influence over the attitudes and behaviors of group members (Whyte 1948, p. 210). Such informal leaders also often acted as carriers of group culture through their telling of group myths and stories and their initiation of jokes and humor that became an important part of group traditions (Miller and Form 1980, p. 410). In these and other ways, they reinforced and fostered the prevailing group culture, which functions as a subculture within the larger organization or society.

An analysis of power (French and Raven 1968), suggests several ways in which informal leaders may influence their groups' cultures. Five sources of power were identified: referent, expert, reward, coercive, and legitimate. Informal leaders are likely to have referent power, which means they are so liked and admired for certain personal qualities that they provide role models for their followers. Informal leaders are also often expert leaders—persons who have expertise that is highly valued by the group. In addition, informal leaders will usually be granted reward and coercive power by their groups; they are expected to enforce group values and norms through rewarding conformity and punishing deviance. The one source of power they lack is legitimate power. However, observations of "gaffers" (glassblowers) at Corning Glass Company showed that some informal leaders can become strong team leaders "even without the formal support of authority" (Whyte 1961, p. 154).

Because the basis for informal leaders' influence lies in embodying existing values and norms of particular subcultures, their influence is probably not transferable to other subcultures. An effective informal group leader in one group may not be equally effective in another. Also, if recognized, plucked out of that subculture, and given formal authority, the informal embodiment leader may have difficulty in becoming equally effective or feeling comfortable as a formal leader. In the 1940s, some U.S. businesses began recruiting supervisors from among union leaders. Some of the union stewards lured by management into supervisory roles experienced severe role conflict and feelings of disloyalty (Sayles and Strauss 1953, pp. 108–10). They found the break difficult and had to change friends. Other stewards turned down management positions because of social pressures from other union members, who framed the shift from union official to supervisor as "selling out." Obviously a shift in values and ideologies was involved. Informal leaders believe in their groups' distinctive ideologies, which may not be easily reconciled with those of other subcultures.

It seems likely that designated, formal leaders of groups, such as managers and supervisors, can also function as embodiment leaders. Although there have been thousands of studies of groups in laboratories and organizations, it is hard to find rich descriptions of what leaders and followers actually do in their groups. Most research has used instruments that describe behaviors in terms of etic categories related to one of the approaches to leadership discussed at the beginning of this chapter. One group of researchers, however, identified a type of leader behavior they called inspirational, defined as "the extent to which a leader *stimulates* enthusiasm among subordinates for the work of the group and *says* things to build their confidence in their ability to successfully perform assignments, and attain group objectives" (Yukl and Van Fleet 1982, p. 89). In studies of four military units, researchers found that inspirational leadership was related to leader effectiveness in both combat and noncombat situations. This form of leadership was inspirational in the sense that it emotionally aroused and heightened motivation among followers.[11] A major consequence of the inspirational leaders' behavior was building confidence—a basic source of emotional strength for soldiers in combat (Yukl 1981, p. 121). These researchers did not describe the cultural aspects of the groups studied, but in all likelihood, the

---

[11]Later research developed a pool of 73 items intended to distinguish transactional from transformational leadership. (The transactional-transformational distinction is similar to that drawn earlier between instrumental and cultural leadership.) Eighteen of these items reflect mostly inspirational leadership but have been labeled as charismatic leadership (Bass 1985a, p. 210), apparently because 2 of the 18 refer to vision or mission. We feel this approach to studying charisma and leadership is not cultural because it fails to address the situations of leaders—most importantly, the cultures which they help to create or maintain. It focuses only on the reported behaviors of leaders or the attributions followers make about leaders. It also fails to measure the traits or actual behaviors of leaders.

groups developed into subcultures over time. With an inspirational leader, these group subcultures were apparently consistent with military values and the goals of the overall organization. Without an inspirational leader, group subcultures may have emphasized other values and goals. One sign of effective embodiment leadership of a small group may be that its subculture reflects and perhaps even exaggerates the overall organizational culture.

Heroic Leadership

While not leaders in the usual sense that they consciously try to influence others, heroes function as embodiment leaders to the degree that others are influenced by their examples. One account refers to them as "corporate right stuff," and thus links them to the men who became the first American astronauts and the film about them.

> Like John Wayne or Burt Reynolds in pinstripes, they create role models for employees to follow. The hero is the great motivator, the magician, the person everyone will count on when things get tough. They have unshakable character and style. They do things that everyone else wants to do but is afraid to try. Heros are symbolic figures whose deeds are out of the ordinary, but not too far out. They show—often dramatically—that the ideal of success lies within human capacity. (Deal and Kennedy 1982, p. 37)

Managers are seldom heroes because heroes are not decisive, but intuitive. "They don't make decisions, except one: does it fit the vision or not?" (Deal and Kennedy 1982, p. 37).

In a brand-new high-tech company, the founders decided to appoint a hero as one of their first tasks. They decided to name a superior inventor as the first chairman of their new company. He was selected, rather than more traditional managerial types, to symbolize the high value the company culture placed on invention. The inventor-hero was given a private laboratory, and during the celebration of its opening, did what an inventor-hero would be expected to do: He made a robot suddenly appear, walk across the room, and turn on the air conditioner. "What would seem to outsiders a joke was in fact a demonstration of faith in the technology to come . . ." (Deal and Kennedy 1982, p. 39). Although the authors don't say so explicitly, it seems likely that this hero-inventor's managerial role as chairman was an entirely symbolic one, and that the real CEO was someone else.

It is unusual for organizations to recognize their heroes by giving them managerial roles. More often, the heroes seem to be specialists whose work is central to the success of the organization. Current company policies that incorporate dual career ladders could be a mechanism to recognize and perhaps foster heroic cultural leadership. We know of one large company, for example, that has the title of corporate scientist. To attain this title is a great honor; the few persons who have it travel to other laboratories in the corporation that ask for their help and advice. In the process, of course, they act as role model for the behaviors of other scientists by personifying the company's cultural values and expectations.

Leadership that Integrates Cultures

Organizations and their environments are multicultural; most have subcultures within them. This cultural pluralism creates a need for some kind of integrating force to keep some degree of harmony and some reasonable balance of power among various subcultures that affect organizational functioning. If internal subcultures are not too diverse, an overall organizational culture may be able to provide sufficient integration. But if internal subcultures are diverse and in conflict, and that diversity is helpful to an organization, or if some subcultures whose cooperation is needed are outside the organization, an integrative form of leadership is needed to manage the diversity. Some integrative leadership involves top managers who pull together diverse interests from inside and outside organizations; this leadership has been described as consensus leadership. Other integration leadership occurs at the workgroup level where immediate supervisors manage to balance conflicting interests; descriptions of transactional leadership fit this latter type of integrative leadership.

Consensus Leadership

Consensus leaders negotiate among groups with diverse values and interests, and by bargaining, trade-offs, and other maneuvers, succeed in incorporating the groups into overall decision making and action (Zaleznick and Kets de Vries 1975, p. 232). Consensus leaders do not seek to homogenize diverse subcultures by changing them or creating a single culture to embrace them all. Rather they use their influence to find workable compromises that allow subcultures to maintain their distinctiveness. They are good listeners, bargainers, and coordinators; actively calculate how to integrate; and act as facilitators of common decisions and as distributors of rewards and punishments. They also are good communicators who can explain different subcultures to each other. They do not seek complete agreement—only enough to deal with problems at hand.

Since there are usually a myriad of outside stakeholders that put pressure on organizations to recognize their particular interests, management must not only find a way to balance inside interests with each other, but also with various outside interests. Employees, stockholders, unions, government agencies, suppliers, vendors, customers and clients, creditors, and members of the surrounding community—all have a stake in the organization, and all in one way or another can, by their actions, disrupt organizational functioning unless some way is found to coordinate and integrate their demands. Consequently, some members of top management must act as consensus leaders who persuade divergent outside and inside interests to cooperate.

Lyndon Johnson provided a prototype for consensus leadership during his tenure as majority leader of the U.S. Senate. He brilliantly brought together highly divergent political points of view, conflicting personalities, and geographically separated constituencies to produce concerted legislative action. He did all of this with a president from the opposing party in the White House. He was widely quoted and admired for using the Prophet Isaiah as his touchstone: "Come, let us reason together." He has been called a "triumphant coalition maker" (Smith 1988, p. 455). Johnson consistently went out of his way to encourage others to incur political debts with him. He had a large accumulation of such debts, and adroitly used them when a consensus could be forged by calling up some of them to back a particular piece of legislation. One of his major tactics was the initial formation of a small clique of legislators with the same limited, but common, concrete goals. Then he would steadily expand this nucleus in order to get a wider alliance and participation in the final decision on legislation and its passage. One factor that aided Johnson was the concrete and explicit ways he demonstrated outcomes from his consensual efforts. Usually goals were in some tangible form, such as legislation passed, appropriations secured, or appointments accomplished.

Another example in the public sector is provided by David Lilienthal, who headed the Tennessee Valley Authority during its formative years in the 1930s. The TVA was a combination of public and private power companies that came together to jointly exploit the potential for hydroelectric power in the Tennessee River basin. The entire effort was intended to bring economic development and prosperity to an underdeveloped region and financial stability to the private power companies there during the bleak years of the Great Depression. The situation has been described as follows:

> The problem of the TVA was only in part that of the application of technology to generate electric power. It was also a problem in rural development and the creation of a new quasi-public institution as an instrument of public policy. If Lilienthal and his associates had had conflictual and competitive relations with the main constituent groups, the enterprise would surely have failed. As it was, it faced the overt hostility of the power-generating industry because it was a source of competition; it could ill afford hostile relations with consumers, landholders, and local politicians. Lilienthal mastered the art of coopting constituents—making them a part of the larger organization identified with the purposes of TVA. This process required consensus in decisions, and participation, bargaining, and negotiation, in which all sides could feel themselves a part of the apparatus in which decisions were made. (Zaleznick and Kets de Vries 1975, p. 232)

Lilienthal knew what he was doing, and was also aware that achieving some measure of consensus by itself was not sufficient; it must be led in a useful direction. He wrote:

> Cooperative arrangements, devices of coordination, and the fullest collaboration among federal and state agencies are characteristic of the TVA's methods of getting the job done, but these methods would go for naught, in our judgment, unless there was central management able to make important decisions and to provide a core of leadership in the region. (Selznick 1949, p. 76)

Pierre Du Pont, who held the Du Pont company together during a time of rapid expansion and family rivalry, is a good example of consensus leadership in the private sector. When Pierre became active at Du Pont at the turn of the century, it was a gunpowder and explosives company. He tried initially to work jointly with two of his cousins, Coleman and Alfred, in running the company. Pierre assumed the position of treasurer, and, with his knowledge of finances, was a key player in the many mergers in which the company was involved in the early 1900s. He constantly negotiated with other powder companies that were for sale, or wished to become part of the larger company, on the conditions and outcomes of their merger. After the merger, he worked to integrate them successfully into the ever-growing company. One result was that the company became a true innovator in organizational design—adopting one of the first divisionalized structures in corporate America (Chandler and Salzbury 1971).

At the same time, Pierre had to deal with family-based threats to the integrity of the company. First and foremost, there was the rivalry between himself and his two cousins, which affected the whole extended family. Alfred was most interested in gunpowder and explosives and soon withdrew to concentrate on that part of the business. Not so Coleman, who became president. Working together, Pierre and Coleman managed to maintain family harmony until 1913, when Coleman decided to resign the presidency. This created an opportunity for Pierre to gain clear control of the company by buying Coleman's stock, a move which other family members—particularly Alfred and William Du Pont—opposed. The result was a protracted lawsuit in which most of the family became embroiled and which Pierre eventually won. With clear control, he could work unimpeded to integrate the various factions into a productive whole (Chandler and Salzbury 1971; Zaleznik and Kets de Vries 1975).

Transactional Leadership

While consensus leaders operate at the top of organizations, other levels of integration leadership are needed to help dissipate conflicts at lower levels and to fashion concerted actions from people and subgroups with divergent interests. To a substantial degree, such leadership relies on conventional social exchange processes. "The transactional leader induces performance among followers by negotiating an exchange relationship with them of reward for compliance" (Bass 1985a, p. 32). In the process, transactional leaders balance and coordinate diverse value systems and interests to achieve some measure of coordinated effort. Often the rewards they administer are nonmaterial; these include feedback, praise, commendations, recommendations for promotion, public recognition, and honors (Bass 1985a, p. 122). Obviously, such nonmaterial rewards are heavily symbolic and their meaning to workers may depend on subgroup beliefs, values, and norms.

An unusual exchange with definite subcultural overtones occurred when a Coast Guard officer named Patterson decided to trade concessions with a group of insubordinate, overqualified, and bored subordinates. In order to do so, he had to gain acceptance from superiors for his unusual plan.

> He sat down with the group and told them he was willing to stake his reputation and military career on their ability to demonstrate the propriety of their work-

saving ideas. He helped them see what was at stake for them. He explained to them that while it seemed silly to these college graduates to keep their hair short and to behave in military fashion when in public, that was the price for having up to two days a week of extra free time. They were willing to take on the challenge. (Wilkins 1989, p. 115)

The group subsequently became the highest performing, highest regarded group on the base—until Patterson left the base and was replaced by another officer.

Patterson was an effective transactional leader not only because he understood the subculture of his subordinates well enough to offer them a reward they valued in exchange for their compliance, but because he was also able to negotiate with his superiors and persuade them that the exchange he proposed to make was consistent with the Coast Guard and base culture. Because the exchanges and negotiations needed to achieve transactional leadership are ongoing, such efforts require continued vigilance or they will be short-lived (Wilkins 1989, p. 117).

Multiplicity of Cultural Leaders

Because cultural leadership can occur in a variety of ways and have a range of consequences, cultural leadership is probably fairly common. Table 7–3 lists four types and ten variants of cultural leadership. Many different persons in each organization have the potential for exercising one or another of the forms of cultural leadership discussed. Some of these leaders are designated to fill leadership roles; others emerge on an informal basis. Some lead followers who are socially and geographically scattered so that some are at a distance; others influence followers they can relate to regularly on a face-to-face basis. Clearly, cultural leadership is not a rare phenomenon.

TABLE 7–3
TYPES AND VARIANTS OF CULTURAL LEADERSHIP

Consequences for Cultures	Variants
Create	Charismatic foundings
	Other foundings
Change	Turnaround leadership
	Transformational leadership
	Reform from within
Embody	Institutional leadership
	Group leadership
	Heroic leadership
Integrate	Consensus leadership
	Transactional leadership

If many organizations lack coherent cultures, it may be not for lack of cultural leadership, but because they have more than one type of cultural leader working at cross-purposes. Although leadership that creates cultures might be expected to face the least threat from competing, incompatible cultural leadership, even new organizations fairly quickly grow their own subcultures and import, along with their new members, elements of divergent occupational cultures. Members of these groups may become potent subcultural leaders. Leaders who attempt to change their organizations' or groups' cultures may be hampered by the presence of other leaders who are functioning as cultural maintenance leaders. Such leaders may not only be present among top management, where rites of degradation can be used to remove those who embody the old culture, but among the subcultural leaders embedded in many work units and informal groups throughout an organization. Leaders who wish to continue and strengthen existing values and traditions find themselves dealing with would-be reformers and countercultures. Leaders good at integrative leadership may find that others wish to fashion a monolithic culture that will dissolve differences.

Which cultural consequences will prevail may depend heavily on followers and situations. Some situations and some sets of followers are ripe for certain types of cultural leadership, but not others. While leaders can influence followers' perceptions of situations by exposing and emphasizing crises and problems, or by emphasizing relative prosperity and the manageability of problems, they cannot stray too far from realities without threats to their credibility and to the futures of their organizations.

However, cultural consequences cannot be dictated by a leader; they must unfold as a product of social processes that involve and engage members of a culture. All cultural leadership entails a coming together of many different elements. Like culture itself, cultural leadership may be more of an emergent and fluctuating phenomenon than past theories of leadership recognize. Designated leaders are not likely to be the only, nor necessarily the most influential, cultural leaders in organizations. Emergent, informal leaders also play a vital role in cultural leadership.

Designated vs. Emergent Leaders

Whether leaders are formally designated to head a group, or emerge informally from within one, creates constraints on their cultural leadership. Designated leaders are appointed, elected, or otherwise formally chosen to assume a position of hierarchical authority. But they are not automatically cultural leaders by virtue of their position; they become leaders only if they succeed in influencing the cultures to which their subordinates or others subscribe. Logically, those who choose designated leaders are likely to prefer persons with attributes that fit with their own cultural values. If the choice process is an election, qualities that are congruent with voters' values will be important. Since voters are also followers, elected leaders have a good chance of being able to exercise cultural leadership. Union members and citizens will follow presidents and elected officials who see the world as they do and who will represent their cherished values and interests. If, on the other hand, the choice is made hierarchically, qualities that mesh with the current values and aims of the appointing authorities will probably be decisive. For example, the type of person chosen as a corporate CEO may depend on whether the current board of directors wants current practices to be continued or drastically changed. Their wishes, however, may not be aligned with those of organizational members. Designated leaders, even though they genuinely share the board's views of the situation, may then face an uphill battle to achieve the cultural consequences the board envisioned.

Emergent leaders are almost automatically likely to be able to influence their groups' cultures because their informal origins mean they already represent group beliefs, values, and norms. Such leaders usually help to express and solidify the substance of existing group cultures. They are unlikely to espouse radically new ideas unless there is some shared sense of crisis that seems to require new solutions. Emergent leaders thus reflect, amplify, and channel social impulses that arise from their followers and their situations.

At-a-Distance vs. Face-to-Face Leaders

Whether cultural leaders operate at a distance from followers or on a face-to-face basis (Dubin 1979) has other implications. Many work organizations are too large for their CEOs and other top executives to exercise face-to-face cultural leadership with more than a handful of senior executives and a small proportion of other employees. As a result, some may only be effective leaders of the top management subculture. Others may be able to forge overall cultures that permeate their organization from top to bottom. One way they may be able to do this is through effects on followers that are recreated and transmitted within groups (Meindl 1990).

Unfortunately, while there are thousands of studies of face-to-face leaders, there are relatively few studies of at-a-distance leaders or leaders at the top of organizations (Hunt 1991). So we have little systematic knowledge of how the two levels of leadership may differ. But it seems highly unlikely from what we know about social processes in general that the ways in which cultural leadership works at a distance are the same as those which work on a more intimate level (Trice and Beyer 1991). Leaders at a distance cannot rely on intimate interactions nor on subtle means of persuasion to influence followers. Their day-to-day behaviors are observable by relatively few in their organization. They cannot provide direct role models for very many followers if they simply quietly go about their business in an unobtrusive way. To communicate their ideas and values to a far-flung group of followers they must engage in dramatic, public acts. John L. Lewis, Lee Iacocca, Steve Jobs, Mary Kay, Tom Watson, Jr., Lyndon Johnson, and most of the other at-a-distance leaders described in this chapter conveyed their visions through bold and dramatic public gestures.

Thus, the personal qualities required to exercise effective cultural leadership on a face-to-face basis and at a distance may be very different. Face-to-face leaders can be low key, considerate, and democratic; they can act largely in a facilitative role, influencing others by their example as much as by direct attempts at persuasion. Leaders at a distance must probably project a more commanding image; followers need to believe they are in control of events. Leaders at a distance probably also need to be more directly persuasive; verbal skills and an air of assurance are therefore more important for at-a-distance cultural leaders.

Of course, the effects of the two levels of leadership also differ. In organizations, leadership at a distance is what influences whole organizations or large subunits, such as divisions. The effects of such leadership will be both direct and indirect. Followers can directly experience its effects through occasional contacts with such a leader, but most of the time the effects will be indirect, with the leadership expressed through strategies, structures, and organizational practices (Hunt 1991).

Balancing Concerns About Cultural Innovation and Maintenance

Although the existing literature on cultural leadership focuses almost exclusively on how leadership can be used to create or change cultures, it is far from clear that this emphasis is driven by the needs of organizations or that it reflects what actually happens. There are several other likely explanations in the cultures of management researchers and practitioners. First, several influential researchers were members of the organizational development (OD) movement (e.g. Schein 1983a, 1985; Bass 1985a), which has ideologies promoting organizational change. Second, U.S. managers seem to be eternally preoccupied with change—probably because of the strong value placed on progress and technology in the general culture. To many managers, the very term *technology* connotes change and progress. This is reflected in recent preoccupations with technology transfer and "high tech." Both are rather universally considered desirable, good, and almost magic routes to prosperity in communities, states, and nations. Third, U.S. managers and management scholars had to make sense of the ascendance of other nations and the relative decline of the United States in the world economy. A rather natural conclusion of such sense making was that something must be wrong and must be changed if the U.S. downturn is to be halted or reversed. Fourth, popular books (Peters and Waterman 1982; Ouchi 1981; Deal and Kennedy 1982) advanced culture as the culprit and the panacea for this decline. Firms with the right kinds of cultures could succeed; others could not. The clear implication was that many firms needed to build cultures or change the ones they had.

It is important to move away from this one-sided and simplistic emphasis on cultural change in organizations. It is doubtful that all U.S. firms need to change their cultures or will be likely to succeed in doing so if they try. Management scholars and consultants have fed this preoccupation with cultural change by focusing on two conceptions of leadership that were developed before the revival of concern with cultures in organizations—charisma (Weber 1947) and transformational leadership (Burns 1978). For example, a recent volume, drawn from papers given at a conference, focuses on charisma (Conger and Kanungo 1988). Also, many of the discussions and studies of charismatic and transformational leadership focus on traits, reported behaviors of leaders, and attributions of followers—probably because this type of study is what the methods perfected earlier in pursuing traditional approaches to instrumental leadership do best. Whether we are considering instrumental or cultural leadership, the traits, reported styles of behaving, and attributes given by followers are not the whole story. There have been very few efforts to incorporate some aspects of the situation into such studies (Ehrlich, Meindl, and Viellieu 1990). But what is most limiting is that studies in this tradition fail to consider how leadership can be important in embodying or integrating cultures.

Practical Disadvantages of Domesticating Charisma

Because this chapter uses charisma as a starting point for analyzing cultural leadership, perhaps some discussion is needed to explain why focusing on charisma as a primary source of cultural leadership organizations is impractical. There are at least four reasons why cultivating charisma may not be practical in most business and other work organizations. First, as already mentioned, genuine charisma is relatively rare. One or another of the factors that produce charisma may be relatively common, but the coming together of all of them is not. The complexity of the phenomenon (Bradley 1987) remains a significant barrier to attempts to cultivate charismatic leadership by such means as training (Sashkin 1988; Conger and Kanungo 1988).

Second, charismatic leadership is risky; the phenomenon of charisma is, at base, irrational. The basis for attraction to the charismatic vision does not rest in rational judgments but in emotional anxieties provoked by a sense of crisis. The radical vision is embraced because people are desperate for a solution (Meindl 1990). In this state they may be attracted to foolish or bad ideas (Musser 1986). Thus, charisma does not always have positive consequences.

Third, when charisma happens, the results are always somewhat unpredictable. They may not be what relevant authorities envisioned or want. Because it results from the coming together of several factors, charismatic leadership is unlikely to be controllable by relevant authorities, such as boards of directors.

Fourth, charisma requires some degree of routinization to stabilize its effects. Intrinsically, charisma is short-lived; it is a transitory phenomenon. Without routinization, the fervor of followers cools and the situation reverts to the status quo (Gerth and Mills 1946).

Training problematic.   Some analysts seem to believe that charismatic leadership is primarily a matter of a leader's exhibiting certain skills or behaviors that can be acquired through training:

> . . . under appropriate organizational conditions (for example when there is a need for organizational renewal or change), it may be possible to train *a corps of managers*

who possess the potential to become charismatic leaders . . . It is . . . our belief that
the training of these *skills* is not different from the training of skills in other leadership programs. (Conger and Kanungo 1988, p. 312 [emphasis added])

Such conceptions of charisma ignore the fact that charisma is a complex social
process. They downplay the crucial role that exceptional personal qualities, a
radical vision, receptive followers, success, and situations of crisis play in the
emergence and effectiveness of charisma.

It is hard to see how, even with careful selection using personality assessment procedures, firms would locate whole corps of managers who possessed
genuinely exceptional personal qualities. Nor does training seem likely to be
able to elicit or develop qualities that are so unusual that "followers experience
a magnetism and a power of attraction that goes beyond their usual experience
and knowledge" (Trice and Beyer 1986, p. 119). Also, exceptional qualities of
charismatic leaders include enduring traits that cannot be quickly assumed or
feigned. Nor are these qualities simply exaggerations or heightened versions of
above-average qualities. Followers must experience the charismatic leader as
truly exceptional, and, by definition, very few can be exceptional.

Other questions must be raised about whether training can stimulate radical visions that will win followers and be successful because they solve existing
crises. Managers can undoubtedly be encouraged to let their imaginations go,
but this does not ensure the radical ideas so generated will be helpful and successful, or that followers will find them convincing. Nor does it ensure that these
managers will have the passionate belief in their ideas and steadfast commitment
to them that charismatics exhibit.

In general, those who advocate the training of managers to be charismatic
seem to wish away the crucial issue of how all the elements of charisma fit together:

> . . . times of crises, distress, and agitation will not necessarily spawn charisma; nor
> is it realistic to argue that charismatics, no matter how potent their endowments,
> can generate relevancy and cogency for their mission without some fit with the
> social situation. (Trice and Beyer 1986, p. 126)

Observations of a very successful, charismatic school superintendent showed that
her charisma was situation-specific; in another job and social context, she was
neither charismatic nor particularly influential (Roberts and Bradley 1988). As
already mentioned, Iacocca, while at Ford, was influential but not charismatic.
It was only when faced with the crisis at Chrysler that his leadership became
charismatic.

Because charisma depends so heavily on the situation, training for charismatic leadership would need to sensitize managers to perceive possible problems
and use them to create a sense of crisis in potential followers. Since problems,
discontents, and conflicts abound in most work organizations, this should not be
too difficult. But stimulating perceptions of crises is a risky business unless leaders have sure-fire solutions. Since the unfolding of charismatic visions is unpre-

dictable, some will fail to solve the problems that have been surfaced and the organization may be left worse off than it was before charisma was attempted.

Routinization essential.   In order for charismatic leaders to have lasting impacts, their charisma must be routinized—it must be made part of the ongoing culture. Routinization is what makes charisma more than a transitory phenomenon. The process of routinization has five elements, the most basic of which is the estab-lishment of some sort of administrative apparatus to carry out the charismatic vision. In practical terms, this often means founding an organization. Charis-matic leaders thus not only create cultures, but the process of routinizing their charisma creates organizations to realize the charismatic vision. Other elements of routinization are: (2) the transformation and transference of charisma to oth-ers through rites, ceremonials, and other cultural forms; (3) the incorporation of the charismatic vision into a written and oral tradition; (4) the selection of a successor who resembles the charismatic; and (5) the continued adherence of the organization over time to the charismatic vision (Trice and Beyer 1986, p. 134).

The successful completion of the routinization process depends heavily on the actions and judgments of a small corps of dedicated followers. Observations of two charismatic leaders and the organizations they founded suggest that char-ismatic leaders risk tarnishing their charisma, and so diluting its power, if they become too involved in the routinization process. Successful routinization of charisma apparently requires that charismatic leaders maintain some distance from most of their followers and from the everyday details of administration (Trice and Beyer 1986). As Weber put it, "the holders of charisma . . . must stand outside the ties of the world, outside of routine occupations as well as outside the routine obligations of family life" (Gerth and Mills 1946, p. 248). Applying this requirement to charismatic organizational leaders implies that they should remain aloof from the most routine aspects of management. They need others they can depend on to do much of the organizing for them. For if charismatic leaders become involved in the mundane details of organizing followers and put-ting their visions into practice, they are likely to reveal qualities damaging to their auras of extraordinariness. As mentioned earlier, this may be very hard for business leaders to do. Another test for a potentially charismatic leader in large organizations is whether he or she can attract and hold followers at a distance, as well as on a face-to-face basis. To do this, the vision that the charismatic ex-presses and comes to symbolize must have widespread appeal and be seen by many followers as having relevance to the crises they perceive around them.

Many current treatments of charismatic leadership ignore the issue of rou-tinization. Perhaps these authors see charisma as a transitory phenomenon that is primarily useful in provoking cultural innovation. Perhaps they do not see routinization as either desirable or necessary. If routinization of charisma is taken into account, the training of charismatic leaders becomes impractical un-less organizations are willing to commit themselves to changing administrative practices, various programs, and policies that function as cultural forms; and to fostering new traditions. Furthermore, they must worry in advance about how they would replace charismatic leaders if they want to transfer them, or if these leaders retire, die, or are hired away. If the organization wants the charismatic mission and the culture that has grown up around it continued, they must be able to select a successor who resembles the charismatic in his or her convictions. The successor must be, in effect, an embodiment leader.

Need for Charisma Exaggerated

Recent analyses have suggested that organizations tend to oscillate between situations of crisis that require cultural change and periods of relative stability and cultural consolidation (Trice 1985; Trice and Beyer 1991). One set of re-searchers described this oscillation as a punctuated equilibrium (Tushman and Romanelli 1985), in which relatively long periods of stability are punctuated by short bursts of change. Even if the rate of change in organizations' environments increases, it seems unlikely that organizations will ever embrace continual change, for continual change would amount to chaos. Thus, the current emphasis on charisma, which is a force for drastic and revolutionary change, seems mis-placed. Even to emphasize transformational leadership is probably to distort the needs and actual practices of organizations.

Managers need to know how to maintain the cultures of their organizations as much as, perhaps more than, they need to know how to change them. A study of firms in the turbulent U.S. electronics industry concluded that people need some sense of stability in the midst of change. Thus, persistent and pervasive cultures can, paradoxically, facilitate change by maintaining "a higher order of stability, in the form of deeply held and slow-to-change values" (Jelinek and Schoonhoven 1990, p. 370). In successful firms, their cultures provided bounda-ries for interpretations and expectations that helped "people to know what to count on, how to make sense of changes, and how to reinterpret their changing organization. Some things—'the fundamentals'—never change, however much products, processes, or organization structure may shift" (Jelinek and Schoonho-ven 1990, p. 419).

The need for embodiment leadership. Because of the radical changes and risks en-tailed, organizations are unlikely to benefit from continuous emphasis on and cultivation of charismatic or transformational leadership. Rather, to realize the benefits of occasional charismatic or transformational leaders, who succeed in instilling new cultural substance into followers, organizations should cultivate embodiment leadership that will carry forward new or transformed cultures and keep them vital.

Such embodiment leadership need not be rigid or inimical to needed adap-tation. Rather it can institutionalize a set of basic, core values that is general enough to serve in many different sets of circumstance and that will give mem-bers a sense of security and continuity. A succession of different change-oriented leaders, each of whom espouses new and different ideas, seems likely to produce so much ambiguity and conflict that members will have difficulty making sense of what is happening. Cynicism and a lack of commitment are likely to result. To ask members to continually change their views of their worlds and abandon commitments already formed seems a sure recipe for their avoiding commitments in the future. Under such circumstances, members may seek coherence and make their commitments elsewhere—for example, to their occupations (Beyer 1990). While occupational subcultures can be positive influences in organizations, strengthening their influence may dilute the influence of managers. For, as described in Chapter 6, one impulse behind the formation of occupational subcultures is for members to establish control over their own work processes. The more control members of the occupation succeed in establishing through their collective efforts, the less control management has. Because members tend to want to follow impulses arising from the growth and expansion of their own technologies and knowledge, occupational subcultures may not be cooperative with some management-initiated change efforts.

The need for integration leadership.   Because occupational and other subcultures are more prevalent in work organizations than organizationwide cultures, the most pressing need in the management of current work organizations is probably for cultural integration leadership. Middle-level managers, in particular, whose units are frequently interdependent with other subunits, could probably accomplish more if they became more effective in exercising consensus or transactional leadership in a way that attends to cultural differences. To do so, they need skills in negotiation. It is interesting to note that courses in such skills are currently very popular in MBA programs and that this topic has been the focus of considerable research in recent years.

A second reason that consensus leadership is needed is to establish the kinds of communication and cooperation with suppliers and customers called for by most quality improvement programs. To do so usually requires dealing with several distinct organizational cultures or subcultures. Managers who try to implement such programs soon find that they must learn to both bargain and listen.

Still another need is for leaders who specialize in being internal integrators who help to manage relations between members of different subcultures (Wilkins 1989). All sorts of liaison roles—internal boundary spanners, project team leaders, heads of task forces and committees, and persons designated as integrating managers—call for some degree of integration leadership by incumbents. Such persons have to understand the subcultures involved well enough to be able to communicate with all and to see possibilities for exchange between them.

Considering Cultural Leadership in General

Although charismatic leadership itself is rare, other types of cultural leadership show many of the same elements. All of the ten elements derived from analysis of charismatic leadership seem pertinent to cultural leadership in general and provide a framework that is useful in comparing types and specific instances of leadership. It is especially noteworthy that cultural leadership that maintains cultures seems to involve many of the same behaviors exhibited by cultural change leaders. "Also, both types of leaders have strong convictions in the ideologies they promulgate and manage to achieve some measure of success in the eyes of followers" (Trice and Beyer 1991, p. 165). These similarities mean that the training intended to produce and encourage charismatic leadership behaviors could be useful if the trainees were sensitized to the needs for cultural maintenance as well as change.

However, cultural leaders who generate cultural innovation and maintenance have different personal qualities. Innovation leaders are more dominant and dramatic; maintenance leaders are more persuasive and facilitative. One must sell new ideas; the other must articulate and make existing ideologies seem vital and appealing. Also, of course, the two types of leadership occur in different kinds of situations. Innovation leadership usually arises when people see themselves as facing difficult problems or crises; maintenance leadership is sufficient when the problems or crises are seen as manageable. Of course, this distinction is highly subjective and thus may depend on how a leader frames and labels the situation.

While the major difference between leadership that produces cultural innovations and that which maintains existing cultures is the nature of the vision or mission articulated by the leader, it seems likely that the vision and situation are often tightly linked. Persons with radical visions see crises as requiring radical solutions; persons who accept the status quo see situations as manageable within it. Leaders are likely to frame situations for followers to fit their visions; potential followers may or may not accept that framing and the associated vision. Without crises, the risks and uncertainties associated with radical solutions make them unappealing. Convinced they are facing a crisis and unavoidable uncertainties, people will accept more risk and be attracted to radical visions that promise solutions.

In a similar way, the administrative actions that leaders take and the cultural forms they employ can be framed differently by them or their followers. The same actions may be presented and seen as a drastic reorientation in one setting and as a relatively minor restructuring in another. New language, symbols, or stories can be presented and seen as inconsistent or consistent with existing ideologies. How actions and forms are perceived may depend on the traditions and history of the organization or group.

> Those that have undergone similar innovations in the past may see the new changes as relatively routine because the ideas and behavioral routines needed to implement them are already present.... On the other hand, organizations and groups that confront change for which they lack relevant skills and experience will more likely define whatever administrative changes they make as innovative. (Trice and Beyer 1991, p. 165)

One factor, however, is less susceptible to multiple interpretations. This is whether activities are directed toward discrediting and destroying elements of the old culture. Full-fledged rites of degradation, in particular, signal that real change is afoot.

Looking at cultural leadership in a more comprehensive way than in past analyses revealed the likelihood that organizations have multiple cultural leaders. The simultaneous presence of many cultural leaders can be seen as a problem and as a benefit. While the presence of cultural leadership trying to achieve different consequences could conceivably lead to stalemate and make establishing an overall culture difficult, it also has certain practical advantages. As already pointed out, organizations need to worry about more than changing their cultures; they also need to find ways to maintain them and keep them vital. Also, organizations have subcultures, which may need different types of leadership at a given point in time.

In addition, broadening the concept of cultural leadership to include both cultural innovation and maintenance has several positive strategic implications. Because most organizations today face dynamic and complex environments, they will need both types of leadership at one time or another. Not only might organizations face times of drastic change interspersed with periods of relative stability, but some may find that certain segments of their environments require change at the same time that others require continuity and relative stability. Having the resources to mount both types of leadership may thus be an important competitive advantage.

Also, as organizations age, they may require different types of cultural leadership (Greiner 1972). Leadership that creates cultures could be followed with embodiment leadership, then turnaround leadership, and perhaps finally integrative leadership as organizations grow and develop from their early entrepreneurial stage through rapid growth to maturity and finally into global enterprises.

SUMMARY

An extensive body of research has explored the instrumental side of leadership. Attention to the symbolic and expressive side of leadership is relatively recent and has focused largely on the leadership involved in cultural change. Leadership requires more than leaders; it is a social process involving leaders and followers interacting in certain situations.

Instrumental theories of leadership and analyses of charisma identified ten elements that can be used to describe cultural leadership. Theories of charisma also indicated that periods of cultural change were often followed by periods of cultural consolidation and maintenance. This suggested a basic dichotomy between leadership that produces cultural innovation from that which produces cultural continuity and maintenance. Within each of these categories, a further breakdown was discerned in actual descriptions of cultural leaders. Cultural leadership can have at least four distinct consequences: it can create, change, embody, or integrate cultures. Other distinctions emerged within all of these types. In addition, descriptions revealed that cultural leaders could be designated or emergent, and could interact with followers from a distance or on a face-to-face basis.

All of these distinctions imply that the presence of multiple cultural leaders in organizations is very likely. Many analysts and consultants are currently emphasizing the development of charismatic leadership. This emphasis is probably misplaced, since attempts to encourage charisma are not likely to be effective and charisma itself is not very practical. Also, organizations need other types of leadership as much as, or more than, they need the drastic changes engendered by charisma. Organizations with different leaders who can engender either cultural innovation or cultural maintenance can have a competitive advantage because such organizations have the leaders they need to change with their environments and cope with the different stages of their own internal growth and development.

8

Cultural Interchange Between Organizations and Environments

Organizations do not exist in a vacuum. Analysts use the term *organizational environment* to refer to everything that surrounds organizations but is not part of them. Their environments include many entities likely to have cultures that can affect the internal cultures of organizations. These include nations, geographic regions, industries, occupations, religions, political parties, and other societal institutions. But organizations are not passive recipients of cultural influences from outside. Through their activities, organizations affect the cultures of entities in their environment by exporting elements of their own cultures. A useful way to think about the reciprocal nature of these influences is as an ongoing interchange across cultural boundaries.

Boundaries Between Organizations and Environments

Although the literature on organizations and management often refers to organizations as if they were concrete, bounded entities, the reality is more complex. Boundaries between organizations and their environments are often fuzzy and quite fluid. "There is no enveloping membrane to separate them from their environments" (Metcalfe 1981, p. 505). The general purpose of drawing a distinction between organizations and their environments is to be able to consider organizations as entities in their own right and to separate those social processes that are supposedly under organizational control from those that are not. Unfortunately, the most straightforward way of drawing organizational boundaries—according to who is and who is not a member—is unsatisfactory because members of organizations live and pursue activities both within their organizations and outside them. A more accurate way of distinguishing between organizations and their environments is to focus on the systems of activities that organizations engage in and over which they have discretion "to initiate, maintain, or end behaviors" (Pfeffer and Salancik 1978, p. 32). The boundary of an organization, then, is where the organization's discretion to control an activity is less than the discretion of some other entity to control that activity.

Also, boundaries of most organizations tend to be quite porous, letting in many different influences. As one analyst put it: " . . . organizations are not fortresses, impervious to the buffeting or the blessings of their environments. On the other hand, organizations are not wind tunnels responding to every perturbation in their context . . . " (Scott 1981, p. 133). The true nature of organizations lies somewhere between these two extremes. Organizations are not closed systems that can operate without considering their environments. Rather, they are open systems dependent on their environments. Their dependence creates reciprocal ties that bind and intertwine organizations with each other and with other entities in their environments. Also, organizations are social systems that have a history and an evolutionary pattern of development. Most important for the purposes of this analysis, organizations are embedded within larger cultural and social systems.

Organizations as Open Systems

Their environments can affect the internal cultures of organizations for two basic and interrelated reasons:

1. organizations are dependent on their environments, and
2. environments pose many uncertainties for organizations.

Organizations are dependent on their environments because they are open systems that must obtain certain inputs from their environments in order to produce outputs and otherwise ensure their survival. Without continued inputs from their environments, organizations would soon use up all of their resources and die. Many of these inputs have cultural content that is thereby brought into organizations.

In addition, organizations must cope with uncertainties that arise from their dependence on their environments and the interactions they engage in with various elements in their environments to satisfy their needs. One source of uncertainty arises from the fact that environments are not static—they change. A second source of uncertainty is environmental complexity. The most powerful forces in the environments of most organizations are other organizations—competitors, customers, suppliers, creditors, governmental regulators, unions, and the like. The greater the range of different entities with which a single organization has to deal, the more difficult it will be to anticipate and attend to all of their expectations and demands. Thus, complexity creates additional uncertainty. A third source of uncertainty is that environments are not dependable. Entities that organizations depend on may fail to deliver what is needed or expected. As occurs with other kinds of uncertainty, people in organizations tend to build into their cultures shared ideas and behaviors to help them to deal with environmentally induced uncertainties. In this way, organizational cultures come to reflect the uncertainties their members perceive in their environments.

In highly developed societies, additional complexities and uncertainties arise because all of the organizations in a particular organization's environment must also depend on their environments—which probably include not only that organization but many others. Thus, the relationship between organizations and their environments is a complex web of interdependencies rather than one-way dependence, or even a two-way interdependence. This complex set of interdependencies can lead to environmental turbulence, in which similar or linked actions by different organizations can cause drastic changes in the environment. (Emery and Trist 1965). The volatility of the stock market following the advent of programmed trading is an example of how such turbulence can arise and increase environmental uncertainties for many organizations. When trading programs include the same triggers for buy or sell decisions, their indirectly linked decisions can cause stock prices to rise or fall to such a degree as to affect the whole market, and, indirectly, the whole economy.

A good illustration of the scope and magnitude or organizational interdependencies is provided by what happened when it seemed that Chrysler Motor Company might fail in the 1970s. The national government was reluctant to let the firm go out of business because so many of its citizens and several of its states depended on the company for wages and taxes. The company's imminent failure had such a large potential impact on the country that Congress took the unusual step of having the federal government back huge loans to the company. In addition, to save the jobs of its members, the United Auto Workers made wage and other concessions to the embattled company. Both the government and unions—elements of Chrysler's environment—recognized their dependence on the auto manufacturer by their actions; without their support, it is unlikely that Chrysler could have survived.

Although our primary focus in this chapter will be on how their environments affect organizations and their cultures, as the Chrysler example shows, this influence does not operate in only one direction. Rather the influence is reciprocal. Organizations not only adapt and change in response to their environments, they also act upon and change their environments. By their actions and by cultural elements they export, organizations affect the cultures surrounding them. In this sense, organizations partially create the environments to which they respond. The reciprocal influence processes between organizations and their environments, in effect, create conditions ripe for cultural interchange.

Historical Factors Underlying
Organization-Environment Interdependence

Modern societies would not be what they are today if organizations as we know them today had not emerged.

> It is only in modern, industrialized societies that organizations dominate the landscape. Their emergence, proliferation, and consolidation as a ubiquitous and a significant building block of society is one of the great social transformations that distinguished the modern from the premodern world. In a quite literal sense, the history of the development of modern society is also a history of the development of special purpose organizations: organizations were both created by and helped to produce these changes. (Scott 1981, 144)

This quote illustrates in a historical sense the reciprocal relationship between organizations and environments: organizations helped to create modern society, but they could not have emerged and survived without the presence of certain resources and cultural elements in the wider society.

To describe in detail the historical codevelopment of organizations and modern sociey is beyond the scope of this book. Briefly, after the feudal period in Europe, many social conditions changed in ways that favored the development of special purpose organizations. Some of these represented changes in social structure: codified law, predictable taxation, military security (Weber 1947); widespread literacy, specialized advanced schooling, a money economy, political revolution, urbanization (Stinchcombe 1965); and increased competition among social classes and other groups for social resources (Scott 1981). Such structural changes grew out of and produced shifts in cultural beliefs and values. Norms changed to favor assigning important roles to anyone who exhibited superior relevant performance rather than to individuals who were born into a particular social status or happened to satisfy idiosyncratic preferences of superiors.[1] There was less consensus among social groups concerning which social goals were most important (Parsons 1966), increased recognition of the rights and interests of both individuals and corporate actors, and greater differentiation within individual and institutional roles. Especially important was the emergence of individualism, because it produced individuals who invested only specific behaviors in the new organizations and were less similar to each other in terms of status and identity than were people in feudal society (Coleman 1974; Simmel 1955; Scott 1981, p. 145). These general social changes increased the motivation of individuals to form and join organizations, and improved the changes that, once formed, organizations could survive (Scott 1981, p. 146; Stinchcombe 1965). As industrialization progressed, advances in technology made possible the increased division of labor, which in turn encouraged the concentration of the workforce in factories. These developments fed the proliferation of organizations.

Human perceptual processes contribute to making the relationship be-

---

[1]In sociological terms, roles began to be allocated on the basis of achievement and universalistic criteria rather than on ascription and particularistic criteria.

tween organizations and environments reciprocal. Environments are not only changed by what organizations do but by how people perceive them. The environment which members of an orgnization respond to and act upon is the environment they perceive. Psychological studies show that people's perceptions are distorted by many factors that can affect how they select and organize information. These include such culturally relevant factors as prior experience, personal values, and motivation. Also, because managers and other members of organizations have limited time and many factors competing for their attention, they may be unable to attend to some aspects of their environments. Thus, for both psychological and structural reasons, the perceptions that organizational members have of their environments will differ in some respects from objective reality. This is the second sense in which organizations create their environments.

Theorists use the term *enacted environment* (Weick 1969) to distinguish the environment that members perceive and act upon from the objective environment. Among the factors affecting what organizational members see in their environments are the internal cultures already present in their organizations. For example, managers of two organizations in the same industry may perceive the same environmental developments as opportunities or threats, depending on whether opportunistic or conservative values predominate in their culture (Jackson and Dutton 1988). In general, since perceptions are very likely to be colored by cultural understandings, organizational cultures are likely to affect how environments are enacted.

As will be illustrated in later sections of the chapter, when the discrepancy between enacted and actual environments becomes too great, organizations may behave in ways that threaten their survival. Organizations that persist in misperceiving their environments are unlikely to survive very long because groups in their actual environments will begin to withhold needed resources if they are not responded to appropriately. Customers can stop buying; banks can cut off credit; voters can defeat bond issues. Thus it is more likely that the enacted environments of most organizations, although not exactly matching actual environments, will bear some resemblance to them. This means that organizational cultures are also likely to reflect some aspects of actual environments; the specific shared understandings that members develop and preserve about how to cope with a particular organization's environment will depend to some degree on what's actually in that environment. For example, some environments are objectively quite friendly and benevolent while others are downright hostile to certain organizations. Such objective differences are likely to evoke very different cultural responses, especially if they persist over time. Local school systems in the United States have been criticized so heavily for so long that their internal cultures are bound to be somewhat defensive.

Cultural Effects of Dependence on Environmental Inputs

Four types of resources organizations obtain from their environments have especially strong implications for internal organizational cultures: human resources, information, technology, and legitimacy. Inputs of human resources affect organizational cultures because those people who are recruited into organizations will bring their cultural understandings with them. The information that organizations collect from their environments affects their cultures because it is bound to contain cultural understandings prevalent in the world outside the organization. The technologies organizations import from their environments partly shape organizational cultures because technologies include not only the hardware used in performing work, but also the understandings embodied in the skills and knowledge of workers, and the characteristics of the objects, including other people and their cultures, on which work is performed (Scott 1981, p. 211). Finally, legitimacy affects organizations' cultures because in order to earn and maintain it, organizations must operate in ways that are congruent with the value systems of the wider society.

Of course, organizations obtain many other resources from their environments—capital and raw materials are examples—that may have cultural implications. Such resources will affect internal organizational cultures through the cultural meanings they carry or through their effects on the four resources already mentioned. For example, as a raw material, coal poses one set of dangers and uncertainties for the organizations using it to generate electricity. The alternative of plutonium and nuclear power poses very different kinds of uncertainties. Both have implications for the meanings organizational members create about their work and their worlds, the technologies organizations employ, the kinds of employees recruited, the information organizations obtain from their environments and how they interpret it, and for the legitimacy they are able to maintain with the wider public.

Two Major Sectors of Organizational Environments

Theorists suggested that it might be useful to distinguish between two types of organizational environments—instrumental and institutional (Meyer and Rowan 1977). Because all organizations respond to both, it may be clearer to consider them sectors of environments. The first, the *instrumental* sector, refers to those parts of the environment with which organizations exchange goods and services for needed inputs. This environmental sector resembles economists' conception of the competitive market and the concept of environment used in the open systems model of organizations. The second, or *institutional* sector, refers to the written and unwritten rules and regulations to which organizations must conform in order to maintain legitimacy in the wider society. In effect, the institutional sector reflects those beliefs, values, and norms of surrounding cultures that are widely shared and relatively codified.

In practice, these two sectors of the environment overlap and the distinction between them blurs. The cigarette companies, for example, might look at all smokers as potential customers who are part of their instrumental environments. But when some of these smokers decide, on the basis of information from medical research, that cigarette smoking is damaging to their health, they may sue for damages to their health or they may join organizations promoting the cessation and even the banning of smoking. In the process, the former smokers and customers move from the instrumental to the institutional sector of the cigarette companies' environment. Similarly, an airplane manufacturer like Boeing may find that how safe its planes are not only affects it sales, but also how closely its products are regulated by the government. Or a company may find, as many of the chemical companies are finding, that products once seen as instrumentally beneficial are redefined as dangers to the public, and thus of major concern to the institutional sectors of their environments. The point here is that organizations must worry about satisfying the demands of both sectors of the environment and that there is often considerable overlap between sectors. Also, there are many institutional pressures for at least the appearances of rationality and efficiency in cultures that emphasize those values.

The distinction between instrumental and institutional sectors reflects the same duality discussed earlier in terms of all actions both saying and doing things. The instrumental sector of the environment attends to what we have called technical consequences; the institutional sector attends to expressive consequences. While no organization can afford to attend to either of these sectors exclusively, the distinction can be useful for comparing types of organizations. It has also helped to sensitize scholars to different dimensions of environments. Table 8–1 illustrates how different organizations may be subject to differing degrees of pressures from these two sectors of their environments. Organizations with environments that have stronger instrumental sectors are likely to be evaluated on the basis of actual outputs. They will reflect the demands of the predominant sector by adopting structures and processes that emphasize efficiency and rationality. Organizations with stronger institutional sectors may experience more pressure to create correct appearances than effective outputs. While such

TABLE 8–1
RELATIVE STRENGTH OF TWO SECTORS OF ENVIRONMENTS

		Institutional Sectors[a]	
		Stronger	*Weaker*
Instrumental Sectors[b]	*Stronger*	Utilities Banks General hospitals	Manufacturing
	Weaker	Mental health agencies Legal agencies Schools Churches	Restaurants Health clubs

SOURCE: Adapted from Scott 1987, p. 126.

[a]Attend primarily to expressive consequences.

[b]Attend primarily to technical consequences.

organizations may be under some pressure to create appearances of efficiency, political and symbolic factors are likely to be more important than rationality in guiding such organizations.

Organizations that face both strong institutional and instrumental sectors have a difficult balancing act. They can vary their attention to demands depending on which sector is especially problematic at a particular time, but this reactive strategy holds dangers of making wrong assessments and being surprised by difficult demands from the other sector. Another strategy they follow is to assign different subunits in their organization responsibility for attending to each set of demands. This is probably what most organizations do. The danger here is that actions taken to deal with one sector may undermine apparent or real performance in the other sector. Organizations for which both sectors are weak do not need to attend to their environments as closely. The chief danger for them is that they may grow complacent and be unaware of impending environmental changes that could make one of their sectors stronger and so change their status.

The interchanges that occur between organizations and the instrumental sectors of their environments involve practical resources, including information, that can be heavily imbued with cultural content. Seven different dimensions of environments that have been identified are reflected in the four cells in the right side of Table 8–2. Three of them—munificence-scarcity, concentration-dispersion, and coordination-noncoordination—describe the availability, location, and control of resources. Munificent environments have many resources available; concentrated environments have many needed resources concentrated in relatively few locations; and coordinated environments are those in which resources needed from the environment are controlled by entities that are structured or connected in systematic ways. Munificent, dispersed, and noncoordinated environments create fewer problematic resource dependencies for organizations than do scarce, concentrated, and coordinated environments.

Five of these dimensions—homogeneity-heterogeneity, stability-changeful-

TABLE 8–2
SOME CHARACTERISTICS OF ENVIRONMENTS

		Problems with Dependencies	
		Few	*Many*
Questions	*Availability*	Munificent	Scarce
About	*Location*	Dispersed	Concentrated
Resources	*Control*	Noncoordinated	Coordinated
	Diversity of elements	Homogenous	Heterogeneous
	Degree of change	Stable	Changeful
Other	*Favorableness*	Benevolent	Hostile
Uncertainties	*Degree of linkage*	Isolated	Interconnected
	Orchestration of actions	Coordinated	Noncoordinated

ness, hostility-benevolence, interconnectedness-isolation, and coordination-noncoordination—are used to describe other uncertainties posed by environments.[2] Homogeneous environments are composed of entities that are similar; stable environments of entities that are not changing; hostile environments of entities that threaten the survival of the organization; interconnected environments of many entities to which the focal organization is linked and whose actions affect the focal organization; and coordinated environments of a set of entities whose actions are orchestrated or structured (Scott 1987, p. 128). Environments that are heterogeneous, changeful, hostile, interconnected, and noncoordinated pose more uncertainties for organizations than those which are the reverse.

It bears repeating at this point that members of organizations respond to the environments they enact. There can be considerable discrepancy between what is actually in an organization's environment and how insiders see and enact it. For example, top management of a Swedish firm that saw itself as making the best electronic calculators in the world didn't notice that computers were being developed by other firms and soon found itself in a crisis (Starbuck, Greve, and Hedberg 1978). This firm enacted a more benevolent and stable environment than it actually faced. This example illustrates that changes in the environment may not affect organizational actions unless important organizational actors perceive them. Similarly, a munificent environment may not provoke actions designed to take advantage of available resources unless organizational members perceive and value those resources. One of the reasons some organizations fail to adapt is that they fail to pay attention to and exploit environmental opportunities (Hedberg, Nystrom, and Starbuck 1976).

Because organizations' awareness and perceptions of their environments are filtered through the cultural beliefs and values of their members, organizational cultures are important determinants of discrepancies between enacted and actual environments. On the other hand, as the Swedish calculator firm found out, environments have the potential of forcing members, in one way or another, to face objective realities. Customers switch to other products; legislation is enacted to regulate firm behavior; competitor firms hire away the firm's most crucial employees. Neither culture nor other factors effecting perception and enactment operate alone in determining how organizations respond to their environments.

Coping with Dependence

When managers sense demands from their organizations' environments, they have three logical options: (1) they can try to adapt their organizations to whatever the environment seems to require; (2) they can try to reduce the effects of

---

[2]Note that the last of these dimensions affects both resources and other uncertainties.

environmentally induced uncertainty through buffering; or (3) they can try to influence their environments in ways that lessen their dependency. In general, managers prefer the latter two options—reducing the uncertainties and demands that environments impose—because uncertainty undermines rational management techniques, because the demands of external entities undermine managerial control, and because too much uncertainty and dependence is inherently stressful. However, sometimes organizations have little choice but to comply with environmental demands. Whichever option or combination of options is chosen, cultural factors are bound to play a role.

How Organization Adapt to Environments

When organizations adapt their internal structures and practices to demands from their environments, they are, in effect, conforming to aspects of the surrounding culture. In this way, cultural elements from the environment are imported into organizations and may influence their cultures. The most obvious instances of conforming to cultural expectations occur when organizations attend to the institutional sectors of their environments. They employ four types of conformity (Scott 1987, pp. 194–98). The first is categorical conformity, in which certain taken-for-granted cultural distinctions or rules provide the "natural" or "obvious" way for organizations to proceed. Voters expect public schools to draw distinctions between students and teachers; businesses customarily have blue-collar and white-collar jobs. The second is structural conformity, which occurs when environmental entities impose certain structural requirements on organizations. For example, all MBA programs accredited by the National Assembly of Collegiate Schools of Business must contain accounting courses and faculty with certain credentials in accounting. The third is procedural conformity, in which environmental entities pressure organizations to carry out their activities in certain specified ways. For example, United Way may require members agencies to use certain accounting and budgeting practices in order to be eligible for United Way funding; the Securities and Exchange Commission requires that corporations release certain information to stockholders and follow certain procedures in annual meetings. Fourth is personnel conformity, in which organizations are expected or required to employ certain kinds of workers to perform certain tasks. The most common of these are licensing requirements for professional employees such as nurses, doctors, lawyers, veterinarians; and for skilled employees such as plumbers, and electricians. By these various types of conformity, organizations align themselves with accepted values and norms and thus legitimate their continued existence.

Of course, as open systems, organizations must also conform in the instrumental sectors of their environments by producing goods or services that entities in the environment value enough to exchange needed inputs for them. In the process, organizations must consider the characteristics of their environments (Table 8–2) when deciding whether to retain or change their markets, products, technologies, structures, and practices.

Organizations must not only maintain their legitimacy with the larger society, they also need to monitor pertinent events in the environment, have available expertise needed to understand those events, and generate repertoires of behaviors to respond appropriately. Some adaptation is facilitated when organizations import new members who bring with them the cultural values and knowledge from the surrounding society. Other adaptation is stimulated by the constant interactions and other ties organizations have with suppliers, customers, regulators, and other entities in the environment. In effect, some amount of adaptation occurs because elements from the environment penetrate organizational boundaries. Such penetration is especially evident when firms relocate and hire employees reared in different regional or national cultures from those of prior employees. One purpose of some relocations may be to seek such differences—for example, when firms relocate to areas where unionism is weak or nonexistent.

Other examples of such penetration are provided by what happened in some of the highly egalitarian organizations like free schools, food cooperatives, and law collectives formed in the 1960s and 1970s. As already mentioned briefly in Chapter 2, these organizations tended to have values and ideologies so in conflict with those of the surrounding culture that they are often referred to as "alternative" organizations. They were, above all, antibureaucratic. They eschewed the need for abstract rules and relied heavily on face-to-face communications as a way to reach collective decisions. There were no hierarchies of authority; rules and written documents were held to a minimum. They managed to buffer themselves from outside influences by accepting for membership only individuals whom they knew embraced their egalitarian ideology. They did not admit strangers into their ranks (Rothschild-Whitt 1979). However, over time, many of these organizations gradually took on bureaucratic features (Newman 1980, p. 159). Their dependence on external funding sources forced them to conform to the expectations of the larger society—especially by the adoption of a distinct hierarchy. Funding agencies expected a clear-cut, specified set of authority relations.

Two studies done in the 1960s dramatized to organizational researchers that business organizations that are structurally adapted to their environments are likely to be more successful than those that are not. In Great Britain, researchers found that firms with more flexible structures were more successful than those with more bureaucratic, rigid structures in rapidly changing industries like electronics (Burns and Stalker 1961). In a study of U.S. plastics and container firms, other researchers found that successful firms matched the complexity of their environments by a concomitant degree of internal structural differentiation (Lawrence and Lorsch 1967). Those facing more complex environments created a larger number of different departments and specialized roles than those facing simpler environments. These and other studies led organizational theorists to what is commonly called the contingency theory of organizational design. In general, it posits that organizations will be more effective if they adapt their structures to fit with their environments and other contingencies they face.

In order to adapt to them, organizations must learn about environmental demands. Members of organizations must scan their environments for information that may be relevant to their activities and welfare. Members of organizations who interact regularly with sectors of the environment are important sources of information on those sectors; they, in effect, act as boundary spanners between their organizations and their environments. Members of purchasing and sales departments are obvious boundary spanners with suppliers and customers, but many other roles and activities include some boundary-spanning activities (Starbuck 1976; Tichy 1981). Because of their interactions with cultures outside the organization, boundary spanners are logical conduits for cultural interchange between organizations and their environments.

When adaptation involves deliberate, internal changes in structure and concrete practices, management soon finds that both internal and external cultures constrain what can be accomplished. Because of the highly visible success of Japanese industry, many U.S. managers and consultants have tried to imitate such Japanese practices as quality circles. They have met with mixed success, probably because of differences between the U.S. and Japanese cultures (Lawler and Mohrman 1987). While certainly a factor that organizations must attend to when adapting to their environments, the topic of crossnational cultural differences is so encompassing that a separate section will be devoted to it later in this chapter.

Of course, adaptations vary in their urgency. Catastrophic or other rapid environmental changes require quick responses, which will nevertheless be somewhat constrained by the values and beliefs of actors in the environment. For example, when Exxon Corporation found itself facing the effects of an enormous oil spill from its tanker *Valdez* off the shores of Alaska, the cleanup and other remedies employed had to conform to the values and beliefs of federal and state officials, wildlife specialists, fishermen, other environmentalists, and affected villagers (Shabecoff 1989; Lemonick and Linden 1989). That they were having great difficulty in complying with the values of all stakeholders became evident when a federal judge rejected Exxon's plea bargain and plan to pay $100 million to settle criminal charges arising from the accident. The judge stated that such a fine was not adequate to achieve deterrence and might send a message that spills are simply one cost of doing business. He added that "his decision was partly in response to growing protests from Alaskans, members of Congress, and prominent environmental groups" (Dolan and Lee 1991, p. A1).

National cultures.   Given the pressures toward conformity, it is not surprising that researchers have found that organizational structures and practices tend to reflect their surrounding national cultures. One observer saw in two French bureaucracies the same individual isolation, emphasis on formal rather than informal relations, concern with status and privilege distinctions, and distaste for face-to-face interactions between authority figures and subordinates that marked the larger French society (Crozier 1964). These behaviors were imported from other

French cultural institutions like the educational system, the national government, and the French labor movement.

Other researchers found that Belgian administrative bureaucracies varied according to Belgium's two regional cultures (Aiken and Bacharach 1979). Each culture is tied to the language spoken in that region. Wallonia's official language is French; Wallonian customs resemble French customs. The cultural values in Wallonia favor impersonal social controls like rules and procedures; accordingly, the Wallonian organizations studied had routinized work activities, seldom short-circuited bureaucratic channels, used formal recruitment and promotion practices, and exhibited little innovation. These findings resemble those obtained in the previously mentioned study of French bureaucracies (Aiken and Bacharach 1979, p. 240). The second region of Belgium is Flanders, where Dutch is the language spoken. This region is adjacent to Holland and has long-standing Anglo-Saxon traditions. In Flanders, cultural values favored practical, informal arrangements, and organizations relied more heavily on interpersonal controls, less on rules and regulations, and did not routinize work to the same degree as organizations in Wallonia.

In a similar vein, two analysts pointed out that cultural values may make such a difference that the direction of relationships between variables may actually be reversed in different countries (Lammers and Hickson 1979). For example, studies discovered a strong tendency on the part of Peruvian workers to react positively to close supervision and production emphasis by their bosses. In contrast, American workers tended to react negatively to close supervision (Williams, Whyte, and Green 1965).

> ... socialization at home, in the community, and in the schools entails in Peru the acquisition of the norm "thou shalt love thy supervisors the more superior they act", and in the U.S.A., the norm "thou shalt love thy superiors the more, the less superior they act." (Lammers and Hickson 1979, p. 408)

National cultures are such important and obvious environmental influences on organizations that a large body of research has accumulated investigating differences and similarities in organizations in different countries. Given the growing importance of global trade, this research is especially pertinent to understanding the challenges facing managers today. The last part of this chapter will summarize some of the concerns and general conclusions from this body of research.

Basic folkways. Some organizational practices are likely to be more tied to the local culture than others. Nontechnical matters relating to the basic stuff of people's lives are especially sensitive to cultural differences. Although not directly work related, these matters inevitably surface within the workplace because they concern universal aspects of human life that cannot be avoided or repressed. For example, eating, sexual attractions, and bodily elimination must be handled somehow within work organizations. They way they are handled will vary according to local folkways—culturally accepted ways of behaving that emerge without conscious design but neverthelesss function as compelling guides to conduct (Sumner 1906).

Eating customs affect organizations in three ways: (1) organizations usually must provide times and places for workers to eat; (2) they may actually provide the food itself; and (3) various work-related social events often involve eating (Humphrey 1979). One of the ways many organizations express cultural values is by whether various statuses of employees are separated in the eating facilities. The executive dining room of General Motors is strictly reserved for the top brass and their guests (Martin and Siehl 1983). To go there is to participate in the aura of power attached to the top management of GM. A former executive reports that high-status executives were expected to eat together in the executive dining room when in town. These lunches were apparently used to conduct business as well as to affirm the status of the attendees—making them, in effect, "power lunches" (DiTomaso 1987, p. 122). Such practices, of course, are not confimed to GM. In its new Saturn plant, where GM management wants to develop a more egalitarian culture than is prevalent in older segments of the firm, employees, managers, and executives eat in the same cafeteria (Treece 1990, p. 59).

An amusing example of how cultural differences can lead to inappropriate behaviors about food involved a visitor from a foreign country who was invited to an executive's home for a social event. During the event, a plate of cookies was passed. In accordance with U.S. customs, the visitor was given the plate first. Apparently in accordance with his cultural expectations and customs, the visitor felt he was expected to clean the plate—so he proceeded "with great effort" to eat all of the cookies himself (Schein 1985, p. 28). Another amusing crosscultural misunderstanding arose when U.S. workers took a recent immigrant from the Philippine Islands out to lunch to celebrate his birthday. In the Philippines, it is traditional for the person having a birthday to invite others to lunch as his guests. Thus, while the U.S. workers planned to treat the Filipino to lunch in accordance with U.S. folkways, he spent the celebrating event in fear because he could not afford to pay for everyone else's lunch (Stuller 1991).

With the recent influx of women into workplaces, many men and women are working together more closely and continuously than in the past. One apparent consequence of this influx is that norms may be changing about what is acceptable behavior between the sexes at work. Uncertainties and conflicts between men and women over expected and appropriate conduct are becoming more evident. For example, the issue of sexual harassment has received increasing attention. A recent *Newsweek* poll revealed that 21 percent of women surveyed reported that they had been sexually harassed at work and 42 percent said they knew someone who had been harassed. "Until just a few years ago, women had no recourse when confronted with unwanted advances or offensive comments by a boss or co-worker" (Kantrowitz 1991, p. 35). But in 1986, the U.S. Supreme Court ruled that sexual harassment was a violation of civil rights; other federal court decisions followed that refined the definition of harassment. Faced with changing social values about how this issue should be handled in workplaces, many employers have formulated sexual-harassment policies to clarify the range of acceptable and unacceptable behaviors. It is an open question whether the attention this issue has received in work organizations will spur a change in so-cial values and behaviors in the general environment so that unwanted sexual comments and advances will also be considered unacceptable in other settings.

Although social values in most societies call for employees to view sexual intimacy as a private matter, sexual attractions occur and often become evident in work settings (Roy 1962; Quinn 1977). More and more women are moving out of sex-segregated occupations and into work arenas where their tasks require close, frequent, and emotionally heightened contacts with men. Under such con-ditions, sexual attractions become especially likely. Sharing excitement over work can easily generalize to sharing excitement over being with one another. Close working relationships between men and women often boil down to choos-ing between "getting closer" or keeping one's distance" (Crary 1987). Even if a partner is held at a distance, some remnant of an original attraction may remain. If the closeness eventuates in an intimate relationship, bystanders tend to assume it is sexual, even if it is not. A well-publicized example is the furor created by the close relationship between William Agee, CEO of Bendix Corporation, and Mary Cunningham, a swiftly promoted and attractive young executive who frequently traveled with him. The widespread gossip about their relationship intensified when, soon after the relationship began, both parties separated from their spouses (Velasquez, Moberg, and Cavanagh 1983). They eventually married. As this case demonstrates, there is a decided taboo against sexual intimacy among co-workers, especially in the top ranks of organizations where it is highly visible and threatens existing systems of power and influence. Peers, supervisors, and other outsiders are often highly critical and punitive when it occurs.

Nevertheless, sexual liaisons are not uncommon in work settings. Interviews with waiting airline passengers who were willing to respond to questions found that over half had observed at least one sexual liaison at their workplace; some had observed more than one (Quinn 1977). The observers reported that when supervisors became aware of the sexual relationship, most ignored it, sometimes with very deleterious consequences. But some supervisors took action by punish-ing one or the other of the partners. A minority of supervisors openly discussed the situation and counseled the involved employees about what to do.

Most managers and other officials are very uncomfortable discussing the possibilities or existence of sexual attractions and relationships in work settings. One reason is that the impersonal norms of bureaucracy and the arch-ideology of rationality make such relationships taboo. But, as women are allowed into worksites that were previously reserved for males, they bring with them the spec-ter of on-the-job romance. Recently, news accounts reported that officials of the National Aeronautics and Space Administration would have to face up to the issue of sexual intimacies on spacecraft (Broad 1992). Because lengthy spaceshift crews have included women, rumors of such possibilities have been around for some time but have been ignored by officials. The issue became hard to avoid when it was announced that a married couple would be on the crew of an upcom-ing mission.

Persons involved in sexual relationships may view them as natural and posi-tive outgrowth of their work. For example, a female consultant, whose performance depended on establishing close relations with line managers, admitted having intimate sexual relations with some of them, saying "our intimacy makes for a better business relationship" (Crary 1987, p. 34). But persons who make such choices run considerable risks, especially if the relationship breaks up—which is very likely. From the reports collected, it appeared that women were especially vulnerable to stigma after the relationship was over, while men who became sexually involved sometimes discovered that personal information garnered from them during the intimacy was misused by their former partners in damaging ways. Also, during the intimacy, both partners face the possibility that the extent of involvement, commitment to, and dependency on the relationship by the other person will change. Coping with these changes is a big problem, especially if a sexual relationship develops. Even nonsexual intimacies are subject to constant realignment and redefinition, just as would happen in nonwork settings (Crary 1987).

Work organizations and their cultures must also deal with such other very private behaviors as bodily elimination. Cultures vary in the degree to which issues surounding bodily elimination evoke either humor or a kind of modesty, including elements of shame, denial, and repression. Privacy, the most basic expression of this modesty, is considered requisite in the restrooms of U.S. workplaces and other public facilities. Other societies do not require the same degree of privacy. In the United States, where walls do not provide total privacy, norms dictate the averting of eyes and avoidance of observing others. The degree of privacy, however, may vary with status. Those in low-status roles may find their privacy is minimal; most U.S. workers share toilet facilities with other employees. High statuses usually carry with them exceptional attention to the privacy of the holder; top executives and deans of business schools usually have private washrooms in their offices. In the military, such norms are recognized even when operating in field conditions. The visit of the top brass calls for the immediate construction of a private latrine so that a field marshall or four-star general "does not have to share the normal communal and semi-public accommodations" (Kiva 1966, p. 56). Organizations such as hospitals, nursing homes, schools, and child-care facilities must also confront issues of privacy surrounding bathing and nakedness, as well as elimination.

Many other folkways impinge on work organizations. The marking of personal events like birthdays and weddings, the celebration of holidays, and gift giving in general are examples of culturally expressive behaviors that occur in most organizations. For example, research in a midwestern U.S. community found that Christmas gifts of money were common from employers to employees, but none occurred from employee to employer. In general, money gifts went from people of higher status to those of lower status—for example, "newsboys, postmen, and delivery men" (Caplow 1982, p. 386). Gifts to relatively high-status persons like physicians, school teachers, and bosses never consisted of money.

Large environmental shifts. Large-scale social changes create shifts in the environments of organizations. Changes in government regulations governing certain industries and companies and changes in the workforce were especially significant in the United States during the 1980s: The federal government deregulated the airlines, banking, and communication industries; and increasing numbers of women stayed in the workforce after having children.

The effects of changes in regulation can be illustrated by what happened in the American Telephone & Telegraph Company, traditionally one of the United States's largest and most benevolent employers. AT&T's benevolent stance toward its employees was expressed by its widely known nickname, Ma Bell. In the early and mid-1980s, the Federal Communications Commission handed down two decrees intended to open the way for competitors and to greatly dilute AT&T's monopoly power. In order to foster competition, the FCC ordered AT&T to divest itself of three-quarters of its assets, including its 22 local operating companies. The huge network that connected telephone lines for both local and long distance calls had to be opened to competitors. The local operating companies (soon dubbed Baby Bells) were spun off as separate entities to compete with one another, with new competitors, and with their parent company. These changes meant that the parent company and the Baby Bells were operating in environments that had shifted drastically from what they were accustomed to. Furthermore, unlike the temporary changes brought on by sudden environmental jolts, these environmental shifts were permanent.

Undoubtedly the most basic change in AT&T's culture followed from losing its monopoly power and facing competition in all of its markets and activities. Management decided that the company had to become leaner and much less protective of its employees if it was to compete successfully with its new competitors. It therefore began a program of personnel reduction, offering 13,000 early retirement packages in 1983 and eliminating 11,000 positions in 1984. These layoffs produced severe shock in the Ma Bell culture (Tunstall 1985). Most employees were not aware of the legal maneuvers that had been going on for years. Suddenly they were told that "Ma Bell doesn't live here anymore" and they could no longer count on lifetime employment. In response "... they spoke in metaphors of personal grief, almost as if they had been deserted or there had been a death in the family" (Tunstall 1983, p. 19).

But layoffs were not enough. One of the central ideologies in the AT&T culture had always been service at all costs. The socialization of all employees instilled a sense of devotion to customer service, measured and symbolized by a quality-of-service index used in the evaluation of performance. Another potent symbol of this ideology was the company legend of Angus McDonald—a 19th-century lineman who bravely fought blizzards to repair broken lines and restore service to customers. This legend implied a "service at all costs" ethic. This ethic, however, did not match the realities to AT&T's changed environment. With competition came greater pressures to provide services at lower costs; AT&T could no longer afford a service-at-any-cost mentality. "We didn't wake up until '85 when the business began to play out ... now we're paying more attention to outside forces; we're totally market-driven, we know what the customer wants, and what our competitors are offering" (Keller and Lewis 1988, p. 62). To survive and continue to prosper, the company had to try to shift its culture to match its new environment.

Another environmental shift having cultural repercussions in organizations is the increasing rate of participation in the workforce of women with infants and small children (O'Connell and Bloom 1987). Cultural values of both individuals and organizations provide important reference points and lenses for interpreting the significance and interconnectedness of such environmental changes (Beyer and Lutze 1990).

> In the case of work-family issues, the values of individuals on the top management team could be crucial in interpreting work-family demands as an organizational rather than a public policy issue, and shared organizational values could strongly affect whether top management views the implementation of work-family policies as likely to affect employee productivity, and other organizational effectiveness criteria. (Milliken, Dutton, and Beyer 1990, p. 101)

Reports indicated that by the end of the 1980s, approximately 3,500 U.S. companies were providing some form of child-care assistance to their employees (Friedman 1989). While this is a substantial number, clearly the larger proportion of employers were not providing such assistance. Societal values and the institutional environment had not changed sufficiently to demand that they do.

Nevertheless, some large companies have responded to the demographic shifts in the workforce and society with programs designed to ease the conflicts employees experience between work and family demands. The Du Pont Company, for example, has a full-time executive whose title is director of workforce partnering. The company has paid out $1.5 million to build and renovate child-care centers; helped to set up a statewide day-care referral service; offers an unusually generous combination of paid and unpaid leave for birth, adoption, or relative's illness; set up 50 "work-life" committees around the country; and is moving toward part-time and flex-time work schedules (Weber 1991). IBM, which tends to keep a low profile about its benevolent activities, recently decided to spend more than $25 million to assist employees with their needs for child and elder care.

Examples of other large environmental shifts include the unexpected appearance of Rachel Carson's book *Silent Spring* in 1962, which immediately put the chemical industry on the defensive and launched the environmental protection movement (Adams 1980); the OPEC cartel's success in controlling the price of oil in the 1970s; deregulation in the airline and banking industries during the 1970s; and the sudden rejection of communist rule by the citizens of Eastern Europe and the Soviet Union in the late 1980's.

The impact of the environmental protection movement is still being felt in many industries in 1991. Automobile manufacturers face new rules for controlling engine emissions by both U.S. and European authorities. Companies scramble to redesign internal-combustion engines to be cleaner, to improve pollution-control devices, and to develop cars powered by natural gas, which burns cleaner than gasoline. GM is working on developing an electric car expected to be ready for the market by 1993. Chrysler is designing a family of cars to run on either methanol, ethanol, gasoline, or a blend of the three (Woodruff and Peterson 1991). Meanwhile the oil industry is working on developing cleaner gasolines.

Bizarre intrusions.   Sometimes, organizations face the unthinkable (Mitroff and Kilmann 1984, p. 2). Someone outside the organization behaves in a bizarre and unexpected manner that intrudes in a damaging way into its domains. During the fall of 1982, the unthinkable occurred to the Johnson & Johnson Company. Someone inserted cyanide into bottles of Tylenol, the company's best-selling product. As a result, five people in different suburbs of Chicago died from ingesting the product. Overnight, a product that had been trusted was invested with an image of death, fear, and unspeakable hostility. Company management responded decisively and in ways that showed concrete concern for the public welfare. The firm acknowledged the enormity of the problem, and responded with a massive recall of the product and intensive examination of its own procedures; its culture dictated that aggressive action was most often successful (Deal and Kennedy 1982, p. 5). Eventually, with intensive advertising of new seals on its bottles, it was able to win back public trust in Tylenol.

The Johnson & Johnson Company's response to the Tylenol poisoning tragedy has become a model for other firms to follow. Many have formulated crisis plans and teams. A crisis manual helped management to cope when the unthinkable happened to Luby's Cafeterias on October 16, 1991. A gunman drove his pickup truck through a cafeteria window in Killeen, Texas and killed 22 patrons and injured another 17 with two semiautomatic weapons. It was the worst mass killing in U.S. history. As soon as Luby's top management learned of the incident, and before they realized its magnitude, CEO Peter Erben left the corporate offices in San Antonio for Killeen. The company's public relations firm was notified and one of its partners flew to Killeen. Other company officials soon joined Erben. The presence of a group of officials on the scene made less panicky and better informed decisions possible. The company quickly took a series of actions expressing concern for the victims and all others affected. It reserved 50 hotel rooms for the families of victims, began accepting donations, promised help to the families of victims, and also promised affected employees they would be kept on the payroll indefinitely. One sign that these actions were viewed positively in the environment was that the company's stock actually took a sharp upturn on the stock market in the days following this awful event (Breyer 1991).

In dealing with its unthinkable event, the Gerber Products Company employed a very different strategy. In early 1986, the company was faced with complaints and rumors that its baby food had glass in it. Although the Food and Drug Administration had been unable to confirm the allegations, they continued to be voiced in the media and among groups of mothers. Gerber decided to take a low-key approach and let the matter "die a natural death" (Bussey 1986, p. 18). Gerber management had already tried the recall approach to deal with an earlier set of complaints in 1984, and felt the recall itself had further damaged consumer confidence in its baby food. The choice to do nothing, however, also involved risks in that, should any glass eventually be discovered in its jars, consumer confidence in the company would be destroyed. The Gerber management was apparently confident of its own quality control and therefore more comfortable with the second set of risks.

In the summer of 1977 the McDonald's Corporation received three letters from an Ohio town inquiring if Ray Kroc, then president of McDonald's, had made sizeable contributions to the Church of Satan. Corporate management had "no inkling they were on the verge of an experience which would persist for three years" (Koenig 1985, p. 9). Soon, however, letters of inquiry and complaint began to arrive from other parts of the country, and when the rumor got to Texas, Oklahoma, and Arkansas, company officials "likened it to an explosion" (Koenig, 1985, p. 10).

Numerous techniques were devised to extinguish the rumor, which was completely unfounded. The company elicited and publicized letters from ministers serving affected areas attesting to Mr. Kroc's integrity. The talk shows on which he was rumored to have said he had contributed heavily to the Church of Satan were rebroadcast by reputable sponsors on local TV and radio stations. The company sent replies denying the rumor and giving detailed explanations to hundreds of inquiries and accusations. But as these steps dampened the rumor in some regions, it flared up in others. Organized newsletters and boycotts against McDonald's broke out all over the country among anti-Satan contingents. Despite subsequent retractions by prominent clergymen involved in spreading the rumor, it proved to be remarkably stubborn. It eventually became national news disseminated by the wire services.

After three years, the Satanic rumor slowly began to burn out as an even more damaging rumor took its place. The new rumor was that McDonald's, as well as Wendy's, put red worms in their hamburgers. The red-worm rumor rapidly gained momentum and posed a new threat to McDonald's reputation. The company tried similar countermeasures—getting specific names and sending letters. They also passed out literature to customers and used the phrase "U.S. inspected ground beef" prominently on all of their hamburger packaging. Finally, as a last resort, the company launched small intense local campaigns where the rumor was strongest. Like the Satanic rumor, the red-worm rumor was slow to die out. No one knows how much these rumors cost the company in lost sales and in expenses incurred in countering them.

Other bizarre events that have threatened company reputations include a religious sect's complaining that Procter & Gamble's logo of the moon and stars was a sign of the devil; an unknown programmer's developing and distributing a pornographic program for the Atari computer of General Custer raping a Native American woman; and some tamperers' inserting Swedish erotica into boxes of Cracker Jack, a children's snack (Mitroff and Kilmann 1984, p. 6). Such bizarre intrusions test corporate cultures' abilities to generate appropriate ways to restore public confidence and maintain positive corporate identities.

Environmental jolts. Bizarre intrusions are not the only instances in which organizations face unpleasant surprises originating in their environments that they cannot avoid or control. Other unexpected events occur that jolt the very foundations of organizations' cultures. Other times, managers of organizations know that something significant is going to happen, but have little way of anticipating exactly how events will occur and how they will affect them. Although organizations try proactively to manage their environments, even the best managements cannot anticipate all of the unusual events that can damage their firms. Thus, they generally must adapt to such events.

A researcher coined the term *environmental jolts* to refer to the effects of a month-long doctors' strike on hospitals in the San Francisco area in May 1975 (Meyer 1982a, p. 515). He defined jolts as "transient perturbations whose occurrences are difficult to foresee and whose impacts on organizations are disruptive and potentially inimical." At the time of his study, doctors were caught in a squeeze caused by their environments; they had just been hit with a 384 percent increase in their malpractice insurance premiums. They went on strike to dramatize their predicament and to force the public and politicians to do something to control insurance costs.

While the hospitals had some warning that a strike might occur, it was still very difficult for hospital administrators to know how best to manage such a situation because it was unprecedented. Hospitals responded quite differently to the strike, depending on their core ideologies. One hospital used the strike as an opportunity to "test members' adaptive dexterity" (Meyer 1982a, p. 531) and ability to innovate. Another simulated the expected impacts on the computer and then simply absorbed the jolt through diversifying services and through self-regulated control procedures. A third decided to "weather the storm" and continue operating as if nothing had happened; reluctant to lay off any staff, it consumed financial reserves to pay them.

Many universities experienced sudden jolts in the 1960s and 1970s, when students demonstrated, disrupted classes, occupied administrators' offices, and destroyed university records and other property. During one week in May of 1970, students at many of the country's colleges were on general strike to protest U.S. military actions in Cambodia, the shootings of student protesters at Kent State University, and alleged police brutality at Jackson State University. In the midst of this environmental turmoil, the State University of New York at Buffalo was choosing its next president. The campus itself was in a state of police-student confrontation for five days. One official involved later pointed to these events as giving the local Buffalo community enhanced influence in the decision about who would be president (Bennis 1979). In practical terms, this meant that relatively conservative, nonacademic values prevailed over those of faculty and students.

Many other forms of environmentally induced jolts occur. Natural disasters such as floods, earthquakes, blizzards, tornados, and hurricanes disrupt organizations' operations and create huge costs. Technological innovations that jeopardise an organization's or even a whole industry's position may surface with little advance warning. In these and many other circumstances that organizations cannot anticipate, their abilities to adapt will be tested. In the process of adaptation, cultural ideologies will likely constrain the options considered.

Buffering

Responding to environmental demands takes time and other resources away from the central production activities of organizations, whether that is producing a play, educating children, curing sick people, or manufacturing household appliances. So organizations may try to avoid or resist some of these demands (Pfeffer and Salancik 1978). Some of these tactics involve acting to change the environment, as will be discussed in the next section of this chapter. An in-between tactic—neither total resistance nor total surrender—is to set up buffers that reduce the impact of the environment on the organization. Organizations can stockpile inventories of raw materials or finished products; they can set up boundary-spanning roles in which certain members filter out for attention only the most relevant or pressing demands; they can even build walls and other barriers to keep out unwanted intrusions. Perhaps the most heavily buffered organizations are highly sensitive military installations like silos for nuclear missiles. Other devices used for buffering include coding and classifying inputs; leveling the flow of inputs or outputs through incentives, advertising, and the like; and forecasting future changes in supply and demand conditions (Scott 1987, pp. 183–84). Most large organizations use most of the buffering devices just mentioned, including some kind of security personnel and receptionists who control who enters and leaves their premises. The major purpose of buffering is to protect the technical core—that part of the organization where goods or services are produced—from environmental intrusions that might disturb production processes.

The degree to which organizations buffer themselves will depend heavily on internal and external cultural definitions of their role in society and of the nature of their environments. Organizations that believe their environments are relatively munificent and stable will likely employ minimal scanning of the environment for danger and threats, and minimal security forces. This was true of public schools in the United States earlier in this century. But, as crime, drug traffic, and other threats made the outside environment more unpredictable and hostile, many schools have had to learn more about crime, drugs, and weapons. Some hire virtual police forces to keep students safe and drug pushers outside school buildings. Others inspect student lockers for weapons.

Some organizations may, for a time, manage to buffer themselves from their environments by minimizing their contacts with any conflicting elements in their environments. Such organizations will need to have relatively modest demands for resources and be able to supply those they need from sympathetic elements in their environments. An observer found that some egalitarian "alternative" organizations founded in the 1960s and 1970s managed to preserve their original ideals. The ones that preserved their ideals had significantly fewer relations with external institutions of any kind than the ones that modified their ideals to conform with environmental expectations (Newman 1980). In effect, they successfully buffered their cultures from their environments. Many religious sects also employ this strategy.

An analysis of the cumulative results of studies of 94 organizations in developing countries suggest that buffering is universal. Results showed that some structures and practices of organizations in these countries fit theories based on Western organizations and some did not (Kiggundu, Jorgensen, and Hafsi 1983). The technical cores of organizations in developing countries was found to be similar to those of Western nations. Apparently Western technical processes of organizing—operating techniques, specialized training methods, computer applications—have been exported to developing nations where they become part of a universal management culture. These elements can be successfully imported and maintained within these cultures because the technical cores of organizations are typically buffered from their environments.

When studies focused on aspects of organizations in direct contact with the environment, results did not fit Western-based theory. "In general, each time the environment is involved, the theory developed for Western settings does not apply, because it assumes contingencies that may not be valid for developing countries" (Kiggundu, Jorgensen, and Hafsi 1983, p. 81). Clearly, one of those contingencies is the differences in culture between developing countries and Western nations.

As the example of egalitarian organizations shows, if organizations wish to differ from the surrounding culture, they must somehow manage to be quite independent of their environments. A study of 34 preindustrial societies found that only a handful had rational production organizations in the sense of social behavior purposefully directed toward explicit, practical objectives and planned in accordance with the best available knowledge (Udy 1959, 1962, 1970). Those found were relatively insulated and buffered from their nonrational cultural environments. They rarely imported new members into their ranks, and rewards were strictly based on evaluative performance criteria controlled by supervisors. Although the report of this study does not provide such detail, it is likely that such organizations survived in their environments by creating most of the resources they needed internally. Historically, utopian groups like the Oneida community and religious sects like the Hutterites and Amish have tried to be collectively self-sufficient. Even so, they are not successful in completely insulating themselves from environmental influences. The Oneida community survived only 30 years (Carden 1969); few utopian communities survive as long. The Hutterites and Amish experience some defections (Peter et al. 1987; Strayer 1991).

A caution must be raised. Buffering is not without risks. Organizations that are too heavily buffered may fail to notice relevant changes in their environment. This may be what happened in the Swedish calculator firm mentioned earlier in the chapter.

How Organizations Influence Environments

Most organizations would prefer to control their own fates; so they don't just give in to environmental demands. They employ many different strategies to influence their environments to be more favorable to them. If they succeed, they manage to reduce some of the uncertainties stemming from their dependencies on their environments. Strategies that help organizations influence environments include growth, diversification, mergers, joint ventures, interorganizational cooperation, contracting, cooptation, interlocking directorates, trade associations, lobbying, and various illegal actions such as deceptive advertising, bribery, and price fixing (Pfeffer and Salancik 1978). Which strategy an organization chooses is likely to be highly dependent on its culture and on the culture of the surrounding community or industry.

For example, not too long ago, hostile takeovers were virtually unthinkable in the U. S. managerial culture. The rash of takeovers that began in the 1980s

> ended long-standing traditions in the business community; they changed the rules regarding the conduct and aims of business; they generated conflict between firms and within firms; [and] they generated conflict between shareholders and management, as these once compatible interests became pitted against each other. (Hirsch 1986, p. 827)

A variety of changes in the environment prepared the way for the takeoever movement. First were a number of so-called friendly takeovers during the late 1960s that turned out to be very conflictual—most notably the merger in 1968 of the New York Central and Pennsylvania railroads. Managers and investors began to see that mergers were never really friendly and that someone had to be clearly in charge of the merged firm (Daughen and Binzen 1971). Later developments included the ascent of free-market values during the 1970s, implemented in the 1980s during the Reagan administration through accelerated deregulation and the relaxation of antitrust prohibitions (Hirsch 1987, p. 23). The latter development meant that firms in the same industry could merge without danger of prosecution.

Looking at the world through the lens of new possibilities, financial analysts detected that U.S. firms were worth much more than their current stock prices if viewed as a bundle of salable assets. All that was now needed to erase the comfortable "gentlemen's agreement" that had once forbidden buying unwilling companies was the development of junk bonds by financial houses and their backing by banks eager to earn high interest. Into this promising arena strode daring entrepreneurs—corporate raiders like T. Boone Pickens—who could obtain the enormous loans needed. When raiders went directly to shareholders and offered them premium prices for their stock, most were in no position to resist. There had also been a significant ". . . shift of share ownership from individuals to institutions who are 'trustees', and especially to pension funds" (Drucker 1986, p. 11), which are duty-bound to realize the highest possible return to their investors.

Whether some specific managerial values had to change before these developments could occur, or whether these developments changed managerial values is not clear. The proponents of the takeover movement found their primary ideological support in one strand of managerial culture—the strong belief in the benefits of a free market. Once underway, the takeover movement changed the culture of U.S. business irrevocably—not so much by making some ideologies more powerful than others, but by making new behaviors available and acceptable. No matter what happens to reverse or moderate these developments, the residues of what occurred in the 1980s will remain as part of the U.S. business culture. Thus, it may be worthwhile to look at this new cultural development in more detail.

Hostile takeovers and other mergers exemplify both sides of the cultural interchange between environments and organizations. The acquiring firm reaches out to change its environment by trying to capture another organization. In the process, the acquirer not only changes the environment of the target firm, but also the environments of many other organizations dependent in one way or another on the target firm—unions, suppliers, customers, and competitors, The target firm can be viewed as having its environment, in the form of the would-be acquirer, making demands to which it must adapt. But as the accounts of takeovers and mergers make clear, the influence processes are not all in one direction. Acquiring firms will also be affected by the acquired firm as they try to manage the newly combined firm.

Hostile takeovers. Takeover bids, if successful, have ominous and wide-ranging implications for the purchased company. Product lines and services may be drastically altered, managerial and employee ranks ruthlessly pruned, accounting systems revamped, and long-standing pension and retirement benefits reviewed. In essence, much that the members have taken for granted is now under question. Strangers are now in control of their company. A whole vocabulary of special terms arose to express the anxieties and attendant sense making provoked by hostile takeovers. Examples drawn from one compilation of these terms are given in Table 8–3.

Inevitably, the cultures of the acquiring and acquired companies must be interrelated in some fashion, and perhaps eventually integrated. Observers of takeovers have portrayed and labeled them as "cultural collisions" (Sales and Mirvis 1984; Buono, Bowditch, and Lewis 1985; Walter 1985). While it is true that the initial impact of the takeover is like a collision—a violent contact between two discrete, ongoing entities—it is the aftermath of the collision that determines the relative success of the acquisition and the continued viability of the merged company. Three types of adaptation can be identified in the events that typically take place after the takeover: exploitation, assimilation, and accommodation.[3]

The first stage in the aftermath of many takeovers is the financial exploitation of the acquired firm by the raider. While there are exceptions, the raider must usually sell valuable parts of the acquired company or use the acquired firm's cash surplus to pay back the large loans that were required to make the takeover possible. In the new language this movement generated, if the raider has been especially astute and has located a "sleeping beauty" who can be overpowered by an "ambush," there will be ready assets that can be immediately plundered. Small wonder that such transactions have been likened to rape

---

[3]Sometimes all three may occur in sequence and thus could be considered stages of an overall process of adaptation. But all mergers do not produce all three types of adaptation and the order in which these types of adaptation occurs probably varies.

TABLE 8–3
EXAMPLES AND DEFINITIONS OF POPULAR TERMINOLOGY USED
TO DESCRIBE TAKEOVERS

Afterflow	postmerger euphoria of acquirer and/or acquiree, usually soon lost
Ambush	swift and premeditated takeover attempt
Barricades	impediments to a takeover (usually lawsuits) raised by the target company
Black knights	unfriendly acquirers drawn to the target by news that the company is already being propositioned by others
Bring to the altar	consummate a merger, usually friendly
Courtship	merger discussions, relatively friendly, between top executives of two firms
Cupid	role played by merger brokers; also called matchmakers
Dancing	preliminary talks and negotiations in a more or less friendly merger
Dowry	outstanding assets that the target may carry into a merger (e.g., low-interest loans, long-term contracts)
Fight letter	strong declaration of target company's opposition to a raider's offer; a gloves-off fight is likely to follow
Friendly offer	merger proposal cleared in advance with the target company's board and top management
Golden parachute	provision in the employment contracts of top executives that assures them of a lucrative financial landing if the firm is acquired in a take-over
Greenmail	a firm's purchase of its own stock, at a premium, from an investor whom it fears will otherwise seek to acquire it or initiate a proxy fight to oust its present management
Hired guns	merger and acquisition specialists, other investment bankers, and law-yers employed by either side in a takeover
Hot pursuit	strenuous campaign by aggressive, would-be hostile acquirer to obtain shares of the target firm
Junk bonds	high-risk, high-yield certificates traded publicly; so-called because they are rated below investment grade
Marbles	advance promise of continued employment for target's executives by the firm's would-be acquirer
Marrying	accomplishing a merger
On the rocks	failed, incompatible merger
Raiders	hostile acquirers, also called pirates
Rape	forcible, surprise hostile takeover, sometimes accompanied by looting of the acquiree's profitability
Saturday night special	a fast and predatory merger
Scorched earth	a policy whereby the target firm would rather self-destruct than be acquired
Sharks	takeover artists
Shark repellant	protective strategies for preventing or combatting a hostile tender offer
Sleeping beauties	vulnerable targets, also called pigeons
Tombstones	advertisements in the financial press containing announcements of in-terest to investors and the business community (e.g., tender offers, stock underwritings)
White knight	acceptable acquirer sought by a potential acquiree to forestall an un-friendly takeover; the preferred acquirer

SOURCE: Adapted from Hirsch 1986, pp. 830–34.

(Hirsch 1986). This stage of the takeover, in effect, ignores the culture of the acquired firm. The acquiring firm's wishes prevail because it has effective financial control. In extreme instances, this type of adaptation may be so ruthless and thorough that the acquired firm's cultures are effectively destroyed. To destroy both a firm's overall culture and all of its subcultures, however, the acquiring firm would have to get rid of most of the acquired firms' employees. Probably most often the overall culture and the managerial subcultures are disrupted, but various employee subcultures remain, with potential to resent and resist the acquiring firm's initiatives.

The cultural rationale supporting takeovers requires the acquirer to go beyond exploiting the assets of the acquired firm. Presumably some other benefits will accrue from the takeover. The acquirer must somehow assimilate what is left of the firm and attempt to run it better than the previous management did. The cultural rationale for takeover implies that corporations under a free market economy must be regarded "more as a salable bundle of liquid assets" than as a generator of goods and services (Hirsch 1986, p. 801). Managers and other employees are not assets because (except in some sports teams) they cannot be sold.

Applying open market principles to firms allegedly helps the economy because it is believed to discipline inefficient or inadequate managements. An implication of this rationale is that managers who allow the market value of their stock to get below the appraised value of the company's assets are incompetent. The acquirers are thus justified in bringing in new management and increasing the surveillance of the acquired company. To accomplish this, large sectors of upper management may be removed. William Agee, CEO of the Bendix Corporation, was "permitted to resign" by Allied Corporation chairman Edward Hennessey when Allied completed its victory over Bendix. President Alonzo McDonald was fired by Hennessey two days later (Sloan 1983; Walter 1985, p. 304). To facilitate such firings, rites of degradation are often used.

In these and other ways, acquiring firms' cultures may assimilate those of acquired ones. In the process, the overall cultures of acquired firms will be weakened by the removal of their top leaders. Indeed, that is often the purpose of their removal: to eliminate the existing subculture of the top management in the acquired firm. Other organizational subcultures, particularly those associated with established and organizationally valued occupations, have a better chance of survival in the acquired organization.

Highly negative emotions generated by the takeover among the employees in the acquired firm often accompany an assimilation process. In one firm, people stood around in shocked disbelief following the takeover's announcement over the intercom. To the observer, they looked like people had looked after they learned President Kennedy had been shot. Later, the employees referred to that day as "Black Thursday." Long-term employees were especially bitter. "Initially, workers experienced shock, disbelief, and grief, as if someone had died in their family; these emotions were followed by resentment, anger, and/or depression" (Sinetar 1981, p. 864).

In order to get beyond these negative consequences, something positive must occur. In some way, if the merged firm is to survive, some type of accommodation must be reached between members of the two firms and their cultures. A culturally sensitive way to begin the process is to employ rites of conflict reduction. Some merger seminars that have been developed provide excellent examples. In one model (Blake and Mouton 1985), a series of fishbowl meetings are held in which sets of managers from the acquired firm and from the new headquarters convene together, surrounded by managers from various other functional elements of both organizations. The latter act as observers and watchers as those in the fishbowl expose their differences and interact to iron them out. Typically, the headquarters staff explains how the acquiring firm usually operates, and then invite managers of the acquired firm to ask questions and comment on how they might accommodate to headquarters' needs by adapting their old procedures to the acquirer's mode of management. This act of invitation symbolizes the acquiring firm's willingness to accommodate in some ways to the culture of the acquired firm. The consultants who run these sessions will try to move both sets of participants toward the identification of common concerns and eventually to submeetings among corresponding managers of similar functional groups in the two companies.

While such rites probably facilitate the accommodation by the acquiring firm of *some* aspects of the acquired firm, analysts conclude that the accommodation process takes a very long time and is seldom complete. A key issue is the cultural compatibility of the two firms—an issue infortunately rarely considered before the merger (Schein 1985, p. 34). If the cultural incompatibility of the two firms is too great, the acquisition may end up a failure. The accommodation required is probably too great. Even when the acquiring organization is determined to make minimal changes in the acquired organization—as occurred when General Electric acquired Intersil—the logic of management cannot leave the acquired firm completely untouched. Concerns about coordination, control, or equity will call for at least minor alterations in the acquired firm's practices. G.E. imposed only one change on Intersil: the original stock option plan was replaced by G.E.'s standard plan. To the engineers and managers at Intersil, however, this was not a minor change; their plan had symbolized the possibility of "big money." Over one-third of them left and G.E. did not get the high-tech expertise and refinements it expected from the acquisition (Magnet 1984). Another possibility is that remnants of the old firms' cultures will persist in the form of powerful subcultures or even countercultures within the merged firm.

In the ideal case, the accommodation process will positively affect the acquiring firm. When Xerox acquired Versatec in 1975, Xerox management retained Versatec's CEO, Renn Zaphiropoulos. He insisted that as long as his company met Xerox's objectives, he should be allowed to run it his own way. Xerox agreed and Zaphiropoulos worked assiduously at maintaining good relations with the parent company while maintaining solid sales and earnings growth. Xerox was so impressed that in 1985, it created a new post for him as corporate director of its Information Products Division (Magnet 1984). In effect, Xerox opened itself to new cultural influences from the cultural leader of the acquired firm.

Few acquiring firms, however, appear able to take such an open stance toward their acquisitions. Most fall victim to overconfidence and arrogance about their own abilities, procedures, and skills. After all, isn't conquering another firm a sign of superiority? Flowing from their assumption of superiority may come miscalculations about operating knowledge of the acquired firm, refusal to learn valuable know-how from the acquired firms' managers, and a tendency to take even greater risks with the next acquisition target. Prevalent cultural definitions of takeovers tend to encourage overconfidence in acquiring firms. Many of the terms used to describe takeovers liken them to military battles, sports contests, or romantic conquests. The prevailing imagery thus clearly envisions the acquirers as winners. The acquired are portrayed as losers, victims, or objects of conquest.

This evocative language provides a way to understand unfamiliar situations fraught with uncertainty for both participants and the wider society. The terms chosen are culturally loaded in the sense that each—although only a fragment of our culture—carries many associated meanings and ideas. Thus they provide a good example of how cultural forms work. It doesn't matter who first used these terms to refer to takeover situations. It may have been journalists rather than participants. Once such language is widely used, it will probably carry meanings into takeover situations even when key participants want to reject the underlying ideas the terms convey. The language has helped to created a cultural definition of the situation that is hard to overcome or resist.

"Friendly" mergers. In situations where hostile takeovers are imminent, companies sometimes seek "white knights" to save them from merging with a company they consider unsuitable or undesirable. While these forced unions might be considered friendly, they turn out to have effects on the acquired firm's culture similar to those of hostile takeovers. This is because of the uniqueness of each organization's culture. While managers in different firms may share many of the same general ideologies and have acquired much of the same formal education and occupational know-how, a unique web of beliefs and practices will be woven by the repeated interactions and practices among a specific set of managers running a specific firm in a specific locale with a specific set of customers, suppliers, and so forth. In effect, what makes each organization's culture unique is that the organization generates a specific context in which new cultural content is invented and more general cultural patterns are adapted and modified.

In supposedly friendly mergers, the adaptation process may not be as traumatic as in hostile ones. The acquirer may refrain from selling off assets of the acquired company if it can afford to do so. The two firms may even agree to operate as relatively loosely linked entities.[4] However, the second and third types of adaptation—assimilation and accommodation—often cannot be avoided.

---

[4]One pair of analysts argues that the acquired firm or unit should be given relative autonomy if the survival of the strategic capabilities on which the acquisition is based depends on preservation of a distinct organizational culture (Haspeslagh and Jemison 1991, p. 143). They advocate considering both needs for autonomy and needs for strategic interdependence in deciding on how closely to integrate the two firms.

A large midwestern manufacturing firm in the United States faced a hostile takeover attempt in 1977 because one of its divisions was unprofitable. To avoid the takeover, management invited a merger with a large conglomerate that it had considered selling out to several years earlier. The hostile takeover bid was indeed made; the chosen "White Knight" countered with a much larger offer and thus rescued the target company from a raider who has a reputation for raping acquisitions (Sales and Mirvis 1984).

The target company soon found, however, that even a friendly merger may involve great cultural clash. The top management of the acquired company had implemented an advanced form of participative management based on "the authority of knowledge . . . the sharing of power and decision making and the commitment that results from effective participation" (Sales and Mirvis 1984). The acquiring conglomerate, and the group vice-president to which the acquired company reported, was dominated by an elitist group of top managers with a "yes-sir" mentality. Procedural differences symbolized these different philosophies. The conglomerate insisted upon monthly reports, two planning meetings per year, and extensive and elaborate financial analyses. The new acquiring managers gave much criticism and few compliments. None of these were part of the accepted ways of doing things in the acquired company, which operated in a much friendlier, informal, and almost familial manner.

In the year following the acquisition, observers detected three social processes that interfered with the two cultures accommodating to one another. Polarization occurred when managers in the acquired company would recognize differences and exaggerate them so as to make them extreme opposites. For example, they saw themselves as "highly participative" and the conglomerate as "extremely autocratic" (Sales and Mirvis 1984, p. 115). Evaluative judgments reinforced these definitions of the situation. The acquired firm was good and the acquirer was bad. Ethnocentrism emerged next; people began to see events in terms of "we" versus "they." The acquired firm felt forced to abandon its cherished ways, even though they were "right." The acquiring firm also felt its ways were right and that the acquired firm was ungrateful. The acquiring firm continued to see itself as a White Knight while managers in the acquired firm tended to forget they had been rescued from a possibly worse fate.

Between 1979 and 1981, a process of accommodation began. The sheer passage of time began to mitigate hostiles and anxieties. In addition, the acquired firm made an important symbolic gesture toward integration by inviting the conglomerate's group vice-president to participate in their search for a new internal executive vice-president. The invitation expressed their own philosophy of participation. Perhaps most important, the hire itself confirmed those values because the person hired subscribed to and had practiced participative management. Over time, the group vice-president became more tolerant of the acquired firm's ideologies. In return, the acquired firm accepted the tough, financial orientation and practices of the conglomerate, including their accounting system, their auditors, and their planning style.

Another friendly merger began when the CEOs of two mutual savings banks met one another at a industry association meeting in the mid-1980s. The banks were not in direct competition and were of similar size and purposes. The CEOs agreed that conditions in their industry made survival difficult for medium-sized banks. They therefore decided that a merger of the two banks would make both more secure. They neglected, however, to assess the compatibility of the cultures of the two organizations. The managerial style in Bank *A* was participative; in Bank *B,* it was authoritarian. In Bank *A,* the CEO was frequently called a "Buddha" and a "good guy"; the other CEO was referred to as "Dennis the Menace" and an "elitist". Accordingly, Bank *A* used more planning, more shared information, more testing of ideas at all levels of management, and consequently had slow decision making. Bank *B* was more oriented to unilateral and rapid decision making by the CEO. Employee eating facilities carried contrasting cultural messages: Bank *A* had "plush and restaurant-like facilities"; those of Bank *B* were "spartan and cafeteria-like" (Buono, Bowditch, and Lewis 1985, pp. 485–86).

Many employees at both banks initially felt favorable to the merger, although support was stronger at Bank *A*. Soon after the merger, however, the employees of each bank saw the other as an "invading army" (Buono, Bowditch, and Lewis 1985, p. 492). Difficulties began even before the merger was accomplished. Personnel in both banks became defensive during joint discussions about which computer system, reporting forms, and operating procedures to use. Clearly, each group had invested their job-related artifacts with cultural meaning. Each group regarded "their way" as better. The situation rapidly became one of competition for positions in the new combined functional areas, even though employees of each bank continued to identify with their prior roles. The actions of Bank *B*'s CEO as the new chief operating officer increased tensions, especially when he violated his promise of no merger-related layoffs. His office came to be known as "murderer's row" as employees, especially those in Bank *A,* attributed the layoffs to him. Bank *B* was increasingly seen as dominant, and the employees from Bank *A* experienced more culture shock because they saw the culture of the merged organization as more similar to that of Bank *B* than to that of their former organization.

Although some analysts have suggested that mergers may eventuate either in integration of the merging cultures or in rejection or even destruction of both cultures, such extreme outcomes seem unlikely. The most likely outcome is some degree of accommodation over time (Berry 1980). How mutual that accommodation is will vary with the circumstances surrounding the merger and how it is implemented (Jemison and Sitkin 1986).

Two possibilities are not addressed by the literature on mergers. One is whether the culture of an acquired firm can eventually prevail in the combined firm. While not likely, such a situation is conceivable if the acquired firm has substantial assets and longevity and the acquiring firm makes little attempt to impose its culture. It is also conceivable if the acquired firm has well-established occupational cultures and much of the value of the acquisition rests on the efforts of employees in those occupations. In mergers where both firm cultures are weak, the outcome is highly uncertain. One possibility is that, to help members deal with such great uncertainty, a new overall culture will develop.

A further complication in mergers is that "many different groups from both inside and outside the firms are involved in an acquisition," yet "few of these have a stake in how the combined firms will be run" or how successful they are after the merger (Jemison and Sitkin 1986, p. 161). Most of these groups focus on economic implications of the merger for the firms or themselves, ignoring the cultural and other "softer, more subtle, and emergent issues of integrating the operations of two businesses . . . " (Jemison and Sitkin 1986, p. 161).

Other strategies.   Various strategies that organizations use to manage dependencies on their environments involve other kinds of linkages with other organizations. These strategies vary in the degree of closeness they create between the linked organizations, but all carry some potential for cultural interchange. One of the closest is the joint venture, in which a new, separate organizational entity, jointly controlled and financed by more than one parent organization, is formed to realize shared objectives.

Joint ventures imply ongoing relations and cooperation over sustained periods that make mutual influences likely. Those managing and working in joint ventures need to be able to communicate with and understand both parent firms and each other. If the cultures involved are highly incompatible, the joint venture is unlikely to succeed. Parent companies will have great difficulty in arriving at shared aims and procedures. Without some consensus, desired outcomes fail to materialize and the joint venture is often abandoned. Despite these likely difficulties, U.S. firms have turned to joint ventures at an accelerating rate to help them remain competitive in fast-changing industries. Three of the computer giants—IBM, Motorola, and Apple Computers—recently announced a joint venture, for example (Ladendorf 1991).

Other, less involving forms of interorganizational cooperation probably require less cultural compatibility, but can also be rendered ineffectual if members diverge in aims and practices. Contracting, cooptation, and interlocking directorates involve relatively few people in interchanges with those in other organizations. While they may also create some measure of mutual cultural influence, it is likely to be more limited in its impact than mergers or joint ventures. The fewer the persons in direct contact with another culture, the less influence the contact is likely to have. Contracting puts mostly salespeople and legal personnel in direct contact; cooptation usually brings in a small number of outsiders to share in organizational decision making or other events; interlocking directorates will involve only one or two members of top management in the mangement of another firm.

Also, less formalized, but regular interorganizational exchanges are common, even among competitors. The term networks is used to describe these systems of "indefinite, repeated transactions" among groups of organizations (Powell 1990, p. 301). Members of networks rely on informal norms of reciprocity to govern transactions; actual exchanges occur through social ties between individuals. They usually involve commodities "whose value is not easily measured. Such qualitative matters as know-how, technological capability, a particular approach or style of production, a spirit of innovation or experimentation, or a philosophy of zero defects are very hard to place a price tag on" (Powell 1990, p. 304). Clearly, such networks require a considerable degree of cultural complementarity. Organizational networks have been documented in such industries as construction, publishing, music, movies, and biotechnology.

Trade associations involve rather indirect interactions of many firms with each other; to the degree that they invest in an independent office staff and executive director, they seem likely to spawn a separate industrywide culture. Such groups, of course, often engage in lobbying on behalf of their members.

All of these strategies involve organizations becoming embedded in networks with other organizations in order to influence them and other sectors of their environments. Like some of the communication interlocks among individuals that allow subcultural formation, networks of organizations provide opportunities for mutual cultural influence. Embeddedness in such networks also imposes new resource and legitimacy constraints on organizations that they must deal with in order to both remain in the network and meet other obligations.

In some countries, bribery of public officials and others who can block or speed transactions is a taken-for-granted way of doing business. Businesspeople who face these realities are likely to decide on the basis of their corporate cultures whether or not they will go along with the surrounding cultures. Those who participate in actions considered illegal in their home countries probably have corporate cultures that are pragmatic and tend to value ends over the means used to reach those ends. Other firms, with strong traditions of honesty, may decide they will not conduct their business differently abroad than they would at home. In general, individuals' propensity to engage in illegal activities can be encouraged or discouraged by the values that are part of the corporate culture. Corporate codes of ethics are empty rituals unless they are backed up by genuinely shared values.

National Cultures as Organizational Environments

The recent emergence of the global economy has alerted managers worldwide to the necessity to enter and compete effectively in national markets other than their own. In the process managers find that they must try to understand the preferences of foreign customers, the regulations and procedures of foreign governments, and the expectations and behaviors of employees from other national cultures. To do this, managers and analysts must decide which features of organizations must be responsive to national cultures, how historical forces may have shaped them differently, and how organizational and employee characteristics differ across national cultures. There is special interest in making these comparisons between the U.S. and Japanese cultures because of the success some Japanese organizations have enjoyed in capturing market share from U.S. corporations in their home market and abroad.

Culture Bound vs. Culture Free

Observers disagree on how closely national host cultures bind and pattern the internal operations of work organizations. One view says that their external, surrounding cultures largely determine organizations' formal structures and internal cultures. It follows from this view that organizations should differ internally in ways that are consistent with differences in the national cultures in which they are located. These differences are expected to arise and persist because of such factors as countries' history and stage of development, natural resources, climate, demography, and cultural inertia (Ronen 1986, p. 86).

The opposing view argues that many of the patterns of organizational characteristics are universal and stem from inherent requirements of organizing or of doing certain kinds of work. This view would hold that differences occur only because of certain factors inherent in the organizations themselves. According to this view, the basic "logic of industrialization" is the same worldwide (Harbison and Myers 1959, p. 117). Industrialization inevitably leads to certain organizational practices, which are culture free in the sense that they arise from the internal makeup and activities of organizations and not from the culture surrounding them. It follows from this view that organizations in different national cultures can be quite similar to each other. A related but somewhat different set of arguments that has been advanced for expecting similarities in organizations across cultures is that cultures themselves are growing more similar over time. Some of the factors expected to contribute to the convergence of national cultures are the diffusion and demands of technology, related educational requirements, the spread of a pragmatic philosophy, and the goals of organizations to adapt and prosper (Ronen 1986, p. 238). Research results, however, have sometimes questioned the notion that using similar technologies creates similar organizational structures (Lincoln 1990). For example, a recent study found that new technologies are often adapted to existing organizational practices rather than the other way around (Child, Ganter, and Kieser 1987).

The convergence argument has two important implications. The first is that it is possible that organizations can be bound by their surrounding cultures yet similar across national boundaries because the surrounding cultures have become similar. The second and more important implication is that organizations themselves are important in changing the surrounding culture. Who develops and uses technology but organizations? Who educates people but organizations? Where is pragmatic philosophy most nurtured and rewarded but in organizations? Also, although organizational goals and adaptations are largely generated internally, they affect the external environment and culture. The convergence perspective, then, provides a potentially fruitful way to consider issues of cultural interchange between organizations and environments and the codevelopment of organizations and societies.

In summary, there are two reasons for arguing that organizations are culture free and therefore similar across national cultures: One is that the processes of organizing and using technologies make certain universal requirements on organizations; the second is that these requirements and other factors are leading to greater similarities across national cultures themselves. The reasons why organizations are bound by their cultural environments and therefore different across national boundaries are simpler: organizational operations are constrained by expectations arising from culture itself and from the same factors, like geography or demography, that give rise to cultural differences.

One way to integrate these two viewpoints is to consider the features of organizations on which each focuses. One analyst suggested that " ... cultural effects will be most powerful in the processes of organization relating to authority, style, conduct, participation, and attitudes, and less powerful in formal structuring and overall strategy" (Child 1981, p. 347). Others have argued that the surrounding culture is most likely to influence those aspects of organizations involving their relations with individuals (e.g., management policies, leadership styles, communication patterns) and least likely to affect machine technologies (production machinery, transportation equipment, data processing systems) (Beres and Portwood 1981). These arguments echo a point already made in the earlier section on buffering—that cultural effects are likely to be greater in those sections of organizations in contact with environments and less important in the technical core because it is usually buffered from the environment (Kiggundu, Jorgensen, and Hafsi 1983). A review of relevant empirical research findings will help to make these distinctions clear. But first we will examine the important role that history plays in the development of distinctive national cultures.

Historical Influences

In and behind the distinctive features of each national culture lies the historical development of its political, social, economic, and other institutions. From these developments emerge distinctive ideologies and cultural forms that persist across generations. Although there is some slippage in them, socialization processes preserve and transmit many elements of cultures and in this way form unique cores of cultural substance that are reflected in subsequent cultural development. Indeed, the continuity of culture is so central that some define culture as " ... beliefs, values, and behaviors which may be directly attributable to contact with the beliefs, values, and behaviors of preceding generations" (Beres and Portwood 1979, p. 139).

A dramatic example of the differences that historical context can have on the culture and functioning of similar organizations is provided by an analysis of the British Royal Air Force and the German Luftwaffe during World War II (Teitler 1981). The German Luftwaffe (air force) was embedded in a national culture that reflected its location in the middle of a continent where it was surrounded and vulnerable to numerous potential enemies. To deal with these dangers, Germany had developed and kept a powerful army constantly trained and ready for swift attack or defense. Ideologies supporting this militant posture included a strong duty to the state and the subordination of individuals to the state welfare. The army, bolstered by the willing members these ideologies made available, became the dominant force in a very powerful and large military. Size and power were seen as the only way to cope with greatest danger of all—having to wage war on several borders at once.

The overall grand strategy of the Germans envisioned swift, powerful, overwhelming might—called a blitzkrieg—that demanded a concentration of modern, mechanized, highly mobile forces. These forces would be spearheaded and dominated by an elite army corps commanding tanks, mobile infantry and artillery, and airplanes. As a result, the planes and their pilots were trained to operate as closely as possible with ground forces and their army commanders. Thus, no independent air force organization was formed. Rather, army commanders allocated Luftwaffe aircraft and personnel piecemeal throughout the army and, to a lesser extent, the navy. Luftwaffe commanders lacked control over their personnel and weapons. Another historical factor underlying these developments was that the Treaty of Versailles banned a German air force; this circumstance also favored embedding the air force in the army because its growth would be easier to camouflage there.

The British Royal Air Force (RAF) grew out of radically different historical circumstances and cultural traditions. England was an island nation with less fear of fighting multiple ground wars. The major reason was that England had developed a powerful navy, which it could use to defend its shores. In addition, England had historically formed coalitions with various European nations to ensure it would not face enemies alone. As a consequence of these strategies, the army had played a relatively minor role in thinking about national defense. During World War I, England had strayed from this overall strategy with disastrous results. After that war, England returned to the strategy of a small army and a large, powerful navy, but now without obligations or tactical commitments to any European neighbors. To this equation was added the possibility of airpower—a force that would make available a speed of response not possible with seapower. The enthusiasts for airpower claimed that, like the navy, an independent air force was a strategic weapon that could practically fight a war on its own. In modeling their air force after their navy, the British therefore gave priority to the heavy, long-range bomber, which could inflict heavy damage at great distances, but was not at all suited to close support of ground or naval forces. A division of labor was created in the RAF, with separate, autonomous commands for coastal defense, for fighters, and for bombers. This gave the RAF commanders relative independence to pursue their long-range bombing strategy without having to respond, as the German Luftwaffe commanders did, to continuous army demands for close support. Ultimately, this close support did emerge within the British air force, but it was important for the success of the overall RAF strategy that it grew from initiatives of its air commanders and not from the dictates of the army or navy.

As this example illustrates, analysis of the historical factors behind organizational differences usually uncovers a complex web of events and circumstances. A somewhat simpler example is provided by comparing the roles of first-level supervisors in French and German industry (Maurice, Sellier, and Silvestre 1984). Becoming a supervisor in a French company is a matter of being appointed to that position by the organization; the supervisor occupies an *organiza-*

tional status. To become a foreman in Germany, the occupant must pass through an apprenticeship that demonstrates technical competence, and must acquire additional expertise through special training; thus foremen in Germany have primarily *occupational* status.[5] Because of these differences in how they gained their status, the authority of the French supervisor derives from rank and that of the German foreman from technical expertise. Other factors strengthening the occupational base of German managers are a traditional emphasis on vocational training in their society, and an ideology that work constitutes a "calling" involving a lifelong commitment to a series of tasks performed for the benefit of the larger society (Hartmann 1959, p. 7). The ways in which managers in these two countries see and enact their roles are profoundly affected by these circumstances. The role of the French supervisor represents a "break [from past work roles] rather than continuity; it means he is entering management (albeit at the lowest level). . . . ". The German foreman, by contrast, can see his or her role as "developing a higher level of training" (Maurice, Sellier, and Silvestre 1984, p. 252). Indeed, because of their strong occupational base and identity, many German managers behave like free-lance professionals (Granick 1962, p. 280). French managers, on the other hand, become bureaucrats—rewarded for seniority, deprived of initiative by endless rules and regulations, but free from personal interference and skilled at resisting their subordinates and maintaining the formalisms that protect them (Crozier 1973, p. 222).

The potency of history is best illustrated by how basic ideological cores of cultures survive even large-scale, revolutionary, coerced social change. The Chinese people in the People's Republic of China have not discarded many traditions and customs rooted in Confucian principles (Shenkar and Ronen, 1987). Nor did the Iranian people discard traditional beliefs as the government of the recent Shah sought to modernize the country. The appeal of the traditional culture became one of the forces contributing to his overthrow. Because of the cultural residues each generation carries as it copes with the present, historical developments must be considered when trying to understand contemporary national cultures. This point is sometimes forgotten by Americans, who are often viewed as an essentially historyless people (Schlesinger 1986), often only too willing to ignore their own past and the ideologies and cultural practices it projects into the present. Such tendencies are very damaging to efforts to understand the effects of culture on human behavior.

Cross-National Comparisons

The dominant research methods and statistics of social science, which are embedded in the ideologies and values of many researchers, are designed to uncover differences. Thus, the literature on similarities among organizations in different nations is much smaller than that documenting differences. These ideolo-

---

[5]The two terms—supervisor and foreman—carry different cultural meanings. A supervisor is a member of management; a foreman is someone who is first among equals. Unfortunately, there is no acceptable gender-neutral term for foreman.

gies and values are so ingrained that the results of a study finding only similarities would be likely to be viewed as inconclusive and therefore unlikely to be published. Despite this bias against finding similarities, the bulk of cross-national comparisons in the organizational literature yields evidence of both similarities and differences. For the purposes of clarity and brevity, the two sets of results will be summarized separately here.

English researchers have been prominent in the efforts to document the presence of structural similarities across organizations in different countries. Their work stems from two sets of studies begun in the 1960s (Woodward 1980; Pugh et al. 1963) that found that some structural features of organizations tended to covary in ways that seemed intuitively sensible. These results were interpreted as providing evidence that organizational size and technology largely determine other structural characteristics of organizations. Later research using the same measures tended to confirm these basic findings for firms in various countries (Hickson et al. 1974, 1981; Child and Kieser 1979; Lammers and Hickson, 1979). A second set of results, using different measures of the structures of state and federal agencies in the United States, also supported the idea that size and technology were important determinants of other aspects of structure (Blau and Schoenherr 1971; Beyer and Trice 1979). Basically, these and many later studies found that larger organizations were more internally complex, with more specialists and subunits, had more rules and formalized procedures, and were more decentralized in their decision making than smaller organizations (Daft and Steers 1986, p. 230). The results for technology were more complex, but are usually interpreted to show that simple or routine technologies tended to be more efficient in more rigid, bureaucratic structures while more complex and nonroutine technologies were facilitated by more flexible, organic structures (Daft and Steers 1986, pp. 256–57).

Relatively early in this stream of studies, the regularities of such results suggested the presence of imperatives that seemed to take effect whatever the surrounding cultural differences (Hickson et al. 1974). But when more results had accumulated, the early position was modified to asking first, how organizations were "like and unlike," and then, "what is the relative weight of cultural versus other influences upon the characteristics of organizations?" (Lammers and Hickson 1979, p. 402). Clearly, something had happened to make the culture-free position in its purest form untenable. A great deal of empirical evidence supporting the opposite, culture-bound, position had been accumulating. Limitations of space prohibit summarizing more than a sampling of the key findings of a large body of cross-cultural research that documents differences between organizations in different countries.

One important series of studies focused on the distribution of authority in socialist and capitalist countries. In the socialist cultures studied—Yugoslav factories and Israeli kibbutzim—prevailing ideologies of egalitarianism favored employee participation and egalitarian decision making. They also led to efforts to apply such tactics as rotating members from one rank to another, or choosing technologies and designing jobs to be rewarding to lower status members. These tactics turned out to be "compromises, at best; they may reduce, but do not eliminate the effects of hierarchy" (Tannenbaum et al. 1974, p. 208). In the capitalist countries studies—the United States, Italy, and Austria—the powerful aspirations of workers to move up the hierarchy and achieve individual success tended to insure the hierarchy's continuance in organizations. While the researchers concluded that hierarchy is inevitable, their results clearly show that its presence and effects are somewhat muted in socialist countries and accentuated in capitalist ones.

Another study of hierarchy found significant differences between French and German firms. As might be expected from earlier descriptions of these two cultures, the French firms had significantly more hierarchical layers, more managerial employees, and a more highly skewed income distribution than did the German firms (Maurice 1979).

A study of international operations uncovered differences in customary management practices among several nationalities (Yamaguchi 1988). In the Japanese and German styles, the CEO and all key people in overseas operations are shipped from home. In the English and French styles, the CEO is a skilled overseas bureaucrat and the staff are locals. In the American style, a highly capable member of the organization, regardless of nationality, is used as the local CEO, and lower levels of management are local.

The most ambitious attempt to compare national cultures used data from two massive surveys of 116,000 employees in a single multinational corporation to investigate the relative positions of 40 countries on 4 value dimensions: individualism versus collectivism, large versus small power distance, strong versus weak uncertainty avoidance, and masculinity versus femininity (Hofstede 1980b). The reported results are very complex because the average positions of all countries for which there were sufficient data were plotted on every pair of these dimensions.

For brevity, these results will be illustrated by defining just two of the value dimensions used and discussing the results relative to them. The power distance dimension deals with the fact that people are inherently unequal. Large power distance means that prevalent cultural values accentuate inequalities, while small power distance means that values deemphasize them. The uncertainty avoidance dimension refers to the extent to which members of a culture are socialized to accept future uncertainties or to try to avoid them. Average responses for each country on these two value dimensions indicated that the Netherlands, Anglo, and Scandinavian countries are similar in having relatively small power distances and weak uncertainty avoidance. In effect, the results indicate that in these countries inequalities are deemphasized and uncertainties accepted. Conversely, Latin, Mediterranean, Islamic, some other Asian countries, and Japan exhibit large power distances and strong uncertainty avoidance. In these countries, the results suggest, inequalities are emphasized and uncertainties avoided. Other patterns of values were: large power distance and weak uncertainty avoidance, Southeast Asia; small power distance and strong uncertainty avoidance, German-speaking countries, Finland, and Israel (Hofstede 1980b, p. 316).

Despite attempts to buttress these results by showing how they correlate with a large number of variables from past research (Hofstede 1980b, pp. 326–

31), these results have been criticized by various scholars. A particularly cogent complaint is that the study lacks "grounding in the context of each nation sampled," particularly the degree to which the values and norms studied are historically embedded in social and institutional developments; thus, the study's results are "no more than suggestive" (Child 1981, p. 332). Another drawback of this study is that it focused on only four sets of values, measured like individual attitudes by questionnaires. The use of questionnaires to measure culture has been criticized for two basic reasons: (1) to the degree that culture is implicit, respondents may not be fully aware of their values and ideologies and thus cannot report them accurately (Schein 1985); (2) the method itself has biasing features—different respondents can have somewhat different understandings of the words employed (despite back translations)[6], cultural tendencies can lead to respondents' either minimizing or exaggerating feelings and positions on numerical scales, and researchers can impose their conceptions on respondents by the questions which are asked and the ways those questions are worded. In addition, data on the levels of agreement across individuals in the same country were not reported for this study; it is conceivable that people in countries with prominent subcultural differences (Belgium or Canada, for example) would exhibit more than one pattern in their values. Thus, it is not clear whether the mean values reported are really accurate representations of collectively shared cultural values for whole countries. Nor is it clear that all important cultural values have been measured; it is certainly conceivable that some national cultures may have values that this research did not consider.

Results from a later study, using both qualitative and quantitative methods, indicated that the values measured in the earlier study are probably *not* the core elements that distinguish one organizational culture from another (Hofstede et al. 1990).[7] In data collected from 20 units of 10 different organizations in Denmark and the Netherlands, values of employees differed more by nationality, age, and education than by organization. What distinguished organizational cultures from each other were "shared preceptions of daily practices" (Hofstede et al. 1990, p. 311). Practices could function as cultural forms by transmitting leaders' values to their organizations' members. Such a process, however, does not explain how and why people who report different practices in different organizations have similar values. The researchers turned to socialization for an explanation. They argued that socialization in basic values occurs early in life and that people's values are therefore rooted in their childhood circumstances (which presumably vary by nationality). Organizational socialization comes later—largely through learning specific organizational practices. If they are right, differing pat-

---

[6]Back translation is a device used to try to ensure that the same meanings are conveyed by questionnaires written in more than one language. It works as follows: A person fluent in two languages translates questions written in language *A* to language *B*. A different person then takes the version in language *B* and translates it back to language *A*. If the meaning is essentially the same as the original version in language *A*, the translation to language *B* is considered accurate and acceptable. If the meaning has changed, more effort is expended to make the translation match the original.

[7]Of course, the etic nature of questionnaires may work against finding such differences, which may require measures more sensitive to context and subtle differences in meaning to detect.

terns of similarities in values would correspond to different sets of childhood experiences and differing sets of patterns of similarities in cultural practices would correspond to different organizational experiences. Other results of this study, however, suggest that socialization into occupational cultures involves the acquisition of both values and practices—in the terminology of this book, of both cultural substance and forms. Thus, this analysis raises as many questions as it answers.

The end product of this large research effort is a qualitative description of 20 cases of organizational culture, a six-dimensional model of organizational culture, and another set of survey items and technologies that can be used to do quantitative comparative research on organizational cultures. The results from this later study are not yet fully integrated with those from the 40-country survey done earlier, and it will be interesting to see how well each kind of data can inform the other. It will also be interesting to see what studies using these methods in other countries and organizations yield. If the qualitative and quantitative data generated can be meaningfully integrated, this new multi-method approach yields considerable promise for future cross-national comparative research of organizational cultures.

The studies summarized are meant only to be illustrative of various types of cross-national research. Large amounts of research have been done, especially comparing attitudes. Most of these studies are subject to some of the same criticisms already discussed. Also, many of these studies do not attempt to measure culture, but assume a distinct culture accompanies the identity of each nation. The other alternative—to collect data grounded in the historical and institutional context of nations as part of measuring their cultures—makes multicultural comparisons very time consuming and difficult. Individual researchers cannot manage to compare more than a few countries; results from different researchers tend to focus on different issues and thus do not cumulate.

It seems fair to summarize the findings on cross-national comparisons by concluding that there are cross-cultural differences among nations that undoubtedly affect organizations in some ways, but that the full range of these differences has not yet been well documented. Neither mangers nor researchers can assume that practices from one country will be automatically acceptable in another; at the same time, there are powerful forces within organizations emanating from the logic of organizing and the technologies employed to produce goods and services that undoubtedly pattern behaviors and perhaps some values and beliefs in similar ways across nations and geographical regions. In effect, organizations are culture free in some respects, but culture bound in many others.

This duality is well-illustrated by the patterns of similarities and differences between U.S. and Japanese organizations. Both countries are certainly well developed and modern, but their unique cultures and histories are reflected in persistent differences in some aspects of their organizations. Because of the great interest in this particular comparison, data on Japanese and U.S. organizations are relatively abundant. It may be instructive to review the major findings from the most reputable of these studies to help readers determine which popular notions contrasting these two countries are upheld by scientific data.

Comparing U.S. and Japanese Organizations

Historical Basis of Ideologies

Differences between U.S. and Japanese organizational cultures have their roots in the differing histories and geographical situations of the two countries. The Japanese culture developed in relative isolation on an island; for an extended period lasting until the end of the 19th century, its borders were effectively closed to foreigners and their influence. One result is a society with homogenous and persistent beliefs and values. By contrast, the dominant U.S. culture developed from a variety of beliefs and values brought by successive waves of immigrants who left their ancestral homes with dreams of greater liberty or fortune, conquered the Native American peoples, and progressively pushed back the western frontier across a vast continent to the Pacific ocean. The result is a pluralistic society with considerable diversity in its traditions, beliefs, and values. Another important historical factor is the different religious traditions of the two countries. To oversimplify somewhat, the Japanese culture has its roots in Confucianism, with added influences from Buddhism. As discussed at some length in Chapter 2, the U.S. culture reflects the Protestant ethic.

One of the legacies of Confucianism, shared by other Asian countries, is that familial relations are the reference point for all other social relations. In effect, relations between parents and children serve as a model for social relations in other social settings. One reflection of this legacy is that Japanese people use social controls very differently than do Americans. An analysis of U.S. and Japanese child-rearing practices, religion, philosophy, and psychotherapy uncovered two basic ideologies regarding social control. The Japanese emphasize secondary control, in which people believe they can ensure rewards and avoid sanctions by accommodating themselves to existing realities, including other persons, and by attempting to devise a "goodness of fit with things as they are" (Weisz, Rothbaum, and Blackburn 1984, p. 955). Such control is consonant with relations within a family. Americans emphasize primary control, in which people believe they will enhance their rewards by influencing and changing what goes on around them. Such controls are consonant with conquering natives and a natural environment seen as impediments to individual aspirations. In effect, U.S. culture shapes its members to want to dominate and control both their environment and other persons; the Japanese culture, on the other hand, shapes its members to be more willing to surrender some personal control so that they can better harmonize with their environment and with other persons. "In U.S. culture the self is all important, and enhancing power for self is the preoccupation; in Japanese culture, harmony is all important and the power of the collectivity and maintaining social order are the preoccupations" (Beyer and Trice 1988, p. 143).

The two countries are similar to each other, and unlike some other countries (for instance, those in Latin America), in giving high status to business, commerce, and work in general. In both the United States and Japan, businesspersons come from a wide range of social origins and backgrounds. Thus, the

American occupation of Japan immediately following World War II acted to reinforce some traditional Japanese values (Halberstam 1986). General Douglas McArthur, Supreme Commander for the Allied Powers, appreciated the Japanese people's desire to work and the dignity they accorded work. He played a prominent role in the postwar rejuvenation of Japanese industry, including the revival of traditional and paternalistic systems of controlling workers.

That historical events both shape and are shaped by culture is illustrated by the effects of the American William Deming and his ideas on quality control on Japanese industry during this period. Deming was persuaded to come to Japan to lecture to Japanese managers on statistical quality control. What was unique about Deming's ideas was his emphasis on the "application of statistical principles and technique in *all stages of production . . .*" (Cole 1979, p. 135 [emphasis added]). This emphasis fit the collectivity-centered ideologies of Japanese management and workers and was translated into their practice of quality circles. In this and other ways, "quality control shifted from being the prerogative of . . . engineers with limited shop experience [as it is in the United States] to being the responsibility of each employee" (Cole 1979, p. 136). The advice of a U.S. expert was given a most profound and consequential thrust by elements in another culture.

Also conseqential has been the differing values that the two cultures place on formal education. The Japanese culture is far more insistent that students make every effort to excel in school. Japanese schools have heavy workloads and long workdays. High school students have especially high levels of mathematical achievement (Cole 1979, p. 184). Behind every high-scoring student, stands "a mother—supportive, aggressive, and completely involved in her child's education" (Simmons 1987, p. 46). Although achievement oriented, the Japanese system avoids direct, interpersonal competition between individual students by using a relatively impersonal, national examination as the basis for ranking students and determining their access to higher education. Once in college or university, however, Japanese undergraduate students do not work nearly as hard as their American counterparts. Their futures are more or less assured once they are admitted to this elite circle. In the United States, by contrast, the competition between individuals for elite status reaches a crescendo in college, as students compete to earn high grades that help to ensure their entry into graduate school or into a desirable job. The educational programs of U.S. universities, especially in their graduate and professional schools, are universally respected and emulated.

Table 8-4 summarizes some of the values we discern in accounts of Japanese history and current practices.

Work-Related Practices

Paternalism.   The familial basis of Japanese work relations was forged in the commercial houses of Japan during the feudal period. Employment in these combinations of homes and workplaces was divided into two categories: (1) apprentices who came from blood kin or friendly families; and (2) servants, who were not considered members of the house and did not enjoy the privileges accorded

TABLE 8–4
CENTRAL VALUES OF JAPANESE CULTURE

High value of work
High value of education
High status for businesspersons
Importance of collectivity
Emphasis on cooperation and harmony
Emphasis on family
Deemphasis on individual
Accommodation to existing realities
Patience
Respect for authority
Long time frame for success

that status. Only apprentices could progress up a clearly defined ladder, and their progress was very slow, foreshadowing such current Japanese management practices as lifetime employment (Cole 1979) and very tall hierarchies (Lincoln, Hanada, and McBride 1986). The two tiers of membership in Japanese commercial houses also foreshadowed dualities in current practice, in which only the employees of certain firms have the benefits of lifetime employment while employees of other firms do not. Also, such benefits have traditionally been conferred only on male workers; Japanese women are considered temporary workers because they are expected to marry and then stay home to raise their children.

Japanese organizations have also traditionally offered many more welfare services and organized activities to their employees than American firms do (Lincoln and McBride 1987, p. 299). Japanese workers expect and like these paternalistic practices (Lincoln, Hanada, and Olson 1981; Whitehill and Takezawa 1968). Rites of passage for new hires often express the parentlike responsibility that Japanese firms take for their employees (Rohlen 1974). In response, Japanese workers often behave toward their supervisors as they would toward a parent. For example, it would not be unusual for a young male Japanese worker to ask his superior for advice about his choice of a wife. He would certainly notify his superior and invite him to the wedding.[8] Observers have repeatedly documented the strong bonds, on and off the job, between Japanese employees and their supervisors (Cole 1971, Dore 1973, Rohlen 1974).

Although paternalistic practices were somewhat prevalent in U.S. industry early in the 20th century (Trice and Beyer 1984b) and some firms had traditions of virtual lifetime employment before the recessions of the 1970s, relatively few U.S. firms have anything like the benefits or felt responsibility for employees that are common in Japan. One reason is that American labor unions saw such programs as undercutting their influence and vigorously fought to control them as part of the union contract.

However, paternalism seems to have positive effects in both countries. A survey of over eight thousand employees in over one hundred plants in the

---

[8]It is highly unlikely his superior would be a woman.

United States and Japan found that employees in both countries who reported higher levels of paternalistic activities by employers also had higher commitment to their organizations than did employees with less paternalistic employers. Job satisfaction and commitment were highly positively related in both countries. Although there has been speculation that individualistic U.S. workers would respond negatively to paternalism by their employers, this survey showed that the positive effects of paternalistic services are nearly identical in the two countries (Lincoln and Kalleberg 1985).

Collective emphasis. The historical roots of Japanese work organizations in feudal commercial houses also led the Japanese to view their organizations as based on collective units, rather than on a system of individual positions. Japanese organizational charts often indicate only one or two of the highest individual positions; the rest of the chart is composed of divisions, departments, and sections, without reference to the individual positions usually found in U.S. organizational charts. Job descriptions often do not exist; responsibility is collective, rather than individual (Whyte 1969, p. 747). " . . . the critical distinction between Japanese and Western social organization turns on the attachments of Westerners to positions or roles within collectivities and the Japanese identification with the group itself" (Lincoln and Kalleberg 1985, p. 34).

The U.S. emphasis on primary control tends to produce people who see their successes as self-made. Such views tend to encourage individual creativity and innovation, but also may produce destructive competition and lack of cooperation. They have been linked to quality problems in manufactured products and low morale (Ouchi 1981). The ideology of primary control also encourages valuing individual careers over loyalty to employers. For example, in the United States, employees may leave their first jobs for no apparent reason a year or two after being hired with no great penalty to their later careers. Japanese employees who did the same thing would be considered "self-centered and disloyal" and would not be considered good prospects by another employer (Weisz, Rothbaum, and Blackburn 1984, p. 966). Although some observers feel this is changing, the felt obligation of Japanese employers has traditionally been reciprocated by great loyalty and fealty from their employees.

Employee participation. Perhaps the clearest expression of the Japanese values toward collectivity and cooperation is the so-called *ringi* system—the way decisions are made in many Japanese organizations. It is a bottom-up system, with heavy emphasis on consensus. Formally, proposals and recommendations originate in the lower and middle echelons of managers, who circulate them for reactions among other managers whose cooperation would be necessary to implement the proposal. Only when agreement is reached at the lower levels is a proposal forwarded to superiors. Managers in each successive level of the tall managerial hierarchy then consider the proposal and either concur or make further suggestions. When they find the proposal acceptable, they sign off on it (Hatvany and Pucik 1981). Eventually proposals make their way to the top of the hierarchy. "By requiring that all decisions go to the top, the chief executive bears symbolic responsibility for every decision, and the organization averts a formal delegation of authority to lower management positions" (Lincoln and McBride 1987, p. 300). The bottom-up initiation possible in the *ringi* system thus generates much networking activity among lower and middle level managers, who must find ways to reach consensus and elicit cooperation from one another to realize their ideas. However, as a practical matter, top managers sometimes have ideas of their own. They can conceivably manipulate the system by planting their ideas with loyal subordinates (Clark 1979).

While it has other benefits, the *ringi* system is a very slow way to make decisions. One of the reasons the Japanese gave for being slow to cooperate with the fast-moving Gulf War in 1991 was that they had not had enough time to reach consensus on the issues involved.

Not only are lower levels of managers allowed more participation in decision making in Japanese companies than is typical in the United States, but ordinary employees are also encouraged to make suggestions through quality control circles. Through meetings of the circles and through many incremental adjustments in their own work behaviors and routines, Japanese workers take responsibility for the quality of the products they produce. In assembly-line operations, individual employees are allowed to stop the line to correct defects. To aid them in detecting problems and making improvements, management trains rank-and-file employees in statistical quality control techniques (Cole 1979).

Work-related attitudes. In general, status distinctions between top managers and regular employees are more muted in Japanese companies than in U.S. companies. Japanese companies do not provide separate dining rooms, parking lots, or pay schedules for executives (Dore 1973). Furthermore, the pay differentials between rank-and-file employees and top executives is much less in Japan than in the United States (Lincoln and Kalleberg 1985).[9] Pay differentials have grown steadily in the United States since 1979, contributing to what *Fortune* magazine has called the "trust gap" (Farnham 1989).

Thus it is perhaps not surprising that relations between management and workers, and worker attitudes toward their organizations, have tended to be more positive in Japan than in the United States. Two surveys of thousands of Japanese and U.S. production workers in 1960 and 1976 showed that (1) Japanese workers put their companies in a much more central position in their lives than did American workers; (2) Japanese workers had greater trust and acceptance of management decisions about practical applications of policies than did American workers; and (3) Japanese workers embraced norms of performing at high levels of work effort and in a cooperative fashion significantly more than did American workers (Takezawa and Whitehill 1981). Although these sentiments did

---

[9]In 1989, the 20 most highly-paid CEOs in the United States earned between $4.8 million and $53.9 million in salaries, bonuses, and long-term compensation (Byrne 1990, p. 57). In Japan, by contrast, the highest-paid employees rarely earn more than 4 or 5 times what the lowest-paid workers earn (*The Economist* 1989, p. 77). Obviously, the ratios in the United States are much greater. A U.S. executive earning $5 milion earns 250 times more than a secretary or janitor earning $20,000. Lowlier executives who earn only $500,000 are still earning 25 times what secretaries and janitors earn.

not change markedly in the period between these two surveys, some observers feel that this pattern may now be changing, as more Japanese workers switch employers. In 1982, only one in four Japanese jobs were filled by someone who had worked for another firm. During 1987 and 1988, half of all vacancies were filled by persons switching employers (*The Economist* 1989, p. 74).

Various cultural strands probably combine to produce the high commitment for which Japanese workers are noted. One manifestation of this commitment is that Japanese workers have traditionally been reluctant to take all of their allotted vacation time (Levine 1981). Other concrete signs of commitment are reports of the willingness of Japanese workers to clean and straighten the work area after their work shift. One story recounts how a Japanese worker in a Toyota plant who failed to correct a defect as the car went up the line later stayed after work, without pay, to fix it (Sengoku 1985).

However, commitment is not equally high in all Japanese organizations. The large companies in core industries, where benefits are better and paternalistic policies are stronger, have more committed employees than do firms outside those core industries. In particular, small companies using batch production methods have lower levels of commitment. Specific practices associated with high levels of commitment among Japanese workers include decentralization, quality control membership, and the practice of *ringi*, (Lincoln and McBride 1987).

A very consistent and important difference between Japanese and U.S. workers is that Japanese workers identify with their organizations while American workers tend to identify more strongly with their occupations. Various practices express and reinforce these differences. Primary among these is the use of *nenko* (seniority) to determine wages in Japan, while many U.S. firms rely on occupational distinctions and merit pay. Historically, the Japanese practice probably originated with the need to train unskilled rural migrant workers who made up the bulk of the labor supply. Since older, more experienced workers were used to train these raw recruits, seniority was rewarded. It is also consistent with the family-centeredness of Japanese culture and the welfare orientation of Japanese employers that employees should be rewarded commensurately as their dependents and other needs increase through their life cycles (Kalleberg and Lincoln 1985). Other practices that reinforce organizational identification in Japan include lifetime employment, hiring of whole cohorts of employees rather than individuals for specific positions, generalized managerial training within the firm, and deemphasis on specialization among managers by rotation through various functions (Lincoln and McBride 1987).

Practices in the United States that reinforce occupational identification include tendencies to change employers, individualized hiring, highly specialized training, and marked divisions of labor and specialization within firms. While exceptions to these practices exist, they are sufficiently common in the United States to lead most employees to see themselves as accountants, nurses, teachers, salespersons or bus drivers rather than as employees of certain organizations. It would be a mistake, however, to assume on the basis of the recent relative success of Japanese and U.S. organizations that occupational identification *per se* is in some way less desirable or leads to inefficiencies. As discussed earlier, German workers also identify primarily with their occupations and German industry is currently very successful.

Labor unions. In addition, the unions of Japanese workers tend to be organized by company rather than by occupation or industry, as are unions in the United States. Most Japanese union functions, particularly the economic ones of bargaining, striking, and grievance handling, are performed within a company-based union. Each union is self-supporting and includes first- and second-level supervisors, and members of the personnel department, as well as blue-collar and white-collar workers. As a result of this structure, Japanese workers see their unions as *inside* their organizations and unions work closely with management, even in high-level strategic planning; most have developed an ideology of mutual cooperation with management, prefer to avoid prolonged conflict, and identify with the interests of the firm (Cole 1985).

Clearly, this structuring of union-management relations opens the door for cooptation by management as well as for productive consultation with union members. Some U.S. firms and industries are moving toward this model, but the traditions of U.S. labor relations have historically been much more adversarial, with U.S. management very reluctant to relinquish any of its control to labor, and U.S. labor very resistant to arrangements conducive to cooptation. Thus, historically there has been very little consultation between unions and management in the United States over strategic issues, and consequently, little appreciation by rank-and-file union members in the United States of the strategic issues that firms face until these issues reach crisis proportions. Whether the recent decline of many U.S. industries is a sufficient crisis to produce substantially greater union-management cooperation in the United States remains to be seen (Kanter 1989). Data collected in the early 1980s indicated that a sample of American union members had significantly less satisfaction with and commitment to their companies than did members of Japanese unions (Lincoln and Kalleberg 1985). Other research in the United States, however, suggests that the union-management climate in a company may affect the commitment of union members to both company and union, with more cooperative climates producing higher commitment to both (Angle and Perry 1986).

Historical differences in the genesis and growth of labor unions in the two countries helped to produce the structural and ideological differences they now exhibit. Because Japan had a labor surplus as it industrialized, the union base in that country was relatively weak. During the pre–World War II period, unions were actually suppressed. Lacking the medieval guild system prevalent in Europe or a generally strong occupational structure, Japan never developed craft unions. Thus, Japanese unions and workers are much more accepting than American ones of managers deciding unilaterally on changes in technology and work content, on assignments to specific jobs, on restructuring of job boundaries, and, generally, of managerial control over work procedures.

A story about a visit by Douglas Fraser, former president of the U.S. United Automobile Workers, to an auto plant in Tokyo illustrates the differences in management-worker relations in the two countries. Fraser was walking through the plant with a few Japanese managers and union officers just as the whistle blew for lunch. What happened next was recounted as follows: "In America, their little group would have been stampeded as the workers scrambled to get away from the workplace and go eat. But here the manager simply raised his hand as if to say stop, and everyone around them stopped" (Halberstam 1986, p. 489).

This story also illustrates the greater deference for authority that is prevalent in Japanese society. One reason that Japanese managers can encourage participation is that Japanese workers are unlikely to demand too much and will be eager to find suggestions with which those in authority will agree. By contrast, U.S. managers may fear that once they give U.S. workers some discretion over decision making, workers will press for even more control and disagree with management over how things are done. These contrasting tendencies arise from impulses rooted in the ideologies of secondary and primary control.[10]

The ways in which unions in the two countries use strikes is a further expression of differing views of control. Japanese unions use strikes symbolically—largely for purposes of publicizing their grievances and thus publicly harassing management. Frequently, strikes occur in conjunction with an annual "spring offensive" that is largely directed toward wage demands. The bigger and more powerful unions synchronize their demands, often selecting one of their number to be most vehement by engaging in a series of one-day strikes to dramatize their collective demands. Because they see themselves as a political force *inside* the company pressing for citizen welfare, Japenese unions rarely prolong strikes beyond one or two days (Dore 1973). However, while not as adversarial as unions in the United States, Japanese unions are militant in their own way; they have succeeded in raising wage levels and engage in more strikes than do unions in West Germany or France (Shirai 1983).

Unions in the United States are more prone to see themselves as adversaries who are *outside* the company and are thus more prone to take confrontational stands vis à vis management. The very phrase *company union* is a derogatory label to United States union members. Unions in the United States have a long-term frame of reference and engage in strikes to achieve a variety of specific demands. Strikes can thus occur at any time of the year in response to any aspect of union concern. Some of these strikes end up being very bitter and prolonged. In general, U.S. unions see themselves as guardians of a wider range of employee rights and benefits than do Japanese unions and believe they must fight management in order to advance their members' interests.

---

[10]An analysis of the way quality circles have been used in the two countries is instructive in this regard (Shea 1986). In Japan, quality circles focus on technical issues related to quality and members receive training in statistics and other technical matters needed to access and monitor quality. In the United States, the focus of quality circles has been broader and much less technical; worker discontents and issues of participation may be raised. Also, U. S. workers are rarely, if ever, given technical training comparable to that received by members of Japanese quality control circles. While the relative lack of mathematical skills of U.S. workers may play a role in these differences, the ideologies of managers, workers, and consultants hired to implement quality control circles in the United States probably made these differences almost inevitable.

Cultural forms.   Finally, Japanese organizations are more likely than most U.S. firms to employ ceremonial activities to strengthen their company cultures. Some of the practices already discussed, such as *ringi* decision making, have expressive and symbolic value, as well as practical consequences. *Ringi* not only symbolizes the ideology of collective effort, but its relatively slow and inclusive process helps to insure the implementation of decisions once they are made. Also notable are the extensive rites of passage that many Japanese companies conduct for new recruits. Such ceremonies can take weeks and symbolize to the recruits and their families that the company greatly values them as new members. Another pervasive ceremonial activity in Japanese corporations is the meeting. Japanese executives and managers meet frequently and for long periods to arrive at the consensus which they expect to accompany all decisions. Such meetings also symbolize the importance given to personal contacts within Japanese companies and society in general (Naylor 1984, p. 36).

Although many U.S. firms have some similar practices, and they have become much more common since the advent of concern about organizational cultures, few U.S. work organizations are as paternalistic as those in Japan. Even fewer manage to achieve the levels of collaboration, cooperation, and harmony that are taken for granted in Japanese organizations. Nor is it clear that U.S. organizations would be successful if they did try to become more like Japanese organizations. While U.S. management and workers can certainly learn some things from the Japanese, specific practices must be seen as cultural forms that may be hard to transplant into a very different national culture.

Japanese employers in the United States.   When Japanese firms began operation in the United States, they were greeted with high expectations. Many of their manufacturing plants were deliberately located in rural areas, where U.S. labor unions were not established and where the local populace, from which they intended to draw their workforces, could be expected to have values more consonant with Japanese values than people living in urban areas. Many U.S. workers and managers were eager to work for the Japanese, not only for lack of other alternatives, but because they believed they would learn superior ways of working and relating to one another. They liked what they had heard about the way Japanese firms treated their employees, and expected to be treated the same way. In some instances, these expectations led to cruel disappointments.

A study of 32 Japanese-owned firms in the United States found that most Americans joined Japanese firms for the apparent professional opportunies (Pucik, Hanada, and Fifield 1989). Instead, the Americans found themselves excluded from decision making, offered little training, and began to doubt their long-term career prospects. The Japanese apparently are not managing their American workers "with the same focus, long-term perspective, and determination they apply at home" (Zellner 1989, p. 42). One former manager at a Honda plant complained he couldn't even order toilet paper without permission from Japanese supervisors. After a Mazda plant in Flat Rock, Michigan, twice lost its top American production and personnel managers, the positions were filled by Japanese.

These discrepancies between expectations and subsequent experiences can be explained in various ways. Clearly many of the aggrieved employees felt that Japanese employers' ethnocentrism leads them to discriminate against non-Japanese employees. Japanese employees, in turn, may have expected more stable economic conditions than they found in the United States, where the government takes a less active role in leveling trends in employment than it does in Japan. Another possible explanation is a lack of cultural understanding. In particular, the U.S. managers may not have realized in advance that the basis of authority and influence in Japanese organizations rests on long-standing associations and embeddedness within social networks. Thus, for U.S. managers the real power within a Japanese firm is essentially out of reach—it lies in interpersonal networks among the Japanese managers that have been built up from the time they joined the firm, fresh out of college (Solman 1991).

Nonmanagerial employees have also been cruelly disappointed by Japanese employers. When the Japanese firm Kyocera acquired another firm in San Diego named Emcon, according to employees, they were promised lifetime employment as long as they did their jobs and did them well. One former employee reported, "Out in the meetings in the parking lot every day they told us you will always have a job here . . . somewhere in the Kyocera family." Eighteen months later, 350 of them were laid off with 10 minutes' notice. A group of the employees subsequently filed suit against Kyocera alleging fraud and breach of contract. The case appears to be headed for the Supreme Court. The attorney in the case, Robert Rothman, commented:

> I think it is a situation that would not have arisen in an American company because I don't think that an American company would have represented to its workers that they had lifetime employment and that they were something other than employees, that is, that they were members of a family, that they were uniting with bonds of love, trust, faith, and honor. (Solman 1991, p. 11).

The suing employees reported they worked like workaholics for the company and felt they were a family until they were fired. Nine years later they still felt angry and betrayed. A two-year study of a Mazda plant in the United States uncovered similar sentiments among U.S. workers and managers there (Fucini and Fucini 1990).

These relatively negative reactions to working for Japanese firms come largely from those who have left their employment. To balance the account somewhat we must look to the results of a study of managers still working for 32 Japanese-controlled firms in the U.S. (Pucik, Hanada, and Fifield 1989). Interviews with more than 50 senior executives plus questionnaire responses from 132 other managers working at these firms revealed a more complex pattern of relations between U.S. managers and their Japanese bosses than are evident from press accounts, which seem to be dominated by the reports of disgruntled former employees. For example, while it is true that some Japanese CEOs did not practice consultative decision making while in the United States, the successful integration of U.S. managers into decision making often depended on the quality of the interactions and the trust they had managed to build between themselves and their Japanese superiors. One of the factors militating against the building of such trust was turnover among the Japanese. U.S. managers who had to confront frequent changes in their Japanese superiors faced additional difficulties in meshing their personalities with their boss's, and in assessing "where the new boss stands" (Pucik, Hanada, and Fifield 1989, p. 49).

Structural Similarities and Differences

Because most cross-cultural research tends to focus on differences between different national cultures, in effect, it focuses on those aspects of culture that are responsive to the divergent forces in a society. The convergent forces, how-ever, should not be overlooked, especially when considering cultures of work organizations. Much managerial and technological know-how used in work orga-nizations has been exported from Western nations to others throughout the world. Indeed, as explained in the beginning of the chapter, the technology of organizing people and other resources to accomplish complex tasks is one of the important building blocks of modern society. Thus, the formal structures of organizations tend to have some commonalities throughout the modern socie-ties of the world.[11]

Since Japan is the most technologically and economically advanced of the non-Western nations, it provides a good test case of theories arguing that pat-terns of organizing are culture free or culture bound. If differences in how firms are organized are found between such an advanced country and other advanced countries, the differences cannot be attributed to less developed technologies or to smaller economic resources. Such differences would support the thesis of culture-bound patterns. Finding that the organizations in two similarly advanced countries are very similar would tend to support the thesis of culture-free pat-terns.

Research comparing the structural aspects of 55 U.S. and 51 Japanese man-ufacturing plants that were similar in size, age, unionization, and basic technolo-gies supports both theories. In some aspects—for example, the effects of size, technology, and other task contingencies—the U.S. and Japanese organizations did not differ. In others they did. Japanese organizations had taller hierarchies, less functional specialization, and less formal delegation of authority but more de facto participation in decisions at lower levels in the management hierarchy. These structures are consistent with the internal labor market processes (lifetime employment, seniority-based promotion) that characterize Japanese companies and the "general emphasis on groups over individuals as the fundamental units of organization" (Lincoln, Hanada, and McBride 1986, p. 361). Also, in Japan, technology had weaker effects on such structural features as departmentalization and decentralization of decision making.

The researchers suggest that as manufacturing technology becomes more

---

[11]Some organizations in developing societies will also exhibit some of these commonalities, but probably not all.

automated and otherwise advanced, workers are separated from direct production tasks. The technology becomes, in effect, more self-contained, and the organization of the factory around it becomes more detached from technological processes and imperatives. Social imperatives can then replace technological ones, and cultural differences will tend to be reflected in structure.

These findings echo the conclusions summarized earlier of other researchers about cross-national similarities and differences. Organizations using similar technologies are most alike in their technical cores and in the structured activities needed to run and manage them. It appears as if technology does to some degree preprogram how it is managed. In other sectors of the organization, or with technology that is less constraining of behavior, cultural differences are likely to influence organizational practices because either people or the environment are the primary sources of uncertainty that must be managed.

Differences in Corporate Strategies

Many observers have remarked upon the relatively short time frame of most U.S. managers. Because of rapid promotions and expectations to be responsive to investors' short-term interests, U.S. managers are often accused of being short-sighted. Japanese managers face different institutional environments that allow them to plan for the long term. The financial markets in the United States almost force U.S. managers to be concerned with immediate profits. If bottom-line performance sags, stock prices will fall and their organizations will become targets for hostile takeovers. Future credit will be jeopardized. They will also personally experience financial losses because of their own stock ownership. They could conceivably be fired. In Japan, many industrial enterprises are better assured of the financial resources they require because they are embedded in supraorganizations, called *zaibatsu*, that include financial institutions.[12] Japanese managers can count on cooperation from their *zaibatsu* partners and thus can often afford to invest for the long term.

The recent histories of the U.S. and Japanese consumer electronics industries dramatically illustrate how differences in time frames can have large-scale consequences. Managers in the United States adopted the usual U.S. business strategy of attending to profits. Thus when Japanese firms entered segments of U.S. markets with specific products at cheaper prices, U.S. electronic firms tended to leave those markets as unprofitable. The Japanese were pursuing a different, more long-term strategy: winning market share. Japanese firms thus took on one product group after another, flooding U.S. markets with products cheaper than U.S. firms could produce. Instead of making investments in new equipment or discovering technological breakthroughs that would allow them to compete at the lower prices, U.S. firms kept retreating until they lost most of the electronic consumer products industry to the Japanese (Chandler 1990, 1991).

Government-industry relations are another important factor underlying

---

[12]Such supraorganizations are forbidden by U.S. antitrust laws, although recent legislation has opened the way for industrywide consortia in some industries.

differences in corporate strategies in the two countries. The Japanese govern-ment has historically played a much more active role in supporting business than has the U.S. government, which is constrained by predominant business ideolo-gies favoring the operation of free markets and opposing any form of govern-ment interference. Japanese government ministries gently pressure industry to cooperate and plan collectively in various ways; for example, they encourage the formation of trade associations and various consortia (Lincoln 1990). Several large industrial-financial combines (*zaibatsu*) that dominiate the Japanese econ-omy maintain close ties with the government. In general, "these patterns of coor-dination among business enterprises and between them and government agen-cies are among the most distinctive features of the Japanese economy today" (Lincoln 1990, p. 266).

Trade officials and businesspersons in the United States deplore another type of cooperative grouping called *keiretsu*, in which Japanese companies linked by financial ties trade among themselves rather than buy from other companies. Such practices, they feel, make it difficult for U.S. firms to compete in Japan. In the United States, such practices would probably violate antitrust laws. To the Japanese, such patterns of mutual shareholding are simply ways to create more stable capitalism and so focus on long-term planning. In response, the U.S. gov-ernment is allowing mergers and strategic alliances among U.S. firms that would have set off alarms in years past. These consolidations are drastically changing the U.S. corporate landscape.[13]

Clearly, cooperative relations among U.S. organizations are becoming more common. They often have a distinctly American twist. The U.S. Air Force re-cently decided to work more closely with its contractors in developing a new supersonic fighter plane. Two different prototypes were developed—each by a different consortium of private firms. The Northrup and McDonnell Douglas corporations joined to produce one prototype; the other was developed by the Lockheed, General Dynamics, and Boeing corporations. The latter won the con-tract (*Austin American-Statesman* 1991). Although the Air Force's close working re-lationship with the contractors apparently helped to produce an aircraft that pleased the military, the expensive competition that was engendered between the two sets of firms may have weakened them financially and precluded invest-ments in other possible innovations.

Both Japan and the United States are very competitive, but cultural differ-ences shape the ways in which competition is practiced. Firms in the United States compete with one another. This internal struggle for dominance is part of the U.S. culture, with its faith in free markets and the capitalist system. It is em-bodied in U.S. laws and regulations, and in managers' ways of thinking. This competitive ethos make cooperation across sectors or organizational boundaries very difficult. Until recently, only great national crises, such as world wars, have suppressed these competitive tendencies. Current competitive pressures from Japan and other countries have given rise to experimentation with consortia and

---

[13]One business magazine recently suggested that U.S. firms are seeking to establish their own versions of the *keiretsu* (Kelly and Port 1992).

joint ventures. But these forms of interorganizational cooperation are still too new in the United States for observers to be able to decide whether they mark a real departure from past practice and whether they can be successful in achieving the aims of their members.

Japan has a culture that promotes cooperation and harmony in internal relations. The Japanese people work together to achieve organizational or other collective goals. The Japanese are also good at competition, but their competition is aimed at realizing collective goals; they see competition as something that is practiced against outsiders, not insiders. Such competition does not destroy internal harmony because everyone in the collectivity can be seen as benefiting from competition aimed at outsiders.

These observations have emphasized the role that cultural factors play in the operation of industries in the two countries. Implicit in them is the question of whether cultural differences may also help to explain the relative recent success of the Japanese and the relative decline of the United States in economic terms. Other differences could be important, and analysts vary in how much weight they assign to culture versus other factors that could account for the success of Japanese industry. But as David Halberstam puts its, " ... the story of Japan's ascent and America's subtle industrial decline seemed ... a drama of the highest order and consequence ... something profound that has taken place so quietly, in much small increments, that it is barely visible to the naked eye ... " (1986, p. 729). Given the stakes in that drama, U.S. managers cannot afford to ignore possible cultural explanations. The challenge for U.S. management is not to try to imitate Japanese practices, but to find ways to capitalize on the strengths inherent in American culture and values.

SUMMARY

Because organizations have boundaries that are fuzzy, fluid, and porous, they are subject to many cultural influences from their environments. Organizations adapt to these influences, buffer themselves from them in various ways, or act to lessen their impacts by taking action that will change their environments.

Because they are open systems that must import resources to survive, organizations are dependent on environments; this dependence poses many uncertainties for organizations. Their environments are changeful, complex, and often not dependable. Complex sets of interdependencies arise among many organizations. As they engage in similar or linked actions, their environments become turbulent, increasing the uncertainty for all.

Modern societies and organizations developed together. The presence of certain resources and cultural elements made the emergence of organizations possible. The development of organizations has fueled the processes of modernization and industrialization throughout the world. Members' perceptions of environments have been important in the founding of organizations and in their adaptation and survival.

Some of the inputs that organizations need from their environment are especially likely to influence their cultures. These include human resources, information, technology, and legitimacy. Environments can be thought of as having two sectors, instrumental and institutional; organizations respond to expectations from both, but the relative strength of pressures from the two sectors varies for different types of organizations. Environments have been described along many other dimensions that are useful in determining the amount of uncertainty organizations face. If the perceptions of organized decision makers' of these dimensions of their environments do not match reality, they are likely to make maladaptive decisions.

Organizations adapt to expectations in the institutional sectors of their environments by categorical, structural, procedural, and personnel conformity. They adapt to the instrumental sectors by providing outputs they can exchange for needed inputs. Examples of organizational adaptation include the ways organizations reflect national cultures, adopt local folkways, deal with large-scale environmental shifts and environmental jolts, and respond to bizarre intrusions into their domains. Organizations also try to buffer themselves from their environments, especially when these are hostile or otherwise threatening. Too much buffering, however, can cause organizations to lose touch with their environments.

Organizations use various strategies to influence their environments. Since the late 1970s, mergers, both hostile and friendly, have been popular ways to try to position firms to influence their environments. Hostile takeovers often involve three types of adaptations between the acquiring and acquired firm: exploitation, assimilation, and accommodation. Friendly mergers may not involve the first, but do involve the other two. The end result of most mergers is a process of accommodation, but sometimes it is a long time coming.

While the culture of the nation in which an organization is located will affect its internal culture, observers disagree on how potent and pervasive these effects are. Historical development within countries appears to be especially important in generating cross-national cultural differences between organizations. Studies of such differences are numerous, but hampered by the difficulties of obtaining both representative samples and of collecting rich, qualitative contextual data. Differences between U.S. and Japanese firms and employees have been heavily studied. They show some similarities and some differences. A central difference, reflecting national culural values, is that Japanese firms emphasize collective effort and welfare while U.S. firms emphasize individual effort and benefits. One result is that firms in the two countries compete differently, with Japanese firms competing with outsiders and cooperating within their own country, while U.S. firms compete as vigorously at home as they do abroad. The U.S. faith in competition and free markets makes cooperation within and between U.S. organizations difficult, but many efforts are underway to foster such cooperation.

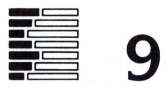

9

Managing and Maintaining Organizational Cultures

The president and vice-president of a new, small computer company in Silicon Valley, here called Falcon Computers, met regularly in what they called value meetings to develop a culture for the company. They excluded everyone else from their deliberations. In a few months they produced a document to express the culture of the company. They distributed the document to middle managers who then met with its originators to discuss and refine it. The document spelled out such things as the proper attitude that should prevail toward customers and colleagues, and how decision making and communication should take place.

Even as the culture statement was being drafted and distributed, however, members detected disparities with actual beliefs and practices. The document advanced the motto, "Attention to details our trademark," yet employees at all levels knew full well that defective computers were being shipped to customers. It said, "We encourage open, direct person-to-person communication as part of our daily routine," but the culture statement itself had been prepared in sessions closed to all but the top two managers and then promulgated rather formally through a chain of command. A trained anthropologist on the staff observed that there was a culture in the firm, but that its "operative values . . . were hierarchy, secrecy, and expediency regardless of what the official document said." (P. Reynolds 1987, p. 34)

Cynical humor became widespread as the disparity between the proclaimed culture and the actual, operative culture was widely recognized. It became "even more grotesque" as the company went into severe decline. As one manager put it, "We do have a zero defect program: Don't test the program and you'll find zero defects." The upshot of "the obvious disparity between official and actual values" was a "culture of hypocrisy that led to commitments by middle managers that they themselves knew would never be met." (P. Reynolds 1987, p. 38)

Despite the ever widening disparity and the worsening financial situation, the value meetings continued. Top management insisted the company needed to have a homogeneous, uniform culture to succeed. It never happened. And only two and a half years after its founding, the company died. (Adapted from P. Reynolds 1987)

This sad story illustrates some of the mistakes that managers can make when they decide to manage their firms' cultures. In order to manage cultures

355

of work organizations successfully, managers must (1) be culturally aware—that is, they must understand and take into account what culture is and how it works; (2) know the cultures they are managing; (3) recognize and use the levers they have available to influence their organizations' cultures; (4) resolve the ethical dilemmas involved in managing cultures; and (5) be clear about whether they seek to maintain existing cultures, change existing cultures, or establish new ones. If managers understand the nature of culture, they will be better able to recognize the opportunities and constraints it poses for managerial action. They will be able to see how ideologies, cultural forms, socialization, subcultures, leadership, and environments channel the cultural and practical directions their organizations might take. They will be sensitive to the serious ethical implications that managing cultures has for members of organizations and for the wider society. They will be prepared to decide whether, in managing their organizations' cultures, they should endeavor to maintain and strengthen what is already present, change an existing culture in substantial ways, or create a new culture in a new organization or within an existing one.

We begin this chapter by addressing the first four of these issues because they apply generally to all attempts to manage cultures. We then discuss factors managers must consider relative to point five—deciding what they want to do about their organizations' cultures. The last half of this chapter deals with issues involved in maintaining existing cultures. The issues involved in the other two kinds of cultural management—changing and creating cultures—are treated in Chapter 10.

General Considerations in Managing Cultures

Understanding What Culture Is and Is Not

Managers who try to manage, change, or establish organizational cultures will surely run into unexpected difficulties and disappointments if they do not understand the nature of culture itself. The account that begins the chapter illustrates some mistaken assumptions that naive managers can easily make:

- that they can unilaterally decide what the culture of their firm should and will be,
- that a single homogeneous culture can be easily created,
- that having such a culture is largely positive and functional, and
- that culture arises from what managers say rather than what they do.

Not a simple tool. Managers make the first assumption when they think about culture as simply another managerial tool at their disposal. This assumption fails to recognize the first and most basic characteristic of culture discussed in Chapter 1—its collective origins. Because cultures emerge from some degree of consensus among people about what their worlds are like and how best to deal with the problems and uncertainties they encounter in those worlds, organizational cultures cannot be imposed from above or manufactured at will. Furthermore, the cultural understandings that members develop and come to share with one another are not like other kinds of ideas—they are emotionally charged, internalized, and important parts of each person's identity. In order to engage members' emotions, cultural understandings must arise from and reflect anxieties and uncertainties that members have experienced or that are part of the organization's history. Without such anchoring in history or present uncertainties, a new set of ideas will seem superficial and irrelevant. Thus, cultures take time to develop. Managing cultures is an ongoing process, and not a one-shot affair that can be accomplished in a short time frame.

Not a monolithic force.   The second mistaken assumption at Falcon Computers was that a single homogeneous culture would make everyone feel and behave in the same way. Managers make this mistake when they think of culture as a monolithic force. Although cultures have at their core substance and forms that are shared, members of a culture are not uniform in the degree to which they personally share in the substance and forms. Individuals vary from each other in the degree to which they subscribe to core ideologies and values and become committed to them. Also, cultures incorporate contradictions, ambiguities, paradoxes, and just plain confusion. Thus, managers need to be realistic about how much behavioral uniformity they can create with culture.

A related factor likely to be overlooked by naive managers as they strive to manage their cultures is the presence of subcultures within their organizations. Cultures arise in all social groups to deal with shared uncertainties, and as we have seen in Chapter 5, if an organization is not brand new, members have probably formed numerous subcultures. Unless an organization is very small, a single culture is highly unlikely. Rather, managers will be coping with a diversity of subcultures.

Not necessarily all positive.   Third, naive managers may also fail to recognize that the shared aspects of culture that produce uniformities have negative as well as positive implications. Managers derive this assumption from recent rhetoric about culture's positive features and come to expect that managing their cultures will be a quick and easy fix for their problems. But, as noted in Chapter 1, cultures also have a negative side. Some dysfunctions are inherent in all cultures and cannot be wished away. For example, sometimes managers want to change what people think or do, but the shared understandings based in past behaviors and the existing culture may stand in the way of people's being able or willing to change. The predictabilities and uniformities built into cultures more often act as constraints on managerial action than as levers for change.

Inherently symbolic.   Fourth, managers who mistakenly assume they can manage their cultures by what they say rather than what they do, fail to recognize the symbolic nature of culture. Their pronouncements may carry one set of cultural values while their behaviors or expectations of others carry a different set of values. Such disparities are especially dysfunctional when they involve top management because they then affect the whole organization. In such circumstances, members of the culture become confused and demoralized. They are likely to respond with either cynicism, as they did at Falcon Computers, or with an advancing of their own subcultural or even countercultural interests. Managers need to understand that employees will pay at least equal attention to what managers do as to what they say. But managers often fail to recognize that their behaviors and the programs they sponsor function as cultural forms that carry unintended messages to organizational members. For example, programs that function as rites of renewal will often disguise difficult problems and defer their solution (Trice and Beyer, 1984a, 1984b). Clearly, the values meetings in Falcon Computers functioned as rites of renewal because nothing really changed as a result of them.

Inevitably dynamic and fuzzy.   Two other characteristics of culture that naive managers may overlook if they treat culture as just another tool are its inevitable dynamism and fuzziness. As pointed out in Chapter 1, culture is not fixed; it is always being constructed and reconstructed. People continuously struggle to establish and maintain order and regularity in circumstances that produce variety, discontinuity, and complexity (Moore 1975, p. 219). The sense-making processes they use inevitably contain many discrepancies between reality and ideologies, and between individuals' and groups' understandings of one another. Nevertheless, people usually manage to achieve some consistency, harmony, and integration in the midst of inconsistencies and ambiguities. The cultures that emerge have traces of both parts of this struggle. Cultures are inherently messy, ill-formed, and often full of contradictions. In addition, the processes of cultural transmission—primarily socialization and cultural forms—are imprecise and cannot reproduce exactly the same cultural substance or forms across generations or even across shorter periods of time. Thus, some variation is also bound to occur over time in any culture. In effect, cultures continually change and are ready to change. This does not mean, however, that managers can easily or automatically achieve control of these change processes. The characteristics of culture that contribute to its internal disorder make cultures hard to manage, in the conventional sense, and make the results of attempts to manage their change rather unpredictable.

Knowing a Specific Organization's Cultures

Managers who try to manage their organizations' cultures need to be not only culturally aware in a general sense, they need to assess their own organizations' current cultures as accurately as they can. Such efforts must be as thorough and ongoing as possible. A one-shot cultural audit will not assure that subsequent attempted interventions will yield desired results. Obviously, efforts to assess culture that are based only on the ruminations of top management, as happened at Falcon Computers, cannot yield an accurate picture of the overall culture and possible subcultures in an organization. All that such ruminations can yield—at best—is a better understanding of the top management subculture. Other organizational members may or may not share the understandings of that subculture. Managers cannot assume they know the whole culture just because they know their own. "If decisions are made on incorrect assumptions about the culture, serious harm could be done to the organization" (Schein 1985, p. 137).

Although they are part of their cultures, managers often have difficulty in surfacing their tacit knowledge of them and in recognizing how various activities express cultural meanings. Also, because cultures are emotionally charged, it sometimes hurts and angers managers to examine their own cultures. They may experience "moral indignation because it [the cultural perspective] challenges their self-image as managers" (Gagliardi 1986, p. 117). Thus, they often turn to outsiders, usually consultants, to help them learn about their organizations' cultures and to advise them how to improve them in directions consonant with managerial objectives. While their use of outsiders can be helpful, too much reliance on them can dull managers' own sensitivities to what they, after all, know better than any outsider. Thus, outsiders should be used to increase managerial cultural awareness and sensitivity, not as a substitute for it. Outsiders should not be expected to discover the substance of a firm's culture unilaterally or to know enough to prescribe cultural interventions unaided. Managers need to work closely with consultants to assure that the latter are not imposing their own ideas on client organizations.

The primary reason that most managers are naive about cultures is that they have only recently attempted to think about them. But managers are, after all, "experts in their own culture" (Gregory 1983, p. 366). Given heightened awareness and some conceptual tools to help them map what they observe and experience, they should be able to become reasonably knowledgeable about their own cultures. As insiders, managers have certain advantages in learning about their cultures:

1. managers know their organizations' histories or are in a position to learn about them;
2. they have access to arenas of decision making and to many of the communications that take place among members;
3. they also have access to at least some of the unguarded and frank informal communications among members;
4. they are in daily and intimate contact with the concrete manifestations of their cultures.

In sum, managers have more data about their organizations than any outsider can have. The reporter of the case that began this chapter might not have known what the significance of top management meetings was to other members of Falcon Computers if he had not been a manager there—an insider—at the time. At the same time, managers lack two advantages that outsiders have in learning about cultures—detachment, and a broad perspective on how cultures work. Without some detachment, managers may project too much of their personal values and understandings into other members of their culture. Without a broad understanding of how cultures work, they may make simplistic assumptions about how to manage them.

Inside sources of information.   As insiders, managers have repeated and continuous access to people and situations that can yield information about their cultures. Some of this information may take some extra effort to collect; some of it is available during their regular routines if they are sensitive observers. For example, managers can search out individuals whose roles regularly expose them to others with expectations that conflict with those of their own organization. Such conflicts create contrasts that bring differences into bold relief; people experiencing such contrasts become aware of what might otherwise be taken-for-granted and unexamined aspects of their own cultures (Louis 1980).

Boundary spanners, in particular, must be sensitive to what outside stakeholders like customers, suppliers, unions, and regulators expect and how those expectations mesh with the cultures of their own organizations. To carry out their duties effectively, boundary spanners must negotiate relationships between inside and outside sets of role-senders—a requirement that is likely to motivate them to learn the basic understandings of each. Purchasing agents, salespersons, public relations and security officers, industrial relations managers, and company lawyers do work that takes them into a variety of settings and events. They thereby gain a broad perspective on their own organizations and have opportunities to compare and contrast the values and practices of a wide sample of people inside and outside their organizations.

Other roles in organizations take their occupants into many different settings within the organization and facilitate social contacts that reveal members' beliefs and values. Various positions within the personnel functions provide such opportunities. The classic study by Melville Dalton (1959) of *Men Who Manage* shows just how wide and deep a personnel specialist's exposure to a company culture can be. While working with a personnel department, Dalton was able to cultivate numerous informants in many sectors of a large company; they were quite willing to tell him about their belief systems, informal cliques and cabals, and widely practiced rituals—some of which were at odds with company regulations and the official culture. Other organizational members in situations of contrast are newcomers. They are therefore "more aware of the understandings associated with both the settings they are entering and the settings they have left than are insiders in either place" (Louis 1985b, p. 134). Tapping the experience and insights of newcomers could thus help managers learn more about their cultures.

In addition, managers can watch especially carefully to see how people react and what they do in situations of crisis and disruption. Major reorganizations, mergers, new CEOs, and acquisitions are among those situations that seem to surface cultural assumptions that people are unaware of when they are conducting business as usual. Even a new member of a workgroup may be a sufficient disruption to make otherwise hidden values and norms evident.

If they want to be more systematic, managers can attempt some kind of audit of their culture (Wilkins 1983b). There are two alternatives, which are not mutually exclusive: managers talk with other members to discuss and try to sur-face underlying values, or they can list and try to interpret the meanings of exist-ing cultural forms. In effect, they can try to learn about the substance of culture directly from what members can tell them, or they can try to learn about it indi-rectly from interpreting what members do.

The process of learning about a culture from what members say is not as straightforward or easy as it sounds. All methods for doing so have drawbacks. The use of questionnaires and other structured instruments to uncover cultural beliefs, values, or norms is disapproved of by many experts on culture. They point out that the structured nature of such instruments presupposes something about the culture, and that these techniques can therefore only discover what those who construct them are aware of and think is important. Questionnaires also tend to tap relatively superficial feelings and attitudes of members rather than their deeply held understandings. They may therefore miss the most crucial aspects of the culture.

To avoid superficiality and gaps, some experts advocate intensive group discussions to bring cultural substance to the surface. However, other problems arise with open discussion among members about their perceptions of values and norms. Such discussions can operate to make the culture seem more uniform than it actually is. It is hard to know whether those participating are reporting what they really think and feel or are, through influence processes emanating in groups, persuaded to express ideas that they do not genuinely hold. Also, such discussions are hard to keep focused, can be very stressful for members, can have political overtones, and can, for all of these reasons, degenerate either into gripe sessions or into efforts to promote certain values rather than to discover the actual ones in use. Although one CEO's reports indicate such sessions were suc-cessful in uncovering a company's values (Burke 1990), it is also possible that they actually functioned to garner support for a managerial code of ethics already envisioned.

Given these drawbacks to direct attempts to surface cultural substance, managers may gain more valid insights from an audit of the cultural forms in use in their organizations. A systematic examination of cultural practices can be used to generate a list of various forms currently in use. These can then be inter-preted for their evident and their hidden expressive consequences. For example, what rites of conflict reduction does the organizations use? Are the consequences of reducing conflict served by meetings and committees? What meanings are conveyed by the ways in which conflicts are reduced in these settings? Also, what stories do newcomers hear about the organization? What conflicts do the stories express and how are those conflicts resolved in the stories?

By asking and answering such questions, detailed behaviors of cultural sig-nificance can be arrayed and given tentative interpretations. Each form must be looked at as but a part of a whole—no one of them will alone provide a master key to the culture. But by "hopping back and forth" between them and by alter-nating observations and interpretations of them (Geertz 1979, p. 239), managers can begin to get a feel for their culture. The tentative interpretations initially generated must be refined and checked through further observations. Managers involved must observe as much as they can of actual behaviors as they unfold during a variety of cultural forms. In this way they can begin to test their interpretations against realities. Only when their observations of specifics and attempts to interpret them yield consistent patterns can managers have some confidence in their interpretations. Discrepancies between interpretations and observations usually indicate that interpretations are incomplete or distorted.

Using outsiders.   We have tried to suggest how managers might read their own cultures because many organizations cannot afford to hire consultants to assist them in this endeavor. For those who can, the different perspectives gained from insiders and outsiders can be beneficial (Evered and Louis 1981; Schein 1985). Some analysts feel that the guidance provided by outsiders can help a group of motivated insiders surface even some of the deeper aspects of their cultures in a relatively short time. The process involves the outsiders, usually consultants, using models and concepts to help insiders become aware of their cultural forms and probe for their meanings. The outsiders help in this process by asking questions and making observations based in a broad knowledge and experience with many organizational cultures. By then extending this process to other groups in the organization, the outsiders can map additional portions of the culture. Since such examinations of culture are often triggered by specific problems or issues, they tend to map only those parts of the culture most relevant to the motivating issues (Schein 1991). Also, they hold much the same potential for mutual influence as if groups of managers met alone. Outsiders may be able to reduce the most blatant of these influences but cannot entirely remove the possibility.

A major difference between a cultural audit conducted by insiders alone and one conducted by a combination of insiders and outsiders is in who puts the pieces together by checking various sets of observations and interpretations against one another. In the former case, insiders are expected to do the "systematic checking and consolidation" (Schein 1985, p. 117) of discrete interpretations that yields a coherent pattern or whole. This task is a formidable one for managers, who have many other jobs to do. When outsiders are involved, they relieve managers of some of this burden and usually play a major role in putting the pieces together. Firms that can afford it usually prefer to use outsiders because of the experience and relative objectivity they bring to this process.

Using Levers to Manage Cultures

Despite the complexities and fuzziness inherent in cultures, managers can gain considerable leverage on managing them if they are alert to the possibilities provided by ideologies, by cultural forms, by organizational socialization, by subcultures, by various types of cultural leadership, and by elements in their environments. Informed opinion and experience suggests that cultures can be managed to an organization's advantage.

> Culture manifests itself through numerous organizational structures; it is made concrete by organizational events. And, thus it can be managed; it can be shifted by changing concrete aspects of an organization's functioning. (Kanter 1984, p. 196)

Managing cultures, however, does not necessarily involve changing them. As we will discuss later in this chapter, managers may also seek to maintain existing cultures or may seek to create new ones. But first, we will discuss certain general features of each of the levers for managing cultures. Later sections in this chapter and in Chapter 10 will treat how the use of these levers may vary in efforts to maintain, change, or create cultures. All of these discussions will summarize points made throughout the earlier chapters of the book. However, we can only illustrate how some of the many issues considered in prior chapters are relevant to managing cultures. Other points covered in prior chapters that are not repeated in what follows could, of course, be relevant to managing cultures in some circumstances.

Ideologies.   Since ideologies comprise the substance of cultures, those who seek to manage cultures often focus on them to the neglect of other aspects of culture. Some practitioners seem to believe that if management can just manage to figure out and promulgate the "right" ideologies, success will follow. One hitch is that what is "right" seems to change with the environment and also with the preoccupations of the business press and popular consultants. Thus, managers who try to follow the conventional wisdom have to keep changing the ideologies they espouse. Such faddishness is, needless to say, not a formula for successfully managing organizational cultures.

Managerial attempts to instill the latest ideology into their organizations cannot succeed unless the ideas involved somehow fit with, not only the current context, but with something in the history of an organization and in the collective experiences of organizational members. Unless faced with a dire crisis, members prefer some measure of continuity. Before they will subscribe to an ideology, it must make sense to them. While new ideas can certainly be brought into organizations and be made part of the accepted ideologies, not all ideas will fit into every organizational culture. Organizational ideologies usually have some features that make them unique to specific organizations. Furthermore, the evidence strongly suggests that a variety of ideologies can form the core of successful organizations' cultures in the same industries at the same time.

Managers must also remember that they should not try to incorporate beliefs and values to which they do not sincerely subscribe into their organizational cultures. If they cannot wholeheartedly subscribe to an ideology, how can they influence others to do so? Their actions, if not their words, are likely to eventually betray a lack of commitment to an ideology.

Top management can also fall into the trap of believing that they alone are the source of distinctive organizational ideologies. Acting on such beliefs, they may cutoff the possibilities for others' helping to shape the culture. Astute managers will instead remain receptive to both the emergence of new cultural themes and ideas and the elaboration and development of old ones that are consistent with desired objectives. They can selectively encourage and reinforce the expression of ideologies that make sense to them. Such cultural infusions from the membership will help to keep the culture relevant and vital to its members.

Cultural forms.   Managers of new organizations need to be aware of the potential and likely effects of cultural forms as they emerge. Managers in existing organizations need to become aware of the many cultural forms that have developed over the years and are currently in use within their organizations. As already discussed, they could attempt to inventory and catalog the forms in use. This will be easier for those forms that are sponsored or initiated through management action. But managers should also be aware that cultural forms can arise informally and spontaneously among organizational members at all levels, and should seek to include in their inventory at least the most potent and widespread of the forms popular among lower level participants.

Since symbols are the most ubiquitous of cultural forms, management might begin an inventory by cataloging them. Many different objects, settings, and actors that people use or encounter in their work setting can serve as valued symbols embued with cultural meaning. When a new restaurant manager decided to occasionally serve beef other than U.S. prime beef on the menu, the assistant manager and other employees were upset by the apparent dilution of this symbol of quality (Whyte 1948, p. 334). The great importance given to this symbol was evidenced by the fact that those employees who prepared and cooked meat were accorded the highest status. When the manager reinstated the earlier policy of serving only prime beef, the emotional disturbances ceased. Work settings and the presence or absence of certain performers or functionaries are also powerful symbols in many organizations. The location of meetings, whether top management attends, who else is invited and attends, what types of questions are asked, and other apparently mundane details carry various meanings that managers can consciously package and manage if they are aware of their potential (Peters 1978, p. 10; Pfeffer 1981a).

The language that people use and don't use also, of course, carries cultural meaning. Around the time of the AT&T breakup, when AT&T management realized that cultural change was needed to cope with a more complex and changeful environment, they eliminated the family-oriented metaphor of "Ma Bell" in their literature and talk (Krefting and Frost 1985, p. 155). This long-standing metaphor carried meanings associated with an ideology that they felt the company could no longer afford.[1] In Western Electric, one of the AT&T subsidiaries, a new image was advanced during management training that was intended to prepare managers for the imminent divestiture of the company. At the end of a speech he gave to the assembled managers, one top-level manager suddenly opened his dress shirt to reveal a T-shirt with the slogan "Lean, Clean, and Mean." This, he announced, was they way the company would have to be in the future.[2]

Stories and other narratives can also be potent managerial tools. Since they record past events, narratives often celebrate and reinforce an existing culture. In Hewlett-Packard (H-P), for example, the story of how Bill Hewlett and Dave

---

[1]Such potent metaphors do not lose their meanings easily and quickly, however. The various regional companies spun off from AT&T in the divestiture are widely referred to as the Baby Bells. All babies, of course, have mothers.

[2]Personal communication to the authors during research interviews conducted in 1982.

Packard founded the company in their garage reinforces values like entrepreneurship, taking risks, and innovation. The story about how H-P avoided mass layoffs by asking everyone to cut their hours reminds employees of the people-centered values within that company's culture (Wilkins 1984). Managers should also be aware of how organizational members can use stories—sometimes to oppose management values and to try to change the culture. John DeLorean used stories like the "refrigerator story" recounted in Chapter 3 to make the then-current values of General Motors management appear ridiculous. Although his attempt to change the culture was not successful, his use of stories to advance countercultural meanings is a good illustration of the potential of stories for inducing changes. One way that stories can become a lever is for management to take dramatic actions to symbolize new or existing ideologies and values and then make sure that stories about these actions circulate through the grapevine. In effect, this is what happened when we heard the story about the T-shirt with its new slogan from several Western Electric managers we interviewed.

Managerial practices are probably the most potent carriers of cultural meaning. As the proverb says, actions speak louder than words. This is because everyone knows that talk is cheap, in the sense that it doesn't require much effort or use up many resources. Actions require a greater expenditure of effort and often involve the spending of valuable resources—time, if nothing else. Therefore, the way managers and other important actors in organizations apportion their time carries cultural messages about what is valued in that culture. Managers who seek to influence their cultures should "be seen as spending a lot of time on matters visibly related to the values they preach" (Deal and Kennedy 1982, p. 169). Another heavily symbolic activity that managers engage in all the time is meeting and talking with people. For example, whom they talk to over the phone and whether they are readily available to others over the phone has cultural meaning. Managers in companies that want to cultivate a participatory and democratic culture must be available to subordinates over the phone and for relatively impromptu meetings. Managers can also signal cultural change by changing customary patterns of action. When the president of a company quickly flew off to consult with an unhappy, but important customer, he communicated that service to customers was to become a central value in that company (Peters 1978, p. 10).

Because managers initiate and supervise many activities and programs that not only achieve practical outcomes, but function as cultural rites or rituals, they need to become aware of the cultural meanings these activities communicate. If they lack such awareness, their activities may act to create cultural confusion and dilute desired cultural ideologies and values (Beyer and Trice 1987). On the positive side, activities and programs that function as cultural rites include many levers to manage culture because they consolidate various cultural forms—each of which can be used to convey desirable new and old cultural messages. It is relatively easy to add, subtract, or change one or more of these forms to make a rite communicate and celebrate desired meanings.

To illustrate, the cultural meanings of an internal appeals committee might be changed by moving its deliberations from near the general manager's office to somewhere on the plant floor and by changing the participants to include fellow-employees as well as members of management. Similarly, the cultural meanings of existing rites of passage could be strengthened by incorporating hitherto neglected sagas or stories about the organization and its early heros. Or a previously moribund Christmas party could be enlivened and made more integrative by having a member of top management dress as Santa Claus and give presents to all assembled—especially if the guest list is changed to include spouses and children (Trice and Beyer 1985).

Perhaps the most direct and obvious set of cultural rites that managers employ to instill desired sets of cultural values are training activities that function as rites of passage. That training has the dual potential of achieving both practical and expressive consequences is generally recognized in management circles. Thus, cultural change efforts usually include some training activities for managers at all levels. What may be less recognized is that these rites can also be used to strengthen cultures even when change is not desired. Such rites can be used to mark any changes in status—promotions, or steps from one skill level to another—and thus as occasions in which members can be reminded of the degree to which desired behaviors conform to desired cultural values. It is also important that the rites of passage used with new recruits are carefully designed to convey desired cultural messages. Managerial inattention to employee orientations, for example, could allow the meanings conveyed in such rites to wander away from desired organizational values.

Other rites that are generally useful in managing culture are rites of enhancement. Since giving rewards is a frequent occurrence in organizations, it is not too difficult for managers to make their conferral into a ceremony. Managers must, of course, be careful about which behaviors they reward in rites of enhancement. Ideally the behaviors rewarded should clearly exemplify desired values and should involve performance that is in some sense extraordinary. Rewarding the wrong behaviors creates cultural confusion. Rewarding ordinary performance in ceremonious ways devalues the meaning of the rewards.

Socialization.   As explained in Chapter 4, the types of socialization used by organizations have different cultural outcomes. Newcomers can be socialized into a rather close conformity with an existing culture, or into an innovative mode that could help to stimulate desired cultural change. Because managers typically have substantial control over which types are used within their organizations, socialization provides them with another available lever for cultural management. Managers, however, have much less control over occupational socialization, and thus often find themselves having to administer their socialization on top of a well-established cultural indoctrination that new members have received in occupational or professional training.

Although rites of passage are perhaps the most important cultural form used in organizational socialization, other rites clearly have potential for socializing members into a given culture. Rites of enhancement tell them which behaviors are valued and will be rewarded; rites of degradation signal when power is being transferred from one group to another; rites of integration show them that there are sentiments and value systems that embrace different groups and their subcultural values; rites of renewal assure them that flaws and faults will be remidied; and rites of conflict reduction reduce conflicts and thus assure members that differences will not lead to destructive aggression. Of course, all of the other cultural forms also convey cultural messages, and socialization is, to a large degree, the process of members' learning the significance of prevalent cultural forms and their meanings.

Role models, leaders, peers, and mentors also contribute to the socialization of members. Only some of these are levers that management can readily employ, and their control over them is limited. But managers can make some role models more prominent than others through such devices as rites of enhancement. Managers can also facilitate the establishment of certain mentoring relationships, and put members in contact with certain peers and leaders by the work groups to which they are assigned. When making such interventions, managers cannot be sure that their intentions will be realized because outcomes are heavily dependent on relationships between other persons. Of course, to the degree that managers themselves serve as role models, leaders, peers, and mentors to some members, their own actions will carry socializing messages to those members.

Subcultures.   Although they are not readily amenable to management control, subcultures do present some levers that managers can employ to manage cultures. Perhaps most basic is that managers have some control over the occupational mix of members in their organization through the choices of products or services they will provide and the technologies employed. Adding or subtracting occupational subcultures will certainly affect the cutlures of the workgroups involved and could even conceivably alter the overall culture. For example, a correctional facility that discharged all of its psychiatrists and social workers would likely change its overall culture to a more custodial than treatment-oriented culture. Conversely, a manufacturing concern that hires a group of researchers may be able to change its culture to a more creative and innovative one.

Managers may also be able to use the subcultures in their organizations to reinforce an existing culture. Insofar as existing subcultural ideologies are consistent with or complementary to the overall culture, their existence buttresses the overall culture. Thus, astute managers will want to find ways to encourage the formation and continuance of such subcultures. One way to do this is to reward and therefore enhance subcultural leaders and exceptional subcultural performance.

Still another possibility is that countercultures can be used as a lever for cultural change. Managers who find themselves facing a crisis requiring drastic change may be able to find countercultures somewhere in their organizations that have developed ideologies and cultural practices that are appropriate for the changes needed. We cannot help but wonder whether GM would be in a better competitive position today if other top managers had listened to and encouraged John DeLorean and his followers.

Leadership.   Most managers probably consider leadership to be the most obvious lever they have to manage their cultures. But, because cultural leadership can take various forms that have different consequences for cultures, managers who wish to exercise cultural leadership need to be clear about what they are trying to achieve and why. They also need to be realistic in their appraisal of what they are likely to be able to achieve, given their situations and their own personal characteristics. But the conclusions of such appraisals are not determined solely by either the situation or by a leader's propensities and strengths. The willingness of followers and the expectations of important actors in the environment must also be assessed. We will discuss some of the issues involved in this appraisal process later in this chapter. On the basis of such appraisals, managers can decide whether they will try to embody, integrate, change, or create a culture.

Because all managers are not naturally cultural leaders, they may need to cultivate not only an awareness of their cultures, but certain sets of behaviors in order to be effective in managing their cultures. Cultural leaders probably need, at a minimum, to be effective role models, create impressions of success and confidence in their followers, be good at articulating beliefs and values, communicate high expectations and confidence in followers, and be good motivators of others. In addition, they need to have strong convictions about what they are trying to achieve and then manage to achieve some measure of success in the eyes of their followers. The rationally oriented behaviors of an effective manager are not sufficient to become a cultural leader. Cultural leaders need to be more like evangelists than accountants (Weick 1979a, p. 42).

Managers also need to recognize that they are probably not the only cultural leaders around. Cultural leadership can occur at all levels of organizations and is not confined to persons in delegated positions of authority. As part of their appraisal of their situations, managers should look for and weigh the influence and aims of other leaders and their subcultures. Situations of great cultural diversity may make certain forms of cultural leadership impractical. In general, managers who would be cultural leaders need to remember that cultural leadership is a process that involves more than leaders. Followers and situations are integral parts of the process.

Environments.   As explained in Chapter 8, organizations cannot survive without their environments, which provide them with the resources they need to continue operating. Although organizational environments are, by definition, outside the boundaries of organizations, they are not totally outside the control of managers. In many ways, managers manage to influence their organizations' environments (Pfeffer and Salancik 1978). To the degree that they are successful in such efforts, managers can use that influence to help them manage their cultures. Managers can influence their environments in two senses: (1) they can influence objective conditions in the environment; and (2) they can influence how members and other stakeholders of their organizations perceive their environments.

Because they make such strategic decisions as what products and services to produce, what markets to enter, where and how to obtain resources, and where to locate facilities, managers choose many of the environments in which their organizations operate. That choice gives them a large measure of, but not unlimited, control over their objective environments. This is because the choices they make at one point in time constrain later choices. For example, when Japanese manufacturers began competing with U.S. manufacturers in the consumer electronics industry, U.S. managers decided to abandon markets they saw as no longer profitable (Chandler 1991). If they had decided instead to take on the Japanese, invest heavily in new technology and training, and compete on the basis of costs and prices, they would have had to drastically change their managerial and organizational cultures. They apparently did not see that as a viable or desirable option. In this example, managers chose to get out of an environment that had changed from benevolent to hostile and from munificent to scarce. By avoiding such drastic environmental change, they could largely maintain existing cultures.

Another prominent example of managers' choosing environments is provided by the wholesale movement of U.S. manufacturing facilities from the North to the South in the last two decades. Motives undoubtedly included the avoidance of employee unions, high wages, and the often antagonistic relations between management and employees prevalent in the North. Southern workers, with different histories and experiences, were expected to make more compliant and willing workers. Southern legislators were expected to keep or enact laws more favorable to business. Lately, the trend has been to locate manufacturing facilities outside the United States. Less developed countries make attractive sites not only because of lower wages, but because of looser regulations on environmental byproducts, worker safety, and other perceived negative effects of business on society.

The choice of product or service and the market segment to be served also importantly affects the culture. Volvo Motors can afford self-managed work teams because the company targets a relatively upscale market. Similarly, Rolls Royces are largely handmade cars. Firms producing less expensive cars cannot afford the same level of labor costs, and so must rely on other devices, like quality circles, to produce some measure of employee involvement while using traditional assembly-line type of production. The resulting organizational cultures will obviously be different.

By attending selectively to some factors in the environment and not to others, and by how they interpret those factors, managers also influence the ways in which people perceive organizations' environments. Managers can frame events in the environment as demonstrating various of the characteristics listed in Table 8–2 (page 306). Competition from the Japanese and other Pacific Rim countries can be framed as creating a hostile or merely a changeful environment. This competition can also be framed as emanating either from relatively uncoordinated, free market forces or from relatively coordinated actions by both governments and private companies. Such framing by managers helps to create and justify certain cultural beliefs and practices.

In the most general sense, the ways in which managers interpret what they see in their environments for themselves and others can be used to justify either cultural continuity or change. If managers want to provoke change, they will frame the environment differently than if they want to maintain existing cultures. By emphasizing discontinuities in the environment, managers can make internal change seem necessary and even desirable. By emphasizing continuities in the environment, they can justify cultural continuity.

Resolving the Ethical Dilemma

The fourth general consideration in any management of organizational cultures in whether such management is ethical. At least three ethical concerns about the deliberate management of organizational cultures have been advanced:

1. that attempts to manage will spoil or pollute the product of indigenous, natural forces (Dorson 1971; Sumner 1906);
2. that those who manage the culture will use it to exploit others (Martin and Powers 1983; Schein 1985; Georges and Jones 1980);
3. that managing cultures is an insidious and subtle way to manipulate people and reduce individual freedom and autonomy (Beyer and Trice 1988, p. 157).

Similar concerns have been voiced about research on cultures and how its results might be used.

Some of the traditions within research on culture spring from ideologies saying that descriptions of culture are, in and of themselves, the appropriate end-products of research on cultures. Those who subscribe to these ideologies seem to view human cultures much as some environmentalists view the natural environment. Human interventions are seen as forces likely to destroy the beauty, purity, and naturally occurring balances that have grown up spontaneously over time. Proponents of these views may or may not be aware that their insistence on simply appreciating and knowing about culture is reminiscent of Social Darwinism, which saw human culture and the organizations within it as a product of gradual development and evolution and in no way the results of human purpose or intellect (Sumner 1906).

Dominant managerial ideologies—particularly in the United States—fly in the face of such concerns. Because of the emphasis in the larger culture on doing and practicality, American managers expect to do something about obstacles to organizational objectives; they believe that's what management is all about. Thus, if Western managers see cultures as affecting what they are trying to do, they will likely try to manage them—either to reduce interference with their objectives or to positively promote those objectives. Rather than disapproving of their efforts, scholars and ethicists might have more impact if they concerned themselves with channeling managerial efforts into what they see as constructive and ethical channels.

There are at least two other reasons that the concerns to keep cultures pristine and natural may be overdrawn. First, these views seem to minimize the effects that leaders have in developing and changing cultures in all settings. Just because a culture grew up over time does not mean that various leaders within that culture did not shape its eventual content and forms. In work organizations, managers are the designated leaders and thus have some socially granted legitimacy for managing their internal cultures. Second, members of organizations are not blank slates that management can write upon at its will. Even lower level participants have sources of power and often quite successfully resist management's attempts to persuade and lead them (Molstad 1988).

This last point is also relevant to the concern that managers will use culture to exploit others, usually employees under their supervision. One extreme form of this view is that all organizational cultures are devices used to legitimate existing authority arrangements and justify relations of inequality and domination "by presenting them as natural, eternal, and unchangeable" (Kan 1989, p. 12). It is not clear from this view what managers need to do about their cultures in order to be ethical. Since people seem to grow cultures wherever they work and interact over periods of time, management can hardly unilaterally disband all cultures in organizations.

Others see the application of knowledge about cultures as inherently exploitative just because it is being used for practical or commercial ends. However, those who hold this view tend to forget that even the academic study of culture, ostensibly for its own sake, often also yields practical benefits for those who engage in it; folklorists and anthropologists make money and gain status from their lectures, concerts, and publishing activities (Jones 1984). Thus managers are not alone in using their knowledge of culture to their own advantage. Again, the solution to the concern seems to lie in guiding the directions that the use of culture takes. The question is not so much who benefits as who might be harmed by managerial efforts to manage culture.

Rephrasing the question in this way leads to the final ethical issue of whether cultural management damages individuals in organizations by forcing them into molds that destroy their individuality and freedom. If cultures have positive benefits to people, like reducing their anxieties, and people therefore have a natural tendency to form cultures, it follows that people will form cultures in organizations whether or not management takes the initiative or otherwise encourages them to do so. This third ethical concern can then be seen to boil down to *which* cultures will influence individuals in organizations—those that management helps to shape or those that emerge from other influences. Also, as chapters 5, 6, and 8 pointed out, in modern societies most people belong to many different cultural groups, both inside and outside their work settings. The cultures of workgroups and community-based groups are not necessarily more ethical or more concerned with individual rights and freedoms than are those promulgated by management. All cultures tend to demand some uniformity of conduct from their members and thus limit individual autonomy. In practical terms, individuals cannot be utterly free and autonomous unless they live without social ties of any kind. But it is also true that some individuals, largely because of social conditions and structures in the wider society, have more opportunities than others to choose their social ties and cultural memberships. Those with more limited choices may end up in organizational cultures that tend to restrict their autonomy and freedom more than happens with the more advantaged members of society.

A related question is whether people are forced to violate their individual values by pressures from within their organizational cultures. There is abundant recent evidence that sometimes they are—that some corporations create cultures that support and encourage unethical and even criminal activities. Recent scandals in the investment industry, in commodities trading, in banking, and in the housing industry seem to indicate that many members of organizations can be persuaded to engage in unlawful behaviors by pressures from peers or superiors. Others in these organizations simply looked away and failed to report what they knew was obviously wrongdoing. Thus, it is clear that managers do not always try or succeed in creating ethical cultures in their organizations.

These are but some of the ethical concerns that may arise in the management of cultures. None have easy or automatic answers. Those who would manage organizational cultures must use their own value systems to determine what is ethical and unethical. Most analysts hope that, in the long run, ethical cultures will also turn out to be the most effective cultures in the sense that organizations with such cultures will survive and prosper. But it would be naive to expect or even hope that such optimism is justified in the short term.

Clearly what is needed is not to focus so much on whether managers should or should not manage their cultures, but on how ethical concerns can be built into that management. If ethical concerns are built in wherever pertinent, cultural management and ethics need not be in conflict.

Choosing Cultural Maintenance or Cultural Innovation

The final general consideration in managing cultures is what that management seeks to accomplish. Considering their aims and their circumstances, managers need to decide whether they should maintain and perhaps strengthen an existing culture, whether the existing culture should be replaced by a substantially different one, or whether a new culture should be established in a new organization or in a relatively free-standing subunit. Because both changing a culture and creating a new one involve establishing something new and different, both entail cultural innovation. At this point, we will focus on what seems to us the main choice managers must make—whether to attempt cultural maintenance or cultural innovation. In Chapter 10 we will address separately the issues involved in the two types of cultural innovation—cultural change and creation.

The line between maintaining an existing culture and cultural innovation is seldom clear cut or obvious. As pointed out in Chapter 7, managers need to work actively to keep an existing culture vital. Otherwise, desired elements in the culture may wither away and disappear over time. Also, cultures do not remain completely static in the absence of management actions to change them. For reasons discussed in Chapter 1, cultures cannot reproduce themselves perfectly over time. They change—usually slightly and gradually, but sometimes more suddely and fairly radically—as new uncertainties arise or the wider culture changes.

Thus, it would be inaccurate to think of maintaining a culture without some degree of change occurring within it. Also, it would be inaccurate to think of all managerial attempts to manage cultures as succeeding in changing them in any substantial way.

Creating a new culture may seem to be a more clear-cut instance of innovation until we remember the potency and persistence of occupational and industry subcultures. The cultures that emerge in new organizations and subunits are likely to have some continuity with members' pasts and do not necessarily develop so as to reflect the intents or ideas of their founders (Martin, Sitkin, and Boehm 1985).

Reasons for cultural innovation.   The decision of whether to attempt cultural innovation should not be based solely on the inclinations of management. Because members identify with their existing cultures, managers need good rationales to convince them that cultural innovation is necessary. One way of proceeding is for managers to assess their current circumstances to see how much innovation they indicate is needed and can therefore justify. Analysts suggest that certain circumstances call for extensive cultural changes: when poor organizational performance can be traced to inept management; when an organization is experiencing either explosive growth or substantial downsizing; when sudden environmental changes occur that cannot be coped with by strongly held and established cultural ideologies and values; when an organization is on the verge of becoming truly large and complex; when demands for services or products either increase or decrease dramatically; and when previously quiet stakeholder groups begin to press for change (Deal and Kennedy 1982; Lundberg 1985b). Reasons for creating new cultures have not been discussed, but it seems likely that if management decides that change is needed but cannot be accomplished within an existing organizational culture, a new organization or subunit will be founded. This seems to be what was involved when General Motors management decided to build what it hoped would be a radically different automobile—the Saturn—in a new plant largely divorced from the rest of the corporation.

Although the previous listing is a good start, it is probably too specific to anticipate all of the situations in which cultural innovation might be advantageous and justified. In order to make a comprehensive assessment, managers need to consider at least five general criteria:

1. organizational performance,
2. the fit between existing cultures and the organization's tasks and structure,
3. the fit between existing cultures and the organization's environment,
4. the fit between strategy and existing cultures, and
5. the characteristics and personalities of top management.

If performance is poor in any important respect, or if the existing culture does not fit current or anticipated tasks, environments, or strategy, cultural innovation may be needed. When more than one of these criteria suggest a different culture is needed, managers can be relatively confident that cultural innovation is desirable. When the indications are mixed, revitalization of existing cultures or changes to just some segments of them may be sufficient.

The last of the criteria—the characteristics and personalities of top management—should be taken into account more as a constraint that might limit efforts at innovation than as an indicator that is or is not needed. As our earlier analysis of cultural leadership indicated, some leaders have personalities and skills that make them ideal as maintenance leaders while others are more suited for cultural innovation. While leaders are but part of the leadership process, they are a very important part of it. Thus decision makers contemplating cultural innovation also need to consider what leadership talent they have at their disposal to help to inspire needed reforms or creation.

Having assessed their circumstances and possible cultural responses to them, managers can then decide how much innovation is required. If only relatively minor changes seem to be needed, then the cultural management effort can be looked at as a revitalization and maintenance effort. If major changes seem necessary, then managers must recognize they are faced with a genuine cultural innovation. Although members of organizations may see both kinds of efforts as cultural innovation or change, and management may decide to so label them, management itself needs to be clear about just how much change it wants. Cultural maintenance and cultural innovation have different implications for managerial actions, as will be delineated later in this chapter and in Chapter 10.

A downside of culture change: resistance.   In his classic guidebook for administrators, entitled *The Prince,* Niccolo Machiavelli wrote in approximately 1513: "It must be considered that there is nothing more difficult to carry out, nor more doubtful to success, nor more dangerous to handle, then to initiate a new order of things" (Machiavelli [1513] 1952, p. 55). His advice is still good.

Two reasons stand out for why cultures are so difficult to deliberately change. First, the intrinsic nature of culture is conservative. Ideologies become emotionally charged and taken-for-granted rationales for accepted behavior. Moreover, the forms that deliver them become familiar and reassuring symbols and rituals to which people become emotionally attached. Although there may be some ambivalences, contradictions, and ambiguities in cultural elements that allow some room for change, people still create strong identities with an ongoing, operative culture. While ambiguities create tensions, they also permit people to interact and get on with their respective tasks without achieving total consensus on all issues. Thus, even ambiguities can be cherished and protected (Meyerson, 1991). A momentum thus grows up in ongoing organizational cultures that make rapid change highly unlikely.

Second, extreme anxieties and uncertainties accompany any substantial culture change. One close observer of organizational life describes cultural change with a metaphor: A trapeze artist has experienced only the left-hand swing of the trapeze and has never leaped through the air to land on the right-hand swing. Colleagues and members of the audience urge him to jump to the right-hand swing for more fame and fortune. "The metaphor helps us to experience in our gut the anxiety associated with change as a real thing, not as an abstract concept.

Asking an organization to change is like asking one to leap through the air, without a safety net, to a swing that one has never tested" (Mitroff 1985, p. 19). Given the choice, most people prefer to avoid such tests.

Research on organizational change has uncovered many reasons people resist change. Managers who contemplate cultural innovation must therefore take these sources of resistance into account in deciding on the costs of the desired changes and the likelihood of success in achieving them. As already mentioned, if the costs and risks of changing a culture are too great, managers may decide they should instead create a new culture. Another alternative is to reconsider whether, with revitalization, new objectives can be accomplished with the existing cultures. The issues surrounding resistance to change will be discussed in more detail in Chapter 10.

Some examples. When organizations have been very successful with one culture, it may be hard for management to recognize that cultural change is needed.

> From 1981 to 1984, People Express Airlines experienced explosive growth and expansion under its charismatic chairman, Donald Burr. His vision was to unleash the entrepreneurial spirit of all employees to achieve exceptional performance. Employees could benefit from their efforts through a generous employee ownership plan and promotion from within. They were given great discretion over how they performed their jobs, often deciding their own hours of work. A key theme of the culture was that administrative staff should be minimal; the managerial hierarchy had only three levels. Managers had to make do without secretaries and expense accounts; they answered their own phones. All employees were expected to do a variety of jobs without supervision—whatever needed to be done. For example, a pilot might manage inventories and collect tickets (Adapted from Byrne 1989, p. 75). Accountants would sometimes come on board to handle ticket purchasing (Perone 1986, p. 10).

The vision that produced this innovative culture and structure was articulated by Burr as follows:

> What we are doing . . . is learning how to unleash the power of the individual in ways that have not been done before and in ways that even we do not fully comprehend. (Hackman 1984, p. 56).

The success of his ideology was evident when People had lower costs than other airlines and thus could offer cut-rate fares that other firms had difficulty matching.[3] Observers were impressed not only by the exceptional performance of the company but by the degree to which its predominantly youthful employees had enthusiastically adopted its culture (Denison 1990).

Like many charismatics, Burr was very successful in winning people over to his ideas; almost overnight People Airlines had a well-established and integrated

---

[3]People Airlines was not the first airline to try this strategy. Southwest Airlines had much the same strategy and ideology and was founded a decade earlier. Its founding and later culture will be discussed extensively in Chapter 10.

culture. Unfortunately, everyone was so convinced by his vision that it blinded them to the need to routinize his charisma as the firm grew (Trice and Beyer 1986). While he admitted "We have to get better organized" and "I'm in meetings so much of the time I can't get any work done," he and his managers failed to act to create more administrative structures and personnel (Hackman 1984, p. 49). One analyst has suggested that the lack of a clerical staff was one of the key problems (DiTomaso as quoted by Perone 1986, p. 10). In effect, the culture and the needs for coordination of tasks became misaligned as the firm grew. Even after People acquired Frontier Airlines, the original company ideologies of minimalist structure and complete faith in people's ability to adapt and manage themselves continued to prevail. The need for structure was ignored. The result was more and more disorganization and stress for individual employees.

Perhaps it was success, perhaps it was the natural outgrowth of the entrepreneurial ideology that led to the decision to expand through acquisition. In retrospect, at least, it is far from clear that this strategy fit the existing People culture with its informal and unstructured management style. Because of the avoidance of division of labor, there were not enough staff specialists in administration to deal with the additional internal and external complexities. The acquisition of Frontier also drastically changed People's environment. Now that they were competing in more than selected pockets of the national market, the large carriers began to view People as a significant competitor. While they had previously more or less ignored and tolerated this upstart airline because it was fairly small, the major carriers now ganged up and resolved to frontally attack People by using its own original strategy. They lowered their fares to a level at which People, with its limited amount of capital and new debt load, could not compete (Byrne 1989).

People Airlines still didn't change; business and profits slumped, the debt of its purchase of Frontier further depressed earnings, and the airline was soon no longer viable as a separate entity. The company and its owner-employees paid a high price for failing to change the culture. It was bought by Texas Air Corporation in 1986 for $200 million—about four dollars a share—one sixth of what the stock was worth in 1983. While different analysts emphasize different reasons for the company's failure, most agree that the lack of management structure was a key factor (Garrett 1989).

Another case history, involving the up-and-down fortunes of the Jaguar car company, is interesting because it involved two changes in culture—one not obviously needed, the other needed. When British Leyland (BL) acquired Jaguar in 1972, it not only reorganized the company, it tried to destroy its culture.

> At one stage Jaguar flags at the entrace to the factory were torn down. Only Leyland flags were allowed to be flown on the premises and telephonists were threatened with disciplinary action if they answered with "Good morning, Jaguar cars." Instead they were supposed to say, "Good morning, Leyland cars," and if any further address was needed, "Large assembly plant number one." Worse still, the then two constituent factories of Jaguar were put into two quite separate organizational units within Leyland—the Power and Transmissions Division and the Body and Assembly Division—hardly an appropriate fate for one of the most famous marquee names in the world motoring industry. (Goldsmith and Clutterbuck 1984, p. 49)

Such actions effectively destroyed the Jaguar identity. They made "Jaguar ... merely a manufacturing location" (Whipp, Rosenfeld, and Pettigrew 1989, p. 570).

BL's downgrading of the Jaguar image and identity was inappropriate, given the prior success of Jaguar cars. The cultural change that BL forced was clearly not dictated by poor performance, but by other factors—perhaps BL's own culture and its preoccupation with controlling its new acquisition. BL was a huge conglomerate that concentrated on high volume and mass production. Jaguar had been a low-volume producer of high-performance cars. The two cultures were obviously incompatible, and BL was not inclined to allow Jaguar enough discretion to continue with its own culture and management style. BL management took control of Jaguar's purchasing, sales, marketing, and finance divisions. They also imposed three major reorganizations and seven different CEOs on Jaguar over a period of eight years. Jaguar did not prosper under its new management or achieve the expanded production BL hoped for. Production of the Jaguar Series III model declined from 32,000 in 1974 to 14,000 in 1980.

Fortunately for Jaguar, a new managing director, named John Egan, and a new executive team were installed in 1980. This group recognized the harm that had been done by the destruction of its traditional culture and the concomitant need to change the culture again. They worked to establish a new culture that contained themes consistent with Jaguar's pre-BL culture. They recreated its craft and skill identity and combined it with a new "can-do" mentality expressed in meeting tight project deadlines (Whipp, Rosenfeld, and Pettigrew 1989, p. 572). In effect, they "honored its past ... returning to [it] for inspiration and instruction" (Wilkins 1989, p. 52), but also remedied its shortcomings by drastically altering the operational ideologies and structure. Finally, they articulated a mission that "through a process of survival, consolidation, and growth, Jaguar's ultimate aim was to become the finest car company in the world" (Whipp, Rosenfeld, and Pettigrew 1989, p. 571). Massive changes over a five-year period accompanied the new mission. Perhaps most important was that the new management negotiated more autonomy from corporate headquarters and government trade officials. "The turnaround in Jaguar's performance thereafter, taken across a range of measures, has been, by any standards, remarkable" (Whipp, Rosenfeld, and Pettigrew 1989, p. 570).

These cases of People Airlines and Jaguar suggest some lessons for managers. They must be both sensitive to situations that may call for cultural change and careful to be sure that a real need for change exists. In both of the cases discussed, management either used poor judgment or did not even stop to assess whether change was needed. Burr and his managers failed to recognize that explosive growth, a new strategy, and a new environment required a change in the company culture. British Leyland failed to realize that it was inappropriate to impose a culture developed to do mass production on a company that was known for limited production, high-quality cars—especially when there was no obvious need for such a drastic cultural change. In both cases, the mismanagement of culture had deleterious effects on company performance.

Together these two case studies illustrate that managers play crucial roles in creating, maintaining, and changing cultures. Since cultural change is usually considered the hardest of the three to accomplish, there are more analyses and written accounts of it than of culture creation or maintenance. From these accounts, a variety of useful considerations emerge that we will integrate and summarize. We will begin with the practical considerations involved in maintaining cultures because this may be the easiest form of cultural management. In Chapter 10, we will examine cultural change and creation as alternative ways to achieve cultural innovation. The various levers for managing culture are interwoven into all of these discussions.

Specific Considerations in Maintaining Cultures

Some organizations are so large and powerful or so lucky that they can prosper without changing their cultures in a substantial way over periods of time. They either do not encounter the circumstances that usually require change, or they are able to manage such circumstances successfully using understandings and behaviors consistent with their existing cultures. AT&T before its divestiture and IBM are examples of two well-known organizations that seem to have maintained discrete cultures relatively unchanged over substantial periods of time. Their past success does not, however, guarantee that their cultures will continue to be equally successful in the future.

Various analysts have observed that organizational success sometimes breeds failure (Starbuck, Greve, and Hedberg 1978; Miller 1990). According to these analyses, success convinces top managers that the ideas and strategies they have used in the past are the right ones, and they therefore stick to them and fail to adapt in the face of changing environments and failing performance. Managers of organizations can become so obsessed with the ideologies they hold that they pursue them even more assiduously. In the process, a dangerous momentum builds that is very hard to resist or reverse. A recent analysis of ITT's performance during Harold S. Geneen's reign concluded: "By concentrating on what it did best, ITT pushed its strategies, cultures, and structures to dangerous extremes, while failing to develop in other areas. Greatness had paved the way for excess and decline as ITT the Builder became ITT the Imperialist" (Miller 1990, p. 7). Thus, maintaining culture has its dangers.

Managers of organizations face a paradox. They want to take advantage of what they have learned in the past and pursue a strategy long enough to realize the gains of past investments and experience. Also, in a cultural sense, they and their subordinates have come to believe in and become emotionally invested in what they are doing. At the same time, they must somehow develop the capability to question whether their past learning fits their present and future circumstances. To fail to do both is to risk what happened to Icarus in the Greek myth. His greatest assest was his wings, but they were made of wax, and when he flew too close to the sun, they melted and he fell to his death in the sea (Miller 1990, p. 3).

One solution to this paradox is what analysts have called punctuated equilibrium—the alternation of periods of drastic change with periods of relative stability (Tushman and Romanelli 1985; Gersick 1991). Most organizations are not engaged in drastic cultural change all of the time. It would be too costly, exhausting, and unsettling to everyone. But they do sometimes change a lot. In between their periods of change, organizations maintain their cultures more or less well. Those that succeed in keeping their existing cultures vital and relevant can realize substantial gains from past learning. Thus, we will offer some suggestions—in the form of aphorisms—about how this might be done.

Karl Weick has alerted organizational researchers to the benefits and dangers of aphorisms in social science. While not as rigorous as formal theories, aphorisms can condense complex understandings and interpretations in a communicable form that preserves much of their content. What follows in the rest of this chapter and in much of Chapter 10 are sets of aphorisms intended to guide managers and others who embark on maintaining, changing, or creating organizational cultures in dealing with what we see as central issues in each of these kinds of cultural management. We have grounded our aphorisms in data and observations where we could, but admit that much of what follows is speculative. We offer them in the following spirit: "Aphorisms can move inquiry along; they can help people see facets of problems they hadn't seen before; they can force people to keep asking questions, possibly improving the quality of the questions that get asked; and they have the obvious advantage of honesty" (Weick 1979b, p. 40).

Here then are some aphorisms that we have distilled from the many sources quoted in this book and from our own research and understandings of organizations.

Don't Assume Continuity; Work for It

As pointed out in Chapter 7, once established, organizational cultures do not always persist and remain vital. Maintaining an existing culture requires that members continue to believe in and be emotionally committed to the substance of that culture. Ideologies, cultural forms, socialization, subcultures, leadership, and environments—all play a role in keeping members aware of and committed to their cultures. Managers can use these levers to create cultural continuity and to revitalize and renew ideologies of the culture that seem to have lost their relevance for present uncertainties or simply have grown stale.

So when managers decide that cultural change is unncessary or undesirable, they cannot afford to ignore their cultures. To ensure that their cultures remain consistent with organizational goals, they must remain aware of and active in managing them. Logically, if they don't see a need for change, they should endeavor to maintain and strengthen cultures already present. In the process of doing so, they will need to consider a number of other issues that are especially pertinent to maintaining cultures.

Respect the Past, but Adapt to the Present

When cultural continuity rather than change is desired, respecting the past is obviously important because it provides the ideological and emotional grounding for the current culture. People often think of cultural elements rooted in their pasts as traditions and come to cherish them because of the continuity they represent (Wilkins 1989).

Ideally, the main criterion for cultural continuity would be the continued viability of a culture's substance—its ideologies, values, and norms. As it happens, cultural forms seem to be more persistent than ideologies. Symbols, language, narratives, and cultural practices persist long after the ideas with which they were first associated.[4] Cultural forms are rooted in personal habits and a myriad of social arrangements, so they do not require conscious attention to continue. People in organizations are hired to do things, and they will therefore act—usually much as they have acted in the past (Starbuck 1983). As they get better at what they do, effects become more pronounced. In this way, traditions and the cultural forms that embody them can become dysfunctional over time.

> Many outstanding organizations have followed ... paths of deadly momentum—time-bomb trajectories of attitudes, policies, and events that lead to falling sales, plummeting profits, even bankruptcy.... Productive attention to detail, for instance, turns into an obsession with minutia; rewarding innovation escalates into gratuitous invention; and measured growth becomes unbridled expansion. (Miller 1990, p. 3)

In the process, other desirable activities are deemphasized and neglected. Obviously, the trick in managing cultural maintenance is to avoid elevating the past into such a sacred position that its lessons are pursued in an unquestioned way to the exclusion of other concerns.

To this end, managers must actively work at keeping existing organizational cultures relevant to the present. They must keep cultural practices in alignment with present circumstances and ideologies by incremental adaptations of their content and forms of expression. Cultural rites that are especially persistent, for example, can perhaps be given updated meanings through the addition or subtraction of some elements. A traditional party can be held in a new setting or incorporate a new tradition, like telling jokes on management. A company saga can be made more relevant to the present by emphasizing some elements and deemphasizing others. New jargon, slogans, and stories can be introduced as attachments to established cultural forms.

---

[4]We will not attempt to resolve the chicken-and-egg issue of whether ideologies give rise to cultural forms or the reverse. Probably both happen.

Adapt Existing Ideologies to Current Challenges and Crises

All ideologies probably have within them some themes and ideas that are more general and worthy of preservation than others. Cultural maintenance should focus on those ideologies that weather well—that inspire commitment from members but are sufficiently general so that they remain relevant as circumstances change. Ideologies that block people from considering any but a narrow range of actions should not be slavishly continued:

> Both organizations and organization theorists can learn a useful lesson from a research project conducted at the University of Paris. During the thirteenth century, the Parisian professors got interested in whether oil would congeal if it was left outdoors on a cold winter night, and they launched a research project to find out. But after much work, they concluded that the question was unanswerable, for they had researched all the works of Aristotle very carefully, and nothing he had written answered this question.
>
> The lesson is, of course, that the Parisian professors were absolutely right: the question *was* unanswerable in their ideological frame of reference (Starbuck 1982, pp. 24–25).

When ideologies have these effects, they interfere with adaptive thinking and behavior. The possible maladaptiveness of ideologies is compounded when one considers the results of research showing that people facing threats and crises tend to become rigid in their thinking and escalate their commitment to past courses of action (Staw, Sandelands, and Dutton 1981; Staw 1976; Starbuck, Greve, and Hedberg 1978). Past ideologies provide ready justifications for such maladaptive behavior.

But ideologies can be made more flexible than many people think. The same ideas can be employed to justify a considerable range of activities if the ideas are rather general and abstract. It is hard to imagine an ideology that does not have, at its core, a rather general principle. Such general ideas usually apply to a variety of situations. For example, the general principle of the sanctity of life can be applied to such diverse issues as abortion, capital punishment, euthanasia, animal rights, and vegetarianism. However, persons who are pro-life on one of these issues are not necessarily pro-life on all of them. This is because the ideology to which they subscribe has been attached to a specific issue, and they believe in this principle only relative to that issue.

Ideologies consist of clusters of interrelated ideas that vary in their specificity. The more general ideas within an ideology form its core; they give more room for interpretation and linkage to a variety of actions than do the more specific ideas at the periphery of a culture. Herbert Kelleher, founder and CEO of Southwest Airlines, advances an ideology of deep concern for his employees' welfare. This ideology permits him to cooperate with or resist unionization depending on how helpful he assesses a specific union as being for his employees (Carey 1988). Attaching his stance on unions to the general ideology of employee welfare enables him to avoid being labeled as either pro- or anti-union. This ideology also helps to justify negotiating with the unions for flexible rules regarding task assignments and work schedules.

The lesson for managers seems to be to resist and downplay the specific prescriptions and proscriptions that get attached to ideologies in favor of keeping them general. While organizational members will need to articulate specific ways to implement ideologies, managers—especially top management—should endeavor to keep emphasizing the general, core ideas of their ideologies. They should avoid becoming too attached to the specifics their subordinates generate. In this way they can keep their own vision clear enough to perceive the unexpected when it occurs and their own commitments general enough so they can support a variety of actions without appearing either quixotic or wishy-washy.

Locate and Reduce Cultural Disparities

Cultural maintenance efforts must recognize that practical actions, the inherent fuzziness of culture, the imperfections of socialization, and multiple demands of environments create internal contradictions and disparities within any culture over time. Such disparities can weaken a culture and perhaps even change it in undesired directions. While some degree of cultural disparity and contradiction will always arise and can be tolerated, managers should beware of inconsistencies and disparities that question the core ideologies. One way that managers can uncover such disparities is through the kind of cultural audit discussed earlier in this chapter. Such audits could be conducted periodically to keep the culture in tune. The initial audit may require considerable effort at consciousness-raising among managers and others engaged in the audit, but the process should become easier as participants become more sensitive to the cultural implications of activities. All kinds of practical programs and activities should be included in the audit. The more complete it is, the better chance there is of uncovering hitherto unnoticed disparities and reducing them.

Perhaps the easiest way that managers can remove or reduce disparities in cultures they wish to maintain is to eliminate and modify practical programs and actions that carry meanings at odds with the culture or with each other. They must also, of course, refrain from adding activities and programs with discrepant meanings. For example, organizations with cultures heavily weighted toward consideration for their employees are likely to send discrepant signals that confuse their employees about the culture if they start mandatory drug testing or use lie detectors during hiring. If employers want to be trusted, they probably must reciprocate by trusing their employees. At a minimum, such discrepancies must be tied to accepted ideologies and values—the importance of safety or security, for example.

Although cultures are inherently fuzzy, their fuzziness can often also be reduced. Top management pronouncements, training, newsletters, and other media of communication can be used to frequently restate and illustrate core cultural beliefs and values. The meanings of cultural forms can be made more evident by those who are sponsoring or participating in them. In general, repetition promotes familiarity and reduces ambiguity; it should help to reduce the fuzziness of culture. Managers, however, should learn to tolerate some fuzziness, both because it is unavoidable and because it has some positive value in helping people to avoid conflicts.

The imperfections of socialization are also inescapable; we cannot create precise social clones with any training, mentoring, or influence processes. But, like fuzziness, imperfections can be reduced by careful, consistent attention to the messages being conveyed in training and in all sorts of cultural communications. Managers also need to pay attention to the messages sent by their own behaviors because lower level subordinates often look for meanings in them and imitate them. Managers may also need to be willing to get rid of employees on whom attempted socialization does not take. If such cases are numerous, managers may need to attend more carefully to their selection processes to try to assure that those who join the organization do not hold cultural values that are greatly at odds with the existing culture. We do not mean to advocate discrimination against any group here—merely that managers use lawful means to screen candidates carefully.

Among the most frequent results of the many different demands that organizations encounter from their environments are multiple, sometimes conflicting goals and the growth of subcultures that deal with different segments of the environment. The issue of subcultures will be dealt with in the next section. Sometimes multiple goals are dealt with by assigning different goals to different groups, but other times the same members are expected to work simultaneously for different disparate goals. A concrete and familiar example may help to illustrate such disparities and how they can be reduced.

In universities, professors are expected to do teaching and research. While these activities are not inherently incompatible—both value scholarship, after all—they are frequently experienced by everyone involved as in conflict because, on a day-to-day basis, faculty must take time from one to do the other. They also embody different sets of values. Science and scholarship have one set of values, as enumerated in Chapter 2. Teaching involves different values and requires different skills—concern for students and some degree of showmanship, for example.

Administrators in research-oriented universities can help reduce the disparities between these two goals by reducing inflated expectations associated with both and making relative priorities clear. They can give their faculty summer salaries to do just their research. They can raise monies to allow faculty to take longer leaves from teaching to do their research. They can arrange teaching schedules to concentrate teaching responsibilities in some quarters or semesters and thus leave others free for research. But above all, they can try to advance ideologies that reconcile the two sets of demands by insisting that good teaching requires proof of adequate scholarship via publication and reward faculty accordingly. They can also try to reduce conflicting pressures on faculty by being sure that administrators concerned with nonresearch activities understand the conflicts that faculty are subject to and not add to them. Somewhat different actions would be appropriate in colleges with cultures that clearly value teaching over research. First, administrators in such colleges should make that set of priorities more evident. Most faculty had Ph.D. training that instilled in them research-oriented values and aspirations. These values should be countered and not reinforced in settings where research must take second place to teaching. Also, in those colleges where resources do not permit much accommodation to research activities, administrators could reduce cultural disparities by having and broadcasting realistic ideologies about the volume and types of research expected of faculty.

Cultural disparities and multiculturalism should not be confused. We recognize that organizations have subcultures and that some degree of cultural diversity may be desirable (Cox 1991). We are not suggesting that all subcultures must assimilate all of the values of the overall culture, although it does seem to us that some compatibility across subcultures on a few core ideologies is worth working for. Without some overreaching general ideologies, organizations do not have organizationwide cultures. Of course, the previous considerations also apply at the subcultural level because subcultures can also have cultural disparities within them.

Manage the Politics of Subcultural Relations

Because cultural analyses of organizations so often emphasize shared values, common traditions, and integrating forms such as symbols and ceremonials, busy managers may fail to realize that most established organizations spawn subcultures within them. As Chapters 5 and 6 pointed out, subcultures form around work units, friendship groups, status levels, occupations, and other factors that accentuate similarities among some persons and their differences from others. Cultural pluralism occurs in workplaces much as it does in larger social units like societies. Because subcultures pursue their own interests, which are supported by their own beliefs, values, and norms, they can be a centrifugal force in organizations. They also can develop into countercultures that actively oppose the overall organizational culture. Another possibility is that conflicts between subcultures will lead to deadlocks in decision making (Zaleznik 1970). Thus, managers cannot afford to ignore their presence.

Probably the best way to think about managing subcultures is as a political process. Experts agree that the successful management of political activity in organizations is necessary for organization effectiveness. The political perspective "emphasizes differences in objectives and preferences of subunits and concentrates on processes by which these differences get resolved"; political tactics include behaviors "that influence, or attempt to influence, the distribution of advantages and disadvantages within the organization" (Farrell and Petersen 1982, p. 405). Subcultures tend to engage in power struggles with one another for organizational resources (Pfeffer and Salancik 1974; Salancik and Pfeffer 1974). Although often carried on below the surface of organizational life, these battles are nevertheless time consuming, destructive of consensus, and damaging to employee morale and commitment. They are often the "least talked about, yet frequently the major absorber of senior management time and resources" (Tichy 1983, p. 397).

Negotiation, bargaining, compromise, accommodation, and assimilation are the basic processes by which the preferences and activities of subcultures are reconciled. As explained in Chapter 5, one way of looking at organizations is as a "negotiated order" (Fine 1984b, p. 240) that emerges from a continuous series of temporary accommodations between negotiations representing various subcultures. From this viewpoint, negotiations are one of the major ways that people work out their relationships within organizations. Continuous observations of managers at all levels in one company showed that they often acted as disturbance handlers and negotiators (Mintzberg 1973, p. 113). Lower level managers played this role more often than those at high levels, probably because of the former's location nearer to the face-to-face interactions from which many subcultures grow.

A study of two psychiatric hospitals observed both horizontal negotiations between groups of physician specialists and vertical negotiations among the different levels of staff. They followed established lines of communication and were patterned, not random. Specific negotiations were contingent on specific structural conditions, especially who talked to whom, when, and what about (Strauss 1978, p. 5).

Also, some negotiations came about in an explicit and structured way while others were set up with practically no dialogue or verbal exchanges. The outcomes of negotiations also varied in their explicitness and specificity. The more implicit and unspecific were referred to as "understandings." The more explicit and specific became "agreements" or "arrangements." In addition, the results of negotiation carried time limits; they were subject to renewal, revision, or to complete overhaul. Thus, they were far from permanent. "Negotiated order had to be worked at, and the bases of concerted action needed to be continually reconstituted. Not only were negotiations continually terminated, but new ones were also made daily" (Strauss 1978, p. 5).

The actual content of bargaining—what are considered mutually acceptable bargaining procedures—can vary for different subcultures in the same organization. For example, in one ward of another psychiatric hospital, negotiations about who was to do what took place quite openly (Schatzman and Bucher 1964). In this unit members could challenge each other, put forward deals, and consummate bargains during meetings. In a second ward, however, negotiations were far more covert, involving behind-the-scenes coalitions and cliques.

It seems likely that internal subcultural norms may vary substantially in many organizations. Thus bargaining techniques that are effective in one situation will not be equally successful in all negotiations between subcultures. Managers must be astute enough to adapt their bargaining tactics to the subcultures involved.

Encourage the Use of Cultural Forms

Cultural forms, in all of their varieties, can help managers to maintain existing, desired cultures. But they can also carry meanings at odds with prevailing cultures. Cultural forms at odds with the desired culture can arise when the cultural meanings of management-sponsored programs and policies are ignored. Consequently, managers should be careful about which forms they employ, sponsor, and encourage. They can also arise among disgruntled groups and countercultures. Young militants in some workplaces were observed to use military garb as an "anti-uniform" that not only mocked the authority arrangements in the organization, but expressed rebellion against society itself (Joseph and Alex 1972). Stories can be used to attack or deny a particular set of norms and values, as was illustrated by the Rumpelstiltskin tale narrated in Chapter 3 (Smith and Simmons 1983). Stories that rather accurately depict the unsavory features of an organization's culture are not uncommon (Wilkins 1984). Managers can best counter such negative cultural messages by astute use of other cultural forms.

Rites can be especially effective in maintaining an organization's culture because they consolidate numerous cultural forms. Managers must recognize, however, that many rites are practical activities that also have expressive consequences. If managers intend to maintain the existing culture, they must therefore assess whether the cultural messages carried by organizational activities and programs reinforce or undermine existing cultural values and beliefs. Because of their intended technical consequences, organizational rites are often designed and carried out by technical experts who are insensitive to what they express. Managers who are less involved with technical details may be better able to detect and assess the cultural messages carried by company programs. When contradictory or inconsistent messages are detected, managers should dismantle or redesign the activities involved to reduce cultural noise. Another reason to assess the cultural messages carried by rites is to preserve and strengthen those that are important expressions of the current culture. Managers who are insensitive to the valuable expressive consequences of some activities and programs might otherwise discontinue them on technical grounds, thereby unwittingly losing their expressive benefits. Only by becoming sensitive to the expressive consequences of all of their programs and activities can managers adequately evaluate which are worth preserving, which need redesign, and which can or should be discontinued (Beyer and Trice 1987).

Different cultural rites are likely to be more useful in cultural maintenance than in cultural change or creation. Rites of renewal and rites of conflict reduction are especially conservative in their latent and manifest consequences and therefore likely to be helpful in maintaining an existing culture. Rites of renewal are conservative because they refurbish existing social structures and improve their functioning. Many structural reorganizations of firms and new programs, such as continuous quality improvement, function as rites of renewal. Although they may be labeled as change efforts by those who foster them, these rites rejuvenate and reinforce existing social arrangements more than they change them. In the process, the status quo is actually strengthened and legitimated.

Rites of conflict reduction are essentially conservative because they function to reduce conflict and aggression that might disturb the status quo. For example, many committees and task forces dissipate discontents simply by airing them (Pfeffer 1981a). Researchers agree that committees are a prime mechanism for managing conflicting interests in organizations (Hickson 1987; Miles 1980).

Research in universities, where committees are abundant, found that they facilitated conflict resolution and decision making (Hickson et al. 1986). An observer of meetings concluded that "... in a fundamental sense their most important function may be to serve as a hemostat[5] in the system to validate the current social structure and to regulate and maintain order" (Schwartzman 1981, p. 80).

Other groups in which having meetings is a prime activity—boards, councils, project teams, and working parties—also function as rites of conflict reduction. They do not need to make substantive changes to reduce conflict; their existence symbolizes a willingness to cope and the stabilizing of conflicting views for a time (Edelman 1977; Cyert and March 1963). Thus, committees that accomplish little in the way of practical outcomes may still be worth preserving.

Other rites of conflict reduction include role releases, status reversals, ritual rebellion, and joking relationships (Trice and Beyer 1988). Role releases involve the temporary abandonment of formalities, norms, and role expectations. Staff parties, company picnics, and other special events can become occasions in which formal norms are put aside to permit persons of various statuses to interact as equals. Even such temporary release can help to dissipate endemic tensions arising from power and status differentials.

Status reversals go further and allow lower status persons "to exercise ritual authority over their superiors; and they, in turn, must accept with good will their ritual degradation" (V. Turner 1969, p. 172). Examples include privates being waited on by officers at Christmas Day dinner in the British Army, managers waiting on the tables of staff waiters during a staff party at a British hotel, and a special day at the Coast Guard Academy when lowerclassmen hazed upperclassmen (V. Turner 1969; Mars and Nicod 1984). Such role reversals provide safety valves for built-up angers and resentments and thereby actually buttress prevailing systems of authority.

Ritual rebellions have similar functions. Their purpose is to openly express the role conflicts that exist between holders of different roles, but in a ritualized way that does not include real rebellion. In effect, they indicate that the prevailing order is strong enough to permit its temporary suspension. The false fights that take place in collective bargaining and the skits that lampoon faculty, political figures, or other superiors at annual dinners and banquets are examples of ritual rebellions.

Joking relationships are equally ritualized but more ongoing than other rites of conflict reduction. They allow people in relationships producing chronic conflict to express their hostilities in ways that are relatively harmless. This is done by framing aggression and insults as playing or joking. The person who is the target of the hostilities is not supposed to take offense. When such relationships emerge, culturally sensitive managers will understand their origins and allow them to continue as long as they appear to release rather than add to hostilities. The tricky part of such relationships is that all parties involved have to understand and be able to accept the rules underlying the ritual. New workers may need time to learn how to cope with such relationships.

---

[5]A hemostat is a clamp or a chemical used to stop bleeding.

In general, managers who seek to maintain a culture will want to support and encourage those cultural forms that help to dissipate cultural strains and those that celebrate positive feelings and accomplishment. Rites of passage, enhancement, and integration are likely to be useful in obvious ways. Rites of passage are, of course, an important part of socialization—those social processes through which cultural understandings are transferred from member to member and, in the process, reaffirmed and renewed. Rites of enhancement are often used to reward exceptional performance of some kind. They signify that *someone noticed and someone cares*" (Kanter 1986, p. 1). An observer of the Honeywell corporation was impressed by the frequent sight of trophies and plaques, and the prevalence of award ceremonies "going on for someone, somewhere" (Kanter 1986, p. 1). Such rites, when they involve public ceremonies and audiences, are also good ways to bind members to the organization and to each other; they can, in effect, also act as rites of integration.

Emphasizing the continuity of current activities with the past history of an organization should also be valuable in maintaining cultures. Stories, sagas, and legends that celebrate a group's history and reaffirm cherished values can be told on all ceremonial occasions to emphasize cultural continuity. Established symbols, from logos to settings, should be preserved as much as possible. When changes become necessary to update or refurbish them, managers should try to discover which aspects of these artifacts have the most central symbolic value. It may be a color of a uniform or a certain style of decor or dress. They can then try to preserve these centrally symbolic aspects in the replacement.

Emphasize Continuity in Socialization

Because much of socialization is "subject to rapid and complete change at the direction of management" (Van Maanen 1978, p. 21), it can be used to either maintain cultures or to change them. As we have seen, its effects depend on the tactics used. The socialization tactics listed in Table 4.1 as institutionalized tend to produce custodial role orientations, meaning that employees so socialized will carry forward and thus continue existing cultural expectations. We will therefore focus here on the four tactics that analysts agree produce a custodial role orientation: collective, formal, sequential, and serial.

Clearly, managers who seek to maintain existing cultures should employ these tactics when possible. New employees should at least be given formal orientation sessions in groups. More extensive group training is even better. Rites of passage are particularly useful. Fully implemented, they typically result in conservative attitudes favoring the continuity and maintenance of existing ideologies and values. "If you review many of IBM's training programs you will find that a very explicit goal and a very explicit part of the program deals with IBM values" (Tichy 1983, p. 401).

The most prototypical instances of rites of passage in work organizations probably take place in military or paramilitary organizations. The socialization tactics used divest newcomers of former roles and symbolically move them into new roles while underscoring continuity of the work culture. For example, not only does police academy training separate recruits from their past worlds by the geographical isolation of training, it also puts them through debasement experiences that make them vulnerable to new work-related ideologies.

Collective formal training can also be used with established employees, of course. Just because managers have no new cultural messages to impart does not mean that such training is wasted. It can be used to update technical skills or impart new ones and also contribute to cultural maintenance by putting that updating into a context of cultural continuity. Participants can be shown how new techniques can be used to better achieve existing aims and values. By restating familiar cultural ideas, such training will serve to mute some of the inconsistencies that arise from imperfect cultural transmission, the presence of subcultures, and the inevitable adjustments involved in dealing with new uncertainties and conflicts. In this way, formal collective training can be used regularly or periodically to revitalize an organizational culture.

To the degree that such training can be employed to prepare people for an accepted and known sequence of roles, its custodial effects will be enhanced. The very existence of such training helps to legitimate the existence of gradations of expertise and status and the movement of graduates from one role to another. If persons who are or have been occupants of the role to be attained actually deliver the training, they will help to ensure that the new occupants do not deviate markedly from what was done in the past.

What if managers do not want a slavish imitation of the past, but still want to preserve the core cultural values? In such situations, managers will probably want to employ some combination of the tactics likely to produce custodial responses with some that encourage more innovative role orientations.

In general, managers need to recognize that socialization is a lifelong process that involves many passages from role to role and from one stage of work life to another. Much of the socialization employees experience as they make those passages is informal and comes from mentors, co-workers, role models, and supervisors. Much of this informal socialization is of great positive benefit to an organization and thus should be encouraged and supported. However, managers should consider how they can make inputs into these processes from time to time to assure that they do not wander away from central aims and values. Periodic training is one way to do this. Another is to create new cultural forms that can be incorporated into socialization efforts. Managers can, for example, engage in dramatic public behaviors that symbolize desired values to provide the stimulus for new stories. Such behaviors also help to create models for others to emulate.

Encourage and Develop Maintenance Leadership

In Chapter 7 we pointed out that cultural maintenance leadership could be of two types: (1) leadership the embodied the essence of the existing cultures and kept it vital; and (2) leadership that integrated diverse interests of subcultures within organizations. The essence of the difference is that embodiment leadership operates in relatively unified cultural contexts while integration leadership operates in organizations fractured by strong subcultures (Trice and Beyer 1991). Which type managers will be able to exercise thus depends heavily on the cultural configuration of their organizations.

Managers in firms that have a predominant overall culture they wish to preserve will want to act as embodiment leaders. Like Tom Watson, Jr., they will want to continue established cultural practices and perhaps add a few new ones here and there that are consistent with them. They will reiterate organizational ideologies at every opportunity and symbolize them by their behaviors. Their preoccupation will be to reinforce the existing cultural values and keep them vital. To do this, they may need, from time to time, to articulate the relevance of the existing culture to current and future circumstances. This may require some invention of new ideological elements that link existing values to new uncertainties and problems. Such inventions differ from ideologies used to change cultures in that they are relatively minor additions and that they are made to seem culturally consistent with the past rather than depart from it.

People Express Airlines was an organization with a prevailing, widely accepted ideology. It consisted of a heavy emphasis upon an abstract ideal of self-management and belief in the power of the individual employees. Consistent with this basic thrust was a persistent insistence that the organization should "... provide each individual with a direct verbal communication link to what's going on and what should be going on" (Hackman 1984, p. 47). The organization must "unleash the power of the individual" (Hackman 1984, p. 45). These ideologies operated in conjunction with a very abstract notion of being people-oriented in all things.

The company chairman consistently reinforced and embodied these beliefs. A charismatic cofounder, he often restated, and through his actions reinforced, a vision shared by practically everyone in the organization. A close observer of the company over a two-and-a-half-year period wrote:

> I could not find a single datum suggesting that alterations in the major tasks and goals of the firm were even considered. On the contrary, the evidence is that the basic vision of the organization has been constantly reinforced, disseminated, and strengthened throughout the life of the firm thus far." (Hackman 1984, p. 48)

Through enormous growth, environmental upheavals, and technological change, the chairman steadfastly adhered to the vision, and by his actions, words, and deeds, became an embodiment of the core values of the culture.

Integration leadership is quite a different enterprise. Although subcultures may at times be neutral to or compatible with one another, they are more likely to have conflicting elements in their ideologies. When those conflicts stem from differences that have value or cannot be avoided, maintaining an organization's cultures consists of reconciling subcultural differences sufficiently so that needed cooperation is achieved despite the differences. This task is probably more difficult than that of keeping ongoing ideologies and cultural forms vital.

One way to look at the integration leader is as a catalyst "... bringing together relevant parties and guiding debate, but never forcing issues in a charismatic way, or relying bureaucratically and rigidly on standard operating procedures" (Pondy and Huff 1985, p. 112). For example, a school superintendent involved in introducing computerization into the curriculum of a school system made use of existing routines that were well established and thus was able to use this change to integrate all segments of the system. His actions emphasized continuity rather than change. He used familiar procedures and existing forms to implement the new technology and establish its place in the system. For example, even when he made public speeches to the staff supporting the computerization of the school curriculum, the speech was done in the context of regularly scheduled events and public addresses. The routine itself "symbolized the unexceptional nature of a change that might otherwise have aroused considerably more attention" (Pondy and Huff 1985, p. 103). Under the umbrella of these accepted procedures, the superintendent integrated diverse subcultures in the school system and successfully implemented the introduction of this technological change into his school system without disrupting the ongoing subcultures within it.

Another prominent feature of integration leaders is that they "must live at the boundary between two or more groups with differing needs and orientations" (Wilkins 1989, p. 186), managing tensions between them and facilitating compromise. The examples of Pierre Du Pont and Lyndon Johnson given in Chapter 7 amply demonstrate these behaviors. Both were realistic politicians adroit at bargaining and compromise.

SUMMARY

Before they can manage the cultures in their organizations effectively, managers need to become culturally aware; they need to know and understand their organization's cultures. They must also recognize and use various levers they have available to influence their cultures and resolve the ethical dilemmas involved. In all of these efforts, they need to recognize and learn to accept that some degree of ambivalence, confusion, and contradiction, is inevitable. Finally, they must decide whether they should try to maintain, change, or create a culture. Given the multiculturalism of most large organizations, managers in them may find they want to do some of all three. We suggest that a primary emphasis should be chosen—that top management must decide what it wants to do about the core elements of the overall culture. This decision should determine the dominant flavor of culture management in that organization. If different types of culture management are needed in different segments of the organization, these should be delegated to different managers, not to the ones leading the dominant culture management effort. To be effective, cultural leadership should convey consistent messages.

Although maintaining cultures carries some dangers, it occurs and is probably beneficial in some circumstances. Organizations seem to alternate short periods of intense change with longer periods of relative stability. Many of the issues involved in maintaining cultures can be distilled into eight pre-scriptive aphorisms:

- don't assume continuity, work for it
- respect the past, but adapt to the present
- adapt existing ideologies to current challenges and crises
- locate and reduce cultural disparities
- manage the politics of subcultural relations
- encourage the use of cultural forms
- emphasize continuity in socialization
- encourage and develop maintenance leadership

They were formulated to condense into a manageable and understandable form the many complexities involved in managing cultures. They illustrate how the various levers available to manage cultures are most likely to operate in maintaining organizational cultures.

The next chapter will offer rather different sets of aphorisms for managers engaged in changing or creating cultures.

10

Changing and Creating Organizational Cultures

When Winton Blount was named postmaster general in 1972, he was charged with making the post office pay its own way. To do so, he needed to discredit and destroy the old ideologies of dependency on Congress and of providing "service, service at all costs" (Biggart 1977, p. 417). To symbolize the new order, he replaced many established symbols and cultural forms with new ones. To signal the change of political status, the 200-year-old name of the post office was changed. A new logo, new typeface for all publications, and new postal colors were put in place. Nationwide birthday parties were held in every post office in the country, and a new stamp was printed with the new logo to commemorate the event. The old seal of the Post Office Deparment, which depicted a colonial rider (Paul Revere), was ceremonially removed and replaced by an eagle poised for flight.

Truncated rites of degradation were used to remove older, up-from-the-ranks managers who represented the old culture. Employees with high seniority were offered a one-time bonus of six months' pay if they would retire immediately. Many took the offer, and subsequent retirement ceremonies helped to communicate that the values of the retiring members were supplanted by a new set of values. With this one stroke, much of the former leadership was destroyed, thus clearing the way for newer employees who might be more receptive to the new culture of self-sufficiency.

An employee newsletter that had been staid and innocuous was drastically changed to vigorously espouse the new ideologies of adaptation to change and cost efficiency. It became a vehicle for advocating and explaining automation, changes in working conditions, and an internal competitive spirit. Recipes gave way to articles applauding post offices that met new efficiency standards—e.g., "What makes Ft. Worth Number one?" (Biggart 1977, p. 420). A management-oriented monthly magazine was initiated and Blount held face-to-face management briefings with field managers in all parts of the country to espouse the new ideologies among management at all levels. (Adapted from Biggart 1977).

Because it entails introducing something new and substantially different from what prevails in existing cultures, cultural innovation is bound to be more difficult than cultural maintenance. Managers who want to change existing cultures need to find ways to incorporate new elements into prevalent ideologies and cultural forms. Managers who want to create cultures need to figure out how to develop and inculcate distinctive sets of ideologies and cultural forms that will fit their circumstances and membership. Whether changing or creating cultures, managers inevitably need to replace some of existing ideologies, symbols, and customs with new ones. Even in new organizations, members do not arrive without cultural baggage from their pasts.

The underlying duality of creation and destruction that is required by innovation is often downplayed by those who preach it. But when innovation occurs, some things replace or displace others. As mentioned briefly in Chapter 9, people often resist such changes. They have good reasons to. It is realistic for people to expect that any change will bring some losses as well as possible gains. Often the losses are more certain than the gains. The successful management of the processes of culture change or creation thus often entails convincing people that likely gains outweigh the losses.

Like the prior chapter, this one will present separate sets of suggestions for managing culture change and culture creation. We will begin by considering how to manage culture change. But first we will discuss a question that is seldom addressed in the literature on organizations—how to think about change itself in a relatively precise way.

Ways of Thinking About Culture Change

There are three basic ways that analysts have considered what cultural change is and what it means. One is to define cultural change by what it is and is not. The second is to describe what appears, from observation, to be qualitatively different types of cultural change. The third is to assess the likely effects of any specific change along dimensions representing specific aspects of organizational functioning. All three really deal with the same important question: When is a culture sufficiently altered so that it makes sense to say it has *changed?*

The answer to this question has practical as well as academic ramifications. To be effective in managing their cultures, managers need to be clear about what the main thrust of that management will be. They need to decide whether their efforts will be directed primarily at cultural maintenance or innovation. If they are not sure, it is unlikely that their subordinates and other stakeholders will receive clear messages of their intent.

A Definition of Culture Change

Discussing culture change can be very confusing unless we define what we mean by change. As described in Chapter 1, cultures are dynamic entities; they naturally give rise to all kinds of incremental changes. Furthermore, as discussed in Chapter 9, attempts to maintain a culture inevitably involve some adjustments in ideologies and cultural forms that could be considered changes. Neither of these forms of change, however, are what most experts and managers mean when they refer to culture change. Most mean something more deliberate, drastic, and profound than incremental changes or cultural adjustments. We will reserve the term *culture change* to refer to planned, more encompassing, and more substantial kinds of changes than those which arise spontaneously within cultures or as a part of conscious efforts to keep an existing culture vital. Culture change involves a break with the past; cultural continuity is noticeably disrupted. It is an inherently disequilibriating process.

Considering what culture change is not is one way to begin the search for a definition. One observer concluded that "... a few examples of new practices here and there throughout an organization do not represent 'culture change'; they need to be woven into the entire fabric of the system" (Kanter 1984, p. 196). Thus, culture change amounts to more than a reduction in litter and vandalism, the promotion of executive health, or the turnaround of an unprofitable two-year history. On the positive side, other analysts suggest culture change is marked by

> ... real changes in the behavior of people throughout the organization. In a technical sense we mean people in the organization identifying with new role-model heroes ... telling different stories to one another ... spending their time differently on a day-to-day basis ... asking different questions and carrying out different work rituals. (Deal and Kennedy 1982, p. 158).

Like the description of culture change that opened this chapter, these analyses make it clear that culture change in organizations is not an easy process; rather it is a difficult, complicated, and demanding effort that may not succeed. It involves not one change, but many changes in many cultural elements so that "... *together* [they] reflect a new pattern of values, norms, and expectations" (Kanter 1984, p. 196). Such concerted, widespread changes don't happen spontaneously. Rather they are planned and consciously carried out—usually at the instigation of top management.

Because it involves such wholesale change, culture change is a relatively drawn out and slow process. The popular press during the 1980s seemed to suggest the possibility that new "designer cultures" could be produced quickly. More cautious thinking has challenged such facile promises, but they have not entirely disappeared. Most experts now agree that culture change usually takes several years to accomplish.

Types of Culture Change

Accounts describe at least three different types of culture change efforts in organizations. Some of these efforts seek to bring about massive changes in whole organizations with as much speed as possible. Others are just as radical, but are confined to only parts of an organization. Still others involve many smaller changes that are spread out over years and decades. The descriptions seem to fall into three basic types: (1) revolutionary and comprehensive efforts to change the cultures of entire organizations; (2) efforts confined largely to changing specific subcultures or subunits within organizations; and (3) efforts that are gradual and incremental, but nevertheless cumulate in a comprehensive reshaping of an entire organization's culture. The changes made at the post office in the 1970s and described at the opening of this chapter exemplify the first type—revolutionary, comprehensive culture change. Efforts that transformed the L-1011 plant at Lockheed, which will be described later in this chapter, exemplify the second type—culture change limited to subcultures or subunits. The last type is exemplified by Cadbury, Limited, the British chocolate confectionery company that continuously and self-consciously modified its culture over a period of almost thirty years to fit its changing environment (Child and Smith 1987).

All of these were planned and conscious change efforts. What makes them different from each other? In a very general sense they seem to differ in terms of the *amounts* of change they involved. It is hard to be more precise because change is such a global and fuzzy concept. Only by breaking down the change process into some of its components can we begin to clarify how much change one particular planned change effort entails as compared to another.

Assessing Amounts of Change

If culture change is viewed as an ongoing process, and not a discrete event or outcome, it becomes easier to disaggregate different aspects of the process. Change processes can be described along four dimensions that help to clarify the amount of change involved in a planned culture change. These dimensions, already introduced briefly in Chapter 7, are the pervasiveness, magnitude, innovativeness, and duration of a change process (Beyer and Trice 1978, pp. 18-20). By analyzing an envisioned change in terms of these dimensions, managers will have a better understanding of the amounts of change they are taking on.

The *pervasiveness* of an envisioned culture change is the proportion of the activities in an organization that will be affected by it. This proportion is determined by at least two factors: how many members are expected to change their cultural understandings and behaviors, and how frequently these changes will call upon them to behave differently in doing their work. For example, when the U.S. Post Office became a public corporation rather than a government agency, all of its employees were affected in the sense that all were expected to be more cognizant of costs and efficiency than in the past. Also, technological improvements and structural reorganizations affected the ways in which the mail was handled and thus the ways in which many employees did their work. Thus, this culture change was a very pervasive one.

The *magnitude* of a change involves the distance between old understandings and behaviors and the new ones members are expected to adopt. Will organizational members see the new desired ideologies and values as close to ones they already hold or as very different and distant from them? Are some existing ideologies and values now so incompatible with the desired culture that members

must stop subscribing to them and put others in their place? In effect, must parts of the existing cultures be destroyed or just displaced somewhat? Looking at the behavioral side, how much replacement or displacement of programs and activities that act as cultural forms is involved? How much will the status quo be disturbed in regard to time allocations, status, power, and other resources? When the post office was reorganized, existing values favoring service to all at any cost needed to be replaced by values favoring the best service possible within budgetary constraints (Biggart 1977). Employees apparently saw this as a change of large magnitude.

Innovativeness refers to the degree to which the ideas and behaviors required by a desired culture are unprecedented or have some similarity to what already happened somewhere. If a desired culture is similar to that used by other groups or organizations, managers and members can adapt what others have learned about how such a culture works. In particular, they can perhaps imitate some of the cultural forms that help to communicate and affirm such a culture.[1] If it is not similar, originality will be required to devise cultural forms with novel content. Also relevant is whether some groups inside the organization already have a subculture similar to the desired culture. If any internal examples exist, managers and other members can learn something from them. But if a totally new and radical culture is envisioned, managers and members must invent new networks of ideologies and values to give it substance. They may also have to invent variations of cultural forms no one has ever tried before. The cultural change at the post office was innovative in some respects but not others. Competitors like United Parcel Service and other delivery firms were already providing high-quality service within financial constraints. These other organizations could serve as models for some of the post office's services. For other services—especially the handling of the regular mail—there were no other providers to imitate or learn from.

Genuinely innovative organizational cultures are rare. But they do happen occasionally. Southwest Airlines seems to have one, which will be described later in this chapter. The defunct People Express Airlines imitated the Southwest Airlines culture in various ways. Current examples of necessarily innovative cultures are those being developed in consortia, like MCC (Microelectronics and Computer Technology Corporation) and Sematech, that have been set up to facilitate research in the semiconductor industry. Because many of their employees are on loan from member firms, managers within these consortia are faced with building organizational cultures that will encourage members of competitive firms in the same industry to cooperate. Furthermore, they must try to build these

---

[1]The imitation of Japanese quality circles provides a well-known example of such cultural borrowing. U.S. users did not invent this cultural form; therefore it was not a totally new cultural innovation. However, the first U.S. users of quality circles did confront a more innovative change than later users because the first users had to figure out how to adapt this cultural form to the U.S. culture. The hazards of borrowing cultural forms are also evident from this example. Most observers agree that quality circles have had only modest success in the United States and have not been successfully grafted onto U.S. organizational cultures (Lawler and Mohrman 1987, Shea 1986).

cooperative cultures in a society in which individualism and competitiveness are dominant values. We know of no models or precedents for these efforts.

Duration refers to how long a change effort is likely to take and how permanent the change will be. While all radical organizationwide culture changes take years, some are more protracted than others. We would expect that culture change in organizations with poor performance or rapidly changing environments would proceed more rapidly than that in other organizations. While management usually intends cultural changes to persist over the foreseeable future, some cultures are temporary—either because they deal with temporary circumstances that are clearly recognized as such, or because they grow up in temporary organizations.

An additional problem faced by the managers of the research consortia already mentioned is that those employees who are on loan from their home companies know their sojourn in their consortia cultures is temporary. Other employees who work directly for the consortia know their cultures will affect them more permanently. Given these circumstances, commitment of employees to these consortia's cultures may vary according to the expected duration of their stay. Those who have permanent status would have greater motivation to become part of the consortia culture than those who are temporary. Fortunately, high commitment to a temporary distinctive culture is possible to achieve. When Peter Ueberroth formed an organization to put on the Olympic Games in Los Angeles in 1984, both he and the employees he hired knew that they were building a temporary organization. Nevertheless they became highly committed to its mission and their culture (McDonald 1988).

Because the four dimensions of change are conceptually distinct, we should not expect any given change to be either high or low on all dimensions. In assessing amounts of culture change, managers will want to especially consider the magnitude and innovativeness of a change; together these dimensions indicate how much the envisioned changes represent a break with the past. If magnitude is high and innovativeness is low or medium, managers are facing a culture change effort. If innovativeness is high, managers may need to create a new culture, especially if the change will also be pervasive. This is what General Motors chose to do in founding the Saturn Corporation. Saturn represents GM's attempt to build cars in what is a radically new way for that company and its employees. If both magnitude and innovativeness are low, managers are dealing with cultural maintenance rather than innovation. The pervasiveness of an envisioned change indicates how comprehensive it will be. High pervasiveness indicates that the whole organization must be persuaded to change; low pervasiveness indicates that the change effort can be targeted to certain subunits or groups. Table 10–1 combines the three types of change discussed in the last section with the four dimensions just discussed. The table shows that different dimensions of change are key indicators of the types of culture change described in the literature. While other combinations of dimensions are possible, these appear to be the most common.

The third type of culture change is the least discontinuous of the three. The

TABLE 10–1
TYPES AND DIMENSIONS OF CULTURE CHANGE

Types of Culture Change	Placement on Dimensions
1. Revolutionary, comprehensive	Pervasiveness: high
	Magnitude: high
	Innovativeness: variable
	Duration: variable
2. Subunit or subculture	Pervasiveness: low
	Magnitude: moderate to high
	Innovativeness: variable
	Duration: variable
3. Cumulative comprehensive reshaping	Pervasiveness: high
	Magnitude: moderate
	Innovativeness: moderate
	Duration: high

culture breaks that occur are numerous, but each is moderate in magnitude. Also, this type of change tends to seek pervasive changes—ones intended to affect virtually all employees to some degree. Because the cultural reshaping occurs gradually, through many changes that accumulate and are internalized over time, this type of change may be easiest to implement and most enduring.

Specific Considerations in Changing Cultures

As in the prior chapter, we will offer sets of aphorisms that distill our understandings of key issues involved in cultural innovation. This section will focus on suggestions for managing culture change. The next section will focus on suggestions for managing culture creation.

Capitalize on Propitious Moments

Culture change is best initiated at propitious moments, when some obvious problem, opportunity, or change in circumstances makes change seem desirable. As described in Chapter 9, by the time that John Egan and his new management team took over at Jaguar, performance was so poor that another cultural change could be readily justified. Many analyses of all kinds of social changes point to the presence of accumulated excesses or deficiencies of the past social order as triggers to cultural revolutions (Lundberg 1985b; Miller and Friesen 1980; Meyer 1982b; Kuhn 1970).

Managers should be cautious not only about whether culture change is appropriate and really needed in terms of the criteria listed in Chapter 9, but also about whether they can persuade members and outside constituents that a culture change is justified. They should not assume that because the need for change seems obvious to them it is obvious to others. Proponents of culture change often need to dramatize the circumstances that call for change to various stakeholders in order to win their support and cooperation. This may require sharing some bad news about the organization that management is reluctant to disclose lest it reflect badly on their performance. Fortunately, any problems that have accumulated can often be blamed on environmental change of some sort (Salancik and Meindl 1984).

At the same time it is probably unwise to fabricate propitious moments:

> It may be possible to manufacture crises, but such attempts are likely to be transparent to employees and thus prove futile. This implies that to initiate culture change, key leaders must have a sense of timing that enables them to seize those opportunities for change that inevitably occur over a firm's lifetime. (Dyer 1985, p. 222)

Opportunities that practically demand culture change—the discovery of a lucrative marketing niche or a new source of venture capital–can suddenly appear in the environment and provide justifications. In addition, "revolutions" may occur that trigger crises and propitious moments for culture change (Miller and Friesen 1980, p. 591). These can be both internal (a coup by "young Turks") or external (nationalization of company property in a foreign country). Research on hospitals caught up in a doctor's strike that constituted a sudden environmental jolt led to the following observations:

> When they are labeled as crises, jolts infuse organizations with energy, legitimize unorthodox acts, and destroy power structures.... [A] hospital's board had long sought to replace the administrator. During the strike he was scapegoated and shortly afterwards he was purged.... By plunging organizations into unfamiliar circumstances, jolts can legitimate unorthodox experiments that revitalize them. (Meyer 1982a, p. 533)

In much the same vein, a study of 26 companies found "... dramatic periods of revolution in which a very great many trends are reversed." According to this analysis, revolutions arise either because many excesses or deficiencies have accumulated during periods of pervasive momentum or because a new strategy requires realignments. A "myriad of structural and strategic reversals" follows (Miller and Friesen 1980, p. 591). The authors liken these developments to revolutions that occur in the development of scientific knowledge, when tradition-bound stages are interrupted by revolutionary breaks (Kuhn 1970). They suggest that organizational breaks come about because of two major forces: shifts in power that permit the emergence of new ideologies, and deteriorations in performance that cause a search for remedies. Together these factors create especially propitious moments to launch pervasive culture changes of large magnitude.

Combine Caution with Optimism

Once they have decided to embark on a cultural change effort, managers need to create an optimistic outlook on what the change effort will bring. While cultures are undoubtedly difficult to change (Uttal 1983; Barley and Louis 1983; Beyer 1981; Martin and Siehl 1983), managers must have confidence that they can succeed or they will likely communicate their doubts to others. A thorough understanding of the various leverage points they have available to them should help to create such confidence. It will also help if they realize that cultures inevitably change anyway, and that it is natural for them as managers to attempt to channel and initiate such change (Jones 1984). Consistency and persistence in their efforts is absolutely essential in conveying optimism and confidence.

One way to resolve doubts about whether an organization's culture can be changed is to realize that the truth lies roughly halfway between extreme views on the subject. Recall that some analysts claim it is practically impossible to change cultures deliberately. According to this argument, cultures are too elusive and hidden to be accurately described, managed, or changed (Uttal 1983). Other analyses, however, imply that cultures can be readily manipulated, suggesting that managers can use direct, intentional actions to change their cultures (Peters and Waterman 1982: Deal and Kennedy 1982; Kilmann 1982). A consensus seems to be emerging that the middle ground between these two viewpoints is realistic. Thus, both caution and optimism are warranted.

A study of innovative programs in local offices of federal agencies showed that changes were better implemented when local agency directors exhibited a positive and supportive attitude toward the changes (Beyer and Trice 1978). When genuine change is sought, "the [job] of the prime movers is not only to 'talk up' the new strategy, but also to manipulate those symbols that indicate commitment to it" (Kanter 1985, p. 361).

Managers must temper their optimism with some caution because culture changes frequently have dysfunctional, unintended consequences as well as functional, intended ones. A classic example from another culture is the increase in warfare that occurred among the Indians of the Northwest following missionaries' successful repression of Potlatch ceremonies. The missionaries forbade these highly competitive rites becasue they involved different tribal chiefs trying to outdo each other in ostentatious destructions of their property. Once the Potlatch was suppressed, these tribes turned to physical rather than symbolic warfare with one another—clearly an unintended and dysfunctional consequence (Dandridge 1983, p. 77).

Another reason to be cautious as well as optimistic is that culture change can provoke substantial amounts of resistance. Some understanding of the sources of resistance may help managers to remove some sources and reduce others. It is hard to see how a change effort that engenders high levels of resistance from many sources will succeed and be functional for an organization.

Understand Resistance to Culture Change

As pointed out earlier, research on organizational change of all kinds has documented many reasons that people resist change. Table 10-2 gives a fairly comprehensive listing of common sources of such resistance. All of them may come into play in culture change efforts. The first, *fear of the unknown,* is what the trapeze metaphor recounted in Chapter 9 is about. But not only are people afraid to try something new, they are also afraid to give up what they feel are proven solutions to their problems. Even if they know such solutions have limitations, they are familiar with the limitations. In effect, to change their cultural understandings or practices is to create new uncertainties—the very thing that they use their cultures to reduce.

Changes in cultures threaten people's *self-interests* because they get certain practical advantages from the status quo. They have economic benefits like salary and bonuses, and they have some degree of status and power—both of which could be decreased or lost in a contemplated change. They may also lose the leverage that their skills and work routines have within their workgroup or the organization as a whole.

TABLE 10-2
COMMON SOURCES OF RESISTANCE TO CHANGE

At the individual level:
   Fear of the unknown
   Self-interest
   Selective attention and retention
   Habit
   Dependence
   Need for security

At the organization or group level:
   Threats to power and influence
   Lack of trust
   Different perceptions and goals
   Social disruption
   Resource limitations
   Fixed investments
   Interorganizational agreements

SOURCE: Adapted from Hellriegel, Slocum, and Woodman 1986; and Daft and Steers, 1986.

Because the substance of their cultures provides accepted ways of perceiving and making sense of their worlds, people are likely to have difficulties in *attending to and remembering* distinctions that do not correspond to their present ideologies. They may simply *delete* any ideas that are not consistent with what they already believe and value. Even if they undergo training and manage to parrot some understanding of new ideas, they may tend to forget those that do not fit into present sets of meanings.

The *habits* that involve accustomed ways of doing things often become cultural forms. Over time, habits come to be invested with accepted, shared meaning. This is especially true in occupations, which often make certain ways of doing tasks into sacrosanct rituals.

In a cultural sense, *people depend on each other* for shared understandings and some degree of emotional support. Thus, individuals may be reluctant to support change efforts until they see others doing so. People vary in the strength of their dependencies; some are relatively more independent. Leaders are those who can persuade the more dependent to follow them.

People with certain personality characteristics will tend to cling to the past for *security*. Dogmatic individuals hold rigidly to existing beliefs and will resent those who question them, especially if the questioners are not part of the existing authority system. Those with an internal locus of control may resent external attempts to change their beliefs and behaviors. Other individuals will resist change because their self-esteem is so low that they have little confidence that they can cope with change.

At a group or organizational level, other factors may come into play. Cultural change may alter existing webs of interdependencies and thus *threaten a group's and even a whole organization's power*. Groups and organizations depend on each other for information and other resources that may be more or less important and valued after cultural change.

Cultural change is especially difficult to achieve in organizations and groups with a history of *mistrust* of their leaders and of each other. Punitive or manipulative management practices will tend to create distrust at both levels. When faced with coercion, people often end up protecting themselves to the detriment of others. When faced with chronic manipulation, they become cynical and try to play the game.

Subcultures lead to *different perceptions and goals* within groups and organizations and thus create barriers to pervasive cultural change efforts. These barriers will be especially severe if the existing overall culture did not encourage communication across departmental and occupational lines and thus allowed these groupings to avoid surmounting their subcultural differences in the past to cooperate with and understand each other.

The expectation of *disruptions to social relations* may also create resistance to cultural change. Over time, people come to value their interpersonal interactions and group memberships in their work organizations. Many depend heavily on their work settings to satisfy their social needs. One of the central functions of culture is to smooth and make such relations somewhat pleasant and depend-able. To the degree that culture change may move people around and change their social interaction patterns, they may be inclined to resist it.

Groups and organizations may want to make changes but *lack the practical and cultural resources* to do so. Cultural change often has economic costs, and the organization may have few financial resources for training, relocation, new tech-nology, or whatever the cultural change envisions. Cultural change also requires some cultural resources, especially cultural leaders with appropriate skills and personalities.

Fixed investments tend to constrain cultural change because they put groups and whole organizations into certain locations using certain kinds of equipment. It costs a great deal to move plants, do extensive remodeling, or change an entire technological approach to production. Yet each of these carries with it certain cultural implications. For example, a plant in a blighted urban area may have difficulty attracting workers with certain levels of training that are needed to use more sophisticated work procedures. A plant with assembly line equipment cannot inexpensively tear it out for more flexible technologies.

Interorganizational agreements are perhaps the most subtle barrier to culture change. Various groups in the environment—customers, suppliers, and even gov-ernment regulators—come to have a stake in how an organization conducts its business; they, too, come to depend on the predictability of certain ways of doing things. Thus, when a group's or an organization's culture changes, all those who interact with it will be affected to some degree by the change. If they see the change as costly to them in some respects, they may use whatever power they have to resist it. Even if they are more favorable or neutral about the change, they may not know how to alter their own interlocked behaviors so that they will not interfere with it. This is why experts say that suppliers and customers must become partners in organizations' quality improvement efforts.

Change Many Elements, but Maintain Some Continuity

Another lesson worth noting from the second culture change[2] at Jaguar is that while the new culture incorporated many new elements, it also preserved some valued elements of the traditional culture that had been displaced. By do-ing this, the new management emphasized the past positive accomplishments of Jaguar alongside its need to make some changes. Members were much less likely to resist the changes because these were not seen as destroying everything they already valued. Instead the new elements of the new culture could be seen as building positively upon some of those values.

One way to honor the past and maintain continuity is to identify the princi-ples that will remain constant "in the midst of turbulence, both internal and external" (Wilkins 1989, p. 56). Hewlett-Packard, for example, has been forced

---

[2]Recall that the first cultural change occurred when its acquirer, British Leyland, tried to sup-press the existing Jaguar culture. The second occurred when John Egan took over and encouraged a revival of elements of that culture.

by its growth to develop large corporate structures that require increased coordination between far-flung operations. Despite these changed conditions, HP management has made substantial efforts to continue the "HP way"—an emphasis on decentralized operations, autonomous management, and the promotion of employee welfare. By increasing the number of meetings and coordinating efforts among division general managers, HP has been able to maintain division autonomy. "By focusing upon what will remain unchanged, and showing that these commitments will be kept inviolate, the company has apparently been able to significantly improve coordination between divisions" (Wilkins 1989, p. 57).

Another way to relate constructively to the past, yet engage in basic change, is to divide the organization's past into specific eras:

> The past administrator of a hospital system had engaged in significant building projects and was regarded by employees as a "brick and mortar man" rather than a healthcare professional. When the new administrator was brought in he quickly sized up the situation and labeled the past era as a "building and development phase." He suggested that the new phase would focus on consolidation and elaboration of the professional skills of the hospital system. Most of the people in the system accepted this labeling of eras. (Wilkins 1989, p. 59)

Of course, changing organizational cultures requires not one change, but many changes in many different cultural elements. In particular, change efforts must encompass both ideologies and the accumulated cultural forms that express them. It is not easy to keep cultural practices and associated meanings consistent with each other and with new ideologies as changes occur. Since ideologies lie at the core of culture, change efforts must be aimed directly at changing "the experiences people have and what they learn from them so that assumptions and core values are altered" (Wilkins and Patterson 1985, p. 289). Detailed studies of cultural change at Jaguar and at a British merchant bank showed that attempts to alter cultures by attending only to cultural beliefs have little success. "Those efforts which are directed towards the essence of . . . values, *as well as* the logics, languages, metaphors or status patterns in which they are embodied promise greater return" (Whipp, Rosenfeld, and Pettigrew 1989, p. 581 [emphasis added]).

One of the main efforts made to change the culture of a large, old public agency—The Metropolitan Sewer and Water District (MSWD)—directly and firmly confronted a prevailing and highly entrenched bureaucratic ideology (Deal and Kennedy 1982, p. 170). In the old culture, "everything was done by the book." When water usage clearly exceeded capacity, political authorites appointed a new general manager. He quickly appointed three major task forces—including one on personnel, thus directly challenging the widely held belief that bureaucratic personnel constraints could not be changed. He also inaugurated a series of weekly staff meetings that directly challenged the old ideology by encouraging direct, informal communications between units that had rarely communicated at all. The task forces acted as rites of creation that expressed new values and, at the same time, devised practical ways to get things done. Managerial training served as rites of passage by which current managers were resocialized to new values, new behaviors, and even new language (Deal and Kennedy

1982, p. 173). To honor the agency's past, the new general manager sent a memo early in the change process promising no firings, layoffs, or pressures to retire—even though the average age of the staff was over fifty-five.

> Six months later no one could doubt that MSWD was significantly different.... There was a clear set of agreed upon priorities, a sense of real urgency in pursuing these priorities, and the beginnings of a "we can make it happen" mentality. Dillon [the new general manager] believed that within one more year of operation in these new modes, the new culture would really take hold. (Deal and Kennedy 1982, p. 174)

Recognize the Importance of Implementation

An informal survey of management consultants found that over 90 percent of American companies have been unable to carry out changes in corporate strategies (Kiechel 1979). This astonishing figure dramatizes the fact that many adopted changes are never successfully implemented. Initial acceptance and enthusiasm are insufficient to carry change forward. Many carefully adopted changes are subsequently abandoned.

Every stage of any change process carries the hazard of omission, abandonment, or return to an earlier stage. A simplified three-stage model of a change process begins with adoption—the decision to make some change. The next stage is implementation—the actions required to put the change in place. The last stage is institutionalization—the persistent incorporation of the change into the daily routines and cultures of the organization (Beyer and Trice 1978). While these stages may overlap, especially in culture change efforts, the model is useful in showing that how thoroughly and well a logically prior stage is executed is likely to affect the next stage. In particular, it suggests that the institutionalization of a culture change effort depends heavily on how well it is implemented.

The Japanese have displayed a greater tenacity and determination to effect desired changes than have American managers. The Japanese take implementation very seriously. While quality circles and statistical process controls did not originate in Japan, they helped to fuel the Japanese manufacturing ascendancy. Japanese managers have adopted and implemented these programs better than American companies do. Recent research on quality circles in the United States shows that they generate initial excitement and enthusiasm, but that U.S. organizations usually falter in implementing them. Managers lose interest and fail to devote the time and training required to support them. The result is that many companies abandon the circles before they can have an impact (Lawler and Mohrman 1987).

Other analyses suggest that their failure may be because the ways in which U.S. quality circles have been implemented send messages to workers that do not reflect managers' beliefs and intentions. Managers in the United States want to use circles to solve quality problems; but they do not expect to relinquish their control over what issues are addressed. Workers in these circles, however, tend to see them as a signal that management will be receptive to workers' ideas for change, including "how people get treated" (Shea 1986, p. 37). These misunderstandings arise because quality circles are advanced by their U.S. proponents as a "multipurpose technology, one that can foster basic organizational change, improve workplace problem solving, alter work relations fundamentally, and not threaten managerial authority" (Shea 1986, p. 36). Such broad and multiple purposes allow mangers and workers to each focus on different aims and can lead to disappointment for both groups.

Both of these analyses suggest that the failure of quality circles in the United States is largely a failure of implementation. Implementation itself usually involves three stages: (1) diffusion of information about the changes to members of the organization; (2) members becoming receptive to the changes; and (3) actual performance or use of whatever is supposed to change (Beyer and Trice 1978). A study of the implementation of policy changes in federal government agencies illustrates these stages. Results showed that greater diffusion led to greater familiarity with the policies, and that both familiarity and diffusion were associated with greater past and expected future use. It seems unlikely that successful cultural change can be implemented by ignoring any of these three stages. Rather it seems likely that sensitive execution at all stages will produce desired understanding and behaviors more uniformly and frequently than less complete and systematic efforts.

The kinds of strategies that can be employed to diffuse a cultural innovation are well illustrated by what happened when Blount set out to change the U.S. Post Office (Biggart, 1977). His implementation strategies employed extensive communications and training. Because unhappy mailers frequently complained to members of Congress, the new United States Postal Service (USPS) created a consumer advocate position in an effort to funnel complaints away from Congress. It also established an Office of Advertising to propagate its new image of autonomy from outsiders and from Congress. At the same time, it dispatched top level executives on media tours to hold briefings in all regions of the country. Finally, training of supervisors focused upon learning new businesslike attitudes and unlearning old practices of relating to employees, customers, and work itself. A large training institute was established in Bethesda, Maryland with a 75-member faculty of specialists in training, development, and technical areas. They trained approximately 20,000 supervisors a year. Also, members of this faculty often went to major post offices and conducted on-site training in decision making directed explicitly at reducing the accumulated emphasis on authoritarianism in the organization.

Despite the many avenues Blount used to implement culture change, critics of the post office see considerable cultural persistence. Many feel the post office has not entirely shed its old ways and that its competitors are still more efficient and businesslike. But it is hard to deny that the post office has changed. What critics see are residues of the old culture. It is unrealistic to expect a complete disappearance of an existing culture without total destruction of the group or organization involved or dispersal of its members. Even then, members will carry much of what they learned in that culture with them as they enter new organizations or join new groups. All culture change is partial; it cannot reasonably be expected to achieve total eradication of a prior culture. Even when envisioned changes are pervasive and of great magnitude, culture change usually amounts to some degree of modification of a culture. Changes that entail innovative responses—unprecedented and genuinely unfamiliar understandings and behaviors—are likely to result in the most radical cultural change.

Select, Modify, and Create Appropriate Cultural Forms

Numerous scholars have suggested that cultural change comes about by managers' employing symbols, rituals, languages, and stories to modify cultural meanings. Some argue that the manipulation of symbols is the "very stuff" of managerial behavior (Peters 1978, p. 10; Schein 1985). The actions of managers can also symbolically legitimate changes in the culture (Pfeffer 1981a; Jones 1984). Their calendar and phone behavior, the apportionment of their time, and their control of settings are powerful symbolic tools managers can use to change organizational cultures. The presence or absence of top managers, the location of meetings, who attends, what types of questions managers ask—all of these act as "mundane tools" that can be consciously "packaged and managed" (Peters 1978, p. 10). Other scholars advise that managers should "be seen as spending a lot of time on matters visibly related to the values they preach" (Deal and Kennedy 1982, p. 169).

Metaphors can also be effective vehicles for change (Krefting and Frost 1985, p. 155). By changing or eliminating long-standing metaphors that depict an old organizational ideology, a culture can be moved toward change. For example, the elimination of the family metaphor "Ma Bell" signaled that AT&T was modifying its protective ideology relative to employees and customers. A new symbol was chosen for the new culture—a globe girdled by electronic communications. Long-standing metaphors can be hard to eradicate, however. As pointed out earlier, the press still regularly refers to the regional companies spun off from AT&T more than ten years ago as Baby Bells.

Devising and promulgating new myths has also been advocated as a particularly effective way to change cultures (Boje, Fedor, and Rowland 1982). Through myths, managers can invent new explanations for the way things are. They can also change existing myths in various ways (Hedberg 1981, p. 12). Ruling myths can be undermined when the actions they support fail to materialize. New leaders and new political coalitions can then discredit old myths as the doubts about them spread. Also, competing myths from outside the organization can be introduced to challenge the old myths.

Although rites and ceremonials can also act as levers for change (Moore and Myerhoff 1977), change is clearly not their usual purpose. They usually maintain and celebrate current, traditional ideologies (Trice and Beyer 1985). For this reason it seems unrealistic to expect that rites composed entirely of forms that express new ideologies will seem appropriate and appealing to members of a culture. Instead, new messages can be combined with accepted, ongoing cultural elements. Either existing rites can be modified to incorporate new values, or entirely new rites that consciously combine elements of the old and the new can be established. "One factor to consider in choosing between these two strategies is the prevalence and vigor of existing rites. If rites are numerous and have many staunch adherents, it may be most practical to try to modify them to incorporate the new values" (Trice and Beyer 1985, p. 391). Because rites typically include many different cultural forms, it is relatively easy to add, subtract, or change some to reach a desirable mixture of the old and the new.

While rites of passage are usually used to maintain the continuity of cultures, these is no inherent reason why they cannot be used to instill new ideologies and values. This will not happen, however, if those managers and staff members who design and carry out the indoctrination and training of new members are adherents of the old culture. Other likely regressive influences are the co-workers recruits encounter when they move into their regular jobs. Thus, it is important to resocialize existing members of the organization as rapidly as possible. One possibility is to use a kind of collective rite of passage, which we call rites of transition in Chapter 3, to symbolically separate key members of the organization from their old culture. Such rites help members to mourn the passing of an old culture as they celebrate the creation of a new one. Rites of transition can help organizations let go of old beliefs and practices and create new ones, permit expressions of anger and grief for the passing of the old ways, move the organization into a transition phase, and position it as a changed entity in its industry and among its stakeholders. The following illustrates all but the last stage of this process:

> A large electronics firm had introduced numerous changes during a two-year period: a new CEO; a new company slogan; and a number of other new values, symbols, and cultural rituals. Again, a management conference was planned, and the process of planning it was filled with tension. Although none of the planners could articulate the main issues, there was a clear sense that the stakes were high. The conference opened with a general discussion of culture and then continued with three successive small-group sessions of thirty participants each. When asked for metaphors to capture the essence of the company, the group overwhelmingly came up with transitive images: afloat in a stormy sea without an anchor, a two-headed animal, and so on. Each group specifically addressed the issue of loss. In the last session, the CEO was present; the word had spread that the discussions were yielding some significant perceptions. The tension in the room was obvious. At one point, the participants were asked to name what they had lost, and these were written on a flip chart. The list included values, symbols, rituals, ceremonies, priests, and heroes. As people contributed specific losses, someone got up and dimmed the lights. The emotion was obviously high. The group then launched into a discussion of the positive features of the company in its new incarnation. The CEO incorporated much of the preceding discussion into an excellent closing speech, and the company moved ahead . . . illustrating the need for, and power of, a transition ritual following cultural change. (Deal 1985, p. 321)

Many companies use management meetings and training with the same aims. These are likely to be most effective when they help to vent and resolve the emotional distress and other conflictual issues involved.

Other possibilities for resocializing members include rites of passage to mark any changes of status of existing members and rites of enhancement that reward those behaviors most in accord with desired ideologies. The latter are likely to be most effective when they reinforce behaviors already instilled in some employees through rites of passage. Of course, all of the other culture forms can also be used to support and facilitate cultural change. Uniforms can be changed, new jargon created, new stories circulated, new songs written, and so on. Readers have probably seen some of these uses and can readily think of ideas for others.

In general, it seems that establishing rites of creation and transition, and new rites of passage and enhancement for individuals may be the best way to begin cultural change efforts. As we have observed in Chapter 4 on organizational socialization, both newcomers and current employees can learn about and be indoctrinated into new understandings with demanding training that readies members for the changes that will be required.

Rites of degradation logically complete this cluster of rites, but probably should ordinarily not follow until members have had a chance to learn the new expectations. Even when a jolt would be desirable to signal that quick change is imperative, and rites of degradation look like a logical starting point, early use may make members of the organization feel that those degraded are being treated unfairly. If firings must take place, it may be better to delay and then gloss over them as quickly as possible (Gooding 1972) while getting on to positive celebrations of new culture.

Rites of conflict reduction and integration comprise the next logical cluster of rites. Together these two rites provide ways to deal with the strains and conflicts generated when new and old cultural values collide and to build cohesion around an amalgam of what is desirable in the new and old. Their creation and modification should probably therefore wait until the exact nature of resultant strains and conflicts is evident. All rites, but perhaps most importantly these two rites, should be designed around the strains, conflicts, and cleavages that often accompany culture change.

Modify Socialization Tactics

Because the primary way that people learn their cultures is through the socialization processes they experience (Van Maanen 1973), if these processes are changed, an organization's cultures will begin to change. We have already discussed the crucial role that cultural forms, especially rites, play in socializing new members and resocializing old ones during a planned culture change. Rites of passage are, of course, the cultural form most directly aimed at socializing people into new roles. One reason that they tend to function to ensure cultural continuity rather than change is that they are often structured as institutionalized tactics (see Table 4.1), which tend to produce custodial role orientations. In work organizations, rites of passage often consist of collective, formal training of a fixed duration that prepares a group of recruits for one of a sequence of established statuses. They may also employ experienced members of the culture to communicate expectations and provide role models, and often endeavor to divest recruits of past identities. It is easy to see how socialization structured in this way is likely to produce cultural continuity.

However, it is far from clear that changing all of these tactics is advisable to further planned cluture change. More individualized tactics (Table 4.1) may produce more innovative role orientations by individual members but are too random and dissimilar in their effects across individuals to be very helpful in instilling desired cultural beliefs and values uniformly throughout an organization. Rather, persons who experience individualized tactics are freer to develop their own ideas about how to carry out their roles. If management already has a set of new cultural ideologies, values, and norms it wishes to instill throughout an organization, some of the institutionalized tactics are still appropriate because a relatively uniform response to socialization is desirable. Collective and formal tactics of a fixed duration can be used to impart new cultural substance in addition to those elements of the old culture that are desirable to retain.

The other three institutionalized tactics, however, must be pruned away or modified substantially. If new recruits have been sought and chosen because they will bring fresh ideas into the organization, any divestiture tactics could work at counterpurposes to such recruiting. Serial tactics could also prove damaging if the experienced members who do the socialization are not proponents of the cultural change. Current members who do such training become role models; they should be drawn from among members who are already committed to the cultural changes envisioned. If old-timers who are uncommitted to the new culture do the socializing, their resistance or ambivalence is likely to be communicated in one way or another to newcomers. If appropriate role models are lacking, it may be better to use outsiders to carry out necessary training until insiders are won over to the new culture. The sequential tactic could also be troublesome in cultural change efforts if changes are likely to alter existing sequences of roles. This part of the content of socialization may thus also require modification.

The individualized tactics of socialization may be most useful to cultural change when management sees cultural change as needed but is not yet sure of its direction. These tactics downplay structured training programs, leaving newcomers to learn their roles by individual experience, improvisation, and trial and error. Their passage into work roles has few clear-cut steps or procedures. Thus, newcomers are relatively free of past expectations that accompanied the role they are assuming.

Although we have focused on the socialization of newcomers, most of the considerations discussed also apply to socialization of present members for new roles and responsibilities or their general resocialization into a desired new culture. Members cannot be expected to change their convictions without some organized presentation and discussion of the new ideas they are expected to internalize. General resocialization efforts usually begin at the top levels of large organizations and work downwards, for it seems unrealistic to expect lower level managers and employees to subscribe to values different from those evidenced by their superiors' behaviors and decisions.

Find and Cultivate Innovative Leadership

Probably the most important quality of an innovative cultural leader is that he or she be able to convince members of the organization to follow new visions. "Members are unlikely to give up whatever security they derive from existing cultures and follow a leader in new directions unless that leader exudes self-confidence, has strong convictions, a dominant personality, and can preach the new vision with drama and eloquence" (Trice and Beyer 1991, p. 163).

During the late 1970s, serious troubles of the Lockheed L-1011 program, a Lockheed Corporation subsidiary, started in its environment. Its sole supplier of engines, Rolls Royce, went bankrupt. In addition, the company became embroiled in an international scandal involving "questionable" payments to high Japanese government officials.

> All told, the program was a financial disaster for the company. It led into a bloody competitive war with McDonnell-Douglas, in which both companies lost immensely. Lockheed's total losses on the program exceeded $2 billion. . . . One Lockheed manager later commented that over the years, the plant had become "an albatross" for Lockheed's top management. It was particularly well known for the autocratic and demeaning style of many of its managers. (Snyder 1988, p. 196)

The turnaround for the troubled program began with the appointment of Dale Daniels as vice-president of manufacturing at the L-1011 plant. Daniels had worked for Lockheed all of his working life, coming up through the ranks as he acquired more education. He had begun in the company as a drill press operator while still in high school, and had subsequently acquired degrees in engineering and marketing. His managerial experience was primarily in aircraft design. Within the first three weeks, he announced his managerial philosophy—a set of beliefs that he had built up from his experience and felt had been tested and proven to work:

- "Don't sell your integrity—it's the only thing that can't be bought."
- "You may be *better* at something than someone else, but you are not *better than* they are."
- When facing persistent difficulties, "attack the problem, not the person."
- There are many different ways to accomplish a given end. "You don't have to make people do things your way to get performance."
- If you want people to tell you the truth, then when they do—and something is going wrong—"don't shoot the messenger." (Snyder 1988, pp. 197–98)

These beliefs contrasted sharply with the existing culture that had been manifested in the program's recent troubles. Daniels communicated his philosophy formally with a memo, but then followed up by roaming the organization and talking to people. He particularly concentrated on those who avoided him. He was, in effect, an evangelist who sought out and converted people. He had strong convictions and confidence in his philosophy, which he communicated to others by his willingness to engage them in discussion and by his own example.

Managers who seek to change an existing culture often have to find ways to discredit and destroy parts of the old culture. One way to do so is to remove prominent persons representing those aspects of the old culture. Their removal has both symbolic and practical consequences. It communicates to other members that certain values and beliefs are no longer acceptable. It also typically eliminates powerful persons who might generate resistance to the new culture. As already mentioned, there are some dangers, however, that firing prominent members of the old culture may cause widespread resentment. Some new CEOs, like Blount in the U.S. Postal Service, used incentives to persuade old-guard members to retire. Others force out those who oppose their managerial ideologies with rites of degradation. They assemble evidence to discredit those they want to dismiss, make it public, and then fire them.

Such actions, which tend to blame the managers being removed for various problems, would not have been consistent with the new philosophy that Daniels was preaching at Lockheed. Thus, when he dismissed the most prominent high-level manager representing the old culture, he went around to all of the key people in the plant and explained that he had not replaced him in retaliation, but because he had been unable to fit in with the new managerial philosophy. In the same way Daniels was able to make over a dozen changes in key management personnel without engendering resentment or opposition.

He also used cultural forms to build positive sentiments among his managers. For example, they were issued special, blue flight jackets to wear while working in the plant. This almost military-style uniform symbolized the managers' importance and the team spirit he sought to foster among them. In a short time, managers were wearing their jackets with pride. The jackets came to represent their strong identification with the Lockheed plant. When managers who had been transferred to other locations came back to visit, they would don their jackets again.

By 1982, the situation at the Lockheed L-1011 plant was greatly improved. Mutual attacks between various departments in the plant had largely stopped. Information on the status of aircraft was much easier to obtain. Managers no longer publicly harassed their employees. The entire plant was on schedule and under budget for the first time in six years (Synder 1988, p. 203).

The numerous and extensive changes entailed in the cultural change at the Lockheed L-1011 plant, or those that occurred at the Metropolitan Sewer and Water District and the U.S. Post Office, did not take place overnight. The manager of MSWD expected the change to take at least a year and a half. The changes at Lockheed took about three years. The turnaround of the gigantic post office culture took much longer. In general, it seems reasonable to expect that cultural change will take longer to achieve in large and complex organizations than in small and simple ones. To produce lasting change, consistent cultural leadership must be sustained over relatively extended periods.

Specific Considerations in Creating Cultures

Creating a culture involves bringing a culture into existence that did not exist before. It inevitably entails innovation in the sense that, although all of the substance and forms that become part of the culture may not be new, they are put together in a distinctive configuration. Every culture is a unique patterning of beliefs, values, norms, and cultural practices.

Analysts have suggested two conceptually distinct ways that new cultures form:

1. Founders and other designated leaders formulate ideologies and forms and then influence followers to adopt them.
2. Ideologies and forms emerge spontaneously as people interact to solve problems of internal integration and external adaptation and are preserved as part of group life (Dyer 1985, p. 210).

The first type of creation is intended and deliberate; the second is inadvertent and occurs naturally. Either type can happen in work organizations, but we will focus more of our attention on the first type, in which managers play the leading roles.

As already pointed out in Chapter 9, it is natural for managers to seek to influence their organizations' cultures. New organizations or subunits present especially fertile ground for such managerial influence. Many observers have documented the strong and lasting influences that some founders have had on the cultures of the organizations they created (Schein 1983b, 1985; Sonnenfeld 1988). But the first type of creation is more than an instance of successful management. It involves cultural leadership, and thus requires the coming together of a leader, followers, and a situation in a mutually reinforcing way. The second type of culture creation probably goes on all of the time in organizations. It probably most often eventuates in new subcultures, but sometimes may create cultural elements that diffuse throughout an organization. In order to diffuse, the cultural elements probably have to be seen by members as relevant to problems that occur throughout an organization.

In the sections that follow, we will use three examples repeatedly to illustrate various issues in culture creation. All involved leaders' formulating ideologies and forms, but all also illustrate the emergent processes by which newly created cultures are elaborated. The first, Southwest Airlines, was founded to capitalize on a unique market niche. This company certainly had a strong cultural leader in one of its founders, but elaborated its culture greatly over time in dealing with persistent threats to its existence. The second, the Saturn Corporation, is a deliberate attempt by GM management to create a new and different culture that may be more successful than its old one in meeting foreign competition. The third illustration, that of two new English universities, involved cultures that were created partially by commissions of distinguished educators and citizens who had been given a mandate to be innovative and then were elaborated by early leaders and faculty (Lodahl and Mitchell 1980).

As before, we will consider the issues involved in managing culture creation through a set of aphorisms that distill what knowledge has accumulated about culture creation and combine it with our own reasoning. Because the literature on culture creation is so sparse, what follows is the most speculative portion of this book.

Discover and Articulate Distinctive Ideologies

Cultures must develop a core set of ideologies that capture members' minds and hearts. Someone in a culture has to originate or recognize ideologies to which others can subscribe, make the ideologies understandable and convincing, and communicate them widely and repeatedly so that others come to share them. Someone has to develop and promulgate what we and others have called a *vision*. Accounts of organizational foundings suggest that early leaders, especially founders, play an important role in establishing the ideological core of their organizations' cultures.

For example, one of the founders and the long-term CEO of Pan American Airlines, was described as follows:

> Juan Trippe set many of the standards of the airline industry, from its romance to its arrogance. He was one of those rare individuals whom one must admire for their courageous determination to challenge prevailing practice and stir the world into new adventure. Trippe conceived and implemented a revolutionary network of international and intercontinental air travel. He was also the genius and energy behind many technological advances, pushing Boeing into providing larger, more efficient jets. (Sonnenfeld 1988, p. 102)

Trippe's vision was to see all of the continents of the world connected by his airline and, in the process, to make international travel ever easier and faster.

Another notable founder who imprinted his organization with his own vision was Edwin Land, the founder of Polaroid. A distinguished scientist with many discoveries and patents to his credit, Land "fashioned a collegial, knowledge-seeking organization with a highly committed workforce" (Sonnenfeld 1988, p. 119). Land explained his own ideology and policies as follows:

> We set out to build a prototype of a corporation where we could have thousands of workers both in school and producing. We were relating the building of profits and growth to advances in science and technology. The leadership becomes a problem only when it atrophies. Leaders must make their jobs grow and not just climb a hierarchy. I never really led a big company. The glory of management is a myth of the business world. This firm was not a hierarchical command structure, but rather was like multiple suns and research satellites." (Sonnenfeld 1988, p. 120)

Other founders who articulated distinctive ideologies have already been discussed throughout the book, especially in Chapter 7. They include Mary Kay Ash, John L. Lewis, Alfred Fuller, and Steve Jobs.

When General Motors executives decided in the mid-1980s that they needed a radically different type of car to compete successfully in the United States and abroad, they opted to found a new, free-standing, relatively autonomous organization to design and build the new car. The new entity—the Saturn Corporation—was GM's answer to concerns about its loss of market share and widespread beliefs that the current GM culture was part of the problem. Thus, one of the motives for founding a new entity and giving it so much autonomy was to establish a new and different culture from that in the parent organization. This was not an instance of changing a culture. Saturn managment was supposed to create a new one—what one reporter called a "clean-sheet approach" (Serafin 1990, p. 16). To separate it from the parent company, GM management chose a rural area in Tennessee as the site of their new venture. In a speech at a conference on economic and community development in Nashville in 1985, the first president of Saturn, William E. Hoglund, set forth a distinctive ideology: "More than anything else, Saturn is an experiment in people-management—in total participation, contribution, and commitment of every person involved: every Saturn manager, machine operator, skilled tradesperson, secretary, and maintenance person is going to be a decision maker" (Hoglund 1986, p. 12).

Although this ideology is radical for the automobile industry in the United States, it bears considerable resemblance to worker participation practices in Scandinavian and Japanese firms. It seems likely that some of the impetus for Saturn ideology came directly from GM's joint venture with Toyota—called NUMMI (New United Motor Manufacturing, Inc.)—because many Saturn managers had spent some time there before joining Saturn. The Saturn ideology differs from that of other GM plants in that it places minimal reliance on robots and automated guided vehicles to achieve high productivity and quality. "Instead, Saturn is pouring its money into people management. It plans to hire exceptionally motivated workers, put them through intensive training, give them more say in how their jobs get done, and pay them a salary plus a performance bonus—just like Saturn executives" (Taylor 1988, p. 69). In addition, Saturn has enacted a new ideology in its relationship with suppliers: they are expected to share risks as well as rewards with the automaker. Saturn is holding them publicly and financially responsible for any quality problems created by materials they supply (Treece, 1991).

The visions that attended all of these culture creations were high on the dimension of innovativeness. All of these founders of new organizations set out to accomplish things no organizations had accomplished before. To a remarkable degree, all of them also succeeded. The Saturn experiment, however, is too recent and too protected from outside observation to be sure of management's success in creating a new culture. Also, the cars being produced are too new to the market to be able to assess their success with buyers.

Recruit Like-Minded People

Founders and other organizational leaders cannot create a culture on their own. They need lieutenants and other followers dedicated to the vision. If they can select people for their organization who already share their views or can be easily won over to them, founders will have allies in their attempts to found a new culture. If they select people, especially for management roles, with contrary or inconsistent views, the organization is likely to receive mixed ideological messages and may never form a single, coherent culture.

A study of two new, innovative universities in England found that their cultures tended to drift away from the founding ideologies after a few years. Both universities embraced ideologies of interdisciplinary study at their foundings. After a few years, the drift away from this ideology was more pronounced at one university than the other. The president of the first university recruited deans primarily on the basis of their stature within their academic discipline. As a result, his deans did not necessarily believe in the interdisciplinary ideal. For example, at the School of Molecular Biology, the trashcans were labelled chemistry—the discipline of the dean. At the other university, the vice-chancellor was more attentive to the ideological leanings of the deans he recruited; only those who sincerely believed in the interdisciplinary ideology were hired. The results of this difference in recruiting were evident in questionnaire data showing that those faculty who had more contact with the deans of the first school were *less* likely to endorse some of the founding ideals; this pattern was not evident at the second university (Lodahl and Mitchell 1980).[3] Also, as it turned out, faculty hired after their foundings did not subscribe to the innovative ideologies of these universities to the same degree that early faculty did. While 100 percent of faculty who joined in the first year agreed that the new university emphasized its differences from traditional universities a great deal, for those who had been recruited seven years later, the percentage was only 40 percent (Lodahl and Mitchell 1980, p. 192). In innovative organizations, the induction of any newcomers can become a force diluting the original ideologies unless they are consciously recruited and selected for their compatibility with those ideologies. As organizations grow and time passes, finding compatible new members may become difficult. Some of the pool of likely prospects is used up and the ideology may no longer have the appeal it had at the time of the organization's founding.

Other constraints can also interfere with this strategy. No doubt in order to gain the cooperation of the United Auto Workers (UAW) with various radical changes in work procedures, GM agreed to recruit the Saturn workforce from current UAW members, including some fifty thousand who had been laid off in various plant closings throughout the country. This gave Saturn a large pool of potential employees from which to recruit a "select breed of ambitious risk-takers" (Taylor 1988, p. 68)—traits apparently seen as fitting with the new desired Saturn culture. Management hoped to generate a list of 40,000 applicants before it filled the first 3,000 jobs in 1990.

Despite plans for careful selection and extensive socialization to follow, GM and Saturn are taking substantial risks to expect workers already indoctrinated in existing GM cultures to be able to develop a new and radically different culture at Saturn. Of course, members of all new organizations bring their past cultures with them, but usually there are many prior cultures respresented in the workforce, and thus no single other culture can operate to dilute or undermine the new culture that management and other members are attempting to create. At Saturn, new workers will bring the old GM culture with them. Under these circumstances, residues of the old GM culture could persist despite management's valiant attempts to create a very different one.

---

[3]Additional information supplied by Lodahl to the authors in a 1991 telephone conversation.

Devise and Use Distinctive Cultural Forms

At Saturn, many symbols of the new culture have already been institutionalized. The Saturn corporate offices in Detroit are open-style cubicles and executives there eat in a simple cafeteria.[4] The plant itself is a symbol of the gigantic commitment the parent company is making and its bet that putting the whole operation in one location will facilitate just-in-time production and other coordination. Saturn has built an enormous factory complex in Spring Hill, Tennessee. Begun in 1985, it is the largest single construction in GM history, covering 3.8 million square feet and extending over a mile in length. All of the essential operations—sheet metal stamping, foundry, plastic-molding unit, interior trim shop, body assembly, and many loading docks—are on this one site. The sheer size of the factory seems to be a symbol that GM thinks it can go it alone—that it has the resources, financial and otherwise, to reestablish itself as the premier auto manufacturer. "No other automobile manufacturer could pile its chips so high or risk so much on a startup operation" (Taylor 1988, p. 69).

The Saturn management ideology expects peer pressures to ensure worker performance. One symbol of this part of the ideology is the absence of time clocks. But perhaps the most potent symbol of the new ideology is that "work teams participate in the selection of both their co-workers and their team leaders" (Newstrom, Lengnick-Hall, and Rubenfeld 1987, p. 121). A third potent symbol was created in 1991 when Saturn replaced, rather than repaired, 1,836 cars it recalled because of bad coolant. This unprecedented action was obviously intended to send a message that Saturn would stand behind the quality of its cars in a way that U.S. automakers had never done before. In addition, in support of the new ideology of holding suppliers publicly responsible for any quality problems their products cause, Saturn's recall letter to car owners "fingered Texaco Refining & Marketing, Inc. as the supplier of the bad coolant" (Treece 1991, p. 38).

In Table 1.1, we listed some of the distinctive ideologies and cultural forms that have grown up at Southwest Airlines. In addition, the founding of the company has been celebrated in the following legend:

> Early in 1967, Roland King consulted Herbert D. Kelleher, a corporate attorney in San Antonio, about legal matters pertaining to the dissolution of a small commuter airline that King headed. But foremost in King's mind was to start still another airline, for he believed that the major cities in Texas needed better air service. When he proposed his idea to Kelleher, the latter responded, rather impulsively, "Roland, you're crazy. Let's do it." They then went to dinner together and sketched out on a table napkin a simple triangle of a three-legged air route between Houston, San Antonio, and Dallas that became the original routes of Southwest Airlines. The napkin is now preserved in a beautiful wooden plaque hanging in Herb Kelleher's office. (Adapted from Freiberg 1987, p. 127)

---

[4]This, of course, contrasts sharply with the plush corporate offices and private dining rooms of GM top executives described in Chapter 3.

This legend is regularly recounted among employees in the company, in company publications, and in press accounts of the company.

Undoubtedly, the actions of Kelleher himself—who was one of the founders of Southwest and became chairman of the board in 1978 and CEO in 1981—provide some of the most potent symbols of the company's ideology. At Southwest, employees are expected to learn more than one job and help one another out when needed. To show his commitment to this ideology, Kelleher often pitches in to help employees as he travels around doing business. These behaviors lead to stories that employees recount to one another. One tells of how Kelleher sat next to mailing operators through one night and late into the early morning doing the same monotonous work they did; others tell of how he got off one of the company planes during his travels and helped ground crews unload the luggage. One Black Wednesday—the day before Thanksgiving and the busiest day of the year—Kelleher worked alongside the baggage handlers until 10 P.M. despite a pouring rain. One of the men he worked with reported, "... he was whipped, he was dragging by the time he left" (Freiberg 1987, p. 203). Also, every month Kelleher personally presents Winning Spirit Awards to nonmanagerial employees selected by peers for outstanding performance.

To symbolize the ideology that work can be fun, employees were encouraged to don fun clothes—tennis shoes, T-shirts, and baggy flowered shorts—during one promotional campaign. Even Kelleher wore them on a business trip to Houston. A researcher who intensively studied the airline concluded:

> The atmosphere at Southwest Airlines shows that having fun is a value that pervades every part of the organization. Joking, cajoling, and prank-pulling at Southwest Airlines are representative of the special relationships that exist among the employees in the company. (Freiberg 1987, p. 234)

The closeness of the relationships among employees is also expressed by the language people use to refer to the company: "... the family metaphor is used by everyone, Kelleher and his staff, the mechanic, pilots, flight attendants, and ticket agents all use it as part of their everyday language" (Freiberg 1987, p. 313). Many other cultural forms used at Southwest Airlines have helped to create a very distinctive culture and committed workforce.

At one of the new English universities founded in the 1960s, a rite of renewal grew up that helped to keep the culture vital and current. Once a year, a group of faculty and the original founder scrutinized a planning document that had been generated at the time of the university's founding and revised it to reflect what had actually happened over the prior year. In this way they were confronted with any divergences between plans and reality. These occasions apparently encouraged broad-ranging and thoughtful examinations of what the organization was about. They probably are one of the reasons that this university was much more successful than the other university studied in sustaining its initial culture (Lodahl and Mitchell 1980).

Socialize to Instill and Sustain Ideologies

At Saturn, the training strategy is to "extensively train core team members and use them to train teammates" (Moskal 1989, p. 30). The centerpiece of the effort is an individualized training plan that assesses each employee's current knowledge and learning speed. To get team members ready to actually build cars, the plan is to give the average worker 300 to 600 hours of training on statistical process control, quality, stress management, general technical knowledge, computer integrated manufacturing, and health and safety. The training also includes lessons in team concepts and leadership skills. The core group of trainers incorporates both UAW-represented and non-UAW employees.

At the innovative English universities, faculty reported that the major socializing agents they experienced during the first three years were faculty meetings and colleagues. During the next four years, the influence of faculty meetings tended to wane while the effects of colleagues increased. In the process, the major influences in socialization became decentralized and moved out of the control of the small group of faculty who had helped to formulate the original ideals of these universities to peer groups through the university. Also, as mentioned earlier, contacts with deans at one of these universities apparently served to dilute rather than reinforce beliefs in the founding ideals.

> . . . as an organization grows, the founder is placed under increasing time constraints and becomes subject to "founder burnout." Structures and pressures must therefore be developed to replace the contact with the founder as a basis of ensuring commitment. Delegation of socialization responsibilities is one possibility, but one that will succeed only if the new contacts transfer the ideals. . . . insofar as delegation of socialization to unreliable hands results in perceptions of the organizational reality that are incongruent with the ideals, it can also contribute to organizational drift." (Lodahl and Mitchell 1980, p. 195)

Managers who want to create new cultures clearly must attend to both the formal and informal socialization that occurs in their organizations. They have considerable control over the ways formal socialization occurs and who does the socializing. When founders participate in such efforts, they seem to have especially strong effects. Although management has less control over informal socialization, managers can shape the direction such socialization is likely to take by the examples they set, by the kinds of people they hire into management ranks and influential staff roles, and by the way they structure their organizations to encourage or discourage social interactions between groups and individuals.

Structure to Influence Subcultural Formation

After a few years, faculty at the new English universities established small disciplinary groups to advise their interdisciplinary schools on such matters as hiring. Since these groups brought together faculty with like interests, they probably easily became subcultures with substantial influence on their members. Because they included even the most junior newcomers to the faculty, these subcultures became important socializing agents. Members shared similar disciplinary training and values and their tasks were discipline-related; thus, interactions within these groups probably served to reinforce disciplinary values rather than the interdisciplinary ideals to which members were now expected to subscribe. Thus, subcultural influences probably helped to dilute commitment to the founding ideals.

Managers at Southwest Airlines and Saturn have been more careful to try to channel and perhaps even dilute the influences of subcultures—especially those that form around distinct occupations. They accomplish this by how they divide tasks among employees. At Southwest, Kelleher has been somewhat able to counter strong trends toward extreme occupational specialization and identity by expecting workers to pitch in and help other employees whenever they can. Mechanics help out baggage handlers when they fall behind; flight attendants help overloaded ticket agents. At Saturn, all employees will be trained to perform a variety of different tasks within their work teams. The idea is that they will be prepared to substitute for one another and will be able to exchange jobs as needed. Job classifications have shrunk from as many as 110 elsewhere in the GM system to only five at Saturn. Workers are called partners and are expected to do whatever teamwork requires. Team leaders will know how to do all of the jobs on their team and will be expected to train new team members. Bonuses are based on extraordinary performance of the team (Gwynne 1990). In this way, Saturn hopes to use subcultural influences as a positive force for employee productivity and performance.

Remain Flexible Enough to Adapt

After their foundings, all new organizations will eventually encounter some changes in their environments. These changes pose various dangers. The more strongly members embrace the new culture, the more danger there may be that its ideologies will prevent members from perceiving the need to change and prevent them from making appropriate alterations in practices. As already discussed in Chapter 9, the structure and practices within People Airlines failed to change appropriately after it acquired Frontier. People tried to maintain an ideology that relied heavily on interpersonal cooperation and individual adaptability with a much larger number of employees, many of whom had never operated within such a structure. Sticking to the founding ideology, Donald Burr and his managers failed to adapt the structure of the firm to its new circumstances.

Thus far, the ideologies of Southwest Airlines have not needed to change to enable it to adapt to changing circumstances. Its dominant ideology grew out of a protracted series of legal battles with competitors and with local governments that sought to put the new airline out of business. Herbert Kelleher—a gifted and determined attorney and the apparent founder of the company culture—personally fought all of these battles all the way up to the Supreme Court of the United States. After a few initial setbacks in state courts, he defeated his adversaries and eventually won the airline's right to fly desired air routes and to occupy Love Field in Dallas. It was in this crucible of persistent attack and defense that the company's predominant ideology of competitive aggression was forged. It is noteworthy that this ideology is more outward-oriented than that which characterized People Airlines.

In 1980, an activist group concerned with aircraft noise threatened Southwest's operations at Love Field. This location was an important competitive advantage for Southwest because it was closer to downtown and cheaper than operating out of the Dallas–Forth Worth Airport, where all of its large competitors had relocated. Despite its relatively small size, the citizens' group was able to marshall formidable support and influence public opinion against Southwest.

> So the war was on. Southwest Airlines, which had always gone into a fight the underdog, persecuted by the bigger airlines, found itself in a different role. The ultimate consumer airline, which had slashed the standard airfare to the markets it served by more than one-third and made air travel more accessible to the masses, was cast as the villain. (Hollandsworth 1986, p. 63)

Once again, Herb Kelleher led the defense and counterattack. Southwest paid for over 66,000 postcards that Dallas citizens sent to the city council with the slogan "Keep Love Alive"; it funded a counter citizens' group called Love's a Good Neighbor. The company also held a gala affair at a local theater to announce that Southwest was immediately purchasing ten new jet aircraft that were more fuel efficient and much quieter, with an additional ten likely to be purchased soon. Kelleher himself lobbied intensively, making deft use of a consultant's report saying Southwest's noise abatement program was the best he had seen at any airport. Kelleher also threatened to close down operations in Dallas (Hollandsworth 1986). Once more Kelleher won; Southwest was still at Love Field in the early 1990s.

The enthusiasm with which Southwest's innovative ideologies are embraced and practiced is not without its dangers, however. Southwest has positioned itself to fly point to point, rather than with a hub system. Kelleher has been quoted as saying, "We don't fly to Dallas because we want to go to New York. We fly to Dallas and Houston because they are worthy destinations in and of themselves" (Jarboe 1989, p. 103). The 1990s brought plans to establish high-speed train travel between the major cities in Texas that could force Southwest to either change this ideology in the future or face sharing its market niche with a new competitor. Also, its fun-loving ideology is not without critics. Not only does it promote ethnocentrism, but some passengers found all of the fooling around and flippancy offensive (Peters and Austin 1985, p. 44).

One way to encourage adaptability is to build some loose coupling into an organization's structure and practices. Loose coupling means that subunits and subcultures do not mesh tightly with one another, permitting each to adapt to different sets of circumstances if necessary. A factory that straddled the Quebec and Vermont borders dramatically illustrates this principle. Similar operations were maintained on each side of the border except that workers, currency, and laws were American on one side and Canadian on the other (Miller 1978, p. 702).

Any disturbances in subcultures that are loosely coupled with each other can sometimes be confined to one subculture, leaving the overall culture and the other subcultures undisturbed.

Another possibility is extreme decentralization. The original and most successful self-help group, Alcoholics Anonymous, has been able to adapt to different national cultures throughout the world and to changing circumstances over the years. It has a very minimal structure composed of relatively autonomous face-to-face groups that form at will and operate very independently of one another. They are held together in the AA organization by their adherence in belief and behavior with the unique ideology of this organization and by members' convictions that their adherence to its principles helps them to maintain their sobriety (Trice and Beyer 1986). The continued ability of AA to adapt could be severely tested by new threats in its environment. Several new competing organizations have formed around ideologies that directly attack core AA principles (Gelman 1991). Apparently some individuals belong to both AA and the competing organizations. They could serve as conduits for the competing ideologies to enter and perhaps change AA. Conversely, they could bring their AA ideas to the new organizations and influence them to become more like AA.

While some industry analysts hope that Saturn's new culture will prove a model for other parts of GM and the industry (Taylor 1988; Gwynne 1990), the extreme decentralization within the parent company, the high level of internal competitiveness among its divisions, and the relative autonomy and geographical isolation of Saturn make such cultural transfer unlikely. Indeed, it is not clear that GM management hopes for such a result. Saturn's identity is being kept so separate from the rest of GM that Saturn advertisements contain no mention of GM (Gwynne 1990). As one close observer of the parent company commented to us, Saturn can be seen as either an extraordinary and wonderful effort, or as an example of a great failure on the part of the parent company to adapt short of expending $6 billion and building a huge new organization (Cameron 1991). Thus, Saturn is a symbol with a mixed message about GM.

Support Innovative Leadership

At the beginning of this section, we listed two ways that cultures form. The first of these is when founders or other designated leaders formulate the elements of a new culture and influence followers to adopt them. The second is when cultural elements emerge and coalesce spontaneously from people's social interactions.

In instances of the first kind of culture creation, management does not usually have to find an innovation leader; instead an innovative founder often finds and recruits other members of management. In these circumstances, those managers who are hired should try to be receptive and supportive to the new culture. The founder needs willing and supportive followers to be able to build a distinctive culture. Managers should be in the vanguard of committed followers in a new organization. They should therefore explore the founders' visions pretty thoroughly before joining a new organization and only join if they find the visions appealing and largely compatible with their own views. If, after joining, they discover serious incompatibilities they need to assess whether continuing to stay is beneficial or damaging to the organization and their own careers. If they are willing and able to function as loyal lieutenants to the founder, managers will find they can have influence by helping to articulate the founder's visions into coherent organizational ideologies and helping to develop and implement supportive cultural forms. Building something new can be exciting and rewarding even if all of the ideas and impetus are not your own.

The core problem in culture creation is to attract and unite a group of followers. Once the founder has attracted a management team, these people can assist in recruiting and socializing other members of the organization. The founder should, however, be a presence in such activities for it is his or her exceptional qualities that help to attract and motivate followers. Mary Kay, Steve Jobs, Juan Trippe, Edwin Land, and Alfred Fuller provide examples of this kind of leadership role in culture creation. As pointed out in Chapter 7, the founders of organizational cultures need not be entrepreneurs who personally start new organizations; the initial CEOs chosen by others to head new organizations can also be founders of organizational cultures.

The second, emergent type of culture creation is exemplified by John L. Lewis, who saw a way to adapt the union movement to external demands by representing noncraft workers. He subsequently took a group of followers with him to found a new union (the CIO) when AFL leadership was unresponsive to his vision. The case of Lewis, however, does not provide a prototype for this kind of culture creation because he ended up founding a new organization. The second kind of culture creation should result in indigenous cultures that emerge and persist in the same organizations in which their members interacted and formulated the culture's core ideas and values. Leaders in this kind of culture creation process could be either (1) informal leaders who emerge to espouse and represent group concerns and values; or (2) formal leaders who are so close and sensitive to a group of followers as to be able to generate new ideologies and cultural forms in interaction with them. Herb Kelleher of Southwest Airlines may be an example of this second type of leader—one who essentially encourages and makes use of indigenous impulses toward cultural creation. Other examples are the Cadbury brothers, about whom the historian Charles Delheim wrote:

> ... the core of the younger Cadburys' thought was their unusual approach to power and authority. ... they rejected the idea that labor was a commodity to be bargained for or a cost to be reckoned with by the capitalist. ... their labor strategy was to elicit commitment rather than exercise control. The interests of capitalist and labor complemented each other. Cooperation was the basis of business. Workers should be led rather than driven, inspired rather than coerced. (1987, p. 26)

Such values enabled them to foster the growth of a remarkably coherent and postive culture among their employees.

Let Go Gracefully

A study of the ways CEOs of U.S. companies leave their high-level positions found four styles of departure: *Monarchs* choose not to leave voluntarily and either die in office or are overthrown; *generals* leave reluctantly and spend their retirement planning a comeback; *ambassadors* retain close ties with the organizations they headed, often acting as consultants and advisors; *governors* willingly serve a limited time and leave to pursue new interests (Sonnenfeld 1988). Perhaps the most interesting findings of this study show that the ways in which CEOs dealt with their impending departure had profound effects on the company culture. Some organizations were literally torn apart by the struggles of their CEOs to hang on. Founder-CEOs seemed to be especially prone to be monarchs or generals who failed to let go gracefully and, in the process, damaged what they had built.

One of the reasons that founders find it hard to let go is that their identities become fused with that of their companies. In the process, they become convinced that their ideologies are the reasons behind their companies' successes. The bigger their successes has been, the more likely that they will want the company they have built to continue the culture unchanged. Signs that time has come to change are ignored. Instead, founders often persist with ideologies and courses of action they found successful in the past. Juan Trippe, the founder of Pan Am, is a prominent example of these tendencies. He gambled on the Boeing 747 and lost when the plane did not perform as expected and incurred large cost overruns. Pan Am's board of directors pressured Trippe to step down; he then succeeded in getting the board to name a longtime colleague, whom only Trippe knew was fatally ill, as his successor. For the position next in line, he pushed someone with little airline experience (Sonnenfeld 1988, p. 104). The result was predictable; Pan Am continued to slide and never recovered. Similarly, William S. Paley founded the Columbia Broadcasting System in 1928 and created such a unique culture within that organization that no one else seems able to run it. After several attempts, he finally retired in 1986, at the age of 85. Less than a year later, he was back at the helm and being given a hero's welcome (Sonnenfeld 1988).

Although not a founder, Harold Geneen, CEO of ITT from 1959 to 1978, was an innovator who led the company during a time of enormous expansion and prosperity. During his reign, revenues grew from $765 million to $22 billion. But by the early 1970s, various actions of the company had garnered it very bad publicity and unfavorable relations with the U.S. and foreign governments. The board of directors began to pressure Geneen to formulate a succession plan. He was very reluctant to let go of his power, however, and tried various maneuvers that were partially successful to delay his retirement. Even after someone else became CEO, he tried to intervene as board chairman. He was eventually barred from attending management meetings without the express invitation of his successor. He managed to stay on the board and kept meddling in ITT affairs until 1983, when he was 73 years old (Sonnenfeld 1988).

One of the commonalities between generals and monarchs is that both fail to groom a viable successor. It appears they are unwilling to even contemplate the possibility of leaving. As a result, the cultures they created are likely to change drastically and painfully when these leaders die or are forced out. Charismatic founders, like Herb Kelleher at Southwest Airlines, become so central to the functioning of their organizations that they pose especially difficult succession problems. Southwest employees have commented:

- "His personality overarches everything. . . . We're always going to come back to him" (Reischel 1985, p. 1).
- "He's the common denominator" (Freiberg 1987, p. 188).
- "He's the spirit . . ." (Freiberg 1987, p. 224).
- "He is the extra ingredient" (*U.S. News & World Report* 1988, p. 55).

As described in Chapter 7, the visions of charismatic leaders will not be fully routinized and continue unless their successor resembles them. In order to ensure that possibility, founders like Kelleher should personally groom their successors—but few actually do so.

In contrast, governors and ambassadors plan carefully for their succession, and thus the cultures they have created have a better chance of continuing. Tom Watson, Jr., who succeeded his father as head of IBM and carefully nurtured the culture his father had created, planned carefully for his own succession. He realized that because his father died, there had been nobody around to dilute his own influence. After talking with other executives, he proposed a rule that executives retire at 60; the rule was adopted in 1966. Watson himself described what followed:

> Within the next few years, plans for an orderly succession had been completed. In 1974, when I reached sixty, I would hand the top job over to Frank Cary who [sic] everyone agreed would make a brilliant and worthy successor. But in 1970, at age 57, I had a heart attack. . . . Rather than bring Cary in ahead of schedule, I asked the Board if I could turn it over to Vin Learson. He still had eighteen months before his sixtieth birthday, and I thought he had done enough for the business that he ought to have the opportunity if he wanted it. Learson served from June 1971 to December 1972. He stepped aside just after he turned sixty and the job went to Cary, as we had planned years before. I remained on the Board of Directors throughout to help maintain stability and continuity. (Sonnenfeld 1988, p. 155)

Cultural leaders who want the culture they have built to last should follow the example of Tom Watson, Jr., rather than the examples of Trippe and Geneen. They need to face up to the inevitability of their eventual succession and plan for it. They need to groom successors who are both carriers of the central tenets of their culture and otherwise competent to manage what the leaders have built. They need to use their power and influence to smooth the transition to their successor. Failure to let go gracefully in favor of a successor who shares the founder's core values can only damage and perhaps destroy the cultural and organizational edifices so carefully built.

Summary

Cultural innovation involves the duality of creation and destruction. Whether old cultures are being changed or new cultures are being created in new organizations, members will need to replace or displace ideologies and customary behaviors they bring from past roles and experiences in different cultures. There is, however, a range of degrees of creation and destruction—of displacements and innovations—involved in what people caught up in them experience as "changes." Because cultures inevitably change incrementally and people within them adjust their behaviors and beliefs in various ways, discussing cultural innovation and change can be confusing if we do not draw a line somewhere to separate substantial changes from minor fluctuations and adjustments. Also, managers need to be clear about which they are attempting because substantial change and minor adjustments in cultures involve different issues and require different behaviors.

Culture change involves a noticeable break with the past; it also inevitably involves changes in both ideologies and cultural forms. Three types of cultural change have been identified: (1) relatively fast, revolutionary, comprehensive change; (2) subunit or subcultural change; and (3) a more gradual cumulative but comprehensive reshaping of a culture. Each of these types has a characteristic pattern along four dimensions of change processes: pervasiveness, magnitude, innovativeness, and duration.

Some of the central issues involved in changing cultures were summarized under eight prescriptive aphorisms:

- capitalize on propitious moments
- combine caution with optimism
- understand resistance to culture change
- change many elements, but maintain some continuity
- recognize the importance of implementation
- select, modify, and create appropriate cultural forms
- modify socialization tactics
- find and cultivate innovative leadership

All included examples of how the levers set forth in Chapter 9 and discussed in more detail in chapters 1 through 8 can be used to change organizational cultures.

Culture creation can occur in at least two ways: (1) at the instigation of founders or other leaders; (2) from the spontaneous interactions of people over time. Founders and other leaders of new organizations can imprint their organizations with their visions and values. While subcultures probably grow up spontaneously within organizations, the cultures so created are not very likely to influence a whole organization's culture. However, newly created cultures will certainly be elaborated and refined through the spontaneous interactions of members.

The issues involved in culture creation were condensed into eight more prescriptive aphorisms:

- discover and articulate distinctive ideologies
- recruit like-minded people
- devise and use distinctive cultural forms
- socialize to instill and sustain ideologies
- structure to influence subcultural formation
- remain flexible enough to adapt
- support innovative leadership
- let go gracefully

Because rich descriptions of culture creation are scarce, these aphorisms are more speculative than those offered for cultural maintenance and change. The aphorisms in this chapter and Chapter 9 are our attempts to distill the insights we gained from trying to digest and integrate the extensive range of materials summarized throughout this book. We hope they provide a useful start toward an integration and synthesis of what scholars and other observers have learned about the cultures of work organizations.

References

ABBOTT, ANDREW
1988   *The System of Professions.* Chicago, Ill. University of Chicago Press.

ABELSON, ROBERT P.
1976   Script processing in attitude formation and decision making. Pp. 33–46 in Carroll, John S., and John W. Payne (eds.) *Cognition and Social Behavior.* Hillside, N.J.: Lawrence Erlbaum.

ABRAVANEL, HARRY
1983   Mediatory myths in the service of organizational ideology. Pp. 273–93 in Pondy, Louis R., Peter J. Frost, Gareth Morgan, and Thomas Vandridge (eds.) *Organizational Symbolism.* Greenwich, Conn.: JAI Press.

ADAMS, GUY B., and VIRGINIA H. INGERSOLL
1985   The difficulty of framing a perspective on organizational culture. Pp. 223–34 in Frost Peter J., Larry F. Moore, Meryl R. Louis, Craig C. Lundberg, and Joanne Martin (eds.) *Organizational Culture.* Beverly Hills, Calif.: Sage Publications, Inc.

ADAMS, J. STACY
1980   Interorganizational processes and organization boundary activities. *Research in Organizational Behavior,* 2: 321–55. Greenwich, Conn.: JAI Press.

Administrative Science Quarterly: Special Issue
1979   24(4), Guest editor: John Van Maanen.

AIKEN, MICHAEL, and SAMUEL BACHARACH
1979   Culture and organizational structure and process: A study of local government administrative bureaucracies in the Walloon and Flemish regions of Belgium. Pp. 215–50 in Lammers, Cornelius, and David J. Hickson (eds.) *Organizations Alike and Unlike.* London: Routledge & Kegan Paul.

ANGLE, HAROLD, and JAMES L. PERRY
1986   Dual commitment and labor-management relationship climates. *Academy of Management Journal,* 29: 31–50.

APPLEBAUM, HERBERT
1981   *Royal Blue: The Culture of Construction Workers*. New York: Holt, Rinehart, and Winston.

APTER, DAVID E.
1964   Introduction: Ideology and discontent. Pp. 15–46 in Apter, David E. (ed.) *Ideology and Discontent*. New York: Free Press.

ARENS, WILLIAM
1975   The great American football ritual. *Natural History*, 84: 72–80.

ARGYRIS, CHRIS
1957   *Personality and Organization*. New York: Harper & Row, Pub.
1964   *Integrating the Individual and the Organization*. New York: John Wiley.
1976   Single-loop and double-loop models in research on decision-making. *Administrative Science Quarterly*, 21: 363–75.

ARORA, SHIRLEY L.
1988   No tickee, no shirtee: Proverbial speech and leadership in action. Pp. 179–89 in Jones, Michael O., Michael D. Moore, and Richard C. Snyder (eds.) *Inside Organizations: Understanding the Human Dimension*. Beverly Hills, Calif.: Sage Publications, Inc.

ARVEY, RICHARD D., and J. E. CAMPION
1982   The employment interview: A summary and review of recent research. *Personnel Psychology*, 35: 281–322.

ASH, MARY KAY
1981   *Mary Kay*. New York: Harper & Row, Pub. Association of American Publishers.

Austin American-Statesman
1991   Air Force picks future fighter: Ft. Worth firm to share in $95 billion Lockheed project, April 24, p. A1.

BABA, MARIETTA L.
1986   *Business and Industrial Anthropology: An Overview*. Washington D.C.: American Anthropological Association.

BACHARACH, SAMUEL B., and EDWARD J. LAWLER
1981   *Bargaining Power, Tactics and Outcomes*. San Francisco: Jossey-Bass.

BALL, DONALD W.
1968   Toward a sociology of telephones and telephoners. Pp. 59–75 in Truzzi, Marcello (ed.) *Sociology and Everyday Life*. Englewood Cliffs, N.J.: Prentice Hall.

BANCROFT, BILL
1986   *Southwest Airlines Celebrates 15 Years of Luv*. Southwest Airlines Corporation, P.O. Box 37611, Love Field, Dallas, TX 75235-1625.

BARBASH, JACK
1967   *American Unions: Structure, Government, and Politics*. New York: Random House.

BARLEY, STEPHEN R.
1983   Semiotics and the study of occupational and organizational cultures. *Administrative Science Quarterly*, 28: 393–413.
1986   Technology as an occasion for structuring: Observations on CT scanners and the social order of radiology departments. *Administrative Science Quarterly*, 31: 78–108.

BARLEY STEPHEN R., and MERYL LOUIS
1983   Many in one: Organizations as multicultural entities. Paper presented at the annual meeting of the Academy of Management, August 14–17, Dallas, Tex.

BARLEY, STEPHEN R., GORDON W. MEYER, and DEBORAH C. GASH
1988   Cultures of cultures: Academics, practitioners and the pragmatics of normative control. *Administrative Science Quarterly*, 33: 24–60.

BARNARD, CHESTER
1938   *The Functions of the Executive.* Cambridge, Mass.: Harvard University Press.

BARNEY, JAY B.
1986   Organizational culture: Can it be a source of sustained competitive advantage? *Academy of Management Review*, 11: 656–65.

BASS, BERNARD M.
1981   *Stogdills' Handbook of Leadership* (revised and expanded edition). New York: Free Press.
1985a   *Leadership and Performance Beyond Expectations.* New York: Free Press.
1985b   Leadership: Good, better, best. *Organizational Dynamics*, 13(3): 26–40.
1990   *Stogdill's Handbook of Leadership: Theory, Research, and Managerial Application.* New York: Free Press.

BASS, BERNARD M., and B. AVOLIO
1985   Charisma and Beyond. Paper presented at annual meeting, Academy of Management, San Diego.

BECK, BRENDA E. F., and LARRY F. MOORE
1985   Linking the host culture to organizational variables. Pp. 335–51 in Frost, Peter J. et al. (eds.) *Organizational Cultures.* Beverly Hills, Calif.: Sage Publications, Inc.

BECKER, HOWARD S.
1951   The professional dance musician and his audience. *American Journal of Sociology*, 57(September): 136–44.
1960   Notes on the concept of commitment. *American Journal of Sociology*, 66: 32–40.

BECKER, HOWARD S., and BLANCHE GEER
1960   Latent culture: A note on the theory of latent social roles. *Administrative Science Quarterly*, 5(2): 304–13.

BECKER, HOWARD S., B. GEER, E. C. HUGHES, and A. M. STRAUSS
1961   *Boys in White: Student Cultures in Medical School.* Chicago: University of Chicago Press.

BELASCO, JAMES, and HARRISON M. TRICE
1969a   *The Assessment of Change in Training and Therapy.* New York: McGraw-Hill.
1969b   Unanticipated returns of training. *Training and Development Journal*, July, pp. 12–17.

BELDEN, THOMAS D., and MARIA ROBINS BELDEN
1962   *The Lengthening Shadow: The Life of Thomas Watson.* Boston: Little, Brown.

BELL, CHARLES G., and CHARLES M. PRICE
1975   *The First Term: A Study of Legislative Socialization.* Beverly Hills, Calif.: Sage Publications, Inc.

BELLAH, ROBERT N., RICHARD MADSEN, WILLIAM M. SULLIVAN, ANN SWIDLER, and STEVEN M. TIPTON
1985   *Habits of the Heart.* New York: Harper & Row, Pub.

BELLEW, P. A.
1984   The office party is one thing at which Silicon Valley excels. *The Wall Street Journal*, 65(49): 1.

BEM DARYL J.
1970   *Beliefs, Attitudes, and Human Affairs.* Belmont, Calif.: Brooks/Cole.

BENDIX, REINHARD
1956   *Work and Authority in Industry.* New York: Harper & Row, Pub.
1970   Industrialization, ideologies, and social structure. Pp. 58–74 in Landsberger, Henry A. (ed.) *Comparative Perspectives on Formal Organizations.* Boston: Little, Brown.

BENGTSON, VERN L.
  1989   The problem of generations: Age group contrasts, continuities, and social change. Pp. 25–54 in Bengston, Vern L., and L. Warner Schaie (eds.) *The Course of Later Life: Research and Reflections.* New York: Springer Publishing.

BENNIS, WARREN
  1966   *Changing Organizations.* New York: McGraw-Hill.
  1979   The Buffalo Search. Pp. 333–431 in Kanter, Rosabeth M., and Barry A. Stein (eds.) *Life in Organizations: Workplaces as People Experience Them.* New York: Basic Books.

BENNIS, WARREN, and BURT NANUS
  1985   *Leaders.* New York: Harper & Row, Pub.

BERES, MARY E., and JAMES D. PORTWOOD
  1979   Explaining cultural differences in the perceived role of work: An intranational cross-cultural study. Pp. 139–71 in England, George W., and Anant R. Negandhi (eds.) *Organizational Functioning in a Cross-Cultural Perspective.* Kent, Ohio: Kent State University Press.
  1981   Sociocultural influences on organizations: An analysis of recent research. Pp. 303–36 in England, George W., Anant R. Negandhi, and Wilpert Bernhard (eds.) *The Functioning of Complex Organizations.* Cambridge, Mass.: Oelgeschlager, Gunn and Hain.

BERGER, PETER L., and THOMAS LUCKMANN
  1967   *The Social Construction of Reality.* 3rd ed. Garden City, New York: Anchor Books.

BERLEW, DAVID E., and DOUGLAS T. HALL
  1966   The socialization of managers: Effect of expectations on performance. *Administrative Science Quarterly,* 11: 207–33.

BERNARD, JESSIE
  1971   *Women and the Public Interest.* Chicago: Aldine.
  1981   *The Female World.* New York: Free Press.

BERRY, JOHN W.
  1980   Acculturation as varieties of adaptation. Pp. 9–25 in Padilla, Amadom M. (ed.) *Acculturation: Theory, Models, and Some New Findings.* Boulder, Colo.: Westview Press.

BETTERHAUSEN, KENNETH, and J. KEITH MURNIGHAN
  1985   The emergence of norms in competitive decision-making groups. *Administrative Science Quarterly,* 30: 350–72.

BEYER, JANICE M.
  1978   Editorial policies and practices among leading journals in four scientific fields. *Sociological Quarterly,* 19: 68–88.
  1981   Ideologies, values and decison-making in organizations. Pp. 166–97 in Nystrom, Paul, and William H. Starbuck (eds.) *Handbook of Organizational Design,* vol. 2. London: Oxford University Press.
  1984   Cultures within cultures: Whose are we talking about? Paper presented at the Annual meeting of the American Institute of Decision Sciences, Toronto, Canada.
  1990   The twin dilemmas of commitment and coherence posed by high technology. Pp. 19–36 in Gomez-Mejia, Luis R., and Michael W. Lawless (eds.) *Organizational Issues in High Technology.* Greenwich, Conn.: JAI Press.

BEYER, JANICE M., ROGER L. DUNBAR, and ALAN D. MEYER
  1988   Comment: The concept of ideology in organizational analysis. *Academy of Management Review,* 13(3): 483–89.

BEYER, JANICE M., and THOMAS M. LODAHL
  1976   A comparative study of patterns of influence in United States and English universities. *Administrative Science Quarterly,* 21: 104–27.

BEYER, JANICE M., and STEVEN LUTZE
1992   The ethical nexus: Organizations, values, and decision-making. Pp. 23–45 in Conrad, Charles (ed.) *The Ethical Nexus: Communication, Values, and Organizational Decisions.* Norwood, N.J.: Ablex Publishers.

BEYER, JANICE M., and HARRISON M. TRICE
1978   *Implementing Change: Alcoholism Programs in Work Organizations.* New York: Free Press.
1979   A reexamination of the relation between size and various components of organizational complexity. *Administrative Science Quarterly,* 24(1): 48–63.
1981   Managerial ideologies and the use of discipline. *Academy of Management Proceedings,* 41: 259–63.
1982   The utilization process: A conceptual framework and synthesis of empirical findings. *Administrative Science Quarterly,* 27: 591–622.
1983   Current and prospective roles for linking organizational researchers and users. Pp. 675–702 in Kilmann, Ralph H., Kenneth P. Slevin, Raghu Nath, S. Lee Jerrell (eds.) *Producing Useful Knowledge for Organizations.* New York: Praeger Publishers.
1987   How an organization's rites reveal its culture. *Organizational Dynamics,* Spring, pp. 5–24.
1988   The communication of power relations in organizations through cultural rites. Pp. 141–57 in Jones, Michael O., Michael D. Moore, and Richard C. Snyder (eds.) *Inside Organizations: Understanding the Human Dimension.* Beverly Hills, Calif.: Sage Publications, Inc.

BIGGART, NICOLE W.
1977   The creative-destructive process of organizational change: The case of the post office. *Administrative Science Quarterly,* 22: 410–26.
1989   *Charismatic Capitalism.* Chicago: University of Chicago Press.

BLAKE, ROBERT R., and JANE S. MOUTON
1983   The urge to merge: Tying the knot successfully. *Management Development Journal,* January, pp. 41–46.
1985   How to achieve integration on the human side of the merger. *Organizational Dynamics,* 13(Winter): 41–56.

BLAU, PETER M., and RICHARD A. SCHOENHERR
1971   *The Structure of Organizations.* New York: Basic Books.

BLAU, PETER M., and W. RICHARD SCOTT
1962   *Formal Organizations.* San Francisco: Chandler Publishing.

BLAU, ZENA S., GEORGE T. OSER, and RICHARD C. STEPHENS
1983   Older workers: Current status and future prospects. *Research in the Sociology of Work,* 2: 101–24.

BLAUNER, ROBERT
1964   *Alienation and Freedom.* Chicago: University of Chicago Press.

BLOOD, MILTON R., and CHARLES L. HULIN
1967   Alienation, environmental characteristics, and worker responses. *Journal of Applied Psychology,* 51: 284–90.

BLUM, ALBERT A.
1961   Collective bargaining: Ritual or reality? *Harvard Business Review,* 39(November/December): 63–70.

BOCOCK, ROBERT
1974   *Ritual in Industrial Society.* London: Allen & Unwin.

BOJE, DAVID M., DONALD B. FEDOR, and KENDRITH M. ROWLAND
1982   Mythmaking: A qualitative step in OD interventions. *Journal of Applied Behavioral Science,* 18: 17–28.

BOK, DEREK C., and JOHN T. DUNLOP
1970   *Labor and the American Community.* New York: Simon & Schuster.

BOLAND, RICHARD J.
1982   Myth and technology in the American accounting profession. *Journal of Management Studies,* 19: 109–27.

BOLAND, RICHARD J., Jr., and RAYMOND HOFFMAN
1983   Humor in a machine shop. Pp. 187–98 in Pondy, Louis R. (ed.) *Organizational Symbolism.* Greenwich, Conn.: JAI Press.

BOLDT, EDWARD P., LANCE ROBERTS, and IAN WHITAKER
1987   The contemporary dynamics of religious defection. Pp. 45–61 in Peter, Karl A. (ed.) *The Dynamics of Hutterite Society.* Edmonton, Canada: University of Alberta Press.

BOLES, JACQUELINE, and A. P. GARBIN
1977   Stripping for a living: An occupational study of the night club stripper. Pp. 226–48 in Gallagher, Bernard J., and Charles S. Palazzolo (eds.) *The Social World of Occupations.* Chicago: Kendall/Hunt.

BOUDON, RAYMOND
1982   *The Unintended Consequences of Social Action.* New York: St. Martin's Press.

BOURNE, PETER G.
1967   Some observations on the psychosocial phenomenon seen in basic training. *Psychiatry,* 30: 187–96.

BOWERS, DAVID
1973   O.D. techniques and their results in 23 organizations. *Journal of Applied Behaviorial Science,* 9: 21–43.

BRADLEY, RAYMOND T.
1987   *Charisma and Social Structure: A Study of Love and Power, Wholeness and Transformation.* New York: Paragon House.

BRADNEY, PAMELA
1957   The joking relationship in industry. *Human Relations,* 10: 179–87.

BRANDES, STUART D.
1970   *American Welfare Capitalism.* Chicago: University of Chicago Press.

BRAVERMAN, HARRY
1974   *Labor and Monopoly Capital: The Degradation of Work in the Twentieth Century.* New York: Monthly Review Press.

BRAYBROOKE, DAVID, and CHARLES E. LINDBLOM
1963   *A Strategy of Decision: Policy Evaluation as a Social Process.* New York: Free Press.

BRETON, RAYMOND
1981   Regionalism in Canada. Pp. 57–79 in Cameron, David M. (ed). *Regionalism and Supernationalism.* Montreal, Quebec: Institute for Research on Public Policy.

BRETT, JEANNE M.
1980   Behavioral research on unions and union management systems. *Research in Organizational Behavior,* 2: 177–215.
1984   Job transitions and personal and role development. *Research in Personnel and Human Resources Management,* 2: 155–85.

BREYER, R. MICHELLE
1991   Cafeteria executives move quickly to protect company's reputation. *Austin American-Statesman,* Friday October 18, p. A9.

BRILOFF, ABRAHAM J.
1972   *Unaccountable Accounting.* New York: Harper & Row, Pub.
1981   *The Truth About Corporate Accounting.* New York: Harper & Row, Pub.

BRIM, ORVILLE
1966   Socialization through the life cycle. Pp. 1–49 in Brim, Orville, and Stanton Wheeler (eds.) *Socialization After Childhood.* New York: John Wiley.

BRINKERHOFF, MERLIN B. and DAVID J. CORRY
1976   Structural prisons: Barriers to occupational goals in a society of "equal" opportunity. *International Journal of Comparative Sociology,* 17: 261–74.

BROAD, WILLIAM J.
1992   Recipe for love: A boy, girl, a spacecraft. *New York Times.* Feb. 11: C1, C9.

BROMS, HENRI, and HENRICK GAHMBERG
1982   *Mythology in Management Culture.* Helsinki, Finland: School of Economics.
1983   Communications to self in organizations and cultures. *Administrative Science Quarterly,* 28: 482–95.

BROWN, L. DAVID
1983   *Management Conflict at Organizational Interfaces.* Reading, Mass.: Addison-Wesley.

BROWN, RICHARD H.
1978   Bureaucracy as praxis: Toward a political phenomenology of formal organizations. *Administrative Science Quarterly,* 23: 365–82.

BROWN, STANLEY
1987   The Japanese approach to labor relations: Can it work in America? *Personnel,* 64(4): 20–29.

BRYAN, JAMES H.
1965   Apprenticeships in prostitution. *Social Problems,* 12: 287–97.

BRYANT, CLIFFORD D.
1972   Sawdust in their shoes: The carnival as a neglected complex organization and work culture. Pp. 180–203 in Bryant, Clifford D. (ed.) *The Social Dimensions of Work.* Englewood Cliffs, N.J.: Prentice-Hall.

BUCHER, RUE, and JOAN STELLING
1969   Characteristics of professional organizations. *Journal of Health and Social Behavior,* 10(1): 3–15.

BUONO, ANTHONY F., JAMES L. BOWDITCH, and JOHN W. LEWIS
1985   When cultures collide: The anatomy of a merger. *Human Relations,* 38(5): 477–500.

BURKE, W. WARNER
1980   Organizational development and bureaucracy in the 1980s. *Journal of Applied Behaviorial Science,* 16: 423–37.
1990   The Tylenol case: How a code can function in an organization. Paper presented at the Academy of Management Annual Meetings, August 13, San Francisco.

BURNETT, JACQUETTA H.
1969   Ceremony, rites and economy in the student system of an American high school. *Human Organization,* 28: 1–10.

BURNS, JAMES M.
1978   *Leadership.* New York: Harper & Row, Pub.

BURNS, TOM
1955   The reference of conduct in small groups. *Human Relations,* 8(4): 467–83.

BURNS, TOM, and GEORGE STALKER
1961   *The Management of Innovation.* London: Tavistock Publications.

Business Week
1984   Who's excellent now? November 5, Pp. 76–88.

BUSSEY, JOHN
1986   Gerber takes risky stance as fears spread about glass in baby food. *The Wall Street Journal,* March 6, P. 27.

BUTCHER, LEE
1988   *Accidental Millionaire: The Rise and Fall of Steve Jobs at Apple Computer.* New York: Paragon House.

BYINGTON, ROBERT H.
1978   Strategies for collecting occupational folklife in contemporary urban/industrial contexts. *Western Folklore,* 37(special issue): 185–212.

BYRNE, JOHN A.
1989   Donald Burr may be ready to take to the skies again. *Business Week,* January 16, Pp. 74–76.
1990   Pay stubs of the rich and corporate. *Business Week,* May 7, 56–66.

CALDER, BOBBY J.
1977   An attribution theory of leadership. Pp. 179–205 in Staw, Barry M., and Gerald R. Salancik (eds.) *New Directions in Organizational Behavior.* Chicago: St. Clair Press.

CAMERON, KIM S.
1986   Effectiveness as paradox. *Management Science,* 32: 539–53.
1991   Personal communication.

CAMERON, KIM S., and ROBERT E. QUINN
1988   Organizational paradox and transformation. Pp. 1–18 in Cameron, Kim S., and Robert Quinn (eds.) *Paradox and Transformation.* Cambridge, Mass.: Ballinger Publishing.

CAMPBELL, J. P., M. D. DUNETTE, EDWARD E. LAWLER III, and KARL E. WEICK, Jr.
1970   *Managerial Behavior, Performance, and Effectiveness.* New York: McGraw-Hill.

CAPLOW, THEODORE
1982   Christmas gifts and kin networks. *American Sociological Review,* 47(June): 383–92.

CARDEN, MAREN L.
1969   *Oneida: Utopian Community to Modern Corporation.* New York: Harper & Row, Pub.

CAREY, CHRISTOPHER
1988   Southwest Airlines sets its own rules. *St. Louis Post Dispatch,* December 25, 1988, pp. 1, 6F.

CARROLL, DANIEL T.
1983   Review of Thomas J. Peters and Robert W. Waterman, Corporate Cultures: The Rites and Rituals of Corporate Life. *Harvard Business Review,* 6(November-December): 78–88.

CARSON, GEORGE
1986   The Fuller Brush man. *American Heritage,* 37(August–September): 26–31.

CARSON, RACHAEL
1962   *Silent Spring.* Boston: Houghton Mifflin Company.

CAUDILL, WILLIAM
1958   *The Psychiatric Hospital as a Small Society.* Cambridge, Mass.: Harvard University Press.

CHANDLER, ALFRED D.
1990   Scale and scope in industry. Paper presented at the Second International Conference on

Socio-Economics, Washington, D.C.: The George Washington University. Sponsored by The Society for the Advancement of Socio-Economics.

1991   Managerial enterprise and competitive capabilities. *Business History,* 34(2): forthcoming.

CHANDLER, ALFRED D., Jr., and STEPHEN SALZBURY

1971   *Pierre S. DuPont and the Making of a Modern Corporation.* New York: Harper & Row, Pub.

CHANDY, P. R.

1991   Chief executive officers: Their backgrounds and predictions for the 90s. *Business Forum,* 16(Winter): 18–22.

CHARNOFSKY, HAROLD

1974   Ballplayers, occupational image and the maximization of profit. Pp. 262–74 in Stewart, Phyllis L., and Muriel G. Cantor (eds.) *Varieties of Work Experiences.* New York: John Wiley.

CHATMAN, JENNIFER A.

1991   Matching people and organizations: Selection and socialization in public accounting firms. *Administrative Science Quarterly,* 36: 459–84.

CHATOV, ROBERT

1973   The role of ideology in the American corporation. Pp. 50–75 in Votaw, Dow and S. Prakash Sethi (eds.) *The Corporate Dilemma: Traditional Values Versus Contemporary Problems.* Englewood Cliffs, N.J.: Prentice Hall.

1975   *Corporate Financial Reporting: Public or Private Control.* New York: Free Press.

1981   Cooperation between government and business. Pp. 487–502 in Nystrom, Paul C., and William H. Starbuck (eds.) *Handbook of Organizational Design.* New York: Oxford University Press.

CHEN, HUEY-TSYH, and PETER H. ROSSI

1980   The multi-goal, theory-driven approach to evaluation: A model linking basic and applied science. *Social Forces,* 59: 106–22.

CHILD, JOHN

1981   Culture, contingency and capitalism in the cross-national study of organizations. *Research in Organizational Behavior* 3: 303–36.

CHILD, JOHN, and JANET FULK

1982   Maintenance of occupational control: The case of the professions. *Work and Occupations,* 9(2): 155–92.

CHILD, JOHN, H. D. GANTER, and A. KIESER

1987   Technological innovation and organizational conservatism. Pp. 87–116 in Pennings, Johannes M., and Arend Buitendam (eds.) *New Technology as Organizational Innovation.* Cambridge, Mass.: Ballinger Publishing.

CHILD, JOHN, and ALFRED KIESER

1979   Organizational and managerial roles in British and West German companies: An examination of the culture-free thesis. Pp. 251–72 in Lammers, Cornelius J., and David J. Hickson (eds.) *Organizations Alike and Unlike.* London: Routledge & Kegan Paul.

CHILD, JOHN, RAY LOVERIDGE, JANET HARVEY, and ANNE SPENCER

1984   Micro-electronics and the quality of employment services. Pp. 163–91 in Mastrand, Pauline (ed.) *New Technology and the Future of Work and Skills.* London: Pinter.

CHILD, JOHN, R. LOVERIDGE, and M. WARNER

1973   Toward an organizational study of trade unions. *Sociology,* 7: 71–91.

CHILD, JOHN, and CHRIS SMITH

1987   The context and process of organizational transformation—Cadbury Limited in its sector. *Journal of Management Studies,* 24(November): 565–93.

CLARK, BURTON R.
1956   Organizational adaptation and precarious values: A case study. *American Sociological Review,* 21: 327–36.
1970   *The Distinctive College: Antioch, Reed, and Swathmore.* Chicago: Aldine.
1972   The organizational saga in higher education. *Administrative Science Quarterly,* 17: 178–83.

CLARK, RODNEY C.
1979   *The Japanese Company.* New Haven, Conn.: Yale University Press.

CLÈVERLEY, GRAHAM
1973   *Managers and Magic.* New York: Dutton.

CLOWARD, RICHARD, and LLOYD OHLIN
1959   Illegitimate means, anomie and deviant behavior. *American Sociological Review,* 24: 164–77.

COHEN, ABNER
1976   *Two Dimensional Man.* Berkeley, Calif.: University of California Press.

COHEN, MALCOLM S., and GEORGE A. FULTON
1987   Unions and jobs: The U.S. auto industry: Comment. *Journal of Labor Research,* 8: 307–10.

COHEN, MICAHEL D., and JAMES G. MARCH
1976   Decisions, presidents, and status. Pp. 174–205 in March, James G., and Johan P. Olsen (eds.) *Ambiguity and Choice in Organizations.* Bergen, Norway: Universitetforlaget.

COHEN, MICHAEL D., JAMES G. MARCH, and JOHAN P. OLSEN
1972   A garbage can model of organizational choice. *Administrative Science Quarterly,* 17: 1–25.

COLE, ROBERT E.
1971   *Japenese Blue Collar: The Changing Tradition.* Berkeley, Calif.: University of California Press.
1979   *Work, Mobility, and Participation.* Berkeley, Calif.: University of California Press.
1980   Learning from the Japanese: Prospects and pitfalls. *Management Review,* 69(9): 22–42.
1985   The macropolitics of organizational change: A comparative analysis of the spread of small group activities. *Administrative Science Quarterly,* 30: 560–85.

COLEMAN, JAMES S.
1974   *Power and the Structure of Society.* New York: W. W. Norton & Co., Inc.

COMMAGER, HENRY S.
1947   *America in Perspective.* New York: Random House.

CONGER, JAY A.
1989   *The Charismatic Leader: Behind the Mystique of Exceptional Leadership.* San Francisco: Jossey-Bass.

CONGER, JAY A., and RABINDRA N. KANUNGO
1988   Training charismatic leadership: A risky and critical task. Pp. 309–23 in Conger, Jay A., and Rabindra N. Kanungo (eds.) *Charismatic Leadership: The Elusive Factor in Organizational Effectiveness.* San Francisco: Jossey-Bass.

CONGER, JAY A., RABINDRA N. KANUNGO and Associates (eds)
1988   *Charismatic Leadership: The Elusive Factor in Organizational Effectiveness.* San Francisco: Jossey-Bass Publishers.

CONRAD, CHARLES
1983   Organizational power: Faces and symbolic forms. Pp. 173–95 in Putnam, Linda L., and Michael E. Pacanowsky (eds.) *Communications and Organizations: An Interpretive Approach.* Beverly Hills, Calif.: Sage Publications, Inc.

CONWAY, JAMES A.
1985   A perspective on organizational cultures and organizational belief structure. *Educational Administrative Quarterly,* 21(4): 7–25.

COOKE, ROBERT A. and DENISE M. ROUSSEAU
1988   Behavioral norms and expectations: A quantitative approach to the assessment of organizational culture. *Group and Organization Studies*, 13: 245–73.

COSER, LEWIS A., CHARLES KADUSHIN, and WALTER W. POWELL
1982   *Books: The Culture and Commerce of Publishing*. New York: Basic Books.

COSER, ROSE L.
1960   Laughter among colleagues. *Psychiatry*, 23: 81–95.

COTTRELL, W. FRED
1940   *The Railroader*. Stanford, Calif.: Stanford University Press.

COWIE, JAMES B., and JULIAN ROEBUCK
1975   *An Ethnography of a Chiropractic Clinic*. New York: Free Press.

COX, TAYLOR, JR.
1991   The multicultural organization. *The Academy of Management Executive*, 5(2): 34–47.

CRARY, MARCY
1987   Managing attraction and intimacy at work. *Organizational Dynamics*, 15(Spring): 27–41.

CROZIER, MICHAEL
1964   *The Bureaucratic Phenomenon*. Chicago: University of Chicago Press.
1973   The cultural determinants of organizational behavior. Pp. 219–25 in Negandhi, Amant R. (ed.) *Modern Organizational Theory*. Kent, Ohio: Kent State University Press.

CULLEN, JOHN B., KENNETH S. ANDERSON, and DOUGLAS D. BAKER
1986   Blau's theory of structural differentiation revisited: A theory of structural change or scale? *Academy of Management Journal*, 29: 203–29.

CUMMING, ELAINE
1963   Further thoughts on the theory of disengagement. *International Social Science Journal*, 15: 377–93.

CUMMING, ELAINE, LOIS R. DEAN, DAVID S. NEWELL, and ISABEL MCCAFFREY
1960   Disengagement: A tentative theory of aging. *Sociometry*, 23: 23–35.

CUMMING, ELAINE, and W. E. HENRY
1961   *Growing Old: The Process of Disengagement*. New York: Basic Books.

CUMMINGS, THOMAS G., and EDMOND S. MOLLOY
1977   *Improving Productivity and the Quality of Work Life*. New York: Praeger Publishers.

CYERT, RICHARD M. and JAMES G. MARCH
1963   *A Behavioral Theory of the Firm*. Englewood Cliffs, N.J.: Prentice Hall.

DAFT, RICHARD L.
1983   Symbols in organizations: A dual-content framework for analysis. Pp. 199–207 in Pondy, L. R., P. Frost, G. Morgan, and T. Dandridge (eds.) *Organizational Symbolism*. Greenwich, Conn.: JAI Press.

DAFT, RICHARD L., and RICHARD M. STEERS
1986   *Organizations: A Micro/Macro Approach*. Glenview, Ill.: Scott, Foresman.

DAFT, RICHARD, and KARL WEICK
1984   Toward a model of organizations as interpretation systems. *Academy of Management Review*, 9(2): 284–95.

DALE, ERNEST
1956   Contributions to administration by Alfred P. Sloan, Jr. *Administrative Science Quarterly*, 1(1): 30–62.

DALTON, MELVILLE
  1959   *Men Who Manage.* New York: John Wiley.
  1962   Cooperative evasions to support labor-management contracts. Pp. 267–84 in Rose, Arnold (ed.), *Human Behavioral and Social Processes: An Interactionist Approach.* Boston: Houghton Mifflin Company.

DANDRIDGE, THOMAS C.
  1983   Symbols' function and use. Pp. 69–73 in Pondy, Louis R., Peter J. Frost, Gareth Morgan, and Thomas C. Dandridge (eds.), *Organizational Symbolism.* Greenwich, Conn.: JAI Press.

DAUGHEN, JOSEPH, and PETER BINZEN
  1971   *The Wreck of the Penn Central.* New York: Little, Brown.

DAVIES, ROBERT J., and NAN WEINER
  1985   A cultural perspective on the study of industrial relations. Pp. 355–72 in Frost, Peter J. et al. (eds). *Organizational Culture.* Beverly Hills, Calif.: Sage Publications, Inc.

DAVIS, ALLISON, BURLEIGH B. GARDNER, MARY R. GARDNER, and W. LLOYD WARNER
  1941   *Deep South: A Social Anthropological Study of Caste and Class.* Chicago: University of Chicago Press.

DAVIS, KEITH
  1953   Business communication and the grapevine. *Harvard Business Review,* 31: 43–49.
  1969   Grapevine communication among lower and middle managers. *Personnel Journal,* 48(4): 269–72.
  1973   The care and cultivation of the corporate grapevine. *Dun's Review,* 102: 44–47.

DAY, MARTIN S.
  1984   *The Many Meanings of Myth.* Lanham, Md.: University Press of America.

DEAL, TERRENCE
  1985   Culture change: Opportunity, silent killer, or metamorphosis? Pp. 292–330 in Kilmann, Ralph, et al. (eds.) *Gaining Control of the Corporate Culture.* San Francisco: Jossey-Bass.

DEAL, TERRENCE E., and ALLAN A. KENNEDY
  1982   *Corporate Cultures: The Rites and Rituals of Corporate Life.* Reading, Mass.: Addison-Wesley.

DELLHEIM, CHARLES
  1987   The creation of a company culture. *The American History Review,* 92(1): 13–44.

DENISON, DANIEL R.
  1984   Bringing corporate culture to the bottom line. *Organizational Dynamics,* 13(2): 5–22.
  1990   *Corporate Culture and Organizational Effectiveness.* New York: John Wiley.

DE TOCQUEVILLE, ALEXIS
  1877   *Democracy in America: The Republic of the United States of America and its Political Institutions.* New York: Barnes.

DITOMASO, NANCY
  1987   Symbolic media and social solidarity: Foundations of corporate culture. *Research in Sociology of Organizations,* 5: 105–34.

DOLAN, MAURA, and PATRICK LEE
  1991   Exxon's spill deal rejected by judge. *Austin American—Statesman,* Thursday, April 25, Pp. A1, A11.

DOMHOFF, G. WILLIAM
  1971   *The Higher Circles.* New York: Random House.

DONNELLON, ANNE, BARBARA GRAY, and MICHEL G. BOUGON
  1986   Communication, meaning and organized action. *Administrative Science Quarterly,* 31: 43–55.

DORE, RONALD
1973   *British Factory, Japanese Factory: The Origins of Diversity in Industrial Relations.* Berkeley, Calif.: University of California Press.

DORNBUSH, SANFORD
1954   The military academy as an assimilating institution. *Social Forces,* 13(May): 316–21.

DORSON, RICHARD M.
1971   Applied folklore. Pp. 40–42 in Sweterlitsch, Dick (ed.) *Papers on Applied Folklore.* Bloomington, Ind.: Folklore Forum Bibliographic and Special Series #8.
1973   *America in Legend: Folklore from the Colonial Period to the Present.* New York: Pantheon.

DOUGHERTY, DEBORAH, and GIDEON KUNDA
1990   Photograph analysis: A method to capture organizational belief systems. Pp. 185–206 in Gagliardi, Pasquale (ed.) *Symbols and Artifacts: Views of the Corporate Landscape.* New York: Walter de Gruyter.

DOUGLAS, MARY
1982   Introduction to grid/group analysis. Pp. 1–12 in Douglas, Mary (ed.) *Essays in the Sociology of Perception.* London: Routledge & Kegan Paul.

DRUCKER, PETER F.
1986   Corporate takeovers—What is to be done? *The Public Interest,* 82: 3–24.

DRUCKMAN, DANIEL (ed.)
1977   *Negotiations.* Beverly Hills, Calif.: Sage Publications, Inc.

DUBIN, ROBERT
1951   Organization fictions. Pp 493–99 in Dubin, Robert (ed.) *Human Relations in Administration.* Englewood Cliffs, N.J.: Prentice Hall.
1979   Metaphors of leadership: An overview. Pp. 225–38 in Hunt, James G., and Lars L. Larson (eds.) *Crosscurrents in Leadership.* Carbondale Ill: Southern Illinois University Press.

DUBINSKAS, FRANK A.
1988   Janus organizations: Scientists and managers in genetic engineering firms. Pp 170–232 in Dubinskas, Frank A. (ed.) *Making Time: Ethnographics of High Technology Organizations.* Philadelphia: Temple University Press.

DUBOFSKY, MELVIN, and WARREN R. VAN TINE
1977   *John L. Lewis: A Biography.* New York: Quadrangle/The New York Times Book Company.

DUNBAR, ROGER L. M., JOHN M. DUTTON, and WILLIAM R. TORBERT
1982   Crossing mother: Ideological constraints on organizational improvements. *Journal of Management Studies,* 19(1): 91–107.

DUNCAN, W. JACK
1982   Humor in management: Prospects for administrative practice and research. *Academy of Management Review,* 7(1): 136–42.

DUNNETTE, MARVIN D., R. AVERY, and P. BANAS
1973   Why do they leave? *Personnel,* 50(3): 25–39.

DURKHEIM, EMILE
1964   *Suicide.* New York: Free Press.

DWYER, TOM
1991   Power and change in organizations. *Human Relations,* 44(1): 1–19.

DYER, W. GIBB
1985   The cycle of cultural evolution in organizations. Pp. 24–41 in Kilmann, Ralph, Mary J.

Saxton, and Roy Serpa (eds.) *Gaining Control of the Corporate Culture.* San Francisco, Jossey-Bass.

Economist, The
1989   Post-workaholism in Japan, March 25, pp. 70–77.

EDELMAN, MURRAY
1977   *Political Language: Words that Succeed and Politics that Fail.* New York: Academic Press.

EDWARDS, PAUL K., and HUGH SCULLION
1982   *The Social Organization of Industrial Conflict: Control and Resistance in the Workplace.* Oxford, England: Blackwell.

EHRLICH, SANFORD B., JAMES R. MEINDL, and BEN VIELLIEU
1990   The charismatic appeal of a transformational leader: An empirical case study of a small, high-technology contractor. *Leadership Quarterly,* 1(4): 229–47.

EISENSTADT, S. N.
1959   Bureaucracy, bureaucratization, and debureaucratization. *Administrative Science Quarterly,* 4(December): 302–20.

EMERY, FRED E., and ERIC L. TRIST
1965   The casual texture of organizational environments. *Human Relations,* 18: 21–32.

ENGLAND, GEORGE W., and RAYMOND LEE
1974   Organizational goals and expected behaviors among American, Japanese, and Korean managers: A comparative study. *Academy of Management Journal,* 14: 425–38.

ETZIONI, AMITAI
1987   How rational are we? *Sociological Forum,* 2(1): 1–17.

EVAN, WILLIAM M.
1972   An organization-set model of interorganizational relations. Pp. 181–200 in Tuite, M. F., M. Radnor, and R. K. Chisholm (eds.) *Interorganizational Decision Making.* New York: Aldine.

EVERED, ROGER
1983   The language of organizations: The case of the Navy. Pp. 125–43 in Pondy, Louis R., Peter J. Frost, and Thomas C. Dandridge (eds.) *Organizational Symbolism.* Greenwich, Conn.: JAI Press.

EVERED, ROGER, and MERYL LOUIS
1981   Alternative perspectives in the organizational sciences: Inquiry from the inside and inquiry from the outside. *Academy of Management Review,* 6: 385–95.

FARAGHER, JOHNNY, and CHRISTINA STANSELL
1975   Women and their families on the overland trail. *Feminist Studies,* 2: 150–66.

FARNHAM, ALAN
1989   The trust gap. *Fortune,* December 4, pp. 56–74, 78.

FARRELL, DAN C., and JAMES C. PETERSON
1982   Patterns of political behavior in organizations. *Academy of Management Review,* 7: 403–21.

FAULKNER, ROBERT R.
1974   Coming of age in organizations. A comparative study of career contingencies and adult socialization. *Sociology of Work and Occupations,* 1(2): 131–73.

FELDMAN, DANIEL C.
1974   A contingency theory of socialization. *Administrative Science Quarterly,* 21: 433–52.
1976   A practical program for employee socialization. *Organizational Dynamics,* 5(2): 64–80.
1981   A multiple socialization of organizational members. *Academy of Management Review,* 6: 309–18.

FELDMAN, DANIEL C., and JEANNE BRETT
1983   Coping with new jobs: A comparative study of new job hires and job changers. *Academy of Management Journal*, 26: 258–72.

FELDMAN, MARTHA S.
1991   The meanings of ambiguity: Learning from stories and metaphors. Pp. 145–56 in Frost, Peter, Larry F. Moore, Meryl R. Louis, Craig C. Lundberg, and Joanne Martin (eds.), *Reframing Organizational Culture*. Newbury Park, Calif.: Sage Publications, Inc.

FELDMAN, MARTHA S., and JAMES G. MARCH
1981   Information in organizations as signal and symbol. *Administrative Science Quarterly*, 26: 171–84.

FELDMAN, S. P.
1987   The crossroads of interpretation: Administration in professional organizations. *Human Organization*, 46(2): 95–102.

FERGUSON, HARVEY
1936   *Modern Man: His Belief and Behavior.* New York and London: Knopf.

FERNANDEZ, JAMES W.
1971   Persuasions and performances of the beast in everybody and the metaphors of everyman. Pp. 38–60 in Geertz, Clifford (ed.) *Myth, Symbol, and Culture.* New York: W. W. Norton & Co., Inc.

FIEDLER, FRED E.
1978   The contingency model and the dynamics of the leadership process. In Berkowitz, L. (ed.) *Advances in Experimental Social Psychology*, Vol. II. New York: Academic Press.

FINE GARY A.
1984a   Humorous interaction and the social construction of meaning: Making sense in a jocular vein. *Studies in Symbolic Interaction*, 5: 83–101.
1984b   Negotiated orders and organizational cultures. *Annual Review of Sociology*, 10: 239–62.
1985   Occupational aesthetics: How trade school students learn to cook. *Urban Life*, 14(1): 3–31.

FINE, GARY A., and SHERRYL KLEINMAN
1979   Rethinking subculture: An interactionist analysis. *American Journal of Sociology*, 85(1): 1–20.

FINHOLT, TOM, and LEE S. SPROULL
1990   Electronic groups at work. *Organization Science*, 1(1): 41–64.

FIRTH, RAYMOND
1972   Verbal and bodily rituals of greeting and parting. Pp. 1–38 in LaFontaine, J. S. (ed.) *The Interpretation of Ritual.* London: Tavistock Publications.
1973   *Symbols: Public and Private.* Ithaca, N.Y.: Cornell University Press.

FLIGSTEIN, NEIL
1987   The intraorganizational power struggle: Rise of finance personnel to top leadership in large corporations, 1919–1979. *American Sociological Review*, 52(February): 44–58.

FORBES, J. BENJAMIN
1987   Early intraorganizational mobility: Patterns and influences. *Academy of Management Journal*, 30: 110–25.

FORM, WILLIAM
1987   On the degradation of skills. *Annual Review of Sociology*, 13: 29–47.

FORTES, MEYER
1962   Ritual and office in tribal society. Pp. 53–89 in Gluckman, Max (ed.) *Essays on the Ritual of Social Relations.* Manchester, England: University of Manchester Press.

FOY, NANCY
1975   *The Sun Never Sets on IBM.* New York: Morrow.

FRANK, ROBERT H.
1987   Shrewdly irrational. *Sociological Forum,* 2(1): 21–39.

FREIBERG, KEVIN L.
1987   The heart and spirit of transformation leadership: A qualitative case study of Herb Kelleher's passion for Southwest Airlines. A dissertation in partial fulfillment of requirements for degree of Doctor of Philosophy, University of San Diego.

FREIDSON, ELIOT
1973   Professions and the occupational principle. Pp. 19–33 in Freidson, Eliot (ed.) *Professions and Their Prospects.* Beverly Hills, Calif.: Sage Publications, Inc.
1982   Occupational autonomy and labor market shelters. Pp. 39–54 in Stewart, Phyllis L., and Muriel G. Cantor (eds.) *Varieties of Work.* Beverly Hills, Calif.: Sage Publications, Inc.

FRENCH, EARL, and HARRISON M. TRICE
1972   The incidence of the emotionally disturbed within the administrative units of a large organization. *Personnel Psychology,* 25: 535–43.

FRENCH, JOHN R. P., and BERTRAM RAVEN
1968   The bases of social power. In Cartwright, D., and A. Zander (eds.) *Group Dynamics.* New York: Harper & Row, Pub.

FRIEDLAND, WILLIAM H.
1964   For a sociological concept of charisma. *Social Forces,* 43: 18–26.

FRIEDMAN, DANA E.
1989   Corporation's stake in the issue of child care and the range of responses corporations have adopted. Talk given at the annual meeting of the Academy of Management, August, Washington, D.C.

FRIEDMAN, STEWART D.
1983   Cultures within cultures: An empirical assessment of an organizational subculture using projective measures. Paper presented at the annual meeting of the Academy of Management, August, Dallas, Tex.

FROST, PETER J., LARRY F. MOORE, MERYL R. LOUIS, CRAIG C. LUNDBERG, and JOANNE MARTIN (eds.)
1985   *Organizational Culture.* Beverly Hills, Calif.: Sage Publications, Inc.

FUCINI, JOSEPH J., and SUZY FUCINI
1990   *Working for the Japanese: Inside Mazda's American Auto Plant.* New York: Free Press.

FUKAMI, CYNTHIA V., and ERIC LARSEN
1984   Commitment to company and union: Parallel models. *Journal of Applied Psychology,* 69: 367–71.

GAGLIARDI, PASQUALE
1986   The creation and change of organizational cultures: A conceptual framework. *Organizational Studies,* 7(2): 117–34.

GAGLIARDI, PASQUALE (ed.)
1990   *Symbols and Artifacts: Views of the Corporate Landscape.* New York: Walter de Gruyter.

GAMST, FREDERICK C.
1977   An integrating view of the underlying premises of an industrial ethnology in the U.S. and Canada. *Anthropological Quarterly,* 50(1): 1–9.
1980a   Toward a method of industrial ethnography. *Rice University Studies,* 66(1): 15–42.
1980b   *The Hoghead: An Industrial Ethnology of the Locomotive Engineer.* New York: Holt, Rinehart & Winston.

GARDNER, BURLEIGH B.

1945 *Human Relations in Industry.* Chicago: Richard D. Irwin.

1946 The factory as a social system. Pp. 4–21 in Whyte, William F. (ed.) *Industry and Society,* New York: McGraw-Hill.

GARFIELD, SIDNEY, and WILLIAM F. WHYTE

1950 The collective bargaining process: A human relations analysis. *Human Organization,* Summer, Pp. 5–9.

GARFINKEL, HAROLD

1956 Conditions of successful degradation ceremonies. *American Sociological Review,* 61: 420–25.

1967 *Studies in Ethnomethodology.* Englewood Cliffs, N.J.: Prentice Hall.

GARRETT, ECHA M.

1989 Up like a rocket. *Venture,* May, Pp. 46–47.

GEERTZ, CLIFFORD

1957 Ritual and social change: A Javanese example. *American Anthropologist,* 59: 991–1012.

1964 Ideology as a cultural system. Pp. 47–76 in Apter, David E. (ed.) *Ideology and Discontent.* New York: Free Press.

1966 *Person, Time, and Conduct in Bali: An Essay in Cultural Analysis.* Yale Southeast Asia Program, Culture Series #14.

1970 The impact of the concept of culture on the concept of man. Pp. 47–65 in Hammel, Eugene A., and William S. Simmons (eds.) *Man Makes Sense.* Boston: Little, Brown.

1971 Deep play: Notes on the Balinese cockfight. Pp. 1–37 in Geertz, Clifford (ed.) *Myth, Symbol, and Culture.* New York: W. W. Norton & Co., Inc.

1973 *The Interpretation of Cultures.* New York: Basic Books.

1979 From the native's point of view: On the nature of anthropological understanding. Pp. 225–367 in Rabinow, Paul (ed.) *Interpretive Social Science: A Reader.* Berkeley, Calif.: University of California Press.

1983 *Local Knowledge: Further Essays in Interpretive Anthropology.* New York: Basic Books.

GELMAN, DAVID

1991 Clean and sober and agnostic. *Newsweek,* July 8, pp. 62–63.

GERSICK, CONNIE J. G.

1991 Revolutionary change theories: A multilevel exploration of the punctuated equilibrium paradigm. *Academy of Management Review,* 16: 10–36.

GEORGES, ROBERT, and MICHAEL O. JONES

1980 *People Studying People: The Human Element in Field Work.* Berkeley, Calif.:University of California Press.

GEORGES, ROBERT

1969 Toward an understanding of storytelling events. *Journal of American Folklore,* 82: 313–28.

GEPHART, ROBERT J.

1978 Status degradation and organizational succession: An ethnomethodological approach. *Administrative Science Quarterly,* 23(December): 553–81.

GERSTL, JOEL E.

1961 Determinants of occupational community in high status occupations. *Sociological Quarterly,* 2: 37–40.

GERTH, HANS, and C. WRIGHT MILLS (eds.)

1946 *From Max Weber.* New York: Oxford University Press.

GILMORE, DAVID D.

1990 *Manhood in the Making: Cultural Concepts of Masculinity.* New Haven: Yale University Press.

GLADWIN, THOMAS N., and INGO WALTERS
1976   Multinational enterprise, social responsiveness, and pollution control. *Journal of International Business Studies*, 7(Fall/Winter): 57–73.

GLASER, BARNEY G., and ANSELM L. STRAUSS
1971   *Status Passage*. Chicago: Aldine-Atherton.

GLASSNER, BARRY, and BRUCE BERG
1980   How Jews avoid drinking problems. *American Sociological Review*, 45(August): 647–64.

GLAZER, MYRON P., and PENINA M. GLAZER
1989   *The Whistle-Blowers: Exposing Corruption in Government and Industry*. New York: Basic Books.

GLEICK, JAMES
1987   *Chaos: Making a New Science*. New York: Penguin.

GLICK, PAULA BROWN
1983   Collective bargaining as a field for anthropological study. *Anthropology of Work Review*, 4: 7–9.

GLICK, WILLIAM H.
1985   Conceptualizing and measuring organizational and psychological climate: Pitfalls in multilevel research. *Academy of Management Review*, 10(3): 601–16.

GLUCKMAN, MAX
1962   Les Rites de Passage. Pp. 1–53 in Gluckman, Max (ed.) *Essays on the Ritual of Social Relations*. Manchester, England: Manchester University Press.
1963a   *Order and Rebellion in African Tribal Society*. London: Cohen and West.
1963b   Gossip and scandal, *Current Anthropology*, 4(3): 307–16.

GOFFMAN, IRVING
1959   *The Presentation of Self in Everyday Life*. Garden City, N.J.: Anchor Books.
1967   *Interaction Ritual*. New York: Anchor Books.

GOLDNER, FRED H.
1970   The division of labor: Process and power. Pp. 97–143 in Zald, Mayer N. (ed.) *Power in Organizations*. Nashville, Tenn.: Vanderbilt University Press.

GOLDSMITH, WALTER, and DAVID CLUTTERBUCK
1984   *The Winning Streak*. London: Weidenfeld and Nicholson.

GOODE, WILLIAM J.
1978   *The Celebration of Heroes: Prestige as a Social Control System*. Berkeley, Calif.: University of California.

GOODENOUGH, WARD H.
1978   Multiculturalism as the normal human experience. Pp. 79–86, in Eddy, Elizabeth, and William L. Partridge (eds.) *Applied Anthropology in America*. New York: Columbia University Press.

GOODING, JUDSON
1972   The art of firing an executive. *Fortune*, October, Pp. 22–30.

GOODSELL, CHARLES T.
1977   Bureaucratic manipulation of physical symbols: An empirical study. *American Journal of Political Science*, 21: 79–91.

GORDON, GEORGE W.
1991   Industry determinants of organizational culture. *Academy of Management Review*, 16(2): 396–415.

GORDON, GIL E.
1979   Looking from the outside in: Management/executive development programs from the employer's viewpoint. *Exchange: The Organizational Behavior Teaching Journal,* Fall: 23–25.

GOULDNER, ALVIN
1957   Cosmopolitans and locals: Toward an analysis of latent social roles. *Administrative Science Quarterly,* 2: 281–306.

GOULDNER, FRED H.
1961   Industrial Relations and the Organization of Management. Unpublished Ph.D. thesis, University of California, Berkeley.

GOVE, PHILIP BABCOCK
1981   *Webster's Third New International Dictionary of the English Language,* unabridged. Springfield, Mass.: Merriam-Webster Publishers, Inc.

GOWLER, DAN, and KAREN LEGGE
1983   The meaning of management and the management of meaning: A view from social anthropology. Pp. 197–233 in Earl, M. J. (ed) *Perspectives on Management: An Interdisciplinary Approach.* London: Oxford University Press.
1989   Rhetoric in bureaucratic careers: Managing the meaning of management success. Pp. 437–45 in Arthur, Michael B., Douglas T. Hall, and Barbara S. Lawrence (eds.) *Handbook of Career Theory.* New York: Cambridge University Press.

GRANICK, DAVID
1962   *The European Executive.* Garden City, N.Y.: Doubleday.

GRANOVETTER, MARK, S.
1973   The strength of weak ties. *American Journal of Sociology,* 78: 1360–80.

GRANROSE, CHERLYN S., and JAMES D. PORTWOOD
1987   Matching individual career plans and organizational career management. *Academy of Management Journal,* 30(4): 699–720.

GRAY, SUSAN, and DEAN MORSE
1980   Retirement and re-engagement: Changing work options for older workers. *Aging and Work,* 3: 103–12.

GREEN, ARCHIE
1965   American labor lore: Its meanings and uses. *Industrial Relations,* 4: 51–68.

GREENHOUSE, CAROL
1985   Anthropology at home: Whose home? *Human Organizations,* 44(3): 261–64.

GREGORY, KATHLEEN L.
1983   Native view paradigms: Multiple cultures and culture conflict in organizations. *Administrative Science Quarterly,* 28: 359–76.

GREINER, LARRY E.
1972   Evolution and revolution as organizations grow. *Harvard Business Review,* 50(July–August): 37–46.

GUSFIELD, JOSEPH R.
1975   *Community: A Critical Response,* New York: Harper & Row, Pub.

GUSTAFSON, CLAUS
1984   Hero-myth and manager descriptions. Paper presented at the First International Conference on Organizational Symbolism and Culture, Lund University; Lund, Sweden, June 27–30.

GUTH, WILLIAM D., and RENATO TAGIURI
1965   Personal values and corporate strategies. *Harvard Business Review,* 43(5): 123–32.

GUYOT, JAMES F.
1977   Prescription drugs and placebos: A new perspective on management. *Personnel Journal* 54(May–June): 67–72.
1978   Management training and post-industrial apologetics. *California Management Review,* 20: 84–93.

GWYNNE, S. C.
1990   The right stuff. *Time* October 29, Pp. 74–84.

HAAS, JACK
1974   The stages of the high-steel ironworker apprentice career. *The Sociological Quarterly,* 15(Winter): 93–108.
1977   Learning real feelings: A study of high-steel Ironworkers' reaction to fear and danger. *Sociology of Work and Occupations,* 4(2): 147–69.

HACKMAN, J. RICHARD
1984   The transition that hasn't happened. Pp. 29–59 in Kimberly, John R., and Robert E. Quinn (eds.) *New futures: The challenge of managing corporate transitions.* Homewood, Ill.: Dow Jones-Irwin.

HADDAD, WILLIAM F.
1985   *Hard Driving: My Years with John DeLorean.* New York: Random House.

HAGE, JERALD, and MICHAEL AIKEN
1967   Relationship of centralization to other structural properties. *Administrative Science Quarterly,* 12(1): 79–84.

HALBERSTAM, DAVID
1986   *The Reckoning.* New York: Morrow.

HALL, DOUGLAS T., BENJAMIN SCHNEIDER, and HAROLD T. NYGREN
1970   Personal factors in organizational identification. *Administrative Science Quarterly,* 15: 176–90.

HALL, RICHARD H.
1986   *Dimensions of Work.* Beverly Hills, Calif.: Sage Publications, Inc.

HALL, RICHARD H., and GLORIA V. ENGEL
1974   Autonomy and expertise: Threats and barriers to occupational autonomy. Pp. 325–29 in Stewart, Phyllis L., and Muriel G. Cantor (eds.) *Varieties of Work Experience.* New York: John Wiley.

HAMMER, TOVE H., and ROBERT N. STERN
1980   Employee ownership: Implications for the organizational distribution of power. *Academy of Management Journal,* 23(March): 78–100.

HARBISON, FREDERICK H., and CHARLES A. MYERS
1959   *Management in the Industrial World: An International Study.* New York: McGraw-Hill.

HARPAZ, ITZHAK
1986   A multinational perspective on the current state of the work ethic. Paper presented at the annual meeting of the Academy of Management, August, Chicago, Ill.

HARRIS, MARVIN
1971   *Culture, Man and Nature.* New York: Thomas Y. Crowell.
1976   History and significance of the emic/etic distinction. *Annual Review of Anthropology,* 5: 329–50.

HARRIS, RICHARD
1973   *The Police Academy: An Inside View.* New York: John Wiley.

HARRIS, STANLEY, and ROBERT SUTTON
1986   Functions of parting ceremonies in dying organizations. *Academy of Management Journal,* 29(1): 5–30.

HARRISON, ROGER
1972   Understand your organization's character. *Harvard Business Review,* 50(3): 119–28.

HARTMANN, HEINZ
1959   *Authority and Organization in German Management.* Princeton, N.J.: Princeton University Press.

Harvard Business Review
1980   It's not lonely upstairs: An interview with Renn Zaphiropoulos. *Harvard Business Review,* 58(November–December): 111–32.

HASPESLAGH, PHILIPPE C., and DAVID B. JEMISON
1991   *Managing Acquisitions: Creating Value through Corporate Renewal.* New York: Free Press.

HATVANY, NINA, and VLADIMIR PUCIK
1981   An integrated management system: Lessons from the Japanese experience. *Academy of Management Review,* 6: 449–80.

HAUG, MARIE, and M. B. SUSSMAN
1969   Professional autonomy and the revolt of the client. *Social Problems,* 17(Fall): 153–60.

HEBDEN, J. E.
1975   Patterns of work identification. *Sociology of Work and Occupations,* 2(2): 107–32.

HEDBERG, BO
1981   How organizations learn and unlearn. Pp. 3–27 in Nystrom, Paul C., and William H. Starbuck (eds.) *Handbook of Organizational Design.* London: Oxford University Press.

HEDBERG, BO L. T., PAUL C. NYSTROM, and WILLIAM H. STARBUCK
1976   Camping on see-saws: Prescriptions for a self-designing organization. *Administrative Science Quarterly,* 21: 41–65.

HELLRIEGEL, DON, and JOHN W. SLOCUM, JR.
1974   Organizational climate: measures, research and contingencies. *Academy of Management Journal,* 17: 255–80.

HELLRIEGEL, DON, JOHN W. SLOCUM, JR., and RICHARD W. WOODMAN
1986   *Organizational Behavior,* 4th ed. New York: West Publishing Co.
1989   *Organizational Behavior,* 5th ed. New York: West Publishing Co.

HENRY, JULES
1963   *Culture Against Man.* New York: Random House.

HICKSON, DAVID J.
1987   Decision-making at the top of organizations. *Annual Review of Sociology,* 13: 165–92.

HICKSON, DAVID J., RICHARD J. BUTLER, DAVID CRAY, GEOFFREY R. MALLORY, and DAVID C. WILSON
1986   *Top Decisions: Strategic Decision Making in Organizations.* San Francisco: Jossey-Bass Publications.

HICKSON DAVID J., C. R. HININGS, CHARLES J. MCMILLAN, and J. P. SCHWITTER
1974   The culture-free context of organizational structure: A tri-national comparison. *Sociology,* 8: 59–80.
1981   The culture-free context of organization structure. Pp. 3–16 in Hickson, David J., and Charles J. McMillan (eds.) *Organization and Nation.* Westinead, England: Gower Publishing.

HIRSCH, PAUL M.
  1986   From ambushes to golden parachutes: Corporate takeovers as an instance of cultural framing and institutional integration. *American Journal of Sociology*, 91(4): 800–37.
  1987   *Pack Your Own Parachute.* Reading, Mass: Addison-Wesley.

HIRSCHMAN, ALBERT O.
  1972   *Exit, Voice and Loyalty.* Cambridge, Mass.: Harvard University Press.

HITT, MICHAEL A., and R. DUANE IRELAND
  1987   Peters and Waterman revisited. *The Academy of Management Executive*, 1(2): 91–98.

HOCART, ARTHUR M.
  1939   Ritual and emotion. *Character and Personality*, 7: 201–11.

HOCHSCHILD, ARLIE R.
  1983   *The Managed Heart: The Commercialization of Human Feeling.* Berkeley, Calif.: University of California Press.

HODGETTS, RICHARD M., and STEVEN ALTMAN
  1979   *Organizational Behavior.* Philadelphia: Saunders.

HOFSTADTER, RICHARD
  1955   *Social Darwinism in American Thought.* Boston: Beacon Press.

HOFSTEDE, GEERT
  1980a   Motivation, leadership and organization: Do American theories apply abroad? *Organizational Dynamics*, Summer, Pp. 42–63.
  1980b   *Culture's Consequences: International Differences in Work-Related Values.* Beverly Hills, Calif.: Sage Publications, Inc.
  1983   The cultural relativity of organizational practices and theories. *Journal of International Business Studies*, Fall, Pp. 75–89.

HOFSTEDE, GEERT, BRAM NEUIJEU, DENISE DAVAL OHAYV, and GEERT SANDERS
  1990   Measuring organizational cultures: A qualitative and quantitative study across twenty cases. *Administrative Science Quarterly*, 35: 286–316.

HOGLUND, WILLIAM E.
  1986   Saturn: An experiment in people management. *Survey of Business*, 21(Spring): 12.

HOLLANDER, EDWIN
  1958   Conformity, status, and idiosyncracy credit. *Psychological Review*, 65: 117–27.
  1978   *Leadership Dynamics: A Practical Guide to Effective Relationships.* New York: Free Press.

HOLLANDSWORTH, SKIP
  1986   The bear and the blonde. *D*, August, Pp. 58–63; 138–46.

HOLZBERG, C. S., and M. J. GIOVANNINI
  1981   Anthropology and industry: Reappraisal and new directions. *Annual Review of Anthropology*, 10: 317–60.

HOMANS, GEORGE C.
  1950   *The Human Group.* New York: Harcourt Brace Jovanovich, Inc.

HORN, J. L., and P. D. KNOTT
  1971   Activist youth of the 1960s. *Science*, 171: 977–85.

HOUSE, ROBERT J.
  1977   A 1976 theory of charismatic leadership. Pp. 189–273 in Hunt, J. G., and L. L. Larson (eds.) *Leadership: The Cutting Edge.* Carbondale, Ill.: Southern Illinois University Press.

HOUSE, ROBERT J., and MARY L. BAETZ
1979   Leadership: Some empirical generalizations and new research directions. *Research in Organizational Behavior,* 1: 341–423.

HOUSE, ROBERT J., and JITENDRA V. SINGH
1987   Organizational behavior: Some new directions for I/O psychology. *Annual Review of Psychology,* 38: 669–718.

HOUSE, ROBERT J., WILLIAM J. SPANGLER, and JAMES WOYCKE
1991   Personality and charisma in the U.S. Presidency: A psychological theory of leader effectiveness. *Administrative Science Quarterly,* 36:364–96.

HOUSE, ROBERT J., JAMES WOYCKE, and EUGENE M. FODOR
1988   Charismatic and noncharismatic leaders: Differences in behavior and effectiveness. Pp. 98–121 in Conger, Jay A., and Rabindra Kanungo (eds.) *Charismatic Leadership: The Elusive Factor in Organizational Effectiveness.* San Francisco: Jossey-Bass.

HOWELL, JANE M., and PETER J. FROST
1989   A laboratory study of charismatic leadership. *Organizational Behavior and Human Decision Processes,* 43: 243–69.

HSU, FRANCIS L. K.
1961   American core values and national character. Pp. 209–33 in Hsu, Francis L. K. (ed.) *Psychological Anthropology: Approaches to Culture and Personality.* Homewood, Ill.: Dorsey Press.

HUFF, ANNE S.
1982   Industry influence on strategy reformation. *Strategic Management Journal,* 3: 119–31.

HUGHES, EVERETT C.
1958   *Men and their Work.* New York: Free Press.

HULIN, CHARLES L., and MILTON R. BLOOD
1968   Job enlargement, individual differences, and worker responses. *Psychological Bulletin,* 69: 41–55.

HUMPHREY, LINDA
1979   Small group festive gatherings. *Journal of Folklore,* 16: 190–201.

HUNT, JAMES G.
1991   *Leadership: A New Synthesis.* Newbury Park, Calif.: Sage Publications, Inc.

HURST, DAVID K.
1986   Why strategic management is bankrupt. *Organizational Dynamics,* August, Pp. 5–27.

IACOCCA, LEE
1984   *Iacocca: An Autobiography.* New York: Bantam.

Institute of Industrial Engineers
1991   Reach the peak: Win the Baldridge quality award. *Managing for Continuous Improvement,* II (Winter): 10.

ISABELLA, LYNN A.
1990   Evolving interpretations as a change unfolds: How managers construe key organizational events. *Academy of Management Journal,* 33(1): 7–41.

JABLIN, FREDERIC M.
1987   Organizational entry, assimilation, and exit. Pp. 679–737 in Jablin, F., L. Putnam, K. Roberts, and L. Porter (eds.) *Handbook of Organizational Communication: An Interdisciplinary Perspective.* Beverly Hills, Calif.: Sage Publications, Inc.

JACKALL, ROBERT
1988   *Moral Mazes: The World of Corporate Managers.* New York: Oxford University Press.

JACKOFSKY, ELLEN F., and JOHN W. SLOCUM, JR.
1988a A longitudinal study of climates. *Journal of Organizational Behavior,* 9: 319–34.
1988b C.E.O. roles across cultures. Pp. 67–99 in Hambrick, Donald C. (ed.) *The Executive Effect: Concepts and Methods for Studying Top Managers.* Strategic Management Policy and Planning: A Multivolume Treatise, Vol. II. Greenwich, Conn.: JAI Press.

JACKSON, JOHN H., and CYRIL P. MORGAN
1978 *Organizational Theory: A Macro Perspective.* Englewood Cliffs, N.J.: Prentice Hall.

JACKSON, SUSAN E., and JANE E. DUTTON
1988 Discerning threats and opportunities. *Administrative Science Quarterly,* 33: 370–87.

JACQUES, ELLIOTT
1951 *The Changing Culture of a Factory.* London: Tavistock Publications.

JAMES, LAWRENCE R., and A. P. JONES
1974 Organizational climate: A review of theory and research. *Psychological Bulletin,* 81: 1096–1112.

JANIS, IRVING
1972 *Victims of Group Think: A Study of Foreign Policy Decisions and Fiascoes.* Boston: Houghton Mifflin Company.
1982 *Groupthink.* Boston: Houghton Mifflin Company.

JARBOE, JAN
1989 A boy and his airline. *Texas Monthly,* 17(4): 98–104.

JELINEK, MARIANN and CLAUDIA B. SCHOONHOVEN
1990 *Innovation Marathon: Lessons from High Technology Firms.* Cambridge, Mass.: Basil Blackwell, Ltd.

JEMISON, DAVID B., and SIM B. SITKIN
1986 Corporate acquisitions: A process perspective. *Academy of Management Review,* 11(1): 145–63.

JERMIER, JOHN M., JOHN W. SLOCUM, LOUIS W. FRY, and JEANNIE GAINES
1991 Organizational subcultures in a soft bureaucracy: Resistance behind the myth and facade of an official culture. *Organization Science,* 2(2): 170–95.

JOHNSON, W. BRUCE, ASHOK NATARAJAN, and ALFRED RAPPAPORT
1985 Shareholder returns and corporate excellence. *Journal of Business Strategy,* 6(2): 52–62.

JONES, GARETH R.
1983a Transaction costs, property rights, and organizational culture: An exchange perspective. *Administrative Science Quarterly,* 28: 454–67.
1983b Psychological orientation and the process of organizational socialization: An interaction perspective. *Academy of Management Review,* 8(3): 464–74.
1986 Socialization tactics, self-efficacy and newcomer adjustment to the organization. *Academy of Management Journal,* 29(2): 262–79.

JONES, MICHAEL O.
1983 Directions in research of organizational folklore. Paper presented at the XI International Congress of Anthropological and Ethnological Sciences, August 20–25, Vancouver, British Columbia, Canada.
1984 Corporate natives confer on culture. *The American Folklore Society Newsletter,* 13(October): 6, 8.
1988 In search of meaning: using qualitative methods in research and application. Pp. 31–49 in Jones, Michael O., Michael D. Moore, and Richard C. Snyder (eds.) *Inside Organizations: Understanding the Human Dimension.* Beverly Hills, Calif.: Sage Publications, Inc.

JONES, MICHAEL O., MICHAEL D. MOORE, and RICHARD C. SNYDER (eds.)
1988   *Inside Organizations: Understanding the Human Dimension.* Beverly Hills, Calif.: Sage Publications, Inc.

JOSEPH, NATHAN, and NICHOLAS ALEX
1972   The uniform: A sociological perspective. *American Journal of Sociology,* 77(4): 719–30.

Journal of Management Studies
1982   Special Issue: *Organizations as Ideological Systems.* Guest Editor: William H. Starbuck.

Journal of Management
1985   Special Issue: *Organizational Symbolism,* 11(2): Guest Editor: Peter J. Frost.

JOYCE, WILLIAM F., and JOHN W. SLOCUM, JR.
1984   Collective climate: Agreement as a basis for defining aggregate climates in organizations. *Academy of Management Journal,* 27: 721–42.

KAKAR, SUDHIR
1971a   Authority patterns and subordinate behavior in Indian organizations. *Administrative Science Quarterly,* 16: 298–307.
1971b   The theme of authority in social relations in India. *Journal of Social Psychology,* 84: 93–101.

KALLENBERG, ARNE L., and JAMES R. LINCOLN
1985   The structure of earnings inequality in the U.S. and Japan. Paper presented at the 80th Annual Meeting of the American Sociological Association, Washington, D.C.

KAN, SERGEI
1989   *Symbolic Immortality.* Washington, D.C.: Smithsonian Institution Press.

KANTER, ROSABETH M.
1968   Commitment and social organization: A study of commitment mechanisms in utopian communities. *American Sociological Review,* 33: 499–517.
1977   *Men and Women of the Corporation.* New York: Basic Books.
1978   The long-term trends in work values. *Daedaus,* 107(1): 51–59.
1984   Managing transitions in organizational culture: The case of participative management at Honeywell. Pp. 195–217 in Kimberly, John R., and Robert Quinn (eds.) *New Futures: The Challenges of Managing Corporate Transitions.* Homewood, Ill.: Dow Jones-Irwin.
1985   Change masters and the intricate architecture of corporate culture change. Pp. 351–368 in Gibson, E. A. (ed.) *Organizations close up.* Plano, Tex.: Business Publications.
1986   Holiday gifts: Celebrating employee achievements. New York: American Management Association. Periodicals Division.
1989   *When Giants Learn to Dance.* New York: Simon & Schuster.

KANTROWITZ, BARBARA
1991   Striking a nerve. *Newsweek,* October 21, Pp. 34–40.

KAPROW, MIRIAM L.
1985   Manufacturing danger: Fear and pollution in industrial society. *American Anthropologist,* 87(2): 342–56.

KATZ, DONALD
1987   *The Big Store.* New York: Viking.

KATZ, FRED E.
1958   Occupational contact networks. *Social Forces,* 37(1): 52–55.

KATZ, ROBERT
1980   Time and work: Toward an integrative perspective. *Research in Organizational Behavior,* 2: 81–128.

KAUFMAN, HERBERT
1976   *The Forest Ranger.* Baltimore, Md.: John Hopkins Press.

KEESING, ROGER M.
1974   Theories of culture. *Annual Review of Anthropology,* 3: 73–97.
1987   Anthropology as interpretive quest. *Current Anthropology,* 28(2): 161–76.

KEIDEL, ROBERT W.
1985   *Game Plans: Sports Strategies for Business.* New York: Dutton.

KELLER, JOHN J., and GEOFF LEWIS
1988   A.T.&T.: The making of a comeback. *Business Week,* January 18, pp. 56–62.

KELLY, KEVIN, and OTIS PORT
1992   Learning from Japan: How a few U.S. giants are trying to create homegrown keiretsu. *Business Week,* January 27: 52–60.

KEMNITZER, LUIS S.
1973   Language, learning, and socialization on the railroad. *Urban Life and Culture,* January.
1977   Another view of time and the railroader. *Anthropological Quarterly,* 50(1): 25–31.

KEOHANE, ROBERT O., and JOSEPH S. NYE (eds.)
1971   *Transnational Relations and World Politics.* Cambridge, Mass.: Harvard University Press.

KERR, CLARK, and ABRAHAM SIEGEL
1954   The inter-industry propensity to strike. Pp. 110–23 in Kornhauser, A., et al. (eds.) *Industrial Conflict.* New York: McGraw Hill.

KETS DE VRIES, MANIFRED F. R., and DANNY MILLER
1984   *The Neurotic Organization.* San Francisco: Jossey-Bass.

KIECHEL, WALTER
1979   Playing the rules of the corporate strategy game. *Fortune,* September, 24, Pp. 110–15.

KIGGUNDU, MOSES N., JAN J. JORGENSEN, and TAIEB HAFSI
1983   Administrative theory and practice in developing countries: A synthesis. *Administrative Science Quarterly,* 28(1): 66–84.

KILMANN, RALPH H.
1982   Getting control of the corporate culture. *Managing,* 3: 11–17.
1984   *Beyond the Quick Fix: Managing Five Tracks to Organizational Success.* San Francisco: Jossey-Bass.

KILMANN, RALPH H., MARY J. SAXTON, and ROY SERPA and Associates (eds.)
1985   *Gaining Control of the Corporate Culture.* San Francisco: Jossey-Bass.

KIMBALL, SOLON T.
1960   Introduction to Arnold Van Gennep, *The Rites of Passage.* Chicago: University of Chicago Press, pp. v–xix.

KIMBERLY, JOHN R.
1979   Issues in the creation of organizations: Initiation, innovation and institutionalization. *Academy of Management Journal,* 22(3): 437–57.

KIVA, ALEXANDER
1966   *The Bathroom: Criteria for Design.* Ithaca, N.Y.: Cornell University, Center for Housing and Environmental Design.

KLEIN, STUART M., and R. RICHARD RITTI
1984   *Understanding Organizational Behavior.* Boston: Kent Publishing Co.

KLOTT, GARY
1985   Accounting roles seen in jeopardy. *The New York Times,* Thursday, February 21, Pp. 22–23, Sec. D.

KLUCKHOHN, CLYDE
1942   Myths and rituals: A general theory. *The Harvard Theological Review,* 35(January): 45–79.

KLUCKHOHN, CLYDE, and DOROTHEA LEIGHTON
1980   *The Navaho.* Cambridge, Mass.: Harvard University Press.

KLUCKHOHN, FLORENCE, and FRED L. STODTBECK
1961   *Variations in Value Orientations.* Evanston, Ill.: Row, Peterson, and Company.

KNOWLTON, CHRISTOPHER
1990   Making it right the first time. Pp. 240–41 in Frost, Peter J., Vance F. Mitchell and Walter R. Nord, (eds.) *Management Reality.* Glenview, Ill.: Scott, Foresman/Little, Brown.

KNUDSEN, KJELL
1982   Management subcultures: Research and change. *The Journal of Management Development,* 1(4): 11–27.

KOCHAN, THOMAS A.
1980a   Collective bargaining and industrial relations. Homewood, Ill.: Richard D. Irwin.
1980b   Collective bargaining and organizational behavior research. *Research in Organizational Behavior,* 2: 129–177.

KOCHAN, THOMAS A., and THOMAS A. BAROCCI
1985   *Human Resources Management and Industrial Relations.* Boston: Little, Brown.

KOCHAN, THOMAS A., STUART M. SCHMIDT, and THOMAS A. DeCOTIIS
1975   Superior subordinate relations: Leadership and headship. *Human Relations,* 28(3): 279–94.

KOENIG, FREDERICK
1985   *Rumor in the Marketplace: The Social Psychology of Commercial Hearsay.* Dover, Mass.: Auburn House Publishing Co.

KORNHAUSER, WILLIAM
1962   *Scientists in Industry: Conflict and Accommodation.* Berkeley, Calif.: University of California Press.

KORSON, GEORGE
1965   *Coal Dust on the Fiddle: Songs and Stories of the Bituminous Industry.* Hatboro, Pa.: Folklore Associates, Inc.

KOTTER, JOHN P.
1982   *The General Manager.* New York: Free Press.

KRACKHARDT, DAVID M., and MARTIN KILDUFF
1990   Friendship patterns and culture: the control of organizational diversity. *American Anthropologist,* 92(1): 142–54.

KRAM, KATHY E.
1983   Phases of the mentor relationship. *Academy of Management Journal,* 26: 608–25.
1985   *Mentoring at Work: Developmental Relationships in Organizational Life.* Glenview, Ill.: Scott, Foresman and Co.

KRAM, KATHY E., and LYNN A. ISABELLA
1985   Mentoring alternatives: The role of peer relationships in career development. *Academy of Management Journal,* 28(1): 110–32.

KREFTING, LINDA A., and PETER J. FROST
1985   Untangling webs, surfing waves, and wildcatting: A multiple-metaphor perspective on

managing organizational cultures. Pp. 155–68 in Frost, Peter, et al. (eds.) *Organizational Culture.* Beverly Hills, Calif.: Sage Publications, Inc.

KREPS, GARY L.
1983   Using interpretive research: The development of a socialization program at R.C.A. Pp. 243–56 in Putnam, Linda L., and Michael E. Pananowsky (eds.) *Communications and Organizations: An Interpretive Approach.* Beverly Hills, Calif.: Sage Publications, Inc.

KROEBER, ALFRED L., and TALCOTT PARSONS
1970   The concepts of culture and of social system. Pp. 85–87 in Hammel, Eugene A., and William S. Simons (eds.) *Man Makes Sense.* Boston: Little, Brown.

KUHN, THOMAS
1970   *The Structure of Scientific Revolutions.* Chicago: University of Chicago Press.

KUNDA, GIDEON
1991   *Engineering Culture: Control and Commitment in a High Technology Corporation.* Philadelphia: Temple University Press.

LACEY, ROBERT
1986   *Ford: The Men and the Machine.* Boston: Little, Brown.

LADENDORF, KIRK
1991   IBM, Apple, Motorola join forces. *Austin American—Statesman.* July 4: A1.

LAKOFF, GEORGE, and MARK JOHNSON
1980   *Metaphors We Live By.* Chicago: University of Chicago Press.

LAMMERS, CORNELIUS J., and DAVID J. HICKSON
1979   Are organizations culture-bound? Pp. 402–19 in Lammers, Cornelius J., and David J. Hickson (eds.) *Organizations Alike and Unlike.* London: Routledge & Kegan Paul.

LANDSBERGER, HENRY
1961   The horizontal dimension in bureaucracy. *Administrative Science Quarterly,* 6(3): 299–331.

LASSON, KENNETH
1971   *The Workers: Portrait of Nine American Job Holders.* New York: Grossman.

LAWLER, EDWARD E., III, DOUGLAS T. HALL, and GREGORY R. OLDHAM
1974   Organizational climate: Relationships to organizational structure, process and performance. *Organizational Behavior and Performance,* 11: 139–55.

LAWLER, EDWARD E., and SUSAN A. MOHRMAN
1987   Quality circles: After the honeymoon. *Organizational Dynamics,* 15(Spring): 42–54.

LAWRENCE, BARBARA S.
1988   New wrinkles in the theory of age: Demography, norms, and performance ratings. *Academy of Management Journal,* 31: 309–37.

LAWRENCE, ELIZABETH A.
1982   *Rodeo: An Anthropologist Looks at the Wild and the Tame.* Knoxville, Tenn.: University of Tennessee Press.

LAWRENCE, PAUL R., and JAY W. LORSCH
1967   *Organization and Environment,* Cambridge, Mass.: Harvard University Press.

LEACH, EDMUND
1964   Anthropological aspects of language: Animal categories and verbal abuse. Pp. 23–63 in

Lennenberg, Eric H. (ed.) *New Directions in the Studies of Language.* Cambridge, Mass.: M.I.T. Press.

1968   Ritual. *International Encyclopedia of the Social Sciences,* 13: 520–26.

1970   *Claude Levi-Strauss.* New York: Viking Press.

1976a   *Culture and Communication: The Logic by Which Symbols are Connected.* Cambridge, England: Cambridge University Press.

1976b   Social anthropology: A natural science of society? *British Academy of Science Proceedings.* 62: 157–80. London: Oxford University Press.

1980   *Claude Levi-Strauss.* New York: Penguin.

LEAVITT, HAROLD J.

1965   Applied organizational change in industry: Structural, technological, and humanistic approaches. Pp. 1114–70 in March, James G. (ed.) *Handbook of Organizations.* Chicago: Rand McNally.

LEEMAN, THOMAS A.

1972   *The Rites of Passage in a Student Culture.* New York: Teachers College Press, Columbia University.

LEMERT, EDWIN M.

1967   *Human Deviance, Social Problems, and Social Control.* Englewood Cliffs, N.J.: Prentice Hall.

LEMONICK, MICHAEL D., and EUGENE LINDEN

1989   The two Alaskas—The oil spill and other effects of industrialization on nature. *Time,* April 17, Pp. 56–57.

LEVINE, SOLOMON B.

1981   Labor regulations. Pp. 52–61 in Richardson, Bradley M., and Taizo Ueda (eds.) *Business and Society in Japan.* New York: Praeger Publishers.

LEVINSON, DANIEL J.

1978   *The Seasons of a Man's Life.* New York: Ballantine Books.

LEVINSON, HARRY, and STUART ROSENTHAL

1984   *CEO: Corporate Leadership in Action.* New York: Basic Books.

LEVI-STRAUSS, CLAUDE

1963   *Structural Anthropology.* New York: Basic Books.

LEIBERSON, STANLEY, and JAMES F. O'CONNOR

1972   Leadership and organizational performance: A study of large corporations. *American Sociological Review,* 37(2): 117–30.

LIKERT, RENSIS

1961   *New Patterns in Management.* New York: McGraw-Hill.

LINCOLN, JAMES R.

1990   Japanese organization and organization theory. *Research in Organizational Behavior,* 12: 255–94.

LINCOLN, JAMES R., MITSUYO HANADA, and KERRY MCBRIDE

1986   Organizational structure in Japanese and U.S. manufacturing. *Administrative Science Quarterly,* 31: 338–64.

LINCOLN, JAMES R., MITSUYO HANADA, and JON OLSON

1981   Cultural orientations and individual reactions to organizations: A study of employees of Japanese-owned firms. *Administrative Science Quarterly,* 26: 93–115.

LINCOLN, JAMES R., and ARNE L. KALLEBERG

1985   Work organization and work force commitment: A study of plants and employees in the U.S. and Japan. *American Sociological Review,* 50(December): 738–60.

LINCOLN, JAMES R., and KERRY McBRIDE
1987   Japanese industrial organization in comparative perspective. *Annual Review of Sociology*, 13: 289–312.

LINCOLN JAMES R., and JON MILLER
1979   Work and friendship ties in organizations: A comparative analysis of relational networks. *Administrative Science Quarterly*, 24(June): 181–99.

LINCOLN, JAMES R., JON OLSON, and MITSUYO HANADA
1978   Cultural effects on organizational structure: The case of Japanese firms in the United States. *American Sociological Review*, 43(6): 829–47.

LINDBLOM, CHARLES E.
1959   The science of "muddling through". *Public Administration Review*, 19: 79–88.
1965   *The Intelligence of Democracy: Decision Making Through Mutual Adjustment.* New York: Free Press.

LINDHOLM, CHARLES
1990   *Charisma.* Cambridge, Mass.: Basil Blackwell, Inc.

LINTON, RALPH
1924   Totemism and the A. E. F. *American Anthropologist*, 26: 296–300.

LIPSET, SEYMOUR M.
1963   *The First New Nation: The United States in Historical and Comparative Perspective.* New York: Basic Books.

LIPSET SEYMOUR M., MARTIN A. TROW, and JAMES S. COLEMAN
1956   *Union Democracy.* New York: Free Press.

LOCKE, EDWIN A. and DAVID M. SCHWEIGER
1990   Participation in decision-making: One more look. Pp. 137–211 in Cummings, L. L., and Barry M. Staw (eds.) *Leadership, Participation, and Group Behavior.* Greenwich, Conn.: JAI Press.

LODAHL, JANICE BEYER, and GERALD GORDON
1972   The structure of scientific fields and the functioning of university graduate departments. *American Sociological Review*, 37(February): 57–72.
1973a   Differences between physical and social sciences in university graduate departments. *Research in Higher Education*, 1: 191–221.
1973b   Funding the sciences in university departments. *Educational Record*, 54(1): 74–82.

LODAHL, THOMAS M., and STEPHEN M. MITCHELL
1980   Drift in the development of innovative organizations. Pp. 184–207 in Kimberly, John R., and Robert H. Miles (eds.) *The Organizational Life Cycle: Issues in the Creation, Transformation, and Decline of Organizations.* San Francisco: Jossey-Bass.

LOPREATO, JOSEPH
1984   *Human Nature and Biocultural Evolution.* Boston: Allen & Unwin.

LORD, ROBERT G., CHRISTY L. DeVADER, and GEORGE M. ALLIGER
1986   A meta-analysis of the relation between personality traits and leadership perceptions: An application of validity generalization procedures. *Journal of Applied Psychology*, 71(3): 402–10.

LORTIE, DAN C.
1968   Shared ordeal and induction to work. Pp. 252–64 in Becker, Howard, Blanche Geer, David Riesman, and Robert S. Weiss (eds.) *Institutions and the Person.* Chicago: Aldine.
1975   *School Teacher: A Sociological Study.* Chicago: University of Chicago Press.

LOTT, ALBERT J., and BERNICE E. LOTT
1965   Group cohesiveness as interpersonal attraction: A review of relationships with antecedent and consequent variables. *Psychological Bulletin,* 64: 259–309.

LOUDON, J. B.
1970   Teasing and socialization on Tristan da Cunha. Pp. 293–332 in Mayer, Phillip (ed.) *Socialization: The Approach from Social Anthropology.* London: Tavistock Publications.

LOUIS, HARRIS, and Associates, Inc.
1978   *The Steelcase National Study of Office Environments: Do They Work?* Grand Rapids, Mich.: Steelcase.

LOUIS, MERYL R.
1980   Surprise and sense making: What newcomers experience in entering unfamiliar organizational settings. *Administrative Science Quarterly,* 25: 226–51.
1981   A cultural perspective on organizations: The need for and consequences of viewing organizations as culture-bearing milieux. *Human Systems Managemen,* 2: 246–58.
1983a   The availability and helpfulness of socialization practices. *Personnel Psychology,* 36(4): 857–66.
1983b   Culture: Yes; Organization: No. Paper presented at the annual meeting of the Academy of Management, August, Dallas, Tex.
1985a   A investigator's guide to workplace culture. Pp. 73–93 in Frost, Peter J., et al. (eds.) *Organizational Cultures.* Beverly Hills, Calif.: Sage Publications, Inc.
1985b   Sourcing workplace cultures: Why, when and how. Pp. 126–36 in Kilmann, Ralph H., et al. (eds.) *Gaining Control of Corporate Culture.* San Francisco: Jossey-Bass.

LOUIS, MERYL R., HARRY Z. POSNER, and GARY N. POWELL
1983   The availability and helpfulness of socialization practices. *Personnel Psychology,* 36(4): 857–66.

LOUIS, MERYL R., and ROBERT I. SUTTON
1991   Switching cognitive gears: From habits of mind to active thinking. *Human Relations,* 44(1): 55–61.

LOVE, RUTH L.
1964   The absorption of protest. Pp. 115–35 in Cooper, W. W., H. J. Leavitt, and M. W. Shelly (eds.) *New Perspectives in Organizational Research.* New York: John Wiley.

LOVING, JR., RUSH
1976   W. T. Grant's last days—as seen from store 1192. *Fortune Magazine,* April, Pp. 109–14.

LOWRY, JAMES
1978   Strategies and stories of the Omaha stock yards. *Folklore Forum,* 11: 29–41.

LUBATKIN, MICHAEL
1983   Mergers and the performance of the acquiring firm. *Academy of Management Review,* 8(2): 218–25.

LUBOVE, ROY
1965   *The Professional Altruist.* Cambridge, Mass.: Harvard University Press.

LUCAS, CHARLOTTE-ANNE
1988   The plane facts: Southwest Airlines and America West try to clip each other's wings. *New Times,* 19(7): 26–28, 30, 32.

LUNDBERG, CRAIG C.

1969   Person-focused joking: Pattern and function. *Human Organization,* 28(1): 22–28.

1981   Characterizing an organization: A metaphor technique for initial assessment. *Journal of Experimental Learning and Stimulation,* 3: 53–56.

1985a   On the feasibility of cultural intervention in organizations. Pp. 169–85 in Frost, Peter J., et al. (eds.) *Organizational Culture.* Beverly Hills, Calif.: Sage Publications, Inc.

1985b   How should organizational culture be studied? Pp. 197–200 in Frost, Peter J., et al. (eds.) *Organizational Culture.* Beverly Hills, Calif.: Sage Publications, Inc.

LUTHAUS, FRED, HARRIET S. MCCARL, and NANCY G. DODD

1985   Organizational commitment: A comparison of American, Japanese, and Korean employees. *Academy of Management Journal,* 28(1): 213–18.

LUTZ, CATHERIN, and GEOFFREY M. WHITE

1986   The anthropology of emotions. *Annual Review of Anthropology,* 15: 405–36.

LYDALL, SARAH

1988   Police-fire feud is set off again by copter death. *The New York Times,* Tuesday, May 3, Pp. 41 and B3.

MAAS, ANNE, and RUSSELL D. CLARK, III

1984   Hidden impact of minorities: Fifteen years of minority influence research. *Psychological Bulletin,* 95: 428–50.

MACHIAVELLI, NICCOLO

[1513] *The Prince* (Trans. Luigi Ricci, revised by E. R. P. Vincent.) New York: New American Li-
1952   brary of World Literature.

MAGNET, MYRON

1984   Acquiring without smothering. *Fortune,* November 12, Pp. 22–30.

MALONE, PAUL B.

1980   Humor: A double-edged tool for today's managers? *Academy of Management Review,* 5: 357–61.

MANNING, PETER K.

1965   *Office Design: A Study of Environment by the Pilkington Research Unit.* Liverpool, England: University of Liverpool Press.

1970   Talking and becoming: A view of organizational socialization. Pp. 239–56 in Douglas, Jack D. (ed.) *Understanding Everyday Life.* Chicago: Aldine.

1977   *Police Work: The Social Organization of Policing,* Cambridge, Mass.: MIT Press.

MARCH, JAMES G., and JOHAN P. OLSEN

1976   *Ambiguity and Choice in Organizations.* Bergen, Norway: Universitetsforlaget.

MARCH, JAMES G., and GUJE SEVON

1984   Gossip, information and decision-making. *Advances in Information Processing in Organizations,* 1: 95–107.

MARS, GERALD

1979   The stigma cycle: values and politics in a dockland union. Pp. 133–58 in Wallman, Sandra (ed.) *Social Anthropology of Work.* New York: Academic Press.

1982   *Cheats at Work: An Anthropology of Workplace Crime.* Boston: George Allen & Unwin.

MARS, GERALD, and MICHAEL NICOD

1984   *The World of Waiters.* London: George Allen & Unwin.

MARTIN, JOANNE

1990   Deconstructing organizational taboos: The suppression of gender conflicts in organizations. *Organization Science,* 1(4): 339–59.

MARTIN, JOANNE
1991   A personal journey: From integration to differentiation to fragmentation to feminism. Pp. 352–66 in Frost, Peter J., Larry F. Moore, Meryl R. Louis, Craig Lundberg, and Joanne Martin (eds.) *Reframing Organizational Culture.* Newbury Park, Calif.: Sage Publications, Inc.

MARTIN, JOANNE, MARTHA S. FELDMAN, MARY JO HATCH, and SIM B. SITKIN
1983   The uniqueness paradox in organizational stories. *Administrative Science Quarterly,* 28(September): 438–52.

MARTIN JOANNE, and DEBRA MEYERSON
1988   Organizational cultures and the denial, channeling, and acknowledgement of ambiguity. Pp. 93–125 in Pondy, Louis, R., Richard Boland, Jr., and Howard Thomas (eds.) *Managing Ambiguity and Change.* New York: John Wiley.

MARTIN, JOANNE, and MELANIE E. POWERS
1983   Truth or corporate propaganda: The value of a good war story. Pp. 93–107 in Pondy, Louis R., Peter J. Frost, Gareth Morgan, and Thomas Dandridge (eds.) *Organizational Symbolism.* Greenwich, Conn.: JAI Press.

MARTIN, JOANNE, and CAREN SIEHL
1983   Organizational culture and counterculture: An uneasy symbiosis. *Organizational Dynamics,* 12(2): 52–65.

MARTIN, JOANNE, SIM B. SITKIN, and MICHAEL BOEHM
1985   Founders and the elusiveness of a cultural legacy. Pp. 99–124 in Frost, Peter J., et al. (eds.) *Organizational Culture.* Beverly Hills, Calif.: Sage Publications, Inc.

Mary Kay Cosmetics, Inc.
1982   Mary Kay Seminar, 1982. Brochure. No place of publication given.

MAURICE, MARC
1979   For a study of the 'societal effect': Universality and specificity in organization research. Pp. 42–61 in Lammers, C. J., and D. J. Hickson (eds.) *Organizations Alike and Unlike.* London: Routledge & Kegan Paul.

MAURICE, MARC, FRANCOIS SELLIER, and JEAN-JACQUES SILVESTRE
1984   The search for a societal effect in the production of company hierarchy. Pp. 231–69 in Osterman, Paul (ed.) *Internal Labor Markets.* Cambridge, Mass.: MIT Press.

MAYO, ELTON
1945   *The Social Problems of an Industrial Civilization.* Boston: Harvard Graduate School of Business Administration.

McCARL, ROBERT S.
1974   The production welder: Product, process, and the industrial craftsman. *New York Folklore Quarterly,* 30: 244–53.
1976   Smokejumper initiation: Ritualized communication in a modern occupation. *Journal of American Folklore,* 81: 49–67.
1980   *Good Fire/Bad Night.* Washington, D.C.: National Endowment for the Arts, Folk Arts Program and Columbia Fire Fighters Local 36.
1984   You've come a long way—and now this is your retirement. *Journal of American Folklore,* 97(386): 393–422.

McCLELLAND, DAVID C.
1961   *The Achieving Society.* Princeton, N.J.: Van Nostrand.

McDONALD, PEGGY
1988   The Los Angeles Olympic organizing committee: Developing organizational culture in

the short run. Pp. 165–77 in Jones, Michael O., Michael D. Moore, and Richard C. Snyder (eds.) *Inside Organizations: Understanding the Human Dimension.* Beverly Hills, Calif.: Sage Publications, Inc.

McFARLAND, DALTON
1962   *Cooperation and Conflict in Personnel Administration.* New York: American Foundation for Management Research.

McGREGOR, DOUGLAS
1960   *The Human Side of Enterprise.* New York: McGraw-Hill.

McHUGH, PETER
1969   Structured uncertainty and its resolution: The case of the professional actor. Pp. 539–55 in Plog, Stanley C., and Robert B. Edgerton (eds.) *Changing Perspectives in Mental Illness.* New York: Holt, Rinehart & Winston.

McKINLEY WILLIAM, JOSEPH L. C. CHENG, and ALLEN G. SCHICK
1986   Perceptions of resource criticality in times of resource scarcity: The case of university departments. *Academy of Management Journal,* 29: 623–32.

MEAD, GEORGE H.
1934   *Mind, Self, and Society.* Chicago: University of Chicago Press.

MEADOWS, PAUL
1967   The metaphor of order: Toward a taxonomy of organization theory. Pp. 77–103 in Gross, Leewellyn (ed.) *Sociological Theory: Inquiries and Paradigms.* New York: Harper & Row, Pub.

MECHLING, JAY and DAVID S. WILSON
1988   Organizational festivals and the uses of ambiguity: The case of picnic day at Davis. Pp. 303–17 in Jones, Michael O., Michael D. Moore, and Richard C. Snyder (eds.) *Inside Organizations: Understanding the Human Dimension.* Beverly Hills, Calif.: Sage Publications, Inc.

MEINDL, JAMES R.
1990   On leadership: An alternative to the conventional wisdom. *Research in Organizational Behavior,* 12: 159–203.

MEINDL, JAMES R., and SANFORD B. EHRLICH
1987   The romance of leadership and the evaluation of organizational performance. *Academy of Management Journal,* 30(1): 91–109.

MEINDL, JAMES R., S. B. EHRLICH, and J. M. DUKERICH
1985   The romance of leadership. *Administrative Science Quarterly,* 30: 78–102.

MEISSNER, MARTIN
1976   The language of work. Pp. 205–79 in Dubin, Robert (ed.) *Handbook of Work, Organizations, and Society.* Chicago: Rand McNally.

MELBIN, MURRAY
1978   Night as frontier. *American Sociological Review,* 43: 3–22.

MERTON, ROBERT K.
1936   The unanticipated consequences of purposive social action. *American Sociological Review,* 1: 894–904.
1968   *Social Theory and Social Structure.* New York: Free Press.
1976   *Sociological Ambivalence and Other Essays.* New York: Free Press.

MERTON, ROBERT K., GEORGE READER, and PATRICIA KENDALL
1957   *The Student Physician.* Cambridge, Mass.: Harvard Press.

METCALFE, LES
1981   Designing precarious partnerships. Pp. 503–30 in Nystrom, Paul C., and William H. Starbuck (eds.) *Handbook of Organizational Design,* vol. I. New York: Oxford University Press.

MEYER, ALAN D.

1982a   Adapting to environmental jolts. *Administrative Science Quarterly,* 27(4): 515–37.

1982b   How ideologies supplant formal structures and shape responses to environments. *Journal of Management Studies,* 19(1): 45–61.

1984   Mingling decision making metaphors. *Academy of Management Review,* 9(1): 6–17.

MEYER, ALAN D., and WILLIAM STARBUCK

1991   Organizations and industries in flux: The interplay of rationality and ideology. Working paper, Graduate School of Management, University of Oregon and Stern School of Management, New York University.

MEYER, JOHN W., and BRIAN ROWAN

1977   Institutionalized organizations: Formal structure, myth, and ceremony. *American Journal of Sociology,* 83: 340–61.

MEYER, MARSHALL W.

1968   Two authority structures of bureaucratic organization. *Administrative Science Quarterly,* 13(2): 216–21.

MEYERSON, DEBRA E.

1991a   Normal ambiguity? A glimpse of an occupational culture. Pp. 131–44 in Frost, Peter, Larry F. Moore, Meryl R. Louis, Craig C. Lundberg, and Joanne Martin (eds.), *Reframing Organizational Culture.* Newbury Park, Calif.: Sage Publications, Inc.

1991b   Acknowledging and uncovering ambiguities in cultures. Pp. 254–70 in Frost, Peter J., Larry F. Moore, Meryl R. Louis, Craig C. Lundberg, and Joanne Martin (eds.) *Reframing Organizational Culture.* Newbury Park, Calif.: Sage Publications, Inc.

MEYERSON, DEBRA, and JOANNE MARTIN

1987   Cultural change: An integration of three different views. *Journal of Management Studies,* 24: 623–48.

MICHELS, ROBERT

[1911]   *Political Parties.* New York: Free Press.
1949

MIEDER, BARBA, and WOLFGANG MIEDER

1977   Tradition and innovation: Proverbs in advertising. *Journal of Popular Culture,* 11: 308–17.

MILES, ROBERT H.

1980   *Macro-Organizational Behavior.* Santa Monica, Calif.: Goodyear Publishing Co.

MILLER, DANNY

1990   *The Icarus Paradox.* New York: Harper Business.

MILLER, DANNY and PETER H. FRIESEN

1980   Momentum and revolution in organizational adaptation. *Academy of Management Journal,* 23(4): 591–614.

MILLER, DELBERT C., and WILLIAM H. FORM

1980   *Industrial Sociology: Work in Organizational Life,* 3rd ed. New York: Harper & Row, Pub.

MILLER, JAMES G.

1978   *Living Systems.* New York: McGraw-Hill.

MILLIKEN, FRANCES J., JANE E. DUTTON, and JANICE M. BEYER

1990   Understanding organizational adaptation to change: The case of work-family issues. *Human Resource Planning,* 13(2): 91–105.

MINTZBERG, HENRY

1973   *The Nature of Managerial Work.* New York: Haper & Row, Pub.

1975   The manager's job: Folklore and fact. *Harvard Business Review,* 53(4): 49–61.

1979a   An emerging strategy of "direct" research. *Administrative Science Quarterly,* 24(December): 582–88.

1979b   *The Structure of Organizations.* Englewood Cliffs, N.J.: Prentice Hall.

MITROFF, IAN I.

1974   *The subjective side of science.* New York: American Elsevier.

1983   Archetypal social system analysis: On the deeper structure of human systems. *Academy of Management Review,* 9(2): 207–24.

1985   Why our old pictures of the world do not work anymore. Pp. 18–44 in Lawler, Edward E., III, Allan M. Mohrman, Jr., Susan Mohrman, Gerald Ledford, Jr., and Thomas G. Cummings (eds.) *Doing Research that is Useful for Theory and Practice.* San Francisco: Jossey-Bass.

MITROFF, IAN, and RALPH H. KILMANN

1975   Stories managers tell: A new tool for organizational problem solving. *Management Review,* (July): 18–28.

1984   *Corporate Tragedies: Product Tampering, Sabotage, and Other Catastrophies.* New York: Praeger Publishers.

1985   Corporate taboos and the key to unlocking culture. Pp. 184–99 in Kilmann, Ralph et al. (eds.) *Gaining Control of Corporate Culture.* San Francisco: Jossey-Bass.

MITROFF, IAN, I., and RICHARD MASON

1983   Stakeholders of executive decision making. Pp. 144–68 in Srivastva, Suresh, and Associates (eds.) *The Executive Mind.* San Francisco: Jossey-Bass.

MITROFF, IAN I., JOHN NELSON, and RICHARD MASON

1974   On management myth-information systems. *Management Science,* 21(4): 371–82.

1981   Job enrichment through symbol management. *California Management Review,* 24(Winter): 24–30.

MOCH, MICHAEL K., and ANNE S. HUFF

1982   Life on the line. *The Wharton Magazine,* 6: 53–58.

MOLSTAD, CLARK

1988   Control strategies used by industrial brewery workers: Work avoidance, impression management, and solidarity. *Human Organization,* 47(4): 354–60.

MONTAGNA, PAUL D.

1973   The public accounting profession. Pp. 135–51 in Freidson, Eliot (ed.) *The Professions and Their Prospects.* Beverly Hills, Calif.: Sage Publications, Inc.

MONTAGUE, SUSAN P., and ROBERT MORAIS

1976   Football games and rock concerts: The ritual enactment of American success models. Pp. 33–52 in Arens, William (ed.) *The American Dimension: Cultural Myths and Realities.* Port Washington, N.Y.: Alfred Publishing.

MONTI, DANIEL J.

1991   The practice of gang research. *Sociological Practice Review,* 2(1): 29–39.

MOORE, DAVID G.

1954   *Managerial Strategies in Organizational Dynamics in Sears Retailing.* Unpublished Ph.D. thesis, Department of Sociology, University of Chicago.

1982   The committee on human relations in industry at the University of Chicago. Pp. 117–21 in *Academy of Management Proceedings.* Kae H. Chung (ed.) 42nd Annual Meeting, New York.

1989   Comments during a symposium on the Committee on Human Relations in Industry at the University of Chicago. Working paper of the Management History Division, William Muhs (ed.).

MOORE, SALLY F.
1975   Epilogue: Uncertainties in situations, indeterminacies in culture. Pp. 210–39 in Moore, Sally F., and Barbara G. Myerhoff (eds.) *Symbols and Politics in Communal Ideology.* Ithaca, N.Y.: Cornell University Press.

MOORE, SALLY F., and BARBARA G. MYERHOFF
1977   Secular ritual: Forms and Meaning. Pp. 3–25 in Moore, Sally F., and Barbara G. Myerhoff (eds.) *Secular Ritual.* Assen, Amsterdam, The Netherlands: Van Gorcum.

MOORE, WILBERT E.
1962   *The Conduct of the Corporation.* New York: Random House.

MOREY, NANCY C., and FRED LUTHANS
1984   An emic perspective and ethnoscience methods for organizational research. *Academy of Management Review,* 8(1): 27–36.

MORGAN, GARETH, PETER J. FROST, and LOUIS R. PONDY
1983   Organizational symbolism. Pp. 3–39 in Pondy, Louis R., Peter J. Frost, Gareth Morgan, and Thomas C. Dandridge (eds.) *Organizational Symbolism.* Greenwich, Conn.: JAI Press.

MORISON, ELTING
1982   Gunfire at sea: A case study of innovation. Pp. 84–95 in Tushman, Michael L., and William L. Moore (eds.) *Readings in the Management of Innovation.* Boston: Pittman Publishing.

MORRILL, CALVIN
1989   The management of managers: Disputing in an executive hierarchy. *Sociological Forum,* 4(3): 387–405.

MORRISON, ROBERT F.
1977   Career adaptivity: The effective adaptation of managers to changing role demands. *Journal of Applied Psychology,* 62: 549–58.

MORTIMER, JEYLAN T.
1979   *Changing Attitudes Toward Work.* Scarsdale, N.Y.: Work in America Institute.

MOSKAL, BRIAN S.
1989   Hybrid incubator hatches workers. *Industry Week,* 15: 27, 30.

MOUND, MICHAEL C.
1978   The concept of status as practiced in business organizations. Pp. 144–51 in Frost, Peter, Vance Mitchell, and Walter Nord (eds.) *Organizational Reality: Reports from the Firing Line.* Santa Monica, Calif.: Goodyear Publishing Co.

MOWDAY, RICHARD T.
1978   The exercise of upward influence in organizations. *Administrative Science Quarterly,* 23: 137–56.

MOWDAY, RICHARD T., LYMAN W. PORTER, and RICHARD M. STEERS
1982   *Employee-Organization Linkages: The Psychology of Commitment, Absenteeism, and Turnover.* New York: Academic Press.

MUHS, WILLIAM (ed.)
1989   *Symposium on Committee on Human Relations in Industry at University of Chicago,* Academy of Management, August 1982, New York.

MUKERJI, CHANDRA, and MICHAEL SCHUDSON
1986   Popular culture. *Annual Review of Sociology,* 12: 47–66.

MUSSER, STEVEN J.
1986   The determination of positive and negative charismatic leadership. Paper presented at the Academy of Management, Chicago.

MYERHOFF, BARBARA
1982   Rites of Passage: Process and Paradox. Pp. 109–35 in Turner, Victor (ed.) *Celebration*. Washington, D.C.: Smithsonian Institute.
1975   Organization and ecstasy: Deliberate and accidental communitas among Huchal Indians and American youth. Pp. 33–67 in Moore, Sally F., and Barbara G. Myerhoff (eds.) *Symbols and Politics in Communal Ideology*. Ithaca, N.Y.: Cornell University Press.

MYERS, RICHARD C.
1948   Myth and status systems in industry. *Social Forces,* 24: 331–37.

NAROLL, RAOUL, and FRADA NAROLL (eds.)
1973   Introduction. Pp. 1–23 in *Main Currents in Anthropology*. Englewood Cliffs, N.J.: Prentice Hall.

NAYLOR, PETER
1984   Bringing home the lessons of Japanese Management. *Personnel Management,* March, Pp. 34–37.

NELSON, D., and S. CAMPBELL
1972   Taylorism vs. welfare work in American industry. *Business History Review,* 46: 1–16.

NELSON, DANIEL
1983   Review of Thomas Peters and Robert Waterman, *In Search of Excellence. Human Organization,* 42(4): 368–70.

NEWMAN, KATHARINE
1980   Incipient bureaucracy: Anthropological perspectives on bureaucracy. Pp. 143–63 in Britan, Gerald M., and Ronald Cohen (eds.) *Hierarchy and Society: Anthropological Perspectives on Bureaucracy*. Philadelphia: Institute for Study of Social Issues.

NEWSTROM, JOHN, MARK LENGNICK-HALL, and STEVEN RUBENFELD
1987   How employees can choose their own bosses. *Personnel Journal,* 66(12): 121–26.

Newsweek
1986   M.B.A.s learn a human touch. June 16, Pp. 48–51.

NICHOLSON, NIGEL
1984   A theory of work role transitions. *Administrative Science Quarterly,* 29: 172–91.

NICHOLSON, NIGEL, and M. A. WEST
1988   *Managerial Job Change*. London: Cambridge University Press.

NIGHTINGALE, DONALD V., and JEAN MARIE TOULOUSE
1977   Values, structure, process and reaction/adjustments: A comparison of English-Canadian industrial organizations. *Canadian Journal of Behavioral Science,* 9(1): 37–48.

NYSTROM, PAUL C., and WILLIAM H. STARBUCK
1984a   Managing beliefs in organizations. *Journal of Applied Behavioral Science,* 20(3): 277–87.
1984b   To avoid organizational crises, unlearn. *Organizational Dynamics,* 12(4): 53–65.

OBERG, WINSTON
1972   Charisma, commitment and contemporary organization theory. *Michigan State University Business Topics,* 20(Spring): 18–32.

O'CONNELL, MARTIN C., and D. E. BLOOM
1987   Juggling jobs and babies: America's child care challenge. Monograph in the Population Trends and Public Policy Series. Washington, D.C.: Population Reference Bureau.

OPLER, MORRIS E.

1938   *Myths and Tales of the Jiccirilla Apache Indians.* New York: The American Folklore Society.

ORBACH MICHAEL

1977   *Hunters, Seamen and Entrepreneurs.* Berkeley, Calif.: University of California Press.

O'REILLY, CHARLES A., JENNIFER CHATMAN, and DAVID F. CALDWELL

1991   People and organizational culture: A profile comparison approach to assessing person-organization fit. *Academy of Management Journal,* 34: 487–516.

Organizational Dynamics

1983   12(2): Autumn.

ORTNER, SHERRY B.

1973   On key symbols. *American Anthropologist,* 75: 1338–46.

ORTONY, ANDREW

1975   Why metaphors are necessary and not just nice. *Educational Theory,* 25(1): 45–53.

O'TOOLE, JAMES

1972   Work in America: Report of a special task force to the secretary of health, education and welfare. Washington, D.C.

O'TOOLE, PATRICIA

1984   *Corporate Messiah: The Hiring and Firing of Million Dollar Managers.* New York: Morrow.

OTT, J. STEVEN

1989   *The Organizational Culture Perspective.* Pacific Grove, Calif.: Brooks/Cole Publishing.

OUCHI, WILLIAM

1981   *Theory Z: How American Business Can Meet the Japanese Challenge.* Reading, Mass.: Addison-Wesley.

OUCHI, WILLIAM G., and ALFRED M. JAEGER

1978   Type Z organization: Stability in the midst of mobility. *Academy of Management Review,* 3: 305–13.

OUCHI, WILLIAM G., and JERRY B. JOHNSON

1978   Types of organizational control and their relationship to emotional well-being. *Administrative Science Quarterly,* 23(2): 293–318.

OUCHI, WILLIAM G., and RAYMOND L. PRICE

1978   Hierarchies, clans, and theory Z: A new perspective on organization. *Organizational Dynamics,* Autumn: 25–41.

OUCHI, WILLIAM G., and ALAN L. WILKINS

1985   Organizational culture. *Annual Review of Sociology,* 11: 457–83.

PACANOWSKY, MICHAEL E., and NICK O'DONNELL-TRUJILLO

1982   Communication and organizational culture. *The Western Journal of Speech Communication,* 46(Spring): 115–30.

PADOVER, SAUL K.

1955   George Washington: Portrait of a true conservative. *Social Research,* 22: 199–222.

PARKER, STANLEY

1982   *Leisure and Work.* Boston: Allen & Unwin.

PARSONS, TALCOTT

1966   *Societies: Evolutionary and Comparative Perspectives.* Englewood Cliffs, N.J.: Prentice Hall.

PASCALE, RICHARD

1984   Fitting new employees into the company culture. *Fortune,* 109(11): 28–40.

PASCALE, RICHARD T., and ANTHONY G. ATHOS
1981   *The Art of Japanese Management.* New York: Simon & Schuster.

PELZ, DONALD C., and FRANK M. ANDREWS
1966   *Scientists in Organizations.* New York: John Wiley.

PERKINS, KENNETH B.
1987   Volunteer fire departments. Community integration and survival. *Human Organization,* 46(4): 342–47.

PERLMAN, SELIG
1949   *A Theory of the Labor Movement.* New York: Augustus M. Kelley.

PERONE, JOSEPH R.
1986   People's corporate style still stands tall. *Newark, NJ Star Ledger,* September, 17, p. E10.

PERROW, CHARLES
1970   Departmental power and perspective in industrial firms. Pp. 59–89 in Zald, Mayer N. (ed.) *Power in Organizations.* Nashville, Tenn.: Vanderbilt University Press.
1972   *Complex Organizations.* Glenview, Ill.: Scott, Foresman.
1979   The sixties observed. Pp. 192–211 in Zald, Mayer, and John D. McCarthy (eds.) *The Dynamics of Social Movements: Resource Mobilization, Social Control and Tactics.* Cambridge, Mass.: Winthrop Publishers.

PERRUCCI, ROBERT
1971   Engineering. *American Behavioral Scientist,* 14(4): 492–505.

PERRY, STEWART E.
1984   San Francisco garbage collectors. Pp. 280–89 in Applebaum, Herbert (ed.) *Work in Market and Industrial Societies.* Albany, N.Y.: State University Press.

PETER, KARL A., EDWARD P. BOLDT, LANCE ROBERTS, and IAN WHITAKER
1987   The contemporary dynamics of religious definitions. Pp. 45–58 in Peter, Karl A. (ed.) *The Dynamics of Hutterite Society: An Analytical Approach.* Edmonton, Canada: University of Alberta Press.

PETERS, THOMAS J.
1978   Symbols, patterns, and settings. *Organizational Dynamics,* 7: 3–23.

PETERS, THOMAS, and NANCY AUSTIN
1985   *A Passion for Excellence: The Leadership Difference.* New York: Random House.

PETERS, THOMAS J., and ROBERT H. WATERMAN
1982   *In Search of Excellence: Lessons from America's Best Run Companies.* New York: Harper & Row, Pub.

PETERSON, W. JACK, and MILTON MAXWELL
1958   The skid road "wino". *Social Problems,* 5(4): 308–17.

PETTIGREW, ANDREW W.
1973   *The Politics of Organizational Decision-Making.* London: Tavistock Publication.
1979   On studying organizational cultures. *Administrative Science Quarterly,* 24: 570–81.

PFEFFER, JEFFREY
1977   The ambiguity of leadership. *Academy of Management Review,* 2(1): 104–12.
1981a   Management as symbolic action: The creation and maintenance of organizational paradigms. *Research in Organizational Behavior,* 3: 1–52.
1981b   *Power in Organizations.* Marshfield, Mass.: Pitman Publishing.

PFEFFER, JEFFREY, ANTHONY LEONG, and KATHERINE STREHL
1977   Paradigm development and particularism: Journal publication in three scientific disciplines. *Social Forces,* 55: 938–51.

PFEFFER, JEFFREY, and GERALD R. SALANCIK
1974   Organizational decision making as a political process: The case of a university budget. *Administrative Science Quarterly,* 19(2): 135–51.
1978   *The External Control of Organizations: A Resource Dependence Perspective.* New York: Harper & Row, Pub.

PFEFFER, JEFFREY, GERALD R. SALANCIK, and HUSEYIN LEBLEBICI
1976   The effect of uncertainty on the use of social influence in organizational decision making. *Administrative Science Quarterly,* 21: 227–45.

PFEIFFER, JOHN
1984   Schlock for sale: A review of *In Search of Excellence. Science '84,* 5(3): 90–94.

PHILLIPS, MARGARET
1991   The cultural contexts of industry: Distinct sets of assumptions in fine arts museums and wineries. Paper presented at the annual meeting of the Academy of Management, Miami Beach, Fla.

PIERCE, JOE E.
1977   Culture: A collection of fuzzy sets. *Human Organization,* 36(2): 197–200.

PILCHER, WILLIAM W.
1972   *The Portland Longshoremen.* New York: Holt, Rinehart, & Winston.

PILLAI, RAJNANDINI, and JAMES R. MEINDL
1991   The effect of a crisis on the emergence of charismatic leadership: A laboratory study. Best Paper Proceedings of the 1991 Academy of Management Meetings, Miami, Fla.

POGGI, GIANFRANCO
1983   *Calvanism and the Capitalist Spirit: Max Weber's "Protestant Ethic".* Amherst, Mass.: University of Massachusetts Press.

POLISOTO, CATHERINE, and ALEJANDRO FERNANDEZ
1987   Visible cultural forms at McDonalds. Working paper # 3, Seminar on Organizational Cultures, School of Industrial and Labor Relations, Cornell University, Ithaca, N.Y.

PONDY, LOUIS
1978   Leadership is a language game. Pp. 87–103 in McCall, Morgan, and M. Lombardo (eds.) *Leadership: Where Else Can We Go?* Durham, N.C.: Duke University Press.
1980   Organizational conflict: Concepts and models. Pp. 473–92 in Leavitt, Harold J., Louis R. Pondy, and David M. Boje (eds.), *Readings in Managerial Psychology.* Chicago: University of Chicago Press.
1983a   The role of metaphors and myths in organization and in the facilitation of change. Pp. 157–66 in Pondy et al. (eds.) *Organizational Symbolism.* Greenwich, Conn.: JAI Press.
1983b   Union of rationality and intuition in management action. Pp. 169–91 in Srivastva, Suresh and Associates (eds.) *The Executive Mind.* San Francisco: Jossey-Bass.

PONDY, LOUIS R., PETER J. FROST, GARETH MORGAN, and THOMAS C. DANDRIDGE (eds.)
1983   *Organizational Symbolism.* Greenwich, Conn.: JAI Press.

PONDY, LOUIS R., and ANNE S. HUFF
1985   Achieving routine in organizational change. *Journal of Management,* 11(2): 103–16.

PONDY, LOUIS R., and IAN I. MITROFF
1979   Beyond open system models of organization. *Research in Organizational Behavior,* 1: 3–39.

PONTELL, HENRY N., LAWRENCE R. SALINGER, and GILBERT GEIS
1983   Assaults in the air: Concerning attacks against flight attendants. *Deviant Behavior,* 4: 297–311.

POPOVICH, PAULA, and JOHN P. WANOUS
  1982   The realistic job preview as a persuasive communication. *Academy of Management Review,* 7: 570–78.

POWDERMAKER, HORTENSE
  1950   Hollywood, the dream factory: An anthropologist looks at the movie-makers. Boston: Little, Brown.

POWELL, WALTER W.
  1990   Neither market nor hierarchy: Network forms of organization. *Research in Organizational Behavior,* 12: 295–336.

PRANGE, GORDON W.
  1981   *At Dawn We Slept: The Untold Story of Pearl Harbor.* New York: McGraw-Hill.

PREMACK, STEVEN L. and JOHN P. WANOUS
  1985   A meta-analysis of realistic job preview experiments. *Journal of Applied Psychology,* 70: 706–19.

PRESTON, PAUL, and ANTHONY QUESADA
  1978   What does your office "say" about you? Pp. 110–16 in Frost, Peter J., Vance F. Mitchell, and Walter R. Nord (eds.) *Organizational Reality: Reports from the Firing Line.* Santa Monica, Calif.: Goodyear Publishing Co.

PREVITZ, GARY J., and BARBARA D. MERINO
  1979   *A History of Accounting in America.* New York: John Wiley.

PRICE, J. L.
  1968   The impact of departmentalization on interoccupational cooperation. *Human Organization,* Pp. 362–68.

PUCIK, VLADIMIR, MITSUYO HANADA, and GEORGE FIFIELD
  1989   *Management Culture and the Effectiveness of Local Executives in Japanese-Owned U.S. Corporations.* Sponsored by Egon Zehnder International, Ltd., Tokyo and the University of Michigan, Ann Arbor. Tokyo: Egon Zehnder International, Ltd.

PUFFER, SHEILA M.
  1990   Attributions of charismatic leadership: The impact of decision style, outcome, and observer characteristics. *Leadership Quarterly,* 1(3): 177–99.

PUGH, D. S., D. J. HICKSON, and C. R. HININGS
  1969   An empirical taxonomy of structures of work organizations. *Administrative Science Quarterly,* 14(March): 115–26.

PUGH, DEREK S., D. J. HICKSON, C. R. HININGS, K. M. MACDONALD, C. TURNER, and T. LUPTON
  1963   A conceptual scheme for organizational analysis. *Administrative Science Quarterly,* 8(December): 289–315.

PUGH, DEREK, DAVID HICKSON, ROBERT HININGS, and CHRIS TURNER
  1968   Dimensions of organizational structure. *Administrative Science Quarterly,* 13(June): 65–104.

PUTNAM, LINDA L., and MICHAEL E. PACANOWSKY (eds.)
  1983   *Communications and Organizations.* Beverly Hills, Calif.: Sage Publications, Inc.

QUAID, MAEVE
  1992   Job evaluation as institutional myth. *Journal of Management Studies,* 29: (forthcoming).

QUINN, ROBERT E.
  1977   Coping with cupid: The formation, impact, and management of romantic relationships in organizations. *Administrative Science Quarterly,* 22: 30–44.

QUINN, ROBERT E., and KIM CAMERON
1983   Organizational life cycles and some shifting criteria of effectiveness: Some preliminary evidence. *Management Science*, 29: 33–51.

RADCLIFFE-BROWN, ALFRED R.
1940   On joking relationships. *Africa*, 13(3): 195–210.
1952   *Structure and Function in Primitive Society.* New York: Free Press.
1964   *The Andaman Islanders.* New York: Free Press.

RAELIN, JOSEPH A.
1987   The '60s kids in the corporation: More than just "daydream believers". *Academy of Management Executive*, February, pp. 21–29.

RAPHAEL, RAY
1988   *The Men from the Boys: Rites of Passage in Male America.* Lincoln, Nebr.: University of Nebraska Press.

REEDER, SHARON J., and HANS MAUKSCH
1979   Nursing: Continuing change. Pp. 209–29 in Freeman, Howard, et al. (eds.) *Handbook of Medical Sociology.* Englewood Cliffs, N.J.: Prentice Hall.

REEVES, WILLIAM J.
1980   *Librarians as Professionals: The Occupation's Impact on Library Work Arrangement.* Lexington, Mass.: Lexington Books.

REISCHEL, DIANE
1985   Herb Kelleher. *The Dallas Morning News*, April 7: 1.

REILLY, R. R., B. BROWN, R. BLOOD, and C. Z. MALATESTA
1981   The effects of realistic previews: A study and discussion of the literature. *Personnel Psychology*, 34: 823–34.

REUSS, RICHARD A.
1983   Songs of American labor, industrialization, and the urban work experience: A discography. Ann Arbor: Labor Studies Center, Institute of Labor and Industrial Relations, University of Michigan.

REUSS-JANNI, ELIZABETH
1983   *Two Cultures of Policing: Street Cops and Management Cops.* New Brunswick, N.J.: Transaction Books.

REYNOLDS, MORGAN O.
1987   Unions and jobs: The U.S. auto industry. *Journal of Labor Research*, 8: 311–15.

REYNOLDS, PETER C.
1987   Imposing a corporate culture. *Psychology Today*, March, Pp. 33–39.

RICHARDSON, F. L. W.
1955   Anthropology and human relations in business and industry. Thomas W. L. (ed.) *Yearbook of Anthropology.* Special publication of the American Anthropological Association.
1961   Talk, work and action: Human reactions to organizational change. Monograph No. 3, Society for Applied Anthropology. Ithaca, N.Y.: School of Industrial and Labor Relations, Cornell University.

RILEY, MATILDA W.
1987   On the significance of age in sociology. *American Sociological Review*, 52(1): 1–14.

RILEY, PATRICIA
1983   A structurationist account of political culture. *Administrative Science Quarterly*, 28(3): 414–37.

RITCHIE, J. B., and PAUL THOMPSON
   1980   *Organization and People: Readings, Cases, and Exercises in Organizational Behavior,* 2nd ed. St. Paul, Minn.: West Publishing Co.

RITTI, R. RICHARD
   1968   Work goals of scientists and engineers. *Industrial Relations,* 7: 118–31.

RITTI, R. RICHARD, and G. RAY FUNKHOUSER
   1977   *The Ropes to Skip and the Ropes to Know: Studies in Organizational Behavior.* Columbus, Ohio: Grid, Inc.

RITTI, R. RICHARD, and JONATHAN H. SILVER
   1986   Early processes of institutionalization: The dramaturgy of exchange in interorganizational relations. *Administrative Science Quarterly,* 31: 25–42.

RITZER, GEORGE
   1983   *Contemporary Sociological Theory.* New York: Knopf.

RITZER, GEORGE, and HARRISON M. TRICE
   1969a   *An Occupation in Conflict: A Study in Conflict.* Ithaca, N.Y.: School of Industrial and Labor Relations, Cornell University.
   1969b   An empirical study of Howard Becker's sidebet theory. *Social Forces,* 47: 475–78.

ROBERTS, E. B., and H. A. WAINER
   1968   New enterprises on Route 128. *Science Journal,* 4(12): 78–83.

ROBERTS, NANCY
   1985   Transforming leadership: A process of collective action. *Human Relations,* 38(1): 1023–46.

ROBERTS, NANCY, and RAYMOND T. BRADLEY
   1988   Limits of charisma. Pp. 253–76 in Conger, Jay A., Rabindra N. Kanungo and Associates (eds.) *Charismatic Leadership: The Elusive Factor in Organizational Effectiveness.* San Francisco: Jossey-Bass.

RODGERS, DANIEL T.
   1978   *The Work Ethic in Industrial America.* Chicago: University of Chicago Press.

ROGERS, EVERETT M., and JUDITH K. LARSEN
   1984   *Silicon Valley Fever: Growth of High-Technology Culture.* New York: Basic Books.

ROETHLISBERGER, FRITZ J.
   1977   *The Elusive Phenomenon.* Cambridge, Mass.: Graduate School of Business Administration and Harvard University Press.

ROETHLISBERGER F. J., and WILLIAM J. DICKSON
   1946   *Management and the Worker.* Cambridge, Mass.: Harvard University Press.

ROHLEN, THOMAS P.
   1973   Spiritual Education in a Japanese Bank. *American Anthropologist,* 75: 1542–62.
   1974   *For Harmony and Strength.* Berkeley, Calif.: University of California Press.

RONEN, SIMCHA
   1986   *Comparative and Multinational Management.* New York: John Wiley.

ROSEN, BENSON, and THOMAS R. JARDEE
   1977   Too old or not too old? *Harvard Business Review,* 55(Nov.–Dec.): 96–106.

ROSENBAUM, JAMES E.
   1979   Tournament mobility: Career patterns in a corporation. *Administrative Science Quarterly,* 24: 220–41.
   1984   *Career Mobility in a Corporate Hierarchy.* New York: Academic Press.
   1989   Organization career systems and employee misperceptions. Pp. 329–53 in Arthur, Michael

B., Douglas T. Hall, and Barbara S. Lawrence (eds.) *Handbook of Career Theory.* New York: Cambridge University Press.

ROSENTHAL, STEVEN M., and ROBERT MEZOFF
1980 How to improve the cost-benefit ratio of management, training and development. *Training and Development Journal,* 34(12): 102–7.

ROSOW, IRVING
1974 *Socialization to Old Age.* Berkeley, Calif.: University of California Press.

ROTHCHILD-WHITT, JOYCE
1979 The collectivist organization: An alternative to rational bureaucratic models. *American Sociological Review,* 44: 509–27.

ROTHCHILD, JOYCE, and A. ALLEN WHITT
1986 *The Cooperative Workplace: Potentials and Dilemmas of Organizational Democracy and Participation.* New York: Cambridge University Press.

ROUSSEAU, DENISE M.
1990 Assessing organizational culture: The case for multiple methods. Pp. 153–92 in Schneider, Benjamin (ed.) *Organizational Climate and Culture.* San Francisco: Jossey-Bass.

ROWAN, BRIAN
1982 Organizational structure and the institutional environment: The case of public schools. *Administrative Science Quarterly,* 27(June): 259–79.

ROY, DONALD
1952 Quota restriction and gold bricking in a machine shop. *American Journal of Sociology,* 57: 427–42.
1953 Work satisfaction and social reward in quota achievement. *American Sociological Review,* 18: 507–14.
1954 Efficiency and the fix: informal intergroup relations in a piece-work machine shop. *American Journal of Sociology,* 60: 255–66.
1960 Banana Time: Job satisfaction and informal interaction. *Human Organization,* 18: 158–61.
1962 Sex in the factory: Informal heterosexual relations between supervisors and work groups. Pp. 44–48 in Clifford D. Bryand (ed.) *Deviant Behavior: Occupational and Organizational Bases.* Chicago: Rand-McNally.

RUNCIE, JOHN F.
1980 By days I make the cars. *Harvard Business Review,* 58(3) May–June: 106–15.

SACKMAN, SONJA A.
1987 Is culture in organizations monolithic or pluralistic? Paper presented at the annual meeting of the Academy of Management, New Orleans, La.

SAHLINS, MARSHALL
1974 *Stone Age Economics.* London: Tavistock Publications.

SALAMAN, GRAEME
1974 *Community and Occupation: An Exploration of the Work/Leisure Relationship.* London: Cambridge University Press.

SALANCIK, GERALD R.
1977 Commitment and control of organizational behavior. Pp. 1–54 in Staw, B., and G. Salanick (eds.) *New Directions in Organizational Behavior.* Chicago: St. Clair Press.

SALANCIK, GERALD R., and J. R. MEINDL
1984 Corporate attributions as strategic illusions of management control. *Administrative Science Quarterly,* 29: 238–54.

SALANICK, GERALD R., and JEFFREY PFEFFER
1974   The bases and use of power in organizational decision-making: The case of a university. *Administrative Science Quarterly,* 19(4): 453–73.
1977   Constraints on administrative discretion: The limited influence of mayors on city budgets. *Urban Affairs Quarterly,* 12(4): 475–98.
1978   A social information processing approach to job attitudes and task design. *Administrative Science Quarterly,* 23: 224–52.

SALES, AMY, and PHILIP H. MIRVIS
1984   When cultures collide: Issues in acquisition. Pp. 107–32 in Kimberly, John, and Robert Quinn (eds.) *Managing Organizational Transitions.* Homewood, Ill.: Richard D. Irwin.

SAMUELSON, SUE
1983   Improving conditions, increasing awareness: An on-site ethnic display. Paper delivered at the University of California at Los Angeles Conference on Myths, Symbols, and Folklore: Expanding the Analyses of Organizations, March 11, Los Angeles, Calif.

SANTINO, JACK
1978   Characteristics of occupational narratives. *Western Folklore,* 37(3): 199–243.

SAPIR, EDWARD
[1915] The social organization of the West Coast tribes. Pp. 26–57 in McFeat, Tom (ed.), *Indians*
1966   *of the North Pacific Coast.* Seattle, Wash.: University of Washington Press.

SAPOLSKY, HARVEY
1972   *The Polaris System Development: Bureaucratic and Programmic Success in Government.* Cambridge, Mass.: Harvard University Press.

SASHKIN, MARSHALL
1988   The visionary leader. Pp. 122–61 in Conger, Jay A., and Rabindra N. Kanungo and Associates (eds.) *Charismatic Leadership: The Elusive Factor in Organizational Effectiveness.* San Francisco: Jossey-Bass.

SASHKIN, MARSHALL, and HOWARD GARLAND
1979   Laboratory and field research on leadership: Integrating divergent streams. Pp. 64–87 in Hunt, James G., and Lars Larson (eds.) *Crosscurrents in Leadership.* Carbondale, Ill.: Southern Illinois University Press.

SATHE, VIJAY
1985   *Culture and Related Corporate Realities.* Homewood, Ill.: Richard D. Irwin.

SAYLES, LEONARD R., and GEORGE STRAUSS
1953   *The Local Union.* New York: Harper & Row, Pub.

SCHATZMAN, LEONARD, and RUE BUCHER
1964   Negotiating a division of labor among professionals in the state mental hospital. *Psychiatry,* 27: 266–77.

SCHEIN, EDGAR H.
1978   *Career Dynamics: Matching Individual and Organizational Needs.* Reading, Mass.: Addison-Wesley.
1983a   Organizational culture: A dynamic model. Working paper, Sloan School of Management, Massachusetts Institute of Technology, January.
1983b   The role of founder in creating organizational culture. *Organizational Dynamics,* Summer, Pp. 13–28.
1985   *Organizational Culture and Leadership.* San Francisco: Jossey-Bass.
1990   Organizational culture. *American Psychologist,* 45(2): 109–19.
1991   What is culture? Pp. 243–54 in Frost, Peter J., Larry Moore, Meryl R. Louis, Craig C. Lund-

berg, and Joanne Martin (eds.) *Reframing Organizational Culture.* Newbury Park, Calif.: Sage Publishing, Inc.

SCHERMERHORN, JOHN R., JR., JAMES G. HUNT, and RICHARD N. OSBORN
1982   *Managing Organizational Behavior.* New York: John Wiley.

SCHLESINGER, ARTHUR M., JR.
1986   *The Cycles of American History.* Boston: Houghton Mifflin.

SCHMITT, NEAL
1976   Social and situational determinants of interview decisions: Implications for the employment interview. *Personnel Psychology,* 29: 79–101.

SCHNEIDER, BENJAMIN (ed.)
1990   *Organizational Climate and Culture.* San Francisco: Jossey-Bass.

SCHON, DONALD A.
1971   *Beyond the State.* London: Smith.

SCHRIER, D. A., and F. D. MULCAHY
1988   Middle management and union realities: Coercion and anti-structure in a public corporation. *Human Organization,* 47(2): 146–50.

SCHULTZ, MAJKEN
1991   Transitions between symbolic domains in organizations. Paper in *Organization,* No. 1, New Social Science Monographs, Institute of Organization and Industrial Sociology. Copenhagen Business School, Copenhagen, Denmark.

SCHWARTZ, BARRY
1983   George Washington and the Whig conception of heroic leadership. *American Sociological Review,* 48(1): 18–33.

SCHWARTZ, HOWARD M., and STANLEY M. DAVIS
1981   Matching corporate culture and business strategy. *Organizational Dynamics,* Summer: 30–48.

SCHWARTZMAN, HELEN B.
1981   Hidden agendas and formal organizations or how to dance at a meeting. *Social Analysis,* 9(December): 77–88.
1984   Stories at work: Play in an organizational context. Pp. 80–93 in Bruner, E. M., and S. Plattner (eds.) *Text, Play and Story.* Washington, D.C.: American Ethnological Society.
1986   The meeting as a neglected social form in organizational studies. *Research in Organizational Behavior,* 8: 233–58.

SCHWARTZMAN, HELEN B., ANITA KNEIFEL, and MENTON KRAUSE
1978   Culture conflict in a community mental health center. *Journal of Social Issues,* 34: 93–110.

SCOTT, W. RICHARD
1981   *Organizations: Rational, Natural, and Open Systems.* Englewood Cliffs, N.J.: Prentice Hall.
1987   *Organizations: Rational, Natural, and Open Systems,* 2nd ed. Englewood Cliffs, N.J.: Prentice Hall.

SCOTT, WILLIAM G., and DAVID K. HART
1971   *Organizational America.* Boston: Houghton-Mifflin.

SELZNICK, PHILIP
1949   *T.V.A. and the Grass Roots.* Berkeley, Calif.: University of California Press.
1957   *Leadership in Administration.* New York: Harper & Row, Pub.

SENGOKU, TAMOTSU
1985   *Willing Workers: The Work Ethic in Japan, England, and the United States.* Westport, Conn.: Quorum Books.

SERAFIN, RAYMOND
 1990   G.M.'s Saturn enters crucial period. *Advertising*, 61(March 5): 16–18.

SERGIOVANNI, THOMAS J., and JOHN E. CORBALLY (eds.)
 1984   *Leadership and Organizational Culture: Theory and Practice.* Urbana, Ill.: University of Illinois Press.

SETHI, S. PRAKASH, HAMID ETEMAD, and K. A. N. LUTHER
 1986   New sociopolitical forces: The globalization of conflict. *Journal of Business Strategy*, 6(4): 24–31.

SETHIA, NIRMAL K., and MARY ANN VON GLINOW
 1985   Arriving at four cultures by managing the reward system. Pp. 400–20 in Kilmann, Ralph H. et al. (eds.) *Gaining Control of the Corporate Culture.* San Francisco: Jossey-Bass.

SEWELL, WILLIAM H.
 1969   The educational and early occupational attainment process. *American Sociological Behavior*, 34(Feb.): 82–92.

SHABECOFF, PHILLIP
 1989   Largest U.S. tanker oil spill spews 270,000 barrels of oil off Alaska. *The New York Times*, Sec. 1, p. 1, March 25.

SHAPIRO, DAVID, and JOAN E. CROWLEY
 1982   Aspirations and expectations of the youth in the United States: Past employment activity. *Youth and Society*, 14(Sept.): 33–58.

SHATTUCK, ROGER
 1980   *The Forbidden Experiment: The Story of the Wild Boy of Aveyron.* New York: Farrar, Straus & Giroux.

SHEA, GREGORY P.
 1986   Quality circles: The danger of bottled change. *Sloan Management Review*, Spring: 33–46.

SHENKAR, ODED, and SIMCHA RONEN
 1987   Structure and importance of work goals among managers in the People's Republic of China. *Academy of Management Journal*, 30(3): 564–76.

SHILS, EDWARD
 1975   *Center and Periphery: Essays in Macrosociology.* Chicago: University of Chicago Press.

SHIRAI, TAISHIRO
 1983   A theory of enterprise unionism. Pp. 117–44 in Shirai, T. (ed.) *Contemporary Industrial Relations in Japan.* Madison, Wis.: University of Wisconsin Press.

SIEHL, CAREN
 1985   After the founder: An opportunity to manage culture. Pp. 125–40 in Frost, Peter J., et al. (eds.) *Organizational Culture.* Beverly Hills, Calif.: Sage Publications, Inc.

SIEHL, CAREN, and JOANNE MARTIN
 1990   Organizational culture: A key to financial performance. Pp. 241–82 in Schneider, Benjamin (ed.) *Organizational Climate and Culture.* San Francisco: Jossey-Bass.

SILVERZWEIG, STAN, and ROBERT F. ALLEN
 1976   Changing the corporate culture. *Sloan Management Review*, 17(3): 33–49.

SIMMEL, GEORGE
 1955   *Conflict and the Web of Group Affiliation.* New York: Free Press.

SIMON, HERBERT A.
 1957   *Administrative Behavior.* (2nd ed.) New York: Macmillan.

SIMONS, CAROL
1987   They got by with a lot of help from their kyoiku mamas. *Smithsonian*, 18(2): 44–52.

SIMPSON, IDA H.
1967   Patterns of socialization into professions: The case of student nurses. *Sociological Inquiry*, 37: 47–54.

SIMPSON, RICHARD L., and IDA H. SIMPSON
1959   The psychiatric attendant: Development of an occupational self-image in a low status occupation. *American Sociological Review*, 24(3): 389–92.

SIMS, CALVIN
1990   Computer failure disrupts A.T.&T. long distance. *The New York Times*, January 16, p. A1.

SINETAR, MARSHA
1981   Mergers, morale and productivity. *Personnel Journal*, November, Pp. 863–67.

SINGER, MARK
1985   Annals of finance: Funny money. *The New Yorker*, April 29, May 6.

SINGER, MILTON
1968   Culture. *International Encyclopedia of the Social Sciences*, 3: 527–43.

SLOAN, ALFRED P., JR.
1963   *My Years with General Motors*. New York: Anchor Books.

SLOAN, ALLAN
1983   *Three Plus One Equals Billions: The Bendix-Martin-Marietta War*. New York: Arbor House.

SLOATE, ALFRED
1969   *Termination: The Closing at Baker Plant*. Indianapolis, Ind.: Bobbs-Merrill.

SMIRCICH, LINDA
1983   Concepts of culture and organizational analysis. *Administrative Science Quarterly*, 28(3): 339–58.

SMIRCICH, LINDA, and MARIA B. CALAS
1987   Organizational culture: A critical assessment. Pp. 228–63 in Jablin, F. M., L. L. Putnam, K. H. Roberts, and L. W. Porter (eds.) *Handbook of Organizational Communication*. Beverly Hills, Calif.: Sage Publications, Inc.

SMIRCICH, LINDA, and CHARLES STUBBART
1985   Strategic management in an enacted world. *Academy of Management Review*, 10(4): 724–36.

SMITH, B. J.
1982   An initial test of a theory of charismatic leadership based on the responses of subordinates. Unpublished Doctoral Thesis, University of Toronto.

SMITH, HARVEY, L.
1962   Contingencies of professional differentiation. Pp. 219–25 in Nosow, Sigmund, and William Form (eds.). *Man, Work, and Society*. New York: Basic Books.

SMITH, HEDRICK
1988   *The Power Game: How Washington Works*. New York: Random House.

SMITH, JONATHAN, KENNETH CARSON, and RALPH ALEXANDER
1984   Leadership: It can make a difference. *Academy of Management Journal*, 27(4): 765–76.

SMITH, KENWYN, and VALERIE M. SIMMONS
1983   A Rumpelstiltskin organization: Metaphors on metaphors in field research. *Administrative Science Quarterly*, 28(3): 377–92.

SNYDER, RICHARD C.
  1988   New frames for old: Changing the managerial culture of an aircraft factory. Pp. 191–208 in Jones, Michael O., Michael Moore, and Richard C. Snyder (eds.) *Inside Organizations.* Beverly Hills, Calif.: Sage Publications, Inc.

SOLMAN, PAUL
  1991   Culture clash, Part 3: Treatment of American employees by Japanese companies. Transcript of MacNeal/Lehrer Newshour, April 3; Educational Broadcasting Corporation. Overland Park, Kans.: *Strictly Business,* Pp. 10–14.

SONG, Y. D., and T. E. YARBOROUGH
  1978   Tax ethics and taxpayers' attitudes. *Public Administration Review,* 38: 454.

SONNENFELD, JEFFREY
  1988   *The Hero's Farewell: What Happens When CEOs Retire.* New York: Oxford University Press.

SONNENSTUHL, WILLIAM J., and HARRISON M. TRICE
  1987   Social construction of alcohol problems in a union's peer counseling program. *Journal of Drug Issues,* 17: 223–54.
  1991   Linking organizational and occupational theory through the concept of culture. *Research in Sociology of Organizations,* 9: 295–318.

SPANGLER, EVE
  1986   *Lawyers for Hire.* New Haven, Conn.: Yale University Press.

SPARKS, P.
  1983   Gossip—How it works. *Yale Review,* 72: 561–80.

SPENNER, KENNETH I.
  1979   Temporal changes in work content. *American Sociological Review,* 44: 968–75.

SPILLAR, KATHERINE, and SHELLY CRYER
  1991   *Empowering Women in Business.* Washington, D.C.: The Feminist Majority Foundation.

SPITZ, BOB
  1986   Mr. America. *Life,* 9(6): 35–42.

SPRADLEY, JAMES P., and BRENDA J. MANN
  1975   *The Cocktail Waitress: Woman's Work in a Man's World.* New York: John Wiley.

SPREY, JETSE
  1962   Sex differences in occupational choice patterns among Negro adolescents. *Social Problems,* 10(Summer): 11–22.

SPROULL, LEE S.
  1981   Beliefs in organizations. Pp. 203–23 in Nystrom, Paul C., and William H. Starbuck (eds.) *Handbook of Organizational Design.* New York: Oxford University Press.

STARBUCK, WILLIAM
  1976   Organizations and their environment. Pp. 1069–1123 in Dunnette, Marvin D. (ed.) *Handbook of Industrial and Organizational Psychology.* Chicago: Rand McNally.
  1982   Congealing oil: Inventing ideologies to justify acting ideologies out. *Journal of Management Studies,* 19(1): 3–27.
  1983   Organizations as action generators. *American Sociological Review,* 48(1): 91–103.

STARBUCK, WILLIAM H., ARANT GREVE, and B. L. T. HEDBERG
  1978   Responding to Crisis. *Journal of Business Administration,* 9: 121–37.

STARBUCK, WILLIAM H., and FRANCES J. MILLIKEN
  1988   Executive's perceptual filters: What they notice and how they make sense. Pp. 35–65 in

Hambrick, Donald C. (ed.) *The Executive Effect: Concepts and Methods for Studying Top Managers.* Greenwich, Conn.: JAI Press.

STARBUCK, WILLIAM, and P. NYSTROM
1981 Designing and understanding organizations. Pp. ix–xxiii in Nystrom, P., and W. Starbuck (eds.) *Handbook of Organizational Design.* New York: Oxford University Press.

STAW, BARRY M.
1976 Knee-deep in the Big Muddy: A study of escalating commitment to a chosen course of action. *Organizational Behavior and Human Performance,* 16: 27–44.
1980 Rationality and justification in organizational life. *Research in Organizational Behavior,* 2: 45–79.

STAW, BARRY M., LANCE E. SANDELANDS, and JANE E. DUTTON
1981 Threat-rigidity effects in organizational behavior: A multilevel analysis. *Administrative Science Quarterly,* 26: 501–24.

STEARNS, CAROL Z., and PETER N. STEARNS
1986 *Anger: The Struggle for Emotional Control in America's History.* Chicago: University of Chicago Press.

STEELE, FRITZ
1975 *The Open Organization: The Impact of Secrecy and Disclosure on People and Organizations.* Reading, Mass.: Addison-Wesley.

STEIN, LEONARD
1971 The doctor nurse game. Pp. 132–43 in Bullough, B., and V. Bullough (eds.) *New Directions for Nurses.* New York: Springer.

STERN, ROBERT, and WILLIAM F. WHYTE
1981 Editor's introduction: Economic democracy: comparative views of current initiatives. *Sociology of Work and Occupations,* 8(2): 139–44.

STEVENSON, WILLIAM B., JANE L. PEARCE, and LYMAN W. PORTER
1985 Concept of "coalition" in organization theory and research. *Academy of Management Review,* 10(2): 256–68.

STEWART, PHYLLIS, and MURIEL G. CANTOR
1982 *Varieties of Work.* Beverly Hills, Calif.: Sage Publications, Inc.

STINCHCOMBE, ARTHUR L.
1959 Bureaucratic and craft administration of production. *Administrative Science Quarterly,* 4(September): 3–21.
1965 Social Structure and Organizations. Pp. 142–93 in March, James G. (ed.) *Handbook of Organizations.* Chicago: Rand McNally.
1983 *Economic Sociology.* New York: Academic Press.

STOGDILL, RALPH M.
1974 *Handbook of Leadership.* New York: Free Press.

STOUFFER, SAMUEL A., LOUIS GUTTMAN, EDWARD A. SUCHMAN, PAUL F. LAZARSFELD, SHIRLEY A. STAR, and JOHN A. CLAUSEN
1950 *Measurement and Prediction.* New York: John Wiley.

STOUFFER, SAMUEL A., EDWARD A. SUCHMAN, L. C. DEVINNEY, SHIRLEY A. STAR, and ROBIN M. WILLIAMS
1949 *The American Soldier: Adjustments During Army Life.* Princeton, N.J.: Princeton University Press.

STRAUSS, ANSELM L.
  1966   The structure and ideology of American nursing: An interpretation. Pp. 132–68 in Davis, F. (ed.) *The Nursing Profession.* New York: John Wiley.
  1978   *Negotiations: Varieties, Contexts, Processes, and Social Order.* San Francisco: Jossey-Bass.

STRAUSS, ANSELM, LEONARD SCHATZMAN, RUE BUCHER, DANUTA EHRLICH, and MELVIN SABSHIN
  1964   *Psychiatric Ideologies and Institutions.* New York: Free Press.

STRAUSS, GEORGE
  1962   Tactics of lateral relationships: The purchasing agent. *Administrative Science Quarterly,* 7(2): 161–86.

STRAYER, KERRY
  1991   Personal communication with second author. June.

STULLER, JOAN
  1991   Personal communication with second author.

SUMNER, WILLIAM G.
  1906   *Folkways.* New York: Dover.

SUNDSTROM, ERIC
  1986   *Workplaces: The Psychology of the Physical Environment in Offices and Factories.* Cambridge, England: Cambridge University Press.

SUTTON, FRANCIS X., SEYMOUR E. HARRIS, CARL KAYSEN, and JAMES TOBIN
  1956   *The American Business Creed.* Cambridge, Mass.: Harvard University Press.

SUTTON, ROBERT I., and ANITA L. CALLAHAN
  1987   The stigma of bankruptcy: Spoiled organizational image and its management. *Academy of Management Journal,* 30(3): 405–36.

SUTTON, ROBERT I., KATHLEEN M. EISENHARDT, and JAMES V. JUCKER
  1986   Managing organizational decline: Lessons from Atari. *Organizational Dynamics,* Spring, Pp. 17–29.

SUTTON, ROBERT I., and MERYL R. LOUIS
  1984   The influence of selection and socialization on insider sense-making. Technical Report 84-6, School of Management, Boston University, Boston, Mass.

SWIDLER, ANN
  1986   Culture in action: symbols and strategies. *American Sociological Review,* 51: 273–86.
  1990   Love and adulthood in American culture. Pp. 120–47 in Smelser, Neil J., and Erik H. Erikson (eds.) *Themes of Work and Love in Adulthood.* Cambridge, Mass.: Harvard University Press.

TAKEZAWA, SHIN'ICHI, and ARTHUR M. WHITEHILL
  1981   *Workways: Japan and America.* Tokyo: Japan Institute of Labor.

TANNEN, DEBORAH
  1990   *You Just Don't Understand: Women and Men in Conversation.* New York: Morrow.

TANNENBAUM, ARNOLD S., BOGAN KAVCIC, MENACHEM ROSNER, MINO VIANELLO, and GEORG WIESER
  1974   *Hierarchy in Organizations.* San Francisco: Jossey-Bass.

TAYLOR, ALEX, III
  1988   Back to the future at Saturn. *Fortune,* August 1, Pp. 68–72.

TAYLOR, ARCHER
  1981   The wisdom of many and the wit of one. Pp. 3–9 in Mieder, Wolfgang, and Alan Dundes (eds.) *The Wisdom of Many.* New York: Garland Publishing, Inc.

TAYLOR, FREDERICK W.
1911   *The Principles of Scientific Management.* New York: W. W. Norton & Co., Inc.

TAYLOR, ROBERT, L.
1979   Chronic epistlitis. Pp. 181–85 in Peters, Charles, and Michael Nelson (eds.) *The Culture of Bureaucracy.* New York: Holt, Rinehart & Winston.

TEITLER, G.
1981   Profession, autonomy and time perspective: A comparative study of the rise of the Air Force weapon. Pp. 373–86 in Lammers, Cornelius J., and David J. Hickson (eds.) *Organizations Alike and Unlike.* London: Rutledge & Kegan Paul.

TERKEL, STUDS
1972   *Working.* Chicago: Avon Printing.

TERRY, W. C.
1981   Police stress: The empirical evidence. *Journal of Police Science and Administration,* 9(1): 61–75.

THOMPSON, JAMES D.
1956   On building an administrative science. *Administrative Science Quarterly,* 1: 102–11.
1967   *Organizations in Action.* New York: McGraw-Hill.

THOMPSON, LAWRENCE C.
1947   The customs of the chapel. *Journal of American Folklore,* 60(Oct.–Dec., #238): 329–44.

THOMPSON, STITH
1946   *The Folktale.* New York: Holt, Reinhart, & Winston.

TICHY, NOEL M.
1973   An analysis of clique formation and structure in organizations. *Administrative Science Quarterly,* 18(2): 194–208.
1981   Networks in organizations. Pp. 225–49 in Nystrom, Paul C., and William H. Starbuck (eds.) *Handbook of Organizational Design,* vol. II. New York: Oxford University Press.
1983   *Managing Strategic Change: Technical, Political and Cultural Dynamics.* New York: John Wiley.

TICHY, NOEL, and DAVID ULRICH
1984   Revitalizing organizations: The leadership role. Pp. 240–64 in Kimberly, John, and Robert E. Quinn (eds.) *New Futures: The Challenge of Managing Corporate Transitions.* Homewood, Ill.: Dow-Jones-Irwin.

Time
1983   Hot 100. July 4, p. 46.

TOLBERT, PAMELA S., and ROBERT N. STERN
1988   Organizations and professions: Governance structures in large law firms. Working paper, School of Industrial and Labor Relations, Cornell University, Ithaca, N.Y.

TRAHAIR, RICHARD C. S.
1984   *The Humanist Temper: The Life and Work of Elton Mayo.* New Brunswick, N.J.: Transaction Books.

TREECE, JAMES R.
1990   Here comes G.M.'s Saturn: More than a car, it is G.M.'s hope for reinventing itself. *Business Week,* April 9, pp. 56–62.
1991   Getting mileage from a recall. *Business Week,* May 27, 38–39.

TRIANDIS, HARRY C.
1973   Work and nonwork: Intercultural perspectives. Pp. 29–68 in Dunnette, Marvin D. (ed.) *Work and Nonwork in the Year 2001.* Monterey, Calif.: Brooks/Cole Publishing.

TRICE, HARRISON M.
1961   Rural reared workers and labor turnover. *Rural Sociology,* 26: 299–305.
1964   The nightwatchman: A study of an isolated occupation. *ILR Research,* 10: 3–11.
1965   *Alcoholism in America.* New York: McGraw-Hill.
1985   Rites and ceremonials in organizational cultures. *Research in the Sociology of Organizations,* 4: 221–70.
1991   Comments and discussion. Pp. 298–309 in Frost, Peter J., Larry F. Moore, Meryl Louis, Craig Lundberg, and Joanne Martin (eds.) *Reframing Organizational Culture.* Newbury Park, Calif.: Sage Publications, Inc.

TRICE, HARRISON M., JAMES BELASCO, and JOSEPH A. ALUTTO
1969   The role of ceremonials in organizational behavior. *Industrial and Labor Relations Review,* 23(October): 40–51.

TRICE, HARRISON M., and JANICE M. BEYER
1982   A study of union-management cooperation in a long standing alcoholism program. *Contemporary Drug Problems,* 11(2): Summer.
1983   The ceremonial effect: Manifest function or latent dysfunction in the dynamic organization. Paper presented at the Conference on Myth, Symbol and Folklore: Expanding the Analysis of Organizations, March, University of California at Los Angeles.
1984a   Studying organizational cultures through rites and ceremonials. *Academy of Management Review,* 9(4): 653–69.
1984b   Employee assistance programs: Blending performance-oriented and humanitarian ideologies to assist emotionally disturbed employees. *Research in Community and Mental Health,* 4: 254–97.
1985   Using six organizational rites to change cultures. Pp. 370–99 in Kilmann, Ralph H., Mary J. Saxton, and Roy Serpa (eds.) *Gaining Control of the Corporate Culture.* San Francisco: Jossey-Bass Publishers.
1986   Charisma and its routinization in two social movement organizations. *Research in Organizational Behavior,* 8: 113–64.
1988   An anthropological approach to conflict reduction. Paper presented at the annual meeting of the Academy of Management, August, Anaheim, Calif.
1991   Cultural leadership in organizations. *Organization Science,* 2(2): 149–69.

TRICE, HARRISON M., and DAVID MORAND
1989   Rites of passage in work careers. Pp. 397–416 in Arthur, Michael, Douglas T. Hall, and Barbara Lawrence (eds.) *Handbook of Career Theory.* New York: Cambridge University Press.
1991   Cultural diversity: Organizational subcultures and countercultures. Pp. 69–105 in Miller, Gale, *Studies in Organizational Sociology—Essays in Honor of Charles K. Warriner.* 10: 69–105. Greenwich, Conn.: JAI Press.

TRICE, HARRISON M., and ROBERT V. PENFIELD
1961   Use of application blank data in a study of job quitting. *Industrial and Labor Relations Research,* Summer Pp. 9–14.

TRICE, HARRISON M., and PAUL M. ROMAN
1971   Occupational risk factors in mental health and the impact of role change experiences. Pp. 145–204 in Leedy, Jack (ed.) *Compensation in Psychiatric Disability and Rehabilitation.* Springfield, Ill.: Chas. C. Thomas.
1973   *Evaluation of Training: Strategy, Tactics and Problems.* Madison, Wis.: American Society for Training and Development.

TRICE, HARRISON, and WILLIAM SONNENSTUHL
1988   Drinking behavior and risk factors related to the workplace: Implications for research and prevention. *Journal of Applied Behavioral Science,* 24(4): 327–46.

TRIST, ERIC L., and K. W. BANFORTH
1951   Some social and psychological consequences of the long-wall method of coal cutting. *Human Relations,* February, 3–38.

TUNLEY, ROUL
1978   Mary Kay's sweet smell of success. *Reader's Digest,* November, 17–21.

TUNSTALL, W. BROOKE
1983   Cultural transition at A.T.&T. *Sloan Management Review,* 25(1): 15–26.
1985   *Disconnecting Parties—Managing the Bell System Breakup: An Inside View.* New York: McGraw-Hill.

TURNBULL, COLIN
1984   Interview with Colin Turnbull. *Omni,* June: 87–90; 124–34.

TURNER, ARTHUR N., and PAUL R. LAWRENCE
1965   *Industrial Jobs and the Worker: An Investigation of Response to Task Attributes.* Boston: Harvard University, Graduate School of Business Administration.

TURNER, BARRY A.
1971   *Exploring the Industrial Subculture.* London: The Macmillan Press.
1981   Some practical aspects of qualitative data analysis: One way of organizing the cognitive processes associated with the generation of grounded theory. *Quality and Quantity,* 15: 225–47.
1986   Sociological aspects of organizational symbolism. *Organization Studies,* 7(2): 101–15.
1990a The rise of organizational symbolism. Pp. 83–96 in Hassard, John, and Denis Pym (eds.) *The Theory and Philosophy of Organizations: Critical Issues and New Perspectives.* London: Routledge & Kegan Paul.
1990b Introduction. Pp. 1–11 in Turner, Barry (ed.) *Organizational Symbolism.* New York: Walter de Gruyter.
1990c (Ed.) *Organizational Symbolism.* New York: Walter de Gruyter.

TURNER, RALPH H.
1969   The theme of contemporary social movements. *British Journal of Sociology,* 20(4): 390–405.

TURNER, STEPHEN
1977   Complex organizations as savage tribes. *Journal of Theory of Social Behavior,* 7(1): 99–126.

TURNER, TERENCE S.
1977   Transformation, hierarchy, and transcendence. Pp. 57–69 in Moore, Sally F., and Barbara G. Myerhoff (eds.) *Secular Ritual.* Assen, The Netherlands: Van Gorcum and Co.

TURNER, VICTOR W.
1967   *The Forest of Symbols: Aspects of Ndembu Ritual.* Ithaca, N.Y.: Cornell University Press.
1969   *The Ritual Process.* Chicago: Aldine.
1970   Betwixt and between: The liminal period in rites of passage. Pp. 354–69, in Hammel, Eugene A., and William S. Simmons (eds.) *Man Makes Sense.* Boston: Little, Brown.
1977   Symbols in African ritual. Pp. 183–94 in Dolgrin, Janet L., David S. Kemnitzer, and David M. Schneider (eds.) *Symbolic Anthropology.* New York: Columbia University Press.
1982   *From Ritual to Theatre: The Human Seriousness of Play.* New York: Performing Arts Journal Publications.

TUROW, SCOTT
  1977   *One L.* New York: Putnam's.

TUSHMAN, MICHAEL L.
  1977   A political approach to organizations: A review and rationale. *Academy of Management Review,* 2: 206–16.

TUSHMAN, MICHAEL L., and ELAINE ROMANELLI
  1985   Organizational evolution: A metamorphosis model of convergence and reorientation. *Research in Organizational Behavior,* 7: 171–222.

UDY, STANLEY H.
  1959   The structure of authority in non-industrial production organizations. *American Journal of Sociology,* 64: 582–84.
  1962   Administrative rationality, social setting, and organizational development. *American Journal of Sociology,* 68(3): 299–308.
  1970   *Work in Traditional and Modern Society.* Englewood Cliffs, N.J.: Prentice Hall.

U.S. News & World Report
  1983   Congress metes out a rare punishment. August, 1, p. 48.
  1988   Proud to serve. March 7: 55.

USEEM, MICHAEL
  1979   The social organization of the American business elite and participation of corporate directors in the governance of American institutions. *American Sociological Review,* 44: 553–72.

UTTAL, BRO
  1983   The corporate culture vultures. *Fortune,* October, 17, Pp. 66–72.

VAN BIEMA, DAVID
  1991   Looking forward to the past. *Life,* October, Pp. 88–91.

VAN DE VEN, ANDREW H.
  1982   The Three Rs of Administrative Behavior: Rational, Random, and Reasonable. Paper presented at the Albany Conference on Organizational Theory and Public Policy, Albany, New York, April.

VAN GENNEP, ARNOLD
  [1909] *Rites of Passage.* Chicago: University of Chicago Press.
  1960

VAN MAANEN, JOHN
  1973   Observations on the making of policemen. *Human Organization,* 32(Winter): 407–17.
  1975   Police socialization: A longitudinal examination of job attitudes in an urban police department. *Administrative Science Quarterly,* 20: 207–28.
  1977   Experiencing organization: Notes on the meaning of careers and socialization. Pp. 15–49 in Van Maanen, John (ed.) *Organizational Careers: Some New Perspectives.* New York: John Wiley.
  1978   People processing: Strategies of organizational socialization. *Organizational Dynamics,* Summer, Pp. 19–34.
  1979   The fact of fiction in organizational ethnography. *Administrative Science Quarterly,* 24: 539–50.
  1982   Introduction. Pp. 7–10 in Van Maanen, John, J. M. Dobbs, Jr., and R. R. Faulkner (eds.) *Varieties of Qualitative Research.* Beverly Hills, Calif.: Sage Publications, Inc.
  1984   Doing new things in old ways: The chains of socialization. Pp. 211–47 in Bess, James L. (ed.) *College and University Organization.* New York: New York University Press.
  1986   Power in the bottle: Informal interactions and formal authority. Pp. 204–38 in Srivastva, S., and Associates (eds.). *Executive Power.* San Francisco: Jossey-Bass.

VAN MAANEN, JOHN, and STEPHEN R. BARLEY
1984   Occupational communities: Culture and control in organizations. *Research in Organizational Behavior,* 6: 287–365.
1985   Cultural organization: Fragments of a theory. Pp. 31–55 in Frost, Peter M., Larry F. Moore, Meryl R. Louis, Craig C. Lundberg, and Joanne Martin (eds). *Organizational Culture.* Beverly Hills, Calif.: Sage Publications, Inc.

VAN MAANEN, JOHN, and GIDEON KUNDA
1989   "Real feelings": Emotional expression and organizational culture. *Research in Organizational Behavior,* 11: 43–103.

VAN MAANEN, JOHN, and EDGAR H. SCHEIN
1979   Toward a theory of organizational socialization. *Research in Organizational Behavior,* 1: 209–59.

VAUGHT, CHARLES, and DAVID L. SMITH
1980   Incorporation and mechanical solidarity in an underground coal mine. *Sociology of Work and Occupations,* 7(2): 159–67.

VEBLEN, THORNSTEIN
1899   *The Theory of the Leisure Class.* New York: Macmillan.

VELASQUEZ, MANUEL, DENNIS J. MOBERG, and GERALD F. CAVANAGH
1983   Organizational statesmanship and dirty politics: Ethical guidelines for the organizational politician. *Organizational Dynamics,* 12(Autumn): 65–80.

VINTON, KAREN L.
1986   Humor in the workplace: It's more than telling jokes. *Small Group Behavior,* 20: 151–66.

VROOM, VICTOR, H., and EDWARD L. DECI
1971   The stability of post-decisional dissonance: A follow-up study of the job attitude of business school graduates. *Organizational Behavior and Human Performance,* 6: 36–49.

VROOM, VICTOR H., and P. W. YETTON
1974   *Leadership and Decision Making.* New York: John Wiley.

WACHTEL, HOWARD M.
1973   *Workers' Management and Workers' Wages in Yugoslavia.* Ithaca, N.Y.: Cornell University Press.

WALD, MATHEW L.
1989   A hitch in plans for nuclear posterity. *The New York Times,* Sunday, February 12, Pp. 24–25.

WALDMAN, DAVID A., BERNARD BASS, and WALTER O. EINSTEIN
1986   Effort, performance and transformational leadership in industrial and military service. Working paper 85–80, School of Management, State University of New York at Binghamton.

WALDMAN, H. BARRY
1980   The reaction of the dental profession to changes in the 1970's. *American Journal of Public Health,* 70: 619–24.

WALENS, STANLEY
1982   The weight of my name is a mountain of blankets: Potlatch ceremonies. Pp. 178–89 in Turner, Victor (ed.) *Celebration.* Washington, D.C.: Smithsonian Institution Press.

WALKER, C. R., and R. H. GUEST
1952   *The Man on the Assembly Line.* Cambridge, Mass.: Harvard University Press.

WALL, JIM
1986   *Bosses.* Lexington, Mass.: Lexington Books.

WALL, TOBY D., NIGEL J. KEMP, PAUL R. JACKSON, and CHRIS W. CLEGG
1986   Outcomes of autonomous work groups: A long-term field experiment. *Academy of Management Journal,* 29: 280–304.

WALLACE, LINDA
1989   The image and what you can do about it in the year of the librarian. *American Librarian,* January, Pp. 22–25.

WALLACE, MICHAEL
1989   Brave new workplace: Technology and work in the new economy. *Work and Occupations,* 16(4): 363–92.

WALLACE MICHAEL, and ARNE L. KALLEBERG
1982   Industrial transformation and the decline of craft: The decomposition of skill in the printing industry, 1931–1978. *American Sociological Review,* 47: 307–14.

WALLMAN, SANDRA (ed.)
1979   *Social Anthropology of Work.* New York: Academic Press.

WALSH, DIANA C.
1986   Divided loyalties in medicine: The ambivalence of occupational medical practice. *Society, Science, and Medicine,* 23(8): 789–96.

WALSH, JAMES P., and LINDA FAHEY
1986   The role of negotiated belief structures in strategy making. *Journal of Management,* 12: 325–38.

WALTER, GORDON A.
1985   Culture collisions in mergers and acquisitions. Pp. 301–14 in Frost, Peter, Larry F. Moore, Meryl R. Louis, Craig Lundberg, and Joanne Martin (eds.) *Organizational Cultures.* Beverly Hills, Calif.: Sage Publications, Inc.

WALTERS, PAT
1978   *Coca Cola: An Illustrated History.* Garden City, N.Y.: Doubleday.

WALTERS, VIVIAN
1982   Company doctors' perception of and responses to conflicting pressures from labor and management. *Social Problems,* 30(1): 1–12.

WAMSLEY, GARY L.
1972   Contrasting institutions of Air Force socialization: Happenstance or bellweather? *American Journal of Sociology,* 78(2): 399–417.

WANOUS, JOHN P.
1977   Organizational entry: Newcomers moving from outside to inside. *Psychological Bulletin,* 84: 601–18.
1980   *Organizational Entry: Recruitment, Selection and Socialization of Newcomers.* Reading, Mass.: Addison-Wesley.

WANOUS, JOHN P., ARNON E. REICHERS, and S. D. MALIK
1984   Organizational socialization and group development: Toward an integrative perspective. *Academy of Management Review,* 9: 670–83.

WARDWELL, WALTER I.
1979   Limited and marginal practitioners. Pp. 230–50 in Freeman, Howard E. (ed.) *Medical Sociology.* 3rd ed. Englewood Cliffs, N.J.: Prentice Hall.

WARNER, W. LLOYD
1937   *A Black Civilization.* New York: Harper & Row, Pub.

WARNER, W. LLOYD, and O. J. LOW
1947   *The Social System of the Modern Factory.* New Haven, Conn.: Yale University Press.

WARNER, W. LLOYD, and PAUL S. LUNT
1941   *The Social Life of a Modern Community.* New Haven, Conn.: Yale University Press.

WATZLAWICK, PAUL, JOHN H. WEAKLAND, and RICHARD FISCH
1974   *Change.* New York: W. W. Norton & Co., Inc.

WEATHERFORD, J. MCIVER
1981   *Tribes on the Hill.* Rawson, Ill.: Wade Publishers, Inc.

WEBER, JOSEPH
1991   Meet DuPont's 'in-house' conscience. *Business Week,* June 24, Pp. 62, 65.

WEBER, MAX
1947   *The Theory of Social and Economic Organization.* A. M. Henderson and T. Parsons (eds. and trans.) New York: Free Press.
1949   *The Methodology of the Social Sciences.* E. A. Shils and H. A. Finch (eds. and trans.) New York: Free Press.
[1904] *The Protestant Ethic and the Spirit of Capitalism.* New York: Scribner's.
1958

WEICK, KARL E.
1969   *The Social Psychology of Organizing.* Reading, Mass.: Addison-Wesley.
1976   Educational organizations as loosely-coupled systems. *Administrative Science Quarterly,* 21(March): 1–19.
1977   Organization design: Organizations as self designing systems. *Organizational Dynamics,* 6(2): 31–46.
1979a   Cognitive processes in organizations. *Research in Organizational Behavior,* 1: 41–74.
1979b   *The Social Psychology of Organizing,* 2nd ed. Reading Mass.: Addison-Wesley.
1982   Management of organizational change among loosely coupled elements. Pp. 375–408 in Goodman, Paul, and Associates (eds.) *Changes in Organizations: New Perspectives on Theory, Research and Practice.* San Francisco: Jossey-Bass.
1983   Letter to the editor. *Fortune,* October 17, p. 27.
1985   Sources of order in underorganized systems: Themes in recent organization theory. Pp. 106–36 in Lincoln, Yvonne S. (ed.) *Organizational Theory and Inquiry.* Beverly Hills, Calif.: Sage Publications, Inc.
1987   Substitutes for strategy. Pp. 221–33 in Teece, David J. (ed.) *The Competitive Challenge: Strategies for Innovation and Renewal.* Cambridge, Mass.: Ballinger Publishers.
1988   Enacted sensemaking in crisis situations. *Journal of Management Studies,* 25(4): 305–17.

WEINBERG, S. KIRSON, and HENRY AROND
1952   The occupational culture of the boxer. *American Journal of Sociology,* LVIII, March: 460–70.

WEISS, CAROL H.
1981   Use of social science research in organizations: The constrained repertoire theory. Pp. 180–204 in Stein, Herman (ed.) *Organizations and the Human Services.* Philadelphia: Temple University Press.

WEISS, HOWARD M.
1978   Social learning of work values in organizations. *Journal of Applied Psychology,* 63(6): 711–18.

WEISS, JOSEPH, and ANDRE DELBECQ
1987   High technology cultures and management: Silicon Valley and Route 128. *Group and Organization Studies,* 12(1): 39–54.

WEISS, MELFORD S.
1967   Rebirth in Airborne. *Transaction,* 4: 23–27.

WEISZ, JOHN R., FRED M. ROTHBAUM, and THOMAS C. BLACKBURN
1984   Standing out and standing in. *American Psychologist,* 39(9): 955–69.

WELLMAN, DAVID
1986   Learning at work: The etiquette of longshoring. Pp. 159–75 in Borman, Kathryn M., and Jane Reisman (eds.) *Becoming a Worker.* Norwood, N.J.: Ablex Publishing.

WESTERLUND, GUNNAR, and SVEN-ERICK SJOSTRAND
1979   *Organizational Myths.* New York: Harper & Row, Pub.

WHARTON, JOSEPH W., and JOHN A. WORTHLEY
1981   A perspective on the challenge of public management: Environmental paradox and organizational culture. *Academy of Management Review,* 6(3): 357–61.

WHETTEN, DAVID A.
1987   Organizational growth and decline processes. *Annual Review of Sociology,* 13: 335–58.

WHIPP, RICHARD, ROBERT ROSENFELD, and ANDREW PETTIGREW
1989   Culture and Competitiveness: Evidence from two mature U.K. Industries. *Journal of Management Studies,* 26(November): 561–85.

WHITEHILL, ARTHUR M. and SHINICHI TAKEZAWA
1968   *The Other Worker: A Comparative Study of Industrial Relations in the U.S. and Japan.* Honolulu: East-West Center.

WHYTE, WILLIAM F.
1943   *Street Corner Society: The Social Structure of an Italian Slum.* Chicago: University of Chicago Press.
1948   *Human Relations in the Restaurant Industry.* New York: McGraw-Hill.
1949   Patterns of interaction in union-management relations. *Human Organizations,* 8(4): 13–19.
1951   *Patterns for Industrial Peace.* New York: Harper & Row, Pub.
1956   Engineers and workers: A case study. *Human Organization,* 14: 3–12.
1961   *Men at Work.* Homewood, Ill.: The Dorsey Press.
1969   *Organizational Behavior: Theory and Application.* Homewood, Ill.: The Dorsey Press.
1978   Organizational Behavior Research. Pp. 129–46 in Eddy, Elizabeth M., and William L. Partridge (eds.) *Applied Anthropology in America.* New York: Columbia University Press.
1979   Review of "The Illusive Phenomena." *Human Organization,* 37(4): 412–20.
1984   Personal communication.

WHYTE, WILLIAM F., TOVE HELLEND HAMMER, CHRISTOPHER B. MEEK, REED NELSON, and ROBERT N. STERN
1983   *Worker Participation and Ownership.* Ithaca, N.Y.: ILR Press, New York State School of Industrial and Labor Relations.

WHYTE, WILLIAM H., JR.
1956   *The Organization Man.* New York: Simon & Schuster.

WILENSKY, HAROLD L.
1964a   The professionalization of everyone. *American Journal of Sociology,* 120(2): 137–58.
1964b   Varieties of work experiences. Pp. 125–54 in Borow, Henry (ed.) *Man in a World at Work.* Boston: Houghton Mifflin.

WILENSKY, JEANNE L., and HAROLD L. WILENSKY
1951   Personnel Counseling: The Hawthorne Case. *American Journal of Sociology,* 57: 265–80.

WILKINS, ALAN L.
1977 Organizational stories as an expression of management philosophy, Ph.D. thesis proposal, Stanford University, June.
1978 Organizational stories as an expression of management philosophy. Unpublished thesis, Business School, Stanford University.
1983a Organizational stories as symbols which control the organization. Pp. 81–93 in Pondy, Louis R., Peter J. Frost, Gareth Morgan, and Thomas C. Dandridge, (eds.) *Organizational Symbolism*. Greenwich, Conn.: JAI Press.
1983b The culture audit: A tool for understanding organizations. *Organizational Dynamics*. 12(3), Autumn: 24–38.
1984 The creation of company cultures: The role of stories and human resource systems. *Human Resource Management*, 23(Spring): 41–60.
1989 *Developing Corporate Character: How to Successfully Change an Organization without Destroying It*. San Francisco: Jossey-Bass.

WILKINS, ALAN, and W. GIBB DYER, JR.
1988 Toward culturally sensitive theories of culture change. *Academy of Management Review*, 13(4): 522–33.

WILKINS, ALAN L., and WILLIAM G. OUCHI
1983 Efficient cultures: Exploring the relationship between culture and organizational performance. *Administrative Science Quarterly*, 28: 468–81.

WILKINS, ALAN L., and KERRY J. PATTERSON
1985 You can't get there from here: What will make culture-change projects fail. Pp. 262–91 in Kilmann, Ralph H., and Associates (eds.) *Gaining Control of the Corporate Culture*. San Francisco: Jossey-Bass.

WILLIAMS, LAWRENCE K., WILLIAM F. WHYTE, and CHARLES S. GREEN
1965 Do cultural differences affect workers' attitudes? *Industrial Relations*, 5(3): 105–17.

WILLIAMS, ROBIN M., Jr.
1970 *American Society*, 3rd ed. New York: Knopf.
1979 Change and stability in values and value systems: A sociological perspective. Pp. 15–47 in Rokeach, Milton (ed.) *Understanding Human Values*. New York: Free Press.

WILLNER, ANN RUTH
1984 *The Spellbinders: Charismatic Political Leadership*. New Haven, Conn.: Yale University Press.

WILSON, JAMES Q.
1983 *Thinking About Crime*. New York: Basic Books.

WILSON, ROBERT N.
1954 Teamwork in the operating room. *Human Organization*, 12(4): 9–14.
1982 Teamwork in the operating room. Pp. 100–106 in Robertson, Ian (ed.) *The Social World*. New York: Worth Publishers.

WILSON, WILLAIM A.
1981 *On Being Human: The Folklore of Mormon Missionaries*. Logan, Utah: Utah State University Press.

WINICK, CHARLES
1976 The social context of humor. *Journal of Communication*, 26: 124–28.

WINSTON, D.
1984 Scut work. *Working Woman*, 9(January): 26.

WISTER, OWEN
1902 *The Virginian: A Horseman of the Plains*. New York: Grosset and Dunlap.

WOODRUFF, DAVID, and THANE PETERSON
   1991   The greening of Detroit: A push is on to make cars more environmentally friendly. *Business Week,* April 8, Pp. 54–60.

WOODS, CLYDE M.
   1972   Students without teachers: Student culture at a barber college. Pp. 19–30 in Geer, Blanche (ed.) *Learning to Work.* Beverly Hills, Calif.: Sage Publications, Inc.

WOODWARD, JOAN
   1980   *Industrial Organization: Theory and Practice.* London: Oxford University Press.

WORTHY, JAMES C.
   1950   Organizational structure and employee morale. *American Sociological Review,* 15(April): 169–79.
   1984   *Shaping an American Institution: Robert E. Wood and Sears, Roebuck.* Chicago: University of Illinois Press.
   1986   *Human Relations at Sears, Roebuck in the 1940's: A Memoir.* Paper dedicated to the development of modern management. David Wren, ed. Norman, Okla.: Academy of Management.
   1989   Comments on the committee of human relations in industry at the University of Chicago. Working paper on the Management History Division, Academy of Management, Pp. 16–22, William Muhs (ed.).
   1991   Personal correspondence, August 5.

WREGE, CHARLES D., and AMEDEO G. PERRONI
   1974   Taylor's pig-tale: A historical analysis of Frederick W. Taylor's pig-iron experiments. *Academy of Management Journal,* 17: 6–27.

WRIGHT, J. PATRICK
   1979   *On a Clear Day You Can See General Motors.* Grosse Pointe, Mich.: Wright Enterprise.

WUTHNOW, ROBERT
   1987   *Meaning and Moral Order.* Berkeley, Calif.: University of California Press.

WUTHNOW, ROBERT, JAMES D. HUNTER, ALBERT BERGESEN, and EDITH KURZWEIL
   1984   *Cultural Analysis: The Work of Peter Berger, Mary Douglas, Michael Foucault, and Jurgen Kurzweil.* London: Routledge and Kegan Paul.

WYNN, ELEANOR W.
   1983   Silicon Valley anthropologist. *Practicing Anthropology,* 6(1): 9–11.

YAMAGUCHI, TAMOTSU
   1988   The challenge of internationalizing: Japan's Kokusaika. *The Academy of Management Executive,* II: 33–36.

YANKELOVICH, DANIEL
   1974   *The New Mortality: A Profile of American Youth in the 70's.* New York: McGraw-Hill.
   1979   Work values and the new breed. Pp. 3–34 in Kerr, Clark, and Jerome M. Rosow (eds.) *Work in America.* New York: Van Nostrand Reinhold.

YINGER, J. MILTON
   1960   Contraculture and subculture. *American Sociological Review,* 25: 625–35.
   1978   Countercultures and social change. Pp. 476–97 in Yinger, J. Milton, and Stephen J. Cutler (eds.) *Major Social Issues: A Multidisciplinary View.* New York: Free Press.
   1982   *Counter Cultures.* New York: Free Press.

YOUNG, ED
   1989   On the naming of the rose: Interests and multiple meanings as elements of organizational culture. *Organizational Studies,* 10(2): 187–206.

YOUNG, FRANK W.

1965   *Initiation Ceremonies: A Cross-Cultural Study of Status Dramatization.* New York: Bobbs-Merrill.

YOUNG, WESLEY O., and LOIS K. COHEN

1979   The nature and organization of dental practice. Pp. 193–208 in Freeman, Howard (ed.) *Handbook of Medical Sociology,* 3rd ed. Englewood Cliffs, N.J.: Prentice Hall.

YUKL, GARY A.

1981   *Leadership in Organization.* Englewood Cliffs, N.J.: Prentice Hall.

YUKL, GARY A., and DAVID VAN FLEET

1982   Cross-situational, multi-method research on military leadership effectiveness. *Organizational Behavior and Human Performance,* 30: 87–108.

ZAHN, GORDON

1969   *The Military Chaplaincy: A Study of Role Tensions in the Royal Air Force.* Buffalo, N.Y.: University of Toronto Press.

ZALD, MAYER N.

1966   Politics and symptoms: A review article. *Sociological Quarterly,* Winter, Pp. 85–91.

ZALD, MAYER N., and MICHAEL A. BERGER

1978   Social movements in organizations. *American Journal of Sociology,* 83(4): 823–61.

ZALESNY, MARY D., and RICHARD V. FARACE

1987   Traditional versus open offices: A comparison of sociotechnical, social relations, and symbolic meaning perspectives. *Academy of Management Journal,* 30: 240–59.

ZALEZNIK, ABRAHAM

1970   Power and politics in organizational life. *Harvard Business Review,* 48(3): 47–60.

1974   Charismatic and consensus leaders: A psychological comparison. *Bulletin of the Menninger Clinic,* 38(May 3): 222–38.

1977   Managers and leaders: Are they different? *Harvard Business Review,* May–June, Pp. 5–16.

1989   The managerial mystique: Restoring leadership in business. New York: Harper & Row, Pub.

ZALEZNIK, ABRAHAM, and M. F. R. KETS DE VRIES

1975   *Power and the Corporate Mind.* Boston: Houghton Miffin.

ZELLNER, WENDY

1989   Help wanted, room to advance—out the door. *Business Week,* October 30, p. 42.

ZERUBAVEL, EVITAR

1979   Private time and public time: The temporal structure of social accessibility and professional commitments. *Social Forces,* 58(1): 38–52.

1981   *Hidden Rhythms: Schedules and Calendars in Social Life.* Chicago: University of Chicago Press.

ZUCKER, LYNNE G.

1977   The role of institutionalization in cultural persistence. *American Sociological Review,* 42: 726–43.

ZUCKERMAN, L. T., and R. A. SAVEDRA

1972   Professional licensing legislation in the United States with an emphasis on social work statutes in California. Mimeographed. Venice, Calif.

ZURCHER, LOUIS A., JR.

1965   The sailor aboard ship: A study of role behavior in a total institution. *Social Forces,* 43: 389–400.

1967   The Naval recruit training center: A study of role assimilation in a total institution. *Sociological Inquiry,* 37(1): 85–98.

Index